MILITARY RECORD OF LOUISIANA

MILITARY RECORD of LOUISIANA

INCLUDING
BIOGRAPHICAL AND HISTORICAL
PAPERS RELATING TO THE MILITARY
ORGANIZATIONS OF
THE STATE

Napier Bartlett

LOUISIANA STATE UNIVERSITY PRESS
Baton Rouge

Published by Louisiana State University Press
Copyright © 1964, 1992 by Louisiana State University Press
All rights reserved
Manufactured in the United States of America
Library of Congress Catalog Number: 64—11967

Louisiana Paperback Edition, 1996
ISBN 978-0-8071-2078-1 (pbk.)

The paper in this book meets the guidelines for permanence and durability of the Committee on Production Guidelines for Book Longevity of the Council on Library Resources. ∞

Published with the assistance of the
Louisiana Civil War Centennial Commission

Sylvan Friedman, chairman
T. Harry Williams, vice-chairman
Elaine Ventress Johnson, secretary-treasurer
Rene' Breaux
Nettie J. Fava
Jesse M. Knowles
Bryan J. Lehmann, Jr.
John Regard, ex officio
Gladys B. Shackelford
Frederic R. Swigart
O. W. (Bill) Welch, honorary

FOREWORD

"It is probably the best Louisiana Civil War book your Commission could reprint," advised Palmer Bradley of Houston, noted collector of rare books about the Confederacy and authority on Confederate matters generally. He was talking about Napier Bartlett's *Military Record of Louisiana,* and because his judgment was so obviously correct the Louisiana Civil War Centennial Commission readily agreed to underwrite the cost of making the book again available to the reading public. Among students of the war the book has long been known as a valuable source, an interesting personal document, and an exceedingly rare item, so much so that in recent years secondhand copies have been about impossible to obtain.

Although the book has been well known, knowledge about its author is relatively scanty. He was born in Macon, Georgia, the son of a physician, and came to New Orleans to study at the University of Louisiana, where he graduated in 1858. He went back to Georgia but in 1860 returned to New Orleans, apparently intending to make the city his permanent home. The records list him variously as a public school teacher, a lawyer, and a journalist, and it is possible that he dabbled in all three professions at the same time.

Thus Bartlett was in Louisiana when the Civil War began. He immediately enlisted, on May 26, 1861, in the elite Washington Artillery, joining as a private and going up later to corporal. As a member of this unit, he traveled to Virginia, where he would spend his war career. He served in some of the principal battles in the Eastern theater, although at intervals he was detailed to special duties in the quartermaster's department at Richmond. He saw a great deal of the war at close range, and like so many sensitive young men of the time he wanted to write about what he had seen.

Apparently Bartlett had long felt an urge to write. At the conclusion of the war he returned to New Orleans and worked as a reporter for various newspapers. He finally purchased the *Claiborne Advocate* of Homer, and was editing that journal at the time of his death in 1876. In between journalistic ventures he tried his hand at writing fiction. Two volumes came from his pen — romantic and frothy productions that caused no more stir than they deserved. Much more satisfying to the author and more successful with the public was *A Soldier's Story of the War*, an engaging account of his own experiences. The reception accorded this work led Bartlett to prepare a larger one, the *Military Record of Louisiana*. In this book he incorporated his previous personal narrative and added a mass of information pertaining to the Washington Artillery and other units. The result was a volume combining autobiography and official data not readily available elsewhere. It was a contribution to both Louisiana and Confederate history, and as such it has had permanent significance and deserves to be read today.

The present volume is for the most part an exact reproduction of the book published in 1875 by L. Graham and Company, 73 Camp Street, New Orleans. In addition to this foreword, a table of contents has been added; photographs bound into the original volume have been omitted (they carried no identification), and a new title page has replaced the old. No attempt has been made to correct the typographical errors or to improve the unorthodox paging, which is evidence that although the various sections of the book were bound together they were printed separately.

In the preparation of this reprint edition two discrepancies

Foreword ix

were noted. One is the title. It appears on the title page as *Military Record of Louisiana;* the binding is stamped *Military Annals of Louisiana.* The other discrepancy is that there are at least two versions of the same work. Both carry exactly the same title page. The major sections and most of the pages correspond. But one volume is thirty-two pages larger than the other: one page was expanded in reprinting; others are completely new. What we have reproduced here is the more complete work — and what would seem to be the second of two editions published in the same year.

The Louisiana Civil War Centennial Commission is happy to have a part in bringing the book before a new audience of readers. It has always believed that its primary function in the Centennial commemoration is to preserve those mementos of a tragic war that should endure in men's minds. We are indebted to Mrs. Edith Atkinson of the Louisiana State Library for providing biographical information about Napier Bartlett, the compiler of this particular inheritance from the war. We are indebted also to the Louisiana State Library and to the Louisiana State University Library for the loan of the single volume of *Military Record* each owns in the preparation of this work.

> T. HARRY WILLIAMS
> Vice Chairman of the Louisiana
> Civil War Centennial Commission
> *and*
> Boyd Professor of History,
> Louisiana State University

PREFACE.

THE papers which follow have all the defects which will be assigned them. They are in no sense complete—they are only fragments. The names of gallant men and the deeds of gallant officers have been omitted, and some companies and officers have been perhaps given more prominence than they deserve.

In spite of these defects in the present plan, the editor has by the advice of old army friends, endeavored to put on record such facts as he can now obtain, with the hope that a more prosperous day and an increasing interest will permit of the publication of a full and complete history. He has invited all to make their contributions and has allowed the men to tell the story of their own regiment and officers, subject to the opinions of a good-natured public, as to whether they have made out their case. Some of the old participants have complied and some have not; and of course the discontent of that class will be greatest who have had no history themselves, or who were too indolent or indifferent to furnish any material for such a work.

The true end of these narratives is to show what the life of the Louisianian was, and the hero or figure head has to be selected, whether the drummer boy or general, whose life or anomalies of temperament furnished the most curious incidents. The writer must have a thread upon which to string his incidents, whether it be furnished by the general who has sent his brigade forward while he makes his headquarters behind the root of a tree, or whether by the soldier who is meanwhile, in obedience to orders, swimming rivers, or charging through wood and field.

These papers are not prepared for those readers who regard all past strugglers in any cause, in the slang of the day, as either played-out "beats" or successful "frauds," and who by their indifference have made the publication of any thoroughly satisfactory work not only ruinous but impossible. But the greatest men are produced in the generation which succeeds and is affected by the struggle—from the youth now growing up, who caught only a glimpse of the crimson stain in the sky, or of the angry glare of the dying fires, as the curtain fell upon the bloody tragedy.

The fresh mind can read with feeling, of brave men who come to the surface in one decade, and of the base and corrupt who get high places in another, where the contemporary regards them both as bores, and sees no points about one or the other. But to one critic, or the other, who thinks the old company and regimental records can be better published than in their present shape, the suggestive inquiry arises: Why have YOU not done so before—why do YOU not do so now?

CONTENTS

Foreword	vii
Preface	xi

I

Confederate Dead, C.S.A., Buried in Virginia	3
Battles in Virginia	8
Biographical and Historical Papers Relating to Louisiana, During and Since the War	20
Organization of the Louisiana Brigades in Virginia	20
The Louisiana Brigades in Virginia and Their Last Commander	24
The Sixth Louisiana Regiment	57
Complete Roll of Fenner's Louisiana Battery	69

II

Louisiana Troops in the West	1
Brigade of the Army of Tennessee	1
The Orleans Guard Battalion and Battery	11
Journal of the Orleans Guard	17
The Thirteenth Louisiana Regiment	21
Orleans Guard Battery	27
Movement of the Orleans Light Horse, and Their First Commander	31

The Twenty-Second Louisiana	35
Memorable Deaths	36
Muster Roll of Captain A. Picolet, Company D, 30th Louisiana Regiment	47
Casualties in 30th Louisiana	48
Third Louisiana Brigade	50
Le Gardeur's Battery	52
Bridges' Battery	53

III

The Trans-Mississippi	1
First Paper	1
Muster Roll of the Consolidated Crescent Regiment	15
Second Paper	17
Third Paper	28
Fourth Paper	33
Sub-Division of North Louisiana	34
Record of the Eighteenth Louisiana Regiment	37
Capture of the Federal Ironclad Gunboat Indianola	45
Louisiana Batteries in Army of Western Louisiana	54
The Twenty-Eighth Louisiana	61

IV

Washington Artillery	iii

Contents

V

Reorganization of the Washington Artillery, Since the War	1
A Soldier's Story of the War	5
Muster Roll of the Washington Artillery of the Army of Virginia	227
Report to Louisiana Legislature of Adjutant General M. Grivot	237

MILITARY RECORD OF LOUISIANA

CONFEDERATE DEAD, C. S. A.,

BURIED IN VIRGINIA.

During the summer of 1875 Maj. EDWARD D. WILLETT, of the 1st Regiment, Louisiana Brigade, in the late war, and now of the house of D. H. HOLMES, occupied a holiday visit to Virginia in going over the old battle fields, in which he and many of his regiment had fought and been wounded. He has since brought back with him many curious mementoes of those now historic fields. Old canteens, cartridge boxes, scraps of shell and stocks of muskets are still to be met with there, and he states although six tons of lead were taken from Spottsylvania alone, bullets are still to be found there and on all of the other " stamping grounds."

Major Willett also brought back with him numbers of photographs representing these localities as they now appear, with maps drawn from his own observations of the position of the Confederate armies, Louisiana troops, etc., and has the most valuable collection of souvenirs of this sort in the city.

At Fredericksburg, the southern portion of Marye's Heights has been turned into a Federal cemetery (which has now about 16,000 corpses) and the stone wall behind which Cobb fought his men has been taken for building a house for the resident sexton. The residence and ground of Gov. Marye changed hands under a succession sale, but the hill still retains the trenches and other memorials of the great battle.

Immediately in front of this hill is the dwelling of a woman, then a social outcast, who remained in it during the battle. She used all of the linen in her house dressing the wounds of soldiers, and finally tore in bandage strips what she wore on her own person. Her services and courage were such that the citizens only know her now for her good actions.

The battle fields generally still retain such landmarks as readily enable the soldier to recognize them. A few more fences have been built and fields have been cultivated.

The battlefield of the 1st La. on Williamsburg Road,* for instance, was waving with a magnificent crop of green corn. But in many of them the topographical features of the ground which caused them to be selected as battlefields have prevented enclosure, and they are now as bare of verdure as when great armies contended for their possession.

At Manassas 300 yards from the station, on the left side going from Richmond, stands a Confederate graveyard containing only one soldier, so far as known, from Louisiana. This graveyard is not in a good condition, but that at Fredericksburg is. This latter contains 16,000 bodies many of which have been brought from the Wilderness and other fields. That at Spottsylvania shows less care. Very few of the bodies of Louisianians who fell in these engagements were reinterred. The graves in Staunton and Richmond are in good condition.

Major Willett's principal task during his travels, was to ascertain the precise locality where the bodies of Louisiana soldiers have been interred in Virginia, and for the time and money he devoted to this work he deserves the gratitude of their surviving relatives and friends. The list we give below:

HOLLYWOOD CEMETERY, RICHMOND.

[The figures denote the regiment and the letter following the company; where neither are given they are unknown.]

J. Abbott, 8th; E. D. Adams, 5th, C; John Adams, John Ayecock, 9th, G; W. C. Akin, 2d, G; G. Allen, 8th, G; W. A. Anderson, 9th; W. Anderson, 9th; M. Angel, S. Antony, 2d, K; J. F. Archball, 3d, G; R. W. Armistead, J. Armstrong, Maj. R. W. Ashton, 2d; J. F. Atkins, 12th, A; W. Auther.

G. W. Bahan, W'n Art.; G. B. Bahan, W'n Art.; — Baker, 15th, H; N. Barham, 8th, C; J. Barnes, 8th, D; F. Bartholomew, 9th, F; R. Base, 9th,

---

*Apropos of this battlefield, the 1st Louisiana captured here the colors of Sickles' brigade. This was in the month of June. In August following Sickles had been again supplied and was making a very pretty showing of them at the 2nd Manassas. The 1st Louisiana did not believe that he ought to be allowed to keep them, and accordingly took them away the second time, and with them a fine battery. These colors were entrusted to an old farmer whom Major Willett hunted up during his visit. The farmer stated that he had kept them until the Federal army had the run of everything and then, fearful of trouble, had carefully torn the captured flags up in small strips, and then not feeling fully satisfied had burnt the rags up.

As for the colors of the First, they met with a still more extraordinary history. In the charge at Gettysburg many of this regiment were captured, including the color-bearer, Clancey. The capture was made at night; and Clancey not wishing to see his regimental flag dishonored, tore it in the darkness from the flag staff, wrapped it around his body under his shirt, and remained with it thus concealed for some months. Clancey reached Richmon safely, and reported back to his regiment. What was his subsequent history or that of the flag he so nobly preserved is not now known.

Confederate Dead, C. S. A.

K; Lieut. J. T. Beach, 5th; J. F. Bearley, A. Bell, 9th, H; W. R. Blackwood, 9th, A; C. Blasingham, 8th; A. G. Blunt, 9th; Lieut. R. W. Boswell, 2d, H; H. T. Bott, 14th, I; V. A. Bourgle, G. Bowlett, W. H. Bradles, 9th; John Bradley, 9th; P. Brandon, 5th, C; J. Branon, 10th, B; J. Brantley, S. Bravaux, 3d; Lieut. J. W. Breimer, R. H. Brawn, 15th, G; W. J Brown, 7th, A; J. Bryant, 7th, D; — Bryant, 2d, F; A. Bunn, 6th, E; H. Burgess, W. Burkley, 10th, D; D. Byrd, 19th, D.

J. S. Cabonis, 9th, F; John Calvin 2d, K; H. Campbell, 11th, F; W. F. Cane, 11th, F; H. M. Canliffs, 8th; D. Carney, P. A. Casbry, A. A. Cavaugh, 5th, B; J. Chamblis. 9th, G; T. Chounacy, 7th, F; H. Clark, 1st, F; W. Clark, 5th, F; B. G. Ceker, 9th, H; P. Coleman, 7th, D; John Connelly, 15th, A; J. B. Connor, 9th, H; J. H. Cooksey, 2d, I; B. Covington, 9th, G; J. H. Crane, 8th; — Cune, 10th.

Capt. Dailey, 1st; Lieut. W. H. Dansbey, 9th, A; C. Darley, 1st F; W. B. Davidson, 9th G; W. Davidson, 7th, B; W. G. Davis, l0th; A. Denson, 9th, C; J. Desmarest, 8th, F; M. Dockery, 14th, F; E. R. Dobson, 14th, H; D. H. J. Domiricky, 1st, A; W. Donell, 1st; — Donohoe, 6th, K; E. Douglass, 2d, G; J. J. Doyle, 9th, B; John Driscoe, 14th, F; M. Duffeys, 6th, K; T. Dupin, 8th; G. Durham, 16th, I.

A. J. Earvin, 2d, H; W. Eason, 9th, A; J. F. Elam, Artillery; M. V. Elder, 9th; John Eatier, Batt., 16 years old.

J. Fairchild, 9th, G; J. Farmer, 1st, D; W. F. Fincker, 1st, F; J. F. Flemming, 7th, K; T. Furlough, 8th, H.

J. N. Galbreth, Washington Artillery; J. P. Garbington, 1st, B; A. H. Gilbert, 6th, A; E. A. Glasscock, 8th, A; M. Golden, 5th, G; H. Goodman, 8th, B; T. Green, 9th; H. Cross, Battalion; Lieut. W. Crossen, 14th; Lieut. W. B. Guess, 2d, A; N. Guira, 15th.

C. Haggard, Artillery; J. Haines, 9th, C; J. O. Haira, 15th, I; A. Harmon, 14th, A; J. Harroett, 10th, A; W. W. Harris, 13th, C; H. S. Hartley, 8th, C; A. M. Hawson, 4th, C; W. G. Hayne, —, I; F. W. Hendricks, J. R. Higginbottam, 8th, E; F. Higginbottam, 8th, E; J. F. Higgs, 5th, B; J. W. Hill, 9th, F; P. Hines, 5th, K; G. Holland, 5th, B; M. O. Hora, 15th, E; Corp'l J. D. Howell, 9th, F; A. J. Hodgson, 9th, I; G. Hudson, 9th, B; J. Hufley, 14th.

J. Ingraham, 2d.

John Jackson, 8th, A; Capt. A. Johnson, 10th; J. W. Johnson, 1st, B; E. A. Johnson, 2d, B; W. Johnson, J. Jones, 4th; M. Jones, W. A. Jones, 14th, I.

M. Kaldy, 14th, A; Thos. Kann, 9th, D; M. Kelly, 14th, A; P. Kerns, 14th, H.

L. Lacoure, 2d, A; S. L. Landrum, 14th, I; E. Lawson, 15th, B; W. H. Lee, 8th, A; Lt. Col. J. M. Legett, 10th; C. K. Leitz, 14th, K; Lt. Col. G. A. Leister, 8th; C. Lindsey, 14th, I; J. Little, Washington Artillery; J. Loften, 8th, F; A. Loper, 8th; Capt. M. Marks; Capt. A. Jonté.

C. Magill, 10th, A; H. Mann, 5th, B; J. Marinay, 1st, D; D. L. Mark, 13th; G. Marston, 2d, C; E. M. Martin, R. Massie, 9th; J. Mayer, 10th, K; A. T. McAllister, James McClinton, Pat. McCormick, 13th; Capt. J. W. McCullock, 2d, K; T. A. McFarlin, 9th, G; R. J. McPherson, 9th, G; Lt. McShell, 14th, D; A. Merrill, 1st, K; J. H. Miller, Artillery; J. D. Mitchell, L. N. Moon, 8th; T. B. Moons, 8th, G; N. Moore, 14th, E; D. T..Moore, Washington Artillery; R. W. Moore, 9th, H; T. W. Moore, 1st, A; E. Moquest, 12th; S. J. Morrell, 4th; H. Morrison, 5th, B; S. Moss, 8th, C; M. Mullen, 10th, A; F. Myers, 7th, E.

B. F. Neason, 16th, H; R. Nicholls, 1st, B; J. Nugant, 9th, A.

J. Olithorpe, 6th, B; R. Oliphant, J. Oliver, 2d, H.

6   Confederate Dead, C. S. A.

W. Page, 8th, B; L. B. Palmer, 9th, F; J. N. Parker, 2d, F; — Parker, 5th, K; J. Pascon, 10th, I; W. Patrick, 3d batt C; J. J. M. Pearson, 9th, G; F. Perry, Artillery; L. H. Philips. 3d, B; D. A. Powell, J. Powers, 9th, I.

T. C. Ragan, 4th batt; S. C. Rawlins, L Rawner, 14th, K; H. C. Richardson, 7, H; James Ripts, J. Ristlett, 10th, D; W. T. Roberts, 8th, B; W. T. Robertson, 3d, H; Lt. I. G. Ross, 9th, I; J. M. Rowler, J. Ruduck, 6th, I.

T. Sanford, 18th, B; J. Z. Saunders, 14th, H; T. Saunders, 2d; C. W. Scarvega, 8th, I; J. C. Scott, 2d, D; A. J. Shackleford, F Guards; G. L. Shiffen, 5th, A; O. A. Shuley, 13th, K; W. Skilman, 9th, A; H. Smith, 12th, C; J. D. Smith, 8th, I; L. J. Smith, 2d; — Smith, 1st, F; H. Smither, Zouaves; H. J. Snyder, 9th, A; S. Stanley, 28th, A; — Stephenson, 9th, H; Srgt. D. C. Sullivan, 7th, H.

L. Taffel, 5th, H, T. F. Tate, 9th; G. Taylor, 9th; J. P. Taylor, 9th, H; B. Thacker, 10th, B; P. Thomas, 14th, K; A. Thompson, 15th, G; A. V. Y. Thompson, 8th, G; Lt. V. Thompson, 14th, I; W. H. Thornton, 9th A; S. J. Tomodle, 8th, I; Jno. Turner, 1st, B; J. D. Tyler, 2d, K.

G. H. W.; G. Wagnon, 13th, G, 22 y's of age; Jno. Wall, 8th, H; T. G. Wall, 5th, C; S. F. Watson, 9th, D; A. B. Wells, 9th, C; H. Wells, 10th, A; J. Wesley, T. R. M. Wharton, 15th; G. W. White, 2d, I; J. Whitehead, 2d, I; A. T. Williams, 9th, B; J. Williams, 7th, I; J. H. Williams, 8th, A; T. W. Williams, 2d; C. Winhart, 10th; W. J. Winlay, 15th; S. F. Winston, 9th, D.

A. Young, 6th, G; Jno. Young, Wheat's Bt; C. S. Youngblood, 2d, H.

OAKLAND CEMETERY, RICHMOND.

Andrew Amans, 9th, B; E. B. Adams, 5th, E.

Daniel Baywell, 15th; W. M. Ballard, 2d, C; P. Baker, 10th, F; — Bashfield, B; J. Blair, 1st, A; H. Barnes, F. Bashall, 13th, B; S. Beck, 9th; A. Bowden, 3d, C; J. M. Bonis, Artillery; E. Brown, 14th; G. Brown, 15th; C. A. Bowling, 1st; John Burke, 7th, B; J. D. Burch, 9th, F.

John Caison, 6th, B; John E. Carter, 9th, H; P. Carlone, 5th, K; — Costover, 10th, I; A. Clisson, 8th, K; W. Connelly, 1st, C; O. Cole, 1st, D.

Jno. Dalery, 14th, B; J. C. Doke, 6th, C; Jno. Doan, 1st, K; D. Dunn, 1st, A; J. H. Dushoney, 2d, H.

T. Fanagan, 2d, I; J. T. Flanagan, 2d, I; W. Fanton, 3d, F; N. Fling, 10th, D; Lt. S. Fischer, 14th, A.

H. L. Garner, 4th, C; C. W. Garters, 2d, K; J. Gray, 1st, I; M. Gabriel, 7th, B; W. M. Garbin, Artillery; Antony George, 10th, C; H. Gilbert, 15th, B.

J. O. Harden, 2d, I; A. H. Henderson, 2d, C; P. Higginbottam, 6th, C; Chas. Honeycut, 6th, A.

J. M. Jackson.

D. E. Kelley, 5th, A; Jno. Kennedy, 25th; W. Kelley, 1st, A; J. G. Kirk, 14th.

S. Lafeter, 14th, E; H. Labon, 14th, B; Mordecia Lancaster, 10th; P. Ledger, 10th, G; A. V. Leonard, E.

Richard Martin, 10th, C; D. Manning, 2d, K; A. T. Mathency, 6th, D; W. McHayne, 3d, A; Francis Merriell, 2d, K; G. W. McGenbry, 14th, A; — McHenry, 8th, G; J. Miller, 6th, G; J. M. McMillan, 8th; Julius McBride, 8th, J. T. McGill, 9th, F; Jno. Moran, 1st; J. M. Morris, 8th; W. W. Morris, 9th; Chas. Mulden, Art'y; M. Meyers, 5th, A; H. M. 1st, K.

G. W. Neale, 9th, B; B. A. Neathery, 14th, A; J. H. Newton, 2d, F; E. S. Newcomb, 7th, I; A. W. North, 9th, E; D. F. Noles, 20th, A. Thos. Offin, 6th, D; J. R. O'Brien, 5th, A. James Patten, 9th, C; John Parker, 9th, E; W. D. Perkins, 10th, E; J. H. Peary, 1st, B. J. L. Ray, 12th; J. Richardson, 14th, I; R. Reilly, 1st, C; P. Richmond, J. Roberts, 3d, B. J. N. Spain, 2d, C; L. J. Spear, 9th; W. S. Smith, 9th; G. A. B. Smith, 6th, K; F. A. Solden, 5th, E; J. Showke, 5th, F; M. Sullivan, 10th, I; S. S. Suttrill, A. John Taylor, 6th, C; J. W. Tassel, 12tb.; A. P. Thomas, 9th, I; J. T. Thompson, 17th, K; J. F. Tooley, 8th, G. W. B. Wade, G; John Wheelery, 6th; B. W. White, 14th, I; N. Wilkinson, 14th, A; J. T. Whiting, 14th; W. G. Willis, 11th, C; W. G. Woodil, 9th, K. R. Yarborough, 9th, A.

FREDERICKSBURG.

J. M. Brown, 15th; S. G. Browning, co, G; N. Bushnell, J. E. Cunningham, 2d; T. C. C-n-der, J. W. Frierson, 2d; G. Fillwer, 2d; Jacob Foster, 2d; Capt. R. P. Harmon, 14; P. Hugh, 2d; Lieut. J. S. Knight, W. M.; J. Montgomery, 8th, F; Jno. Mordecia, 7th, H; Lt. J. A. Murphy, 8th, A; Lt. J. M. Posey, 2d; A. H. Price, co, I; C. A. Prox, co, A; L. H. Robison, E. W. Stevens, 8th, E; Jas. Tronzber, 15th; R. H. W, 2d; Sgt. H. L. Williams, co. E.

SPOTTSYLVANIA.

Lt. D. Burweigh, Madison Artillery; G. P. Baskens, 8th, F; C. H. Clifton, 9th, D; Albert Dudenheim, 8th, B; Lt. A. Durham, 8th, C; Adjt. J. Finley, 14th; R. H. Humphreys, J. Levy, 7th, C; Jno. Lowe, 7th, G; A. W. Logan, 9th, D; Col. Bruce Manger, 5; Srgt. Jno. Mulroon, 6th, I; M. McFeeley, 8th, I; E. S. Pervis, 5th, E; Shields, 5th, E.

STANTON.

Martin Blackley, 7, B; Chris. Carrol, 14th, F; Th. H. Herrin, 8th, D; H. W. Jeffries, 10th, D; Srgt. H. King, 9th, E; Lt. W. Mills, 9th, A; E. G. Murphy, 14th, D; G. W. Story, 9th, F; E. L. Stephens, 9th, C; Michael Stevens, 10, C; W. H. Wynne, 9th, F.

MANASSAS.

W. T. E. Rowls, 8th.

BATTLES IN VIRGINIA.

Casualties in Louisiana Regiments and Batteries on the Rappahannock.

CASUALTIES OF NICHOLLS' SECOND LOUISIANA BRIGADE, IN THE BATTLES OF MAY 2 AND 3.

General and Staff—Wounded: Brig. Gen. T. F. T. Nicholls, severely, left leg amputated.

FIRST LOUISIANA REGIMENT, MAJ. JAS. NELLIGAN, COMMANDING.

Field and Staff—Wounded: Major Jas. Nelligan, slightly in thigh.

Company A, Capt. Alex. Boarman, commanding—Killed: Private E. M. Pennell. Wounded: Privates E. S. Mason, S. Bledsoe, H. Schroink and Sergeant W. J. Jones. Missing: Privates A. Bertin and B. S. Day.

Company B, Captain Sam. H. Snowden, commanding—Killed: none. Wounded: Lieut. H. C. Gill, Privates M. Lyles and A. C. Turner. Missing: Private J. M. Duncan.

Companies C and D, Captain A. N. Cummings, commanding—Killed: Private G. G. Moore. Wounded: Captain A. N. Cummings, Sergeant Farmer, Corporals Hope, Rhodes, Myers and Curran; Privates T. Holt. J. Callerny, J. Maloney, McMullins, B. Dunne and O'Neil.

Company E, Captain Thomas Rice, commanding—Killed: none. Wounded: 10. Missing: 3. Wounded: Captain Rice, slightly; Lieut. Kernion, since dead; Lieut. J. Maskew, Corporal Weldon, Privates Meagher, J. Powers, J. Brady, W. E. Duismore, J. McManus, T. Piggott. Missing: J. Gleason, W. Moore, P. O'Rejly.

Companies F and G, Capt. E. D. Willett, commanding—Killed: Corporal G. F. Werlein. Wounded: Privates G. Angel and Barth. Missing: Sergeant P. H. Raymond.

Companies I and K, Captain Charles E. Cormier, commanding—Killed: Sergeant Danziger and Private Geo. F. Driver. Wounded: Privates J. Issis and R. Baum. Missing: Capt. C. E. Cormier and Private Tripple.

SECOND LOUISIANA REGIMENT, COL. J. M. WILLIAMS, COMMANDING.

Company A, Captain J. W. Brown, Jr., commanding—Killed: none. Wounded: Capt. J. W. Brown, severely; Lieut. W. H. Noel, slightly; Lieut. A. W. Hammond, seriously, arm amputated; Second Lergeant Wm. Hollan, severely; Fourth Sergeant F. P. McKinney, slightly; Privates W. P. Cannon, Jr., severely; John Coley, slightly; J. Desleuches, slightly; J. T. B. Hudson, M. Fitzgerald, J. C. Fowler, severely; Wm. Key, H. M. Levy, J. W. Manny, slightly; Wm. Meadows, severely; J. Stokes, badly; J. B. Tucker, slightly.

Company B, Captain James F. Utz, commanding—Killed: Color Sergeant A. S. Odom. Wounded: Lieut. F. C. McRae, slightly; First Sergeant A. Crawford, slightly; Privates W. G. Loyd, slightly; John W. Powell, severely; C. C. Grissom, severely; J. H. Cluney, slightly; J. W. Leatherwood, slightly. Missing: Thomas Kearney and A. P. Williams.

Company C, Lieut. N. L. Hartly, commanding—Killed: Privates Grammont, Filhool, Stephen H. Pace. Wounded: Lieut. R. G. Cobb, slightly; Corporal J. T. Godley, slightly; Privates J. H. Brook, severely; J. H. Madden, L. Dyolous, W. T. Theobolds, slightly; J. J. Haynes, G. C. Dawkins, slightly. Missing: Lieut. J. M. Harris, Privates P. G. Oates, G. L. Gullay, T. H. Blakely, W. Holman.

Company D, Capt. Jas. S. Ashton, commanding—Killed: Privates Jas. E. Cunningham, Jr., Jacob F. Foster and John Whitten Frierson. Wounded: Privates W. R. K. Hogana, Isaac Hayes and John Henerick, since dead; Joe Casparey, severely; James L. Boone, John DeWitt, C. C. Reynolds, W. T. Riggs, severely; W. W. Ashton, slightly; Corporals W. F. Rembert and R. H. Riggs, very slightly. Missing: Sergeant H. J. Wells, Privates J. B. Gardner and D. G. Marshal.

Company E, Capt. L. G. Picon, commanding—Killed: None. Wounded: First Lieut. J. M. Batchelor, slightly; Second Lieut. J. M. Lewis, slightly; First Sergeant W. A. Deloach, slightly; Second Sergeant A Korber, slightly; Privates A. Coulon, slightly; R. J. Marshal, severely; G. Gauthier, slightly; G. P. Chaffant, slightly. Missing: Corporal H. Cunningham, Private O. A. J. Moore.

Company F, Capt. M. C. Redwine, commanding—Killed: Sergeant G. B. Bernard. Wounded: First Lieut. W. P. Posey, severely; Capt. Burrel Stuart, slightly; Privates G. W. Bishop, slightly; C. Lewis, slightly; J. P. Tatum, slightly; F. Kurty, severely. Missing: Second Lieut. A. P. Racine.

Company G, Capt. James Jones, commanding—Wounded: Sergeants C. T. Bradley and M. J. Matthews, severely; Private T. H. Brock, slightly.

Company H. Capt. G. L. Fortson commanding—Wounded: Second Lieut. C. A. Mallory, Privates C. C. Davenport, J. Oliver, T. H. Youngblood, C. S. Youngblood, J. G. Golden, B. F. Whatley, W. H. Davis, J. C. Williams, J. R. Johnson, P. G. Cassidy, J. B. Brodbeck, J. M. Bushong, Sergeant T. G. Small. Killed: D. C. Dunn.

Company I, Captain A. S. Blythe, commanding—Killed: R. B. Miller and T. P. Riordan. Wounded: W. C. Cooksey, A. N. Brown, T. N. Bolin, J. N. Jeter, N. Copeland, J. E. Simmonds, C. F. Thompson. Missing: Corporal B. B. Carter, Private J. P. Kendric.

Company K, Lieut. C. M. Farris, commanding—Killed: Corporal R. T. Denning. Wounded: Second Lieut. J. W. Hoard, First Sergt. J. R. Wright, mortally; Corporals L. W. Herring and R. M. Autrey, Privates J, W. Reid, D. F. Sut, F. C. Greenwood, Felix Wilson, J. W. Green, John Wright. Missing: J. T. Davidson.

TENTH LOUISIANA REGIMENT.

Lieut. Col. J. M. Legget, killed, and Major H. D. Monier, wounded.

Company A, Captain I. L. Lyons, commanding—Wounded: First Lieut. D. Mahoney, Sergt. T. McGuire, Privates J. Conway, P. Collins, J. Ford, M. Gilbert, P. Hammond, J. L. Kil. Killed: M. Flanagan.

Company B, Capt. C. Knowlton, commanding—Wounded: Privates P. Burk, D. Kessener, R. Carpenter. Missing: P. Stevenson.

Company C, Capt. T. N. Powell, commanding—Wounded: Corpl. Monahan, J. Gill, J. C. Mady. Missing: Garrety.

Company D, Capt. E. Welbre, commanding—Wounded: Privates W. Buckley, W. H. Crew, J. Carroll, C. Nash. Missing: Sergeant J. Wilson, Private J. Cunningham.

Company E, Lieut. Chisholm, commanding—Killed: Color-bearer, J. Anderson, Privates E. McBride, T. C. Anslem. Wounded: Sergeants R. B. Reaves, J. Bass, Privates J. Cronan, J. Westfall and McCoy. Missing: Private P. Moran.

Company F, Captain Pagruce, commanding—Wounded: Lieut. C. Cooper, Sergeant G. Parks, Privates H. Tetchy, J. Ulmer, J. Campbell, J. Edgar, Edgecomb, J. Quigeley. Missing: Privates C. Ross, P. Barrar.

Company G, Capt. C. Marmillion, commanding—Wounded: Capt. C. Marmillion, Lieut. Kendall, Sergeant C. Constard. Killed: Private Bergearn.

Company H, Captain L. Gastranski, commanding—Wounded: Capt. L. Gastranski, Sergeant E. Roubbau, Corporal McCasley, F. Ruffeatz. Privates M. Masterson, J. Henry, C. Jacob, J. Wolf. Killed: J. Burk, C. Guerrette, Gilless. Missing: A. Dayton.

Company I, Captain A. Jonte. commanding—Wounded: Capt. A. Jonte, Privates A. Babiron, Jean Marie. Killed: Sergeant Burnon, J. Humagall. Missing: A. Galiz.

Company K, Captain A. Penodin, commanding—Wounded: First Lieut. E. A. Seaton, Second Lieut. J. Ryan, Sergeant Kerinan, Corporal S. Mogent, Privates M. Ryan, J. Moyless, J. E. Stringer, H. Moss, J. Redfall, J. Truhan, J. Moreau, J. Eglinter. Killed: Sergeant J. Reeves, F. Lark. Missing: Sergeant H. Fleshman.

FOURTEENTH LOUISIANA REGIMENT—LIEUT. COL. D. ZABLE, COMMANDING.

Company A—Killed: Private W. Cotton. Wounded: Private Dan Green, Owen Quin, S. G. Wilson. Missing: Privates P. W. Boyle, W. McClellan, L. Newcomer.

Company B—Wounded: First Lieutenant Jno. H. Hood, Corporal McFee. Privates W. Smith, Henry Reese and James Hetherton. Missing: A. Kinsley, J. Weinn, Omer Burt.

Company C—Wounded: Capt. J. W. T. Leech, Corporal John Buckley. Privates C. Sullivan, Jas. Nolan. Missing: John King, Jas. Nolan.

Company D—Wounded: Sergeants D. Markey and R. S. Gardner. Privates M. Galvin, F. Pecquery, F. Stadte, N. Shaft. Missing: G. Coulin, T. Fowler, John Hughes, Con. Mellon, J. Sullivan, F. Strop, P. McGowan, Jr., and W. R. Mitchell.

Company I—Wounded: Lieut. Wm. Hoffman; Corporal Gookey; Private H. Murphy. Missing: Sergeant E. D. Bolger and Private John Moriarty.

Company F—Wounded: Lieut. Wm. Grossler; Sergeants W. Holliday and L. Metrille. Privates W. W. Butler, J. F. Bender, P. Fox, M. Kelger, J. M. Whalin. Missing: J. Roman.

Company G—Wounded: Corporal F. McNellis; Privates J. Brunan, William Miller, M. Keough. Missing: None.

Company H—Wounded: Sergts. C. McDougal, J. Gunsenhouser; Corporal T. Crough; Privates D. Kane, M. Saller, F. Havers and Jas. McCullough.

Company I—Capt. G. H. Pouncey, commanding—Wounded: Sergt. J. Pope; Privates W. Gaffing and C. Allen; Corporals H. Scarborough and John Holland. Killed: Corporal Taylor.

Company K—Wounded: Sergeants McEbeny, J. Weeble, F. Soutry; Corporals E. T. Hale, P. Schlesinger; Privates H. Smith, J. F. Scruggs, M. Clark.

FIFTEENTH LOUISIANA REGIMENT, COL. EDMUND PENDLETON, COMMANDING.

Field and Staff—Wounded: Col. Edmund Pendleton, in hand; Lieut. Col. L. McGoodwin, in hand and thigh; Sergeant Major Haskins, in ankle.

Company A—Killed: Privates F. Hoffman, P. Burns and Whittle. Wounded: Sergt. R. Lente, severely. Missing: Private E. Cain.

Company B—Killed: Privates Walker, Finnegan, West and Brake. Wounded: Sergt. Henricks, Corporal McArthur, Privates Conway, Brennan, Fitzgerald, Huffy, Russell. Missing: Private Peters.

Company C—Killed: Private Brown. Wounded: Lieut. Erwin, seriously in right arm; Lieut. Gross, slightly; Sergt. Hanck, Sergt. Dupuy, Privates C. Viger and P. Smith. Missing: Bernard O. Badeau and P. Badeau.

Company D—Killed: Private H. Johnson. Wounded: Lieuts. Powers and Lockwood, Sergts. Simcox and Duffy, Privates Reiley, Klech, Cann, Leharvey, Fauning and Gorivan.

Company E—Killed: Lieut. Haynes, Sergt. Paul. Wounded: Privates Cormandy and Brown. Missing: Corporal Burke.

Company F—Killed: Sergt. Roe. Wounded: Sergts. Roden and C. Clendenning, Corporal Winn, Privates Knight and Donley. Missing: Corporal Holleway, Privates Carroll and Flynn.

Battles in Virginia. 11

Company G, Capt. Wm. C. Michie, commanding—Killed: Sergt. McElwee, Corporal Tucker and Private Bigger. Wounded: Capt. W. C. Michie, slightly; Lieuts. Bowman and Davenport, Sergeants Wynn and Brown, Corporal Aldridge, Privates Lott, Carroll, England, Dawson, Merrillian, Braddock, Cannedy, J. W. Mygatt, Crawford, Womack. Missing: Private Manning.

Company H—Killed: Private Wm. Wolf. Wounded: Capt. J. F. Witherup, Lieut. Blackstone, Corporal D. Venet. Missing: Privates McPherson, McGainer, F. Barnett.

Company I—Kiiled: Privates D. Hogan and E. Clark. Wounded: Lieut. Brown, Sergeant Transler, Sergeant Napier, Corporal Trisler, Privates Tiller, McClure, Manning, Groer, McQuade and Shae.

Company K—Wounded and Prisoners: Sergeant Brown and Private Keefer. Wounded: Sergeant Buck, Corporals Salvis and Dillon, Privates Arnauld, Cunningham, Hoff, Heno, Mengis, Norris and Rank.

GRAND RECAPITULATION.

1st Louisiana Regiment		50
2nd	do. do.	126
10th	do. do.	86
14th	do. do.	81
15th	do. do.	104
General Staff		1

Grand total of killed, wounded and missing....448

THE WASHINGTON ARTILLERY.

List of Killed, Wounded and Missing in the Battalion Washington Artillery.

First Company—Killed: Sergeant W. H. West, Corporal T. J. Lutman, Private J. E. Florence. Wounded: Corporal C. A. Everett, prisoner. Captured: Capt. C. W. Squires, Lieut. Edward Owen, Lieut. John Galbraith, Sergeant W. T. Hardie, Privates R. Alsobrook, H. B. Berthelot, J. B. Ozant, Wm. Fellowes, Jr., J. R. Harby, M. E. Harris, James M. McCormack, A. Micou, J. Myers, N. B. Phelps, E. Peychaud, C. Peychaud, P. Siebrecht, T. S. Turner, Samuel Turner, Van Vinson. Drivers Captured: John Eshman, John Hock, James Kennedy, P. Rierson, E. W. Smith.

Second Company—Wounded: Lieut. J. B. DeRussey, Privates Barton Kirk, Phil. Van Collin. Captured: Privates H. D. Summers, Wm. Giffin, H. D. Coleman.

Third Company—Wounded: Corporal R. P. Many and prisoner, Privates L. Adam, O. Frank. Captured: Sergt. John T. Handy, Privates W. P. Noble, Benjamin Dick.

Fourth Company—Killed: Corporal L. L. Lewis. Wounded: Corporal J. Valentine, artificer F. Callahan, driver J. Anderson.

PIECES CAPTURED.

First Company—One 12-pound Napoleon, one 3-inch rifle.
Second Company—One 12-pound howitzer.
Third Company—One 12-pound Napoleon, one caisson.
Fourth Company—One 12-pound Napoleon, one 12-pound howitzer.

CASUALTIES OF THE 10TH LOUISIANA FROM MAY 5TH, 1864, to 1865.

Battle of the Wilderness, May 5th, 1864.

Company A, Captain I. L. Lyons, commanding—Killed: Private Tom. Newman. Wounded: Lieut. T. Barron, Privates M. Stanton, P. Stanton.

Company B, Lieut. H. Eustis, commanding—Wounded: Private Dan. Kearney. Missing: Sergt. Tom. Whalen, Privates Pat. Mahan, Mike Osborne.

Company C, Capt. James Scott, commanding—Killed: Private Michael Leddy. Missing: Jno. O. Molly.

Company D, Capt. Ernest Webre, commanding—Killed Pat. Mullins. Wounded: Privates Ed. Wynne, Andy Moffitt, John Holland, Dan Rogers, Corpl. G. Tally.

Company E, Capt. Sam. H. Faulkner, commanding—Killed: Pat. Kear, Pat. Kane. Wounded: Sergt. T. N. Taylor, Privates J. Shilbert, James Moore.

Company F, Capt. A. F. Pagnier, commanding—Killed: Private J. Myer. Wounded: Privates Martin Cusack, J. Herbert.

Company H, Capt. Leon Jastremski, commanding—Wounded: Sergt. Wm. Cunningham.

Company I, Capt. P. Leclaire, commanding—Wounded: Corpl. A. Jean Marie, Private S. Pisani.

Company K, Capt. August Perrodin, commanding—Wounded: Sergt. Jos. Harring, Private Jos. Strange. Missing: Privates Thos. E. Stringer, Jos. Richard, George Lalonde, John Toomey.

Battle of Spotsylvania, May 12th, 1864.

Wounded: Major Thos. N. Powel, Lieut. and Ensign T. G. Boykin. Missing: Adjt. H. Pierson, Asst. Surg. Henry Shiff.

Company A, Capt. I. L. Lyons, commanding—Wounded: Capt. I. L. Lyons, Private Jno. Lafferty. Missing: Lieut. Dan. Mahoney, Ord. Sergt. Wm. McMullen, Sergt. J. Dellahanty, Privates G. W. Loomer, Jno. S. Kail, Henry Scott, Thos. Doyle, Dan. Dailey, Wm. McGuire, Jas. Conway, Wm. Hackett.

Company B, Lieut. H. Eustis, commanding—Missing: Ord. Sergt. Dan. Tierney, Private J. Moran, Phil. Ryan, P. Doyle.

Company C, Capt. James Scott, commanding—Killed: Private Jno. Henry. Missing; Private Jas. Gannon, P. Monaghan, P. Carroll.

Company D, Capt. Ernest Webre, commanding—Wounded: Capt. E. Webre. Missing: Private C. Narshtedt, Jno. Saunders.

Company E, Capt. Sam. H. Faulkner, Commanding—Killed: Private J. Cronan. Wounded: None. Missing: Lieut. Chas. A. Chisholm, Privates Jno. E. Bell, James Moore, Chas. Reily, Corpl. Geo. Perkins.

Company F, Capt. A. F. Pagnier, commanding—Wounded: Capt. A. F. Pagnier. Missing: Privates F. Springis, F. Smith, Sergt. J. Newcomb.

Company G, Capt. Chas. B. Marmillion, commanding—Wounded: Lieut. T. Louis Mills, Robert Fortier. Missing: Ord. Sergt. H. Danten, Privates A. Bejeau, J. Kenner.

Company H, Capt. Leon Jastremski, commanding—Missing: Capt. L. Jastremski, Ord. Sergt. E. Ronbleau, Sergts. Wm. Cunningham, J. McCasland, Corpl. Z. Bond, Private A. Brignac, Robt. Linder,

Company I, Capt. P. Leclaire, commanding—Killed: Capt. P. Leclaire. Missing: Ord. Sergt. A. Purkel, Sergt. C. Mahoney, Privates F. Manchini, Paul Moreau, J. G. Metilino, Philip Miller, Louis Bonette.

Company K, Capt. August Perrodin, commanding—Missing: Capt. A. Perrodin, Lieuts. E. A. Seaton, T. Rycon, Ord. Sergt. Jno. Courville, Corpl. Louis Nugent, Privates M. Marcautil, Ben. Elender, Walter F. Moss, Jos. D. Granger, Jos. Kennedy.

Battles in Virginia.

Malvern Hill, July 1st, 1862.
Col. EUG. WAGGAMAN, Commanding.

Field and staff—Missing: Col. Eug Waggaman.

Company A, I. A. Cohn, commanding—Killed: Privates Con. Hollerand, Michael D. Mullen, John McGee, Charles McGill, William Voorvart, George Wolf. Wounded: Private Patrick McLaughlin, Frank Powell, Thomas M. McGuire, Geo. Seymour, Patrick Tansey, Martin Gilbert. Missing: Lieut. Isaac L. Lyons, Sergeant Patrick Barron.

Company B, Capt. Henry C. Marks, commanding—Killed: Capt. Henry C. Marks, Sergt. V. Harrison, Privates Charles Gordon, A. Roach. Wounded: Privates Patrick Doyle, John Moran, John Smith. Missing: Robert Bracken, Richard Carpenter.

Company C, Capt. Thos. N. Powell, commanding—Killed: Privates John Higgins, John Mangan. Wounded: Serg't Owen Connelly, Priv. Henry Boigar, Corp'l James Gill, Corp'l James Gallagher, Priv. John Lavin, Pat. O'Brien. Missing: Priv. Michael Moffit, Michael Kennedy.

Company D, Lieut. Sam. May, commanding—Killed: Sergt. Wm. Donovan. Sergt. Martin Ready. Wounded: Private Edward Wynne, George Tate, John Nash. Missing: Private Dominick Owens, Sergt. Wm. H. Parker, Private Thos. Ryan.

Company E, Capt. S. Cucullu, commanding—Killed: Corporal John Walton, Sergeant Henry Jackson. Wounded: Sergeant Eug. A. Dickey, Private Wm. C. Hosea.

Company F, Capt. John M. Leggett, commanding—Killed: Sergt. Paul Moreau. Wounded: Corporal John Richards, Fred. Prietz, Michael Faller. Missing: John McFadden, Charles Broglie.

Company G, Capt. Chas. B. Marmillion, commanding—Killed: Private John Edgar. Antonio Riola. Wonnded: Serg't H. Herrero, Private A. Bejean.

Company H, Capt. Wm. Barnett, commanding—Wounded: Sergt. Adam Conrad, Private Z. Borne, Jonn Owens.

Company I, Lieut. A. Jonté, commanding—Wounded: Andrew Leary, John Gustin. Missing: Privates Joseph Cortez, Francois Randy, Philip Locker, Antonio Ruiz, Guilarmo Geromini,

Company K, Capt. A. Petrodin, commanding—Wounded: Corpl. Wm. Durio, Private Patrick Coynes, James Moyles, Jos. D. Fargue. Missing: Private Jas. McKinney·

Battle of Cedar Run, August 10th, 1862.
Lieut. Col. WM. B. SPENCER, Commanding.

Company C, Capt. N. Powell, commanding—Killed: Corporal Edward Martin, Private Pat. Feeny, Wm. Quinn, Michael Slavin. Wounded: Serg't Thos. Ford, Private Daniel Curran.

Company D, Capt. Ernest Webre, commanding—Wounded: Corpl. Simon Kennear.

Company I, Capt. Henry D. Monier, commanding—Wounded: Andre Nicole. Missing: Jules Delherbes.

Manassas, No. 2, August 28th, 29th and 30th, 1862.
Lieut. Col. WM. B. SPENCER, Commanding.

Field and staff—Killed: Lieut. Col. Wm. B. Spencer. Wounded: Adg't Henry Puissan.

Company A, Capt. J. A. Cohen, commanding—Killed: Capt. J. A. Cohen, Corpl. Thos. White. Wounded: Sergt. Daniel Mahoney, Privates Charles

H. Cross, Martin Gilbert, Peter Hammond, William Hackett, Hugh Larkin, Patrick Stanton, Frank Powell, Martin Welsh. Missing: Lawrence Keighan.

Company B, Capt James Buckner, commanding—Killed: Private John Little, David Quirke, P. Townley, Robert Wilkenson. Wounded: Sergeant Thomas Hunt, Privates R. Carpenter, Richard Doyle.

Company C, Capt. Thos. N. Powell, commanding—Killed: Lieut. Eugene Janin, Priv. John Conner. Wounded: Capt Thos. N. Powell, Sergts. Owen Connelly, Michael Garrithy, Michael Hussey, Privates John Foy, Michael Counor, Pat Cheevers, Jas. Gannon, John Moore, J. N. Whitlow.

Company D, Capt. Ernest Webre, commanding—Killed: Corpl. John Livick, Priv. Con. Murphy. Wounded: Corpl. Tim. Kelly, Dan. Lockerbic.

Company E, Capt. S. Cucullu, commanding—Wounded: Capt. S. Cucullu, Color Bearer Robert Strom, Sergt. Wm. Carmichael.

Company F, Capt. Albert F. Pagnier, commanding— Wounded: Priv. Frank Barthel, John Campbell, Dennis Hayes, Henry Meyers, Jean Moisan, Sergeant Aug. Lasere.

Company G, Capt. Chas. B. Marmillion, commanding—Wounded: Bernard Lafargue. Missing: Anton Wagner.

Company H, Lieut. — Adam, commanding—Killed: Scrgt. Adam Conrad, Privates Theodule Cambre, John Cochrane. Wounded: Privates Dan Dean, Alceste Brignac, Wm. Beadle, John Gillis.

Company I, Capt. Henry D. Monier, commanding—Wounded: Lieut. Peter Leclairc, Nicole Danilovich, Antonio Jacques. Missing: Privates David Torrenelle, Paul Moreau, Serg't Francisco Brescianini

Company K, Capt. Aug. Perrodin, commanding—Killed: Sergt. Pierre Vincent, Private David Hargrove. Wounded: Lieuts. Isaac Ryan, O. Prudhomme, Privates Joseph L. Ryan, Fred. Sark, Pat. McCormick, Wm. C. Boland. Missing: Sergt. Henry A. Fleshman, Corpl. I. C. Ruchenbach.

Battle of Sharpsburg, Md., September 17th, 1862.

Capt. HENRY D. MONIER, Commanding.

Company A, Ord. Sergt. Dan Mahony, commanding—Killed: Private David Holmes. Wounded: Private George Seymour. Missing: Privates Thomas Hammond, John Dolan.

Company B, Capt. Chas. Knowlton, commanding—Wounded: Capt. Chas. Knowlton, Sergt. Robert Bracken, Private Phil. Ryan.

Company C, Ord. Sergt. J. Scott, commanding—Killed: Serg't Martin Durkin.

Company D, Lieut. Sam. May, commanding—Killed: Sergt. Jos. Joyce, Privates Peter Collins, Henry Friday, Edward Hassey. Missing: John Saunders.

Company E, Lieut. Chisholm, commanding—Killed: Color Bearer Robert Strom, Corporal John Sloan, Private Charles Easman. Wounded: Corpls. Pat. Kean, Elisha McBride, Private John Moulzer. Missing: Priv. James Sheffield.

Company F, Lieut. Chas. Cooper, commanding—Killed: Louis Arons, Henry Jones, James McFadden, Fred. Preitz. Wounded: Sergeant James Newcomb, Corporal Edward Edgecomb. Missing: Corpl. James Edgar, Private Gus. Boorhead.

Company G, Chas. B. Marmillion, commanding—Killed: Privates Juan Tacon, Victor Nunenmacher. Wounded: Capt. Chas. B. Marmillion, Lieut. S. Herrero, Serg't Alexander Romain, Corpl. Hypolite Austin, Priv. Lewis Long. Missing: Privates Jugal Constantine, Max Miller.

Battles in Virginia. 15

Company H, Capt. Adam Alexander, commanding—Killed: Capt. Adam Alexander, sergt. John Thompson, Private John Watson. Wounded: Corp'l Fred. Brogan, Privates John P. Usher, Mike Gavin.

Company I, Lieut. A. Jonté, commanding—Killed: Serg't Alex. Feuga, Privates C. Salonicho, George Zapf. Wounded: Sergt. A. Baldoni, Privates F. Lappi, G. Juliani, O. Paoli Aguis. Missing: G. Mariotte, C. Vallesariz.

Company K, Lieut. Isaac Ryan, commanding—Killed: Corpl. Joseph Augé, Privates J. H. Jackson, Jas. McKinney.

Battle of Fredericksburg, December 13th, 1861.

Company E, Killed: Corporal Charles Eilert.

Company F—Wounded: Sergeant Frank Rasche, Privates F. Barthel, Michael Reinhart. Missing: Private Francois Martin.

Company H—Wounded: Mike Masterson.

Company I—Wounded: Serg't C. Mahoney, Priv. A. Baleron.

Company K—Wounded: Private L. Courville.

Battle of Chancellorsville, Va., May 2d and 3d, 1863.

Lieut. Col. J. M. LEGGETT, Commanding.

Field and staff—Killed: Lieut. Col. J. M. Leggett. Wounded: Major Henry D. Monier.

Company A, Capt. I. L. Lyons, commanding—Killed: Private M. Flannagan. Wounded: Lieut. Daniel Mahoney, Sergeant T. M. McGuire, Corpl. John Ford, Privates James Conway, P. Collins, M. Gilbert, P. Hammond, John Skail.

Company B, Lieut. H. Eustis, commanding—Wounded: Sergeant D. Kearney, Privates P. Burke, D. Kessener, R. Carpenter. Missing: P. Stevenson.

Company C, Capt. Powell, commanding—Wounded: Capt. Powell, Corpls. J. Gill, P. Monoghan, Priv. John O'Mally. Missing: Sergt. M Garrity.

Company D, Capt. E. Webre, commanding—Killed: Wm. Buckley. Wounded: Sergt. John Tulley, Privates J. Burnett, Jas. Carroll, W. H. Crew, C. Narshtedt. Missing: Sergt. J. Wilson, Priv. J. Cunningham.

Company E, Capt. Sam. H. Faulkner, commanding—Killed: Color Bearer James Anderson, T. C. Anselon, E. McBride, C. Bobo, J. Moran, J. M. Campbell. Wounded: Sergeants I. N. Taylor, R. B. Reeves, John C. Bass, Corporal P. Kean, Privates J. Westfall. J. Cronan, P. McCoy.

Company F, Capt. A. F. Pagnier, commanding—Killed: Lieut. Charles Cooper, Sergeant Charles Ross, Corpls. G. Parks, Henry Leichy. Wounded: Corporals E. Edgecomb, J. Edgar, Privates J. Campbell, R. Lubeight, J. Quigley, J. Ulmer. Missing: Private P. Barran.

Company G, Capt. C. B. Marmillion, commanding—Killed: Private J. Bergeron. Wounded: Capt. Chas. B. Marmillion, Lieut. L. H. Kendall, Sergeant C Constant.

Company H, Capt. L. Jastremski, commanding—Killed: Corp'l C. Jacob, Private J. Burk, J. Wolf, A. Dayton, Jno. Gillis, C. Gueret. Wounded: Capt. L. Jastremski, Sergt. E. Roubleau, Corpls. A. Keller, A. McCasland, T. Rafftery, Privates P. Havery, M. Masterson, J. Henry.

Company I, Capt. A. Jonté, commanding—Killed: Capt. A. Jonté, Sergt. J. Bremont, Private J. Fumagali. Wounded: Corp'l A. Jean Marie, Priv. A. Balleron. Missing: Corp'l A. Galli, Private Sesto Pisani.

Company K, Capt. A. Perrodin, commanding—Killed: Sergeants H. A. Fleshman, Jas. Reeves, Privates J. Moyle, Fred. Sark. Wounded: Lieuts.

E. A. Seaton, Isaac Ryan, Sergeant B. Kirkman, Corporal L. Nugent, Privates J. Trahan, T. E. Stringer, J. Reeves, M. Ryan, W. F. Moss, G. Kanghfall, J. Ellender, J. Maran.

Battle of Gettysburg, July 1st and 2d, 1863.

Company A, Capt. I. L. Lyons, commanding—Killed : Corporal E. Webb, Privates B. Conway, W. McDermott. Wounded : Sergeants C. Briggs, G. W. Loomer, Corporal J. Ford, Privates J. Conway, D. Daley, T. Doyle, J. Gillion, J. Kane.

Company C, Capt. C. Knowlton, commanding—Wounded : Lieuts. H. Eustis, R. Bracken, Sergt A. McDonald, Privates P. Madden, J. O'Grady, C. Ryan.

Company C, Capt. James Scott, commanding—Killed : Privs. J. Vandergriff, P. O'Brien. Wounded : Captain J. Scott, Sergts. Thos. Kahoe, F. Kelly, M. Hussey, J. Gallagher, Corp'ls P. Laffy, W. Lawless, Privates M. Maloney, T. Logan, M. Kennedy, P. Higgins, F. Gallagher, T. Flynn, P. Cheevers, P. Carroll, Henry Boigar, J. Keegan.

Company D, Capt. E. Webre, commanding—Killed: Corpl. G. Petrovich, Private J. Cunningham. Wounded : Lieut. S. H. May, Sergeant J. Tully, Corp'l S. Kennear, Privates J. Connor, D. Farrar, C. Narshtedt, M. Stappleton. Missing : Private J. Burnett.

Company E, Capt. S. Faulkner, commanding—Killed : Corp'l J. Sheffield, Privates E. Conner, G. Zwiegler. Wounded : Capt. S. Faulkner, Sergeant I. N. Taylor, Corporal E. Beard, Privates J. Westfall, J. Jarnagen, J. Bobo,

Company F, A. F. Pagnier, commanding—Killed : Privates P. Turquais, A. Berthancourt. Wounded: Sergeant August Saucier, Corporal P. Tapie, Privates J. Newcomb, J. Caudidi, P. Barran. Missing : Privs. Fred. Smith, C. Schwartz.

Company G—Killed : Privates J. Wilder, B. Lafargue, A. Lopez. Wounded : Sergt. H. Dantin, Privates M. Miller, J. Lima, A. Constancia. Missing : L. Courajoux, M. Castanio, S. Estrado, L. Gros, H. Austin, C. Fassaldatto.

Company H, Capt. L. Jastremski, commanding—Killed : Sergeant F. Webber, Corporal F. Brogan. Wounded : Capt. Jastremski, Sergts. J. P. Usher, W. Cunningham, Private C. Holmes. Missing : Corpl. T. Raftery, J. Burke.

Company I, Capt. P. Leclaire, commanding—Wounded : Privates J. Delherbes, P. Miller, F. Manchini, A. Ruiz, V. Allis, Corp'l A. Galli, Serg't J. G. Metalieno. Missing : A. Stallbaumer, D. Gelancovich. C. Dondaro, N. Danilovich,.

Company K, Capt. A. Perrodin, commanding—Killed : Privates J. Reeves, J. Regan. Wounded : Serg't J. G. Harrington, Corpls. L. Nugent, A. Lalonde, Privates J. Toomey, J. L. Strange, Geo. Lalonde, P. Sherry. Missing : Privates L. Couville, J. Granger, E. Linder, R. F. Pierce.

Battle of Payne's Farm or Moore's Run, Va., November 27th, 1863.

Lieut. Col. HENRY D. MONIER, Commanding.

Company A, Capt. I. L. Lyons, commanding—Killed : Private H. Larkin. Wounded : Private M. Stanton. Missing : Private P. Stanton.

Company B, Capt. C. Knowlton, commanding—Killed : Private D. McCarthy. Wounded: Capt. C. Knowlton,

Company C, Capt. J. Scott, commanding—Killed : Private J. Lavin. Wounded : Privs. Pat Higgins, Wm. Lawless.

Company D, Capt. E. Webre, commanding—Killed : Serg't J. Tully. Wounded : Privates W. H. Crew, J. Stephen.

Company E, Capt. S. Faulkner, commanding—Wounded: Color Bearer T. G. Boykin, Sergeant I. N. Taylor, P. Kean, P. McCoy.

Company F, Capt. A. F. Pagnier, commanding—Wounded: Corporal G. Malone.

Company G, Capt. C. B. Marmillion, commanding—Wounded: J. Baker, A. Constancia.

Company H, Capt. L. Jastremski, commanding—Killed: J. O'Donnell. Wounded: M. Masterson.

Company I, Capt. P. Leclaire, commanding—Wounded: Lieut. G. Sauvé, Private L. Bonetti.

Company K, Capt. A. Perrodin, commanding—Killed: Private J. Moreau. Wounded: Privates Y. Lebleu, T. E. Stringer.

Battle of the Wilderness, May 5th, 1864.
Lieut. Col. HENRY D. MONIER, Commanding.

Company A, Capt. I. L. Lyons, commanding—Killed: Private T. Newman. Wounded: Lieut. P. Barron, Privates M. Stanton, P. Stanton.

Company B, Lieut. H. Eustis, commanding—Wounded: Private D. Kearney. Missing: Sergeant T. Whalen, Privates P. Mahan, M. Osborne.

Company C, Capt. J. Scott, commanding—Killed: Private M. Leddy. Missing: Private J. O'Mally.

Company D, Capt. E. Webre, commanding—Killed: Private P. Mullen. Wounded: Serg't J. Holland, Corp'l E. Wynne, Privates A. Moffatt, D. Rogers.

Company E, Capt. S. Faulkner, commanding—Killed: Private P. Kean. Wounded: Sergeant I. N. Taylor, Privates J. Shibert, J. Moore.

Company F, Capt. A. F. Pagnier, commanding Killed: Private J. Myer. Wounded: Privates M. Cusack, J. Herbert.

Company H, Capt. Jastremski, commanding—Wounded: Serg't W. Cunningham.

Company I, Capt. Leclaire, commanding—Wounded: Corp'l A. Jean Marie, Private S. Pisani.

Company K, Capt. Perrodin, commanding—Wounded: Sergeant J. G. Harrington, Private J. L. Strange. Missing: Privates G. Lalonde, J. Richard, T. E. Stringer, J. Toomey.

Battle of Spottsylvania, May 12th, 1864.
Lieut. Col. HENRY D. MONIER, Commanding.

Field and staff—Wounded: Major T. N. Powell, Ensign T. G. Boykin. Missing: Adjt. H. Puissan, Surgeon H. Shiff.

Company A, Capt. I. L. Lyons, commanding Wounded: Capt. Lyons, Private J. Lafferty. Missing: Lieut. D. Mahoney, Sergeants W. McMillan, J. Dellahauty, Privates G. W. Loomer, J. Skail, H. Scott, T. Doyle, D. Dailey, W. McGuire, J. Conway, W. Hackett.

Company B, Lieut H. Eustis, commanding Missing: Serg't D. Tierney, Privates J. Moran, P. Doyle, P. Ryan.

Company C, J. Scott, commanding Killed: Private J. Henry. Missing: Privates P. Monaghan, P. Carroll, J. Gannon.

Company D, Capt. E. Webre, commanding Wounded: Capt. E. Webre. Missing: Privates C. Narshtedt, J. Saunders.

Company E, Capt. S. Faulkner, commanding Killed: Private J. Cronan.

Missing: Lieut. C. Chisholm, Corporal G. Perkins, Privates J. E. Bell, J. Moore, C. Riley.

Company F, Capt. A. F. Pagnier, commanding Wounded: Capt. Pagnier. Missing: Serg't J. Newcomb, Privates A. Springer, F. Smith.

Company G, Lieut. T. L. Mills, commanding Wounded: Lieut. T. L. Mills, Private R. Foster. Missing: Serg't H. Dantin, Corp'l J. Kenner, Private A. Bejean.

Company H, Capt. L. Jastremski, commanding Missing: Capt. Jastremski, Sergts. E. Roubleau, W. Cunningham, A. McCasland, Corpl. Z. Borne, Privates A. Brignac, R. Linder.

Company I, Capt. P. Leclaire, commanding Killed: Capt. Leclaire. Private J. G. Metilieno. Missing: Sergts. A. Purkel, C. Mahoney, Corp'l P. Miller, Privates L. Bonetti, P. Maureau, F. Manchini.

Company K, Capt. A. Perrodin, commanding Missing: Capt. Perrodin, Lieuts. E. A. Seaton, J. Ryan, Serg't J. Courville, Corp'l Louis Nugent, Privates B. Ellender, J. D. Granger, J. Kennedy, W. F. Moss, M. Marcantel.

Flank Movement, May 19th, 1864.

Company C—Missing: Private J. O'Mally.

Company D—Killed: Private G. Tate. Missing: Private J. Sanders.

Flank Movement, June 3d, 1864.

Company C—Wounded: Corpl. C. Hammerick. Missing: Private M. Gorman.

Company F—Wounded: Private J. Labranch.

Company K—Wounded: Private J. Strange.

Battle of Monoccacy, Md., July 9th, 1864.

Company A—Wounded: Lieut. P. Barron.

Company C—Wounded: Corpl. C. Hammerick.

Company F—Wounded: Private Geo. Malone.

Combat near Cedar Creek, August 12th, 1864.

Company F   Wounded: Privates M. Cusach, F. Bartel.

Combat near Leetown, August 25th, 1864.

Company B—Killed: Private R. Doyle.

Company D—Killed: Private D. Rogers.

Company E   Wounded: Sergeant J. M. Bass.

Battle of Winchester, September 19th, 1864.

Field and staff Wounded: Col. Eug. Waggaman, Ensign T. G. Boyken. Killed: Lieut. and Acting Adj. H. Eustis.

Company A—Missing: Sergt. J. Ford, Private P. McLaughlin.

Company B—Killed: Private Hugh Hall.

Company C—Wounded: Sergt. P. Moran.

Company D—Killed: Private A Moffatt.

Company E—Missing: Private T. McCoy.

Company F—Missing: Sergeant F. Jorger.

Company G   Wounded: Lieut. P. Guzman.

Company H—Missing: Sergt. J. P. Usher.

Company I   Killed: Private V. Allis.
Company K   Missing: Private A. Lalonde.

Battle of Fisher's Hill, September 22d, 1864.

Company C—Missing: Lieut. L. F. Garic.
Company D—Missing: Sergt. J. Wilson, Privates O. Krauser, J. Connor.
Company F—Wounded: Ord. Sergt. J. Ulmer.
Company G—Missing: Private H. Prieur.
Company I—Wounded: Corpl. A. Jean Marie. Missing: Corp'l A. Galli.
Company K—Missing: Private J. H. Lindsay.

Battle of Cedar Creek, October 19th, 1864.

Field and staff   Missing: Major T. N. Powell.
Company A—Wounded: Capt. I. L. Lyons.
Company C—Wounded: Capt. J. Scott.
Company E—Wounded: Ord. Sergt. W. Carmichael. Missing: Private E. Stappleton, P. McCoy.
Company F—Killed: Private J. Labranche. Missing: Private F. Rasch.
Company G—Missing: Private T. Williamson.
Company I—Missing: Corporal. S. Ferri.
Company K—Missing: Sergt. J. G. Herrington, Privates Oliver R. Moss, N. D. Orcut.

Attack on Fort Steadman, March 25th, 1865.

Company C—Wounded: Sergt. T. Ford.
Company D—Wounded: Sergt. J. Wilson.
Company G—Missing: Privates T. Williamson, J. Edgar.
Company H—Wounded: Private P. Havery.
Company K—Killed: Lieut. Isaac Ryan.

Petersburg, April 3d, 1865.

Killed: Major T. N. Powell.
Company G—Missing: Private H. Prieur.

BIOGRAPHICAL AND HISTORICAL PAPERS RELATING TO LOUISIANA,
DURING AND SINCE THE WAR.

Organization of the Louisiana Brigades in Virginia.

HAYS' BRIGADE.

What was generally known as Hays' brigade was organized at Centreville with the 6th, 7th, 8th and 9th Louisiana regiments and Wheat's Battalion. Gen. Walker (afterwards killed), was its first commander, but gave place soon after appointment to Gen. Dick Taylor. The latter was transferred to the Trans-Mississippi at the time of the Seven Days' Fight, in the summer of 1862. Col. Seymour was the commander of the brigade in this prolonged engagement and was killed at its head during the struggle of the second day. He was succeeded by Gen. Hays, who became identified with it until 1864, at which time he was made Division General and sent to the Trans-Mississippi. Col. Penn, the officer next in rank, who had previously and afterwards been in command of this brigade, was also promoted to a generalship and assigned, and the two brigades were merged together. Thus consolidated they remained under Col. Waggaman until the close of the war.

NICHOLS' BRIGADE.

W. E. Starke, Colonel of 52nd Virginia in 1861; appointed Brigadier General July, 1862; killed in the battle of Sharpsburg, September 17th, 1862.

Francis T. Nichols, Captain of Company—in 8th Louisiana; promoted Colonel in 1862; appointed Brigadier General in December, 1862, and lost left arm; disabled in the battle of Chancellorsville by loss of left leg, May 2d, 1863.

L. H. Stafford, Colonel 9th Regiment; appointed Brigadier General in August, 1863; killed in the battle of Wilderness May 5th, 1864

Z. Yorke, Colonel of the 14th Louisiana; appointed Brigadier General May, 1864; disabled in the battle of Winchester by loss of left arm Sept. 19, 1864. At the same time the 1st and 2d Louisiana Brigades were consolidated and placed under command of Gen. Yorke. Col. Eugene Waggaman remained in command after the releiving of Gen. Yorke until the surrender.

Mandeville Marigny, appointed Colonel March, 1861; resigned July, 1862.
Jules C. Dennis, appointed Lieutenant Colonel May, 1861; resigned December, 1861.
F. Dumonteil, appointed Major May, 1861; resigned December, 1861.
Albert Fabre, appointed Adjutant May, 1861; resigned December, 1861.
Eugene Waggaman, elected Lieutenant Colonel January, 1862; appointed Colonel August, 1862.
Wm. H. Spencer, elected Major January, 1862; appointed Lieutenant Colonel July, 1862, and killed in the battle of Manassas, No. 2, August 30th, 1862.
John M. Leggett, appointed Major in July, 1862; appointed Lieutenant Colonel in December, 1862, and killed at the battle of Chancellorsville May 3d, 1863.
Henry C. Monier, appointed Major December, 1862, and Lieutenant Colonel in May, 1863.
Thomas N. Powell, appointed Major in June, 1863, and killed at the battle of Petersburg April 3d, 1865.
Henry Puissan, appointed Adjutant in June, 1862.

Co. A (Shepperd Guards).

Alfred Phillips, Captain; resigned January, 1862.
J. A. Cohen, 1st Lieutenant; elected Captain January, 1862, and killed in the battle of Manassas, No. 2, August 30th, 1862.
Isaac L. Lyons, 2nd Lieutenant; elected 1st Lieutenant in January, 1862; appointed Captain in September, 1862; wounded at battle of Cedar Creek.
Maurice Grunewald, 2d Lieutenant, jr.; resigned December, 1861.
Michael Carroll; elected 2d Lieutenant, jr., in December, 1861; appointed 2d Lieutenant in January, 1862, and resigned in November, 1862.
Daniel Mahoney; appointed 1st Lieutenant in November, 1862; wounded at Chancellorsville.
Patrick Barron; appointed 2d Lieutenant in November, 1862; wounded at Wilderness, Monaccacy and at Petersburg.

Co. B (Derbigny Guards).

Lea Bakewell, Captain; resigned August, 1861.
E. W. Huntington, 1st Lieutenant; elected Captain August, 1861, and resigned in January, 1862.
E. T. Fellowes, 2d Lieutenant; elected 1st Lieutenant August, 1861, and resigned in January, 1862.
Henry C. Marks, 2d Lieutenant, jr.; elected Captain in January, 1862, and killed in the battle of Malvern Hill July 1st, 1862.
James Buckner; appointed 1st Lieutenant in January, 1862; appointed Captain in July, 1862, and Regimental Quartermaster in December, 1862.
James Knowlton; appointed Captain in 1863; badly wounded and crippled at Mine Run.
Horatio Eustis; appointed 1st Lieutenant in 1863; killed in the battle of Winchester September, 1864.
Robert Bracken; appointed 2d Lieutenant in 1863.

Co. C (Hewitt Guards).

Richard Hewitt, Captain; resigned October, 1861.
C. Conrad, 1st Lieutenant; resigned October, 1861.
Thomas N. Powell, 2d Lieutenant; elected Captain in February, 1862; appointed Major in June, 1863.
Eugene Janin, 2d Lieutenant, jr.; elected 1st Lieutenant in February, 1862, and killed in the battle of Manasss, No. 2, August 31st, 1862.

James Scott; appointed 1st Lieutenant in November, 1862, and Captain in June, 1863; wounded at Gettysburg.
Louis F. Garic; appointed 2d Lieutenant in November, 1862.

Co. D (*Hawkins Guards*).

Chas. F. White, Captain; resigned October, 1861.
E. Williams, 1st Lieutenant; elected Captain in November, 1861 and resigned in September, 1862.
Ernest Webre, 2d Lieutenant; elected 1st Lieutenant November, 1861, and Captain in September, 1862; badly wounded at Gettysburg.
— Hawkins, 2d Lieutenant, jr.; elected 2d Lieutenant in November, 1861, and resigned in September, 1862.
Sam. H. May, elected 2d Lieutenant, jr. in November, 1861, and appointed 1st Lieutenant in September, 1862; badly wounded in the shoulder at Gettysburg.

Co. E (*Swamp Rangers*).

James Dickey, Captain; resigned December, 1861.
Albert Fabre, 1st Lieutenant and Acting Adjutant, resigned December, 1861; wounded at Manassas.
S. Cucullu, 2d Lieutenant; elected Captain in February, 1862, and resigned in November, 1863.
— Merrill, 2d Lieutenant, jr.; resigned in October, 1861.
Sam. Faulkner; elected 2d Lieutenant, jr., in October, 1861; 1st Lieutenant in February, 1862, and Captain in November, 1863; wounded at Gettysburg.
Chas. A. Chisholm, elected 2d Lieutenant in February, 1862, and 1st Lieutenant in November, 1863.

Co. F (*Louisiana Rebels*).

John M. Leggett, Captain; appointed Major in July, 1862.
Ernest Cucullu, 1st Lieutenant; resigned in May, 1862.
Ernest Miltenberger, 2d Lieutenant; resigned in October, 1861.
Albert F. Pagnier, 2d Lieutenant, jr.; elected 2d Lieutenant in November, 1861; 1st Lieutenant in May, 1862, and Captain in July, 1862; wounded at Spottsylvania.
Gus Taney; elected 2d Lieutenant, jr., in November, 1861, and resigned in February, 1862.
Albert Scanlan; elected 2d Lieutenant, jr., in February, 1862, and killed on picket April 3d, 1864.*
  *Scanlan was foreman in the Picayune office before the war.
Charles Cooper; elected 2d Lieutenant, jr., in June, 1862; 1st Lieutenant in July, 1862, and killed at the battle of Chancellorsville on May 3d, 1863.
Paul Guzman; elected 2d Lieutenant November, 1862.

Co. G (*Orleans Rangers*).

Edward Crevon, Captain; resigned December, 1861.
Arthur Raymond, 1st Lieutenant; resigned December, 1861.
John P. Montamat, 2d Lieutenant; resigned September, 1861.
Adolph Revoil, 2d Lieutenant, jr.; resigned December, 1861.
M. Arthur Guerin; elected 2d Lieutenant, jr., in September, 1861, and Captain in December, 1861; resigned June, 1862.
S. S. Rivas; elected 1st Lieutenant in December, 1861; Captain in June, 1862, and appointed Captain Commissary in July, 1862.
C. B. Marmillion; elected 2d Lieutenant in December, 1861; 1st Lieutenant in June, 1862, and Captain in July, 1862; wounded several times.
Chas. Bechnel; elected 2d Lieutenant, jr., in December, 1861; resigned in June, 1862.
Thos. Louis Mills; elected 1st Lieutenent June, 1862; wounded at Spottsylvania.

Louis H. Kendall; elected 2d Lieutenant June, 1862; wounded at Gettysburg.
S. Herrero; elected 2d Lieutenant, jr., June, 1862; wounded in three places at Sharpsburg.

(Co. H Orleans Blues).

Wm. H. Barnett, Captain; resigned January, 1863.
Charles Roussel, 1st Lieutenant; resigned September, 1862.
Emile A. Bozonier, 2d Lieutenant; resigned November, 1861.
Richard Clague, 2d Lieutenant, jr.; resigned January, 1862.
Victor Lobit; elected 2d Lieutenant, jr., November, 1861; resigned December, 1861.
Adam Alexander; elected 2d Lieutenant in January, 1862; appointed 1st Lieutenant in September, 1862; and killed in the battle of Sharpsburg on September 17th, 1862.
Leon Jastremski; appointed Captain in November, 1862; wounded at Chancellorsville.

Co. I (Orleans Skirmishers).

Eugene Waggaman, Captain; elected Lieutenant Colonel in January, 1862; badly wounded at Winchester September 19th, 1864.
Alphonse Canonge, 1st Lieutenant; resigned in March, 1862.

Henry D. Monier, 2d Lieutenant; elected Captain in January, 1862, and appointed Major in December, 1862; wounded at Chancellorsville.
Paul Forstall, 2d Lieutenant, jr.; resigned in May, 1862.
Alphonse Jonté; elected 2d Lieutenant in January, 1862, and appointed Captain in December, 1862; killed at the battle of Chancellorsville May 5th, 1863.
Henry Puissan; elected 1st Lieutenant in May, 1862, and appointed Adjutant in June, 1862, with rank of Captain; wounded at 2d Manassas.
Peter Leclaire; appointed 2d Lieutenant in August, 1862; 1st Lieutenant in December, 1862; Captain in May, 1863, and killed at the battle of Spottsylvania May 12th, 1864.
George Sauvé; elected 2d Lieutenant in August, 1863; badly wounded in the battle of the Wilderness.

Co. K (Confederate States Rangers).

Wm. H. Spencer, Captain; elected Major January, 1862; appointed Lieutenant Colonel August, 1862.
Michel Prudhhomme, 1st Lieutenant; died on the Peninsular in November, 1861.
E. A. Seaton, 2d Lieutenant; elected 1st Lieutenant in January, 1862; died in Fort Delaware in 1864.
Louis Prudhome, 2d Lieutenant, jr.; resigned November 1861.
Auguste Perrodin, elected Captain in January, 1862.
Octave Prudhomme, elected 2d Lieutenant in January, 1862.
Isaac Ryan, elected 2d Lieutenant, jr., in January, 1862; killed at siege Petersburg.

THE LOUISIANA BRIGADES IN VIRGINIA AND THEIR LAST COMMANDER.

*Journal of the Tenth Louisiana.**

In the hall of an elegant residence on St. Charles street hangs a massive basket-hilted sword, richly mounted in silver and bearing evident signs of considerable antiquity. Many dents hint that it has seen rude service, has been often used for the straight thrust or down cut, or perhaps in private quarrels in tierce and parry. The soldier who brought it here was a Spanish Commandante. Possibly the blade has received the ice-brook temper of Toledo and been used in the Moorish wars when Christian fought against Paynim, or perhaps in some of the Indian fights mentioned in the early annals of this State. Whatever its previous history its next possessor, after the death of the Commandante, was a distinguished senator, who terminated in a duel a brilliant political career. Its present owner carried it in Lee's and Jackson's battles, cutting his way with it in the desperate bayonet charge at Malvern Hill, into the enemy's line, but having to lose it at last, and only recovering it by a sort of romance accident. It was last used at Lee's surrender, when the then commander of the Louisiana Brigades ordered his men to ground arms. But it finally came back to its old resting place, and there it hangs now a little rusty and half forgotten by the lucky owner, who survived to bring it home, or only referred to when, with slippered feet and surrounded by friends he tells of former encounters, or of some imminent peril in the deadly breach. It is pleasant to record that its present possessor, too modest to allow of mention of his name, is one of the happy Sinbads who survive their shipwrecks, and who live to enjoy gaily the honors and emoluments which better

*In the facts given in this paper Major E. D. Willett, and Captains Manning, I. L. Lyons, Puissant, A. S. Bythe and other officers of the Louisiana Brigade have been consulted. The narrative is especially indebted to Capt. Henry Monier, who on many occasions was in command of the 10th regiment, for a clear and carefully prepared journal of the war. Nearly the whole of this has been quoted with scarcely any change. The company rolls, casulties, etc., are contributions from the same hand.

days bring with them in the pleasant company of their families and friends.

Sinbad, if the truth was known, probably went, like Capt. Cook, on one voyage too many, which he had no opportunity afterward of relating; just as has happened to Dr. Livingston and the balloon men of recent date; and just as happened to many a famous old campaigner and soldier, who pushed their fortunes too far. Destiny affixes the word "Danger" to some men's career; peril follows them and hangs the Damocles sword over their heads, and the best fortune they can hope for is the sudden dramatic death which Cæsar asked, and which, as if his prayer had been answered, he with the last hundred of the Cæsarian name and blood ultimately encountered.

Still a few of the danger seekers are permitted not only to hunt for the bubble reputation at the cannon's mouth, but to bear the prize away; to return home and "hang the old sword in its place;" and crowned with bays and substantial honors, to forget the hailstorm of bullets and the whirlwind of battle.

There were forty officers allowed to a regiment at one time, and of these 31 of the 10th were killed or wounded. The regiment lost 12 color bearers by death on the battle field, 6 alone at Chancellorsville, and 20 wounded. The following officers are known to have fought all through and survived the war: Waggaman,* Lyons, Mahoney, Janin, Buckner, Knowl-

---

*Waggaman is the great-grand son of Baron de Bruner, a Commandante of the Province of Louisiana in the days of Spanish and French domination, and is the son of Senator Waggaman, who for six years represented this State in the United States Senate. In 1843 one of the much talked of events of the day was the death of the Senator in a duel growing out of the bitterness at the time of political strife. The spot where he with so many others fell a victim to honor is still pointed out at the Oaks.

After graduating at St. Mary's College, in Baltimore, the war found him assisting his mother in the management of the large estate left by his father. But fate had not destined him for this quiet life. The storm which was then lowering over the country, at once suggested to a man of his active and stirring disposition, the career and field in which his talents would find their fullest exercise. With the first note of alarm he set to work to organize a company in Jefferson Parish, among the sons of neigboring planters. As horses were there easily to be obtained and every one accoustomed to travel mounted, the organization almost necessarily took the shape of cavalry. But horses at the commencement of the war were not what horses became afterwards, and the exigencies of the incipient Confederate government did not admit of the necessary transportation to the scene of service. The company after having learned the cavalry drill and secured their cavalry outfit, were unwilling to attach themselves to any other arm of service, in spite of a strong effort upon Waggaman's part (and with probably some after regrets of their own) to induce them at once to enlist as infantry. Finding himself now alone he joined Col. Mandeville Marigny in organizing his regiment, together with Captains Alfred Philips, I. L. Lyons, Cohen, and others.

As for Capt. Phillips he was a favorite of fortune. He was well educated, handsome and single; elected a professor in the University of Louisiana, and taken as a partner

4

ton, Eustis, Brocken, Scott, Garcia, Webre, May, Faulkner, Chisholm, Gusman, Kindall, Herero, Jastremski, Monier, Puissant, Saucier, Perrodin, Prudhomme; nearly all of these received one or more wounds. Without having authentic data at hand for the other regiments, it is believed that their casualties were equally great.

This statement is made now because the time has arrived when, from policy, a dispostion is shown to speak of those who served in the late war as the refuse of society, and the officers as "commanders of 60 roustabouts who served through the war without receiving a scratch."

The 10th regiment, in the month of July, proceeded to the "Peninsula" and remained on Warwick River near Lee's Mill during the dreary year which followed the commencement of the war, and which period of weariness and despondency and absolute loathing of life the old soldier remembers with more horror and disgust than the misery he ever after experienced from hard marching, cold, hunger and all his other ills put together.* The time, too, devoted to acquiring the first lessons

---

of Christian Roselius, the most prosperous member of the New Orleans Bar. But all of these advantages and a fortune of $200,000 besides, did not keep him from dying a young man in the summer of 1875.

January 26.—Secession of Louisiana, and Montgomery Convention, shortly after. Each State called on for a quota of troops.

Mandeville Marigny was commissioned among others to raise a regiment of infantry. Col. Marigny was a gentleman of tall commanding figure, and probably at that time one of the best specimens of the French Creole (before broken with age), in physique, general appearance, manners, accomplishments, that the State has produced. His father who resigned a title to become an American, was old Bernard Marigny, who once owned, besides other possessions, one-half of the land upon which New Orleans is built, and who spent a $500,000 plantation in hospitality to Louis Phillippe and his suite, when the latter was traveling as an exile in this country. The King of the French showed his gratitude after his accession, to the extent of having Bernard's son entered as a pupil in a French Military School, and the talents of Mandeville secured him subsequently advancement and position in the French army. He afterwards returned to Louisiana, and was received with great honor by the people of his native city, who besides other testimonials of their esteem elected him to several profitable offices. His popularity soon enabled him, after receiving his commission, to obtain as many companies as was necessary to make up his regiment. From those that offered at Camp Moore the companies as *given on page* 250 were selected.

*July 29th—Regiment departed for Virginia by the Jackson Railroad.

August 3—Arrived in Richmond after a fatiguing journey; received with great honor by the citizens and Confederate authorities. Camped at the Fair Grounds. The testimonials of favor here shown by ladies and citizens were remembered by the old soldiers as among the pleasantest souvenirs of the war.

August 18th—Ordered to the Peninsula.

August 23d—Marched—the first one made—under heavy rain from Williamsburg to Eutopia Bluff, on the James. Roads made slippery by the rains, and marching very severe on raw troops. Temporary Camp for a portion of the regiment. The right wing sent, under Lieut. Col. Dennis, six miles below the Bluff.

Sept. 13th—Left wing proceeds to Lee's Mills and go into camp. Joined a few days after by the right. Men set to work at constructing fortifications and building corduroy roads. Spades and pickaxes so disgustingly plentiful that the mere sight of them was enough to send men to the hospital. The fortifications finished, winter quarters were built, and pronounced by Magruder to be the best in his army. Meanwhile steady drills, parades, guard duty and frequent expeditions to innumerable points, with a view to deceiving the enemy.

in military discipline, the establishment of attachments and friendships, and in understanding individual eccentricities in a military organization formed a very trying period, and until the details in the life of a soldier had become a pleasant habit, instead of an irksome task, there was no comfort or happiness for either officers or men. They each had to learn to work and pull together. Fortunate indeed were those officers, who succeeded in maintaining discipline and good understanding, at an early day, in their companies, and who, instead of making the hearts of men sore by galling and needless tasks, could while away the long hours not occupied in duty in their tents, with such stray volumes as chance would send in their way.

From this monotonous and half solitary life Capt. WAGGAMAN was one day aroused by an incident as pleasing as it was unexpected. He was now informed that the vacancy in the office of Lieut. Colonel* had been supplied with his name. He was the best officer for the situation and the men knew and recognized the fact.

About the same time McClellan arrived in the Peninsula, and the first shot fired was directed upon the redoubt in which the 10th Regiment had been stationed.† The position of

---

*Lieut. Michael Prudhome dies and his body sent to St. Martin's Parish.
Jan 15th—Reorgainzation, Waggaman elected Lieut. Colonel; W. H. Spencer, Major.
March 31, 1862—Picket duty at Young's Mill. McClellan advances with 120,000 men. A wounded scout reports the enemy two miles distant. Position taken on the high grounds around Warwick Court House. The gleam of the enemy's bayonets now first seen glistening in the forest, and the command given to load. It is answered with a yell. The men very much disgusted at being ordered from headquarters to fall back.
April 5th—Drew's Battalion fire a shot. Furious cannonade from the Federals which is responded to—loss in the regiment 20. The next day some firing and both armies for some days after remain in the same position.
The 10th and Drew's Battalion under Gen. McLain.
April 16th—The enemy capture a dam which they break and attempt a crossing. Checked in their first assault. On attempting a second the 10th came to the front at a double quick. Cheers and yells of the latter are followed by a wavering and a falling back of the Federals across the dam after a loss of 500 on their part.
May 3d—Retreat to Richmond commenced. The 10th Regiment take an active hand in the battle at Williamsport. Sent to guard a road south of Petersburg.
May 6th—Move all night and at noon; following day, bivouac at New Kent Court House near the Chickahominy. After some marching and countermarching camp until May 13, at which time Col. Marigny, who is disgusted at the favoritism shown at Richmond, to his prejudice, is sent to organize the cavalry of Mississippi and Louisiana. Col. Waggaman takes command of the 10th.
June 2—A. P. Hill sounds the preluding note to the Seven Days Fight.
June 9th—Battle of Malvern Hill. Ordered forward in the final desperate charge. Waggaman in command.

†April 6th—While company F (Orleans Rebels) was out on picket Lieut. Alfred Scanlan of said company at a late hour proceeded to make the rounds on the skirmish line. He mistook his way, got beyond the line into the woods, and was finally hailed and challenged by a sentry. Discipline was then very rigid—the men raw in military experience, and his response when he answered back was not heard by the sentinel. The sentinel (poor Hays

Magruder's forces was critical now. Upon a slender line of 11,000 extending from Warwick River to the York, the whole of McClellan's army were moving. This was the period when the shallow rivulet known as Warwick River, not ordinarily more than 18 inches deep, was dammed up in such a way as to make it a line of defence, and to render it so deep that men were not unfrequently drowned in its accumulated waters. This also was the time when stove pipes were transformed into Quaker guns, and every artifice used to deceive the enemy. Finally the army of Johnson arrived only to return again to Richmond, and shortly after the joy-awakening intelligence was received that the Louisiana troops were to be put in motion. Then commenced the first of those marches which carried the Pelican standards through the fights around Richmond, through the valleys, over the mountains, and across the rivers of Virginia, and into so many dangers that the old soldiers not unfrequently have forgotten their details, and can only remember in a general way that some fifteen or twenty fights or skirmishes occurred during a given month or around a particular locality.

We need not dwell in detail therefore on their services on the Chickahominy, in whose dense swamps the men were for weeks encamped. But in the storming of Malvern Hill the 10th Louisiana, that day commanded by Col. WAGGAMAN, were undoubtedly the heroes. These men were the last that were ordered up to the frowning guns of McClellan's almost unassailable position, and the only ones that succeeded in penetrating the enemy's lines.

A daring attempt in the first place had been made to flank Malvern Hill; but this movement had been met by a superior flanking party of the enemy. The brigade now pressed forward across the open field fronting Malvern Hill,

---

of Co. F) did as he had been instructed to do, fired, and hearing a groan, ran forward. Reaching the spot and bending over to see his victim he recognized in the dying man the face of a gallant officer, who had won the esteem of his men by his soldierly bearing and amiable manners. The sentinel was still standing silent and motionless when the sergeant, alarmed by the shot brought out the picket line. Litters, tender care, and the surgeon's art proved of no avail. He sank rapidly and his body still lies where his comrades put it in the little church grave yard near Lee's Mills. Scanlin before the war was foreman of the Picayune office.

with the ardor of young soldiers panting for their first laurels, and ignorant of the madness which had doomed so many of their number to cruel wounds, or certain death. As they advance the troops on the flank give way, though all of Semmes' brigade continue on gallantly, in spite of the waning light. When within five hundred yards of the Federals, the brigade reformed, and the desparate cry rung out : "Fix bayonets, —CHARGE"—commands almost equivalent to a death sentence. But with the natural ardor of the troops from the Pelican State the men labored up the crest of the plateau immediately in front of 33 pieces of Artillery. Up the hill they go at a double quick, Col. WAGGAMAN jumping imprudently far in advance of the regiment, but the men tearing on after him. On the last fifty yards of the charge comes the strain. It lasts but five minutes. In that time 127 men are lost out of 272. So withering was the storm of shell and bullets with which they were received, that at one time they walked over a whole regiment who were lying down, colors and all, and who appeared in the dusky twilight to be so many corpses. Onward still the little band pursued its way, although unsupported by the other troops, until it crossed bayonets with the Federal infantry. It thus happened (one of the rarest occurences of the war) that the whole of the 10th Louisiana engaged in a bayonet struggle along almost their entire line, with a force fifteen times greater than their own number. The advanced line of the Federals having been driven back the 10th finds itself among their canoneers. While Dean, a brave Irishman, was receiving his death wound at the side of the leader of the 10th by a bayonet through the neck, the latter succeeded in knocking up the muskets in his immediate front and in cutting a path as far as the second line of the enemy's artillery.* His death seemed inevitable. Cries of " Kill him," " Bayonet him," sounded on every side. His command, which it may be said,

---

*Major Chase, who constructed the principal Fort at Pensacola. stated in a report made to Washington, that the charge of the Louisianians at Malvern Hill was more desperate though less known than that of the allied troops at Balaclava. The chances of surviving the fight were so few that during the night, after the enemy had withdrawn, some of Waggaman's friends went to look for his body.

in passing had been ordered forward by a military error, and never for a moment had a ghost of a chance of success, were of course nearly all either killed or captured by the formidable infantry line in their immediate front. Those of the 10th who succeeded in stumbling back over the bodies of their fallen comrades, owed their escape to the darkness. The Colonel of the 10th was captured (along with Capt. Isaac Lyons). That night tired and worn out they supped off of the bleeding beef allowed the prisoners, and slept on the piles of shucks which their captors awarded them—perhaps as a compliment to their gallantry—and were shortly after sent off with the transports to the North. They remained prisoners for a considerable time at Fort Warren, near Boston, and having met sympathizing friends in Baltimore did not fare badly.

As to what occurred among the Louisiana troops during the subsequent months, the following memoranda, taken from the accurate and interesting manuscript of Capt. Monier, will show:

July 7th—The troops placed in the breast-works about Richmond.

July 29th—The Louisiana troops organized into brigades and put under A. P. Hill. The 10th sent to Rocketts and put under command Gen. W. C. Starke—a thirty years resident of the Crescent City—along with the 1st, 2nd, 9th and 15th, together with Coppen's Zouaves and the Chasseurs à Pied. Gen. Starke had been a large cotton dealer in New Orleans, knew the habits and character of his troops and was well suited to his position.

July 31st—Brigade under command of Col. Stafford start by the cars to reinforce Jackson. Bivouac at Gordonsville to right of the railroad.

August 2d—Camp 4¼ miles from town near a saw mill.

August 6th—Move forward, and at break of day, on the 9th, through Orange Court House, and then cross the Rapidan. After picketing and counter marching, halt near Cedar Run, at the foot of Slaughter Mountain. At 6¼, P. M., after harassing and rapid marching, the brigade is led to with in a mile of Jackson's battlefield. The brigade stacks arms to rest in a wood; ten minutes after, started forward on the double quick, until they came to a stubble field where wheat was in the shock ; formed and advanced through a bloody cornfield where a battle had just been fought; then through a wood and then into another field. Here they were exposed to a galling fire, until darkness ended the combat and permitted them to rest where they had fought.

The day after Companies C and F picketed under Capts. T. Q. Powell and A. F. Payonier, and held their ground against a Federal advance with a loss of 4 killed and 3 wounded.

August 11th—After lighting camp fires the brigade falls back to the Rapidan. Cross at sunrise, near Liberty Mill. Bivouac at Orange Court House (12th). Pitch camp at Gordonsville. Brigade here attached to Jackson's old Stonewall division, under command of Gen. Talliaferro.

August 20th—Break camp.

August 26th—Picket at Manassas Junction—right under Maj. Spencer, left under Capt. John M. Leggett. Commissary stores exceedingly plentiful here and could be obtained by the car load. Any one who wanted clothing and something to eat had only to break open a box, case or barrel and help himself, taking care to destroy what he could not carry off. Often in after days when the men were hungry and badly shod, the recollection of the immense stores here destroyed recurred to their mind.

August 28th—Sharp engagement, until sunset, along the Warrentown Turnpike, at which time it became severe until 9; Talliaferro and many field officers wounded. Starke placed in command of the division, Stafford of the brigade.

August 29th—The woods to the front blue with Federals. Capt. Perrodon's company (K) picketed and hold their ground until the commands 'fall in," "fix bayonets," are given. The men answered it with a yell, and started off on a double quick on their own impulse. They carried everything before them, even the second line of the Federal reserve. Lieut. Thos. Mills, of Co. G, captured a piece; great numbers of killed strewed the field and 500 prisoners were captured. The 10th was relieved at sundown by the brave Col. Forno with the 1st and allowed to go back and rest a little before the approaching decisive battle. As the Louisianians marched back they were complimented by Old Stonewall and greeted along the line by prolonged cheers.

August 30th—A hard day's work from sunrise (at which time the men fell in and commenced double quicking) until late at night. Jackson, whose situation was now extremely critical, ordered them to hold the railroad embankment at all hazards, and they held it with the loss of many of their men, including Col. Spencer. He is succeeded, during 1862, in command of the regiment, by an excellent officer, Capt. H. D. Monier. So desperate was this day's fight that at one time the Confederate and Yankee standards were not 20 feet apart. Then ammunition became scarce and the brigade fired with the care of old hunters. Finally, as the enemy were once more advancing, the ammunition gave out. It was here that the Louisianians laid down their muskets and drove back the Federals with rocks. At this moment Barksdale's troops came up and hastened their flight.

The Brigade now marched a little distance towards the ammunition wagons, when Jackson rode up. His simple words of "Louisianians I need you once more" made the men forget all of their weariness, and back they went over the railroad and into the woods. Here they obtained ammunition by removing from the killed and wounded of the enemy, who had previously held this ground, their ammunition pouches. As the men pressed onward and formed themselves for a charge a tremendous yell and a deafening rattle of artillery greeted their ears. The North Carolina troops whom the 2nd brigade had come to support, had just captured a splendid battery. This ended the fight for them, and the men slept where they were. Killed: Lieut. Col. Spencer, Capt. Cohen and Lieut. Janin. Wounded: were Capts. Cucullu and Terrill, Adjt. Tiersan and Lieut. Peter Leclaire.

Sept. 1—Heavy fighting for the brigade about Germantown.
Sept. 2—Battle of Oxhill—Picket the Fairfax Road.
Sept. 5—Cross the Potomac at White's Ford. Sept. 6th—Camp 3 miles beyond Frederick.

While pasing through this city, the first the Confederates had seen for many months well stored with every sort of supplies, some of the roughs gave way to brutal excesses, which led to charge being made to Gen. Jackson of maltreatment of ladies by a gang of miscreants. Gen. Jackson thereupon ordered the 2d Louisiana Brigade to be marched to town for identification, for an obvious reason, as the guilty parties had been described as foreigners. Gen. Stark, who was sensitive to the reputation of his brigade, refused to obey, as casting a stigma on his command, unless the order was made general for the other troops at the time in town. Stark was thereupon placed under arrest. Investigation meanwhile shewed that the malefactors came from Jackson's old Stonewall brigade. The guilty parties however, owing to the lapse of time or opportunity, were never punished. As for Starke, he enforced orders so rigidly that some of his officers were put under arrest for neglecting to keep their men in ranks.

Sept. 10th—Brigade marched to Harper's Ferry.
Sept. 15th—The white flag waves from Bollivar's Heights; 11,000 men and great quantiy of arms and stores surrendered.
Sept. 16th—Cross at Shepherdstown and take place in line of battle at Sharpsburg on the extreme left. Heavy shelling from sundown till late at night.
Sept. 17th—Terrible cannonade at dawn, and musketry fire; the line thrown in great confusion by an overwhelming Federal advance. Gen. Starke takes Gen. Jones' place, who has been carried from the field, and while endeavoring to restore the line of battle is shot from his horse. Stafford takes his place and orders the brigade to charge and avenge his loss. Drives the Federals into a cornfield 500 yards beyond the Hagerstown Road. Here the men are assailed by a desperate fire, rear and flank, and are driven foot by foot; reinforced on the edge of a wood they again shove forward and drive the Federals, until they are in turn reinforced. The brigade now marched by the left flank to right of Stuart, and face the enemy who are there massed. The brigade holds its ground with desperate tenacity. At 10½ they are being forced back and send to Early for assistance. They are now reinforced and drive back the enemy in a charge. The report of Capt. Henry D. Monier, then in command of the 10th regiment, shows a casualty of 71 men and 4 officers out of 207 muskets and 11 officers.

In the Hollywood Cemetery the body of Gen. W. E. Starke now rests. He was killed in Sharpsburg while endeavoring to stay the flight of a brigade of troops from his native State, (Va.) This brigade had been exposed to a terrible fire and had become demoralized. Thereupon Gen. Starke, abandoning for the time the command of the Louisiana brigades, who were ordered up to support the former, seized the colors of the Old Dominion and ordered a charge along his whole line. These colors were waving over him when he met death like a true son of the Old Dominion and of his adopted State. In the same railing sleeps the body of his son, the gallant Adjt. of the 59th Va.

During the desperate fighting which has been briefly shown in the journal of Major Monier, Col. Seymour who had been in command of the First Louisiana Brigade, had been killed and Gen. Nicholls dangerously wounded. A word of biography about two gallant officers whose names are respected as much as any that Louisiana contributed to the war, will not be seen without interest by the reader.*

Col. Isaac G. Seymour was unanimously elected commander of the 6th La. He was with his regiment in the battle of Manassas, was assigned charge of the rear guard at Johnson's

---

*For the gallant services of Gen. Hays and other officers not now mentioned, the reader is referred to foregoing chapters of this work.

retreat to Richmond, and was with Jackson in his most brilliant campaign. He fought the First Louisiana Brigade for two days at Richmond; at Gaines' Mills he was struck by two minie balls and instantly killed.

Col. Seymour occupied a position in New Orleans for integrity and ability which few citizens have equaled. After fighting in the Indian and Mexican wars, and after having been for six years elected Mayor of Macon, Georgia, Col. Seymour became editor of the New Orleans Bulletin, and remained its proprietor until the time of his death. It was conducted after his election to the command of the 6th, by his son Major Wm. J. Seymour (until suppressed by Butler), assisted by our oldest and most reliable commercial writer Mr. J. C. Dennies. A curious circumstance attending Col. Seymour's death, was that the acting editors were sent for many months to prison at Fort Jackson for writing and publishing an obituary notice in which Col. Seymour was said to have soldiered and died from a sense of duty. His son Major Wm. J. Seymour became afterwards Chief of Staff of the 1st Louisiana Brigade.

Apropos of journalism, it may be said here that scarcely any one was connected with newspapers during and previous to the war, but what did more or less military service, and many of them did not discover that the pen was mightier than the sword until the struggle ended. In the latter class was Colonels Jos. Hanlon, J. O. Nixon, Majors Israel Gibbons, Dan. Scully, Judge Burwell, Jack Wagner, Baker, Quintero, and many others whose names are not now recalled.

Gen. Francis P. Nicholls, who lost two of his limbs while leading on the Louisiana, troops in Virginia, was born in Donaldsonville, Parish of Ascension, on the 20th of August, 1834, and was the son of Thomas C. Nicholls, one of the judges of the Court of Errors and Appeals in this State. He died in 1846, and in 1852 was followed by the General's mother. This lady was Louisa H. Drake, the sister of Joseph Rodman Drake and the author of the "Culprit Fay," one of the most exquisite poems ever composed by American genius.

The future General had five brothers and two sisters. The

elder two of the brothers gained great distinction in the Mexican war, in Blanchard's company of Louisiana Volunteers, and were favorably mentioned in the military reports of the day. The appreciation of the citizens of Ascension, was shown by the presentation to each of the brothers of a sword upon their return

Gen. Nicholls entered West Point as a cadet in 1851, and in 1855 when he graduated, he was assigned to duty as Brevet 2d Lieutenant in the 2d U. S. Artillery, stationed in the Everglades of Florida. He was thence transferred to the 3d U. S. Artillery as 2d Lieutenant and remained in it—stationed at Fort Yuma on the Colorado River—until October 1856; he then resigned and returned to Louisiana.

Having received his license at the bar he commenced practising law in Ascension. After a few months he removed to Assumption and formed a partnership with Alphonse Gentile, under the name of Gentile & Nicholls. This firm was dissolved the next year. He then formed a partnership with his brother Laurence D. Nicholls, under the name of L. D. & F. T. Nicholls. The General in 1860 married Miss Catharine Guion, of Lafourche, and is now the happy father of six children.

At the breaking out of the war, his brother in Ascension, and the General in Assumption, organized together a company from the two parishes, which went to Camp Moore under the name of the Phœnix Company. It afterwards became company "K" of the 8th Louisiana Regiment, with Francis as Captain, L. D. Nicholls 1st Lieutenant, Victor Saint Martin, 2d Lieutenant and Benjamin F. Birdsall as Junior 2d Lieutenant. When the company was thrown into the 8th Regiment, the General was elected Lieutenant Colonel of the Regiment. His brother became Captain of Company "K," and the other officers rose each one step, Martin being elected as Junior 2d Lieutenant. Captain L. D. Nicholls was afterwards killed in the battle of Gaines' mills in the "Seven Days Fight" before Richmond, Victor Saint Martin became Captain, and was killed at Gettysburg; Lieut. Birdsall was killed at the battle of 2d Manassas.

Lieutenant Whit. Martin resigned, returned to Louisiana and organized a company which was thrown into the 26th Louisiana Regiment. He became the Major of the 26th, and was killed at the siege of Vicksburg. These deaths and changes caused vacancies which were filled by Williams Sims, Frederick Duffel and Dodridge Smith.

Captain Sims was for a very long while at Johnson's Island a prsisoner. They were all good officers. The 8th Regiment was at Mitchell's Ford in reserve at 1st Manassas, and under fire, but not actively engaged. It went into the Valley of Virginia in the Spring of 1862 under Gen. Jackson's command.

At the first serious fight in the Valley (that of Winchester) the 8th was on the extreme left of our line. In attacking the enemy's position and charging, the General was shot in the left arm and his elbow shattered. The arm only was amputated. The wound however was so serious that the following week he came very near dying.

On the day of the amputation, our army fell back, and he was left in the hands of the enemy. Nicholls was then exchanged at the end of September, 1862, and was immediately promoted Colonel of the 15th Louisiana, a new regiment made from a battalion and two detached companies.

A few days afterwards however, he was appointed Bigadier General and assigned to the 2d Louisiana Brigade, then at Skin Run's Neck near Fredericksburg. The Brigade was composed of the 1st, 2d, 10th, 14th and 15th Louisiana Regiments. It was part of the force which, under Gen. Jackson, turned the enemy's flank near Chancellorsville. During the night of Saturday and just after Gen. Jackson was wounded, the enemy opened a very heavy artillery fire down the Plank Road on which his Brigade was. A shell passed through and killed his horse, and in passing out took off his left leg entirely, just at the ankle.

On recovering from his wound, which when healed incapacitated him for active service in front, he was assigned to the command of the Lynchburg District, and there remained until August, 1864. He was now ordered to the Tras-Mississippi as Superintendent of the Conscript Bureau of that Department, with headquarters at Marshall, Texas. He was acting as such at the end of the war,

On his return home, he resumed the practice of his profesion and is still engaged in it.

The officers of the 8th Regiment, were : Henry B. Kelly, Colonel; Francis T. Nicholls, Lt. Colonel; John B. Prados, Major; T. D. Lewis, Adjutant.

The officers in the re-organization of the Regiment in 1862, were: Henry B. Kelly, Colonel; F. T. Nicholls, Lt. Colonel; T. D. Lewis, Major.

Col. Kelly is now practising law in New Orleans.

Major Lewis afterwards became Colonel of the 8th, and was killed at Gettysburg. Alcibiade DeBlanc, of St. Martin, was Colonel at the close of the war.

Capt. William Sims is now at Donaldsonville. Lieutenant Frederick Duffel at the same place.

Capt. William P. Harper of the 7th Louisiana Regiment, afterwards Sheriff of New Orleans, was the Acting Assistant Adjutant General of the Brigade whilst Gen. Nicholls had command, Lieutenant Samuel C. Hipburn his Aid-de-Camp. Capt. Victor Saint Martin of Company " K," 8th Louisiana, acted as Assistant Adjutant General for a short time.

Major Frank Rawle now a prominent broker in New Orleans, was the Brigade Quartermaster.

J. M. Goodman was Quartermaster of the 8th Regiment.

Dr. Semmes, a brother of T. J. Semmes, was Surgeon, and John E. Duffel the Assistant Surgeon.

The other Surgeons of the various Louisiana Regiments, so far as known, were: Drs. Stevens (2d), Assistant Surgeon Martin (7th), Dr. Davis (9th), Dr. Smith (10th), Dr. T. S. Taney, afterwards Surgeon of the Brigade (15th), Dr. White. Dr. Egan of Louisiana (Regiment not known) was killed in the discharge of his duty at Sharpsburg. Dr. Sauve was wounded at Winchester. Another Surgeon, name not known, was killed at Martinsburg.

After Gettysburg, eighty Surgeons, left in charge of the wounded, found themselves herded together at Fort McHenry, in a suffocating manner, and compelled at times to do menial duty. When they afterwards went back, they were ordered to examine the Richmond prisoners, and they then made oath that the inmates of the latter fared infinitely better than had the Surgeons left behind in the cause of humanity.

Three other New Orleans physicians, Drs. De Blanc, Chastant and Fomento (the latter at the Louisiana Hospital), were Confederate Surgeons.

WAGGAMAN commanded the Louisiana Brigades in the Valley campaigns of 1864, and his conduct is always spoken of with feeling by the surviving veterans, when leading his men in the victorious charge, rolling the first line back upon the second, and capturing artillery; or lastly at the Winchester battle of the 19th September, when victory definitely turned her force against the Confederates, he was seen wounded and struggling like a maniac, with his 'bridle-reign between his teeth, to stay the waning fortunes of the Confederacy.

He is then remembered when the "All is lost" of a great battle was heard, and nothing was seen but flying cavalry, wagons and ambulances—as covering the route of the Confederate army; and shortly after, at Fisher's Hill (where the Southern Cause was so desperate that not one man could have escaped if properly pursued) as doing his duty, even while suffering with an inflamed wound.

In the well known raid to Washington which Early made during the seige of Petersburg, WAGGAMAN'S command took an active part. Early's corps gave the enemy an eternal cleaning out at Martinsburg, and one of the incidents of the campaign, was the bivouac of the Louisiana Brigade at Chrystal Springs, Montgomery Blair's well known residence near Washington. At one time it looked as if the Crescent City Regiments would stack arms in the National Capital, and give a point and emphasis to their 1500 miles march, by serving that city as the Romans did Carthage. And had the right move been made, had there not been a delay of three days on the part of Early in commencing the attack, according to the Federal authorities, Washington would undoubtedly have been captured.

The Valley campaign was the turning point of the war. There was an extraordinary amount of strategy and hard marching developed and but little victory. So desperate was the race between the opposing armies at one time to reach Martinsburg first, that sometimes the hostile columns would be marching by parallel roads not over half a mile apart. But the fiat had gone forth that Ilium was to be destroyed, and the heroic valor of no corps or commander could save her.

Thus weary weeks and months of hard fighting rolled on, bringing Plutonian shadows for some and promotion to others. Sixteen battles and fights had been fought, and in one of them (Winchester) every single officer on horseback had been wounded.

The ranking Generals Hays, Starke, Nicholls and Yorke, having been killed, crippled up, or assigned to other duties, and at the time, when death seemed more probable than distinction or promotion, WAGGAMAN was still at the head of the Louisiana troops,* with Alcibiade DeBlanc as the ranking officer of Hays' Brigade. None envied such honor at the time. The truth was that the life of an officer on horseback, or a flag bearer was not then thought to be worth a week's rations, and promotion only brought to mind the Trappist maxim " Brother, thou too must die."

In the following February the Brigades were ordered to the Petersburg line at Hatcher's Run, and there, like many other

---

*The gallant Col. Peck who preceded Waggaman in rank, had been made a General and been sent elsewhere. He died since the war. He was a man not only worthy of remembrance for what he did, from a soldier's sense of duty, but was a remarkable man in other respects. He was nearly six feet and a half high, and though of a daring nature never received a wound during the whole war. He rode a horse equally large and stout in proportion. His brother who was the Porthos of the Confederate army, was six feet nine inches high, and lost his life in consequence of his extraordinary statue—that is by having his head shot off. Gen Peck was in command of the Louisiana Brigades during much of the war, greatly distinguishing himself at the Monoccacy in Early's raid, and Hatcher's Run. He was a man of such modest nature, that although a speaker of sentiment and fire, and possessed of considerable wealth and influence, his name never appeared before the public. When he died, none of the journals knew that Louisiana had lost one of her bravest and most distinguished sons.

gallant veterans, were compelled to realize slowly, step by step, day by day, the destruction of long years of hope and the certain death of those patriotic dreams, which had for many years hovered around the Southern soldier's pillow.

On the last of February the men took their final position in the breastworks about Petersburg. Immediately to the rear of their position was the Dædalus labarynth of underground roads and passage ways, cut for the purpose of sheltering the soldiers in marching, from the never ceasing rain and hail of enfilading bullets, and which rendered it at the same time, difficult for even the experienced, with no Ariadne's clue, to find entrance or exit. Nearly touching the right was the site where the Confederate fort had been blown up by undermining—the final burying ground of hundreds of brave men.

A week before the final *coup* was given to Secessia, Waggaman was summoned at night to a Division Council of war, in which the question of making an offensive movement and the capture of the opposing fort by a storming party, was discussed. It was here that a high tribute was paid to the courage of the Louisiana Brigades, when an assault upon Grant's lines had been determined upon, and the duties of the various officers assigned. "On account of the valor of your troops" said Gen. Evans, "you will be allowed the honor of leading off in the attack. This you will make with unloaded arms." This honor of course meant that the Louisiana troops were, as had happened in nearly every battle before, to be the Forlorn Hope, to suffer the brunt of the attack; or in other words that they were to be allowed the same opportunities for distinction, that David permitted Uriah, when in love with the latter's wife.

At three o'clock in the morning, Waggaman who had been watching all night, silently awakened his men and moved forward, outside of the breastworks. In so doing his command during the darkness and confusion, was cut in two by the marching of other Confederate commands. He passed out through Grace's Salient to the objective point of the Federal works and the key of their position, towards the guns of Fort

Steadman. Though the men had been quietly awakened and preparations had been made as noiseless as possible, no advance of the sort could of course be undertaken without something of the confused hum, which always indicates that a camp is in motion, or that some great movement is on foot. As the column pushed forward, it had to contend with the darkness and the boggy soil, and at one time the command seemed in danger of being entirely cut up, in the general mixing up of regiments, and in the treacherous character of the ground. Waggaman himself had to be extricated from the mud of a ditch, by a private who succeeded in reaching the opposite bank first and in extending him a helping hand. Reaching the outer edge of the Fort, the men following, their officers rushed forward through an embrasure of Fort Steadman and fought their way inside. The situation was fearful for several moments. As they jumped into the enclosure where its defenders were now fully awake and stirring, such was the excitement and desperate energy of the struggle, that the combatants fought as was afterwards said "as if they had drank two quarts of brandy." The fort was finally carried, though it was rough and tumble fighting; the opposing soldiers being locked together like serpents. It was a little before sunrise as they entered the Fort, with just sufficient light to enable them to see their way. As the defendants refuse to surrender they were knocked in the head with the musket or bayoneted by the assailants.*

The guns were finally captured, were ordered to be turned on the other fort, and the Louisianians emerged forth to attack another redoubt; but they had now lost more than half their original number and were no longer able to take the initiative. Besides, after the Louisianians had captured the fort, each command commenced diverging in the prescribed direction previously arranged, and the daylight revealed their weakness. The enemy at first panic stricken, discovered their small number and rallied; and now circling around them with

---

*Bresman was one of the Louisiana Brigades who were bayoneted in the storming of this Fort, and who, though run through the abdomen, recovered.

a crushing force drove them back to Fort Steadman, the point whence they had emerged. In other words the 2d Corps consisting of 6000 men, found itself opposed by the whole of Grant's army.* The day was lost, the assaults of the Confederates were repulsed, and the final order from Gen. Gordon at length came of *sauve qui peut.* Immediately after the disaster when the troops had retired inside of the lines, Col. Waggaman meeting Gen. Evans and solicitous for the honor of his men, inquired if the Louisianians had done their duty? His answer was " They did."

But the end of all things comes at last, and it was so even with the siege of Petersburg. A week after the preceding attack (April 1st) a few random shots and a gradually increasing fire, hinted that the day of the great struggle had come—that Lee's army had slept their last night around Petersburg. Indeed before midnight of the same day the firing and booming of the guns had extended along the whole line. This of course compelled the men to remain awake at their post expecting the final attack. At day-break on Sunday (April 2nd) the enemy made an attack upon the Confederate lines and pierced them in three places. They throw themselves upon the Louisiana Brigades at Graves' Salient but are there successfully repulsed. Then the Louisianians are ordered to assist Cook in a desperate attack which he sustains at the Crater. The Confederates were not at this point able to dislodge the Federals from the hold they had obtained. They however succeeded in keeping them hemmed in the Salient and prevented them from advancing. This the Brigade continued doing during the 22 hours which this long battle lasted. At nightfall, Gen. Lee had been driven to the inner line of Petersburg, and this position was irretrievable.

*Some of the soldiers of the other Confederate Brigades showing a disposition to return, the commander of the Brigade prevented this by drawing his revolver and compelling them to halt. An officer with some of his followers rode up and asked why his men had been stopped. He continued expressing his views in a dictatorial way and assuming a general authority. The commander of the Louisiana Brigade who had been the only lucky officer who had accomplished his work, losing all patience, excitedly collared him, with the remark, that he was not fit to command any body or anything and thrust him aside. Immediately after, shouting to his men that now was their time, Waggaman lead them forward in the last attack of the occasion.

The silence which followed was one of the most striking incidents of the day. Nothing now was heard but the occasional stamp of a picketed horse—the faint rattling of a cannon carriage in the direction of Petersburg, or the indistinctly heard tramp of large bodies of men. On the breastworks the sentinel stood motionless, the moonlight flickering on their bayonets thus deceiving the enemy. To-night is the last guard-night upon these ramparts; on the morrow the camp and battle-field will be sufficiently deserted for the ploughman to re-commence his labors, and the old uniform and battle-flag will then be traditions of the past.

At 10 o'clock, P. M., the Brigades retreated in perfect silence, still leaving behind active sentinels upon the breastworks, who were to rejoin the main body at the Petersburg bridge. This latter was crossed by part of the Louisiana troops a little while before it was blown up. The rest of the march to Appomattox C. H. was made with the usual amount of skirmishing by day and fighting by night, the Brigades acting as the rear guard. The rations were reduced down to a biscuit and an ounce or so of bacon, and every hour added to the difficulties of the situation.

The Brigades on the retreat had an opportunity allowed them of distinguishing themselves by the manner in which they checked pursuit, thus giving Gen. Lee's army an opportunity of filing by. So hard pushed was the rear guard, that they would not unfrequently be pressed by the Federals to within twenty yards and be entirely flanked, and then have to run back under a close range fire of the enemy. For the skill with which he performed this part of a perilous duty, Captain Blythe, of Claiborne Parish, is frequently spoken of by his men.

When the Brigade reached the Long Bridge, the measured step of the men produced a vibration or swing that threatened to destroy them by snapping the bridge's timbers. They now showed a passive proof of courage and discipline, by promptly halting at the word of command, instead of giving away to panic, until the vibration had ceased and the Brigade could break step.

Their last attack was made on the day of Gen. Lee's surrender. The men, when ordered to move forward, had to march over a freshly ploughed field half a mile wide, and their courage found it difficult to sustain itself against pure exhaustion. However, they remained true to their colors, and though meanwhile, exposed to a heavy artillery fire, and although the Federals were sheltered behind a fence, they boldly drove them into the adjoining woods. They were just upon the point of laying hold of the batteries which had hitherto been enfilading the Confederate lines and which the Brigades had already driven from position. In the moment of victory, and while they were capturing the colors of a regiment from a flag-bearer (who already was run through with a bayonet,) came the command " Fall back." " What did it mean ?" asked the men of each other ; and as they lay down on the ground to rest like troops flushed with victory, who had successfully accomplished their task, a whisper, so strange that it might have started in the air, said that the Brigades would never charge any more, and that Lee's army had surrendered. Men looked at each other forgetful of rank, and stared hard at the brazen mouths of the artillery, the signification of whose movements every old soldier knew, and which had been previously parked on Appomattox Hill. These were now passing around, and the abandonment of such a position could have only one meaning. Every moment the whisper became louder. Every additional manœuvre proved that what had thus far been a rumor, was an undisputed certainty. And now came the agonized look, which the brush of Salvator Rosa could never paint—the gaze of despair which settled like a cloud on powder stained faces, and which said that the bloody tradegy was ended, their four years struggle had been useless, and that having appealed to the arbitrament of the sword, the only thing to be done was to accept the result with the best grace they could. The cup had been drained—the last act of the drama had arrived. The situation simply was that every cartridge had been fired; 140,000 Federal soldiers stood in easy cannon range according the honors of war, and that the grand old man, whose name history will ever perpetuate, could no longer lead them.

The concluding incident of the war, so far as concerns this narrative, was that just as our men grounded their arms, and the old veterans marched past the triumphant Federal army, it gave the Louisiana troops a soldier's salute with their arms, and showed by their demeanor, by the absence of scornful laugh or word, their respect for the Pelican Brigades.

JOURNAL OF MAJ. MONIER, FROM SHARPSBURG TO APPOMATTOX.

Continued from Page 32.

Sept. 17th, 1862.—At the close of the battle of Sharpsburg we are sent from the field, two miles to the rear for ammunition. Remain there until 7 o'clock P. M. Then sent to support some artillery in rear of Sharpsburg Stayed there one hour and came back to the woods near the springs. Slept here all night.

At 3 o'clock next morning, go to the front and take the same position we previously occupied in the line; then throw out a line of skirmishers and remain there until midnight, when we begin retreating. Cross Potomac at Shepherdstown, at about break of day. Take position on the hill on the right of town. At 9 o'clock A. M., fall back about two and a half miles. Camped in the woods at 4 P. M. Return to Shepherdstown to support Gen. A. P. Hill. At dark fall back to Opequan river, 6 miles from Martinsburg and camp; we remained in this camp until the morning of the 23d of September, when we crossed the Opequan river, passed through Martinsburg, and camp about one mile from town, to the left; stayed there until the 25th of September, then marched to Bunker Hill.

Oct. 18th.—March to Martinsburg and camp.
19th.—Destroy the Baltimore and Ohio Railroad.
23d.—Returned.
24th.—March to Elizabeth Farm, near Ripley, and camp there.
Nov. 1st.—Within seven miles of Winchester.
4th.—March to Whitepost, passing through Berryville and camp near town.
8th.—Pass through Winchester; camp seven miles from Bunker Hill. Picket the roads to Martinsburg and Jordan Springs.
22th.—At sunrise we break camp, pass through Winchester, and taking the valley main turnpike, move up passing through Kernstown.
23d.—Pass through Middletown and camp near Strasburg.
24th.—Pass Strasburg and Woodstock, and camp one mile from this place.
25th.—March through Edenbury, then to and through Mount Jackson, and camp half a mile from this place, south of the north branch of Shenandoah river.
16th.—Pass through New Market, then filing to the left, cross the Massahutten Mountain. Camped for the night on the bank of the Shenandoah river.
27th.—Enter the Blue Ridge Mountains at Thornton Gap. March all day over mountains. At dark, camp at the foot of a mountain near a small village.

Nov. 24th.—Move at sunrise. March until about 3 o'clock, P. M., to within 5 miles of Madison Court House. 25th, march through Madison. Crossed Rapidan River at Liberty Mill and camp within 6 miles of Orange Court House. Passed through Orange; take the plank road to Fredericksburg and camp in the evening about 8 miles from the Court House.
29th.—Pass by Fredericksburg, leaving it on our left, and camp 8 miles from it at dark.
30th.—March to within two and a half miles of Guinea Station, on the Richmond and Fredericksburg Railroad. Remain here until spring.

CAMPAIGN OF 1863.

April 28th, 1862.—Left camp and proceeded to Port Royal, a town on the bank of the Rappahandock River; arrive at dark and camp two miles from town.
29th.—Return to Camp Seymour.
30th.—At break of day march for Fredericksburg; camp two miles beyond town. Camp on the Fredericksburg and Orange C. H. plank road.
May 1st.—Arrive on Brock Road; follow it to the old turn-pike leading to German ford; take the pike, move about two miles and form line of battle in the woods on the right of the road. Remain here about half hour, then form line on the left of the pike, advance and strike the enemy's flank and rear and drive them back two miles, capturing 4 pieces of artillery and a number of prisoners. At dark move to the front on the plank road and form line of battle at the left of road and rested all night on arms.
At day-break the next day we advance in line on the Wilderness; march about half of a mile and then moved by the left flank about 500 yards; then moved by the right flank and advanced to the top of a hill. Meet the enemy; severe fighting. Our brigade being outflanked, fall back to the wooden breastworks previously erected by the Yankees. In the evening ordered to charge a battery posted on a commanding position and supported by two lines of infantry; we boldly advanced to the assault, but want of support forced us to fall back to our original position. Remained here all night. 10th La. act as skirmishers.
May 4th.—Same position. The balance of the brigade has moved to the right to build breast works.
5th.—The enemy has recrossed the river. We are sent 6 miles from battle-field to camp. Go to Hamilton Crossing and camp. Resume the usual duties of camp life.
June 5th.—Move, taking the road for Spottsylvania Court House, passed through this place and after a tramp of 18 miles rested for the night.
6th.—At 8 o'clock, A. M., we marched about two miles, but returned to cook rations. At 2, P. M., we resumed march and camp at dark.
7th.—Moved at day-break; crossed the Rapidan River at Sommerville ford; camp on the south bank of Cedar River, to the right of the Orange and Alexandaia Railroad.
8th.—Marched at 6 o'clock, A. M., on the road to Culpepper Court House.
10th.—At 2 o'clock, P. M., we marched about 10 miles on the Sperryville pike.
11th.—We move at 4 o'clock, A. M., passed through Woodville, Sperryville and Little Washington.
12th.—Resumed the march, passing through Flint Hill, Gaines Cross Road and Front Royal, crossed the Shenandoah River.
13th.—At break of day moved on the road to Winchester and came in sight of the enemy 3 miles from town at about 10 o'clock, A. M.; formed line of battle in a wood on the left of the road and remained there until dark.
14th.—Changed position and came in view of town.
15th.—At sunrise, near Jordan Spring, met the enemy moving by the right flank about two hundred yards from our line; we moved by the left

flank at double quick time, and after a race of about 200 yards we faced into line, jumped over a fence, fired into the enemy and charged them, completely routing them, capturing about 200 prisoners, one stand of colors and killed and wounded quite a number. (Stand of colors captured by Jos. Moreau, private of Co. C, 10th La. Regt.) At 3 o'clock, P. M., camped near battle field.

16th. At 11 o'clock, A. M., marched about one mile, then returned from whence we had started.

At 2 o'clock, P. M., passed through Brucetown and went to the left of Smithfield and camped.

17th. Moved at sunrise; at 2 o'clock, P. M., passed through Shepherdstown, crossed Potomac and went 2¼ miles from Sharpsburg and camped.

19th.—Same position.

20th.—Moved at 9 o'clock, A. M., passed through Sharpsburg and formed line of battle, half-mile east of town and remain thus all day.

21st.—Same position.

22nd.—Six Companies, A, B, E, D, G and K of the 10th La. Regiment went on picket on Antietam Creek, about half mile from camp.

23d.—Moved forward, camped in half-mile of Pennsylvania line.

24th.—Resumed the march at sunrise, cross Pennsylvania line, and camped two miles south of Chambersburg.

25th.—Same position.

26th.—Moved forward at 8 o'clock, A. M. 3 o'clock, P. M., went to camp.

27th.—At 7 o'clock, A. M., went to camp 4 miles south of Carlisle.

28th.—Remain in camp.

29th.—At 12 o'clock in the day marched back; camped in 5 miles of Shipperburg.

30th.—Resumed march at dawn and camp 4 miles beyond Scotland.

July 1st.—At 7 o'clock, A. M., move on the Baltimore turnpike, arrive at Gettysburg and form line of battle one mile on left of town (marched 30 miles).

2d.—Moved forward, crossed a creek and attacked the enemy.

3d.—Fought all day; remain in line of battle part of night; between midnight and dawn moved to the right.

4th.—Remained in sight of Gettysburg all day; at dark began retreating; march all night.

6th.—At 7 o'clock, A. M., resumed retreat, camped one mile beyond Waynesboro.

7th.—Move at 8 o'clock in the morning, going through Latinsburg and camped, 2 miles from Hagerstown, until the 10th of July at sundown; then march through Hagerstown and go to camp 3 miles beyond the Williamsport road.

11th.—Went and took our position in the line of battle; build breastworks.

12th.—Remain in the trenches.

13th.—At 6 o'clock in the morning the regiment went on picket one mile from the line; skirmish all day with the enemy; at 11 o'clock P. M. fall back, marched all night, at daylight passed through Williamsport and crossed the Potomac at this place, joined the brigade one mile from the river, then marched on to Martinsburg pike and camped 4 miles from town. Remain here until 2¼ o'clock, P. M.

15th.—When we move, march through Martinsburg and go to camp near Darksville. Remain at this place July 16th, 17th, 18th and 19th.

20th.—March to and through Martinsburg, and destroy at this point the Railroad; at night camp in wood west of track.

21st.—Finished destroying the railroad; we fell back to our old camp near Darksville. (This day Brigadier General Alfred Iverson, from Georgia, was temporarily assigned to the command of our brigade.)

22d.—Marched at 6 o'clock in the morning; passed through Darksville, Bunker Hill, and came to camp about 3 miles of Winchester.

23d.—Resumed the march at sunrise; passed through Winchester and over Front Royal road; marched to the rear of Front Royal; kept moving to and fro until midnight; rest for the night at the edge of town, after a march of 25 miles.

24th.—Move at daylight; march through Front Royal to the Luray Pike; camp about half a mile from Milford; march 12 miles.

25th.—Move at 5 o'clock A. M.; march 8 miles on the Luray turnpike. Camp.

26th.—Same position; inspection by Gen. Iverson.

27th.—March at 4 o'clock in the morning, cross the Blue Ridge mountains at Thornton Gap and go to camp, having marched 16 miles.

28th.—At 5 o'clock A. M., move to and through, Sperryville, and go and camp in 12 miles of Mason's Court House.

29th—At 5 o'clock A. M., within 5 miles of Madison C. H.

31st.—March through Madison C. H. and camp 4 miles beyond town, on the road to Gordonville.

August 1st.—March at sunrise, pass Milford and Liberty Mill, and take the road to Orange Court House; camp 4 miles from town at Camp Montpelier. Pass the residence of President James Madison. In this camp we drill. A regular corps of sharpshooters is organized, with target shooting.

Sept. 17th.—Form line of battle a mile and a half beyond Orange Court House, in a field on the left of the old turnpike. The Yankees make some demonstration at the ford on the Rapidan river.

18th.—Remain in line until 1 o'clock P. M. March through Orange Court House and camp on the hill east of town.

21st.—At break of day we again pass through Orange Court House and go to Morton's Ford on the Rapidan river to meet the enemy, who is reported crossing in force. Arrived there at dark, form line of battle parallel with the river. Work all night erecting breastworks. The next morning at 11 o'clock, move about 400 yards to the woods in rear of Gibson's house, and camp. We remain 15 days in this camp, drilling and picketing the bank of the Rapidan, from Morton's Ford to Mountain Run.

Oct. 8th.—At 4 o'clock P. M., march to Pisgah Church, about 6 miles of Orange Court House and camped. Next day, move forward at sunrise, passed through Orange Court House; cross the Rapidan river at Union Mills and camp at Jack's Shop, 8 miles from river.

10th.—Pass by Madison Court House, leaving it on our left, and camp 8 miles from town.

11th.—Camp 4 miles of Culpepper on the right of the turnpike.

12th.—At sunrise move forward, leaving Culpepper on our right, cross Hazel river by fording; pass through Jeffersontown, and halt three-quarters of a mile beyond town. The cavalry are fighting, the Yankee's trying to effect a passage. At dark we resume the march, cross the Rappahannock river, and camp near Warrenton Springs.

13th.—March to and through Warrenton and camp a mile and a half from town.

15th.—Pass over Gen. Ewell's farm and camp 2 miles from Bristow Station. on the Manassas and Culpepper Railroad.

17th.—At sunrise cross the railroad and form line half mile from Bristow Station. Stack arms and tear up the track.

18th.—Same thing.

19th.—Retreat, following the railroad and come to camp within 2 miles of Rappahannock river.

20th.—Cross river and camp 2 miles from the banks.

22d.—Retreat to Brandy Station and go into camp, 2 miles on the left—built winter-quarters.

Nov. 6th.—Go to Kelly's Ford on the Rappahannock, it being reported the enemy are attempting a crossing at his place. Arrived there at 9 P. M., finding everything quiet; to-morrow will move back toward our camp.

7th.—Breaking camp. At daylight arrive within 2 miles of Culpepper, form line of battle and build breastworks. At dark fall back, cross Rapidan river at Raccoon Ford and camp 1 mile from river

8th.—Return to our old camp near Morton's Ford and to rear of Gibson's farm.

9th.—Pisgah Church; camp in the wood about ¼ mile in front of Church, on the right of the Old Orange and Fredericksburg turnpike.

12th—Camp near Mountain Run, 2¼ miles from Rapidan river.

13th.—March about midway between camp and the river, form line of battle and build breastworks; came back to camp at dark. Stay in the place eleven days, during which time, we picket, by details, Mine Run.

26th.—At daylight march 200 yards beyond Zoar Church and picket several roads.

27th.—At dawn took position on the breastworks in front of our camp near Mountain Run ; at 9 o'clock A. M. cross over the works, take the road to Bartlett's Mills, cross Mine Run at this place and go to James Farm; met the enemy. Form line at the edge of wood by the road edge and parallel with it,. and throw up wooden works. Remain there until 3 o'clock P. M., when we move forward, drive back the enemy's skirmishers, and attack their line. Arrive in a lane leading from the main road to Squire Gaines' house and hold the position until dark, when we fall back to our works. Johnson's division alone, to which we belonged, held in check and defeat the whole of French's Yankee corps; loss slight. At 9 o'clock P. M. fall back to the other side of Mine Run in the direction of Zoar Church and camp.

28th.—March to Zoar Church and build breast-works perpendicular to the road leading to Morton's ford. The next day stay behind the trenches until dark; 10th and 1st La. Regts. went on picket in front of Mrs. Dare's farm on the right of the road and 2 miles from the church.

30th.—At 8 o'clock relieved from picket; find the remainder of the Brigade building earthworks diagonally to the former line about 1¼ miles from church. Worked all day. At ten o'clock, P. M., we were ordered to fall in. Move by the right flank, marching inside the line of works. As we move we keep up the fires which the other troops build.

Dec. 1st.—At dawn rest ¼ mile from Mine Run and Zoar Church road. At 9 o'clock cross Mine Run, march about one-half mile, come back and re-cross the run, go to Zoar's Church and take the road to Morton's ford. At 8 o'clock, P. M., arrive in the works formerly occupied by Rhode's Division in rear of Buckner's House, one mile from Rapidan River. The next day at about 11 o'clock, A. M., march back to our old camp near Mountain Run. Remain here twenty days picketing Mine Run.

23d.—Move at sunrise and camp in the woods in front of Pisgah Church, between Mountain run and the old Fredericksburg and Orange C. H. turnpike. Here we build winter quarters.

31st.—Go on picket to Rapidan from Morton's ford to Mountain Run. Picket five days and return to camp.

Jan. 20th, 1864.—Again on picket; remain seven days and come back to winter quarters.

Feb. 6.—At two o'clock, P. M., march to Morton's ford to support the picket, the Yankees are coming. Arrive there at dark, too late to do anything. Gordon's, Walker's and Stewart's Brigades had driven the enemy back. Go to rest for the night on the road leading to Gibson's house in front of our old camping ground of September 1863.

Feb. 7th.—Fall back to breast-works and remain there until next morning, when we return to winter quarters.

CAMPAIGN OF 1864.

April 30.—Move from winter quarters near Pisgah Church and go to camp 1¼ miles from Morton's ford on Rapidan River.

May 4th.—At 12 o'clock, M., cross Mine Run and camp on the right of the old turn-pike about 1 mile from Locust Grove.

5th.—Move on the turn-pike at sunrise ; march about 5 miles and arrive in a dense wood on left of the road ; form line of battle and manœuvre to and fro in the wood until 10 o'clock; when we meet the enemy and drive them from our front. We were however flanked on the left and at one time were nearly surrounded. Finally get out of the scrape and fall back about one-half a mile and throw up works.

6th.—Work all day fortifying our position.

7th.—Work all day ; at 8 o'clock, P. M., move to the right of the line, following the breast-works; march all night.

8th.—At 7 o'clock, A. M., resume the movement to the right down the Spottsylvania road ; at sunset support Rhode's Division then fighting. At midnight take position on line and erect earthworks.

9th 10th and 11th.—Work all the time fortifying the line and occasionally skirmishing with the enemy.

12th.—In the morning a very heavy fog. The enemy, taking advantage of this, advance in 4 lines of battle and charge Jones' front, taking possesion of their works; charge our front,but we keep them at bay ; then they come in our rear, flank and front. We hold our ground to the last. Being overpowered ; we fall back to the second line, having been engaged all day. At dark we charge our old position without success. Fall back to second line and work all night.

13th.—Go to the rear for rest.

14th.—Same position.

May 15th.—Go back to the front, in breastwork on the left of Gordon's Brigade.

16th.—Slight demonstration by the enemy ; move to the left about 400 yards.

17th.—Same position.

18th.—Assault by the enemy on our front ; drive them back, inflicting upon them very heavy losses.

19th.—Enemy having disappeared from our front, at 1 o'clock, P. M., we move forward and meet them entrenching about 7 miles from Fredericksburg. Attack them and fought till dark ; then fell back to original position.

20th.—All quiet.

21st.—Move on Spottsylvania C. H. road, to the right of the line ; reach Telegraph road and camp.

22d.—March at 4, A. M., reach Hanover Junction and camp.

23d.—Move towards North Anna river on the right of Fredericksburg R. R. Bivouac in woods all day. The enemy reported to have crossed above ; we return to camp at Hanover Junction.

24th.—Move early in the morning to the front; kept in reserve. After dark, march to the right, formed line on Central R. R., and rest for the night.

25th.-26th.—Work all the time at fortifying our line.

27th.—Moved to the right between Fredericksburg and Central Railroads, cross South Anna river and camp for the night about 10 miles from Richmond on the Hanover C. H. road.

28th.—Marched at daylight towards Richmond ; turn to the left, take the road to the Old Church in search of enemy ; halt in woods about 4 miles from Mechanicsville, and 8¼ miles from Richmond and camp.

29th.—Deployed in line to the left of the road and throw up breastworks.

30th.—About 1 o'clock, P. M., went to the right along the works, cross over, went through field to Mechanicsville pike, retained as reserve, supporting Rhodes' Division then fighting, rest there for the night.

31st.—Work at fortification, skirmish with the enemy in the evening, move on to the left at the old position of the 29th inst. Kept moving to and fro all night.

June 1st.—At 3 o'clock A. M., heavy skirmishing. At 3 o'clock, P. M. relieved and sent to the right on Mechanicsville pike; sharp skirmishing, heavy fight on the left.

2d.—Take position on the right of Mechanicsville turnpike.

3d–4th–5th.—Same position.

6th.—The Yankees gone from our front; we move forward about 4 miles and find the enemy entrenched behind a swamp; skirmish and manoeuvre until dark, when we return to our old position.

7th.—Move out to the front; skirmish all day; in afternoon return to breastworks.

8th.—Same position.

9th.—In the evening move to the right, to Gaines' farm, and go about one mile to the rear.

10th–11th–12th.—Same position.

13th.—March at 4 o'clock, A. M., via Ellyson's Mill to Brook turnpike, on to the road to Louisa Court House; at a point about 20 miles from Richmond, we camp.

14th.—Move at sunrise in the direction of Louisa C. H. March about 19 miles and rest for the night.

15th.—Resume the tramp at 6 o'clock, A. M., pass through Louisa C. H. and camp near Spring Bottom, near Mechanicsville.

16th.—March at sunrise, pass through Mechanicsville and Charlottsville and camp for the night 5 miles from latter place.

17th.—March to the cars; there being no room, we move down to North Garden depot to await transportation.

18th.—Take the cars at 9 o'clock, A. M., at 2 o'clock, P. M. arrive in Lynchburg. Go to the Fair Grounds to rest, in the evening go to the front form line of battle to the left of the pike and throw up breastworks.

19th.—Move forward in pursuit of the infamous Hunter; pass through New London and meet the Federal rear guard about 2 miles from Liberty; route it and camp at the outskirts of town.

20th.—Move early in the morning, reach Buford Gap; skirmish with enemy's rear guard, having driven it back; rest here for the night.

21st.—At sunrise move in the direction of Salem, pass through Big Lick, about 2 miles from Salem, move off towards Falling Rock and camp.

22d.—Same position.

23d.—March at daylight and come to camp on a fine creek 4 miles from Buchannan.

24th.—At 3 o'clock, A. M., cross James river; pass Buchannan, rest two hours at Natural Bridge (Rockbridge County) and went to camp eleven miles from Lexington.

25th.—Move at break of day; at 10 o'clock, A. M. pass through Lexington. Jackson's old corps filed in the cemetary and march by the grave of the Great Chieftain with reversed arms, then go about six miles from town, halt and cook rations; move again at sunset and rest for the night about 25 miles from Stanton.

26th.—March at 6 o'clock, A. M., rest 2 or 3 hours during the heat of day; in the evening march about 5 miles and camp.

27th.—Move at 3:30 o'clock, A M.; at 10 o'clock, A. M., camp 2 miles from Stanton.

28th.—March at daylight; pass through Staunton, cross South Fork and camp near Mount Crawford.

29th.—Move at sunrise; pass through Mount Crawford. Harrisonburg, and camp near Lacey's Spring.

30th.—Start for the march at 4:30 o'clock, A. M., pass through New Market, Mount Jackson and camp on the outskirts of the last named place, near the Shenandoah river.

July 1st.—Resume the march at 3:30 o'clock, A. M., pass through Edenburg, Woodstock and camp on Fisher's Hill, 2 miles from Strasburg.

2d.—Move at sunrise; pass through Strasburg, Middletown, Newton and Kernstown and camp 1¼ miles from Winchester.

3d.—March at daylight; pass through Winchester; meet the enemy at Bunker Hill, who retreated; pass through Darkville; in the evening drove the Yankees from Martinsburg, capturing all their Commissary and Quarter-Master stores; camp 1 mile beyond town.

4th.—March at 3 o'clock, P M., on the Harper's Ferry road and camp about 4 miles after passing the Shepherdtown road.

5th.—Move at daylight on the Shepherdstown road, pass through town, cross Potomac river and camp on the canal about 9 miles from Harper's Ferry.

6th.—At 7 o'clock, A. M., met the enemy about 5 miles from Harper's Ferry; drive the enemy to Maryland Heights.

7th.—Remain all day in sight of the Heights, skirmish with enemy; at 8 o'clock, P. M. fall back, pass through Rouseyville, Md., and camp a while to rest.

8th.—At 7 o'clock, A. M., move forward and camp on the left of the pike, 8 miles from Frederick City.

9th.—Arrive at Frederick City, rest near town until 3 o'clock, P. M.; move forward, cross to Monocacy creek, strike the 6th Federal corps on its left flank; drove them to Monocacy Station; here rout them. Rest on battle field for the night.

10th.—March at sunrise on National pike; go to camp 4 miles from Rockville.

11th.—Resume the tramp; pass through Rockville, go on picket 1¼ miles from town on the Baltimore and Rockville road, to protect the safe passage of our wagon train. March again in the evening and join the command at Blair's mansion, 4 miles from Washington City.

12th.—Move forward at sunrise and form line of battle on the left of the pike 2 miles from the city. At dark, begin retreating. March all night.

13th.—At daylight, pass through Rockville and halt to rest a while on the road to Edward's Ferry, 9 miles from Rockville. Resume the march in the afternoon and march all night. Reach Potomac river at break of day.

14th.—Rest on the bank of the river until our train has crossed. Ford the river and camp at Big Spring, 2 miles from Leesburg.

15th.—Same position.

16th.—March at daylight, pass through Leesburg, take road to Berryville, pass through Hamilton, and Snikersville. Cross Mountain at Sniker's Gap; cross Shenandoah river at Sniker's Ferry and camp on the banks.

17th.—Resume retreat at sunrise; come within one mile of Berryville. Then ordered back to picket the rear. Heavy skirmishing in the evening.

18th —At 10 o'clock, P. M., relieved of duty by Evan's troops. Go back about two miles to rest, but are immediately summoned to the front, the enemy having effected a crossing. Drive them back with great slaughter. Camp near Wilson's farm for the night.

19th.—Same position.

20th.—Resume retreat at 10 o'clock, A. M., pass through Berryville, Milwood; go within 2 miles of Newton, turn off to the left and go to camp within 5 miles of Front Royal

21st.—March at daylight on the back road to Middletown; pass through town and camp in woods on the outskirts of it.

22d.—Move at sunrise up the Valley pike; cross Cedar creek and form line of battle near Strasburg. In the evening guard a ford on the creek, near the Massahutton Mountain.

23d.—Same position.

24th.—March at daylight, pass through Middletown, Newtown and meet

the enemy near Kernstown. We attack him and drive him through Winchester, toward Bunker Hill. Camp 3 miles from Winchester.
25th.—March at 5 o'clock, P. M. to camp at Bunker Hill.
26th.—March at 6 o'clock, A. M. to Martinsburg; camp one mile beyond town: go to work destroying the Ohio and Baltimore R. R.
27th.—Same position.
28th.—Move across the Opequan and camp.
29th.-30th. Destroy railroad to within a few miles of Harpers Ferry.
31st. March soon in the morning. At 10 o'clock A. M. go to camp near Darksville.

August 4th Cross Potomac river at Shepherdstown; pass through this town, take the pike to Shepherdstown and camp 1¼ miles from this place.
5th. Move at 5 o'clock, A. M.; cross Potomac river at Shepherdstown, pass through Sharpsburg, form line of battle on Antietam creek, to the right of the town; drove in the Yankee cavalry and rest there for the night.
6th. At sunrise, move on the Hagerstown road; turn to the left at cross road; take the road to Williamsport; pass this place, recross the Potomac river and camp at Falling Waters.
7th.---March at 7 o'clock, A. M.; pass through Martinsburg and go into camp at Darksville.
8th.---Same position.
9th.---Left camp at 1 o'clock P. M.; go to Bunker Hill, where we bivouac for the night.
10th.---Move at sunrise up the Valley pike; took the road to Jordan spring; pass this place and camp half way between the Berryville and Winchester pike and the spring; at dark go on picket to the spring.
11th.---March at sunrise and form line on the left of Winchester at 11:30 o'clock A. M.; move by the left flank in parallel line with the Main valley pike to protect our train; reached Newtown; form line west of town, about 1 mile from it; skirmish with enemy: at dark fall back near town and bivouac.
12th.---Move at sunrise; pass through Middletown, cross Cedar creek and go to the old position at the ford, near Massahutten mountain; skirmish with the enemy; in the afternoon our sharpshooters driven back; at 8 o'clock P. M. fall back through Strasburg and go to Fisher's Hill, in the breastworks.
13th-14th-15th-16th.---Work all the time at fortifying our line of defence.
17th.---Move forward at daylight; pass through Strasburg, Middletown, Newtown and Kernstown; meet the enemy at this place, engage him, and drive him through Winchester towards Berryville; camp near Winchester.
21st.---Move forward at sunrise; pass through Charlestown, and camp at the edge of town, in a fine oak forest.
22d-23d.---Same position.
24th.---Move to the front formed line of battle; at dark go in picket near Bolivar Height.
25th.---March at daylight to Leetown; pass through town; meet the enemy about 1 mile from it; attack and drive him through Shepherdstown, across the Potomac; camp at dark, 1¼ mile from town.
26th.---March at 1 o'clock P. M. and go to camp near Leetown.
27th.—March in the morning and go to camp near Bunker Hill.
28th.—Same position.
29th.—March at 11 o'clock A. M. on the road to Smithfield; meet enemy near Opequon river; drove him back through Smithfield and beyond; return at dark to camp near Bunker Hill.

30th-31st-September 1st.—Same position.
2d.—March at 10 o'clock A. M. toward Summit Point; finding no enemy,

came back and pass through Brucetown, and camp 1 mile from town and 6 miles from Winchester.
3d.—At sunrise move toward Bunker Hill, but soon return to camp; at dark march to and through Winchester, and went to camp 1 mile from town, on the Front Royal road.
4th.—At dark pass through Winchester and camp on the left of the pike, 1 mile from town.
5th.—Go on the Pughtown road, about 2 miles from Winchester, to picket.
6th-7th-8th.—Same position.
9th.—In the evening march back to camp near Brucetown.
10th.-11th.-12th.—Same position.
13th.—About 9 o'clock A. M. pass through Brucetown; go to Opequon creek; skirmish with enemy and drive them back; at dark return to camp.
14th-15th-16th.—Same position.
17th.—Move at 3 o'clock P. M. to Bunker Hill.
18th.—March at sunrise; pass through Darksville and Martinsburg; meet the enemy 1 mile beyond the latter place and drove him across the Opequon; then return to Bunker Hill.
19th.—Move in morning; arrived near Winchester, formed line and charged the enemy; drove them back with severe losses; the cavalry giving way on the left forces us to fall back; retreat to Middletown and camp.
20th.—Resume retreat; pass through Strasburg and take position in the works on Fisher's Hill.
21st.—Skirmish with enemy.
22d.—Skirmish from morning till 4:30 o'clock P. M.; enemy having flanked the left of our line, the troops give way; our boys remain bravely in the works until all others had left, then withdraw and fall back to within 1¼ miles of Edinburg.
23.—At daylight resume retreat, passing through Edinburg, Mount Jackson; form line of battle 2 miles from the pike, on Rood's Hill.
24th.—Begin falling back, skirmishing all the while; pass through New Market, near Lacey's Spring, turn off toward the mountain, and camp near Keezeltown.
25th.—Move at daylight; pass through Keezeltown, cross Shenandoah river at Port Republic; go to camp at Brown's Gap, near the Furnace.
26th.—Same position.
27th.—Move forward; meet the enemy near Weer's Cave; drive them back and camp.
28th.—March at 10 o'clock A. M.; camp 2 miles from Waynesboro.
29th.-30th.—Same position.

October 1st.—Move at daylight on the road to Valley pike, near Mount Sidney; camp near Mount Crawford.
2d-3d-4th-5th.—Same position.
6th.—At sunrise resume marching; pass through Harrisburg and camp on left of the pike, 2 miles from town.
7th.—March at daybreak; pass New Market, and camp 1 mile from said town, on road to Jordanville.
8th-9th-10th-11th. Same position.
12th.—Move at sunrise down the Valley pike, pass through Mount Jackson, Edinburg, and camp 1 mile from Woodstock.
13th.—Resume march at 6 o'clock A. M.; pass through Woodstock; arrive near Strasburg; leave this place to the right; go to Cedar creek; meet the enemy and drive them back; at dark fall back to our former position on Fisher's Hill.
14th.—Move to the front of our works on the hill, overlooking Strasburg; skirmish with Federal cavalry; at dark fall back to the hill.
15th-16th-17th.—Same programme.
18th.—At dark move noiselessly in the direction of Massahutten moun-

tain, followed the base of the same, cross Shenandoah river, and rest near Cedar creek, on the enemy's left flank.

19th.—Surprise the enemy's pickets at Cedar Creek; waded the stream, formed line immediately, and charged the enemy; we drive them from the camp, capturing 1900 prisoners, 18 pieces of artillery, a great many wagons and ambulances, and most all of their ordnance, quartermaster's and commissary stores; we forced them back beyond Middletown. In the afternoon was driven back; fell back to Fisher's Hill; march all night; in morning pass through Edinburg, Mount Jackson, and go to old camp near New Market.

21st-22d-23d-24th.—Same position.

25th.—Change camp about 1 mile; go near the north branch of Shenandoah.

26th.—Same camp; temporary consolidation of the Louisiana Regiments; 10th and 15th Louisiana regiments organized into the company known as Company D, York's command.

27th-28th-29th-30th-31st. November 1st-2d-3d-4th-5th-6th-7th.-Same camp; daily drills and parades.

8th.---Go to camp, 4 miles above New Market, on the right of the Great Valley pike.

9th.—Same position.

10th.—March at sunrise down the pike; passed through New Market, Mount Jackson, Edinburg, and camp 1 mile of Woodstock.

11th.—Move at 6 o'clock A. M.; march through Woodstock, Strasburg, Middleton, and camp 1 mile of Newton.

12th.—Skirmish all day with enemy near town; at dark fall back to Fisher's Hill.

13th.—Resume retreat at sunrise; pass through Woodstock and camp near Edinburg.

14th.—Move at 6 o'clock A. M.; pass through Edinburg, Mount Jackson, New Market, and go late to camp.

15th-16th-17th-18th-19th-20th-21st.—Same position.

22d.—March to Rood's Hill to support our cavalry, which had been driven back to Mount Jackson; drove the enemy back, re-established our cavalry line of pickets, then returned to camp.

23d-24th-25th-26th-27th-28th-29th-30th. December 1st-2d.--Same position, &c.

3d.—Move to change camp; march about 1 mile up the valley and camp.

4th-5th. Same camp.

6th.—March at sunrise up the valley pike; pass through Harrisonburg, Mount Crawford, and camp near Mount Sidney.

7th.—Took the road to Waynesboro, arriving within 1¼ miles from town, at dark; embark on the cars and proceed to Richmond.

8th.—Arrive at Richmond at 10 o'clock A. M.; march to the Petersburg depot, take cars, go to Petersburg, and camp in Law's brigade quarters; again move to the right of the line and occupy Davis' quarters.

9th.—Go to extreme right of the line to re-establish the cavalry picket line, and reconnoitre the position; return to Davis' quarters at dark.

10th-11th-12th.—Same camp.

13th.—Organize a camp on the extreme right, near Hatcher's Run, 1 mile in rear of Burgess' Mill; here build winter quarters.

February 5th.—Fought the enemy on the north of Hatcher's Run; at dark return to camp.

6th.—Fought the enemy south of Hatcher's Run, near Armstrong mill; kept him in check.

7th.—Worked all day fortifying; at dark returned to camp.

March 12th.—Left winter quarters near Burgess' Mill, on Hatcher's Run, ann go in the breastworks in front of Petersburg, near the Crater.

13th.—At dark move about 700 yards to the left, and take the position formerly occupied by Grace's brigade.

14th to 24th, inclusive.—Remain in same position, skirmishing with the enemy.

25th.—At about 2:30 o'clock in the morning, move by the left flank and take a position on the left of Evan's brigade; at dawn cross the breastworks at Grace's salient; move forward, capturing the Yankee pickets, and assault and take possession of Fort Steadman, &c.; capture 4 guns and 3 mortars and nearly the whole garrison. An advance is now made towards battery No. 5 and arrive within 300 yards of it. Here the confident progress was arrested by large reinforcements reaching the enemy. Lee orders a retreat, which is executed under a terrible fire of artillery and musketry. At about 10 o'clock both armies occupy their original position (order of attack), the corps of sharpshooters, Louisiana brigade, head of attacking column.

29th to 31st, inclusive.- Same position and all quiet.

April 1st.—At 10 o'clock P. M. grand demonstration by the enemy; heavy shelling and skirmishing, which lasted the whole night.

2d.—At break of day move to the right to drive the enemy, who has forced a portion of our line; after several charges, recapture about 200 yards of our works, but fail to drive him away. [The Louisiana troops while hemming in the corps, which had succeeded in effecting an entrance at the Crater, had to remain passive while under a galling fire during a large portion of the 22 hours battle. Their lines were enfiladed, and the only chance for any preservation of life whatever, was in closely hugging the coins of vantage about the breastworks. All of the men killed were shot through the head, and frequently the men, in order to tell what was the force of the storm of battle, would hoist a cap on a pole and count the number of bullets it received in a given time, just as the steamer tells of the number of feet it is drawing by its lead soundings. As to what this bullet fury amounted to, the following incident will suffice :

During the quiet days of the occupation of Petersburg, the officers and men had been accustomed to attend church service on Sunday. The last battle about Petersburg occurred on Sunday, and at about 10:30 A. M., Col. Waggaman, who had frequently attended on these occasions with Powell, the son of the well known old Surveyor of the same name, by way of inquiring what was the hour, jocularly asked if they would yet have time to get to church. "Hardly," said Powell, consulting his watch, "unless we leave quickly." He had scarcely finished speaking before a bullet came along which caused his instantaneous death. His comrades could hear it crash in passing through his head. His expression did not change until he had lost his last drop of blood. His father's death, doubtless brought on by he loss of his promising son, followed soon after.] At half past 1 o'clock, on the morning of April 3d we evacuated our position on the line of Petersburg, cross the Appomattox river and relocate on the Woodpecker road, towards Amelia Court House, and camp after marching 10 or 11 miles.

4th.—At daylight move on the Hickory road, recross the Appomattox river, and camp 2½ miles from Amelia Court House.

5th.—Pass through the Court House and march towards Burksville.

6th.---Retreat, all the time fighting the enemy, on the left of the road leading to Burksville; being closely pressed, we fall back across the road, where we are confronted by another line of the enemy's troops; we retrace our steps and meet our troops; ordered at the bridge to defend its passage, but before reaching it are ordered to fall back; at dark, ordered to support one piece of artillery, posted on a road, to defend any approach in our direction, whilst the army retreats to Farmsville; remain in the position until 9 o'clock, when we resume the retreat and meet the main body of our army at High Bridge; rest there and then march to Farmsville, where we bivouac until daylight,

7th.---Cross Appomattox river; form line of battle on the hills bordering the river; at 8 o'clock A. M. begin skirmishing and build breastworks with

fence rails, expecting an attack in force; remain there until our train had passed, then move by the left flank on the right of the road leading to Appomattox Court House, now and then halt and form line of battle.
10th.---Surrender.
13th.---Left Appomattox Court House.
16th.---Left City Point.
21st.---Transferred from the United States transports to the steamship Atlanta, and left Fortress Monroe at 2 o'clock P. M. on our way home.

[Lieut. Col. Monier (for with this latter title he came home after Appomattox), here ends a journal which is as remarkable for the patient indifference or forgetfulness of the hardships which the brigades must have endured, as for the enumeration of the marches, military movements, and continual encounters to which they were every day exposed. The journal gives enough to show what was done and no more. If any more remarkable career of service during the whole war can be found than is contained in the simple journal of these brigades, it has thus far failed to meet the present writer's eye.]

  Reader, one sigh for the gallant Tenth —
   One sigh for the fallen brave;
  Their tale is told, their deeds at length
   But a line in history crave.

  Where are the dead, and who have wept?
   Full many are their graves;
  Alas! who comes where they have slept,
   Alone, where the willow waves?

  Far from their homes, in a distant clime,
   Most from beyond the sea;
  Unknown their fate, untold by time,
   Buried in mystery.

  From the Rhine and Rhone, from foreign land,
   From Northern icy shore;
  Their hearts beat warm, a noble band,
   For the Southern cause full sore.

  From Britain Isle, from sunny France,
   From Erin dear they came;
  And fiercely fought the North's advance,
   And for our Southern fame.

  Devoted to death for Southern right,
   Fighting in Freedom's cause;
  Can country e'er their deeds requite,
   Or honor by the laws?

  No more exists the gallant Tenth,
   With us no more in name,
  But though extinct and gone in strength,
   Shall perish not in fame.

THE SIXTH LOUISIANA REGIMENT.

The 6th Regiment of Louisiana volunteers, composed of the companies as shown below, was organized at Camp Moore, on the 23d of May, 1861. Col. I. J. Seymour, a veteran of the Florida and Mexican wars, was elected Colonel; Captain Louis Lay, of the Violet Guards, Lieutenant Colonel, and Captain S. L. James, of the Irish Brigade, Major. On the 11th of June the Regiment started for the seat of war in Virginia, and, on arriving at Manassas, were immediately sent to the front. It there occupied the advance posts, under General Ewell, until the approach of the enemy, when it fell back to the Bull Run line.

During the fight of the 18th July, the Regiment was in reserve, and was not called into action. On the memorable 21st of July, the position occupied by the Regiment was not attacked, and a movement on the part of Ewell's command, contemplated by General Beauregard, was not executed, in consequence of the disappearance or the courier bearing the order.

On the organization of the army of the Potomac, this Regiment, with the 7th, 8th and 9th La. and Wheat's Battalion, formed the 8th Brigade of that army, under General Walker. General Taylor was afterwards assigned to the command of the Brigade, and on the retreat from Manassas, for a long time protected the line of the Rappahannock.

The history of the 6th Regiment from this time was identified with that of Jackson and Ewell. On the death of Colonel Seymour, at Cold Harbor, the command devolved on Colonel Strong. He also met the death of a soldier at the battle of Sharpsburg. The command then devolved on Colonel Monaghan, its last commander, who was killed at the head of his regiment.

The muster roll given below represents the regiment at the commencement of the third year of the war.*

---

*At the departure of the regiment Dr. McKelvey was surgeon and remained so during the first and second years of the war; Lieut. Lewis Graham was also Adjutant during the first and second years of the struggle.

STAFF.

Col. W. Monaghan. Lieutentant Colonel J. Hanlon. Major W. H. Manning. Surgeon W. A. Robertson. Assistant Surgeons C. H. Todd, J. M. Maxwell. Quartermaster J. A. Reed. Commissary J. G. Campbell. Adjutant John Orr. Sergeant Major J. Tobin. Quartermaster's Sergeant M. Egan. Commissary Sergeant C. Moran. Color Sergeant P. Bogler. Hospital Matron M. S. Hill.

COMPANY A—(Sabine Rifles.)

Captain J. F. Philipps. Lieutenants, E. C. Kosh, J. S. Gilbert, J. S. Weymouth. Sergeants, E. J. Richelberger, J. C. White, W. Beard, W. B. Cuddell. Corporals, F. F. Gilbert, J. F. Brolton, T. J. Gilbert, R. A. Maines.

Privates—H. Bath, A. M. Bright, J. H. Briggs, J. Bently, J. Butts, H. Carlin, J. B. Carley, J. Curtis, T. M. Cook, R. D. Carson, G. W. Carson, S. T. Dickerson, T. L. Davis, J. Davis, J. A. Dean, A. M. Peason, H. S. Fritz, O. P. Freeman, R. M. Gilbert, A. M. Gilbert, C. J. Gilbert, J. M. Gully, J. D. S. Goodwin, C. C. Hayslip, S. B. Hodges, J. Howard, W. A. Hays, C. Honeycut, G. Heath, W. D. Jordan, W. R. Johnson, C. Kalker, W. C. Lee, W. H. Low, J. H. McCabe, S. W. Morris, J. Martin, J. P. McGough, B. F. Pearson, J. C. McLemone, W. Pugh, W. Patterson, T. Province, H. Reynolds, J. H. Reynolds, P. P. Roach, J. Shepherd, B. J. Smith, R. W. Sibley, B. O, Scarborough, A. J. Traylor, J. Thomas, R. Ursery, Y. Ursery, S. B. Wininger, S. Wineberg, W. B. Williams, T. P. White, J. R. Traylor, S. Traylor, M. L. Taylor, S. T. Taylor, B. B. Thompson.

COMPANY B—(Calhoun Guards, N. O.)

Captain Thomas Redmond, Lieutenants Archibald Duncan, H. Long, H. Muldowney; Seargeants P. Flannegan, T. Cassey, J. K. McGuinness, Edward Shaw, W. Kennedy; Corporals M. Freret, J. Ricker, John Killacky.

Privates—C. Adams, T. Brett, C. Brown, T. Byrnes, R. Boyne, M. Carlos, D. Curry, W. Coffee, T. Clayton, W. Cooney, T. P. Cavanagh, B. Collum, C. Devon, J. Donavan, B. Dunn, J. Devine, J. Doyle, P. H. Ennis, T. Flannagan, John Fay, P. Foley, T. Gaffney, J. Good, R. Grimstead, M. Gohan, J. Gallaher, M. Hughes, P. Aughes, G. Hughes, M. Hanley, J. Hart, J. Husselby, R. Hines, W. Henry, S. Jenkins, S. Keiger, J. Kesla, A. Kennedy, J. Kain, J. Kegan, F. Lynch, P. Lawler, T. Long, L. Miller, J. Mack, E. Murdock, J. Maloney, C. Murphy, J. Murphy, J. Mehan, J. McClung, P. McGuin, J. McDonough, P. McEvoy, M. McDonald, J. O'Bryan, J. Ryan, T. Quinally, J. O'Reedy, J. Rafferty, L. Schidell, M. Shanaghan, M. Tiner, J. Sullivan, P. Ward, J. Wilkinson, J. Walker.

COMPANY C—(St. Landry Guard, St. Landry Parish.)

Captain L. A. Cormier; Lieutenants P. Scott, F. O'Reilly, L. E. Cormier; Sergeants A. Phiel, G. W. Hanna, A. Lacomb, H. Graham, H. O. Tubre; Corporals E. Lafleur, F. Kirol, A. Young, U. W. Fisher.

Privates—W. Arden, A. Andrus, A. Barton, M. Bushnel, C. S. Belbow, C. Baddeau, M. Bolendorf, M. Bihm, A. W. Blair, W. W. Bowen, A. Bertrand,' R. Curtis, T. Craig, D. Cunningham. T. N. Cheiner, J. Cox, F. M. Drinkard A. Disbert, L. T. Darby, W. Douglas, P. Derosier, B. Fontenot, J. Fitch, O S. Fontenot, E. Fontenot, M. Fontenot, P. H. Fontenot, M. Ford, J. B. Fusilier, G. P. Gordon, J. S. Gale, L. Gleary, C. J. Going, Z. Guillory, A. Guillory, J. D. Hain, W. Hebert, F. Hardy, J. H. Hull, C. Humble, F. Sacob, B. Johnston, P. Jackson, A. Lacomb, P. Lambert, A. Lawney, W. Labarge, E. Lejeune, J. Lejeune, J. Mulholland, J. Morris, J. Mullen, L. Meriviere, A. McKinney, L. McGee, A. Manuel, T. N. Overall, W. R. Olds, T. O. Connor, J. Porter, L. Pitre, A. Quintard, C. N. Richmond, L. Richard, J. R. Scott, B. Savant, J. Sam, A. Schenk, O. Smith, T. Smith, J. Steven, F. N. Stout, P. Y. Simpson, L. Fessenden, J. Otrainor, J. B. Vidrine, H. Vable, A. Vable, E. W. Winkler, A. Winkler, H. Young.

COMPANY D.—*(Tensas Rifles—Tensas Parish.)*

Captain B. F. Buckner. Lieutenants, W. H. Gibson, J. G. Davs. Sergeants, J. Coleman, W. R. Wood, L. N. Coffey, James Mildoan. Corporals, W. E. Trahan, J. C. Allen.

Privates—E. Allen, J. Bonnily, K. M. Burodyne, T. H. Chew, J. A. Guillard, J. Donoho, L. Farnhan. C. Drank, P. F. Ford. J. K. Guilbert, J. M. Guilbert, C. B. Green, B. C. Guire, Thos. Hays, W. Harris, J. C. Hilliard, J Isenhard, M. Kelly, J. C. King, I. S. Lee, H. L. Lilly, P. Meinhart, J, L, Nevers, A. S. Nealhery, J. U. Paxton, S. D. Pitman, A. Phillip, A. Reinfrank. C. Reinhart, J. M. Rosson, Alex Reed, J. S. Riley, Tim Sullivan, J. H. Smeje, T. H. Woodward, Wm. Wheelan, Wm. Weldons, Mich Welsh, W. T. Wells, R. White.

COMPANY E—*(Mercer Guards, New Orleans.)*

Captain, J. J. Rivera; Lieutenants, Robert Lynne, Geo. Lynne; Sergeants, W. Lacklin, W. Strohfeldt. Robert Black, T. T. Byrne.

Privates—J. T. Aitkens, J. W. Brady, Joseph Burci, Henry Burgess, W A. Beard, N. Buckholtz, M. C. Cullen, J. F. Carney, Wm. Elmore, M. L. Gleeson, H. C. Hall, F. Cane, C. Moran, J. Moran, W. Murdock, A. F. Moynan, James Madden, J. H. Murray, F. Rosch, D. Romer, J. H. Smith, J. Shannon, E. Sattele, J. P. Skalon, R. Alexander, N. Brugniens, P. Burci, W. Burns, Gus. Cenas, Delaney, C. Deisler, M. Donnolly, M. Driscoll, M. Evans, E. Gorman, D. Hutchings, W. Hutchings, E. Harney, I. Hayes, B. Hubert, Kane, James Kelly, H. R. Kelly, Kelly, J. Murphy, S. Moore, W. Meisner, M. Obermeyer, John Park, A. Palmer, R. Robertson, John Robinson, E. M. Rusha, C. Sherwood, John Wills, Wm. Wills, D. Williams, J. Williams.

COMPANY F—*(Irish Brigade, New Orleans.)*

Captain, M. T. Connor; Lieutenants, J. O. Martin, J. Orr, M. Murray; Sergeants, J. J. Conway, M. Long, J. Ward, M. J. Edwards, T. Bone; Corporals, E. Gready, R. Cahill, W. Phair, J. Murray.

Privates—J. Adams, J. Brainard, T. Bowe, J. Burns, A. Cahill, P. Cummins, P. Dunn, D. Carroll, P. Canahler, L. Flanagan, M. Flanagan, J. Fitzgerald, F. Fairot, D. Floiery, B. Fox, W. Fox, P. Gannon, E. Green, Gallagher, M. Hogan, S. Hill, S. W. Hill, J. Hanby, P. Holland, M. Hays, H. Hall, D. Haley, J. Johnson, M. Joyce, T. Keane, R. McGee, R. Murphy, J. Murphy' P. McCormick, M. McCormick, M. Moran, W. Murray, M. Murray, B. McCoole, W. Mooney, M. Nolan, W. O'Brien, T. O'Brien, Jas. O'Neil, P. O'Mara, H. Phew, J. Poolta, D. Porer, D. Rionda, M. Riley, Pat. Ross, John Ryan, J. South, W. South, P. Sweeney, M. Sinault, M. S. Walsh, H. Walsh, C. White. Jno. Wheelon, F. Austin.

COMPANY G.—*(Pemberton Guards, New Orleans.)*

Captain, Frank Clarke; Lieutenants, Jeff. Van Benthuysen, John Shay; Sergeants, Philip Bolger, Andrew Hill, Jno. A. Shiver, Jno. Brunning, A. A. Steinnitz, Jno. Klopher; Corporals, A. Bock, A. Beach, G. Dick.

Privates—J. Abel, H. Boelte, F. Dorsing, T. Daegner, A. Elkins, H. Englehardt, P. Fitzpatrick, P. Ford, J. Fraid, W. F. Hugden, H. Husselman, P. Knapp, P. Lievre, M Lush, J. Lorentz, F. Lorentz, J. McDonnough, A. Miller, F. O. Rourke, Jno. O. Reilly, L. Pfister, N. Peters, J. Renicke, J. P. Rogers, H. Smith, James Smith, John Smith, F. Schwenterman, F. Spers, L. Shaw, W. Thers, C. Waldman, J. Vogler, J. Weik, C. Wagner, E. Weigert, John Weis, Fred. Wolf, A. Young. Musician—H. Huschky.

COMPANY H.—*(Orleans Rifles, N. O.)*

Captain, Charles Pilcher. Lieutenant Thomas Lucas. Sergeants, Williams Rourke, C. Meyers, H. C. Hiedelberg, M. J. Kennedy, D. Crawford. Corporals, Louis Bertand, Ford, Rosse.

Privates—H. Brabas, T. Connell, J. Flynn, H. Grubble, John Joy, F. Koesner, H. McCance, R. Carr, P. Duffee, E. Farrell, H. Leman, W. Jackson, W. Lyle, J. F. Morris, A. McAllese, P. Clark, C. Flohr, N. Pigenshne, L. Houston, F. Kelly, J. E. Laingriage, J. F. Michell, J. Mayee, C. Olding, J. Quinn. W. Ryan, M. Rabbuck, J. Richardson, H. S. Safford, H. Steuart, G. Singleton, J. F. Shannon, N. Scofield, F. Stern, J. A. Schrieber, J. Singrey, —— Templeton, C. Turner.

COMPANY I.—*(Irish Brigade, N. O.)*

Captain, B. T. Walshe. Sergeants, P. Byrnes. J. Mulrooney, D. Fitzgerald, J. Buckley.

Privates—J. Clancey, J. Cahill, N. Conner, B. Clarke, J. Clarke. J. Condon, P. Denavan, John Donahoe, T. Davis, M. Dabis, E. Fitzgerald, T. Flynn. T. Flanagan, E. Gunderson, T. Hughes, W. Hart (1), W. Hart (2), William Knox, J. Keefe, Richard Kelly, J. Kellecher, J. Lewis. P. Murphy, M. Moffat. C. Managan, J. Mullen. J. Maguire, J. McCarthy, R. Nolan. M. Rooney, J. Riley. D. Ryan, J. Sullivan, R. Tobin, M. Walsh.

COMPANY K.—(Violet Guards.)

Captain, Geo. P. Ring. Lieutenants, Samuel O. Kirk, Edward Flood, Peter Hare. Sergeants, J. H. Agaisse, W. Harding, B. W. Seales, P. P. Hickey, W. Halpin. Orderly Sergeant, John Cahill. Corporals, M. Smith, P. Healey, T. Maher, Edward Burns.

Privates—T. Bartley, M. Clarke, D. Curry, J. W. Coleman, J. Coleman, C. Comfort, J. Conley, C. Delmore, P. G. Dunn, D. Driscoll, L. Durr, G. Estlow, J. Finnegan, T. Fitzgerald, P. Finnegan, G. Graham, G. Grasser, G. Gaisser, M. Hughes, T. Hughes, J. Hurley, W. Higgins, E. Hoolahan, O. Hearty, W. Henry, A. Hutchings, J. Kingston, M. Kerwin, W. Lucas, P. Madden, E. Manning, P. Matthews, T. Murphy, G. Murphy, H. McGurty, C. McMahon, J. McAdams, M. McCue, W. McCluskey, M. Niess, M. Plunhartt, G. C. Russel, J. Russel, D. Ryan, M. Sullivan, M. Shay, D. Shay, T. Wallace, M. Wilson, L. Walch, J. M. Walsh, P. Wagner, W. Wibell, J. Waldron, John Waldron, M. Young, D. Singleton, J. Nunon.

CASUALTIES UP TO 13TH DECEMBER, 1862.

WINCHESTER, May 25, 1861.

Killed—Major McArthur, Privates Ed. Butt, E. Doyle, T. Murphy, S. Newport.

Wounded—Capt. J. Hanlon, Sergeant D. Horrigan, Corporals C. Drady, J. Maher, Privates J. S. Gibbert, A. S. Neathery, E. Allen, R. Cahil, P. Caughlin, L. Pfister, A. Weik, E. Clarke, T. H. Flanagan, P. Frazier, N. Magner, R. Tobin, J. Finnegan, J. Shepherd, J. Killacky, M. Wheelan, W. Fox, R. Murray, J. O. Reiley, H. Englehart, P. Donavan, E. Fitzgerald, P. Gleason, C. McAuliff.

PORT REPUBLIC, June 8, 1861.

Killed—Captain I. A. Smith, Sergeant D. A. Fitzpatrick, Corporal Montgomery, Privates J. Croak, M. Murray, J. Smith, M. Murray, C. Euth, Noonan, D. Fitzpatrick, A. Benito, F. Gallagher, T. Kane, J. McCormack, D. Mullen, C. Sponhammer, T. Windsor, J. Gallagher.

Wounded—Lieutenants J. O. Martin, T. P. Farrar, Sergeants J. C. White, J. Agaisse, D. Fitzgerald, Corporal J. Ward, Privates R. M. Gilbert, M. R. Speight, J. McCarthy, J. H. Myers, J. Wade, E. Fontenot, J. Donahoe, M. Casey, J. Fitzgerald, P. O'Rourke, J. Shannon, W. Flood, M. Wilson, M. Young, W. Higgins, P. G. Dunn, H. K. Goldsby, J. A. Dean. J. Kesler, J. Fox, W. Smith. L. Metevier, W. H. Corcoran, E. Grady, A. Zang, T. Connell, M. Davis, T. Hughes (Co. I), W. Henry, T Hughes (Co. K), J. Finnegan, P. Madden.

COLD HARBOR, June 27th, 1861.

Killed—Col. I. G. Seymour; Sergeant B. Stagg; Corporal Torhill; Privates J. Cassidy, T. Connors, A. D. Cassidy, Otto Luderf, J. Hale, M. Lyons.

Wounded—Lieutenants C. M. Pilcher and B. T. Walshe; Sergeants E. O. Riley, W. Harding; Color Sergeant J. Heill, Turner, M. Conroy; Corporals M. J. Edmond, A. Bock, P. Nealey, L. Hentz; Privates J. K. McGinniss, J. Keegan, H. Schiller, A. Ryan, G. Singleton, A. Tinley, J. Higgins, J. Hurley, L. Walsh, D. Shay, P. Ward, J. Gallagher, R. White, W. Reilley, J. Lorentz, D. Ryan, H. McGurty, J. Coleman, J. Torpey.

CROSS KEYS.

Killed—C. M. Smith.

LEE SPRINGS.

Killed—S. T. Reilley.

MALVERN HILL, July 1st, 1862.

Killed—Lieutenants S. D. McCauley, G. Frances; Privates M. Campbell, Z. Meyers, P. Higginbotham, J. Adams, J. Leggerton, J. Cullen, J. Sugre, J. Flemming.

Wounded—Captain D. Buckner; Dr. W. A. Robertson; Sergeants J. Brunning and Myer; Privates M. Hughes, M. Sloan, M. Hogan, W. Mooney, A. Beach, Fegenshee, McCance, J. Richardson, D. Corfatt, D. Curry, C. Delmas, C. Hayslip, M. McDonald, P. Meinhart, F. D. Cummins, D. McCann, J. Fitzgerald, F. Lorentz, T. Lucas, S. Murray, J. Delaney, W. McCluskey, D. Driscoll, B. Burns.

CEDAR RUN, August 10th, 1862.

Wounded—P. M. Kelley.

BRISTOW STATION, August 22d, 1862.

Killed—Sergeants M. J. O'Connor and Weiss; Privates B. Merthin, A. Zang, J. Phillips, W. Little, A. Mayer, J. Nolan, P. Frazer.

Wounded—Corporal M. Smith; Sergeant G. G. Kruse; Privates B. F. Pierson, B. Fontenot, T. Hayes, M. Welsh, N. Bucholz, F. Kane, P. Roe, M. Lusk, H. Schmidt, W. Knox, D. Murphy, E. Hoolahan, P. Lambert, S. J. Reilley, O. B. Green, F. Rosch, W. Murdock, W. Phair, J. Vogler, E. Schwenterman, M. Moffat, M. Shay.

MANASSAS (2), August 28th, 29th and 30th, 1862.

Killed—Lieutenant Healey, Sergeant S. Leslie; Privates, E. Dillon, H. Gleeson, E. T. Harney, J. Connoly, J. McGovern.

Wounded—Corporals, T. P. White and Kennedy; Privates, R. Ursery, F. Lawler, E. Weighart, T. Flynn, R. Nolan, P. P. Roach, P. Foley, J. W. Brady, J. Cahill, T. Wallace, P. P. Hickey.

CHANTILLY.

Killed—Corporals, L. Curtis and Roose; Privates, S. Jones, J. Williams, C. Vincent, P. McCormack, D. Havigan, J. Brason.

Wounded—Major W. Monaghan; Captain Rivera; Lieutenant G. P. Ring; Sergeants, E. Richelberger, —— Pfeil, R. Black, J. J. Conway; Privates, J. R. Gilbert, D. R. Thompson, J. Venoy, A. G. Swan, J. C. Hilliard, T. Sullivan, W. Strohfeldt, D. Brenan, S. Hill, T. Bowe, J. Condon, H. Manning, J. Graham, J. M. Gully, S. B. Winegar, J. Reddy, O. S. Fontenot, W. R. Olds, J. K. Gilbert, A. S. Nethery, H. G. Lilly, E. Grady, J. Murray, J. McDonough, M. Rooney, W. Higgins, N. Hunkett.

SHARSBURG, September 17th, 1862.

Killed—Colonel Strong: Captain Calloway, Captain H. M. Ritchie, Lieutenant M. Little, Lieutenant G. Lynne; Sergeant G. W. Joyner; Privates, E. Sloan, P. Oger, W. Mansell.

Wounded—Captain M. O. Connor, Captain G. P. Ring, Captain F. Clark; Lieutenant J. O. Martin, Lieutenant John Orr, Lieutenant C. H. Smith, Lieutenant Heintz, Lieutenant I. A. Reed; Sergeants, J. C. White, J. N. Cuffey, A. Hill, J. A. Schreiber, Turner, P. Carr, P. Burns, J. McGuire; Corporals, J. T Balton, L. Heintz. Privates, A. Cox, T. J. Gilbert, T. McCook, S. W. Morris, T. F. Gilbert, J. R. Traber, P. Ursery, R. A. Maines' W. W. Fisher, Wells, Coleman, V. L. Farnham, J. Smith, G. Cenas, G. P. Purcy, F. Rustin. M. Harkin, M. Sinnott, P. Tewhey, J. Carroll, J. Weiss, Meekler, Safford, G. Dunn, P. Burns, M. Sullivan, K. Comfort, P. Manning, Harding.

FREDERICKSBURG, December 13th, 1862.

Killed—Rungenberg.

Wounded—Captain Buckner; Sergeat W. Wood; Corporal F. Gilbert; Privates, T. Quinnally, J. Ryan, J. Kane, J. Keegan, J. Gallagher, J. Morrisson, W. Weible.

MUSTER ROLL OF CO. G, 1ST LOUISIANA REGIMENT,
FROM AUGUST TO OCTOBER, 1861.

Captain T. M. Dean; First Lieutenant E. D. Willett; Senior Second Lieutenant J. A. Blaffer, resigned October 14th, 1861; Junior Second Lieutenant A. N. Cummings; First Sergeant A. J. McAlpine; Second Sergeant W. Wilson; Third Sergeant George Richardson; Fourth Sergeant ———; Corporals R. E. Garnier, W. L. Doyle, H. Healey, W. D. Jones; Musician, W. H. Clark.

Privates—M. Crawley, G. B. Anthony, R. A. Cannell, D. DaSilva, John Bader, P. W. Carroll, L. F. Degray, L. H. Baker, F. Casserino,* Thomas Fitzgerald, John Begley, E. Cleve, J. S. Gerson, S. Benson*, Charles Collins, W. Hayeman, John Brennan, W. Connery, R A. Edwards, S. Brown, John Corcoran, Thomas Fitzgerald, W Henney, J. D. P. Jones, W. C. Lee, Jr., M. Hertz, Charles H. Leonard, C. M. Hillburn, James F. Lyman, John Meehan, S. M. Kell, J. A. McDonald, M. O'Rorke,* J. T. Kelly, M. McGregor, R. E. Patteson, J. Pendergast, R. S. Pruith, H. Prieur. P. H. Raymond, C. W. Reade, L. A. Richardson, Charles Roberts, B. Saphier, Robert Sanders, L. Schernger, H Schanb; F. Stubin, Abbt. Sturm, D. E. Sullivan, W. L. Thompson, William Tracy, George Werlein, P. Wiegel, L. E. White, George Wilson, B. Woolf.

Transferred to Company K, Captain Frost, September, 1861, J. M. Coy; transferred to Company D, Captain Nelligan, September, 1861, Patrick Corbine, Charles Padden, Thomas Pilkington, H. E. Himan.

I certify, on honor, that this muster roll exhibits the true state of Captain Deane's Company G, 1st Regiment, Louisiana Volunteers, for the period herein mentioned.

Lieutenant E. D. WILLETT, Commanding the Co.
November 1st, 1861.

ROLL OF CAPTAIN E. D. WILLETT, COMPANY G, 1st REGIMENT LA. VOLS.

FOR THE MONTH OF FEBRUARY, 1864.

Captain E. D. Willett, First Lieutenant M. O'Rourke, detailed as conscript officer at Mobile, Orderly Sergeant M. Hertz, Second Sergeant R. E. Garnier, Third Sergeant F. Casserino.

Privates—S. M. Benson, J. Bierman, E. Clerc, absent wounded, on furlough; P. W. Carroll, W. Conery, W. L. Doyle, detailed at Jackson Hospital, Richmond, Va.; D. H. Da Silva, absent on furlough; R. A. Edwards, absent, wounded; J. Mehan, detailed at Stanton Hospital; J. Pendergast absent, wounded, R. E. Patteson, R. S. Pewett, L. A. Richardson, D. E. Sullivan, detailed as Quarter Master Sergeant; R. Sanders, discharged February 27th, 1864.

I certify on honor that this Muster Roll exhibits the true state of Capt. E. P. Willet's Company G, 1st Regiment La. Vols., for the period herein mentioned.
P. H. CAVANAUGH,
Lieut. Commanding Company G.

*Elected Lieutenant, April 30th, 1862.

MUSTER ROLL OF THE DONALDSONVILLE ARTILLERY.

Captain, V. Maurin ;* promoted to Major of Artillery in 1864.
First Senior Lieutenant, William C. Lawes, resigned.
First Junior Lieutenant, Lestant Fortier, resigned.
Second Senior Lieutenant, M. Cazares, resigned.
Second Junior Lieutenant, R. P. Landry ; promoted to Second Senior Lieutenant in 1862 ; promoted First Junior Lieutenant in 1862 ; First Senior Lieutenant after the battle of Gettysburg ; promoted to Captain, in command of the Company, at the surrender.
First Junior Lieutenant, Camile Mollere ; promoted from Sergeant.
Second Senior Lieutenant, Hubert Trille; promoted from Sergeant at Gettysburg.
Second Junior Lieutenant, Antonio Sanchez ; promoted from the rank
Artificers—Bienvenue Cire, J. Oubre.
Bugler—J. N. Brand.
Commissary Sergeant—Aime Richard.
Orderly Sergeant—Clement Israel.
Sergeants—Tip Landry ; J. T. Blorrin ; John T. Landry ; Arthur Echavaria ; Oscar DeMesme, killed at Petersburg.
Corporals—Thomas Morelli, wounded at Gettysburg ; Horace Rougean, killed at Petersburg ; Thomas Byrne, Eugene Kerprotte,* H. Acasta,* A. M. Sobral, Ed. Terriot.
Privates—William V. Parks ; Pierre Ramirez, discharged ; Andre Suarez, wounded at Petersburg ; John Suarez ; P. S. Brand ; Charles Pidoux ; T. Babin ; J. G. Dugas ; J. B. Gaudet, wounded at Gettysburg ; Adolphe Grilhe, wounded at Fredericksburg ; L. Guidry ; J. O. Herbert; L. D. LeBlanc, lost a foot at Fredericksburg ; R. Suarez, J. O. Delmer ; D. Arcenaux ; T. Herbert, wounded at Sharpsburg ; N. Pleasancia, wounded at Chancellorsville ; Adolph Landry, discharged ; James Landry ; Henry Loeb ; John Richard ; Desire Landry, discharged ; Octave Landry ; S. Landry ; William Dalga Dafferes ; H. Duffel, Jr. ; Octave LeBlanc ; C. LeBlanc, discharged ; Jules Guedry ;* Louis Lacroix, discharged ; M. Ramirez ; Peter Hoplin ; Collins Southerland ; Octave Dupas, missing at Gettysburg ; William Ely* ; C. Savoie ; Ed. Newchurch, wounded at Petersburg ; Henry Newchurch, wounded at Petersburg ; S. Blanchard ; Gabriel Kling ; Abraham Klotz ; Evariste Aucoin ; D. Molere ; Ernest Monot ; William Marks ; Armas Friche ; Paul Humbert ; Emile Bergeron ; Octave Boudro ; Michel Morin ; Mathieu Morin ; Ed. Morin ; Herman Landry ; William

Kuhn, killed near Gordonsville; T. Viala; Ernest Hidalgo; Joseph Stanley, killed at Beaver Dam; L. Linossier, killed at Fredericksburg; A. Melancon, killed at Sharpsburg; J. Wagner, killed at Sharpsburg; Desire Tiroir, killed at Five Forks; John Hernandez, wounded at Frazier's Farm; R. Gaillard, died in Richmond; D. Shure, died in Fredericksburg; Caville LeBlanc;* S. Lyon, discharged; R. Winchester, discharged; J. Winner, lost his arm at Sharpsburg; Arthur Comstock, wounded at Petersburg; Julien Levy; Ernest R. Lynn; Albert Scmidt; L. Querolle; John Mioton; William F. Laresche, wounded at Petersburg; J. Eckleburg; Paul Drouilhet; James Carroters; Mike Joyner, wounded at Williamsport; Wm. Hart; Robert Chase, wounded at Harper's Ferry; James McCoy; H. C. Furry;* F. Fedderly; L. Walfrom; M. Flannigan; S. Murphy; G. Epinger; Wm. Williams; Eugene Cooley, wounded; Cyrille Decoux, wounded twice; Alexander McCullough; * Louis Comes; * Fustave Boudro;* William Delesternier;* J. Choinier;* Eugene Hardie, murdered since the war; H. Templet; C. Templet; E. Mataye; Seymour Mioton; Henry Nicaud; Rodolphe DeBlanc; T. Bynum; Tim Bohen; McEroy;* J. Bloom;* James Cellett, died in Richmond; Alfred Gauthreaux; A. Perrez, wounded at Fredericksburg; J. Wagner, killed on the Potomac; E. H. Levy, wounded at Petersburg.

* Died since the war.

CRESCENT RIFLES—COMPANY A.
(Co. B, Dreux's La. Battalion.)

Captain, S. W. Fisk; killed as Colonel 25th Louisiana.

First Lieutenant, Thad. A. Smith; Captain Sept. 13, 1861.

Second Lieutenant, N. T. N. Robinson; promoted to Captaincy in calvary service.

Second Lieutenant, T. A. Fairies; 1st Lieutenant Sept. 13, 1861; afterwards Major of Artillery, Trans-Mississippi.

Sergeants—M. C. Gladden, 1st Sergeant, promoted and killed in 1st La. Infantry; W. E. Huger, 2d Sergeant, wounded, 1st Lieut. Sept. 13, 1861; afterwards Lieutenant in 1st La. Regulars; D. D. Logan, 3d Sergeant, died in Virginia; W. M. Bridges, 4th Sergeant, promoted Lieutenant 1st La. Regulars, and Captain of Artillery.

Corporals—William Norcom, 1st Corporal, and afterwards Lieutenant and Aide-de-Camp to Gen. Barton; W. G. O'Regan, 2d Corporal; W. P. Clark, 3d Corporal, afterwards Adjutant of 14th La., and severely wounded; S. R. Garrett, 4th Corporal, afterwards Lieut. of Artillery. Privates—Columbus H. Allen, afterwards Adjutant and 1st Lieut. in Edmonston's Battalion, wounded at Shiloh as Aid de Camp of Gens. T. C. Hindman and R. G. Shaver; Captain of Ordnance and in charge of first arms sent to Trans-Mississippi; C. M. Allen, promoted Lieut., dead; H. T. Axon, dead; C. H. Aby, F. W. Ames, F. A. Armstrong, O S. Babcock, H. C. Brown, J. S. Beers, jr., F. W. Baker, dead, Geo. Brady, F. W. Brady. R. H. Benton, W. W. Buford, A. L. Bynum, dead E. O. Cook, Herbert Copeland, F. O. Claiborne, killed at Vicksburg as Captain Light Battery, J. F. Claiborne, dead, S. W. Cetton, George G Cooper, promoted 1st Lieutenant La. Regiment, John Cantley, B. A. Connelly, J. H. Didlake, killed in 6th La. as Lieutenant, E. T. Eggleston, B. C. Elliott, N. C. Folger, jr, dead, F. G. Folger, dead, H. W. Fairchild, Walton Fry, T. F. Gwathmey, A. Goodriche, S. Gregory, S. F. Green, F. M. Hall, Samuel E. Holt, dead, J. B. Hazzard, Abner Hammond, Charles J. Howell, Robert Howe, C. L. Huger, afterwards Lieutenant in La. Regulars, W. H. Houck, I. R. Harby, Jackson, John Johnson, George C. Knox, O Kettleson, J. G Lallande, J L. N. Logan-George H. Law, James Lingan, promoted Captain Battalion Sharpshooters, Warren Lockett, Jos. Lewis, H. T· Coffee, A. Soniat, Julius Keifer, Ed. Montgomery, dead, J. Mussleman, W. Morgan, jr., William McVicker, jr., W. B. McGaughy, T. Micon, A. G. Morse, W. L. Murphy, Joseph Murphy, John R. Miott, dead, P. T. Minor, promoted to 2d Lieut., dead, W. W. Mather, T. C. Newcomer, dead, J. B B. Neale, promoted Major in Ransom's Cavalry, George Norton, promoted Captain 13th La., F. N. Ogden, afterwards Lieut-Colonel of Cavalry, John Patton, dead, George S. Pettit, J. G. Poindexter, jr, J. B. Poole, dead-R. A. Phelps, afterwards Lieutenant of Artillery, dead, E Phelps, U. H. Pearce, Chas. Palfrey, Win S. Robinson, S. M. Roberts, E. L. Ross, W. F. Roath, J. C. Riley, T. M. Ryan, promoted Captain in 20th La. and killed at Murfreesboro, Clarence Rivers, killed, H. S. Smith, J. P. Smith, J. M. Schmidt, killed, W. H Shaw, T. C. Salter, A. L. Stuart promoted to Captain in 13th La., B T. Stewart, A P. Simpson, dead', afterwards Captain in 14th La., John F. Simpson, Lieut. in 14th La., Louis Skeels, Lieut. in 13th La., killed, W. E. Starke, killed in Virginia as Brig Gen., Robert Urquhart, J. D. VanBenthuysen, promoted Captain in 6th La., dead, T. W. Warren, J. R. Walker, George Walker, A. S. Watt, S. M. Wilkins, dead, M. M. Mann, W. H. Keen, F. C. Zacharie, afterwards promoted to Colonel 25th Consolidated Regiment.

Mustered into Confederate States' service and left New Orleans April 15th, 1861. There were four companies of Crescent Rifles. Company A was of Dreux's Battalion; Companies B and C were in the 7th La. Harry Hays was the first Captain of Company B. Company D was with the Crescent Regiment. Gen. Gladden, Colonel, in the Mexican war of the Palmetto Regiment, was the first Captain of the Company; and it received its organization from him. He was promoted to the Colonelcy of the 1st La. Regulars. He was killed at Shiloh, after being promoted to Brigadier General. The Company which had been mustered in for one year's service, at the expiration of that time either obtained promotions or were distributed among the other regiments, at the option of the men.

COMPLETE ROLL

OF

FENNER'S LOUISIANA BATTERY,

From the time of its Organization, May 16th, 1862,

UNTIL THE SURRENDER OF GENERAL TAYLOR, AT MERIDIAN, MISSISSIPPI, MAY 10, 1865.

Charles E. Fenner,* Captain; Thos. J. Duggan,* 1st Lieut.; W. T. Cluverius,* Jr. 1st Lieut.; E. Montgomery,* 2d Lieut.; G. P. Harris, Jr. 2d Lieut., discharged for disability; C. J. Howell,* Jr. 2d Lieut; Frederic Ernest,* 1st Sergeant; S. R. Garrett, 2d Sergt., commissioned as Lieut. in Faries Louisiana Battery; J. F. Early,* 3d Sergeant; S. H. Copeland, 4th Sergt., discharged Aug., 1864; A. P. Beers, 5th Sergt., commissioned Lieut. in Gibson's Louisiana Brigade; E. W. Finney, 6th Sergt., transferred to Richmond Howitzers; R. Woest,* 7th Sergt. Promoted to Sergeants—L. John Gill,* J. Carley,* C. Young,* R. Howe.* Quartermaster Sergeants—L. Steadman, discharged for disability, H. C. Walker,* G. Sumerall; W. Woelper,* 1st Corporal; J. K. Renaud,* 2d Corporal; J. H. Kennard, 3d Corporal; P. T. Minor, 4th Corporal, commissioned Lieut. in Gibson's Brigade; H. W. Palfrey, 5th Corporal; W. M. Brunet, 6th Corporal, killed at New Hope, May 25th, 1864. Promoted to Corporals as vacancies occurred—P. J. McGrath, wounded New Hope, May 25th, 1864; J. H. McDaniel, Commanding Lieut. in Gibson's Brigade. Corporals, J. H. Holmes,* D. B. Rindle;* F. M. Hall,* B. Cosby, discharged on disability; R. W. Benbury, wounded at Atlanta, (disabled); J. T. Davis, transferred to the Navy; B. N. McCarty,* J. F. Muse,* J. McGregor, W. J. Salter, wounded July 2d, 1864, disabled; A. David, A. H. Clark,* T. Murphy, killed, February, 1865. Privates, H. S. Addison,* C. Ahern,* J. Augustin,* T. J. Beck,* Baggett, discharged on disability; J. B. Seers,* C. Buhler,* C. A. Bessac, on detached duty time of parole; T. B. Bodley,* A. Bowman,* E. A. Brandao,* R. A. Bridgins, killed at New Hope, May 25th, 1864; Jos. Bridgins,* John Bridgins,* A. Britton, discharged for disability; B. T. Brunet,* R. H. Brunet,* T. W. Buddecke,* W. W. Bufford, C. C. Burns, L. Burnel,* R. H. Burton, detached; F. W. Bartels, detached; T. W. Brammes, supposed to have been killed; J. Beylle,* P. Callahan,* W. Campbell, detached Ord. Sergeant and Artillery; W. S. Campbell,* F. Carroll,* J. P. Casey,* F. S. Carey, G. P. Childress,* M. B. Childress,* A. B. Clark,* R. R. Conningworth,* J. D. Conway,* W. Conrad.* W. H. Cook,* W. B. Cooper,* J. B. Cooper,* J. J. Corprew, detached, wounded May 25th, 1864; W. Corprew, detached to Ordnance Department at Resacca; S. W. Cotton, discharged for disability; J. Crawford, discharged over age on expiration of term; R. H. Crawford, detached; W. S. Crawford,* T. Cusack,* J. S. Clark, sick in hospital; P. C. Clark,* E. David, discharged for disability; L. Desforges, detached; G. W. Dicks,* J. Dirker,* G. Douglass,* J. Duggan, commissioned as

---

* Paroled at the general surrender.

Quartermaster; W. Chap. Duncan,* G. T. Dunbar, detached; E. O. Eaton, wounded May 25th, 1864, New Hope, paroled at Selma; J. T. Eggleston, commissioned Lieut. of Marine; F. Enders, detached; R. Erichson,* H. W. Fairchild,* G. M. Fisher,* Chas. V. Fisher,* wounded at Resacca; C. N. A. Fitzenriter,* T. Flanagan, detached; F. G. Folger, detached; G. L. Folger,* N. C. Folger, on furlough time of parole; R. B. Ford,* R. P. Ford, missing, (supposed to have been killed); G. W. Fry,* J. J. Gidiere, detached; H. R. Giffney, H. Guider, detached and after commissioned; J. J. Goode, P. Graham, killed May 12th, 1864; A. Grivot,* S. B. Gill,* S. Green, commissioned Lieut. in Forrest's Cavalry; T. F. Gwathmey, detached; G. E. Haller,* A. E. Hammond,* J. B. Hayes, detached; G. H. Helm, transferred; A. D. Henriquez,* H. H. Hester,* J. Henley,* J. Hibben,* J. H. Hollingsworth,* G. Horton,* W. F. Hosmer,* Jos. P. Hornor, J. S. Hudnal,* D. Hughes, sick in hospital; A. H. M. Hunter,* L. C. Ivy,* B. F. Jonas,* F. P. Jones, A. P. Joyner, E. Judice, killed at Mt. Pleasant; J. F. Kay, died in hospital; W. H. C. Laade,* C. A. Lagroue,* W. H. Layton, killed at Jackson; L. C. Levy, on sick furlough; W. Lindsay, J. J. Link,* R. Little, discharged over age;. J. O. Locke, died at Marietta; J. L. N. Logan,* L. P. Long.* C. Lauber, wounded at Resacca; W. Lockett, A. Magnon, B. Maguer, died at Marietta; G. Mather,* H. C. Martin,* E. T. Manning, discharged for disability; H. L. Manning, transferred to navy; A D. Macaulay, discharged for disability; A. McCartney, A. McLean, paroled Richmond March 2d, 1865, drowned attempting to-cross Lake Pontchartrain in an open boat; P. J. McGuire, wounded at Atlanta and detailed; R. McNair, sick in hospital; G. Miller, John Miller, died at Jackson, Louisiana; J. E. B. Miller, transferred to the navy; H. G. Morgan,* T. C. Morrison.* C. Mount, discharged under age; F. Mullen, killed at Resacca; L. P. Murphy, detailed on secret service; John Murphy, killed at Port Hudson; D. M. Murphy,* Jos. Murphy, wounded at New Hope, disabled; J. Hyes Myers, W. R. Norcom, commissioned Lieut. on Barton's Staff; T. C. Newcomer, detached; J. W. Noyes,* S. J. Pecot,* J. T. Pecot,* wounded; G. S. Petit,* C. M. Perrin,* H. Pearson,* J. L. Pierson,* T. Porteous,* J. W. Person, commissioned Lieut. of Privateer; I. T. Preston, killed at Murfreesboro; L. Prophet,* J. W. Ramsey, transferred to the navy; T. C. Raby,* T. Reid, W. E. Rees,* J. G. Reeve, J. R. Redmond, absent, sick; J. L. Risk, absent, sick; W. H. Rogers, detached; E. D. Ross, commissioned Lieut. in Gibson's Louisiana Brigade; Ross, discharged for disability; T. Seaton,* H. Seibert,* J. L. Simmons,* W. H. Shaw, J. F. Shaw,* J Lewis Sharkey, J. J. Sharkey,* M. Sharkey,* T. L. Shute, transferred to Bradford's Scouts; W. R. Skelton,* E. Smith,* M. Smith,* A. B. Sparks, killed at Jackson; H. C. Stannard, sick in hospital; H. St. Germain, prisoner of war; G. M. Steirer,* T. J. Stewart, detached; F. M. C. Swain,* L. Skeels, commissioned Lieut. in Gibson's Louisiana Brigade, killed; H. S, Smith, transferred to the navy; W. W. Thompson, M. L. Thompson,* Mac. Thompson, H. J. Thomas, N. N. Trotter,* W. T. Vaudry,* G. Voorhies,* P. J. Vigo, prisoner; H. D. Wall,* L. H. Walker, Q. Waterman, transferred to the navy; S. Waters, detached; O. Weise, E. G. Wells, sick in hospital; Wilson, discharged for disability; S. Wilkins,* A. L. White,* T. J. Wells,* T. McK. Whiteman,* P. Work, discharged for disability; Artificers—J. Weingartner, sick in hospital; H. C. Kennedy, detached; W. T. J. Kerwish, transferred to the navy; H. Nathan, sick in hospital; Private—W. H. Renaud,* Artificers—J. W. Steele,* C. A. Smith.*

List of men temporarily assigned to duty in Fenner's Battery, paroled at Meridian, Mississippi, May 10th, 1865.

C. Bevans, N. Burns, J. Curran, J. Cowan, H. Folwell, A. V. Gusman, J. Moran.

* Paroled at the general surrender.

LOUISIANA TROOPS IN THE WEST.

BRIGADE OF THE ARMY OF TENNESSEE.

After the retreat from Corinth to Tupelo, Miss., the brigading of troops from the same State, under instructions from the War Department, was commenced. At this time the following regiments composed the Louisiana contingent in that army :*
The First Louisiana Regular Infantry, under command of Col. D. W. Adams, who as Lieut. Colonel had succeeded Col.

---

*Apropos of the Louisiana troops in the West and of those which finally joined them at Mobile was the 28th Louisiana, which went out a short time after the Confederate Response call of Beauregard, and which was placed at Vicksburg under Pemberton. Col. Thomas (now of Ascension) was its first Commander ; but Allen becoming too crippled to longer command the brigade known by his name, Col. Thomas became one of his successors and J. O. Landry became Colonel of the 28th.

As digressions in a book about curious incidents, and gossip about men and places, are sometimes the most readable part, a word about the last mentioned name, now held by one of our best known public men, will not be read without interest.

The Landry family, which dates back to the French and Spanish occupation of the country, is probably the most numerous of any in the State—the blood of the first settler flowing in the veins of fully 2000 of his descendants. The parish in which it is established bears his name, and a large portion of it was given the family as a Spanish grant. The name has given to the State Trasimond Landry, for Lieut. Governor, J. Aristide, a member of Congress, Narcisse, a distinguished soldier at Chalmette, Amadeo, one of the city fathers of New Orleans and Chairman of the Finance Committee, and Theodule, as a Surveyor General. In the Confederate War, R. Prosper Landry was Captain of the gallant Donaldson Artillery of Lee's army.

Of Col. J. O. Landry, now Administrator of Commerce of New Orleans, it may be stated, by way of showing that races do not degenerate in this climate, that the present representative of the old Norman name is over six feet in stature, robust and red faced in proportion, and is physically one of the most powerful men in the State.

Col. Landry went into the Confederate service as Lieut. Colonel of the 28th Louisiana, carrying with him five companies from his own parish, and as many blood relatives as the Chief of a Scottish Clan.

A. H. Gladden (promoted to a Brigadiership and killed at Shiloh). Gladden's regiment had served with distinction at Pensacola and had been transferred in time to take part in the battle of Shiloh.†

The numbering of the regiment gave rise subsequently to much confusion, owing to the fact that another regiment commanded by Colonel (afterwards General) Grey was formed in the Trans-Mississippi with the same name (28th), neither regiment, in the disordered condition of the State and the absence of all facilities for communication, knowing anything, at the time of organization, of the existence of the other. As other regiments however had meanwhile been organized and numbered, they both retained the same name until the end of the war.

The command from Camp Moore was sent to Vicksburg, and suffered all of the miseries incident to that long and memorable siege.

As a curious illustration of what fighting amounted to there, the following is, in substance, quoted from Mrs. Dorsey's excellent Life of Gov. Allen:

"The Federals having discovered the weakness of the fortifications in front of the 21st called for a hundred volunteers, to each of whom a $300 bounty and a discharge were offered. They obtained the men, but were saved the necessity of making out the discharges. That is, ninety-seven men were killed before reaching the ditch, two fell inside of it, and one man alone managed to get back."

At the battle of Chicasaw Bayou, Landry's command were placed in Thermopylean style, at a narrow neck of firm land, across which the Federals were about marching, in greatly superior numbers. He was ordered to hold his ground at all hazards. This, his regiment did, and so desperate was the work, for six hours, that the two forces were not twenty feet apart when the 28th was relieved.

When Breckenridge made his attack on Baton Rouge, Col. Landry, who was serving on military commission, patriotically accompanied that General, who had been deprived by sickness of the attendance of some of his staff, as one of his aids. This expedition was made brilliant by some of the most desperate fighting of the war.

Col. Landry was paroled at the surrender of Pemberton at Vicksburg, and was exchanged some thirty days after. He then took command of the 22d at Enterprise and reported to Maj. Gen. Dabney H. Maury at Mobile. He there took charge of the fortifications around Mobile and was afterwards sent out on picket duty to Pollard Station to check Federal raids. He remained at Mobile until the surrender of that town at the close of the war. He has since held the position of City Controller, and is now one of the City Administrators.

† Probably as varied a career of service as any seen by any soldier from this State was that of Capt. Wm. Taylor Mumford, the host now of the City

The Eleventh Louisiana, Col. S. F. Marks, which had honorably participated in the campaigns of the Western army, distinguishing itself at Belmont and Shiloh.

The Twelfth Louisiana, Col. S. M. Scott, which had also meritoriously served in the same campaigns.

The Thirteenth, Col. R. L. Gibson,* which had been similarly situated.

The 16th,† Col. Preston Pond.

The 17th, Col. Hurd.

The 18th, Col. Mouton.

The 19th, Col. B. L. Hodge.

The 20th, Col. Reichart.

Hotel, who went out as Second Lieutenant in Hebert's Regiment of Artillery. The Major served with distinction at the capture of New Orleans, was made prisoner and had the same luck happen to him at the siege of Vicksburg, while serving as a staff officer. He did good service in the Western campaigns, in the battles of Tennessee and Georgia, and was captured for the last time at the siege and fall of Mobile.

*Gen. Gibson entered the army with a great reputation for literary attainments, having carried off the valedictory at Yale, graduated in the Law Department of the State University, and having served as *attaché* a year at the American Legation at Madrid. He commanded the rear guard of the Western Army the first day of the retreat from Nashville, and was then sent to Mobile. He was assigned the conduct of the operations (near the water battery of the Spanish Fort) with a division of infantry and forty pieces of artillery, including his own brigade and Col. Patton's 22d Louisiana Artillery. In the race of '74 he was elected to Congress.

†E. John Ellis, Esq., was elected 1st Lieut. St. Helena Rebels early in the summer of 1861. This company was mustered into the 16th Louisiana Infantry, under the command of Col. Preston Pond. It participated in the battle of Shiloh, and in all of the subsequent movements of the Western army under Gens. Johnson and Bragg. On the reorganization of the army, Ellis was promoted Captain. He was in the engagements at Murfreesboro, Tenn., and Chickamauga, and Missionary Ridge, in which latter battle he was made prisoner, in a hand to hand fight with the enemy. He was imprisoned at Johnson's Island for the remainder of the war, and paroled in July, 1865. Since the war he has, with his partner, Gov. McEnery, occupied a leading position at the bar, been elected to Congress, and holds a position in the public mind for honesty, capacity, and past discharge of duty second to that of no one who has been entrusted with similar high positions.

These were all new regiments, which had been hastily raised and hurried forward to the army, where they were reinforced by the 25th, Col. S. W. Fisk, commanding.

Besides these infantry regiments, a battalion of infantry, which had been stationed at Columbus and Fort Pillow, was augmented by several independent companies and constituted the 21st Louisiana, under Col. Kennedy.

These regiments composed all the organized bodies of Louisianians serving as infantry in the Western Army, if to them were added the three companies of Clack's Battalion of Confederate Guards. The Battalion of Orleans Guards had disbanded, many members joining the Orleans Guards Battery, Capt. Ducatel, or the Washington Artillery, 5th company—the two Louisiana batteries.

At the time of the arrival of the troops at Tupelo, Miss., the older regiments had been much worn in service and diminished by sickness and casualities in battle, during a service of six or eight months, active campaigning, in the winter and spring. The new regiments, on the other hand, recruited mostly from the country districts had fallen, to a great extent, victims to the unwholesome location of Corinth, and its fatal effects.

In this condition were these regiments, when Gen. Bragg took command of the army and commenced a re-organization, preparatory to carrying the summer and fall campaign into Kentucky, and by the time the forces were transferred to the neighborhood of Chattanooga, and ready for the onward march, the formation of the Louisiana troops had undergone considerable change in perfecting the State organization. Leaving undisturbed the 1st and 12th regiments, the old 11th had been disbanded, and a battalion of two companies of sharpshooters had been formed under command of Maj. Austin,* and the balance

---

*Jas. B. Lingan, Esq., (grandson of the Gen. McC. Lingan, killed in the now almost forgotten political disturbance in Baltimore in 1812) was with this organization. After following the fortunes of Dreux's Battalion to Pensacola, in April, '61, he was with that officer in the fatal reconnoissance on the Peninsula, which led to the death of the first volunteer battalion leader from the State. Lingan came home with others of his command

of the regiment was distributed among the other regiments. Clack's Battalion had been also disbanded and similarly distributed, but on the eve of the march, under orders from Richmond, it was re-organized, and together with the 18th and Crescent Regiments,† was transferred to the Trans-Mississippi

in charge of the casketed corpse of Dreux and took part in the funeral —the great sensation pageant of the day. Lingan was afterwards elected 2d Lieutenant of Cannon Guards, in Marks' 11th Regiment and was with the first troops that disembarked with the invading army of Kentucky. The 11th had a hot time of it at Belmont, having to cross the river to the support of Cheatham, but after a variety of vicissitudes, came off with a number of prisoners and a standard of colors Gen. Polk would have promoted him for his part in capturing these, but for Lingan's honesty, who declined the proffered advance in rank, on the ground that some other comrade was really entitled to the honor. He served in the Sharpshooters after its organization, as Captain of a company, and was looked on as one of its most efficient officers.

After the battle of Chickamauga and Missionary Ridge, his command having been shattered by casualties in battle and reduced to scarcely more than a corporal's guard, he accepted a staff position under Lt. Gen. Polk and served under Col. T. F. Seviere (now of Sawanee College, Tennessee) as Asst. Adjt. General. Just before the close of the war he was ordered to Richmond as bearer of dispatches, and was assigned to duty as Asst. Com. of Exchange, under Col. Robt. Oulde, by Gen. Breckenridge, at that time Secretary of War.

†This was commanded (together with a brigade in the last part of the war) by Col. Bosworth, who went out with it at the time it left the city, as Major, at which time it numbered over one thousand men. In the fight which immediately followed its arrival at Shiloh, at a critical portion of the day's fighting, it struck Prentiss' Brigade on the flank, and compelled its surrender, in reply to a call from Bosworth, who had been galloping on ahead, in advance of his men, answered by a downward motion of his sword on the part of the Federal officer in command. Bishop Polk happening to pass in that direction, Bosworth, forgetting his hearer's cloth, inquired how he was to fence in the whole d—d batch. The Bishop replied by referring him to an Aid, repeating meanwhile, mechanically, Bosworth's exact phrase.

Col. Bosworth was with the regiment in its marches (as given elsewhere) in the Trans-Mississippi. He was of too impatient and vehement a temperament to get along always, without some stormy episodes, at Dick Taylor's headquarters and elsewhere, in the generally mixed-up condition of things which then existed; he, however, arrived at the honor of commanding a brigade, and has since been named President, by his old Crescent Regiment, of the Benevolent Association of the same name.

Department. The 4th, Col. H. W. Allen, and 17th had been previously detached at Corinth and ordered to Vicksburg.

The Kentucky campaign was now inaugurated, and the Louisianians first took up their line of march as a State brigade, under command of Brig. Gen. D. W. Adams, recently promoted and assigned to this duty.

As now constituted, it consisted of the 13th, Col. R. L. Gibson; 16th, Col. Gober; 19th, Capt. commanding; 20th, Col. Reichart; 25th, Col. S. W. Fisk, and the 5th Co. Washington Artillery, as well as the battalion of sharpshooters under Major J. E. Austin.

As such its organization continued until the end of the war. It participated in the battles of Perryville, Murfreesboro, Chickamauga, Missionary Ridge and in nearly all of the engagements during Johnson's retreat through Georgia. It bore a prominent part in the battles under Hood of the 28th and 31st July, 1864, in front of Atlanta, as well as at Jonesboro and Nashville, in Hood's Tennessee Campaign. At the battle of Franklin it was held in reserve.

Its active career on the field terminated with the defence of Spanish Fort near Mobile.

The brigade surrendered and was disbanded at Meridian, Miss., May 9th, 1865, being then embraced in the command of Lieut. Gen. Dick Taylor. It remained during its whole military history constituted as it originally was as a brigade, if we except that the 1st Louisiana Regulars, the 4th Louisiana Infantry, 4th Louisiana Battalion, under Col. McEnery,* and

---

*Governor McEnery was born in 1833 at Petersburg, Va., and came to the State when a child. He spent a year in college at South Hanover, graduated in law at the University in New Orleans in '53, and in '57 was given the lucrative appointment of Land Register, which position he ultimately lost by stumping the State for Douglas. He went out to Floyd's assistance in West Virginia as an Infantry Captain, and was then sent to Savannah and Charleston, this latter city being saved by the timely arrival of his battalion at the battle of Secessionville. This fact was recognized by Gen. Evans, who in a general order declared that the service rendered by this battalion was so great that they merited a formal commendation before the whole of his troops. The Federal General at the time had captured

30th† Louisiana were joined to it before the commencement of the Georgia campaign under Johnson. At its surrender the brigade was commanded by Brig. Gen. R. L. Gibson and consisted of Austin's Battalion, the 13th and 20th Regiments consolidated, Col. F. A. Campbell, the 1st Regulars, 4th Battalion, 4th Regiment, 20th, 16th, 19th and 25th consolidated, under Col. F. C. Zacharie,‡ comprising in all about 250 rank and file.

With the 22d at Mobile was Capt. Samuel Barnes in command of a battery of Cohorn mortars at Mobile; at which

Fort Secessionville, when McEnery arrived with 200 men, regained possesion of the Fort, and finding three gunners among his men, held 10,000 Federal troops at bay until Confederate reinforcements could arrive. Had Secessionville fallen it would have involved the loss of Charleston. The battalion was received with great honor afterwards by the ladies and citizens of that important seaport. McEnery's Battalion was also at Jackson, Miss., Chickamauga (with Wilson's Georgia Brigade), Dalton, Resaca, and he was twice wounded. In 1866 he was a member of the Legislature, and in 1872 was (though never permitted by the administration at Washington to perfom the duties of the office) elected Governor of Louisiana.

†Leon Bertoli, now City Administrator, who went out with the Orleans Guards and who was afterwards with the 30th Louisiana, is an honorable instance of the Confederate volunteer, of intelligence and capacity, who fought until too badly wounded to be of much service to himself or to the Confederacy. He went through all of the battles of the army of the West until the autumn of 1864 when he was maimed in his right arm by the explosion of a shell, and lost entirely his hand.

‡Col. Francis Charles Zacharie, the son of the well known merchant of that name, succeeded to the command of the 25th Regiment upon the deaths of Cols. Fisk and Lewis, and among a variety of other brilliant services in Virginia, the West and the Trans-Mississippi, commanded the Regiment in the charge of Breckenridge's Division, on the 2d of January, 1863, and was present at Murfreesboro, when the 25th lost 287 out of 457 men. After the battle of Spring Hill he was detached and guarded a body of 1600 prisoners during a march of 600 miles, in midwinter, and with small-pox prevalent as one of the least evils. Zacharie boasts the honor of having studied at Mount Pleasant Military Academy, New York, graduated at Trenton, New Jersey, and at the Louisiana University. Since the war he has been twice elected to the Legislature and counted out, and failed by only a few votes of obtaining the last Congressional nomination, over Gibson. He is now devoting his time to the profession of law.

place he was shot through the head by a ball which passed to one side of his nose and which came out at a correspondingly opposite point of the skull. His recovery was regarded as but little less than miraculous.

Another battery was there commanded by Maj. Richard Bond, who had been with Majs. Mumford, Squires and Hayes detailed to the Trans-Mississippi, to organize the Artillery of that department, afterwards recalled to their command, when the siege of Vicksburg commenced. Mumford then became Adjutant on the staff of Gen. Edward Higgins, commanding all of the Artillery. This was organized into a brigade, consisting of the 1st Louisiana Regulars, 1st Tennessee Regular Artillery, 7th Louisiana Battalion, commanded by Col. Fred. Ogden, 22d Volunteer Louisiana, 23d, and the Bladen Artillery of Miss., a light battery. The line of batteries was five miles long, and there were in position 28 Columbian rifles and 10 inch mortars.

Another actor upon this arena was Richard Agar, an officer of the British army, who on first visiting America brought along his uniform for the purpose of assisting at the reception of the Prince of Wales. He entered the 1st Louisiana Artillery as Lieutenant, served with it through the war and is still of this city.

On General Gibson's staff was Captain Hugh H. Bein, Adjutant General, Captain Stewart, Inspector General, Captain Norton and Captain Eustis (now of the house of Baldwin & Co.) as staff officers. The Senator of the same name from the parish of Orleans (Eustis) was upon Magruder's staff.

AUSTIN'S BATTALION.

The Louisiana Battalion of Sharp Shooters was organized at Camp "Lookout," near Chattanooga, Tenn., in August, 1862, from the 11th Louisiana Regiment, then disbanded by an order of the War Department. Major J. E. Austin was ordered to organize a battalion under the special Act of Congress, providing for sharpshooters.

The order gave him liberty to pick about two hundred men from the 11th Louisiana Regiment, the remainder of which was to be distributed between the 13th and 20th Louisiana Regiments.

This battalion was organized just prior to Bragg's movement into Kentucky and its first brilliant service was at the battle of Perryville.

Gen. Adams was ordered to attack the enemy in a thickly wooded eminence in his front, and was moving forward across a broken but cleared ground, to do so, Austin's Battalion occupying the extreme right of the brigade.

The enemy were formed in eschelon by brigades, but the first line of that formation was not discovered until Adams' Brigade had almost passed beyond it, and then it was only perceived on the right owing to the irregular topography of the country. As the brigade was moving forward in line of battle, Austin's Battalion was seen to change front, form to the right in double quick time and quit the main line of battle. Adams being in the centre of the brigade, was astonished to see this eccentric movement, and sent a staff officer to at once order Major Austin to bring his battalion back into line. But the staff officer had barely reached the Major with the order, when the battalion opened a terrific fire on the enemy's right flank and rear.—The enemy were completely surprised. They were evidently watching the Confederates in their immediate front, and had no knowledge of the presence of a force on their flank. The attack was so sudden, furious and dashing that a whole Federal brigade was put to rout, across the field with immense slaughter; Col. Jewett, of the 15th Kentucky regiment was killed on the spot, and Col. W. H. Lyttle, of the 99th Ohio, afterwards Gen. Lyttle, the author of the famous, " I am dying, Egypt, dying," was dangerously wounded and captured. The Federal line that was routed was lying down behind a stone wall, waiting for an attack in front, and as Austin's Battalion swept by the flank, Major Austin perceived from his position on horse-back, the enemy to his right not above 50 yards. Both bodies discovered each other about the same time; but Austin's Battalion being in motion, changed front so rapidly and precipitated itself upon the rear and flank with such impetuosity, that the line of the enemy broke in inextricable confusion and melted away in fearful slaughter. This movement of Austin's Battalion was a brilliant tactical manœuvre on the field and saved Adams' Brigade; for if it had moved with Adams' Brigade forward to attack, in front, the refused flank of the enemy, it would have been at the mercy of the enemy, who would have fallen upon it, front and rear.

Gen. Adams rode to Major Austin on the field and complimented him in the highest terms and said: " Nothing but such a brilliant success could excuse an officer for taking his command from the main line without orders." In his report also of this engagement from Bryantsville, Ky., Gen. Adams makes a special mention of Maj. Austin for conspicuous courage and skill, and of the gallantry of his battalion.

This battalion stood foremost in the army of Tennessee as a battalion of Sharp-shooters, distancing all competitors in drill and manœuvre, and took the palm at Tullahoma in March, 1863, in the celebrated drill of Hardee's corps over all others. This was at the same time that the 13th and 20th (consolidated) drilled in presence of Hardee, Breckenridge and others, against the celebrated 17th Tennessee regiment, and achieved a victory.

As to the condition of arms and accoutrements the commanding General in an order dated Tullahoma, March 22d, 1863, says : " At the inspection of arms, the General commanding found only Austin's Battalion in perfect order. The appearance of the guns does high credit to the commander and his officers, as well as to the privates."

THE ORLEANS GUARD BATTALION AND BATTERY.

ORGANIZATION AND MUSTER-ROLL.

The following is the complete list of the officers and men who went out with the above organization:

BATTALION.

Leon Queyrouse, Major; E. Puech, Adjutant Major; Dr. Ferrier, Surgeon; A. Pitot, jr., Sergeant Major; Alphonse Tertrou, Quartermaster; Victor Labatut, Color Bearer.

COMPANY A.

Captain, Chs. Roman.
1st Lieutenant, J. B. Sorapuru; 2d Lieutenant sr., T. Moreno; 3d Lieutenant, T. O. Trepagnier.
1st. Sergeant, P. A. Judice; 2d, E. Villere; 3d, L. Menard; 4th, V. Prados; 5th, J. R. Toleando.
1st Corporal, P. L. Bouny; 2d, W. H. Hewitt; 3d, Commissary, Oscar J. Forstall; 4th, R. Fernandez.
F. S. Coiron, P. A. Vienne, O. Morel, E. Collon, J. Aldige, Just· Andry, A. V. Angiboust, A. Beaudet, J. A. Belaume, J. Bermudez, F. E. Bernard, D. Bienvenu, F. Blois, L. Boudousquie, G. Bryan, A. Bussae, E. Bertus, E. Cassard, C. C. Crawford, A. Cruzat, L. Cucullu, G. B. Cury, A. Darcantel, V. David, jr., E. DeArmas, F.|DeArmas, H. DeBuys, A. Delery, G. P. Devron, E. Ducatel, L. Duffel, A. D. Dugue, E. Dupre, A. D'Hebecourt, E. Duplantier, G. Fecel, E. Fixary, U. Forestier, L. Forestier, A. Forstall, Octave Forstall, Ernest Forstall, Theobald William Forstall, L. Fortin, F. Gaiennie, P. Ganel,

A. Gardere, G. Del'Isle, jr., S. Gerard, E. Glenny, A. Grima, E. Harris, R. A. Hebrard, M. E. Hernandez, E. Hoa, C. V. LaBarre, Jules Larose, C. E. LeBlanc, Euge ne LeBlanc, E. B. Livaudais, L. A. Livaudais, E. Malus, E. Miltenberger, A. Morel, O. M. Opdenweger, G. Pascal, E. Peychaud, A. Peychaud, jr., C. Philippi, G. Pitot, W. Pilard, J. J. A. Plauche, L. A. Polk, H. Rousselin, F. A. Rasch, L. Rocquet, C. H. Taney, A. Tournemire, C. Trouard, T. J. Verret, James Vienne, J. G. Vienne, J. C. Villars, J. A. Webre.

COMPANY B.

Captain, Eugene Staes.

1st Lieutenant sr., E. DeBuys; 2d Lieutenant jr., O. Carriere; 3d Lieutenant sr., P. O. Labatut.

1st Sergeant, Louis Arnauld; 2d, G. Porce; 3d, A. Hincks; 4th, V. Labatut; 5th, L. DeBuys.

1st Corporal, Emil Carriere; 2d, H. Ferrand; 3d, F. Perry, jr.; 4th, J. E. Villavaso.

P. E. Crozat, Ernest Bourges, T. Libois, A. G. Romain, F. Arnand, E. S. Audler, G. Aguillard, F. Avegno, E. Arcenaux, John Archinard, E. Auzoat, N. Bienvenu, jr., S. Blassman, H. C. Barnett, E. R. Barnett, J. A. Bordnzat, M. F. Bouis, H. Boisblanc, Hte Bienvenu, H. C. Benit, A. W. Brette, Chs. Beaulieux, D. Conturie, Ls. Courcelle, H. Chagnon, J. Colla, T. N. Cobb, H. Y. DeMahy, P. E. Durand, Paul J. Davon, H. Daspit, O. J. Delery, T. I. Danziger, Chs. Liard, L. J. Even, L. E. Fazende, Emile Fortin, Ex. Guerin, B. Genois, E. Hirch, F. Jorda, Albert Johns, L. P. Harang, A. Kilshaw, B. P, Leefe, P. Lacoste, B. Lacoste, E; E. Livaudais, P. J. Lefevre, Louis Gregoire, John Lefevre, Chs. Laferriere, Gus. Luminais, A. Lusto, E. Lamouta, D. C. Levy, V. Martin, Chs. Marine, Hy. Maurras, Alex. McArthur, F. Nicaud, E. Nicaud, F. Marcotte, J. D. Olivier, A. Pechier, A. Pochee, Louis Piderit, Jas. Rennie, Jos. Schrempp, Emil Villavaso, L. Villavaso, Justin Wolkart, Jules Volkart, A. G. Wagner, L. A. Gaillard, A. E. DeBlanc, F. M. Campbell, Chs. Jumonville, Hy. Bonneval, Francis Lafayette, O. Andry, M. Cousin, O. Andry, Debouchel Prosper, Constant Cazeaux.

COMPANY C.

Captain: August Roche.
1st Lieutenant: Fred. Thomas; 2d, EugeneTourne; 3d, Lucien Charvet.
1st Sergeant: A. Granpre; 2d, E. Barbier; 3d, A. Luminais; 4th, V. Pujos, jr.; 5th, A. Gonzales.
1st Corporal: F. Greig; 2d, A. Galot; 3d, J. E. Dutillet; 4th, L. Courtin; Sappers: A. R. Blair, Tambour: Delimage; Treasurer: George C. Brower.
A. Aubert, S. Alexander, O. Aymes, Js. H. Brown, O. L. Blean, R. Bachemin, L. Bertol, F. Brugier, F. Cavaroc, A. Castanedo, E. P. Barlin, A. Kadroy, A. Caranovas, C. Cavelier, G. Dockter, H. Delasey, E. Dumas, J. Dumas, F. Dupre, L. Dessin, E. Dejean, P. E. Dugue, H. Ferriot, O. Fellon, E. Fagot, C. Gessler, Arthur Grailhe, J. A. Girod, W. H. Guinaud, J. B. Jacquin, E. Jastram, E. Krost, T, Kaes, F. Labauve, N. Labarthe, J. H. Laudon, R. Legier, A. Lange, P. Lemaitre, L. Leefe, Chas. Longuemere, jr., A. Lebesque, J. B. Levesque, J. D. Levesque, V. Lobit, A· Montamat, Arthur Morehead, J. Noblom, A. Olivier, J. Ollie, P. Pousson, Ernest Robin, L. Rivierre, J. Roche, E. Robert, Edward Ruffier, E. Rosiere, L. Sibeck, Leonce Soniat, O. St. Alexandre, L. Smith, P. Sarrazin, H. Tronchet, E. Treme, J. T. Thibodeaux, J. L. Vincent, H. Viavant, E. Duval, H. L. Frebourg, C. H. Franck, Paul N. Lacroix, J. B. Delahoussaye, G. A. Callery, Alfred A. Fuselier, C. H. Hinclay, B. DeMonford, C. A. Grevenberg, G. Rosiere, J. E. Santon, A. R. Blais.

COMPANY D.

(DeClouet's Guards.)

Captain: Charles Tertrou.
1st Lieutenant: Paul DeClouet; 2d, Alfred Voorhies; 2d, B. De St. Clair.

1st Sergeant: A. L. Tertrou; 2d, Adelma Broussard; 3d, Charles Guilbeau; 4th, Alex. DeClouet; 5th, Charles Gueriniiere.

1st Corporal: Edmond LeBlanc; 2d, Jules Broussard; 3d, Louis Comeau; 4th, J. S. Robichaud.

J. B. Angell, Louis Allemand, Ozeme Allemand, Dazincourt Babineau, Euze Broussard, Alphonse Broussard, Alphonse Bulliard, E. Bernard, M. Bienvenu, S. Bienvenu, J. B. Barras, Numa Bienvenu, C. Babineau, A. Bienvenu, V. Bueche, C. Breaux, S. T. Bienvenu, C. Badon, D. Badon, C. Broussard, F. O. Champagne, E. C. Caillier, N. J. Caillier, Adolphe Castille, Joseph Colette, Pauline Cormier, S. A. Coudroy, Ferdinand Colette, L. Comeau, Valiere Campagne, S. David, Alcide Dupres, J. C. Dupuis, Desire Dugas, John Devalcourt, Jacques Delhomme, J. B. Dautreuil, Antoine Frederic, Homere Gautier, Daniel Green, Julien Guilbeau, Jules Guilbeau, Sosthene Guilbeau, Anatole Gautier, Destival Gantreau, O. P. Guidry, Aug. Guilbeau, Emile Guilbeau, J. P. Guidry, John Jackson, Robert Jackson, Jules Jamard, Arville Hollier, Henry Religare, Numa Landry, Ant. Latiolias, Edmond Latiolais, Edmond Laperuse, Antoine Lasseigne, Alexandre Lasseigne, C. Landry, A. Leblanc, Arville Leblanc, Desire Leblanc, J. Melancou, J. H. O'Brian, Alcee O'Brian, Paul O'Raurke, Numa Patin, Ernest Patin, Adolphe Patin, Alfred Patin, Jules Patin, Auguste Patin, Felix Potier, Louis Roger, Charles Savoie, Ozeme Semere, Bernard Chevalier, Nicholas Thibodeau, Joseph Thibodeau, R. Thibodeau, Edouard Thibodeau, Homere Thibodeau, Ludger Webre, Cesaire Webre, Alcide Webre, Jules Webre, Alexandre Woltz, Amade Woltz, Vincedt Barras, Aurelian Barras, Jules Barras, Ernest Fontenette, Julien Patin, Aurelien Gautreau, Jacques Menard, Henry Comeau, Aristide Dugas.

BATTERY.

Captain, Henry Ducatel; First Lieutenant, Sr., F. Livaudais; First Lieutenant, Jr., M. A. Calongne; Second Lieutenant, Sr., G. Legardeur; Second Lieutenant, Jr., F. Lange; Surgeon, Auguste Capdeville.

First Sergeant, E. H. Reynes; Second Sergeant, A. P. Faurie; Third Sergeant, A. Arroyo; Fourth Sergeant, N. Delery; Fifth Sergeant, C. Weysham; Sixth Sergeant, H. Huard; Seventh Sergeant, A. Baudeon; Eighth Sergeant, J. W. Mader.

First Corporal, A. Bertus; Second Corporal, B. Tremoulet; Third Corporal, E. Deverges; Fourth Corporal, G. Fortin; Fifth Corporal, A. De Rosenon; Sixth Corporal, C. De Armas; Seventh Corporal, J. B. de Mahy; Eighth Corporal, F. Duplessis; Ninth Corporal, S. P. Lamon; Tenth Corporal, L. A. Lange; Eleventh Corporal, L. O. Moreau; Twelfth Corporal, H. I. Nores.

1st Artificier: A. Zamit; 2d, O. Livaudais; 3d, S. P. Martinez; 4th, T. Trepagnier; 5th. P. Roman; 6th, T. Buisson. B. Buisson, jr., N. P. Boulet, E. Buisson. A. Buisson, A. Bougere, J. A. Bonafon. A. Bosonier, jr., H. Bachemin, J. Brandin, A. Bachemin, P. Clerc, A. Charbonnet, E. Coignard, C. B. Coignard, J. A. Charbonnet, G. Clauss, J. B. Casanova, Placide Canonge, sr., H. Canonge, O DeGruy, A. Devoe, Lebreton Deschapelles, E. Deblanc, C. Degruy, E. Dupre, L. Dolhonde, A. Durel, Wm. Delahay, A. Daquin, B. E. Dejean, M. T. Ducros, V. Ducros, L. O. Desforges, A. W. Duplantier, C. R. Egelly, J. Esclapon, E. Elysardi, E. Foulon, E. Funel, A. Gamotis, L. A. Guillet, J. Gaillard, P. Grima, N. Gonzales, Jos. Garidel, V. Gaudin, A. Gangloff, E. A. Guibet, J. Glynn,jr., E. C. Haydel, D. Halphein, O. L. Kerniou, T. S. Kennedy, O. Le. Blanc, E. Laroque Turgeau, H. Lobit, E. Laforest, A. Lauve, A. Lelong, A. LeBeau, A. F. Lynn, J. Lemarie, V. J. Lauzainghein, P. Lagrange, A. Lorreins, O. Lauve, H. Legendre, J. Montreuil, J. Miltenberger, H. Mioton, G. Montegut, O. Menard, C. McMurdo, E. Montreuil, F. Marquez,jr., L. Mauberret, G. W. Nott, A. A. Oehmichen, G. Oemichen, J. B. Pelletier, A. Paul, A. Pellerin, S. Phillpot, J. L. Percy, Alex. Prados, E. C. Reggio, J. Rivero, A. R. Roux, A. N. Ruch, P. Roubieu, G. Sauve, P. Sarpy, Chas. Souchon, H. Tremoulet, O. Tremoulet, C. M. Tarut, J. H. Tirado, P. A. Tabary, E. Thomas, A. Tiroux, Paul Viallon, Jules Verret, J. A. Vignaud, C. F. Verbois, E. Ver-

gnes, John Wilson, A. Willoz, V. Willoz, R. Wiltz, A. B.
Wickes, D. Wildt, A. Weysham, C. Weysham, C. Zapata.
31 drivers and 1 trumpeter.

Losses of the Orleans Battalion on the 6th and 7th April, 1862.

Company A—S. Gerard, L. Forestier, E. Leblanc, B. Martel.
Company B—G. Porée, J. Archinard, D. Coutourie, P. Dubouchel, J. Schrempp. Company C—A. Gallot, A. Fleury, J. B. Jaquin. Company D—C. Broussard, A. Lasseigne, P. Rourke.

Wounded and Missing.

Company A—Lieut. J. Moreno, P. A. Vienne, P. Ganel, O. M. Opdenmeyer, C. Phillippi, J. A. Rasch. Company B—none. Company C—E. Robin, G. C. Brower, P. A. Lacroix, F. Cavaroc. Company D—P. L. Declouet, J. Delhomme.

Wounded.

V. Prados, J. S. Coiron, B. Bienvenu, G. Bryand, N. Forestier, W. Forstall, R. A. Hebrard, E. Hernandez, G. Pitot, P. Judice, L. Menard, A. d'Hebecourt, C. V. Labarre. Company B—F. Percy, Th. Dubois, A. G. Romain, F. Arnoud, E. S. Audler, E. Arcenaux, H. Boisblanc, H. DeMahy, Ch. Diard, L. E. Fazende, L. A. Gaillard, L. Gregoiro, E. Jorda, J. Lefevre, E. Tafonta, P. J. Daron, Marine, P. Lacoste, Wolcart, E. Villavasso. Company C—V. Lobit, H. Tronchet, P. Sarrazin, H. Ferriot, A. G. Callery, J. Thibodeaux, L. B. Delahoussaye, Ch. Gessler, E. Robert, H. Hertzog, E. Ruffier, E. Delimage. Company D—Ch. Tertrou, P. Babineau, G. Broussard, S. Bienvenu, T. N. Champagne, J. Guilbeau, J. H. O'Brian, Ch. Lavoie, B. Savalier, A. Wiltz.

Missing:

Company A—Lieutenant Trepagnier, Company B—P. Leefe, C. Cazeauz, P. J. Lefebvre, F. Marcotte, A. Poche, L. Villavasso. Company C—P. A. Thibodeaux, F. Brugier, E. Fagot, J. Alexander, A. A. Fusselier, L. Schmidt. Company D—A. Declouet, H. David, A. Patin.

JOURNAL OF THE ORLEANS GUARD

DURING THE MOVEMENTS PRECEDING AND FOLLOWING THE BATTLE OF CORINTH.

April 2d—Orders given by Major Queyrouze* to the Battalion to be ready at the first signal, with five days' rations and one hundred rounds of ammunition.

3d—At 4½ began to move, with very little baggage and no rations, towards the enemy. At 10 o'clock, P. M., camped about two miles from Monterey, by the side of the 18th Louisiana.

4th—In the morning heavy rain. Left camp and halted about half a mile from Monterey. Let Monterey on the right and halted on a hill half a mile further. At 1 P. M. a few pieces of meat and biscuits were distributed to the men, with recommendation made to eat but the fraction. During the halt, the battle flag of Gen. Hardee's Division was paraded in front of the Battalion so that it could be recognized on the battle field. The Battalion resumed its marching order, the Crescent Regiment to its left, the 18th Louisiana to the right. Met a cavalry officer exhibiting Gen. Polk's Division battle flag for recognition before going into battle; halted for an hour, awaiting orders and listening to the musketry. Received orders to bivouac in the neighboring woods, at about six miles above Monterey.

5th—Heavy rain. Resumed marching at 6½ o'clock, here and there coming across dead horses and pools of blood. Towards 2 o'clock our light baggage was abandoned on the road and muskets were loaded. At 3 o'clock Gen. Bragg passed near the Battalion and was received with cheers. His answer was that he would soon give us work. Slept on our arms, formed in column, until 6 o'clock the next morning.

At 4 o'clock camped in the woods, near the Tennessee River.

---

*The Battalion of Orleans Guards left under Beauregard's ninety day call, with a following of 411 men. Major Queyrouze, the head of an old commercial house which still commands the trade of the Coast and French parishes, went out at the head of these, and did good service in fitting out his Battalion and leading them on the field. He took part in the battle of Shiloh, and received a wound whose duration more than covered the term of enlistment for which he had abandoned his business.

6th—At 5 o'clock ordered into line of battle; marched to and fro until 8, through woods and fields. At about half-past 8 passed through the abandoned camp of the 6th Iowa. Found there a bountiful supply of bread, hot from the oven, any amount of provisions, wine, fruits, and other delicacies; enough altogether to feed ten regiments. Halted there for a half hour. Passed soon after to another camp, abandoned by its occupants at our approach, not without their firing a parting volley. The Crescent at this camp diverged (owing probably to the dense woods) from the line of march of the Orleans and 18th Louisiana. After half an hour's march further on, just as it was preparing to assault another camp, it was assailed by a brisk musketry fire, which proved to be from the 6th Kentucky and a Tennessee regiment. These troops, at sight of the blue uniform brought out from New Orleans, mistook the Battalion for the enemy. Two men were killed by this error.

At five o'clock joined the 18th La. in a ravine, about half a mile from the Tennessee river. Remained exposed to the enemy's fire from the plateau of the hill in front of its line of battle, and to the shells of the enemy's gunboats.

The Battalion here awaited the order of General Preston Pond, who stood twenty yards off; the enemy meanwhile was a half mile from the Tennessee river, which they had fortified. They were now awaiting our attack, having already repulsed that of the 16th La.

The cry of "Forward, the 18th!" was now heard on our right. "Follow me," was given in the well known voice of Col. Mouton. Then the regiment disappeared as it charged up the hill, and we could only judge by a lugubrious concert of cannon and small arms that their attack had commenced. It had charged full. of fire, and its ranks well dressed. When we next saw it, it was mutilated, cut to pieces, leaving behind it a path of blood. Men could be scarcely recognized. Their shirts were covered with blood and their faces disfigured with hideous wounds. At this point, Major Queyrouze gave the order to charge to the Orleans Battalion. This was promptly obeyed, men moving forward, as if they were a machine, to the top of the plateau. The command of " fix bayonets " was given, and this was answered by the men with a hurrah. Then they moved forward on a double-quick, under a galling fire. The battle flag fell from the hands of G. Poree, the color-bearer, who was shot dead. Before touching the ground it was caught by Gallot, who was shot dead through the head; then seized by Coiron, whose arm was shattered while holding it. The fourth standard bearer was Percy, who was also wounded. The fifth time it was seized, without ever having touched the ground, by a soldier, whose name is now unknown.

At forty paces from the enemy we opened fire. This lasted for a few moments, after which they were driven from the field. The tramp of a large body of men was now heard. While we were expecting our total destruction, the division reached the field, with the blue flag and white center *ovale*, which had previously been pointed out as indicating Hardee's command.

These troops nobly avenged the losses which had been inflicted on the Orleans Guards and 18th La. regiments. Among these losses were Major Queyrouze and Captain Charles Tetrou, Lieutenant Moreno, and twenty-five per cent. of our number wounded or stretched dead on the field. Captain Charles Roman ‡ succeeded in command. The attack having been overpowered by a battery of six pieces and the superior infantry force of the enemy, the order for retreat was given. Although the enemy could easily have captured the whole command, they made no attempt to follow.

At 7 o'clock the remains of the Battalion received orders to form as a picket guard. During the ensuing night the enemy fired an occasional bomb to keep our troops awake.

With this Battalion marched Father Turgis, a priest who had seen soldiering in his day, and who was still enough of a trooper to enjoy the incense of battle almost as much as that of the altar. He shared the hardships of the men, followed them into the thickest of the fight, and administered the rights of religion to the wounded of both armies. His time with the Great Archer came, too, at the close of the war, and his body was followed to the Esplanade-street Cemetery by the largest funeral procession of ladies and gentlemen on foot ever known in the city. He was a man who was excellent company for any one, and frank enough in his exhibition of character to escape any charge against him of hypocrisy.

Doctors Capdevielle, McGuire and Ferrier discharged their duty toward the sick.

The following day, rain at 7 o'clock in the morning. A detachment was sent on the battle-field to bring in our wounded, but owing to the enemy's shells could recover only two bodies.

April 7th, moved at 6¼ A. M., without food, under a heavy fire of the enemy. Gen. Pond, commanding the 16th Regiment, took another direction. During the next two hours our only incident, beside alternate marches and halts, was the finding, as we traversed an abandoned camp of the enemy, a half-barrel of wet hard-tack. This was our only food for the

---

‡ Le capitaine Charles Roman, qui nous avait conduits au feu depuis que le Major Queyrouze avait été mis hors de combat, nous donnes l'ordre, qu'il avait reçu, de rentrer dans notre ancien camp, à un mille et demi de Corinthe. Digne remplaçant du bon et brave Major Queyrouze, qui nous avait donna l'exemple du sang froid à la bataille du 6. Le capitaine Roman devait, jusqu' à notre retour à Corinthe, marcher à notre tete.—[Correspondence New Orleans Bee, from a translation of which most of this account is taken.

day. The failure, however, was not the fault of our quartermaster, Alfonse Tertrou, but to Bragg's order to abandon our wagons on account of their having become stuck in the mud at Monterey.

The remainder of the day we were united with the 18th, under Col. Mouton.

The colors of the Battalion were now put upon the breast of Private Fenot. As the blue color of our uniform was not in the odor of sanctity with Confederate sharpshooters, the men were ordered to turn their uniform wrong side outwards, thus giving them the appearance of going to a masquerade ball. As we marched on, Beauregard passed us; he was received with an immense cheer. He said to us as he passed, "Forward, fellow soldiers of Louisiaaa! one more effort and the day is ours." Mouton repeated the same cry, and we rushed forward to where the fighting had already commenced.

Col. Mouton was wounded at the first fire, and was succeeded in command by Col. Alfred Roman. At a moment of hesitation in our ranks, under a heavy fire, Beauregard rushed forward, and seizing the colors, shouted, "forward!"

He was relieved by Col. Numa Augustin, his Aid. The standard finally passing into the hands of Major Ernest Puech, who planted it in the ground until the line was reformed. The battalion and the 18th suffered enormous losses. Lieutenants Trepagnier, Declouet and Moreno were wounded, and our losses, altogether, with those of the preceding day were 33 per cent. of our whole number in line.

8th—13th. During the following five days the troops fall back to original camp, at Corinth. Previous to starting on this retreat the firing recommenced in front of us—one of the shots ricocheting over the battalion, and taking off the legs of a tall Texas cavalryman, who was seated twenty yards behind, on a waggon. Bivouacked at Monterey. Heavy rain during the night; the ground saturated with water.

On the second day of the march, the men began to travel barefooted, on account of swollen feet. The only food obtained was found by the wayside; no rations being issued during the retreat. Arriving at Corinth, the dreary place seemed like paradise; our tents were palaces, and old friends whom we rejoined we hugged like brothers.

THE THIRTIETH LOUISIANA REGIMENT.

MUSTER ROLLS OF THE OFFICERS AND MEN.

Lieut. Col. Thomas Shields, killed July, 1864; Major Charles J. Bell, killed 28th July, 1864; Capt. A. Picolet, promoted Maior 28th July, 1864; Lieut. F. O. Trepagnier, Captain, 1864, commanding the Regiment at surrender; A. Q. M. C. F. Krule; Assistant Surgeon, W. W. Cross ! Adjutant, B. C. Cushman*; Chaplain, F. Turgis; Sergeant Major, E. R. Barnett; Orderly Sergeant, John Flinn; Ensign, L. Trinquieri, Quartermaster Sergeant, F. A. McConnico, wounded.

COMPANY A.

Captain O. F. Valette, wounded; First Lieutenant, H. Fortier, killed July 28th, 1864; Second Lieutenant, C. E. McCarthy*, Junior Second Lieutenant, J. A. Ruiz*; Orderly Sergeant, F. Fortier*; Sergeants Nicklaus, P. Gravois*, L. Comeau, wounded; W. Schabel*; Corporals L. Roger, H. O'Brien*, P. A. Coudray, wounded August, 1864; D. Planchard.

Privates: C. Aikman, wounded; O. Allemen, killed; Jas. D. Augustin, J. B. Angelle, C. Berthaut, E. Barras, A. Barras, V. Barras, P. B. Bethancourt, W. Broadtman, D. Badon, C. Breaux*, F. Borgne, H. Comeau, wounded; N. Cailler, died from wound; W. A. Chambers*, A. Carraras , J. C. Dupuis*, H. David, A. David, L. David*, P. David·, S. David, H. Dudley, L. Duvillier, J. Esnard, H. Gauthier, A. Gauthier, J. P. Guidry*, O. P. Guidry, D. Green*, A. Gautheaux, killed July, 1864; J. Guilbeau*, F. H. Guillott; J. J. Guillott*, J. Guillaume, died in hospital; H. Hatters, J. Hatters*, B. Henry, L. Hymel, G. Hull*, A. E. Hotard, J. Janmar, P. Jones*, R. Kramwerer, wounded; E. Laperuze*, H. R. Lorio, N. Landry*, A. Lormand, T. Lejeune, H. N. LeBreton, killed 1864; U. Loupe, N. Minot, F. Myers, E. H. Magnon, L. J. Pisere, A. L. Planchard, died May, 1864; T. A· Ruiz, G. Roubic, J. Spencer*, H. Sarazin*, P. Shaffer, E. Schremppe, N. Tisdale, J. Thomas*, W. Thompson, J. Webre, J. Wolkart, A. Zimmerman, E. Nuer, J. Winterhalter.

---

*Taken prisoner.

COMPANY B.

Captain H. P. Jones died 20th November, 1864; First Lieutenant N. B. Baker, killed, June, 1864; Second Lieutenant L. J. McNeil, Jr.; Second Lieutenant R. McNeil, Orderly Sergeant J. W. Cook*. Sergeants D. McGregor killed July, 1863; J. W. Wilson killed August, 1864; M. McCaffery*; J. H. Drillion. Corporals—W. Dalton,* H. Buckhardt, wounded, August 1864; Hy. Cushing, killed, December, 1964; J. F. Burkel*. Privates—R. Aikman, J. Burtus, J. L. Bremner, D. Bailey, killed, July, 1864; J. A. Breaux*; C. Breaux, E. Barley, K. Babin, L. A. Collier*; A. Conway, J. Donner, V. Devauselle, J. Donnóvan*; M. J. Doyle, Chas. Felieck*; J. E. Grimes, O. Hield, R. Hackmen, Sam. Hirsch*. Chas. Jolly*; John Kreigger,, Jas. Keating, Jas. Leissence*; L. Laurence*; A. D. Landry*; S. Lacroix, died; H. Lerry*; J. E. Morisson, wounded; John McDermot*; T. McNamus, R. Cherry, M. Gharra, C. L. Petit, died; K. Rodi, A. Steele, J. H. Fabing*, W. E. Todd*; J. B. Thuilier, A. Vilneuve, A. Waggatha*; G. Weightman*; A.F. Wiliiams, R. Barry, H. Fick, wouuded; M. M. Firth, killed; T. Friar, W. Heath, G. S. Hale, John Moriety*; R. A. Walters, wounded.

COMPANY C.

Captain R. T. Boyle; First Lieutenant H. C. Wright°; Second Lieutenant D. C. Byerly; Junior Second Lieutenant W. B. Chippendale, killed, July 25th, 1864. Orderly Sergeant A. G. Kane°. Sergeants F. A. Vierling, E. Delaupe, killed, 28th July, 1864; W. H. Tolson*; T. O'Keefe, wounded, 28th July, 1864. Corporals A. Barker°; A. Landry, killed, July 28th, 1864; P. W. Kelly°.

Privates: Charles Allietz°; Fred Barrett, Charles Barrett, Geo. Beckenkohler°! E. Blanchard, W. J. Boyd, D. Blanchard°: Andry Cass, killed, July 28th, 1864; J. M. Coos°; J. T. Danos, J, A. Dacons, John Farley, C. C. Farmer. Gus Faw, J. B. Faw°; M. Fritx Gibbons, Dan Flinn°; G. B. Freman, J. E. Guin, S. D. Harris°; T. D. Harris, A. Sacobs, T. J. Johnson, wounded, disable: W. J. Johnson, J. E. Keirnan°; E. Lally, wounded, July 28th, 1864, T. J. Lawler, died in hospital; John Lopue, killed; S. E McCormic°. J, E. Tittlemeyer, Chas. McClarey°; John Murphn, Mike O'Brien. killed, July 28th, 1864; Hy. Polson, Geo. Tosey, Hp. Rednouer°; S. Stinson. died in hospital; Peter Wirtz, killed, July 28th, 1864. J. E. Wuerstell, died from wound.

COMPANY E.

Captain C. W. Cushman, killed December 15th, 1864; First Lieutenant A. D'Apremont;° Second Lieutenant M. Boland, died; Junior Second Lieutenant U. Landry; Sergeants M. A. Campbell,° Charles King, — Gossen ;°

°Taken prisoner.

Corporals Fred Hirt, killed July 28th, 1864; P. Belsom, W. J. Ross, wounded; Joseph Sabine.

Privates William Bambery, killed December 17th, 1864; Clinton Bell,° M. K. Chandler,° Oct. Constant,° Louis Dalon,° Bernard Ditté,° Henry Durosse,° Herman Dohmier, Ambrose Forbes, Alceé Gainnie,° George Gevy,° Desire Gravois, Lewis Hass,° William Hack, John R. Hebrard, J. O. Hebert,° Thomas Hebert,° Murat Landry, William H. Lewis,° N. Mahan,° E. Maher,° Peter McGee, John Poché,° Victor Paillote,° George Smith,° William A. Smith,° Forrest Uzee,° Joseph Stromyer,° David Wild.

COMPANY F.

Captain F. O. Trepagnier; First Lieutenant Charles Diard; Second Lieutenant Frank Greig;° Orderly Sergeant A. Luminais;° Sergeants L. J. Vienne,° E. Rosiere,° O. J. Delery, L. A. Livandais; Corporals A. Grailhe, Henry Delery,° S. J. Blosman,° H. D. Canning,° E. Anderman,° A. Allen, killed July 28th, 1864; T. Adam, killed July 28th, 1864; S. Alexander, discharged; J. Albert, C. Blache, L. Bertholi, wounded August 25th, 1864; V. Berthelotte, J. L. Bourgeois,° George B. Bryant,° J. H. Brown,° Henry Barnett, Jules Bayhi, killed July 22d, 1854; Anselme Bayhi,° Gus V. Bayhi, killed; H. C. Benit,° E. Burthe,° L. Burthe,° C. Betat, wounded; Paul Blanc,° H. Baudier,° P. Bondonsquie, A. Castanedo, C. Cavelier,° E. Choxnayde,° M. Cantrelle,° L. A. Clairin,° E. Dejean,° E. Dumas, E. Duguy, E. Drouilhet,° F. L. Duplessis, killed July 27th, 1864; V. David, J. Evard,° Numa Fazende, Edmond Fazende, Dorsino Fazendo,° H. J. Terriot,° G. Froisy, H. F. M. Fortier, Jules Fécel, F. Guerin, died from wound; A. E. Garcia, Louis Gauchey,° Charles Giesler,° A. Grandpré, Alexander Humphreys,° A. Jorda,° Charles Laterriere, F. Labauve,° Numa Labarthe, killed July 28th, 1864; Gus. Le Breton, Ang. Lisbony, P. N. Lacroix, killed July 28th, 1864; Louis Leefe, wounded; J. A. LeBlanc, Edgar Luminais' wounded; John Lefebvre,° Jules E. Livandais, John E. Livandais,° Joseph Lecorgne,° Benjamin Leefe, wounded; Alexander McArthur,° D. Mayronne, wounded; O. Mayronne, A. Matherne, wounded; C. Minvielle, killed July 28th, 1864; A. Morehead,° E. Nicand, C. Ollié,° A. Ollivier,° O. M. Opdeniveyer,° A. Péna, C. Philippi, F. Percy,° L. Rideau, J. Reinne,° H. Rousselin,° F. Rome,° F. Rapp,° G. A. Reggio, J. J. Roche,° Paul Sarazin, woanded; P. Scioneaux, killed; P. Saulet,° F. Froxler, Louis Troxler, wounded; Aug. Troxler, Jules Vinet,° J. C. Villars,° Gaston Villars,° A. Verret, T. J. Verret,° A. D. Voisin, J. S. Vincent, Charles Willoz, wounded; Joseph Zerinque, killep July 3d, 1864; Felix Zerinque,° Edmond Zerinque, killed July 28th, 1864; Fortuné Zerinque, wounded; L. P. Harang, J. N. Elliott, E. Mondeil, Peter Forshee, H. Gaccon, Jean Marie, V. B. Sebley, Richard Stanford.

°Taken Prisoner.

COMPANY G.

Captain, L. P. Becnel, wounded July 28, 1864, died August 2d, 1864; First Lieutenant, B. Haydel; Second Lieutenant, A. D. Bougere; Second Junior Lieutenant, L. Becnel; Orderly Sergeant, O. Roussel°, Sergeants, Emile Boyer, Honorat Bodrigue°, Aristide Oubre°, Frank Webre, wounded; Corporals, M. Laurent°, wounded July 28th, 1864, and left on the field; Antoine Becnel°, Victor Hymel°, Adam Gnedry°, O. Belsome°, O. Benoit, M. Boudreax, Emile Boudro, Gaspard Boudro, Louis Boudro°, Chas. M. Boudro°, O. Bourgeois°, T. Brou°, Ed. Chaix, wounded; C. Cazeaux, E. Champagne°, F. Champagne°, E. Chiasson°, A. Clement°, Jos. Faude, Ernest Haydel°, T. C. Healey, H. Hertzog, W. C. F. Hosea, S. Hymel, Ulysse Jacob, John Kealy°, E. Levert°, L. Lario, C. Naguin, E. Nicolle°, T. Nicolle, wounded; F. Nicolas, J. B. Nicolas°, T. Porthier, L. Riviere, Edgard Rodrigue°, F. Rodrigue, J. E. Santon°, Sullivan Streck°, F. Schexnaydre°, J. Schexnaydre, Octave Schexnaydre°, Ozeme Schexnaydre, F. Schexnaydre°, G. A. Sykes, J. Tanzin°, U. Tauzin, A. Toups°, E. Toups, F. Toups°, O. Usée, D. Vicario, John° Walton.

Paroled as Prisoners of War at Meridian, Miss., on the 4th Day of May, 1865.

Captain F. O. Trepagnier. 1st Lieutenant B. Haydel, 1st Lieutenant Chas. Diard, 2d Lieutenant L. J. McNeill, Jr. 2d Lieutenant Robert McGill. Assistant Surgeon W. W. Cross. Chaplain J. F. Turgis, Ensign L. Trinquiery. Sergeants J. H. Orillion, Emile Bougere, F. A. Vierling, H. Nickglus, L. A. Livaudais. Corporals D. Planchard, B. P. Leefe, Louis Hymel.

Privates E. Legendre, D. Fazende, E. Fazende, G. A. Harrison, A. Knoblock, E. B. Livaudais, E. Hotard, J. Morierthy, A. Roth, A. Humphreys, R. Hackney, E. N. Rothe, U. Jacol, J. O. Riuct, W. J. Johnson, A. Webre, R. Kammerer, E. Winterhalter, A. Lawrence, E. Boudro, E. Levert. A. Blanchard, T. McManus, D. Badon, C. Naguin, J. Bremner, A. Phelps, O. Brand, F. Patterson, A. Comey, T. J. Roask, A. Castanedo, C. Schexnaydre, V. Derouseselle, J. E. Skipper, G. Farr, U. Tanzin, F. H. Guillot, T. Troxler, M. Garcia, A. P. Voisin, A. A. Graudpre, J. J. Walker.

I certify the foregoing to be a correct roll of the officers and enlisted men of the 30th La. Regiment of infantry, C. S. A., who were present and were paroled as prisoners of war at Meridian, Miss., on the 4th day of May, 1865, in pursuance of terms of agreement between Major General E. R. S. Canby, U. S. A., and Lieutenant General R. Taylor, commanding department Alabama, Mississippi and East Louisiana, at Citronella, on the 4th day of May, 1865.

F. O. TREPAGNIER,
Captain Commanding 30th La. Vols. Inft.

°Taken Prisoner.

Military Movements of the Thirtieth Louisiana.

The (20th) Sumter Regiment having evacuated New Orleans at the time of its capture in 1862, was ordered to Camp Moore. During the evacuation many of the men were separated from the command, and when it arrived at Camp Moore the Regiment was incomplete and had to be reorganized.

Several detached companies joined the Regiment at that time; one company composed of the remnants of the Orleans Guard Battalion, Capt. Louis Fortin, whose term of service (90 days) had expired; the Algiers Guard, Capt. Norbert Trepagnier, and one company of Miangohara's Battalion, Capt. A. Picolet; one company from Lafourche, Capt. de LaBretonne, and one company from Iberville, Capt. Bevan.

The command thus organized was designated as the 30th Regiment Louisiana Volunteers, G. A. Breaux, Colonel; Thos. Shields, Lieutenant Colonel; Chas. J. Bell, Major; B. C. Cushman, Adjutant.

In 1863, the Regiment still being incomplete, was reduced to a Battalion of seven companies, under command of Thos. Shields, Lieutenant Colonel, and Charles Bell, Major, and was designated as the 30th Battalion Louisiana Volunteers.

The 30th Louisiana took part in the battle of Baton Rouge, and after the engagement was ordered to Port Hudson, where it remained for nearly a year, defending that position when first bombarded by the enemy's fleet.

In June, 1863, Maxey's Brigade, of which the 30th formed part, was ordered to reinforce Gen. Joseph Johnson, near Jackson, Miss., and the command marched from Port Hudson to that point, and formed part of the army operating in the rear of Vicksburg.

Retreated to Jackson, Miss., after the fall of Vicksburg and defended that position. Was ordered to Mobile and stationed some time at Fort Gaines, Ala. Took part in the campaign under Gen. Polk against Gen. Sherman, when the latter invaded Mississippi, in 1863. Was sent back to Mobile, and shortly after was ordered to reinforce Gen. Bragg, at Missionary Ridge, but did not reach destination in time and was stopped at Dalton, Ga., the evening of the battle; was stationed at that point about two months, forming part of Quarles' Brigade, and was ordered back to Mobile, Ala.

In the month of June, 1864, the battalion was ordered to reinforce General Jos. E. Johnson, then disputing the advance of General Sherman, in Georgia. Joined the Army of the West at New Hope Church, and was transferred to Gibson's Louisiana Brigade; took part in the numerous engagements that followed, and lost very heavily, especially in the attack near Atlanta, on the enemy's left, July 28th, 1864, when three-fourths of the battalion were either killed or wounded. Among the killed were Lieutenant Colonel Shields and Major Bell.

From that time the battalion was much reduced in numbers, and next took part in the campaign of General Hood, in Tennessee. Major Picolet being in command of the battalion—took part in the battles of Franklin and Nashville, losing many men. It was captured at latter engagement, the position occupied by the battalion being flanked by the enemy.

During the retreat that followed, it formed part of the rear guard, and again lost several men by capture, including Major Picolet.

The remnants of the battalion retreated to Tupilo, Mississippi, and remained from that time until the surrender, under command of Captain F. O. Trepagnier, of Company F (Orleans Guards), the senior officer present.

From Tupilo the battalion was sent to Mobile, Alabama, and defended Spanish Fort during the seige of that position. It retreated to Meridian, Mississippi, at the evacuation of Mobile, Alabama, and was surrendered by General R. Taylor, in May, 1865.

ORLEANS GUARD BATTERY.

This command, which left New Orleans on the 15th March, 1862, proceeded to Grand Junction, Tenn., with a battery of eight guns (bronze 6-pounders and 12-pounder howitzers), the private property of the command, where it received its complement of horses and was equipped for the field.

It took part in the operations of the Western Army; was engaged at Farmington, Perryville, Murfreesboro, Mount Look-Out, and Chicamauga, when, by request of Gen. Beauregard, the command was ordered to Charleston, S. C., where it did duty until the evacuation of the city, in March, 1865.

On the march to make a junction with Gen. Lee, the Battery took part in the battles of Averysboro and Bentonville.

The following was the organization of the Battery at the date of its surrender under Gen. Joseph E. Johnson, at Greensboro, N. C., in April, 1865: G. LeGardeur, Jr., Captain; N. O. Lauve, First Lieutenant; T. Trepagnier, Second Lieutenant; Jno. Glinn, Junior Second Lieutenant; Arthur Durel, Sergeant Major; E. Coignard, Quartermaster Sergeant; Chas. B. Coignard, Alphonse Lauve, E. A. Guibet, E. Deverges, Sergeants; V. Gaudin, A. Lalande, M. L. Fotier*, J. Lemarié J. B. Cassanova, A. A. Ruch, L. Percy, A. Thiroux.

The Battery numbered 103 members. All of the commissions dated from July 15th, 1863.†

---

* Fortier was killed in a battle a week or so preceding the surrender.

† Among other artillerymen who rose to distinction in the Army of the West was Major B. F. Jonas, who served as a private soldier in Fenner's Battery until made Adjutant of Artillery in Gen. S. B. Lee's command, in Hood's army. He was also with Col. Beckham and Lieut. Col. Hoxton, and was entered on the rolls at Dick Taylor's surrender. He has since attained position at the bar and been promoted to high honors in the city and State government.

Acting with the forementioned troops from Louisiana at Vicksburg was Col. Fred. Ogden's Battalion (the 7th), until after the surrender. Col. Ogden was then ordered to assist in organizing a body of cavalry for Gen. Polk's Division. This having been done, he was assigned to Wirt Adams' Brigade, with orders to report to Forrest. He was with the latter command when it was surrendered at the close of the war.

General Orders Relating to the Surrender of Western Troops at Mobile.

General Orders No. 3.

HEADQUARTERS BATTERY GLADDEN,
MOBILE BAY, April 11th, 1865.

COMRADES: Mobile is about to be evacuated. It is no fault of ours. The enemy, with his large fleet, idle at this moment, has not dared to approach within range of our battery. Your officers have confidence in you, and in our holy cause. We must be soldiers to the last. The memorable words of our great General in Chief, R. E. Lee, should guide us now, and always: "Take new resolutions from the fate which our enemies intend for us; let every man devote his energies to the common defense. Our resources, wisely and rigorously employed, are ample, and with a brave army, sustained by a determined and united people, success, with God's assistance, cannot be doubtful. The advantages of the enemy will have little value if we do not permit them to impair our resolution. Let us oppose constancy to adversity, fortitude to suffering, and courage to danger, with the firm assurance that He who gave freedom to our fathers will bless the effort of their children to preserve it."

I know that there are no cowards or faint-hearted among you. It is easy to be gay and confident after victory; none but the really brave and true are firm and obedient under misfortune. Prove yourselves noble men and gallant soldiers. Do not only imitate the example of the thousands who have sacrificed their all, and who still keep on devoting every thought and pulsation to the holy cause of freedom, but surpass them in devotion and courage. Remain, Southern soldiers, come what will. There is no reason to be dependent. It is believed that Gen. Lee has gained a great victory over the enemy. It is by his orders that we will concentrate under his banner, and fight out the great fight against Yankee despotism. On this occasion we will be the last to leave, and have been selected to form the rear guard, an honor of which we should be proud. We will soon be with Taylor and Forrest, who have never known defeat.

RICHARD C. BOND, Maj. Commanding.

General Orders No. 3.

HEADQUARTERS VICKSBURG, MISS.,
May 2d, 1865.

To the officers and men of the First Louisiana Regulars (artillery) First Tennessee Artillery, Twenty-second Regiment Louisiana Volunteers, Twenty-third Regiment Louisiana Volunteers, Eighth Louisiana Battalion:

General Orders.   29

Before severing my official relation to you, and in the absence of either of the generals commanding the department, it becomes on my part a duty to acknowledge, in accordance with the expressed will of Congress, the distinction which the steady courage and cheerful endurance of danger of one and all acquired for you, during the severe attack and bombardment of the city in May, June and July, 1862. Occasion was taken at that time to eulogize your conduct, and it is proper to repeat now that the gallantry and devotion to duty then displayed were worthy of praise.

As your then commanding general, I hereby authorize you to inscribe on your banners the well-known name "Vicksburg." May your deeds continue to brighten more and more the halo of renown which now surrounds this name.   M. L. SMITH, Maj. Gen. Comdg.

HEADQUARTERS MAURY'S DIVISION,
Six Miles East of Meridian, Miss.,
May 7th, 1865.

SOLDIERS: Our last march is about ended. To-morrow we shall lay down the arms which for four years we have borne to defend our rights, to win our liberties. We know, the world knows, and history will record that we have borne them with honor. We now surrender to the overwhelming power of the enemy, which has rendered further resistance by us hopeless and mischievous to our people and to our own cause. But we can never forget the noble comrades who have stood shoulder to shoulder to this moment, the noble dead who have been martyred, the noble Southern women who have been wronged, and are unavenged, or the noble principles for which we have fought.

Conscious that we have played our part like men, confident of the righteousness of our cause, without regret for our action in the past, and without despair of the future, let us to-morrow, with the dignity of veterans who are the last to surrender, perform the duty which has been assigned to us.   DABNEY H. MAURY,
Major General C. S. Army.

HEADQUARTERS GIBSON'S BRIGADE,
NEAR MERIDIAN, MISS., May 8th, 1865.

FELLOW SOLDIERS: For four years you have shared together the fortunes of war. In the bivouac, on the march, amidst the shock of battles, throughout all the eventful scenes of this revolution, you have been fully tried, and now retire with the consciousness of having performed your whole duty faithfully, of having achieved a character for discipline, for soldierly training, for valor, and for intelligent and devoted patriotism, of which you may be justly proud.

There is nothing in your career as soldiers to look back upon with regret; our banners are festooned with the emblems of every knightly virtue. The past at least is secure.

You have the right to face coming events with calmness, and not without hope. Never permit a fated mistrust of your country and countrymen to enter your minds. Bravest in time of war, show yourselves the most orderly and generous while peace endures.

Comrades! forget not the good and true men who have fallen. No sculptured marble may perpetuate the recollection of their service, but their names shall be enshrined in the remembrance of their grateful countrymen. and you will bear them ever fresh and green in your hearts.

Erase from memory every unkind thought towards those who still stand beside you. You separate, not as friends merely, but as brethren, whom mutual trials, common hopes and aspirations, and equal hardships and disasters have made kinsmen. You must rely one upon another.

Rising from the command of a company and regiment in the brigade, I have known many of you from the commencement of the struggle, have been with you, and leave to each one of you at parting, the tribute of my admiration and affection, and the invocation that the God of our fathers may bless you.

Farewell.

R. L. GIBSON, Brigadier General.

MOVEMENT OF THE ORLEANS LIGHT HORSE, AND THEIR FIRST COMMANDER.

No account of the Louisiana Volunteers in the Confederate Army that omitted mention of the Orleans Light Horse and Captain Thomas L. Leeds would be correct. This troop was organized early in 1861—J. McD. Taylor, a well-known merchant of New Orleans, being chosen Captain; Thomas L. Leeds, First Lieutenant; W. A. Gordon, Second Lieutenant; George Foster, Third Lieutenant. For various reasons, several months elapsed without prospect of active service on the part of the troop; but when, in the fall of that year, it was known that the Federal army was being largely increased, steps were taken to place the Light Horse on a war footing. As it was beyond the power of Captain Taylor to devote the necessary time to the management of the command, he requested the acceptance of his resignation. To fill this vacancy, each of the officers was advanced a grade; and Mr. Leeds Greenleaf elected Third Lieutenant. From this moment the history of the Orleans Light Horse is connected with the name of its new leader.

It can hardly be deemed out of place, in this connection, that a few words should be said of Capt. Leeds—the first in rank in his company, and the first whom Death numbered on his list. Descended from Puritan stock of the "straightest sect," and inheriting the rigid virtues of his ancestry, no man drew sword in the war with clearer views of the duty of a citizen to his country. Accustomed from early years to define his position whenever necessary, and entertaining the most generous ideas of what was due to others, his character combined those better qualities which we are generally agreed to attribute to the higher classes of the South. Shortly after his return from a Northern college, he assumed his share of the control of the most important foundry in the South, and helped his business with that steady energy which afterwards proved of such service to his command. By nature and by education he was fit to be a leader of men. Proficient in manly exercises, a good swordsman and horseman, and handsome withal, he was the beau ideal of a calvary soldier.

When Captain Leeds assumed command of the troop, he devoted his time and exertions to improve its drill and discipline; and in a few weeks it had acquired a most creditable proficiency. During the winter of 1861-'62, the United States Government prepared a great land and naval force to operate against New Orleans; and there seemed to be reason to believe that mounted troops were called for in the vicinity of the city. In March, 1872, General Beauregard issued a call for volunteers from the extreme Southern States of the Confederacy, to reinforce his army, then being gathered at Corinth. Among the commands that determined to answer that call was the Light Horse; and, owing to the care and management of Captain Leeds and his officers, it was not difficult to swell the ranks to such a number as to justify a departure for the seat of war. No sooner had the members of the troop signified their readiness for active service, than it was evident of what material the commander was made. Owing to his personal influence, the necessary equipments were procured, and the steamboat General Quitman chartered to carry the Light Horse to Memphis. Situated as Captain Leeds was —an active partner in a large establishment then bending all its energies to the preparation of material of war—his presence was of the greatest value to the cause of the Confederacy, and his delicate health certainly did not justify active participation in the fatigues of a campaign. But his ardent nature looked lightly upon any sacrifice of personal ease when the good of the country was at stake. His action, in this matter, was undoubtedly influenced by the most exalted motives.

On the 29th of March the last man and horse were embarked, and a start made; but owing to an accident which occurred that night, the boat was obliged to return for repairs, and it was not until the 30th that the Orleans Light Horse left never to return. During the trip to Memphis, no exertions were spared by the Captain and his officers to fit the men for active service; and drills on the roof of the boat served to pass the time. Whilst occupied in teaching his men the details of their new career, an accident to the Captain brought a recurrence of a former physical trouble, and reduced him to a condition of great danger and pain. On his arrival at Memphis, he consulted a surgeon, who advised quiet. But such counsel was of no avail; and on Sunday, the 6th of April, the troop, with the Captain at his post, left on the cars for Corinth, which was reached the next morning at daylight. The second day's fighting at Shiloh was in progress; but it was incumbent upon the troop to go into camp before attempting a move of any kind.

The first duty assigned the Light Horse was to guard the prisoners taken the day before; after that came an expedition towards the battle field, for the purpose of recovering stragglers, to furnish information of the condition of the roads leading to Corinth, and to enable the Commanding General to ascertain the position of the enemy's outlying forces

As soon as these first duties had been performed, Captain Leeds determined to fix the status of his command—as, up to this time, he had not been attached to any particular corps. After considerable exertion, he succeeded in procuring an order detailing the troop to serve as escort to General Leonidas Polk. This end attained, the Captain, in spite of his illness, busied himself with the condition of his men, and endeavored to make it as perfect as constant drill and strict discipline could accomplish. But his spirit was stronger than his body. At first he was able to mount his horse and conduct the drills, but by degrees his complaint overcame him, and he was forced to confine himself to his camp and then to his tent. For a little while his condition now seemed to improve; but the nature of the malady was too deep-seated. His rapidly failing strength warned his friends that it was imperative his services should be, for a time, lost. A consultation of surgeons resulted in his being ordered to New Orleans. The decision, however, came too late. On the journey South it became evident to Lieutenant Greenleaf, his kinsman, who accompanied him, that the end was near. He stopped at Jackson; and there, on the 24th of April, 1862, died Captain Thomas L. Leeds, as much a victim of the war as if he had been killed in battle. No purer, truer man laid down his life a sacrifice, for his country and his honor, in all the Southern army.

After the death of Captain Leeds the command devolved upon Lieut. W. A. Gordon, now a prominent member of the bar of this city. Sergeant H. Thornbull was elected Jr. 2d Lieutenant to the vacancy caused by the promotion of Lieuts. Foster and Greenleaf. When Lieutenant Foster resigned from the troop and was assigned to duty in the Department of Mississippi, Sergeant Lallande became Junior Second Lieutenant; and, on the resignation of Lieutenant Thornhill, Sergeant J. C. Patrick was made Junior Second Lieutenant. After the Kentucky campaign, Sergeant P. M. Kenner was elected Junior Second Lieutenant; Captain Gordon having resigned, and was succeeded by Lieutenant Greenleaf, who retained command of the troop until the final surrender of General Johnston's army at Durham Station, in North Carolina; at which time the Lieutenants were—First Lieutenant, P. M. Kenner; Second Lieutenant, E. M. Morse; Junior Second Lieutenant, Ar. Hopkins Lieutenants Lallande and Patrick having, in the meanwhile, been assigned to other duty.

From the time when the Light Horse first entered into active service as the escort to Lieutenant-General Polk at Corinth, to the termination of the war, they participated in all the great actions of the Western Army. At Perryville, Murfreesboro, Chickamauga, Missionary Ridge, Resaca, Kennesaw, New Hope Church, Atlanta, Franklin, Nashville and Bentonville, besides the countless minor affairs and movements of the army, they had a part. To General Polk and his successor, Lieut.-General A. P. Stewart, they were the constant attendants. The duties devolving upon the Light Horse consisted not only of the regular duties of an escort troop, but of arduous and dangerous services in the field. As occasion required, they were compelled to perform scout service; and, on many occasions, their duties led them in rear of the enemy's lines. The loss of the troop, in proportion to the losses experienced by similar commands throughout the service, was heavy; and the last man of the Confederate Army killed on this side of the Mississippi, was John H. McKnight, an original member of the Orleans Light Horse.

MUSTER ROLL.

Captain, T. L. Leeds.
First Lieutenant, W. A. Gordon.
Second Lieutenant, George Foster.
Second Junior Lietenant, Leeds Greenleaf.
Surgeon, W. C. Nichols.
Sergeants—J. F. Pollock, Q. M. Sergeant; E. K. Converse, Orderly Sergeant; C. D. Lallande, 2d Sergeant; Fred. Freret, 3d Sergeant; H. Thornhill, 4th Sergeant.
Corporals—J. N. Jackson, 1st Corporal; Jules Robelot, 2d Corporal; Ar. Hopkins, 3d Corporal; Ed. Hobart, 4th Corporal.
Acting Commissary Sergeant—W. A. Bell.
Privates—James Adams, C. Armstrong, E. Boisblanc, C. T. Beauregard, H. F. Bonfanti, F. K. Byrne, Hardy Bryan, L. A. Buard, W. H. Brenham, M. G. Campbell, H. N. Crumborn, P. J. Christian, H. S. Carey, A. J. Claiborne, J. Clough, R. H. Davis, J. W. Dowsing, W. W. A. Freret, F. B. Fleitas, T. W. Foley, St. Leon Fazende, L. H. Gardner, A. H. Gunnison, R. S. Griffith, C. Gallwey, J. O. Hardin, C. A. Hildreth, Martin Hayne, F. Harrison, C. M. Hite, J. M. Kennedy, P. M. Kenner, F. Landreaux, L. Lange, J. H. McKnight, W. C. Mitchell, C. C. Mitchell, T. P. May, F. P. Montz, E. M. Morse, Opedenweyer, B. F. Peters, J. C. Patrick, jr., J. W. Parsons, A. W. Roundtree, E. T. Robinson, Bernard Riley, J. W. Simmons, W. N. Shaw, James J. Stewart, H. S. Sprigg, Chs. Shalley, F. Seiler, F. E. Trepagnier, Rob't Urquhart, jr., A Viavant, T. H. Williams, J. C. Walker.
Blacksmith, Con. Murphy.
Trumpeter, A. H. Phar.
Saddler, G. Eberley.
Farrier, E. Smith.

THE TWENTY-SECOND LOUISIANA.

The 22d Louisiana (sometimes called the 21st), after reorganizing at Camp Moore, was sent to Vicksburg; and its history, until the fall of that city and the surrender of the Confederate troops as prisoners of war, was principally the same as that of every other regiment at that point. It took part in the movement to Snyder's Bluff, on the Yazoo, as well as in the hotly contested battle of Baker's Creek.

After the surrender, the 22d, together with the 23d and fragments of four or five other Louisiana regiments, were gathered together at what had been an old camp near Enterprise, Miss. The first commander of the 22d had been Colonel Higgins. At the reorganization, it stood—
I. W. Patton, Colonel; E. S. Landry, Lieutenant Colonel (afterwards put in command of the 28th)*; and with George Purvis, Captain of the Scotch Guards (and afterwards with Wash. Marks), as Major.† The latter afterwards became Lieutenant Colonel.

After leaving Enterprise, the regiment went to Mobile, and was marched into the breastworks in the rear of the latter city. Afterwards they were placed at Spanish Fort. Upon the fall of the fortifications at that point, the regiment was marched, via Cuba Station, to Meridian, where it was paroled at the surrender.‡

A large number of prominent citizens connected with this command still survive. One of the best known of the companies was the Perseverance Guards, composed, almost exclusively, of firemen from No. 13.§

---

*John Plattsmier was Lieutenant-Colonel, at one time, of the regiment, and surrendered with it at Meridian.

† Major Purvis, whose abilities as a builder and contractor were fully recognized by the military authorities, as well as his military services were, during the siege of Vicksburg, by the 22d, was afterwards placed as managing man for furnishing substance and commissary stores for the Sub-Department of Mississippi. What his duties amounted to may be judged of when it is stated that he daily—or, rather, nightly, as he commenced work at midnight—scalded and butchered a thousand hogs, and baked up a corresponding amount of bread.

‡ The names of the companies which composed this command, and their organization, will be found [Adjutant-General's report] at page 254 of this work. For other reference, see heading, "Army of the West."

§ The Fire Companies that went into service, with various regiments, were Perseverance Company A (Company B remaining behind for home duty— Captain Tenbrink commanding); Violet Guards, composed, principally, of No. 12's men; the American Rifles, formed, principally, from No. 5 and American Hook and Ladder; Washington Light Infantry, formed from No. 20.

Its first Captain was John Rareshide (since dead), who was succeeded by David H. Todd (brother-in-law of President Lincoln), its last commander. Sergeant Daniel Owens was of this command; and John Fitzpatrick (clerk of the Superior Criminal Court; Lieutenants P. H, Savage, John Curry, Michael Smith, C. G. Hersey; also Mike Brennan. Ordnance Sergeant, and Henry Taylor, Orderly Sergeant. Until the fall of the city, Perseverance Guards were stationed at the various forts that guarded the coast.

MEMORABLE DEATHS.

CAPTAINS FORTIN AND VIENNE.

The similarity of fate which these two gallant soldiers, Capt. Fortin and Capt. Vienne (his successor) met, may be ranked among the singular coincidences of the war. But that the facts are well authenticated, they would appear on a par with the story of guns loaded precisely in the nick of time by shots fired into them by the enemy. The circumstances referred to were as follows:

Captain Louis Fortin, the commander of the Orleans Guards, had escaped unharmed the dangers which beset the Western Army, until it had long been at Atlanta; and even then escaped the fierce fire which killed their heroic Colonel, Thomas Shields, and nearly all of their commissioned officers, and which numbered among its victims a very large proportion of the command. But the shears of destiny which cut short the thread of life of so many on the 28th, were only suspended in his case until the following 14th. Two days preceding his death, Capt. Fortin, sympathizing with his men in their mortification at the mismanagement which had allowed them and the 30th to be almost destroyed, made the following address:

Atlanta, Georgia, August 12, 1864.

Fellow-soldiers in suffering:—It is now two years and a-half since you left your homes. Since then I have been constantly with you---sharing your good and bad days, your rejoicings and troubles. When the time should approach in which your cause ought to triumph; when the dream which I have so long caressed, of sending you back to your families should be realized, I see my dearest hopes depart. I have seen you fall, mutilated and sacrificed, in an unnecessary attack. To you who are no more, happier days await you in a better world---you have dearly bought them. To you, poor, wounded comrades, who were abandoned and left behind in the battle-field, heaven send you a prompt return to our midst. Your captain will await you with widespread arms. For you who still remain, shall be all my cares, all my solititude and friendship. LOUIS FORTIN, Capt. Comn'dg Orleans Guards.

None of these generous wishes were to be fulfilled. The 14th came;

and of all the days of the siege, it was quietest along the line. It was indeed so quiet (for an armistice had been agreed on) that the Federals fired only one shot; this shot, however, was aimed by the Grim Archer himself—and Fortin fell mortally wounded.*

The circumstances attending the death of this brave officer were curious enough; but the effect was heightened by what happened to his successor.

On the 25th of the same month, Lieutenant A. J. Vienne, who now became Captain, reached Atlanta from Montgomery, where he had been confined after receiving a serious wound. His arrival or promotion meant death for him. Shortly after entering camp, he received his death wound within a few paces of the trenches, or near the spot where Fortin had been shot. On this day, as had been the case on the 25th, there had been a total suspension of hostilities. The only cannon ball from the enemy fired during the day, struck Vienne in the head and scattered his brains.

The remains of Captains Fortin and Vienne were conveyed from Atlanta, through the care of Father Turgis, the Chaplain of the regiment, and interred in the St. Louis Cemetery, in their respective family tombs, where they still rest but a few feet apart.

The body of Captain Becnel, of the Thirtieth Louisiana, killed

---

*Captain Fortin was born on the 26th of November, 1829, in the parish of St. James, in this State, and was the son of Charles Fortin, a sugar planter. In 1843, Louis Fortin entered Jefferson College, in the parish of St. James, the then leading institution of our State, where so many of our Creoles were educated. On his withdrawal from college, after receiving a brilliant education, he made a traveling tour in the United States, visiting the principal cities. On his return, he devoted his time to the study of Medicine, which he would have continued in Paris had not the war broken out. Fortin was refined and elegant in his manners and bearing, and had always been accustomed to the ease enjoyed then by almost every Creole family. All of this, however, did not prevent him from sacrificing family ties and future hopes. He abandoned his studies to take part for years in the weary marches and battles which terminated in his death. He started from this city as a private on the 18th of March, 1862; and through his bravery and evenness of character, soon gained the esteem of his officers and comrades. The promotion of Fortin to the captaincy of Company F, which took place after the battle of Shiloh, was a just recognition of the services he rendered in the different positions he filled, and was a just reward to commanding traits of character shown in the hour of peril. His devotion was great to his company, and his attachment to his comrades so strong as to induce him to refuse higher positions tendered him.

before Atlanta, was also brought back by Father Turgis, and his remains sent to his family in the parish of St. John the Baptist.

LIEUT. COL. CHAS. D. DREUX.

He left this city on the 11th of April, 1861, with about one hundred and five of the finest young soldiers that ever marched to confront an enemy. His was the first volunteer company that left Louisiana. Its departure from the city drew to the lake end of the old Pontchartrain a large crowd of the first ladies and gentlemen of the city; and as the steamer bore away with this heroic freight, sorrow moistened eyes that looked for the last time on many forms that graced her decks. Snowy handkerchiefs, wet with tears, waved a last farewell to the Orleans Cadets. But amid the gloom that settled over the young soldiers, one face peered eagerly into the future; there was one form beckoned forward by an unseen hand. This was Charles D. Dreux. No evil star hovered on the horizon ; no cloud threw its shadow upon his hopes.

At Pensacola he soon saw that the situation afforded little scope for military enterprise. Frowning Pickens stood far out on the other shore; Pensacola bay swept between the opposing forces; and war there was reduced to artillery duels between heavy siege pieces, at a distance of at least two miles. The active theatre of war was Virginia, and Dreux yearned to go there. All obstacles were surmounted by the vigor of his efforts and influence, and at length the order was obtained. In Virginia he commanded a battalion of the flower of the youth of Louisiana, consisting of the Crescent Rifles, Orleans Cadets, Louisiana Guards, Grivot Guards and Shreveport Grays. His fine presence, admirable self-posession, dauntless bearing, together with his high military qualities, won for him the love and affection of his men and attracted the attention of his superior officers. He was assigned to service under Gen. Magruder.

On the 5th of July, 1861, Lieut. Colonel Dreux, with about one hundred and fifty picked men, left camp at Young's Mill and made a reconnoitering movement toward Newport News, where the enemy were reported throwing up works and making preparations for an advance. When about seven miles out from camp, his command encountered a considerable force of the enemy, and at the first fire he was killed. He fell in the prime of youth, while all the starry graces of young manhood were glittering about him. When he received his mortal wound, he dropped to the ground so noiselessly and slowly, that the soldier on the right whom he touched did not know he was dead. One account represents him as leaning against a tree, with arms akimbo, at the time that the Federal scouts, a few paces in front, suddenly revealed an ambush by their fire. After his death, his body was placed on horseback, supported by one of his late command; and then it was hardly known that the officer upon whom so many hopes had been placed was no longer among the living. His body now reposes in the St. Louis Cemetery, adorned by a simple monument.

ADVENTURES OF A ONE ARMED SCOUT.

Cicero M. Allen enlisted in Company A, Crescent Rifles, on the 15th of April, 1861, for Pensacola. From this point they were ordered to Virginia, and stationed at Young's Mill, on the Peninsula. Nothing important occurred here, except the skirmish near Newport News, and much hard marching in sand ankle deep, night and day; and with no rest for the wicked, or anybody else. In the skirmish at Newport News Dreux was among the first killed. Allen and his twin brother, together with Bailey P. Vinson and McVickor, participated in this fight, and carried Dreux's body from the field. A small wagon was then obtained, in which was placed the body of Col. Dreux and those of the other members of the Battalion who had been killed (Private Hackett of the Shreveport Grays, and others whose names are not known), and William Beaufort of the Crescent Rifles, wounded.

In February, 1862, Allen was promoted First Lieutenant in Colonel Edmonston's Battalion ; but threw up his commission to join a company of Louisiana Cavalry, raised in Carroll parish—the Briarfield Rebels, of Phifer's Battalion—just as they, with other Confederates, were evacuating Nashville. He did duty with this company up to the time of his last capture, and participated in most of the cavalry fights that occurred.

At Britton's Lane, Tenn., the Confederates, under Gen. Frank Armstrong, had a hard fight with the Federal Cavalry. Allen was wounded and his horse killed in the charge, and he himself made prisoner. He was carried to the Federal Hospital, and had the wound in his arm, of which he never afterwards recovered the use, dressed. This having been done, Allen walked out of the building. The surgeon, then busily engaged with his patients, had rode to the hospital on an elegant gray horse, which he conveniently hitched outside. Allen, catching sight of this, leaped into the saddle and rode rapidly off. The shades of night soon after coming on, he safely made his way through the enemy's lines.

At Farmington and Shiloh he was actively engaged, and in the latter engagement he carried the battle flag of his regiment until ordered by General Hindman to replace his twin brother, who had been detached, on the evening of the battle, to act as aide-de-camp to General R. G. Shaver, commanding Hindman's old Brigade of Hardee's Division, and who had been severely wounded. Here Allen displayed his soldierly qualities, and the brothers were complimented for good conduct. After this battle small fights occurred so constantly that they were almost of daily occurrence.

At Ponchatoula, La., where the Briarfields, with two companies from the first Mississippi Cavalry, Col. Pinson, had been ordered from North Mississippi, with the view of picketing and watching the enemy, who were threatening to advance on Port Hudson, Allen was elected 2nd Junior Lieutenant. His first affair was with a small tin-clad Federal gunboat, the Lafitte, which had been prowling around the Amite river for the purpose of reconnoitering. With a small force of his company and detachments from other camps, he attacked this boat, and made matters so uncomfortable that the Lafitte, in her efforts to get away, run on a stump, and was abandoned and blown up.

It having been discovered that she had a splendid globe-sighted rifled gun on board when she went down, several officers, among them Allen, managed to get possession of a small schooner, and recovered the gun. This was accomplished by one of the men diving down and placing a slip-knot around the piece. Allen was now left, with a detail of two men, to bring the schooner and gun to where the piece could be shipped to Port Hudson. While passing through Lake Maurepas, he was intercepted by a yawl boat filled with nine Federals. Allen quickly run his schooner into a small bayou near by; and, jumping ashore, prepared an ambush. The Federals meanwhile came up, confident of an easy prize. As they did so, they received a well directed fire from Allen's small force, which effectually closed the career of one Sergeant Kline. The balance hastily tumbled from the boat into the water, from which they emerged to enter the woods. There they were speedily attacked; and, after retreating through the marsh for nearly a mile, the white flag was hung out. Allen, fearing to disclose his real force to the enemy, gave the command to "Cease firing;" then, calling upon several imaginary companies to "Halt," boldly marched forward and received the surrender of the whole party. This consisted of two lieutenants and five privates. Single handed, and after divesting the prisoners of their arms and moving them to a convenient distance from the stack of guns, he ordered his *two* men up, and marched his prisoners on board of the schooner and then to camp. Gen. Frank Gardner, who was then commanding at Port Hudson, sent an order complimenting Lieut. Allen on his gallantry.

While the Company was doing duty at Ponchatoula, Allen took eight men, crossed Lake Maurepas in a yawl, and leaving the boat in one of the numerous bayous (near Pruniere), waded with his men waist-deep through the swamp marsh. He here crossed the railroad to Lake Ponchartrain, and there discovered two Federal schooners lying at anchor. He now found a little dug-out, boarded the two schooners, made prisoners of the crews, and got away with his prizes to Madisonville. The one on which Allen remained was safely brought to shore; and a grand blow-out with the large quantity of fluids and commissary stores on board, testified to the success of the expedition. The second schooner, owing to the ignorance of the four men in charge about the management of the centre-board, drifted to far to the leeward, and was recaptured by the Federals.

On another occasion, while scouting with his command, he discovered a picket of Federal Cavalry (1st Texas Regiment), which he quickly charged. After killing three men and wounding another, he captured the balance. He had many such affairs, and invariably handled his men so as to scarcely ever have one hurt.

The Briarfields did some fine service during the siege of Port Hudson, and were notably prominent in an attack on a Federal wagon train, which Colonels Powers and Logan captured. The advance guard in this affair was commanded by Allen's twin brother, who, though only a private, had been mistaken for the Lieutenant by Col. P., who ordered him to take a detachment and fight the enemy when met. The brother, thinking there was a chance for a joke, and seeing his opportunity to get a little surreptitious glory, rode rapidly off, and was soon engaged with the enemy. Lieut. Allen, however, came up in time to pitch in on the flank of the Federals and do excellent fighting with his detachment. The skirmish resulted in the capture of one hundred wagons, four mule teams, forty old prisoners, with twenty of the enemy killed and wounded. When the affair was over, and Lieut. Allen discovered the ruse adopted by his brother to get command of the advance guard, his rage knew no bounds. An excited interview occurred between him and his brother, which was finally settled amicably by an agreement that the latter should get a transfer to some other regiment.

At daylight one morning the Colonel sent an order to Allen to take a detail of men and pursue and capture some seven deserters. This

Allen did. After marching over forty miles in one day, the Mississippi river was reached, only to find that the deserters had taken refuge on the gunboat Rattler. While resting from the long ride, and squatted on the side of the road, much disappointed at his poor success in recapturing the missing men, an old lady came riding by in her carriage. She speedily informed them that the crew of the Rattler were daily in the habit of landing in Rodney and holding high revel in the street, boasting, at the same time, of their ability to thrash any number of buttermilk cavalry, and do it with cornstalks. Allen thereupon camped in the woods near Rodney. A watch was stationed in the graveyard just above town; and during the entire night the sentry's "All's well," as the boat's bell struck the hour, was heard by the picket concealed behind a time-worn tombstone. Sunday morning, at ten o'clock, a considerable stir was visible on board the gunboat. Soon three boats shot out from her side, filled with gaily dressed officers and marines. These soon after landed; and it now became evident that cornstalks would have to come into play. Allen now mounted his men and ordered his few followers forward, and rushed into the town at a gallop. The popping of pistols soon demonstrated that the work had begun. The Federal Captain and his Lieutenant were evidently men of pluck; and quickly getting their men into the church, attempted to barricade the doors. But this move was foiled by the rapidity with which Allen dismounted his men, and, pistol in hand, led them into the building. As he forced his way in, a marine met him, and their pistols went off simultaneously. The shot of the marine cut through Allen's hat, and a piece of percussion cap struck him across the nose, causing it to bleed profusely. But, on the other hand, the marine was shot through the body and fell in the aisle of the church. Meantime, the Confederates had entered through another door, and the close proximity of the muzzles of their carbines decided the marines in surrendering. The number of prisoners taken were fifteen marines, and the Captain and First Lieutenant—the enemy having three killed. This little affair happened while church service was being performed and a congregation assembled for worship. It need hardly be stated that a terrible commotion existed for a brief period, particularly among the fairer portion of the worshippers. Allen withdrew in safety with his prisoners, notwithstanding the battery promptly opened fire upon the town.

After a series of adventures and much hard fighting, Lieut. Allen at last fell into the hands of the enemy, while on a scout in the Federal lines, and was taken on board the steamer Iberville. While surrounded by his guards, Allen leaped from the deck of the steamer; and, after desperate struggles in the water, being greatly retarded by his broken arm, which was then unhealed, and notwithstanding the volley fired at him, made his way to the bank, and thence to camp.

On the hurried retreat from Colliersville, Tenn., by the Confederates, the Briarfields were ordered to the rear, to hold the Federals in check until the balance of the command could effect a crossing at a difficult ford on the Coldwater river. Here, with his small command, Allen made a most obstinate defence; until the Federals, discovering the smallness of his force, charged in largely superior numbers. They actually rode over Allen, he having been thrown from his horse; and again he fell into their hands. He was then placed on the cars, *en route* for the old Capitol Prison. The night was pitch dark, and the train dashing along at the rate of thirty miles an hour. This, however, did not prevent Allen, when near the city of Baltimore, from snatching the guard's overcoat and leaping from the cars. He soon met with some noble-hearted Southern ladies, who aided him in crossing the lines.

Once again was he captured before the final close of the war, and once again did he escape. He reached the Confederate lines to find the struggle ended. Hoping it would be continued on the Trans-Mississippi side, he made his way to Alexandria, to find there also that the war was nearly over. The Confederacy he loved so well was in its death throes The South had played and lost, and the curtain fell; the great tragedy of the Southern struggle was ended.

Sadly retracing his steps, Allen reached New Orleans, promptly entering the business walks of life. He endeavored to build up his shattered fortunes; and, meeting with success, he embarked, in conjunction with Capt. J. Frank Hicks, in cotton planting, near Lake Providence, where he died. His remains are now interred in Greenwood Cemetery.

Col. Valery Sulakowski.

The sternest and (according to many) best disciplinarian in the Confederate army, was Col. Valery Sulakowski, a Polander by birth, who went to Virginia in command of the First Polish Regiment, or Fourteenth Louisiana. His character embodied the idea of abstract military rule as much so as Victor Hugo's heroes in "Ninety-Three" do the irreconcilable combative forces of the French Revolution. As an officer on duty, he was the incarnation of military law—despotic, cruel and absolutely merciless. On the other hand, no regiment, in its wants, was better looked after, or obtained more regularly its requisitions. He secured order among the wildest body of soldiers that took part in the Virginia campaigns. For recklessness, the Zouaves, Tigers, and Guerrillas were all constant subjects of conversation around camp fires; but as will soon be shown, the establishment of discipline was child's play with the others compared with what it was in the Polish regiment.

At the same time, it is but just to state, it proved itself splendid fighting material on many a hard fought field, and no men knew better how to die gallantly in their tracks. It went into the Seven Days' Fight with nine hundred men; and in one fight at Frazer's Farm (known to the combatants as the "SlaughterHouse"), it lost thirty-three men out of a company of forty-two—nine of them being shot dead on the spot; or, in other words, "only nine men came out without bullets in their hides. The regiment was tetotally ruined for months, from the number of killed and wounded; and there was not left, after the fight, a decent company."

The Fourteenth, after organizing at Camp Pulaski, started to Virginia in August, 1861. Capt. Wm. Swan was for some months connected with it, and Judge Cooley, since killed in a duel, was one of its first captains. Major Wm. H. Toler followed its standard until disabled.

The Polish regiment was composed of men of all nationalities—mostly of foreign birth. The Irish were largely represented. There were, however, French, Germans, and men from every State, and, among Americans, the steamboat element predominated. Having different languages and usages, and with no previous experience of discipline, it was a work of great difficulty to bend the necks of a thousand robust, passionate men to the life of a camp. However, no serious incident occurred until the regiment had been embarked on a train of cars to Virginia, and had half way reached what was afterwards to be the burying ground of most of their number.

At the intermediate point, (Grand Junction, Tenn.,) a detention occurred, and the men, wearied with confinement in crowded cars, were marched into a temporary camp. The first order, however, given by the commanding officer was that every grocery and coffee-house should be closed, and that guards be stationed at each to prevent the soldiers from obtaining liquor. Major Toler, as officer of the day, executed the order. The trouble, however, was that the men, while on the cars, had had no coffee, whisky being issued instead, and those who did not drink gave their share to the others. This prohibitive order gave great offence. It was soon found impossible to execute it, as the men would penetrate through rear entrances, over roof tops, and would get in by the backways. They soon obtained a superabundance of liquor, and the officers on the spot could not make their authority heeded.

Another account given of the affair was that two barrels of bad whisky had been smuggled on board of the cars before reaching Grand Junction. The *emeute,* aside from the effects of the liquor which the soldiers obtained, was the result of the dissatisfaction which prevailed in every regiment before their organizations had been satisfactorily completed.

This regiment, at the time, had not received its full complement of guns, had no ammunition, and but few bayonets. The arms were at first in the hands of the guards, stationed at one drinking saloon, who in the first place undertook to arrest the rioters. This was at the command of Captain Myatt, (since dead,) a very brave officer, and afterwards three times wounded at Gaines' Mill—once while being carried off the field in a litter.*

The row having commenced, a soldier named Joe Johnson, ran a bayonet through one of the rioters. The guards were now overpowered and the guns taken away. Meanwhile, in the streets, four hundred yards distant from camp, a Lieutenant fired a pistol at the rioters, and this was followed by two or three shots from other officers. The fury of the men who were there gathered exceeded all bounds. The officers who had fired were driven into the hotel of the town, followed by a company who wore Zouave caps. The doors of the hotel were now barred on the inside, but the enraged soldiers, not to be baffled of their prey, set fire to the building in several places, although the hotel was filled with two or three hundred women and children, and other spectators. This fire was extinguished by the steady men who had been kept out of the row. Meanwhile the fight was still going on in camp, where it amounted to a general rough and tumble promiscuous fight among the men.

Major Toler, who was present on the occasion, says it was the most

---

*Myatt was desperately wounded each time, and one shot broke the bones of his arm so badly at the elbow, that the surgeon deemed it prudent to have it amputated. Myatt was so afraid that it would be done that he slept with his revolver under his pillow, and threatened the life of any one who came about him with chloroform. His arm, however, was saved by a resection of the elbow—that is, by cutting out the bones about the joint—the first case that occurred. He went back with his lame arm to the army and remained to the last.

desperate situation he was ever placed in; that three times his life was saved, from blows aimed at him, by attached friends among the mutineers themselves. All restraint and order had ceased to exist, when Sulakoski appeared on the scene, at the hotel, with a revolver in each hand, and made his voice, which was of extraordinary power, heard above the uproar. He was a man of commanding presence, six feet high, and his features, always stern, were now distorted and livid with passion, and absolutely devilish in their expression. His lips had become blue with rage, and the rattlesnake glance of his eye so terrible that the men who caught it stopped and listened, as he shouted, "Go to your quarters." These words, sometimes pronounced with a frightful imprecation, with revolver upraised, were followed by an almost instantaneous discharge, where there was any hesitation or reply given back. Peter Moran, still living, was shot down, but jumped up, spit out a tooth or a bullet, and swore that he was "not dead yet." An excellent Sergeant, who had been assisting to restore order, was shot dead, through failure to heed the command. His wife came to hand just in time to see him die. Col. Sulakoski afterward showed her great kindness, and assisted her with money to get home.

In short, there were seven men killed, powder-burned; and nineteen wounds inflicted, before both the turbulent and orderly classes discovered that it meant equal death to all not to yield instant obedience.

Sulakowski afterwards bitterly reproached some of his officers with neglect of duty; the Franco Guards, though composed of fine material, were distributed among the other companies; and the Catahoula Guerrillas, taken into the regiment. Sulakowski's course afterwards abounded with incidents of a similar character. His soldiers, who did not love him, regard him as one of the most provident and efficient commanders they ever had, spite of his despotic character. This personal trait, indeed, they soon saw redounded to their advantage, when their regiment would come in competition with others in the Confederate army, about camping grounds, supplies or similar subjects of contention. It was his impatience of any will but his own, which virtually ended his military career. Other men were promoted over him, and it was doubtful whether other Colonels to any brigade, to which he might have been appointed, would have served under him.

The regiment was sent to the Peninsula, and Sulakowski constructed some of the most remarkable fortifications there. The 14th had the finest winter quarters, for they were all built by military rule, there were in Virginia. When the men were not working they were drilling.

Sulakoski was succeeded by Dr. R. W. Jones, who fought the command through the Seven Days' Fight. He, in turn, was succeeded by Col. Zebulon York, afterwards Brigadier General. Lieut. Col. David Zable was the last commanding officer. After the Seven Days' Fight, the 14th was merged into the Louisiana Brigades, and their marches and further adventures will be found in the account of the Louisiana Brigades in Virginia. As for Sulakoski, he threw up his commission, accompanied by a bitter address to his regiment, after a year's service. Though afterwards in command on the Gulf coast in Texas, he accomplished no result corresponding to his natural force of character. With more moderation and a better balanced judgment, he would, had he lived, have arrived at high military distinction. His last appearance before the public of this city was on the occasion of the visit of the Duke Alexis to New Orleans, whom Sulakowski bitterly denounced in a placard, and whom the fierce Polander would probably have assaulted in the streets, but for the remonstrances of his friends and the surveilance of the police. Colonel Sulakowski died in this city a year ago.

Among the officers of the 14th still living, whose names can now be called to mind, were Captains Zimmerman and J. W. T. Leech, Lieut. John Simpson, and Adjutant W. P. Clark.

MUSTER ROLL OF CAPTAIN A. PICOLET, COMPANY D, 30TH LOUISIANA REGIMENT.

Captain A. Picolet, wounded July 28th, 1864; promoted to Major; assigned as Assistant Provost Marshal at Mobile, Ala. First Lieutenant E. N. Ganuchean, promoted to Captain; taken prisoner at Nashville, Tenn., and retained in prison until the surrender; twice wounded. Second Lieutenant P. D. Sourdes. Third Lieutenant Auguste Maurrs, promoted to First Lieutenant; taken prisoner at Port Hudson; detained at Johnson's Island and Fort Delaware until the end of the war. First Sergeant F. M. Dutra, Third Sergeant Felix Balat, Fourth Sergeant Fernandez Anselmo. First Corporal Leon Ferrer, Second Corporal Marcelina Garcia, Third Corporal N. Paiquerre, Fourth Corporal F. Kessler.

Privates—Jose Baldor, Jose D'Farias, Philip Fernandez, Isaac Kahn, L. Meyer, Tainie Pryol, T. A. Rodriguez, Miguel Scamin, Juan Miller,

Andre Beltran, Joe Dickermann, C. Luders, Pedro Olivera, Candido Raby, Aug. Rodriguez, Juan Treveno, T. M. Adams, Victor Clavier, Amedee Fagot, Manuel Trachin, Bernard Miller, Pepe Coll, Ernest Rivet, T. M. Reeves, T. M. Ybarra, J Bourdin, A. C. Hevison, Jose Abal, Charles Burns, T. W. Causey, C. W. Cuck, Joe, Gaff, G. W. Maloney, August Salas, Felix Thomas, A. Wirtb, Louis Rousseau, D. Fremont, Robert Sandford, Manuel Rivas, John Burns, Louis Cosfus, L. C. Causey, F. Dupree, M. Leonard, W. Miller, Frand Silva, S. Farranelli, Louis Verdier, F. Everett, James Rodriguez, L. L. Armstrong, Jacob Bardier, V. Cardenas, Ura Carinas, George Hollsteon, Luke W. Pyburne, John Shannon, James Wiggins, Eugene Martin, Francis Shields, Jose T. Ramon, Eugene Cuezer, discharged, Joe Tamboury, discharged, Joseph Guillot.

I do hereby certify that this Muster Roll exhibits the true state of Captain A. Picolet's Company D, of the 30th Regiment of Louisiana Volunteers, from February to April, 1864.

E. N. GANUCHEAU, First Lieutenant Commanding Co.

CASUALTIES IN 30TH LOUISIANA.

Lieut. Colonel Thomas Shields, killed at Atlanta, July 28, 1864; Major Charles J. Bell, killed at Atlanta, July 28, 1864; Assistant Surgeon W. W. Cross, wounded at Atlanta, July 28, 1864; Ensign L. Trinquierri, wounded at battle of Baton Rouge, and twice at Atlanta; Captain Norbert Trepagnier, disabled from wound received at battle of Baton Rouge, and retired from service; 1st Lieutenant A. D'Apremont, wounded and taken prisoner at battle of Baton Rouge, exchanged, and taken prisoner at battle of Nashville; Adjutant B. C. Cushman, taken prisoner at Port Hudson, and detained in prison until the surrender; Captain O. F. Vallette, wounded at Atlanta; First Lieutenant H. Fortier, killed at Atlanta; Captain H. P. Jones, died Nov. 20, 1864; First Lieutenant N· B. Baker, killed near New Hope Church, June 3, 1864; Captain R. T. Boyle, wounded at Atlanta and detached on special duty; First Lieutenant H. C. Wright, taken prisoner at Port Hudson, exchanged in 1865, and killed near West Point, Miss., April, 1865; Second Lieutenant Daniel C. Byerly, disabled from wound received at Atlanta, retired, and killed in New Orleans by H. C. Warmoth; Junior Second Lieutenant W. B. Chippendale, killed at Atlanta; Captain C. W. Cushman, killed at Nashville, Dec. 15, 1864; Second Lieutenant M. Boland, died in 1864; Junior Second Lieutenant J. U. Landry, wounded at Atlanta and taken prisoner at Nashville; Captain Louis

Army of the West.

Fortin, killed at Atlanta; Captain James Vienne, killed at Atlanta; Captain F. O. Trepagnier, wounded and taken prisoner at battle of Shiloh, exchanged five months later, and wounded at Atlanta; First Lieutenant Charles Diard, wounded at battle of Jonesboro, August, 1864; Second Lieutenant Frank Greig, taken prisoner at Nashville; Captain L. P. Becnel, wounded at Atlanta, and died from his wounds, August, 1864; Second Lieutenant A. D. Bougere, wounded at battle of Jackson, Miss.; Captain A. Picolet, wounded at Atlanta and taken prisoner near Nashville; Captain E. N. Ganucheau, wounded at Atlanta, and wounded and taken prisoner at Nashville; First Lieutenant Auguste Maurras, taken prisoner at Port Hudson and detained in prison until the end of the war; Sergeant O. J. Delery, wounded July 28, 1864: Numa Fazende, wounded July 28, 1864; G. Froisy, died from wounds received July 28, 1864; Charles Giesler, wounded at Nashville; John C, Livaudais, wounded at Atlanta, and taken prisoner; C. Ollie, wounded July 28, 1864; F. Percy, died in prison; P. Saulet, wounded at Atlanta; Auguste Troxler, wounded at Atlanta; Bachelot Zeringue, killed at Vinney Station; E. D. LeBreton, taken prisoner at Macon, Ga.; Sergeant F. A. McConnico, wounded at Atlanta; T. J. Johnson, wounded at Kennesaw Mountain; Joseph Coll, wounded at Atlanta; C. Betat, wounded at Atlanta; Louis Troxler, wounded at Atlanta; R. Kammerer, wounded at Atlanta; H. Ferriot, wounded at Atlanta; H. Buckhardt, wounded at Atlanta; L. Bertoli, wounded at Atlanta; L. Comeau, died from wounds received at Atlanta; P. A. Condroy, wounded at Atlanta; C. Ackiman, wounded at New Hope Church; O. Alleman, killed August, 1864; M. Callier, killed at Atlanta; A. Gantreau, killed at Atlanta; J. Guillaume, died in hospital; H. N. LeBreton, killed July 28, 1864; A. L Planchard, drowned in Mobile Bay, May 7, 1864; Sergeant C. McGregor, killed July 28, 1864; Sergeant J. W. Wilson, killed August 31, 1864; Corporal Hy. Cushing, killed Dec. 16, 1864; D. Bailey, killed July 26, 1864; S. Lacroix, died in hospital; J. C. Morrison, wounded Aug. 31, 1864; C. L. Petit, died in hospital; A. Steele, died in hospital; A. Villeneuve, died in hospital; H. Fick, wounded June 29, 1864; M. M. Firth, killed Dec. 15, 1864; R. A. Walters, wounded; Corporal A. Landry, killed July 28, 1864; Andy Cass, killed July 28, 1864; F. Chandoir, wounded July 28, 1864; E. Lally, wounded July 28, 1864; J. J. Lawler, died in hospital; John Logue, killed June 24, 1864; Mike O'Brien, killed July 28, 1864; S. Stinson, died in hospital; Peter Wirtz, killed July 28, 1864; J. E.

Wuenstell, died from wound, July 16, 1864; Corporal Fred Hirt, killed July 28, 1864; Corporal W. T. Ross, wounded; William Bamberq, killed Dec. 17, 1864; Murat Landry, wounded; Sergeaht C. Rosiere, wounded; A. Allen, killed Dec. 15, 1864; P. Adam, killed July 28, 1864; Jules Bayhi, killed July, 1864; Gus V. Bayhi, killed July 28, 1864; F. L. Duplessis, killed July 28, 1864; F. Guerln, died from wound; Sergeant Frank Webre, wounded at Nashville; Corporal M. Laurent, wounded July 28, 1864; Edward Chaix, killed July, 28, 1864; F. Nicolle, wounded at Baton Rouge; Juan Trevinio, wounded July 28, 1864; Philip Fernandez, wounded at Nashville; Pepe Coll, wounded July 20, 1864; A. Lange, wounded at Baton Rouge and Nashville; A. Landry, killed July 28, 1864; P. N. Lacroix, killed July 28, 1864; O. Mayronne, wounded July 28, 1864; C. Minville, killed July 28, 1864; Paul Sarrazin, wounded at Atlanta; P. Scionneau, killed July 28, 1864; Charles Willoz, wounded July 28, 1864; J. C. Villars, wounded at Baton Rouge; E. R. Barnett, wounded at Baton Rouge; Joseph Zeringue, wounded July 28, 1864; Edmond Zeringue, killed July 28, 1864; Fortune Zeringue, wounded at Atlanta; Lieut. Ruiz, wounded at Atlanta and taken prisoner at Nashville.

THIRD LOUISIANA BRIGADE.

The Third Louisiana Brigade was organized early in the war at Vicksburg, and placed under the command of General Martin Luther Smith. With the artillery, it held this important post against the successive attacks of Williams, Grant and Sherman.

It afterwards became part of Smith's Corps, under the command of Brigadier-General S. D. Lee. Upon his promotion to Major General, it was assigned to Brigadier-General Shoupe, who afterwards became chief of staff of the Army of the West.

After the fall of Vicksburg, Brigadier-General Henry Watkins Allen became its head; and he, being shortly thereafter elected Governor of Louisiana, Brigadier-General Allen Thomas was assigned to the command. At this time the Brigade was composed of the 17th, 26th, 27th; Thomas' 28th, the 31st, and Weatherly's Battalion of Sharpshooters; and comprised about four thousand men.

General Thomas is a native of Maryland. Among the earliest settlers, the family name has included many distinguished men in that State, and has been identified with her prosperity from the time of

Calvert to the present day. [Hon. Philip Frank Thomas, Secretary of the Treasury under Buchanan; elected to the U. S Senate in 1865, and not permitted to take his seat on account of sympathy with the South; and now on the Committee of Ways and Means in the Lower House—is of the same family.] General Thomas himself is a graduate of Princeton, and was admitted to the Maryland bar. In 1856 he became connected, by marriage, with one of the oldest Creole familes of Louisiana (the Bringiers), and since that time has been a resident of the State.

In 1860, having been appointed Colonel by Gov. T. O. Moore, he assisted Brigadier General Pratt in organizing troops in Western Louisiana. This work accomplished, he joined the Confederate service, and was elected Major of a Battalion, which was afterwards merged into the 28th Louisiana. Of this Thomas was elected Colonel. Shortly afterwards the regiment was ordered to Vicksburg, where it remained until the town was surrendered.

As its final investment, during the determined charges of the 22d of May, he was placed in command of Baldwin's Brigade—Gen. Baldwin having been wounded early in the action. During the remainder of the siege Thomas had charge of a Brigade of Louisianians.

When Sherman made his disastrous attempt to turn Vicksburg by the right flank, Thomas was sent forward, on the evening of the last day, to make a reconnoissance of the enemy's position and force. Being unable to accomplish this before night, he bivouacked in a woods on the enemy's front. Early the next morning, having deployed his men as skirmishers, and being protected by the nature of the ground, he succeeded in checking the enemy's advance until the arrival of the Divisions of C. L. Stevenson and D. H Maury.

In the second day's fight, he commanded a Brigade on the left, which did efficient service on the enemy's flank. After the fall of Vicksburg, with Gen. H. W. Allen, he collected and organized the paroled prisoners west of the Mississippi.

When General Polignac was sent by the Confederate Government to France, he succeeded to his (Gen. P.'s) Division, in Buckner's Corps, holding the Confederate front of the Trans-Mississippi, with headquarters at Alexandria. There he remained until the army was ordered to take up the line of march to Texas. The surrender of General Lee occurring shortly afterwards, General Thomas' command, with the forces of that department, surrendered, among the last of the Confederate troops, commanded by General E. K. Smith.

LE GARDEUR'S BATTERY.

FROM FEBRUARY, 1865, TO SURRENDER.

Captain G. Le Gardeur, jr., First Lieutenant N. O Lauve, Second Lieutenant T. Trepagnier, Second Junior Lieutenant John Glynn, jr. Sergeant Major Arthur Durel, First Sergeant Charles Coignard, Second Sergeant E A. Guibet, Third Sergeant A. Lauve, Fourth Sergeant E. Deverges Gunners V Gaudin, A. Lalande, J. Lemarie, Lucien Fortier, killed at Eveysborough, N. C Quarter Master Sergeant Ernest Coignard, Bugler A. Vial, Guidon G. Montegut, Saddler S. E. Dubuisson, Blacksmiths P. E. Retif and A. Keelay, Wheelwright C. V. Gillet, Teamsters P. Saucier and G Stephanus, Ambulance Driver S. P. Lamon, Corporal Caissions J Casanova, A. Ruch, L. Percy (hand shot off at Aveysborough), H Thiroux.

Privates—H. Allison, A Bozonier (arm shot off at Aveysborough · killed in New Orleans 14th September), H. Broker, Jas Brandin, Paul Brelet, Charles Barriere, M. Blakemore, V. Coignard, P. Capdevielle, G. Cruzat, William Delahaye, L Dolhonde, P Ducatel, C. Delahoussaye, Emile Durel, Robert Druhan, A. Feyne (wounded at Aveysborough), A. Gangloff, F. Gonzales,Alphonse Guibet, E Guidry, A. Gaillard, Jules Gerard, A. Gardere, P. Guerin, T. Green, Alphonse Gamotis, A. Hoover, Edward Harris, J. Kirgman, W. Kingman, Paul Lagrange, Arthur Liveaudais, Leon LeGardeur, Henry Lobit, Leonce Lange, D. Ludevig, A. Lapice, Philip Lavergne, Leon Mauberret, Frank Marquez, H. Milleudon, E. J. Moss, S Mouillard, J. Martine, W. McMillan, G. Oehmichen, N. Olivier, A. Pitot, E. Pitot, J B Pelletier, Mike Preto, J. B Philbet, L. Peschier, Alce Piseros, John Pemberton (wounded at Aveysborough), Edgar Pilie, Arthur Roux, E. Roux, A. Retif, E. H. Reynes, T. Robert, Paul Roman, Ed. Roman, P. Saucier, C. Soeger, Paul Sarpy, Charles Souchon, G. Stephanus, O. Simoneaux, Leon Sere, Felix Sauve, J. Sheridan (wounded at Aveysborough), F. N. Sharp, Robert Taney, P. Triche, S. Toca, J. Tobin, J. Umaran, A. Vial, Jules Verret. W. B. Wickes, C. Whitner, Leon Wiltz, William Walsh, A. V. Wogan, Hy. Willoz, C. Weysham, A. Zamit, A. G. DeLisle, J. Ferguson, Victor Decoux, W. Forstall, A. Kelly, A. Wolf, Paul Roman (transferred to Dew's Cavalry), S. A. Dugan, Theo. Johnson, William Olivier, Pierre Saucier, John Sherrer, Alfred Thiroux, S. P. Lamon.

A. DUREL, Sergeant Major.

BRIDGES' BATTERY.

Captain William M. Bridges assumed command of this Company (Company D, composed of Louisianians transferred from Companies A, B and C of the South Carolina siege train, under Major E. Manigault) December 3, 1863, according to Special Order No. 270, Headquarters Department South Carolina, Georgia and Florida, by command of Gen. Beauregard. It was known as Company D; and served both as heavy artillery and infantry, up to February 7, 1865. It took part in several engagements, and in the continual bombardment of Charleston, James Island, Secessionville and Stone River; and worked at the first fortification of Battery Haskel. On February 9th, 1865, as per Special Orders No. 32, the Company was ordered to proceed to Georgetown, and report for duty to Brigadier General J. K. Jackson, commanding, to relieve Ward's Light Battery. By command of Lieutenant-General Hardee, it was known as Bridges' Louisiana Battery.

MUSTER ROLL

Captain William M. Bridges, First Lieutenant J. G. Vienne, Senior 2d Lieut. R. Painpare (killed near Sumpter, S. C.) Junior 2d Lieut. A. Damarin, Surgeon D. T. Pope, Sergt-Major J. Songeron, Q. M. Sergeant J. P. Marchand (died since the war), Sergeants A. Lamothe, E. G. Durel, P. O. Peyroux, N Landry, Corporals E. Villavaso, A. Durel, A. Rocquet, A. Vean, J. M Villavaso, E. Landry, V. LaBranche, Bugler J F. Planchard (died since the war), Artificers G. Berlucheau, T. A. Bienvenu, Teamsters M. K O'Neal, C. A. Lepage (died since the war), H. L. Noves.

Privates—L. G. Arnoult, G. M. Beck, N. Bel, D. Bienvenu, N. Bienvenu, jr., A. Boisblanc, H. Bonneval (died since the war), B. G Boulet, A. J. Camus, Paul Darby, A. DeGruy (died since the war), J. A. Duchanfour, Hy. Dupre, Charles D. Delery, J. L. Esneault, Samuel Farge (died since the war), A. D. Fagot (wounded), James Fahey, Octave Forstall, Paul Forstall, Anatole Forstall, H. Flotte, Charles Fleischman (died since the war), H. V Garidel, J. Gerard, John G. Guerin, S. Gonzales (died since the war), J. A. Hincks, Charles F. Jumonville, Chevalier Jumonville, Raoul Jumonville, Paul Jumonville, E. Lafonta, A. Lamothe, Leon Lamothe (died since the war), Alfred G. Lanaux, S. Lanaux, O Legier, A. Lipinski, E. E. Livaudais, D. C. Levy, Charles LeBreton, J. Masicot, E Malue (died since the war), J. Meunier, A.

Michot, G. A. Meillenr, N. J. Maxwell, G. W. Nott, Edgar Nott, A. Ochmichen, J. A. Peyroux, M. A. Peyroux, T. A. Peyroux, Paul Poincy, Ben Poincy, William Relf, L Rocquet, D. D. Rogers, W. Rogers, James D. Saul, J. H. Starr, A. Seurentine, T Sommereau, Charles Sylva, L. Soniat, C. L. Turgeau, Octave Toca, Richard Joutant Beauregard, J. T. Villars, Adolphe Villars, Albert Villars, Cyrille Villere, J. Vigo (wounded).

I certify that the above is a correct muster roll of the Company.

J. SOUGERON, Sergeant-Major.

THE TRANS-MISSISSIPPI.

FIRST PAPER.

Though Virginia was the most frequent battle ground of the Confederate struggle, and the arena for brilliant achievement from all portions of the South, it still was not upon her soil that the events which most affected the action of the drama were performed. Lee's victories were, judged by the final result, in reality merely details or delays. At New Orleans, Vicksburg and Atlanta, Secessia was receiving the fatal stabs which made the scene at Appomattox only a foregoing act of the tragedy.

The portion of the struggle which occured in Louisiana, the sacrifice of New Orleans through the inattention and indifference of Davis and Benjamin—the arrival of Butler—the hanging of Mumford—Grant's wonderful canal for changing the bed of the Mississippi—the famous Red River expedition—the battles of Mansfield and Pleasant Hill, were all incidents too much impressed upon the minds of the people to need more than a casual allusion. It was one of the mournful incidents in the State's history, that the prominent actors in this quarter were Lovell, who had no means of doing anything if he had had the ability; Pemberton worse than useless; Smith amiable but purposeless, and Magruder whose otherwise brilliant reputation for generalship, was somewhat tarnished by the repulse of the Confederates at Malvern Hill. Taylor had gained an advantage over the enemy under Gen. Jackson by disobeying orders, and was equally fortunate at Mansfield by a similar course.

The only officer who gained great popularity and the confidence of the people was Henry W. Allen, crippled in both legs at the battle of Baton Rouge, and afterwards made Governor of the State. Though a man with a good deal of rhetorical nonsense, exploded medieval sentiments, which appeared absurd in this age, he yet had the great manly qualities of undaunted courage, incorruptible honesty and unceasing activity in laboring for the people. He had the same admiration for the feudal heroes (and more enthusiasm), as Napoleon or Mme. Roland for those of antiquity; in every other respect he was thoroughly American in character, and was probably the most useful governor Louisiana has ever had. He was indeed the guardian angel of the poverty-stricken people of this State, and by his honesty and energy in using her credit for the purchase and distribution of supplies was the means of arresting untold misery.

And apropos of the great final suffering, one of the most curious features of the war in Louisiana, was the enormous loss of property and the wonderful exhibition made of the productiveness of the soil, not to speak of the destruction of the immense quantity of products on the levee at the capture of the city. When it became known that the Federal fleet was ascending the Mississippi above New Orleans, a simultaneous column of smoke ascended from almost every cotton plantation along that river; and on many of the pyres thus kindled, each planter had sacrificed a half million dollars. In the cultivation of sugar as much as two and a half millions had been invested by one planter alone (who had commenced life without means), and that this interest suffered may be guessed from the following statement of another of his class:

" I commenced making sugar fifteen years ago. The crop in one or two seasons, went up to 400 hogsheads. In '57 I made 3,000 hogsheads. In '62 my largest crop was in the field. . At that time the Union troops took possession. I lost my crop, over 300 negroes, whose cost was $500,000, and all of my cattle, carts mules, harness and horses. Butler returned them to me, but 120 of my negroes, from exposure and dissipation, had to be sent to my hospital, and the stock was broken down or lost. The black frost set in, my loss was over $600,000 and I did not make enough, nor the planters generally through the State, to pay expenses."

Utter want and misery came at last for all. At Vicksburg, people of wealth, when they burrowed in caves to escape shot and shell and cut habitations in the hill-sides, similar to those of Petræa, carried thither their carpets and pianos; but with thousands of delicate women, the day came for wandering around the country as helpless refugees, or of staying at home and receiving the visits of the demons known as Swamp Angels. Of what families suffered outside of the military seizures and destruction of property by war, the following will serve as an instance:

At Island No. 40 a gang of fifteen thieves came over and carried off everything that was portable. They robbed Mr. R. S. Saunders of $1,000 of property and Dr. Bateman of a similar amount. "Are you Confederate or Federal soldiers?" was asked. "We are neither; we are money boys." One of the villains proposed to fire into the parlor windows. Dr. Bateman was awakened at night by a pistol presented at his head. He boldly denounced the gang and threatened a retaliation and punishment, which eventually was carried out. The thieves were soon after attacked and driven to the woods, or under cover of half submerged thickets, or else killed.

But this article proposes rather to give some of the adventures of the Regiments and prominent actors therein who went from this city. Of these we know of none who made a greater figure in Texas than our well known townsman, Maj. Bloomfield.

Maj. BENJAMIN BLOOMFIELD was in the Washington Artillery at the commencement of the war, but was taken from that corps and assigned to duty by Magruder as a Captain of Artillery. Before, however, he had reached the front, Magruder placed him upon his staff, and he remained with the latter as his "Familiar" in all of his subsequent campaigns. What Magruder thought of him will be seen from the following report of that General:

"I cannot express too strongly my estimate of the services rendered by my Chief Quartermaster, Major Bloomfield. Soon after he took charge, he introduced order, promptness and economy in the management of his department. The scarcity of supplies and materials was so great as to make it almost impossible to procure them. The genius, energy and extraordinary industry of Major Bloomfield, however, overcame all obstacles and enabled the army of the Peninsula to march and fight with the regularity of a machine.   *   *   Maj. Bloomfield was sent by General Lee to Richmond on important business (the communication to Mr. Davis of full information as to Gen. Lee's plans) and returned in time to render me good service."*

The services here referred to were in accompanying Magruder on the battlefield during the Seven Days' Fight—Major Bloomfield being the only officer, besides Col. Chilton, present —and in conveying confidential messages between Magruder, Lee and other generals.

When Gen. Magruder came South to take command of the Trans-Mississippi Department, after the last named fight, he sent Bloomfield with artillery, stores and an immense military train by the overland route, together with a considerable military retinue to meet him (Magruder) in Texas. This journey of 2000 miles was much of it made on foot, and as all sorts of supplies had to be gathered up on the way, at Vicksburg, Alexandria and other points, for the defence of the new department, the journey was not completed until Christmas Eve following.

In Texas Major Bloomfield was Magruder's intimate friend and most confidential adviser, and though there was a small military row whenever the two men came together (for which Magruder had a certain fondness with nearly all of his officers) he never allowed Bloomfield to go from his presence. It was

---

*When Johnson came to the Peninsula orders were given by him to an engineer to have two or three bridges built over Black River for the retreat of his troops and *impedimenta*, as occasion might require. About a week after he was not a little disgusted at finding that nothing had been done beyond making requisitions for a certain quantity of spikes, nails, &c., and Magruder recommended him to try Bloomfield, which was accordingly done. The same night the woods along the banks of the river resounded with the axes of a regiment of woodcutters, working by the light of huge fires, and although the smoke from these was an immediate mark for the shot of the enemy, the *impromptu* bridges were completed by daylight, ready for the retreat if necessary.

as quartermaster that Bloomfield published in Confederate days the "Quartermasters' Guide" and the "Paymasters' Guide," the only books of the sort used until the Confederate Government took the matter in hand, and it would have been well if the opening instructions had been always remembered by the sub-quartermasters: "The duties of a quartermaster," says the "Guide," are to supply the wants of his Division, Brigade or Regiment and to treat every soldier with whom he may have business as 'some one's absent darling,' whose comfort and health are dependant on his exertions."

Bloomfield had control of all of the railroads in Texas, and it was by the care he had taken at the time of Banks' Red River advance, in organizing depots of supplies for the dispersed regiments, that the Texas troops were concentrated and enabled to make such connections as to reach Mansfield on the day when that battle came off, or rather on the day when these troops forced the enemy to battle. In fact, so close was the connection that Magruder had scarcely finished swearing at Bloomfield, for not *knowing* positively whether they actually had come up in time, when the news reached his headquarters that everything had been worked according to programme, and that Banks had left behind his wagon train without his expected load of cotton.

One of Bloomfield's most meritorious services was in getting in blockade goods for the supply of the department, which of course meant the obtaining of the necessary quantity of cotton from the people of Texas. However, the latter never failed to respond, and either through her own ports, or the neighboring territory of Mexico, the needful supplies were not often lacking.

THE CRESCENT REGIMENT left New Orleans in March '62 and thirty days after took part in the battle of Shiloh, losing 30 killed and 14 wounded. After leaving Corinth, it was disbanded and the regiment merged into the 18th. One of the causes of this was that a very large number of the young men who went out in this Regiment were accomplished accountants and were immediately detailed to the number of 300 to clerical duties. In September, Captains H. B. Stevens and W. C. C. Claiborne, Jr., went on to Richmond and showed to the War Department the injustice of the proceeding, and obtained an order for a re-organization of the Regiment.

The Regiment was now transferred from Adams' Brigade to the Trans-Mississippi, and subsequently took part in the engagements at Labadieville, Camp Bisland, in which there were 15 men killed, and heavy skirmishing all of one day. At Avery's Island, a section of Corney's, the St. Mary's battery and companies A and H were put to guard that point, under Capt. Stevens.

After its ranks had been largely recruited, it took part in the batttle of Mansfield, where nearly all of the troops who made the front attack were literally mown down—where the three field officers, Col. Beard, Lt. Col. Clack and Major Canfield were killed, and all of the Captains present, excepting Claiborne, were killed or wounded. Part of the regiment meanwhile had again been captured by the 18th, and went into battle under its colors. In this fight the 18th suffered with equal severity. Col. Armand, the only field officer, was killed and nearly all of the line officers were killed or wounded. In Stevens' Company of 18 men, 7 were shot dead and 5 were wounded. Capt. Stevens himself carried off four bullet marks and his orderly sergeant sixteen. The brave Gen. Mouton, the Commander of the Brigade, here lost his life with two or three of his staff officers.

On the following day the Crescent Regiment was equally badly used up and met afterwards with severe handling at Mansura, near Simsport, when Taylor followed close upon the retreating columns of Banks. It took part in the affair at Berwick's Bay, and remained in that neighborhood afterwards until the close of the war.

The old Crescent office, of which Col. J. O. Nixon was the generous and princely proprietor and last editor, gave to the journalistic world the names of Gen. Nicaragua Walker, Judge Semple, Jack Wagner, T. D. Van Horn and King (afterwards the founder of the Times), Wm. R. Whitaker and a good many others. In the days when this paper flourished on St. Charles street, in the old building where curious observers can still faintly trace the words "Crescent Office" on the brick wall, Maddox was at the helm and Lewis Graham was foreman. Judge G. H. Braughn was the roller boy, improving his time in solid reading, running to fires with engines and finally becoming an infatuated amateur of the stage. He responded to Beauregard's call for volunteers and went out to the war as Lieutenant in the Crescent Regiment; but this was a long time after when he had already made his mark as the principal accountant in a large business house, studied law, and figured prominently in politics besides.

Once in Secessia he shared the hardships, triumphs and battles of the regiment—rose to be Captain of his Company, and filled with ability various posts for which his administrative talents led him to be selected; such for instance as the offices of Judge Advocate, Provost Marshal in St. Martin, or commander of the post at Nachitoches. Towards the close of the war he was put to organizing a Reserve Corps and with this broke up the contraband trade that had previously been carried on by the lakes and bayous west of the Mississippi.

BRAUGHN'S luckiest exploit was the capture of the heart and hand of a wealthy and beautiful lady of that country—the daughter of Hon. Edward Simon, lawyer and planter of St. Mary, who in his best days had sat upon the Supreme Bench of the State.

Capt. BRAUGHN'S good fortune followed him after the war. He devoted his time closely to law and immediately gained a large practice; he took an active part in all of the Clubs and organizations which interested the town, and became in most of them their leading spirit, especially in the entertainments given for charitable purposes, in which he showed histrionic talents of the highest order. Other honors followed him; he was elected Senator and served his time in the Legislature, and in 1875 was appointed Judge of the Superior Criminal Court. During his occupancy his decisions and charges were as carefully written out, in the opinion of the bar, as those of any of our Judges who have yet held the scales. He failed to act in accord with the dominant party, was removed, and has since devoted himself to law.

One of the best hearted and bravest soldiers who went out from this city during the war and who lived to get back again was Lt. Col. HYATT, of the Consolidated Crescent Regiment. This was composed of the Response troops, Confederate Guards and other Battalions, whose organization as they went out is given on page 151. Lt. Col. A. W. HYATT was twice wounded in the leg, once at Shiloh and once at Mansfield, and served faithfully, though the head of a family left behind in New Orleans, and though a man of strong domestic attachments, and without ever obtaining a furlough, until the dreary close of the war. During that wearisome period he kept a journal of the movements of his command, and of personal incidents which gives an excellent idea of what soldiering amounted to in this State. We make a few extracts:

April 3d, 1862—The Response troops leave Corinth.

April 6th and 7th—Arrive at Shiloh. Engage in battle of the same day and of the following. Return to New Orleans wounded a month after going out. Compelled before my wound is healed to report back, in consequence of the capture of the Crescent City.

May 1st—Confederate Response Battalion transferred to 1st Florida Battalion.

July 14th to August 28th.—Transferred to 25th Louisiana. Reclaimed by Major Clack (August 19th) and leave Chattanooga for Meridian via Mobile. Three happy days in the last place. Of all infernal, nasty, stinking, Godforsaken places Meridian is the worst.

August 3d to September 11th.—Pass through Jackson, Tululu (by wagons) and Monroe for Columbia.

Sept. 19th—Grounded on a steamboat at Catahoula Shoals and take to a flat boat.

Sept. 19th.—Start for Alexandria with two wagons for sick and baggage, and then on to Gordon's Landing on Red River. Down with raging fever and all day exposed on the top of one of the wagons for ten hours to terible shaking and a burning sun.

Sept. to Oct. 4th.—Down the Atchafalaya into the Teche, through Franklin, New Iberia, Thibodaux to camp near Donaldsonville. The march from Chattanooga has thus lasted nearly three months.

Oct. 10th.—The men—Co. A, now 33d Louisiana—are in a most deplorable state of destitution. The night is cold, the wind extremely high and two-thirds of the command without blankets, shoes or tents. For the last week it has rained every night, and the exposure is causing great sickness. Lieut. J. M. Bonner sick with bilious fever.

Oct. 14th.—Attack of chills and fever. Feel as if pressed between the cylinders of a sugar mill.

Oct. 25th, 26th.—Enemy passing up the river, and fight constantly expected. Cold intense and food scarce. At one time had to march and leave behind what we had half cooked.

Oct. 27th.—The ball opened by batteries of both sides. We advance almost into the middle of a superior body of the enemy and lose one-half of the 18th and Crescent Regiments in killed wounded and prisoners. After various manoeuvres, which last twenty-two hours, arrive at Thibodaux the following day. Col. McPheeters killed—a good officer and gallant soldier.

Oct. 31.—The whole army will be sick if not soon sheltered. Had no shade for five days from the sun though shade trees were all the time in sight.

Nov. 6th.—Tried to keep up on the march to Iberia but sent to the hospital with fever. The post surgeon refuses to give the convalescents anything to eat, until he learns the fate of some missing spoons.

Nov. 9th.—Back to regiment. Col. Clack tenders his resignation as commander of the 33d.

Nov. 12th, 13th.—Firing from enemy's gunboats, which is replied to.

Nov. 24th.—The Yellow Jackets (Fornet commanding) separated from the Confederate Guard Response and Col. Clack reinstated.

Dec. 23d.—Picket at Dautrives Sugar House near Grand Lake.

Jan 3d, 1863.—Rain all day. The ground of the tents too muddy and wet to lie down in.

Jan 7th.—Word brought to Gen. Mouton of the passage of the obstructions by the enemy, and all cotton is fired and sunk. As the report was false, there was considerable feeling among the owners about the loss of the cotton.

Jan. 21.—Major Clack arrested Capt. Hugh W. Montgomery for failing to arrest a sergeant who had been carried off in a wagon. The sergeant had the leave of his Captain, but no surgeon's certificate, and the man was too sick to wait, the driver refusing to bring him back.

March 1st.—Lieut. Bonner put in command of Avery's Island where we now are. March to New Iberia and thence to Charanton. Bivouac at midnight on fence rails.

April 2d.—A tremendous mystery. Capt. M. Caufield was discovered majestically sleeping on a matrass bed with a lace fringe pillow. Nobody saw the soft things come in at night and the lucky rascal remained snugly muffled up on purpose to keep from telling which of the sympathyzing fair ones had sent it in.

6th.—The ladies have made our time pass like a holiday or pic-nic. Back to Avery's Island.

10th.—The Battalion has three companies, a band, the only one in the Department, and is splendidly drilled, with intelligent and gentlemanly officers.

27th.—Party at Mrs. Thompson's. One of the brass buttoned guests got drunk and made an ass of himself. The women have spoiled us. One of them sent me a rocking chair.

13th.—March to New Iberia and go to Charenton in a boat. A general break down and succession of accidents on the way, such as running aground, breaking down the boat chimneys, and so on. March all night through heavy rain, arriving at Franklin at day light. There the enemy attack us in the fortifications three times and are repulsed—just below Camp Bisland on the Teche.

14th.—Battle of Franklin. Battalion deployed as skirmishers, with Gray's 28th La. on our left, Col. Raley's Texas mounted infantry on the right. We are ordered to charge and the prettiest fighting I ever saw was done here. The Battalion highly complimented by Gens. Gray and Taylor. I captured four prisoners. The troops ordered to fall back to Generett's after a march of 26 miles in fifteen hours, with a battle on top of it The feet of the men all swolen and nothing to eat.

15-24th.—The fall back continued, full tilt to Alexandria. Camped last night in a cow pen, much to the disgust of the men who would have preferred a wood 400 yards further on, which would have kept off the dew.

B

29th.—Called on Gov. Moore, who was hospitable enough to give us a good drink of whiskey, and supper.

May 4th, 1863.—Cockafare's Place on Clear Creek, 20 miles from Alexandria.

6th.—Reach Paul's at dark. News of a digraceful occurrence reached us to-day: It was of the shooting and wounding of an officer after he had surrendered. The excuse given was that the prisoner was upon the opposite side of the bayou, and his captor did not have time to wait. Don't know on which side the shooting was done. but the act was cowardly and base, and meets the scorn of every soldier.

8th.—Alexandria surrendered. March to Cane River—the old bed of the Mississippi. Artillery and baggage crossed during the night. A regular race from the enemy. Feet sore, dust intolerable and not allowed to ride a horse which belongs to me. Completely broken down, and secretly envious of my colored cook who rides my horse for me. When we halt, we squat ourselves down, no matter where—in the sand, in the mud, anywhere—and our only hope is that the halt will last fifteen minutes. At night you fall down too tired to be careful of selections, and go to sleep with one blanket, without taking off clothes, shoes or cap. The men, who would crack their jokes on the way to the Old Nick, nevertheless retain their spirits.

9th.—Cross Cane River and take a swim.

10th.—Cross Cane at Duplex. Pass through Natchitoches, which is quite a town, with its galleries crowded with pretty women, and camp, having now retreated 280 miles.

20th.—Right about! Camp at Mme. Plauché's. The enemy has returned to Washington, La., with 8,000 bales.

Our Major is a pretty smart man. Lt. Bonner, tired of packing his own blankets, placed them in the carry-all. The Major ordered the driver to put them out. He has no principle about dividing fodder for the horses, each of which ought to have nearly two bundles. And yet when he draws for himself and officers, he orders the hostler to give three bundles to his own (the Major's) mare, one to the Adjutant's horse, and one to Preaux, The Adjutant swears he be d—d if this thing shall be stood.

23d.—At Jos. Texada's plantation, 15 miles from Alexandria.

24th.—Camp as provost guard at the Alexandria C. H. Coffee sells for $4.50 per pound, whiskey $35 per gallon, boots $100.

July 10th.—Suicide of Lieut. Jas. DeLahanty by jumping in the river. Sold his effects for $214, and turned the money over. Enemy's gunboats capture four or five boats in Black River. Our conscripts are worthless, the majority of them desert.

Aug. 19th.—Camp at Dupre's, 21 miles from Opelousas, at which (21st) we purchase some real Havana Cigars and French Brandy.

August 22.—After a severe march from Aleaxndria reach our destination, which is Vermillion Bridge. The Crescent and 18th are on either side of us.

August 23d, 27th.—Move 22 miles towards New Iberia. Our Major lost his way in the Prairie and made us march in a circle for three miles. Once we interrupted a fight between two bulls, one of whom charged the regiment and put a large part of it to flight. We are sent in this direction to quell mutiny in Selby's Texas Brigade. A box of blacking is worth $1 00. Given up smoking because of the scarcity of tobacco. Great hospitality among the ladies of this place.

August 31st.—March to Newtown, 22 miles, in 6½ hours. Order read for the consolidation of regiments.

Sept. 2d.—Arrive at Camp Hunter.

Sept. 9th.—Camp Pratt, (10th) Camp Taylor, 17 miles distant. Suffering with fever. Got all of my wife's letters out and read them through. These did me more good than all of the medicines, but since then Sergt. Garner has seen a Lieutenant from New Orleans who brings word that my family are in destitute circumstances. My position was never so trying as now.

10th.—Letters from home that all are in good condition. Send back $714 and letters by Mrs. Stafford.

17th.—March to Carrion Crow Bayou and am allowed, as a sick man, to sleep under the baggage wagon during a heavy rain.

19th.—Ville Platte. Left Washington this morning.

20th.—The old military road.

21st.—Retrograde, or rather advance 6 miles beyond Ville Platte (22). March to Mandeville. Mouton's Brigade present for duty, numbers 300. The men are dissatisfied at consolidation and at the idea of being taken to Texas.

26th.—Morgan's Ferry. Marched yesterday 18 miles—road dusty and water scarce.

29th.—Yesterday evening we were all sitting around a big fire under the trees in a drizzling rain when the long roll was beat. The Battalion fell in, crossed the Atchafalaya, and took position on the left of Spait's Brigade. After marching a mile down it was found impossible to advance on account of the now heavy fall of rain, and had to halt in the road for the night. The only thing to be done was to pull down some fence rails, as the ground was covered with water, and find what comfort we could in wrapping ourselves in wet blankets.

30th.—Move towards Mrs. Sterling's plantation. Gen. Green and Semmes' Battery taking the straight road and Spait's Brigade and our Battalion diverging to make a flank attack. At one o'clock we were in their rear, and found them camped in Mrs. Sterling's Sugar House and the negro quarters. Making now a vigorous attack we drove them from cabin to cabin and finally forced them to take refuge behind the levee. Here they poured in a fire sufficiently destructive to make us much less impetuous than we had been at the commencement. The gallant Major Boon however coming up at this moment on the Federal flank gave a finishing touch to the fight by a general charge. The affair was so badly managed on our part that our loss was 100 in killed and wounded, where it ought not to have been a tenth of the number. Bonner was struck in the hip and badly wounded in the arm; Sergts. Smith and Hudwell were wounded. We had 1500 men who were not engaged, as they did not come up in time. The enemy fought bravely and lost 40 killed and over 400 prisoners.

The march during the day was over slippery roads, with rain still falling and the movement was almost at a double quick. There was no plunder or swag to capture, and the men are generally of the opinion that such sort of expeditions do not pay.

It was still raining when we returned, and the roads were so slippery that one could not walk ten steps without falling down. I fell down a dozen times myself, and there were none who were not covered with mud. No place to sleep, nothing to eat and the rain descending in torrents. It's a nice sort of man that can stand this sort of thing and not loose his temper. Kelso is completely stove up—there's nobody to help put up a tent or make a fire, and the fact is our mess is in a regular fix.

Oct. 3d-8th.—Bell Cherry Springs. March on the Simmsport road 13 miles 5th, Camp at Moreauville. 6th, Camp on Bayou Rouge. 8th. Big cane ; Camp in a perfect swamp with Walker's Division. There will be at least 50 cases of fever to-morrow. We marched 300 miles last month, and none of us can see what this eternal movement is for. This is what is called strategy by some. We have evidently, a military genius in this Department. Old Kirby has a little too much on his hands, taking care of three States (even with the assistance of his immense staff) and at the same time watching over a bran new wife and going to pic-nics and blackberry and crawfish parties. Gen. Taylor is a very quiet, unassuming little fellow, but noisy on retreats, with a tendency to cuss mules and wagons which stall in the road.

9th.—Engagement yesterday between the 2nd La. cavalry and the enemy at Vermillion Bridge. Capt. Squires desperately wounded. Camp at Evergreen, after 12 miles march.

11th-20th.—We take the Huff Pine River Road, and pass Holmesville, to Mandeville.

21st.—Horses galloping, mules trotting, tents struck and everything in commotion. There's to be a fight or a foot-race.

22nd—Leave camp in a devil of a hurry. Col. Lain skirmished with the enemy and is supposed to have been captured.

25th.—Holmesville. Enemy skirmish with our pickets.

Nov. 14th.—Simmsport. Consolidated with the 18th La.

15th.—Our Brigade crosses the Atchafalaya on a raft planked over. 18th, Camp on Black Lake. Our batteries engage the gunboats.

21st.—Semmes' battery fired 30 shots into the Black Hawk and burnt her to the water's edge.

Dec. 12th.---March through two days rain to Simmsport. Roads fearfully muddy—the mules are worn out and every now and then, over goes a wagon.

13th.—A regular hailstorm. 18th, Pass Marksville and Pineville, opposite Alexandria, *en route* for Monroe

25th.—Camp in Jackson parish, and have a sort of Christmas affair. The boys of the different regiments, go around visiting each other, and Cols. Grey, Armant, Beard, Maj. Canfield and Capt. Claiborne make us speeches.

29th.—Have come to Monroe, where we meet Col. Zacharie and other friends. We have a ball at night, and find at its close, my hat and overcoat stolen. Weather bitter cold, and all of our tents left behind. One blanket on frozen ground is too ridiculously thin!

[The Federal campaign of '64 in the Trans-Mississippi, may be generally stated to have been the concentration of 45,000 men at Shreveport, in three bodies, coming by different routes. The first of these landed at the mouth of Red River under General Smith, captured Fort DeRussey and Alexandria, and caused Taylor to fall back to near Shreveport. Banks meanwhile advanced up the Atchafalaya, joining Smith, while Steele was at Camden, 100 miles above, moving southward. The battle of Mansfield was brought on, to obviate the danger of the general junction of Federal troops, and because at the particular time of attack the various Federal divisions were not in supporting distance of each other. It was a complete route of the enemy at Mansfield ; at Pleasant Hill the result was more doubtful ; the Confederates fell back twenty miles after the fight.]

Jan. 1st, 1864. At Monroe. The ponds frozen and the boys sliding on ice. Arrived here from camp on Ouachita River. The ground too cold to lie down. Pitiable at night to see them nodding around camp-fires with only one blanket. This is soldiering, this is.

9th,—Camp 7 miles from Bastrop, and 13 from Monroe, march the coldest thirteen miles we have yet traveled.

11th.—After passing through Bastrop, camp at Knox Ferry on Bayou Bartholomew. Nothing seen but ice.

12th-31st.—A half a dozen changes of camp. Read "Ivanhoe" during a march of nine miles, and did not feel too tired to forget to sympathize with Rebecca, whom Ivanhoe, if he had been a decent man, would have married. Brigade crosses the Ouachita moving towards Alexandria.

Feb. 4th.—March to Vernon and have a ball, and Vernon knows how to give a lively ball, too.

5th-18th.—Through Lewisville, Winnfield and Pineville on the road to Alexandria. Dinner at John Kelso's with actually oyster soup, pickled salmon, real coffee and wine ; which all got in somehow by blockade.

March 3d.—Enemy capture Harrisonburg with four gunboats and two transports containing a brigade of infantry, Polignac and the Texans defended it.

March 7th.—John Paul shot for desertion. Ball given at the Ice House in Alexandria, on opposite side of the river. A considerable stir in town about rumors of the enemy.

March 14th.—Big excitement. Fort DeRussey captured by the enemy's cavalry. We fall back and all the steamboats are loaded with government stores. We cross the river.

15th. Leave for Grand Ecore. A Yankee gun boat is firing at the Frolic, who has had to let go a steamboat she had in tow after setting her on fire. The people seemed to have cooled down a little, at least those who got on our boat.

21st.—The deuce to play now in Natchitoches, and everything has to be moved. Terrible excitement—everyone on the skeedaddle.

23d.—March 23 miles to camp near Beesley's, through Red River mud.

24th.—Soaking rain. Camp at Churchville.

29th.—After camping near Old River and picketing at Stevens' Saw Mill, pass through Bellwoodville.

30th.—Fort Jessup.

April 1st.—Face to the right about and my company pickets the road. No fires, and pass a miserable night in the cold.

2d.—Skirmish by Col. Bush's 4th Louisiana Cavalry near Pleasant Hill, which place we reach.

4th.—Rained all day. Have had no tents during the march. Nothing but bulk beef, corn bread, dirt and sore feet. Camp five miles from Mansfield. Wounded two years ago to a day.

8th.—The line of the battle of Mansfield has just been formed; 100 cavalry charge our line; our regiment sends them back. My company had the honor of opening on the enemy, who came within 20 feet of us. Minnie balls like hail. The fire of the enemy was so terrible that almost every man in the direct attack of Mouton's Brigade was struck with a bullet. All of the troops in front would have been shot down but for the timely turning of the enemy's flank by the troops sent by Taylor to get around them.

Mouton was killed at the head of his brigade. Armand at the head of his Creoles received three wounds, the last one killing him dead while waving his sword. The men of Mouton's Brigade charged at a double quick for twenty-five minutes. Out of 2,200 men it lost 762, principally in a ravine where the Federals had been driven and where the Brigade was, torn to pieces by grape and canister at close range.

Gen. Taylor sat with his leg crossed on his saddle, smoking a cigar. It was generally agreed among the mounted officers that they would fight on horseback. The fire was so hot that some of them had to lead their troops on foot.

April 9th.—Was wounded yesterday in one of the most terrible charges of the war. Shot through and through the thigh of my left leg. Col. Armand charged a battery over a field a quarter of a mile in width, with my company. We lost 29 killed and wounded out of 42. Nunez, the last officer left, was badly wounded in both legs and back. At Pleasant Hill the enemy are again worsted to day, and are now in full retreat towards Natchitoches, burning their wagons and trains. Chas. Hardenburg, who was also wounded at Mansfield, in the same room with me at Dr.|Gibbs. Gen. Green is killed in an attack on the enemy's gunboats, and we could have better lost any other man in the Department.

25th.—Suffering from fever and secondary hemorrhage of wound. Col. Clack died yesterday.

May 9th.—Kirby Smith defeats Steel in Arkansas and captures his guns and stores. Enemy still below at Alexandria surrounded by our forces.

15.—Poor Felix Nunez! The Doctors are cutting off one of his legs above the knee, and he cannot survive. He was wounded in both his legs and in his back besides. Few could undergo his sufferings with more fortitude.

19th.—He is burried next to the grave of Lieut. Horton. Write a letter to his wife.

June 5th.—Now at Camp Eggeling, Avoyelles parish. Came here with Judge Braughn, via Shreveport, Alexandria and Doud's Ferry.

8th.—Move to Mansura. Two gunboats and a battery come up the river and engage our command. Result, one of our pieces was captured, and the other bursted.

14th.—After camping at Cowville and Fort DeRussey, came to Marksville. Made Lieutenant-Colonel here of the Confederate Guards' Response Battalion.

20th.—The Crescent Regiment leaves for Shreveport. Our pleasant associations with the 18th also cease.

28th.—Assigned to duty as President of a Court Martial. Leave for McNutts' Hill with Captains Stevens, Ross and Damaron. We put up at the Ice House at $20 a day each. Government owes me $700, but cannot get a dollar. Capt. T. W. Abney is Judge Advocate.

Aug. 5th.—Camped at Pineville August 1st, and then came to Trinity---a town which has four rivers within its limits. There was not a grain of corn from Alexandria to Lake Catahoula; my horse lived on the grass which is excellent. Only one or two farms on the road.

30th.---A project for crossing the Mississippi in Franklin parish has been abandoned. We are at Turkey Creek in this parish, and are starting for Missouri, via Monroe. Swapped my horse for a dun-colored one of Bowie's, having a black mane and tail, white feet and white spot in forehead, and marks of a sore back. Gave him $600 to boot.

Sept. 12.---Arrive at Monroe. Fairchild and John Ray are calculating to start a paper at this place. Spend a pleasant day at Capt. J. M. Bonner's place.

Sept. 22nd.—Court Martial dissolved. The Consolidated Crescent Regiment moving from Alexandria toward Monticello, Ark., where the rest of the troops now are.

Oct. 2nd.—The Regiment at Monroe is ordered back.

6th.---Col. Bosworth sick. Am in command of the Crescent Regiment.

18th.—Leaving Monroe the Regiment marched past Sulphur Springs Phioles, Farran's, Columbia, Black Bayou, Centreville, Trout Creek, Clear Creek to Alexandria. Crossed the Ouachita at Columbia and Little River at Le Croix Ferry—the latter on a pontoon, the wagons forded it a mile higher up.

Nov. 11th.—Duboc executed for desertion—171 men detailed through the Department.

20th.—Wrote letter 23 to my wife. Regiment camped near Alexandria at Camp Buckner.

They remained there with but little additional incident until the close of the war.

MUSTER ROLL

OF THE

CONSOLIDATED CRESCENT REGIMENT.

A. W. Bosworth, Colonel, commanding 2nd Louisiana Brigade; A. W. Hyatt, Lieut-Col; J. J. Yarborough, Major; Wm. H. Wall, Adjutant; R. T. Gibbs, Surg'n; Jas. A. Cruikshank, Ass't-Surg'n; S. P. DuBois, A. Q. M.; M. Foley, Ensign.

Company A.—J. M. Bonner, Captain; J. W. Hardie, 1st Lieut; H. C. Mooney, 1st Lieut.; S. Allston, 2d Lieut.; J. J. Horan, 2d Lieut.

Company B.—W. B. Spencer, Captain; A. H. Thigpen, Captain; W. R. Jackson, 1st Lieut.; J. E. Zachary, 1st. Lieut.; A. J. Fortson, 2d Lieut.

Company C.—Wm. C. C. Claiborne, Captain; L. H. LeGay, 1st Lieut; C. G. Southmayd, 1st Lieut., A. A. A. G. 2d Louisiana Brigade; J. J. Auburtin, 1st Lieut.

Company D.—W. J. Self, Captain; E. D. Beard, 1st Lieut.; W. M. Prothro, 2d Lieut.

Company E.—E. F. Moore, Captain; F. H. Thompson, 1st Lieut.; C. O. Webb, 2d Lieut.; W. J. Campbell, 2d Lieut.

Company F.—H. E. H. Buck, Captain; G. H. Sutherlin, 2d Lieut.; T. J. Foster, 2d Lieut.

Company G.—C. Hardenburg, Captain; N. C. Forstall, 1st Lieut.; A. Muir, 2d Lieut.

Company I.—Wm. J. Calvit, Captain; John M. Barrett, 1st Lieut.; M. Neal, 1st Lieut. R. Hart, 2d Lieut.

Company K.—Jno. Houston, Captain; J. B. Johnson, Captain; M. D. Lindsay, 1st Lieut.; W. L. Robertson, 2d Lieut.

Company L.—J. M. Fain, Captain; W. H. Rogers, 1st Lieut.; L. A. Santon. 2d Lieut.

Company N.—D. Collie, Captain; J. T. Carey, 2d Lieut.; D. Peters, 2d Lieut.

Company O.—H. B. Stevens. Captain; G. W. Tyson, 1st Lieut.; J. B. Rosser, 2d Lieut.; H. N. Phillips, 2d Lieut.

Company P.—L. D. DeBlanc, Captain; L. P. Fournett, 1st Lieut.; L. Fontelieu, 2d Lieut.; A. Maraest, 2d Lieut.

MUSTER ROLL CO. A, CONFEDERATE GUARDS RESPONSE,

REPORTED APRIL 30TH, 1862.

F. H. Clack, Captain, elected Major, March, 1862. Geo. P. MacMurdo, commissioned Captain, March 9th, 1862. A. W. Hyatt, 1st Lieutenant, wounded April 7th, 1862, and at Mansfield. J. M. Bonner, 2d Lieutenant. J. W. Hardee, Jr., 2d Lieutenant, wounded April 1st, 1862. J. F. Mollere, 1st Sergeant. J. S Tharp, 2d Sergeant, detached as brigade commissary. A. P. Bennett, 3rd Sergeant, detached to printing office. J. B. Lyman. E. E. Sinclare, 4th Sergeant. Thos. McIntyre, 5th Sergeant. J. C. Cooper, wounded and left on battlefield, April 7th, 1862. L. M. Brisbin, musician. Jno. Schneider. W. H. Adams. J. T. Adams. L. D. Allen, Chas. C. Bryan, wounded April 6th, 1862. Jas. Bogart, wounded April 6th, 1862. John Beard, discharged June 17th, 1862. J. B. Burgess, wagoner. W. W. Brisbin, detailed at printing office at Corinth. D. P. Bly, discharged June 14, 1862. J. L. Berry, batallion baker. F. A. Bennett. P. D. Collins, H. C. Clarke, discharged June 4th, 1862. J. H. Cohoun, wounded April 6th, 1862. Michael Cailey. F. R. Cottom, wounded. Jules Coste. M. Dugan. Wm. Dunn. P. P. Dowler. J. Dobson, wounded April 6th, 1862. C. W. Daniels. Geo. H. Dugger, wounded May 6th, 1862. D. R. Elliott. Thos. Enright. C. W. Feeney, wounded April 6th, 1862. John Finney, Jno. E. Florence. M. L. Gilder. Wm. Golmin. Fred Goodwyn. John J. Horan, wounded April 6th, 1862. M. Hayes. E. P. Houstin, discharged May 27th, 1862. Dan Hutchins. A. Hopkins. D. A. Holmes, wounded and left on the fieldof battle April 7th, 1862. P. Kingsbury Jno. Killahn. J. W. Keene, detached to sappers and miners. J. M. Kokernot, detached as Beauregard's orderly April. 1862. H. Lein. W. R. Mathus, wounded April 6th, 1862. P. H. McDermott, wounded April 6th. 1862. J. J. McFarland, discharged June, 1862. D. R. Monroe. Henry Miller. Ben R. Miller. Wm. Mathes, W. C. Monroe, detached May, 1862. Jas. Mudford. C. L. Martin, wounded April 7th, 1862, and reported dead. Wm. Malloy. J. R. McCormick. Hugh Mullin. Jas. McCreary, wounded April 6th, 1862, and died 18th. Thos. McDonald. Fred Morell. Jno. McFarlane. G. Nish. Thos. North, wounded April 6th 1862. Frank Patton. H. W. Porter. S. A. Page, discharged May, 1862. J. S. Rivers, 4th Corporal, discharged May, 1862. R. E. Rivers, 2d Corporal, discharged May, 1862. Jno. Roach, 3d Corporal. R. Rizeau. H. J. S. Roberts, detached. M. Sheridan. Jacob Sample. Thos. St. Clair. C. H. Stroudback. Geo. Stelhe. Geo. Thomas. John H. Weaver. Jno. Watson. Wm. Watson, discharged May 1862. N. J. Wilson. J. S. Walker. O. H. Williams. Phil. Winfree, discharged May, 1862. G. W. Verlander. A. J. Vandergrief, discharged June, 1862. Wm. Bogart, wounded April 6th. A. Binny, discharged 1862. John Clabby, discharged 1862. John Donnelon, discharged 1862. Wm. Gaylord, discharged 1862. Geo. Haller, wounded, discharged 1862. C. L. Holmes, discharged 1862. Jno. H. Harris, wounded and discharged 1862. W. O. Hyatt, discharged 1862. R. Lemon, wounded and discharged 1862. Geo. Parks discharged 1862. W. H. Smith, discharged 1862. R. Sands, discharged 1862. R. Pollard, Sergeant-Major. H. W. Chandler. J. P. Butler. Pat. Coffee, killed April 6th, 1862.

[In the fight at Farmington on the 22d of May, 1862, private Jas. W. Price, of the Crescent Blues, Crescent Regiment, now a well known manufacturer of this city, was crippled in one of his arms for life and discharged. Price, thereupon, joined the Washington Artillery and with the remaining hand did as good duty at priming his gun as any man in the army.]

THE TRANS-MISSISSIPPI.

SECOND PAPER.

On a certain day in September 1863, Gen. Kirby Smith's headquarters had gathered around it the usual crowd of staff officers, schemers and projectors, as well as a small number of originators who had some practical plans to offer. Among others was a captain twenty-two years of age, seeking his first interview, and whose chances of obtaining a favorable hearing, judging from his youthful appearance, were the most unflattering of any one present. He was, however, contented to remain awaiting his turn among the last, and ultimately succeeded in obtaining the coveted hearing. His plans are submitted; the hoped for results are minutely detailed, and the practical workings of the proposed system accurately specified. The advantages of the new system appear so obvious and his ideas are so evidently those of a man familiar with workshops and the business concerns of life, that before he has proceeded far he is interrupted by the General, who jumps up and slaps him on the back, with the exclamation, "Why sir," "you are the man for whom I have been looking for a year. Call upon my Quartermaster; if your proposals seem as sensible to him as they do to me, after close examination, you shall organize your bureau, get all you want, and be made a Major besides."

The second interview proved equally satisfactory as the first; the Captain was made a Major, and remained in charge of the transportation bureau until the close of the war.

The Confederate officer thus introduced is E. A. BURKE, the present Administrator of Improvements in New Orleans, and at present regarded as one of the most sagacious leaders of the Conservative party. His organizing capacity has been his success—his readiness in handling large moneyed interests.

The right man to provision or clothe an army, make the proper distribution of trains of wagons and transportations, or properly dispose of the products of a large scope of country, or of a dozen commercial centres, is not always easy to be obtained. At least such was Napoleon's idea, who may be said to have given the word "organize" its modern meaning.

Maj. BURKE was born in September, 1841, in Louisville, Ky. He came of the same Irish stock in South Carolina (the State into which his family first immigrated) as that which produced Jackson, Calhoun and many other names which have become famous in American history. His ancestors were for three generations Irish officers in the British army. The last one of the three (the grandfather) became attainted in the Irish rebellion, and was glad enough to sacrifice a large landed estate in Galway and Limerick to the preservation of his head. However, he found some amends in inducing a lady, with whom he had long been in love, to share his flight to the nearest seaport. There a ship was obtained and the parties united in marriage just before the setting sail of the vessel. However, these ancestral recollections or traditions amount to but little in a Republican country, and the Major, aside from the satisfaction he feels in coming of good Irish stock, prides himself more upon having earned his living in a red flannel shirt as a common laborer when necessity demanded it, or upon his having a constitution capable of enduring any fatigue, natural activity and energy, than upon any past family greatness.

Major BURKE's father successfully established himself as an architect and builder in Louisville, and many of the finest buildings in that city were designed and constructed by him. He was able during his prosperous days to give his son all of the advantages of education. This halcyon period, luckily for the son, did not always last.

During vacations young BURKE had been, to keep him out of mischief, put in a telegraph office, and the idle acquirement he now found would enable him to continue his studies and give him his first chance in life. When his small earnings became exhausted, not wishing to be a burthen on his family, he took a situation, at a wayside station, as telegraph operator and express agent. At fourteen he was in charge of a construction train, superintending thirty laborers, and thenceforward his advancement to situations of trust and responsibility was rapid. He had opportunities given him of mastering the carrier system of the United States, the working of railroad companies and their management, and he profited by them; he familiarized himself with laborers and mechanics and learned to understand their wants and ideas. While in charge of a wrecking train (disposing of cars and freight which had been ditched) or as a freight conductor, calculating the power of his engines, the amount of freight which could be moved from one centre to another, or while keeping all of his faculties on the strain to see that each car load was properly distributed at the various stations, he was learning the same sort of lessons that the educated soldier or sailor learns, or in other words acquiring the most useful discipline and experience which is taught in life. When at fifteen Maj. BURKE had learned by his quickness and ability to take charge of a lightning passenger train, he had acquired more than if he had at that age graduated at college, or poured for years over musty Latin and Greek text books.

During this period when he would be sent off to different points, or when opportunities were offered him of visiting his family and relations who were now established in New Orleans, he became intatuated with this State, like everyone who has ever once visited it, and formed such friendly ties as ultimately induced him to come here and reside.

Meanwhile he had been promoted to the place of division superintendent. He left this to take a still more lucrative situation on the then proposed road from New Orleans to Texas. This was at the time when the city was dreaming of broad gauges, rapid connections, and as the road was never completed his hopes were of course fallacious. He met however with better success on the Texas Central, and was on the track of prosperity when the war broke out. Then like every one else he hastened to take his place in the ranks to put on the uniform of a private Confederate soldier (in the 1st Texas cavalry).

It is not necessary to follow minutely in his campaigns through Arkansas, Missouri, Louisiana and Texas. A soldiers first and last battles are alone remembered by even himself.

By merit he won his way upward as corporal, sergeant and lieutenant, until the battle of Galveston where the success of the engagement depended mainly upon constant communication and prompt co-operation between Confederate land and naval forces. The duty of securing this result was assigned to BURKE and was successfully performed. For his services in that campaign he was complimented in general orders and promoted to a Captaincy.

The Major meanwhile was seeing every description of the miscellaneous and sometimes incongruous duties which Texas cavalry were then called upon to perform; such, for instance, as the service on board of Confederate gunboats, where cavalmen with their spurs on were made *impromptu* marines, and would be called on to explode a steamer, or capture such a vessel as the Harriet Lane by boarding; a thing actually done by Commodore Smith, who led the way for his cavalrymen with a cutlass between his teeth, in spite of the hammock nettings which had been triced up about the Harriet Lane's deck. Another curious feature of the Texas service was the re-capture of one of their lost batteries by mounted Texans, with no other weapon than the lasso, which every *ranchero* and Texas cattle farmer know how to swing. So quickly and adroitly was this performed that the guns were out of sight before the astonished Federals knew what had been done.

Another curious feat was a charge made through the shallow water about Galveston Island, where the men waded knee-deep with scaling ladders in their hand, and had to mount the wharves and make good their landing against opposers who occupied a firm footing.

After the capture of the Federal fleet, he was assigned to the work of collecting the captured stores and was placed in charge of Federal prisoners. One of these, an engineer named

Stone, who visited the city since the war, on the Wilderness, called on the Major and thanked him for kindness shown him and other compulsory guests. His imprisonment had resulted in the following little romance:

After the battle of Galveston a flag of truce boat under the charge of Governor Lubbock, went to the Westfield, then the Federal Commodore's ship, and Stone was allowed to go on board with the Confederate party. While there he employed his time in writing letters home, and was so occupied when the truce boat, forgetting all about him, returned to the shore. Stone being a man of high sense of honor, insisted on returning and ultimately reached land in a small scull boat which had been furnished for that purpose. This act of honor saved his life, as was soon shown by the result. For it had been previously arranged to blow up the steamer then aground. The slow match having been set, the officers and men of the Westfield entered a long boat and pulled away to some distance, to witness in safety her destruction. But the slow match was unusually long in reaching the powder magazine, and the Federals returned to place another. Just as they had re-entered the Westfield, the explosion took place, and Commodore Renshaw and other officers and men shared the fate of the doomed vessel.

As for Stone himself he won the love, while in Burke's charge, of a lady in Houston, and the again lucky engineer succeeding in carrying her off, when he was exchanged, as his bride.

For his services about Galveston Maj. Burke was highly complimented by Gen. Magruder in general orders, promoted to a captaincy, as stated before, and assigned to duty with Bankhead's brigade. This he was now ordered to fit out in first class style for an advance into Missouri, through Indian Nation, Magruder at the same time remarking that he had boosted him to the first limb: "You must climb higher, if you, can by your own effort."

The hint about zeal in his new work proved altogether unnecessary. BURKE obtained the proper authorization and lost no time in making a raid on Bloomfield's quartermaster stores at San Antonio, of which he captured one-half, and relieved Capt. Wharton at Houston to the same extent, picking up meanwhile as he went a magnificent ambulance and field train, where anything on wheels was to be found. In short, he succeeded in getting away with army funds, caps, jackets, shoes and dead loads of army stores. Sometime after the brigade had left for the Indian Territory and Magruder had forgotten all about the order, news was brought of a Federal advance. This led Magruder to call out his Texas reserves, and he one day spent his time in pacing up and down at headquarters, and at the same time making the proper dispositions for his army. Magruder's orders to his subordinate officers all of a sudden received a rude jar from a casual inquiry, which was made by one of his staff officers, as to the way he intended to feed and clothe his new troops. This interruption he immediately scouted by referring with great satisfaction to his accumulation of stores at San Antonio and Houston. "But there are scarcely any stores left, General. Your new quartermaster of the Indian Nation Brigade has carried, at least half of them, off." Magruder spent some time in discrediting the whole statement; but as the fact dawned dimly upon his astonished senses, he cursed out Bloomfield, ordered BURKE to be immediately arrested, and made the air blue with his maledictions upon quartermasters in general.

While the order of arrest was being made out and Magruder was storming around like an enraged lion, he all of a sudden stopped short as if at some sudden recollection, and said to his adjutant "Tear up that order, BURKE only obeyed instructions about fitting out that Brigade; the only trouble after all is that he fitted it out too d—d well. Let him go—he'll do."

It was following this period that Maj. BURKE becoming wearied with the monotomous life of a Brigade Quartermaster, obtained a thirty days furlough, and determined to try his chances, for a bolder throw in the battle of life, by an interview with Gen. Kirby Smith. His daring suggestions at this audience were nothing less than the reorganization of the whole field transportation service of the Trans-Mississippi, the founding of permanent workshops and foundries, the substitution of good wagons for those which had been hastily gathered up immediately around Gen. Smith's army from the plantations, and the employment of detailed colored mechanics and trained labores from the army. His system of making the whole department a vast Confederate workshop, and of caring for condemned stock was reported to Richmond and became the basis of the organization of the Field Transportation Department of the Confederacy. The Confederate Commissioners sent out to suggest improvements and reorganization through the South, so reported it back—that the plan approved at Richmond had already been long since anticipated in the Trans-Mississsippi. Such indeed was its success that the Eastern side of the river was soon drawing its supplies from the Western; and at the time of the surrender over 600 wagons and 4000 sets of harness were being made up every month in the woreshops organized by Major. BURKE.

Shortly after the colapse of the Confederacy and the final surrender of General Smith, Major BURKE, who was on his staff as Chief of the Bureau of Transportation, determined to accompany his old leader to Mexico, partly actuated that way by friendship, but principally because a general apprehension was at the time felt of a rigorous policy on the part of the Federal Government towards their late opponents. Upon reflection however he decided to remain in the South and share the common lot of his fellow soldiers. He thereupon borrowed a small sum in gold for travelling expenses, succeeded in making his way to Houston and subsequently to Galveston.*

---

*In the latter city he considered himself fortunate in obtaining a situation at $75 a month. But his talents and his reputation for business energy came to his aid; he was advanced to the charge of the cotton shipping of the house of T. H. McMahan & Gilbert, the largest commercial firm in Galveston, and much of the success obtained by this firm immediately after the war was due to his administrative ability.

Subsequently Maj. Burke, after establishing himself in business on his own account, accumulated no inconsiderable fortune in a short time. But with American fatality, pushing his ventures too far, he found himself so deeply embarrassed that there was nothing before him but to assign his property, for the benefit of his creditor's, and start for a new field. He had

Burke was finally appointed to a situation on the Jackson Road, which in a short time made him the responsible business man of this great artery of New Orleans trade. In this work his skill was so evident as at once to secure for him the confidence of the public and general managers of the company.

His prominence in business matters was soon equaled by that which he acquired in matters relating to the public welfare. The protecting of the accumulated wealth of the city by promoting all new improvements suggested in the Fire Department occupied his attention and he made earnest efforts to

---

only an insignificant store of money, and this was all spent (partly in assisting comrades as unlucky as himself) the first week after his arrival in New Orleans.

The dark days were heavy upon him now; like many an other gallant officer and soldier, and the old possessors before the war of great riches, the whilom Major had to wander around the streets seeking for employment, and not unfrequently anxious about his next meal or lodging-house. One day after being for many hours without food, and still unwilling to be a burthen upon his friends, he chanced upon the marble-yard of Newton Richards, and after thinking long and half despairingly of the chances one has to regain his former level, when adversity sets heavily in and we commence going down hill, his attention was attracted by the satisfaction the man seemed to find in his work; a feeling of envy was awakened that the marble-clipper should have a field for the display of his abilities. With somewhat the same sentiment among the tomb-stones that Hamlet expressed to the grave diggers, the Major entered into conversation, and began to think— instead of getting off a soliloquy upon death—of what would be the chance of a new artificial stone then introduced by Poursine. An idea half formed, that the use of the artificial and natural stone could be advantageously combined, induced him to ask for employment of his new acquaintance. "You want to have a situation in a marble-yard ? So you shall," said the marble man looking rather contemptuously at Burke's careful dress; "So you shall," (here he encouragingly laughed in Burke's face,) "if you feel like pitching in with a mallet and chisel. There's a vacant slab there over by that colored brother. If you beat him at chipping off, I'll raise your wages at the end of the week, a half a dollar a day more.".

The Major however coolly took off his coat and went to work, though with somewhat of a sore spirit and very soon after with still sorer hands. He earned his week's wages, however, honestly enough, and invested part of his earnings in a red flannel shirt. His wages were raised by the extra half dollar previously promised, and he had made so much progress as a stone mason that he was set to work building the stone fence which is still to be seen on Esplanade street in front of Capt. Sinnott's residence, and which the Major probably looks at very hard when he passes in that direction. He remained in this kind of labor long enough to catch the attention of the leading men interested in the business, and at last succeeded in organizing it into a combined Natural and Artificial Stone Company. However the paralysis of business, which for some years has made a new building almost as rare here as in Venice had set, in and though a good salary had been promised him as superintendent, he soon resigned it to disembarrass his friends of needless expense. Besides other parties were now offering him the railroad employment for which he had long been wishing.

combine the advantages of the paid and volunteer systems, as well as to perpetuate the Charitable Association, designed for the protection of the orphans and widows of firemen.

In the Advisory and Central Committees in the struggle of the last few years to get the State back to a better government, he has always enjoyed the confidence of the old citizens and been kept actively employed. In the campaign of '72 he was nominated by the Democratic and Liberal parties for the office of Administrator of Improvements, but owing to unfortunate divisions, the Republican candidate succeeded to the office, and Burke's present promotion to this important Bureau was not obtained until the following election in 1874.* But in both political races he was on the Committees appointed to conduct the campaign and devoted to them his most unremitting attention. Few, not practically familiar with the conduct of public affairs know what unremitting watchfulness is neccessary for such labor, and how much the success of any cause is dependent on the political sagacity of the men selected for such duty. One or two instances immediately pertinent to the matter in hand will suffice.

A curious feature of the campaign of '72, was the fact that the Governor and Lieutenant-Governor (Warmoth and Pinchback) had, though elected on the same ticket, quarreled and each was striving to maintain or gain control of the political machinery of the State. Should by any accident the Governor be away from the State for a single moment, and the Lieut-Governor remain behind, then Pinchback would have been vested with full executive authority.

Such being the case, a conspiracy was formed by Chandler, then Chairman of the National Central Committee, with the Customhouse officials at New Orleans, based upon the fact that *both* the Governor and Lieutenant-Governor were absent from the State—were both watching each other with suspicious eyes in New York. The precise plan was that Pinchback

---

*It was in every way creditable to him, that in a contest of great severity he received within 1300 votes of his distinguished competitor, Gen. Beauregard, of a total Conservative vote of 23,000.

D

should at once travel back over the intermediate 1400 miles and arrive in Louisiana first. He was then to promulgate a new election law, call for the impeachment of Warmoth (then acting with the Conservatives), and in other words formally turn over so much power to his party that it could not have been driven from office by any result of the election. This scheme almost succeeded.*

In the election which followed, the Customhouse officials with the assistance of the military and the Administration at Washington, returned their candidates as elected, without regard to the actual elections returns, which they never succeeded in obtaining. But a desperate effort however, had been made to secure these by the Administration party, and Mechanics' Hall in which the three or four wagon loads of returns had been deposited, had been carefully guarded with soldiery. Maj. Burke however, with a select party of friends succeeded in entering, secreting the returns in bootlegs and about their clothing and in removing the last one of the returns to the Major's room before the loss was suspected. These were

---

*Warmoth, while expecting an interview with his Deputy Governor was astonished to discover that he had set out for Louisiana some hours previous by the shortest line train. Meanwhile the Conservative State Central Committee saw their danger and were at a loss how to prevent it. After anxious deliberation the matter was placed in the hands of Major Burke, and he authorized to use all fair party stratagems to delay the culmination of the conspiracy.

It was now a game in which the Lieut. Governor had twenty-four hours start on one side and Maj. Burke on the other, a knowledge of the telegraph and railroad systems as profound as that of Morphy over the laws of chess. Warmoth was apprised and put in telegraphic report, and special relays of trains prepared at a half dozen points for his coming. Meanwhile every railroad route was guarded. A dozen different emergencies were provided against, by the happening of which Pinchback would be delayed in his journey, or any blunder on his part have been taken advantage of. Meanwhile Maj. Burke remained at the telegraph station, hour after hour, with his fingers on the telegraph keys. It was like a mesmeric exhibition, where the operator was putting one patient, or city after another under his spell and bidding them look on every train and seat until Pinchback's precise presence was known. Finally the exact car was discovered and when Pinchback neared Canton, a dispatch was sent which in no case was to be delivered to any one but the dusky Lieutenant Governor in person. This direction was carried out—the dispatch was delivered to the party for whom it was intended, but before he could return to the car the train had gone. He had got left. Warmoth meanwhile made the quickest trip South ever yet achieved, and succeeded in easily reaching the State in advance of Pinchback.

preserved, turned over to the Mitchell Returning Board, and were finally transmitted to Washington City for the Louisiana case.*

In the subsequent compaign, it was largely due to his finesse that the white population weve not deprived of the right of carrying arms. The police, anticipating the arrival of a considerable quantity of these in the city, had made preparations to have them taken from the train and the particular cars which contained them, when they should arrive. This danger was however anticipated, and next day the police discovered that by a singular coincidence the cars containing these arms had been so injured as to require the transfer of cargo to other cars whose numbers they did not have. The guns safely reached their owners.

In the uprising of the people that ensued on the 14th, these were used with such precision, as for a time prevented the police from becoming dangerous to the political liberties of the citizens.†

---

*One of the current jokes of the day was that Marsh Stoddard, the seat of whose pantaloons may be roughly compared in size to a bake-oven, was assigned to the task of carrying off the returns from the Third Ward (the largest in the city) and such important country parishes as Caddo, St. Landry and Claiborne, while Jim Houston, the smallest of the co-laborers, was assigned such apocryphal returns as those from the recently created parishes of Vermillion, Webster, or Grant, whose list of voters, as the joke was, altogether hardly filled an ordinary fob pocket.

†One more instance of his sagacity will suffice: It had been anticipated that the Federal troops would arrive in New Orleans and act as a support to the party in power in carrying out their measures, however unpopular they might become; and so close was the calculation made by the leaders on both sides, that the troops were on their way to New Orleans and would have arrived in time to have prevented any popular uprising. There was thereupon some proposal made of burning a bridge over which the military train would pass, which Burke opposed as the guardian of the road's property. He pointed out so many less destructive ways of detaining the train, that it did not greatly surprise him to hear that the workmen on the road had shortly after commenced raising (a work previously contemplated) the road bed. The troops were promptly set to work at replacing the rails, when they arrived at the first obstruction; but this finished, so many other replacements were found neccessary. that there was no chance for them to get the train to the city. Neither Burke nor the head workman (who knew nothing of what was going on, understands now whence came the order.

The most arduous public work in the campaign of '74 was the revision by Major E. A. Burke, as a leading member of the State Central Committee of the Registration lists and the organization of a board which succeeded in detecting 5,200 fraudulent registrations. This gigantic

Maj. Burke in the election which followed, was triumphantly elected to the position of Administrator of Improvements which he has since held.

THIRD PAPER.

Hon. Louis A. Wiltz, when the war commenced, was in his eighteenth year. He joined one of the companies of the Orleans Artillery, and had the honor of a Captaincy of a Third District Company conferred upon him. Wiltz at first consulted only his modesty and lack of years, and refused to accept the proffered responsibility. He was, however, overruled by the other officers of the new company.

He was assigned to the Chalmette Regiment, commanded by Col. J. Szymanski, and stationed at Quarantine. Wiltz's father was also a captain in the same regiment, but his health succumbed before the prevalent diseases of this malarious post, and his father was sent home. Louis received dispatches of a mournful character from the city, and was placed in the cruel position of deciding between his duty as a soldier and that of a son. He remained until remonstrated with by his brother officers, and then went to pay his last visit to his father. The old man gave him his final blessing, and noticing his embarrassment, told his son not to linger, but to leave a younger

---

work was alone made possible by a close examination and visit to every house in the city; by obtaining maps and plans of the same, and by prompt inquiry after registry as to the correctness of any given place of residence.

The value of such services to the cause of good government may be guessed at but not now explained. Suffice it to say that the tricksters were only beaten by a vote of mojority, 3600.

brother, and get back to his command. It was a sundering of the strongest of earthly ties; but the sacrifice was made. The same day, the last which left his father on this earth, found him working his way down the river in a skiff, purchased for the occasion.

Meanwhile the Federal fleet had entered the Passes, the regiment of Szymanski was the first captured of the Louisiana troops, and Forts Jackson and St. Philip were immediately bombarded. When Wiltz and his friend had proceeded twenty miles below the river they met the Federal fleet coming up. This news was of vital importance; there was no time to lose. They immediately landed, and promptly conveyed the intelligence to Fort Chalmette of the near approach of the enemy.

In the resistance which then ensued, Captain Wiltz lent his best aid to the last effort of the Confederate army to retain the city.

Wiltz reached New Orleans to find his father dead and about being buried. The day after, he left the Crescent City, to return no more until after the surrender of the last Confederate forces.

His adventures now carried him into the cavalry of the Trans-Mississippi Department, and found him in command of a body of scouts from different regiments. He succeeded, in this way, in acquiring a knowledge of the movements of the enemy and in making many prisoners. It also gave him an opportunity of showing the natural humanity of his disposition by the uniform kindness which he showed to those who fell into his hands, at Mansfield and other similar battles. He even, on one occasion, went so far as to give away his blanket for the benefit of a badly wounded prisoner, who' expended his gratitude for the favor he received in curses, though finally in thanks.

In Banks' advance upon Shreveport, Wiltz was picked out by his colonel to cross Cane river, at Monette Ferry, and bring precise information of the whereabouts of the enemy. This he was proceeding to do, when, all of a sudden, while advancing in the dark, the party found themselves surrounded by a Yankee regiment. There was a sudden shout to "surrender," and a volley which laid two of his men low (who were only twenty yards in advance of the Yankee cavalry), warned them that there was no time to lose. All were captured except Wiltz, who, by desperate riding, managed to escape the bullets which were fired at him, and in putting the river between himself and his pursuers. Subsequently he captured several prisoners by himself, and once, while commanding the advance pickets on the Teche, he succeeded, with a company of Texans, by stratagem, in capturing from a Federal regiment two hundred head of cattle, besides many prisoners. One of his last feats was in holding his ground with twelve men, in Patterson, against three companies, in defence of the life of a citizen, which at that time was threatened.

After the war (in 1867) when twenty-four years of age, he was elected a member of the House of Representatives, from the Ninth District, and served his term.

Here he labored hard to defeat Conway's school bill, which would have imposed a million dollars of extra taxes upon the people, and did succeed in neutralizing its worst tax features.

In one of the closing struggles of the season, when the dominant party showed a determination to force the election bill through, Wiltz and the generous Clarence Pratt (afterwards killed in a duel) by their labors and energy kept his friends together, and prevented the necessary suspension of the rules. The Republicans contended that the bill had twice passed its readings during the day. The assertion was combatted so resolutely, and passions were excited to such a pitch that the attempt had, for that session at least, to be abandoned. A persistance would have led to bloodshed. His course in uniformly opposing all of the infamous grants and monopolies which were forced through the Legislature by Radical majorities and weak-kneed Democrats, was such as to secure his election, in spite of his extreme youth, to the Board of Aldermen, and, subsequently, an unanimous call to the Presidency of that

Board. The same year witnessed his unanimous nomination for Mayor, though the election was afterwards postponed by the action of the Legislature. Though again nominated and elected in 1870, Mayor Wiltz was arbitrarily counted out, and the election set aside. In 1872 he was returned and took his seat, and in spite of stormy clamors and tremendous pressure, succeeded in discharging his duties under the most trying municipal administration the city had yet witnessed.

He was a candidate for nomination for a second term, and was generally known to be the choice of a large part of the white citizens of New Orleans. The vote by which he was first nominated, was, in consequence of some blundering in calling the correct count annulled, when, by some adroit rival movement, a new ballot resulted in his defeat. He had a right to insist upon the first ballot, and was urged to do so by hundreds of justly indignant friends. Again, for the sake of harmony in the party, he magnanimously declined to claim the nomination—so announced his resolve to the public, urged all his friends to support the whole ticket, and until the close of the polls on election day, spared neither pains, time nor influence in swelling a reforming majority.

Mr. Wiltz is now Director of half a dozen Insurance and Railroad Companies, President of a Fire Company, manager of the branch depository of the State National Bank, and holds a seat as a member of the State Legislature.

On that memorable day in Louisiana history, the 4th of January, when the U. S. soldiers, with loaded muskets and fixed bayouets, entered the Legislature and caused members to be taken from their seats, Mr. Wiltz, who had been elected speaker, thus protested against this invasion of the people's rights: " Our brother members have been seized and torn from us—troops march up the hall, and the chair of the Speaker of the House of Representatives is now surrounded. I call upon the Representatives of the State of Louisiana to retire."

The Speaker, who had conducted himself with nerve and self-possession, left, followed by the Conservative members, and the military remained in possession of the building.

The exertions of Mayor Wiltz in philanthrophic enterprises are well remembered, and especially his solicitation and distribution of charity to fifty thousand sufferers from the overflow. The public believed that their contributions would be honestly disposed of, and to justify this confidence he called to his aid true and good men like himself, with whom he organized plans of relief that were eminently successful. Through their combined exertions the effects of the most destructive flood ever known in the South were averted.

The political course of the Mayor, even after events had proved its wisdom, was made the subject of comments that were unfair, censorious and unjust. Coming from members of his own party and reiterated with unfriendly persistance, these unfair censures were keenly felt by those who knew how little they were deserved. At their request he carefully prepared a full vindication of his course. This was exhibited to many of those who had repeated the complaints made against him. They and all others who read it pronounced the defence complete and the wisest and ablest members of the party approved his course as that of a sagacious magistrate, a good citizen, a patriot and a thorough Democrat. The defence was intended for the public, but he declined giving it for publication, as it necessarily contained statements which would have disturbed to some extent the harmony of the party. What was conceded then by the sagacious few has become the prevailing sentiment of the masses of the Democratic party, and in spite of the rigid ordeal through which he has passed, he has seen the purity of his course and the honesty of his motives vindicated in the minds of all who know him.

Though not elected to the office of Speaker under the final Compromise of parties, Mr. Wiltz was nominated in a caucus by the strict men of the Democratic party, and still continues to command their entire support and sympathy.

FOURTH PAPER.

The subject of the Trans-Mississippi Department should not be dismissed without a word about Red River and the Crescent Artillery, who, upon the Confederate side, did nearly all of the fighting which has ever yet occurred upon that crooked stream. This Artillery Company was upon the "Louisiana" until she was blown up at Fort St. Phillip, and the command taken prisoners. The officers having been carried to Fort Warren, and exchanged at Richmond, were ordered to Vicksburg, and finally placed at Fort De Russey, on Red River, where they encountered the Federal gunboat "The Queen of the West," which, after a sharp fight, was captured. The "Queen" was immediately ordered to be repaired by General Taylor, and placed under command of Captain James McCloskey. The "Webb" was put under command of Captain Charles Pierce, with Thomas H. Handy, our well-known merchant, in command of troops and artillery. These boats were then ordered to go to the Mississippi River and fight the "Indianola." They left the fort on February 22d. They met the "Indianola" on the night of the 24th at Joe Davis' plantation, and they fought and captured her after a fight of 45 minutes.

In a report of this fight, General Jos. L. Brent (now of the Ashland plantation) mentioned for meritorious conduct Lieut. Handy, and gave a point to his praise by furthermore adding that "for honorable service, I make you prize-master of this boat."

The Crescent Artillery, on the 4th of May, having been placed on the "Grand Duke" and "Cotton," fought the "Albatross" on Red River, at Fort De Russey. The "Albatross," however, was lucky enough to make her escape. At the final surrender of Fort De Russey, when hemmed in by General Smith, the command were taken prisoners along with the other gallant defenders of that post.

Among other well-known river men who were on the "Grand Duke" and "Cotton," as officers and pilots, were Rush Splan

E

Dick Britton (the steamboat agent), and Captain Jim White (now master of the "Katie"). When the "Webb" ran past the city of New Orleans, after the surrender (a very exciting event at the time), she was commanded by Captain Read (now engaged with the Mexican border expedition at the mouth of the Rio Grande), with Charles Pierce (still on the river), as her pilot.

SUB-DIVISION OF NORTH LOUISIANA.

On the 9th May, 1862, Col. Frank A. Bartlett received information from Capt Corbin, who commanded the pickets at Caledonia, (near the Arkansas line on Bayou Macon, and six miles from Bunch's Bend on the Mississippi river) that the enemy had surprised his guard and crossed Bayou Macon in force at Williams' plantation. Collecting every available man who could be spared from guarding the railroad crossing at Delhi* and the Court House at Floyd, Col. Bartlett, at once marched to meet the

---

*Capt. J. W. Blanks, one of our best known and most popular steamboatmen, was a Lieutenant in a Caldwell Company, served for three years in this and other portions of the State, but did not have the fortune to get into any of the larger battles; or in other words, he resembled the old lady who played whist all her life and never had the luck to have in her hand a trump. He was marching around from pillow to post and doing good service, during all of the war, and every day thinking that a fight would come at last; and as badly scared a good many times as if he had been in one. Once while commanding a little boat called the Homer, he narrowly escaped being gobbled by the Yankee gunboats, together with Gen. Price and staff who were on board. Capt. Fred Blanks, now the President of the Ouachita Packet Company, was out with a Company which went from Carroll.

enemy. His force when united to Corbin's, numbered only 85 men, while that of the enemy was two regiments of cavalry numbering in the aggregate, about 500 men. The encounter occurred on the evening of the 10th May, at a point a little distant from Lane's Ferry. The Federals were ambushed successfully and driven back in confusion, leaving thirteen dead and twenty-six prisoners. The next morning the Federals retired to the Mississippi river, considering their escape from so overwhelming a force as miraculous. The Confederate commander, knowing the enemy had divided their troops, by the spirit of his attacks, and the superior marksmanship of his men, had convinced them that they were confronted by at least a division of Taylor's army. From that day he acted upon the offensive, and some detachment of the force under his command inflicted loss and annoyance upon the enemy on the Mississippi river, capturing prisoners, supplies and war material.

Being reinforced about the 1st of June by a regiment of Texas infantry—the 13th—under the gallant Col. Crawford, he made a raid upon the town of Lake Providence.

He first improvised a bridge of logs at Caledonia and crossed the Bayou Macon upon it on the 10th. Marching rapidly east, he surprised and captured the Federal picket at Bunch's Bend and from thence pushed on without a moment's delay towards Lake Providence. Almost every hundred yards of this march was disputed by bodies of the enemy's cavalry, but nothing could withstand the charge of Lieut. John McNeil's squadron of Caper's Battalion. Each stand that the enemy made, ended in a route, and at Baxter's Bayou, where they had cut down and set fire to the bridge, our boys carried it by storm, although it was in a blaze and sunk, at its middle, below the surface of the water.

At Tensas river, when almost in sight of the coveted prize, for which they had started out, the bridge was entirely destroyed. It was obviously, time to return, which the expedition did, bringing off a large amount of stores and a number of prisoners, nine splended army wagons and 36 mules, besides, destroying much of the enemy's property. Bartlett's loss was 3 killed and 7 wounded.

Six or eight months after the Sub-District of North Louisiana was broken up its final quarters being in Minden.

Among the brilliant actions which deserve to be recorded in the history of the Sub-District of Louisiana, was the successful defence of Fort Beauregard, by Col. G. W. Logan, which occurred on the 8th, 9th, 10th and 11th of May, 1863. Although but partially supplied with guns and ordinance Col. Logan drove back some four or five of the enemy's gunboats, which for four days bombarded him incessantly. He did not waste a single shot, but when his 24 pounder gave tongue, there was blood spilled on board of the gunboats, as the numerous graves at Brushley bayou indicated after they retired. Major Eugene Soniat of Col. Logan's Regiment was distinguished on this occasion for his coolness and courage, and greatly assisted his commander by his councils.

During the closing month of war, Carriere and Capt. Martin Gilloire, who had made an organized resistance to the conscription act for two years with great determination, were killed in the Teche country. They served as scouts or spies for the Federal army, with a band of fifty men, and at the time of their death encountered a party of Confederates who attempted to arrest them for still continuing to live and act as jayhawkers. It was while resisting this arrest that the two men were killed.

On May 6th, occurred the surrender of Dick Taylor, of the Department of Alabama, Mississippi and East Louisiana at Meridian. His force was estimated at 7000 men, though a number, greatly larger presented themselves for parole. These latter, when their names failed to appear upon the surrender roll, were marked "deserters" and were seized by Confederate soldiers, ridden on a rail, and had their heads shaved in penitentiary style.

RECORD OF THE EIGHTEENTH LOUISIANA REGIMENT.

The 18th Louisiana Regiment, which was temporarily organized at Camp Moore with eight companies, completed its full organization in December, 1861, at Camp Benjamin, on Gentilly road, near New Orleans, by the addition of Company I, Captain Joseph Collins, and Company K, Captain Lastrapes. Company I, the third company of the Orleans Cadets (the first having gone out with Captain Chas. D. Dreux; the second being in the 5th Louisiana, also in Virginia) had been in service in the State since the 19th of June, and took rank as the first or right company; and Company K was newly formed from the parish of St. Landry. Being brigaded with the Sixteenth, Seventeenth, Nineteenth, and Twentieth, under command of Brig.-Gen. Daniel E. Ruggles, the regiment left New Orleans about the 17th of February, 1862, for Corinth, Miss., organized as follows:

Colonel, Alfred Moulton.
Lieutenant-Colonel, Alfred Roman.
Major, Louis Bush.
Company A—Captain Druilhet, St. James Rifles.
Company B—Captain Hugh L. Garland, of St. Landry.
Company C—Captain Wood, Nachitoches Rebels.
Company D—Captain Hayes, of St. Mary.
Company E—Captain Mire, Chasseurs of St. James.
Company F—Captain Wm. Mouton, of Lafayette.
Company G—Captain J. K. Gourdain, Lafourche Creoles.
Company H—Captain Henry Huntington, of Orleans.
Company I—Captain Joseph Collins, Orleans Cadets.
Company K—Captain Lastrapes, of St. Landry.

At Corinth, the regiment was ordered to the Tennessee River; and at Pittsburg Landing drove off two of the enemy's gunboats, the Tyler and Lexington, unsupported by any artillery. In this first engagement the loss of the regiment was nine killed and twenty-two wounded; while that of the gunboats was seventy killed. The regiment bivouacked that night in and around the little log church which afterwards gave its name to the battle of "Shiloh."

It took part in the battle of Shiloh, in Pond's Brigade, Ruggles'

Division; and lost, in killed and wounded, two hundred and eighteen, or almost half the number of men in line—Colonel Mouton himself being wounded in the face. Remained in Corinth, taking part in all the engagements of the siege, until the evacuation. It was then ordered to Tupelo.

Colonel Mouton having been appointed Brigadier-General after the battle of Shiloh, Lieut.-Colonel Roman having been appointed on the staff of General Beauregard, and Major Bush having returned to Louisiana to organize a regiment of cavalry, and the reorganization of the twelve-months' troops having taken place, the regiment began its second year's service, with the following named officers:

Colonel, Leopold L. Armant of St. James.
Lieutenant-Colonel, Joseph Collins, of Orleans.
Major, William Mouton, of Lafayette.
Company A—Captain William Sanchez.
Company B—Captain
Company C—Captain Cloutier.
Company D—Captain Ben. S Story.
Company E—Captain Alex. S. Poché.
Company F—Captain A. Pope Bailey.
Company G—Captain J. K. Gourdain.
Company H—Captain Paul B. Leeds.
Company I—Captain John T. Lavery.
Company K—Captain James Hayes.

It was ordered to Pollard, Ala., where it remained, with the 19th Louisiana and 29th Alabama, under command of Colonel Tatnall, of the latter regiment, until about the 1st of October, 1862; when it was ordered to the Trans-Mississippi Department, reporting to Brig.-General Mouton at New Iberia. Soon afterwards it marched to Berwick's Bay; and, on the 26th of October, at Labadieville, about fourteen miles from Thibodaux, the 18th Regiment, the Crescent Regiment, and Ralston's Battery,* under command of Colonel Armant, with less than five hund-

---

*A much larger quantity of the artillery used in the Confederate Army, than is generally supposed, was made in New Orleans, in hastily constructed works. Edmund M. Ivens, a manufacturer of this city, claims to have made sixty pieces, with gun carriages, battery wagons and everything attached to them, except the horses. The metal for the guns was obtained by recasting the bells from the churches, plantations and other sources. Dr. Palmer's church contributed one, and more than a hundred were obtained from all sources. These guns were hurried forward as soon as made, and some of them did service in the battle of Belmont a few days after their manufacture.

red men and four pieces, fought the brigade of General Weitzel, which had come out of New Orleans. Colonel Armant succeeded in holding the enemy in check for several hours; he only fell back when his canister and case shot had given out. The last shot fired by the last piece in action was a round shot, while the enemy were only a few yards distant. Our loss in this affair was heavy, several having been taken prisoners; among others were Captain Ben Story, of the Eighteenth, and Captain Ralston, of the artillery. Colonel McPheeters, of the Crescent, was killed; Lieut.-Col. Collins, of the Eighteenth, wounded. The enemy's loss was greater than the numbers opposed to him. Returning to the Bayou Teche, the regiment was largely recruited from the Camp of Instruction, near New Iberia.

It took part in the affair of the 14th of January, 1863, when the enemy came up the Teche above Pattersonville.

In April, 1863, Banks having advanced from Berwick's Bay, by land, with a large force (estimated at 18,000), and sent 12,000 in transports up Grand Lake to take our troops in the rear, the Eighteenth, holding, with the Crescent Regiment and Faries' (Pelican) Battery, the extreme left of the line, fought him for two days from behind hastily thrown up breastworks, until compelled to fall back, to prevent being cut off by the troops who had gone up the lake in transports and landed at Mrs. Porter's place, near Franklin.

At this battle—known as "Bisland," from the name of the owner of the place upon which our lines were made—the entire Confederate force consisted of about 5,000 of all arms: and the estimated loss of the enemy was over 4,000 in killed and wounded. Retreating as far as Nachitoches, the regiment returned, and was present at the recapture of Brashear City, with all Banks' commissary, quartermasters' and ordnance stores, and heavy baggage, which had been left to facilitate the pursuit of our little army.

In August, the regiment camped in the vicinity of Vermillionville, the brigade consisting of the 18th Louisiana (Mouton's) Colonel Armant; *28th Louisiana, Colonel Henry Gray; Crescent Regiment, Colonel A. W. Bosworth; Yellow Jacket Battalion, Lieutenant Colonel Fournet;

---

*Major Wilbur Blackman was Adjt.-General of this command, and acquired enough military glory to be several times elected to the House and Senate of this State. He was a prominent candidate for the office of Governor in 1872, though a young man. Since that time he has devoted himself to the practice of law in Alexandria.

Beard's Battalion, Lieutenant-Colonel Beard; Clack's Battalion, Lieutenant-Colonel Clack.

In September, the brigade, with Waller's Battalion (Texas Cavalry), crossed the Atchafalaya at Morgan's Ferry, and captured about 400 prisoners at Bayou Fordoche, the enemy retreating to the cover of his gunboats at Morganza.

In October, the 18th Regiment was consolidated with the Yellow Jacket Battalion, and was afterwards known as the Consolidated Eighteenth Regiment, and was officered by Col. L. L. Armant, Lieut.-Colonel Joseph Collins, and Major Paul B. Leeds (afterwards of the staff of General E. Kirby Smith). During the winter, the brigade, under the command of Colonel Henry Gray, marched to the Arkansas line on Bayou Bartholomew, returning, in February, 1864, to Pineville, opposite Alexandria, on Red River.

On the 8th of April, the army having fallen back to Mansfield before Banks' advancing force, halted and gave him battle. Mouton's Division, consisting of his brigade and Polignac's Texas brigade, on the left of the line, made the decisive charge of the day. Mouton's brigade was composed of the 18th Louisiana, 28th Louisiana and Crescent Consolidated Regiment, Col. Beard. The loss of the Regiment, in this battle, was 96 killed and wounded. General Mouton, its first Colonel, was killed, and also its Colonel, Leopold L. Armant, who fell while gallantly leading the charge; Colonel Beard, of the Crescent, Lieutenant Colonels Walker, of the twenty-eighth, and Clack, of the Crescent, and Major Canfield, of the Crescent, were killed, and the brigade was left in command of Lieutentant Colonel Joseph Collins, of the Eighteenth, who had his horse shot from under him—Captain Wm. C. C. Claiborne, commanding the Crescent Regiment. These two regiments continued the pursuit of the enemy, and held the left of the line against the fresh army corps brought up. Marched next day to Pleasant Hill, about twenty miles, and got into that fight about sundown.

The following description of Banks' advance and defeat, is extracted from Mrs. Dorsey's " Recollections of Henry Watkins Allen :"

" In the month of March, 1864, General Banks made his famous raid up the valley of the Red River. General Taylor, stationed at Alexandria, had been advised in February, by secret information sent him from New Orleans, of the probable Federal plan of attack, by one division under A. J. Smith, from Vicksburg, and General Banks from New Orleans, who was to march up through the Teche country. Taylor immediately notified General Kirby Smith of his suspicions of this attack, and Smith began to concentrate his troops to meet the attack, if so made.

" Smith's department was very large, and so desolated in Arkansas and Louisiana, that in order to subsist the troops, it was necessary to scatter them; so the forces were scattered over Louisiana and Texas. Shreveport and its vicinity was the central point in this widely-scattered circle of troops. Upon the reception of Taylor's information, Smith began to draw in his forces.

" General A. J. Smith came up the Red River, Banks advanced up the Teche. It was estimated by us that Banks had a force of forty thousand men, and a co-operating navy of sixty gunboats and transports, 'and a legion of camp-followers and speculators,' in his train. The Federals captured Fort DeRussy, an inferior earthwork below Alexandria, and then marched unchecked up the whole valley of the Red River, until they reached Mansfield, a small town between Shreveport and Natchitoches. Taylor had fallen back before the Federals, skirmishing every day, until he found himself here almost at the doors of Shreveport, within a day's march of the Texas border.

" Taylor resolved to make a stand, and sent a despatch to Smith, at Shreveport, to that effect. Taylor had 9000 men at Mansfield. He selected his ground as well as he could, about a quarter of a mile from Mansfield. The country here is hilly, and heavily wooded.

"The line of battle was single. Mouton commanded his own brigade, with Polignac's in the centre. Majors, with his cavalry dismounted, formed the left wing. De Bray, with mounted cavalry, was posted on the extreme right. Churchill and Parsons, with Missouri and Arkansas troops, acted as reserves, stationed three miles in the rear. The public road, by which the Federals were advancing, ran over a very steep hill. They had posted one of their best batteries (Nims'),—the same battery that Allen had rushed upon, captured and lost, after being wounded at the battle of Baton Rouge,—upon the top of this high hill. Taylor rode along this line, and when he passed Polignac, he called out, "Little Frenchman, I am going to fight Banks here, if he has a million of men!" Taylor now ordered Mouton to advance until he engaged the enemy. Mouton led the charge of infantry. By agreement, all the Confederate officers retained their horses, which was one reason why so many of them were killed in this famous charge. Mouton charged down a hill, over a fence, through a ravine, then up a hill right in the teeth of the guns. The charge lasted twenty-five minutes. The men were moved forward at double-quick, exposed to a terrible fire all the time, especially whilst in the ravine, between the woods and the hill, upon which the Federal batteries were stationed. The exposure to grape and canister was dreadful; many Confederates fell here. The men were nearly breathless when they struggled up the ravine. Mouton commanded them to throw themselves prostrate a moment, to recover breath. Then they sprang up, and rushed on to the attack. The officers fell fast. Armand, at the head of his Creoles, had his horse killed, and received a shot in the arm. Starting to his feet, after disengaging himself from his dying steed, he ran on by the side of his men, waving his sword in the other unwounded hand. Again a shot struck him—he fell—a wound through both thighs. He raised himself again, on his wounded arm, and, half-reclining, with the life-blood pouring in torrents, he still waved his sword, and cheered on his Louisianians. They responded with a cry of vengeance. Another shot struck Armand in the breast,—the gleaming sword dropped from the cold hand. Armand lay dead. The Eighteenth Louisiana rushed on. Polignac led his troops gallantly. Mouton was always in the front. The guns were taken after a desperate struggle. The Federals broke and fled. Mouton pursued: he passed a group of thirty-five Federal soldiers; they threw down their arms in token of surrender. Mouton turned, lifting his hand to stay the firing of the Confederates upon this group of prisoners: as he did so, five of the Federals stooped down, picked up their guns, aimed them at the generous Confederate: in a moment, five balls pierced the noble, magnanimous breast; Mouton dropped from his saddle dead, without a word or a sigh. The Confederates who witnessed this cowardly deed, gave a yell of vengeful indignation, and before their officers could check them, the thirty five Federals lay dead around Mouton. The chase of the Federals was continued a mile and a half by this division, then the reserves under Walker and Churchill took up the hunt, and drove back the enemy to Pleasant Hill. Half way between Pleasant Hill and Mansfield, there was a creek of pure water, for which there was a heavy fight. It ended in the Confederates *retaining possession of the water*, on whose margin they bivouacked that night,—Major General N. P. Banks' assertion to the contrary notwithstanding. Mouton had (2,200) twenty-two hundred men in this charge; he lost seven hundred and sixty-two. Five officers were killed, amongst them Taylor, of the Seventeenth Texas, a much-beloved officer. It was the musket-fire from the enemy on the left of the ravine, and the grape and canister in it, that killed most of Mouton's men. Mouton said to Polignac, previous to the attack, "Let us charge them right in the face, and throw them into the valley.'

"The Battle of Mansfield was fought on the 8th of April. It was a day of fasting and prayer, specially ordered by General Smith, and spent by most of us, ignorant of the contest that was transpiring, on our knees before our altars. Taylor now pressed his success. He had captured an immense wagon-train—two hundred and ninety-five wagons, filled with most valuable stores; had taken Nim's Battery of six guns, which Allen had such cause to remember; had also captured twenty two guns on the road. The 'Grand Army' fled in wild confusion. At Pleasant Hill the Federals were re-enforced. Taylor engaged them again, with Walker and Churchill's Divisions. The fight was heavy; and night fell on 'a drawn battle;' but the Federals retreated under cover of darkness, and Taylor camped on the battle-ground. That night General E. Kirby Smith joined him."

Colonel Gray, having been promoted, assumed command of the brigade as Brigadier-General. It was then composed of the Eighteenth, Colonel Collins, Twenty-eighth, Colonel Thomas Pool, and Crescent Regiment, Captain Claiborne commanding. It continued operations around Alexandria while the enemy was shut up therein, building a dam on the falls, to let his fleet out; following him to his crossing on the Atchafalaya, at Simmsport, and giving him the last fight at Yellow Bayou. In this affair, the Eighteenth was on the extreme right, (Captain Wm. Sanchez, commanding,) and with the Thirty-second Texas, Colonel Wood, turned the enemy's left. While on the extreme left, between the road and the bayou, a gallant little company, Captain William's engineer troops, composed of old soldiers of the Eighteenth, Crescent and Twenty-eighth, with a vigorous fire, checked his advance up the road.

In the Fall it marched to Camden, Arkansas: back to Minden, La., and in February camped on Bayou Cotile, near Alexandria. During the stay at Camden Brigadier General Henry Gray was elected to the Confederate Congress, and Colonel Joseph Collins, who had been recommended for promotion, assumed command of the Brigade, until the return of Col. A. W. Bosworth's Crescent Regiment.

A new organization of Brigades was about to be effected. Collins Brigade to consist of the Eighteenth, Twenty-eighth and Eighth Louisiana Dismounted Cavalry, Colonel Ben W. Clark, of West Baton Rouge, when the news of Lee's surrender closed the history of the war, and the Consolidated Eighteenth Louisiana Regiment surrendered at Nachitoches, on the 9th of June, 1865, being probably the last organized troops of the Confederacy who laid down their arms.

Colonel Joseph Collins was twice wounded, at Shiloh and Texana. Major J. Kleber Gourdain, who was wounded at Shiloh, was killed at New Orleans on the 14th of September, 1874. Captain Wm. Sanchez, who went out as Sergeant-Major of the regiment, commanded it in the last engagement, as its senior Captain.

Among the other officers, who surrendered, were Captains Alexander Poché, Ben. S. Story, H. N. Jenkins, (with thirteen of the original members of his company, the Orleans Cadets,) C. M. Shepherd, of St. James, L. Becnel, of St. John the Baptiste, A. Castille, of St. Martin; Lieutenants Octave Jacob, Septime Webre (who left his right arm at Mansfield,) V S. Bourque, of St. Landry, (who lost a leg in a gunboat skirmish on Red River, near the mouth of Cane River, with a detachment of the regiment then supporting Cornay's Battery,) the St. Mary Cannoneers, (in which the gallant Cornay himself was killed); Alfred St. Martin, (who succeeded Sanchez as Sergeant-Major until appointed a lieutenant—a soldier who had never been off duty for a single day during the war); Sheldon W. Clark, Charles L. Cobb and Charles E. Cautzon, of the Orleans Cadets, Thomas Bellow, of St. James, L. C. Villere, of Orleans.

Among the officers killed at Shiloh were Captains Henry Huntington, Wood, of Natchitoches, and Lastrapes, of St. Landry. Lieutenant John M. Young, of the Orleans Cadets, was wounded and taken prisoner; Lieutenant Gautreaux, of Lafourche, was wounded and died at home of his wounds. Lieutenant Dudley Avery was severely wounded.

Captain John T. Lavery, of the Orleans Cadets, was wounded at Mansfield and died a few days after.

CAPTURE OF THE FEDERAL IRONCLAD GUN BOAT INDIANOLA.

On February 14th, 1863, Colonel Charles Ellet, commanding the Federal ram, Queen of the West, engaged Fort DeRussy, a Confederate post on Red River, then garrisoned by a weak detachment under the command of Captain John Kelso, of Rapides. Two thirty-two pounders were in position, forming a water battery, and a shot from one of these guns cut the steam pipe of the Queen. She was then abandoned by the Federals and taken possession of by the Confederates. She was a wooden boat of the ordinary Mississippi type. The machinery was protected in front, the rear and on both sides, by bales of cotton, extending as high up as the passenger deck. Above, there was a plank bulwark, easily penetrated even by small arms, extending around her gun deck and pierced with embrasures for guns. The armament consisted of a thirty-pound Parrott gun, mounted on her open and unprotected bow, outside of the cotton bulwarks; and five light field pieces on her gun deck, concealed only, and not protected, by the plank bulwark. The bow had been built solid, so as to make her a ram.

The Webb was the only other available gunboat—if she could be called one—which the Confederates possessed. She had been used before the war for towing vessels to and from New Orleans. The only protection was a few bales of cotton, placed in front of her boilers. The rear and sides were totally unprotected.

The military situation was this: The Union forces had wrested from the Confederates the Mississippi river, from St. Louis as far down as Vicksburg, which place was then being attacked by General Grant; and from its mouth as far up as Port Hudson, this latter then being besieged by General Banks. So that the Confederates held only that small section of the Mississippi between Vicksburg and Port Hudson. This section was vital to the Confederate cause, as it was the only outlet through which to communicate with the Eastern and Western States, and by which supplies could be poured into Vicksburg and Port Hudson.

About the time of the capture of the Queen at Fort DeRussy, the Federal ironclad Indianola passed the Southern batteries at Vicksburg: and thus took possession of the Confederate section of the great river. The Indianola was a formidable gunboat. She mounted, forward, two eleven-inch guns; and, astern, two nine-inch guns. These pieces were protected by two iron casemates, impervious to any but the heaviest artillery; and the hull was sheathed in iron plates. The boat was propelled by two wheels and two propeller screws.

Major-General Richard Taylor, commander of the Army of Western Louisiana, appreciating the vital urgency of retaining possession of the section of the Mississippi river between Vicksburg and Port Hudson, thereby securing communication with Richmond, had begun, with the most limited resources in material and skilled labor, to arm the Webb and some ordinary cotton boats. The capture of the Queen added tenfold to his strength, and enabled him, when he learned that the Indianola had passed Vicksburg, to issue the following order:

HEADQUARTERS DIST. OF WEST. LOUISIANA,
Alexandria, La., Feb. 19, 1863.
Special Orders No. 49.]

* * III. Major J. L. Brent will take supreme command of the two gunboats, the Queen of the West (Captain James McCloskey, commanding), and the Webb (Captain Charles Pierce, commanding). He will apply to Major W. M. Levy, commanding post at Fort DeRussy, for such aid and assistance as he may require to fit out the expedition in the shortest possible space of time; which aid will be rendered by Major Levy to the extent of his means. As soon as the boats are ready for service, Major Brent will proceed down Red River (taking with him, if deemed advisable, the steamer Grand Duke) and into the Mississippi, in search of the enemy's gunboat. In the event of her capture or destruction, Major Brent will act in accordance with the verbal instructions of the Major-General commanding, or in such other manner as circumstances may dictate.

By command of Major-General Taylor :

E. SURGET, A. A. General.

When, five days after her capture, the Queen, in obedience to the above order, steamed away from Alexandria, mechanics were still at work on her, and were carried as far down as Fort DeRussy ; and this notwithstanding her repairs had been pursued day and night, great fires having been built at night to afford the necessary light.

At daylight on the 22d of February, Major Brent had completed the organization of his expedition, and steamed from Fort DeRussy down the river. The officers and crews were entirely new to the boats and to each other. The artillerists saw for the first time the guns they were to man and use; the engineers and pilots for the first time took control of the machinery, moving the boats towards the enemy as rapidly as steam could take them.

The 22d of February was a busy day for officers and men. The guns were manned and the magazines opened ; and by evening the bow guns of the Webb and the Queen had been fired, and each man had been taught the place he was to occupy in action. Signals were arranged to summon the men to quarters; and great excitement was produced by the signal being sounded at midnight, and every man being turned out, while the magazines were opened and ammunition brought on deck. These precautions were not only prudent, but were indispensable.

There were seventy-five men on the Queen—sharpshooters and artillerists. The were drawn from the 21st Tennessee Volunteers, Lieut-Colonel Burnett's Battalion of Texas Sharpshooters, and the 3d Maryland Artillery. The captains of the guns were volunteers, who had never seen the guns or detachments before they sailed. It was almost equally as bad on the Webb. Lieutenant Thomas H. Handy, of the Crescent Artillery, who commanded the troops on board, had under him some of his own men, some Tennesseeans and some Marylanders—about sixty in all.

The Webb carried on her bow the most formidable gun of the expedition : a banded and rifled thirty-two-pounder, shooting an eighty-pound projectile. It was fired for the first time at the mouth of Black river, and the gun carriage worked badly and with difficulty.

On leaving Red river, the expedition was joined by the steamer Batey, sent out from Port Hudson with two hundred men, under Lieutenant Colonel Brand. The Batey was not a ram, carried no heavy guns, and relied on the gallantry and pluck of the men to carry the enemy by boarding, if an opportunity occurred.

The expedition entered the Mississippi, at night, prepared for action, as far as practicable under the circumstances. At the mouth of Red river parties were met who had seen and been on board the Indianola.

When the expedition sailed, General Taylor and his officers were under the impression that the Indianola was a wooden boat, of the type of the Queen. Such was the information received from Vicksburg and Natchez. A paper in the latter city described her as "an old Cincinnati tub." On reaching the mouth of Red river the expedition learned, for the first time, the character of the boat they were seeking. A well-known and reliable planter said he had seen all the Federal gunboats that had passed his plantation, having been aboard most of them ; and that the Indianola was superior to all others. He described her iron casemates and heavy guns, and declared, as his belief, that the Confederate gunboats would certainly be destroyed if they engaged her.

After wooding, the Queen and the Webb steamed up the river in pursuit of the Indianola. When Natchez was reached, the whole city turned out to greet the boats. Making a stop there for the purpose of procuring coal, which was much needed for the Queen, as she only had such coal as had been captured with her, the officers and men were much cheered by the energy displayed by the people in furnishing and hauling the fuel free of charge. Further information concerning the formidable character of the Indianola was also obtained.

The expedition sailed from Natchez in the evening, and was forced to proceed slowly to economize coal and to get wood, which was found in very small quantities.

On the next day, the 24th of February, about 12 o'clock, the expedition reached Berry's Landing, above Rodney.

After consideration the Confederate commander determined to overtake and attack the enemy at night. He was inclined to this decision by the reflection that, as he was compelled to run into the Indianola to ram her, his greatest peril would arise from her heavy guns, one shot alone from one of which would destroy either one of his boats; and it was supposed that the firing of the guns would be less accurate by night than by day.

A careful noting of the time when the Indianola passed the various points on the river, showed that since she had left Natchez she had made only two miles and a quarter an hour. This slowness was attributed, in part, to the two coal barges she had lashed on her sides. As the speed of the Confederates was over five miles per hour, it was determined to overtake the Indianola that night, between 8 and 9 p. m., at a point about thirty-two miles beyond.

A delay took place in the evening, owing to the fact that the cotton on board the Queen was set on fire by the discharge of small arms, which were being fired and reloaded to be ready for action. The fire ran along the upper tier of cotton, and but for prompt action would have encircled the Queen with a belt of flame. Some of the bales were thrown overboard. The cotton was tied with rope, and had been baled for years The bagging was torn and full of holes, out of which projected thousands of little tufts of cotton, as inflammable as gunpowder.

The Queen, upon which was Major Brent, commanding the expedition, led the advance, five hundred yards ahead of the Webb, while the Batey, over two miles in the rear, was lashed to the Grand Era, the tender of the expedition.

About 9:40 p. m. the enemy was seen by the Queen about one thousand yards distant, and the Webb was signaled to prepare for action. The Indianola was hugging the Western bank of the river, with her head quartering across and down the stream.

Not an indication of life appeared on the Queen, as, under full head of steam, she steamed towards the Indianola. Grim and silent, her lights obscured, her machinery at rest, she abided the shock. Soon the long line of the coal barge was disclosed, extending from forward of the bow of the Indianola to nearly abreast of her wheel. The Queen trembled with the excess of steam, produced by weighting down the safety-valve and opening wide the throttle-valve, as it drove her onward with with prodigious speed.

When within five hundred yards of the enemy, the ardor of the men could hardly be restrained. The guns were loaded and run in battery, and permission to fire clamored for; but the vast importance of traversing the intervening distance without drawing the fire of the huge Dahlgren guns, was too apparent to be disregarded.

When one hundred and fifty yards distant, Major Brent ordered the pilot to steer the Queen so as to strike the Indinola close to her wheel, and to pass the rear of the coal barge. He then directed Captain McCloskey to open fire, which he immediately did with his three forward guns.

Just before the Queen dashed on her, the Indianola backed, and thus interposed the coal baage to receive the tremendous onset. But nothing could effectually stop it. The bow of the Queen went crushing through the barge, and was not arrested until it struck the iron plates of the Indianola. The force of the blow deeply indented her sides, and disabled the engine that worked her wheels.

When the Queen attempted to back out, after her blow had been delivered, the severed sections of the barge and its load of coal closed on her and held her in its jaws, fast against the sides of the Indianola. She remained in this situation for more than a minute, until the current of the river floated off one section of the barge, and she slowly backed out, still, in part, checked by the other section. Whilst in this position Sergeant Langley, of the 3d Maryland Artillery, in charge of the thirty-pound Parrott gun on the exposed bow of the Queen, fired one round with the muzzle of his gun over the side of the Indionola; but the shot only indented the forward casemate.

The sharpshooters of the Indianola kept up a continuous but inaccurate fire, which was replied to.

As the Queen backed clear of the Indianola, the Webb dashed past at full speed. When within seventy-five yards of the enemy, she received fire from his eleven-inch guns in the forward casemate. One of the huge shots passed just in front of the bow of the Webb, almost grazing it; the other flew wide of its mark. Thus narrowly escaping destruction, the Webb delivered her blow well forward on the Indianola, but slightly glancing, so that she shot forward, passing across and in contact with the bow of the Indianola, and under the very muzzles of the guns which had just been fired. She collided with the coal barge on the opposite side, and with such force as to break its fastenings and set it adrift.

The result of the first charge of the Confederate gunboats was to strip the enemy of his two protecting barges, and disable the machinery that drove his two paddle-wheels; thereby impairing the precision and rapidity of their future movements.

Why the Indianola failed to fire on the Queen on the first onset, or to use her two nine-inch guns in the rear when the Webb, as she ascended the river, ran within fifty yards of her, is incomprehensible.

The Queen, swinging round rapidly as the Webb bore away, again dashed on the Indianola, which, slightly turning, received the blow at an angle instead of a square, and suffered but little injury.

As the Queen backed out, the Indianola opened on her with the two nine-inch guns in her stern casemate. The range was so close that the flames of the gun touched the bow of the backing ram, and the heat from them was perceptible on board. One shot struck the shoulder of cotton bales on the right side of the Queen, carrying off ten or a dozen bales. The other, a shell, entered the front port-hole on the left side, struck the chase of a twelve pound brass gun, and exploded, killing and wounding six men, and disabling two pieces of artillery.

The Queen ran up stream a little way, and then descended, with fearful momentum, for her third onslaught. She escaped the fire of the huge guns, and struck the Indianola on her right side, just in the rear of her wheel. The blow was fairly delivered, and was received without any movement on the part of the Indianola. The bow of the Queen crushed the frame and loosened some plates of armor.

As the Queen backed out, the Webb came rushing down stream with tremendous rapidity, and, by a singular coincidence, struck the Indianola in the same place the Webb had last struck her. The timbers were broken in and the iron plates pushed aside; and the sharp bow of the Webb, rising up as it struck, seemed as if it would pass through its enemy. The Indianola would probably have been sunk outright, but the frail bow of the Webb was staved in, and a portion broke off about fourteen inches above the water line.

Captain Pierce and Lieutenant Handy, realizing the situation of the Indianola, but ignorant of their own broken bow, rapidly turned and gallantly ran towards the enemy to deliver a third blow, which would doubtless have sunk the Webb, when voices from the Indianola announced her surrender, and that she was sinking. A hawser was thrown on board, and the Webb began towing her ashore. The hawser parted; and, before the Webb could regain her prize, the Batey, ignorant of the state of affairs, gallantly bore down on the Indianola. The men prepared to board her, when her surrender was announced. Lieutenant-Colonel Brand jumped on board and received the sword of Lieutenant Brown, her commander.

After her third charge, the Queen was much dilapidated. The loss of a portion of her cotton caused her to lean over so that it became necessary to throw cotton off from the other side to right her. The machinery worked slowly and badly, and three of her five guns were unserviceable. Still she was brought round, and headed for a fourth charge on the Indianola, when the latter's surrender was announced.

Lieutenant-Colonel Brand, disclaiming any right to the prize, turned the Indianola over to Major Brent, who appointed Lieutenant Thomas H. Handy prize-master, as a reward for his gallantry and skill. Lieut. Colonel Brand embodied his disclaimer in an official report made by him to General Pemberton.

The Indianola was found in a sinking condition, with the water all over the holes through which it entered. The officers and crew were taken off as fast as possible. Seeing that she must inevitably sink, Major Brent determined to remove her from the western bank of the river, where she was only a few miles from General Grant's army, to the eastern bank, then in possession of the Confederates. Accordingly, strong hawsers were passed under the Indianola, and each end lashed to a Confederate boat on either side. Thus supported she was carried across the river; but when within fifty yards of the eastern bank she sank on a sand-bar, and remained with her gun-deck out of water: thus losing to the Confederates the enormous value of her capture.

A single shot of any one of the four casemate guns of the Indianola, striking the Webb or the Queen fairly, would have destroyed it. The cotton bales, so far from affording protection from guns of that character, augmented the danger. The bow of the Webb was grazed, and another shot passed just over her, breaking the hand-railing around the upper-deck. The Queen was exposed, in addition, to the hazard of its cotton being fired, which might have happened not only from the explosion of the enemy's shells, but from her own fire. The accidental firing of the cotton early in the evening, as before described, acted as a warning; and precaution was taken to keep the cotton wet with water, which was renewed during the action. The Indianola suffered no injury from the guns of the Confederates. Lieutenant Handy fired an eighty-pound shell from his rifled thirty-two-pounder, at a range so close that the flame from his gun reached the enemy's iron casemate; yet the iron armor was only indented, not broken. So completely was she protected, that she lost but one man, and had none wounded.

It is impossible, in a narrative like this, to describe the acts of gallantry and courage exhibite in this action. General Taylor took care that a record of the names of the officers and men should be made; and we conclude this article by publishing his order, and the list officially reported in obedience to it:

HEADQUARTERS DIST. OF WEST. LOUISIANA,
Alexandria, La., March 1, 1863.

General Orders No. 13]

The Major-General commanding has the pleasure to announce to the troops under his command, the complete success of the expedition fitted out at these headquarters for the capture of the Federal ironclad ram Indianola. To the gallantry and skill of Major J. L. Brent, commanding the expedition; of Captains James McCloskey and Charles Pierce, commanding, respectively, the Queen of the West and the Webb; and to the brave officers and men serving under them, is the country indebted for the surrender of one of the most formidable of the enemy's vessels, fitted out by them at enormous expense, provided with the most destructive appliances of modern warfare, and believed by them to be impregnable—an achievement which will not suffer by comparison with the most brilliant naval exploits upon record.

The commanding-general regrets his inability to make special mention, in the limits of a general order, of the officers and men, to whose heroic conduct and hearty co-operation, with their commanders, this signal success is attributable. As every one connected with the expedition did his duty, and his whole duty, the commanding-general has directed Major Brent to prepare, and he will officially publish, a list of all the officers and men comprising it, in order that their countrymen may know to whom thanks are due for these happy results.

By command of the Major-General:

E. SURGET, A. A. General.

List of Officers and Men of Major-General Taylor's Gunboat Expedition, made out in pursuance of General Order No. 13.

Queen of the West—James McCloskey, Captain Commanding; Capt. Carnes, 21st Tennessee, commanding Sharpshooters; Captain J. H. Hutton, Chief of Artillery; Lieutenant Miller, 21st Tennessee; Lieut. Doolan, Adjutant of Lieutenant-Colonel Burnett's Texas Battalion of Sharpshooters; twenty-five volunteers from Burnett's Battalion; Sergeant E. H. Langley and twelve men from 3d Maryland Artillery. The following named officers volunteered and acted in the capacities set opposite their names: Captain C. H. White, Ordnance Officer; Captain Touk, Lieuts. C. Stanmeyer and Fisk, Captains of Guns; Lieut. K. R. Hyams, Quartermaster and Commissary. Pilots L. Milligan, W. Melloy, W. Dunbar and Frank Littrel. Mate W. H. Parker. Engineers J. R. Allaboy, Chief, E. Wood, J. Crawford, T. Montrose, O. W. Daniel.

Webb—Charles Pierce (a civilian), Captain; Lieutenant Thomas H. Handy, commanding troops on board; Lieutenant Rice and his company from 21st Tennessee; Acting Lieutenants Prather, volunteer, in charge of two light guns, and Charles Schuler, in charge of one gun; detachment of men from Crescent Artillery; twelve men from 3d Maryland Artillery; Mate Norman White; Pilots Elijah Pierce, Frank Smith, Charles Oakey and O. S. Burlett; Engineers Hugh Daly, Chief, George Marsh, Richard Stockton, J. E. Compton, W. Kerrish.

[*Note.*—The various detachments have been so scattered, that it is impossible to procure the names of all the men.]

J. L. BRENT, Major Com'dg Expedition.

J. W. Mangum, Capt. and Adj't of Expedition.

LOUISIANA BATTERIES IN ARMY OF WESTERN LOUISIANA.

The field artillery of this army was quite numerous, and frequently exceeded twenty batteries. In March, 1863, it was placed by General R. Taylor under the command of J. L. Brent; and, after the battles of Mansfield and Pleasant Hill, it was organized into a regiment commanded by Major Brent, promoted to Colonel; Major T. C. French, promoted to Lieutenant-Colonel; and Captains O. J. Semmes and T. A. Faries, promoted, respectively, to Major. Lieutenant J. B. Tarleton, of Cornay's Battery, was assigned as Adjutant, and Captain G. L Hall as Quartermaster and Commissary, of the Regiment. This organization was composed of batteries from Louisiana, Texas, Arkansas and Mississippi. Among the Louisiana Batteries were the following:

The St. Mary Cannoneers, or Cornay's Battery.—Its organization was as follows: Captain F. O. Cornay, First Lieutenants M. T. Gordy and J. B. Tarleton, Second Lieutenants Oscar D. Berwick and Oliver H. Jones. The battery first did duty as part of the garrisons of the forts between the mouth of the river and the city of New Orleans; and proved itself faithful, obedient and courageous, under the most trying circumstances.

After the defeat of General Banks at Mansfield and Pleasant Hill, and his evacuation of Natchitoches, General Taylor placed this battery on Red river, just above the lower mouth of Cane river, with orders to blockade the river against the Federal fleet. The battery had no earthworks or protection of any kind. In the evening of the 26th of April, 1864, three Federal gunboats and two transports engaged the battery, and one gunboat succeeded in running by. The transport Champion No. 3, loaded with two hundred negroes, taken from the plantations along the upper Red river, was attempted to be convoyed past the battery by these gunboats, under the personal supervision of Rear-Admiral Porter. When one gunboat had gone by, the remaining two—one of which was the Cricket, Admiral Porter's flagship—engaged the battery, while the Champion attempted to pass the battery under cover of the fire of the two gunboats. The Champion was struck in her boiler by a solid shot from a twelve-pound gun of the battery, and in a moment was enveloped with hot steam and vapor. This, probably, was the most fatal single shot fired during the war, as it caused the death, by scalding, of two hundred and twenty people. Every human being on the Champion, except three, perished.

The Cricket, the other gunboat, and the remaining transport, declined further fight, and ran up the river. The Champion was captured, brought to shore, and the dead buried. The inhumanity of rushing unarmed people into the midst of a battle, and exposing them to the frightful disaster that overtook them, is not chargeable to the Confederates, who were blockading the river against the retreat of Admiral Porter's fleet, and who were engaged in actual combat with armed gunboats.

On the morning of April 27th, Admiral Porter, with the Cricket and other gunboat, convoying the transport Champion No. 5, again undertook to run by the battery. After a short engagement, in which the Cricket was badly damaged, its guns disabled and silenced, and its crew decimated by the rapid and precise fire of the battery and the sharpshooters supporting it, the two gunboats ran by the battery, declining all rurther fight, and ingloriously abandoning their convoy, Champion No. 5, which fell a second prize to the Confederates.

It was in this apparently unequal combat—of four light field pieces against gunboats thinly armored, but mounting powerful guns—that the gallant and heroic Captain F. O. Cornay fell, instantly killed by a ball from the gunboats, while directing the fire of his superb battery. No better eulogy can be pronounced upon him and the St. Mary Cannoneers than the official report of Rear-Admiral Porter, describing this engagement, and addressed to the Secretary of the Navy. In the report he represents this four-gun field battery as being a battery of sixteen heavy guns, in position; and says that the fire to which he was exposed was the heaviest he had ever undergone.

Lieutenant John B Tarleton, of Cornay's Battery, when the Field Artillery was organized, after battle of Mansfield, into a regiment, was assigned to Colonel Brent as Adjutant; but, immediately after the death of Captain Cornay, was relieved from staff duty, and ordered to the battery. He was not the ranking lieutenant, but he assumed command, owing to the fact that First Lieutenant M. T. Gordy, just before the opening of the Mansfield campaign, had been placed under arrest; which arrest continued until the campaign was terminated, and General Taylor was relieved by General Kirby Smith of the command of the Army of Western Louisiana.

The St. Mary Cannoneers participated in nearly all the engagements along the Teche, and in most of those occurring in the Mansfield cam paign, ending in the bloody affair at Norwood's, on Bayou de Glaise.

At Mansura it took an active part in the engagement brought on by Major-General Wharton, commanding the Cavalry Corps; in which thirty-two Confederate guns were used, belonging to the Battalions of Majors O. J. Semmes and T. A. Faries, and to the reserve Battalion of Major C. W. Squires—all commanded by Colonel J. L. Brent.

When General Wharton had accomplished the object of his demonstration, he withdrew his right, passing to the rear of his left; and Cornay's Battery was the last kept in position on the left, to cover its withdrawal. General Banks maneuvered to turn the Confederate left, and to strike the Evergreen road, which was General Wharton's line of retreat. For that purpose masses of artillery and infantry rapidly advanced to strike the Evergreen road.

The St. Mary Cannoneers, commanded by Lieutenant J. B. Tarleton, who possessed all the qualities that make a soldier illustrious, held their position with tenacity, firing on the enemy until the latter was within three hundred yards of the battery. The command to withdraw being given, the battery limbered to the rear as steadily as if on parade, and began its retreat at a walk. The fire of the enemy's sharpshooters and two or three batteries reached far beyond them. The steady and soldier-like movement, the absence of nervousness and confusion in executing that most difficult and hazardous movement—of withdrawing before an attacking enemy—bespoke the soldiers who had become veterans, and officers who were worthy to command.

It chanced that this interesting exhibition of soldierly qualities attracted the observation and admiration of the artillery commander, who felt constrained, in his official report to the commanding general, to mention what would seem to be, to the casual observer, an ordinary incident in a soldier's life, and which would otherwise have been lost. But, in fact and in truth, when rightly understood, it was the stamp and seal of perfect soldiership, performing its duty alike in defeat as in success; and which, in this case, bore fruit; for the rear guard of cavalry and infantry, already in a certain degree of confusion—not unnatural where a defence had been pushed to so perilous a verge—became steadied by witnessing the unbending discipline of the battery, and checked the advance of the enemy.

The Pelican Battery—After the promotion of Captain T. A. Faries to Major, this battery was organized as follows: Captain B. Felix Winchester, Lieutenants J. Richard Winchester, Stephen R. Garrett, O.

Gaudet and Louis Armand. This batttery was principally recruited on the Mississippi coast; and it participated in every campaign south of Red river. It 1863 it was brought over the Lafourche, and placed on the Mississippi river, engaging gunboats and transports, and blockading the river.

It was a singular incident in the history of this battery, that it was placed on the Mississippi river in signt of the homestead of the young Winchesters (the two lieutenants in the battery), and that the echoes of their guns shook the house in which they were born. It was fought *pro aris et focis ;* which never had cause to be otherwise than proud of the young champions defending them.

It is hardly possible, in a book like this, to give a detailed account of the campaigns of this battery, or even a summary of its most important actions. To do either would involve almost a complete narrative of the military operations of the forces under Major General Taylor.

After the evacuation of the Lafourche country, this battery was one of the principal instruments used by General Alfred Mouton in the defence of the Teche. At one time it would be protecting the Confederate gunboat Cotton; at another, abiding the attack of the heavy pieces of the enemy's gunboats; again it would be fighting, now with the rear-guard and then with the advance, or holding, with feeble support, a position of vital importance (as on the left at Camp Bisland, during the fights of April, 1863). Then the scene of duty would again change, and it would be traveling northward, crossing Red River and marching to Harrisonburg, with General Polignac, to take part in the defence of that place against the Federal ironclads from the Mississippi

This battery indeed was composed of the finest *personnel*, and illustrated every quality of soldierly dash, endurance, gallantry, steadiness and discipline—that homely quality, without which the others are of little avail. It was at Mansfield and Pleasant Hill, but was held in re serve. It also took part in numerous skirmishes, engaged gunboats on Red river, and took part in the warm attacks at Mansura and Moreauville. Its record is without a blemish.

The Confederate Regular Battery.—Captain O. J. Semmes. After the promotion of Semmes, John Thompson Mason Barnes was Captain, Lieutenants J. A. A. West, J. W. Boyle, M. T. Fauntleroy and George E. Strawbridge. This was a battery of the regular Confederate Army, but it was principally recruited in Louisiana. It performed distinguished service in Louisiana, beginning in the attack on Baton Rouge, made by

General Breckenridge. It participated actively in all the campaigns mentioned above, and always served with great distinction. It was emphatically a fighting battery, and is endeared to the people of Louis. iana by the courage and endurance it always displayed. Captain (afterwards Major) O. J. Semmes, has won, by constant and gallant services, a claim on the esteem and gratitude of the State. Captain J. T. M. Barnes was a gallant and devoted soldier—tested an hundred times under fire.

West's Horse Battery.—Captain J. A. A. West, Lientenants John Yoist, William H. Warren and J. Lyne. This battery was organized and equipped late. It reported at Mansfield for duty one hour before the battle opened, and was held in reserve. It was attached to Major Semmes' Battallion of Horse Artillery, and fought at Pleasant Hill, advancing and firing while under fire. It participated in many skirmishes while in pursuit of Bank's retreating army.

When Banks was cooped up in Alexandria, waiting until the Red river was dammed so as to enable Admiral Porter to float his ironclads over the falls, General Taylor dispatched the cavalry to get on to Red river below Alexandria, so as to blockade it and break up Banks' communication with New Orleans.

West's Battery, then under command of Lieutenant John Yoist, was placed on the river not far from Chenyville, and performed one of the most remarkable feats of the war. On the 3d of May, 1864, the U. S. Transport City Belle, having on board the 120th Ohio, came up the river, intending to join General Banks, who was then at Alexandria. The battery, supported by General Baylor and his Texas Brigade of Cavalry, acting as sharpshooters, opened fire on the City Belle. The third shot from his rifled gun exploded the boiler of the boat, and she was run ashore on the opposite, or northern, bank. Lieutenant Yoist ran two of his pieces by hand to within two hundred yards of her (for the river is very narrow there), when she surrendered.

The battery consisted of four guns—two ten pound Parrott guns, and two twelve-pound Howitzers. After the fight, they were divided: one section above and the other below, both on the southern bank of the river, and about three miles apart.

At sunrise on the 5th of May, 1864, the U. S. Transport Warner, convoyed by the gunboats Signal and Covington, each carrying eight twenty-four pound guns, came down from Alexandria and attempted to run past the battery. They succeeded, with some loss, in running past the upper section, the Warner in lead; but soon encountered the lower section, commanded by Lieutenant Lyne. So effective was his fire, that in a few moments the Warner surrendered, notwithstanding the heavy fire of the gunboats on Lieutenant Lyne's section. On the surrender of the transport, the two gunboats retreated up the river, and sheltered their sixteen guns behind a bend, where the Confederate guns could not strike them.

When the transport and two gunboats ran by Lieutenant Yoist, commanding the upper section, he, unwilling to give up the chase, limbered up and continued the hunt down the river. He shortly came up with the gunboats, who were throwing shells at Lieutenant Lyne at long range. Lieutenant Yoist unlimbered and ran his guns by hand out upon the open bank, within three hundred and fifty yards of the enemy, and opened fire, giving his attention first to the Covington.

Here occurred a marvellous episode in this wonderful campaign.

These two gunboats, attacked from above and below by the two sections of the battery, which fired with great rapidity and accuracy, attempted to escape first by running down the river towards New Orleans, and then up towards Alexandria. Col. Baylor's Sharpshooters joined in, and aided in the extraordinary result. Finally, a shot from the battery exploded the boiler of the Covington, and she was got ashore on the northern bank, fired and abandoned by her crew, and shortly after was blown up.

The rifled ten-pound Parrotts were then moved by hand to within two hundred yards of the Signal, and she, with officers and men, surrendered.

These boats were of the class called tinclad—that is, sheathed with iron sufficient to turn a rifle shot, but not able to resist field artillery.

This result established the blockade of Red river, cutting off General Banks, communication for fifteen days. It was only raised by the retreat of his whole army, aided by Admiral Porter's ironclad fleet.

This battery participated in the balance of the campaign.

Benton's Battery.—Captain F. O. Benton, Lieutenants J. D. Gritman, W. P. Douglas, S. D. Brown and J. F. Bussey. This battery was organized early in the war, but was never properly equipped or disciplined until it was placed in the Artillery Camp near Alexandria, where, in February, 1864, it ran the risk of being disbanded. Captain Benton devoted himself earnestly to its improvement; so that, when it joined the forces under General Taylor, the change for the better was remarkable. It was particularly distinguished in a series of skirmishes above Lecompte and near the Bayou Bœuf. In these actions Captain Benton showed himself a gallant and courageous officer. At Polk's Bridge he held his position so tenaciously, and the enemy advanced so close on him, that he drove them back with canister, at short range, after his supports had retired.

This is an incomplete sketch of some of the Louisiana Batteries. Others that were engaged in North Louisiana are excluded for want of proper data. It would not be proper to conclude a sketch of this kind without referring to batteries from Texas, Arkansas and Mississippi, comrades of Louisiana soldiers in many a hard fight. There is the Val Verde Battery, Captain T. D. Nettles; the gallant Captain M. V. McMahon, especially conspicuous at Mansfield, and, with Lieutenant E. Fontaine, at Monette's Ferry; Captain J. G. Moseley's, Horace Halderman's, H. C. West's, Battalions (afterwards Captain B. F. Wade's Battery), and several others.

Those who have supplied the facts for the foregoing narrative were not unmindful of these, their brethren. They cherish them in their affection and memory, and regret that they cannot recount their deeds in defence of Louisiana.

THE TWENTY-EIGHTH LOUISIANA.

Before day on the morning of the 8th of April, 1864, orders were received at the headquarters of the 28th Louisiana (Gray's old regiment, then commanded by Colonel William Walker) to prepare for marching. The Confederates had been resting for a day or two a few miles north of Mansfield, after the fatigues of a long retreat. It was generally believed among the soldiers, that, when they resumed the line of march, it would be towards, instead of from, the enemy. So when, on the morning named, they turned face towards the south, and began to retrace their steps, there was little or no surprise; every man felt that there was soon to be a battle. All were cheerful, and some even gay—memorably so those two noble and gallant officers, Gen. Mouton and Col. Armand, who, before the sun went down, were cold in the embrace of death.

A short distance south of Mansfield, in the edge of a woods, and near a large open field, the troops were drawn up in battle array. While in that position, there were continued appearances of cavalry on the brow of the hill, about three-quarters of a mile in front, who were evidently reconnoitering. Not long after several companies of cavalry descended the hill at a gallop, in perfect order, upon our left. General Mouton commanded in person—his old regiment (the 18th) holding the position on the left. His orders were for the men to hold their fire until the enemy were within forty yards. Notwithstanding, our men fired too soon; but not without effect. The beautiful order of the cavalry was suddenly broken up, riderless horses were scampering over the field, and many of the enemy were lying dead and wounded on the ground.

This little skirmish produced great enthusiasm. General Mouton, with his powerful form raised to its full heighth in his stirrups, and with hat in hand, added to it. He swept along the command crying, "Louisiana has drawn the first blood to-day, and the victory is ours."

After this the troops were moved still further to the left, in the edge of the woods, and near an open field. They were soon halted and rested, under a slow but continued and harmless fire from batteries and sharpshooters stationed in the woods beyond the field. It was not long until Lieutenant-Colonel Milton—who took out company A from Bienville parish—was ordered, with skirmishers, to charge through the field towards the enemy. With a handful of men from each company, he dashed up the hill in front of his men, and his powerful voice was heard rising above the battle, urging his men onward. The whole command followed, in a double quick, up hill and over the field, towards the enemy concealed in the woods. In the meanwhile it was subjected to the fire of the Federals during the entire charge. Many gallant men fell before they saw the foe amongst them. Lieutenant-Colonel William Walker, commanding the 28th, was mortally wounded, and expired in Mansfield, at the residence of a relative, after suffering in great agony.

Major W. F. Blackman signalized himself for gallantry and daring. The soldiers having commenced to waver in their long up-hill charge, the Major dashed for the colors, grasped them, and rode immediately upon the ensconced enemy. He thereupon wheeled and shouted to his men to come to their colors. This they did with a will. A captured soldier of the Federals afterwards stated that not less than two hundred shots were fired at Blackman, when he was not more than fifty yards distant. He escaped unhurt.

After reaching the brow of the hill and the woods, the 28th was ordered to lie down behind an intervening fence. It did so just in time to escape a most severe fire of small arms, grape and shell. After resting a little, it was ordered to charge; and the fence went down with a crash. The regiment precipitated itself upon the Federals. They fell back in confusion to the woods, and thence into another open field, where they reformed. The Confederates were ordered to pursue, but became entangled and scattered in the woods, and the line began to waver. Lieutenant (afterwards Captain) Kidd, of Jackson parish, seized the colors of the 28th and bore them far into the field in front of the enemy; and then called upon the men to follow. They rapidly did so, and captured the batteries in front of them, and all the horses of the dead and wounded Federals. The pursuit became general, and before sundown there was a general rout.

The officers of the 28th, besides those named, who gallantly bore their part in this battle, were Major (afterwards Colonel) T. W. Pool; Captain Brice, of Bienville parish (since a member of the Legislature from that parish); Captain Hines C. Mitchell (now a representative from Claiborne parish); Lieutenant William Lewis, of Company C, from Jackson parish; Captain T. W. Abney, Captain Lewis, of Winn parish, and others.

The 28th Louisiana Regiment was formed almost entirely from North Louisiana, and did gallant service in the Trans-Mississippi Department. It was known as Gray's Old Regiment—General Henry Gray having been its first commander.

WASHINGTON ARTILLERY.

RECORD OF NEWLY ELECTED FIELD, STAFF AND COMPANY OFFICERS.

The following is the record of officers and veterans of the battalion of Washington Artillery, reorganized for visiting the Centennial Exposition in 1876:

FIELD AND STAFF.

Col. J. B. Walton, Colonel of the Washington Regiment in Mexico, (see p. 10, part 1.)—Left the city as Major of the Battalion in 1861. Promoted Colonel and Chief of Artillery of the Army of the Potomac. Assigned as Chief of Artillery of Longstreet's corps. Appointed by the Secretary of War in 1864 as Inspector General of Field Artillery. Recommended twice by Generals Beauregard and Longstreet for promotion as Brigadier General of Artillery. Colonel Walton is now engaged in the auctioneer and appraisers business in this city. (See reports in body of this work.)

Major W. J. Behan*—Left with the Battalion in 1861 as 2d Sergeant of the 4th Company. Was promoted 2d Lieutenant of his Company in 1862. Served through the war and surrendered at Appomattox Court House. Major Behan had the

---

* Col. W. J. Behan was born in this city and is of Irish extraction. His father was an architect and builder here for many years, and added enough to the architecture of the city to make some of his old friends remember him for a long time to come, without putting up tombstone monuments. Besides what is stated above, the son never lost a day's service from any cause whatever, and had the honor of participating in every march, skirmish and battle of his battery, and every campaign of the grand old Army of Northern Virginia. During all of that time he distinguished himself for his attention, vigilance and watchfulness over his command, and for the care he manifested for their comfort and welfare—a no small recommendation, when it is remembered the amount of suffering that private soldiers (who could then do little more for themselves than a flock of sheep) had to undergo, where their officers were remiss or careless

honor of placing the last gun in position at Appomattox, being one of a battery captured the morning of the surrender from the Fifth New York Artillery by Johnson's Maryland cavalry, Major Behan joining in the charge. The two guns having been turned over to Major Behan, he placed one in position, and was just in the act of firing it, when an Aid from General Lee rode

in looking after their supplies. Lieutenant Apps was in this company, and merited the compliment due to a faithful and at the same time a thoroughly prudent, cautious officer. Behan fought with his battery with signal success from Bull Run to Appomattox, and assisted greatly in making the Fourth Company batteries respected by every corps with whom they served. He showed as quick an eye for military position as he has since for opportunities in the mercantile world, and was reputed to be one of the best officers for sighting a gun there was in the Virginia army. An evidence of this was that at Maryland Heights he sighted the very gun wihch killed General Bayard, of the Federal cavalry.

In the affair referred to above at Appomattox, Colonel Behan was in the act of firing, when one of General Lee's staff rode up and ominously shouted: "Don't fire those guns; we have surrendered."

Behan returned home, the youngest officer of the Battalion, and showed himself at the close of the war as daring and active as a business man as he had been as a soldier, chartering ships laden with the produce of the country for the Antilles, or Spanish Main, and, generally learning a great deal about the management of monopolies in countries, where, if the merchant does not take the first price offered, he never after is honored by receiving a renewal of more than one-half of the original offer. However, experience came at last—foresight and quickness told their story, and he one day discovered that he had the Midas-gift which converts everything into gold, or its greenback representative, and that his friends and old comrades looked to him as to a leader.

Thus, though just entering his thirties, he has established himself among our most sagacious merchants, and is looked upon as a rising man of the day. So much so that when the people in '74, wearied beyond endurance by past election frauds and those about to be perpetrated, armed and organized to prevent it, Behan was put in command of a regiment of the citizen militia. When, on the 14th of September, it came to the wager of a battle, he led the regiment which decided the fortune of the day.

The reputation which he has since obtained as a clear-headed actor of great industry and determination, and his readiness to lavish his own means, instead of drawing on others, has attracted towards him our laboring and industrial population, and ardent men of all classes, and made him the popular favorite of the day.

up and announced the surrender. Major Behan is a member of the firm of Behan, Thorn & Co.

Adjutant W. M. Owen—Left as Adjutant; promoted Major of Artillery in 1863, and assigned to Preston's Division, West Virginia, as Chief of Artillery; reassigned as Major to Washington Artillery in 1864; promoted Lieutenant Colonel of Artillery, and assigned to the command of 13th Virginia Battalion of Artillery at Petersburg; surrendered his Battalion at Appomattox. Wounded at Petersburg. Now agent of Messrs. Bliss, Bennet & Co., of New York.

Quartermaster John N. Payne—Left as private of the 1st Company, and promoted to Sergeant. Subsequently assigned to the command of Byrne's battery, attached to Morgan's cavalry in 1864. Was wounded at Saltville, and surrendered at Appomattox. Now of the firm of Messrs. Payne, Brooks & Co., wholesale grocers, New Orleans.

Commissary John Holmes—Left as private in the 3d Company. Was shot in the leg and disabled, at Sharpsburg, from further duty. Is now the proprietor of Pork Inspection Warehouse, of New Orleans.

Ordnance Officer W. B. Krumbhaar—Served as private in Slocomb's 5th Company, afterwards promoted Captain of Artillery in the Trans-Mississippi Department, under General Holmes. Now of the firm of W. B. Krumbhaar & Co., and owners of the Penn Cotton Press, New Orleans.

Surgeon Thomas G. Aby—Left as private and promoted Sergeant of 1st Company. Continued his study of medicine in camp, and passed examination before the Medical Examining Board, and appointed Assistant Surgeon to the Battalion. Now practicing his profession at Monroe, Ouachita parish.

Sergeant-Major E. I. Kursheedt—Left as private of 1st Company. Appointed Corporal, and promoted to Sergeant-Major on the promotion of C. L. C. Dupuy; promoted as Adjutant, vice Owen, promoted. Wounded at Sharpsburg and Fredericksburg. Now of the firm of Kursheedt & Bienvenu, Camp street, New Orleans.

COMPANY OFFICERS.

Captain M. B. Miller,* Company A—Left the city in 1861 as Captain of the 3d Company, and was specially mentioned in General Lee's report for gallant conduct with his battery at Sharpsburg. Promoted Major of Artillery in 1864. Served during the whole war. Led off 45 of his command (by cutting the traces of his battery horses and mounting his men) over the mountains, at Lee's surrender, to Johnston's army. Now engaged in the sugar business in New Orleans.

Capt. Eug. May, Company B—Left as private in the 5th Company, and served with gallantry during the whole war, surrendering at Meridian, Miss., with the 5th Company, Washington Artillery battery. Now with the firm of Messrs. Wheelock, Finlay & Co., New Orleans.

Captain John B. Richardson,† Company C—Left the city as

---

* "Old Buck," as he is familiarly known among his command, had the good fortune, though noted for being a hard, stern officer, to retain his popularity through the war. His voice (which he had cultivated while engaged in the sugar business on the levee, in shouting to and cursing at roustabouts), was about the loudest and harshest there was in the army, and a little more so on big battle days, when all of a soldier's natural combativeness came to the surface. In very hot places, he would give his commands in his old levee style of getting out freight, and would talk of "rolling out" the guns as if he was the mate of a steamboat, ordering forward so many hogsheads of sugar. Major Buck came back home pretty well grizzled about the jaws, from eating sheet-iron crackers, and is at his old business of sugar weighing on the levee. He extends to his friends a hospitable hand (as large as a Honeysuckle ham), and is looked on by his comrades as one of the bravest and best men in the command.

† Three excellent officers, whose soldierly conduct suggests an additional passing note, were Captain Richardson, Lieutenant DeRussey and Lieutenant Brittain. Neither of these had any pretensions to brilliancy or were distinguished for more than ordinary accomplishments. They were all three, however, possessed of those sober, steady qualities which commanded the respect of their men, and which gave them the same weight in the Virginia campaigns as they do in the battle of life elsewhere. Generally the characters of the men were ranked according to their approach to a high standard of morality or Christianity, and all the more so as the war dragged along, and the volunteers, while tortured by every misery, were compelled to show their generousness or selfishness, and all of the bad and mean qualities which lurked in their nature.

Junior 1st Lieutenant of the 1st Company. Transferred as Captain of the 2d Company, June, 1862. Had his horse shot under him at the first battle of Manassas, and surrendered at Appomattox Court House. Now cashier of the firm of C. A. Whitney & Co.

Junior 1st Lieutenant Frank McElroy,* Company A—Left the city as 1st Sergeant 3d Company. Promoted 1st Lieutenant in 1862, and commanded the two pieces of the Washington Artillery which made so gallant a defense at Fort Gregg, Petersburg. Now connected with the mechanical department of the Bee.

Senior Lieutenant Andrew Hero, Jr.,‡ Company A—Left the city as 2d Sergeant of the 3d Company. Promoted 2d Lieutenant, May, 1862. Promoted Captain of the 3d Company, 1864. Wounded at Sharpsburg and Petersburg. Now a Notary Public in this city.

---

* Frank McElroy was the lively and jovial man of the Battalion, and probably never suffered a day from mental depression during the war. He had an excellent voice, and there were but few towns in General Lee's line of march which were not made familiar, through him, of old New Orleans fireman choruses. (For full account of his services at Fort Gregg, see p. 216.)

‡ Senior Lieutenant Andrew Hero, of Company A., joined the Artillery previous to the war, when a boy, and distinguished himself by his quickness, usefulness and fondness for everything relating to the Battalion—to such an extent that his comrades elected their youngest and smallest member to the rank of Corporal; partly as a joke from his boyish appearance, and partly from his thorough knowledge of the details of the organization. He proved himself the most active and vigilant Corporal the Battalion ever had—a good deal on the rat-terrier order; thoroughly lynx-eyed, and as sharp as a brier. When the Battalion went out he had reached the rank of 2d Sergeant of the 3d Company, and his smartness and working talent, as an accountant, soon made him almost indispensable in a position of a much higher grade. He was made Lieutenant in May, 1862, and, on the promotion of Captain Miller to his majority, he succeeded to the command of the 3d Company.

At Sharpsburg, the 3d Company, to which he was attached, was ordered into a broken gap, or crevasse, in General Lee's line, where the enemy's fire was so withering that it seemed that no living thing could stand before it.

2d Lieutenant George E. Apps, Company A—Left the city as 3d Sergeant 4th Company, and afterwards promoted to 2d Lieutenant. Horse shot under him at Gettysburg; surrendered at Appomattox. Now of the firm of Messrs. Apps & Korndoffer, cotton brokers, New Orleans.

Lieutenant William Palfrey, Company B—Left as private in the 4th Company. Promoted in 1863 Lieutenant of Confederate States Artillery. Served through the siege of Vicksburg. Now cashier of New Orleans National Bank.

Lieutenant W. T. Hardie, Company B—Left as private of 1st Company. Wounded at the first battle of Fredericksburg; promoted Sergeant; captured while on escort duty with President Jefferson Davis en route South. He is now of the firm of John T. Hardie & Co.

Senior 1st Lieutenant C. H. C. Brown, Company C—Left as Sergeant of 1st Company; promoted 2d Lieutenant May, 1861; was severely wounded, left on the field and captured at Get-

---

Five batteries had preceded the 3d Company of the Washington Artillery in attempting to get a foothold, but the cannoniers had been killed or driven off. To prevent a repetition of this disaster, the last named battery drove to the fatal crest at a full galop—as fast as lash and spur could carry the lumbering and bounding guns and ammunition carriages. Without halting, and at imminent risk of capsizing with the cannoniers upon them—the pieces were wheeled into position, and in less than two minutes after, had opened a fire. This stopped, at this point, the breach in the Confederate line; but in five minutes after, the enemy's marksmen had shot down eight of the gunners and seventeen horses of the 3d Company. The men were indeed picked off so fast that distinguished officers, who had been brought by the crisis to this point, jumped down and assisted with hands and shoulders at the guns—Longstreet among the number. Captain Hero was badly wounded while working away at one of these pieces, and was flung across an empty caison on his way to the rear, with not much idea of his ever turning up alive. He, however, lived to take part in the subsequent battles of Lee's army, to get wounded again while standing on the breastworks in the final assault upon Petersburg, and to obtain (what he probably valued more than any other of his soldiering experiences) the hand of one of Virginia's daughters, who had nursed him during his sickness. He now stands in the front rank of cautious and painstaking notaries of the city.

tysburg. Now of the firm of J. M. Sandidge & Co., cotton factors, New Orleans.

Junior 1st Lieutenant George B. DeRussey, Company C—Left as private of 1st Company. Promoted Sergeant, and afterwards 2d Lieutenant in 1862. Wounded at Chancellorsville in 1863. Served during the war and surrendered at Appomattox. Now a prominent cotton weigher of New Orleans.

2d Lieutenant D. Kilpatrick—Joined in 1862. Taken prisoner at second battle of Fredericksburg. Wounded at Petersburg. Now of the firm of Jackson & Kilpatrick.

Sergeant W. A. Collins, Company A.—On the march from Orange Court House to Raccoon Ford and thence to Richmond, such a stalling of caissons and pieces took place as old soldiers never saw before or after. The wheels of the pieces actually dragged through the mud and would not revolve. It took the whole of a very tempestuous night to go eight or nine miles, and the movement could not have been made at all except by double, or rather treble teaming; that is, instead of the usual four horses, twelve were attached to a piece. The men got no rest at all that night. They halted behind an old barn (on a tobacco plantation) filled with staves, and spent their time in splitting up tobacco sticks, preparatory to kindling fires, and destroying their gun carriages and exploding the caisons, in case the enemy should appear. Sergeant W. A. Collins had charge of this work, for which his business experience and mechanical turn well adapted him.

The truth was that many of the ablest workers in this corps of artillery—a service which depends for its value upon the pride and intelligence of the men as much as upon that of the superior officers, were the individual privates and non-commis-officers. Success was due to the constant interest they took in the care of the horses, pieces, implements and ammunition. Excellent instances of this assertion were Sergeants Pettis, Ellis, Coyle, Randolph, Fuqua and De Blanc. Men like these had each to be a cook, woodcutter or dishwasher, in their individual capacity, make the details, and (when it came to greasing the pieces, digging fortifications and packing ammunition chests,) had, besides, to show brilliant examples of hard work.

Sergeant P. O. Fazende is worthy of mention as a cool soldier, present in every engagement of his command, and as representing the stock of the original settlers (through the Chevalier Fazende, one of the first four Administrators of New Orleans) who peopled Louisiana when she was a French province. He went out when 17 years of age, and was several times slightly wounded. At Gettysburg his piece was disabled (with nearly every man and horse attached to it), and had to be left between the lines after Pickett's repulse. This did not prevent Sergeant Fazende from returning with more men and horses, and from recovering the disabled gun. He was taken prisoner at Drury's Bluff, and succeeded in making a daring escape (by way of Canada). He reached Niagara when Messrs. Clay and Holcomb were there, endeavoring to arrange the terms of a treaty, and made himself sufficiently useful to be several times sent from the Canada side into the Northern States on secret service. When he returned to Richmond he brought important dispatches, and was honored by the Secretary of War with a complimentary pass to every part of the Confederacy. Sergeant Fazende is now a sucessful note broker of the city.

H. M. Isaacson—Orderly Sergeant of Company A, ranking Captain in the first year of the war, and one of the most active organizers of the Battalion in its early history. His usefulness and knowledge of the work in hand at the reorganization, led to his prompt assignment by his old comrades to the arduous post in which he had first made his reputation.

H. Dudley Coleman—Orderly Sergeant Company A. He was but little more than an awkward, unformed boy during the war, with no more opportunities for distinction than that of every soldier who simply did his duty. He, however, showed enough character to secure the esteem of his army friends, establish himself in business, and obtain a leading position as a merchant and upright citizen.

A LAST CHAPTER PLACED FIRST.

REORGANIZATION
OF THE
WASHINGTON ARTILLERY,
SINCE THE WAR.

In the years immediately following the termination of the war the Washington Artillery still retained its old autonomy as a benevolent society or association. Partly owing to military rule, partly to a disinclination to bear arms under State governments whose policy was foreign to their sympathies, the reorganization into Batteries and Companies was not attempted until ten years after the close of the struggle.

In the month of July, 1875, the general aspiration for a better feeling at the various celebrations of the anniversary of American Independence, and the honorable part assigned Confederate soldiers at the centennial celebration of the battle of Bunker Hill in Boston awoke a responsive throb.

On the 22d of July a meeting of the surviving members of the companies of Washington Artillery who served in the Virginia and Western Armies, was called, and a formal organization at this and subsequent meetings acted upon. The object set forth in the meetings was to take part as a Battalion in the National Centennial of the following year. The Battalion was divided into three batteries and these, after according the commanding officer who might be elected, the privilege of appointing his Staff, elected their Field and Company Officers. The names given below represent the present organization of the Battalion:

FIELD OFFICERS (ELECTED).

J. B. WALTON..Colonel.
W. J. BEHAN...Major.

STAFF (APPOINTED).

1st Lieut. W. M. Owen...Adjt. and Chief of Staff.
1st Lieut. John N. Payne...Quarter-Master.
1st Lieut. John Holmes...Commissary.
1st Lieut. W. B. Krumbhaar...Ordnance Officer.
Thos. Y. Aby..Surgeon.

NON-COMMISSIONED STAFF (APPOINTED).

E. I. Kursheedt...Serjeant-Major.
W. H. Ellis..Q.-M. Serg't.
M. W. Cloney..Commissary Serg't.
O. F. Peck..Ordnance Serg't.
Frank P. Villasana..Chief Bugler.
J. W. Dempsey..Artificer and Armorer.

COLOR CORPORALS.—H. F. Wilson, W. C. Giffen, Gus. J. Freret.
COLOR GUARD.—A. H. Peale, J. W. Parsons, C. C. Lewis, Geo. W. Dupre.

STANDING COMMITTEES.

FINANCE.—Major W. J. Behan, *Chairman;* J. M. Seixas, P. O. Fazende, C. L. C. Dupuy, W. G. Coyle.

UNIFORM AND EQUIPMENT.—W. M. Owen, *Chairman;* J. D. Edwards, W. B. Krumbhaar, Jno. B. Richardson, B. T. Walshe.

ARRANGEMENTS.—H. Dudley Coleman, *Chairman;* F. N. Thayer, C. H. C. Brown, O. S. Babcock, Frank McElroy.

ORGANIZATION.—A. Hero, Jr., *Chairman;* T. L. Bayne, D. M. Kilpatrick, Wm. Palfrey, Jno. W. Emmet.

INVESTIGATION.—Jos. H. DeGrange, *Chairman;* Geo. W. Dupre, John R. Porter, Wm. A. Randolph, F. F. Case.

Company A.

OFFICERS.

Captain...................M. Buck Miller.	4th Sergeant...................O. S. Babcock.
Sr. 1st Lieut...............Andrew Hero, Jr.	5th Sergeant...................John R. Porter.
Jr. 1st Lieut...............Frank McElroy.	1st Corporal...................E. L. Mahen.
2d Lieut.......................Geo. E. Apps.	2d Corporal.....................E. O. Cook.
Orderly Sergeant........H. Dudley Coleman.	3d Corporal..................W. W. Charlton.
2d Sergeant....................W. A. Collins.	4th Corpora!....................G. Leefe.
3d Sergeant....................P. W. Pettis.	

PRIVATES.

Adam, L. A.	Cautzan, W. H.	Langdon, Tom	Stocker, C. H.
Andres, F. M.	Cowand, A. S	Labarre, L. V.	Smith, J. H.
Aime, Gus.	Cloney M. W.	Leverich, C. E.	Seichsnaydre, L.
Andress, S. S.	Carter, T.	Luria, A.	Seicshnaydre, A.
Bartlett, Napier	Dempsey, J. W.	Leefe, Gus.	Selph, C. R. McRae,
Brewer, Wm. P.	Ellis, W. H.	Michel, Jr., P.	Shaw, F.
Benton, J. P.	Forshee, J. M.	Miller, Louis	Shecker, J.
Brodé, F. A.	Guillotte Hy.	Madden, J. J.	Treme, J.
Ballauf, R.	Gerard, L. M.	McDonough, B. A.	Tew, W. A.
Charlton, Geo. W.	Holmes, W. H	O'Neal, W. T.	Ulrick. F.
Clark. E. A.	Harrison, S.	Peck, O.	Whittington, J. B.
Carey, Thos.	Jagot, Jas.	Rousseau, J. A. A.	

Company B.

OFFICERS.

Captain......................Eugene May.	3d Sergeant...................... Gus. Micou.
Sr. 1st Lieut..................Wm. Palfrey.	4th Sergeant...............Ant. Sambola.
Jr. 1st Lieut.................W. T. Hardie.	1st Corporal.................. Jno Meux.
2d Lieut......................M. J. Bebee.	2d Corporal..................Robt. Strong.
Orderly Sergeant..........F. L. Richardson.	3d Corporal..................C. W. Witham.
1st Sergeant.................R. McMillen.	4th Corporal................W. D. Henderson.
2d Sergeant.................. C. C. Cotting.	

PRIVATES.

Abbott, Jno.	Carpenter, J. D.	Hews, E. L.	Miller, Henry
Bryan, J. A.	Crawford, Geo.	Holmes, Jno.	Oliver, Wm.
Bayne, T. L.	Cowan. Chas.	Jones, G. R. P.	Peale, A. H.
Belsom, Dransin	Cowan, E. A.	Kent, John R.	Seixas, J M.
Belsom, Felix	Davidson, Jno.	Kenner, Minor	Steven, Wm.
Brewerton, E. W.	DeGrange. J. H.	Laffington, A. M.	Thayer, F. N.
Bridge, B.	Dugan, Jos. H.	Lamare J. M.	Tynan, Wm.
Blaffer, J. A.	Eschelman, B F.	Legaré, J. C.	Turpin, E. S.
Bartley, Jno.	Freret, Gus. J.	Levy, L L.	Villasana, F. de P.
Bloomfield. Jas.	Fox, C. W.	Marsh, J. B.	Walker, G,
Bruce, Robt.	Giffen, W. C.	Miller, Jno.	Webre, Jules
Byrne, Chas. M.			

Company C.

OFFICERS.

Captain................John B. Richardson.	4th Sergeant...................T. O. Fuqua.
Sr. 1st Lieut..................C. H. C. Brown.	5th Sergeant...................F. A. Behan.
Jr. 1st Lieut............Geo. B. De Russy.	1st Corporal...................John Bozant.
2d Lieut...................D. M. Kilpatrick.	2d Corporal...................Ed. Collins.
Orderly Sergeant............H. M. Isaacson.	3d Corporal.................. H H. Marks.
2d Sergeant............John R. McGaughey.	4th Corporal..................Ed. Peychaud.
3d Sergeant..................Chas. Palfrey.	

PRIVATES.

Augustus, E. D.	Emmett, Jno. W.	Kelly, D. M.	Pinckard, W. F.
Brinsmade, A. A.	Edwards, J. D.	Lobrano, P.	Randolph, W. A.
Baker, H. H.	Egan, Pat	Lobdell, A. G.	Rodd, Jno. R.
Bradley, J. S.	Fagan, J.	Lund, J. R.	Roebuck, J J.
Bartlett. F. A.	Florance, H.	Lewis, C. C.	Roach, Louis
Coyle, W. G.	Fazende, P. O.	Lehman, C. L.	Von Colln, P.
Cronan, D.	Falconer, W. R.	Leahy, P.	Walshe, B T.
Carter, Thos.	Gessner, Geo.	McCormick, J.	White, D. Prieur
Case, F. F.	Guillotte, L. E.	McCarthy.	Wilson, H. F.
Dupuy. C. L. C.	Hufft, Bern'd	Metzler, J.	Zebal, H. L.
Dupré, Geo. W.	Harris, Chas.	Payne, E. C.	Zebal, L. E.
Drew, E. S.	Jones, A. C.	Pierson, J. G.	

A SOLDIER'S STORY OF THE WAR.

INTRODUCTORY.

LIKE many better soldiers, when I came back from the war, I determined at once to adapt myself to the changed condition of things in the South and not to waste any time or weary the patience of friends with fighting over old battles. I kept my resolution for more than thirteen years after my first battle. Still one cannot always be discreet—some experiences, like the secrets told of the ears of Midas by the whispering reed, will have expression.

What I have now to say is what is being said by the fifty thousand soldiers from this State who wore Confederate uniforms during the war—by the fifty thousand refugees who went from this city after its capture—in fact, is the same story that will be talked over by forty millions of people North and South, or so long as the present generation shall remain alive. Secessia, amid her desolation, looks to the old battlefields, as the Sphynx does towards the ruined cities of Egypt; and whether we will or not, in our dreams or daily ideas we are constantly hearing the command to "March;" to pack up our slender baggage and go vagabondizing from one miserable town to another searching food, shelter and rest for your tender ones, if you are a woman ; or, if a man, to take your place in line of battle, and receive the bullet that has already been moulded for your breast. The old ideas cannot be rubbed out—will come back; some unseen influence will march you over the well-tramped, fenceless, grassless and herbless fields—through the forests whose trees have been cut down or completely killed by the volleys of musketry.

Do not these fancies come to all of us? Do not some of our old men who dry up and drop off, and tearful-eyed women who still pray for shelter and protection from beggary—do not the surviving soldiers who find it hard to cope in skill or robust health with younger rivals brood over these memories?

My excuse for writing this narrative is that I never at first intended it; I thought only to pass a wearisome hour in a letter to an old friend. Once commenced, I could not end; at the same time many old comrades, the subject once suggested, begged me if I proposed writing about the war at all, to take for my theme the soldiers who went from Louisiana.

I have tried to do this, though at the same time attempting only a rough military narrative. I want only to try and show how large bodies of our young men went through the transformation of the citizen into the soldier. How we learned and became reconciled to the rough life of camp; consented to new ways of thinking and living, and suffered, as it were, a general breaking up and wreck of our previous identity and existence.

A story of such great changes in worldly circumstances, of any class, ought to have its charm, if properly brought out; the charm that we find in Crusoe, in the Blythedale visionaries who renounced the luxuries of civilization and became farmers, in the nun who buries herself in the cloister, or in a St. Francis who renounces his riches and weds himself to poverty. You will perhaps not care for the dull details of a soldier's life in itself; but when it is added that it embodies the experience of many men of well known names who have since made themselves distinguished in industrial enterprises, in positions of trust and responsibility, and as worthy and virtuous citizens every way, their marches will not be without interest. Some of us too, have seen the world outstrip us in the struggle for existence; our rough life in the army has made us duller than rival applicants or contracted for us bad habits, and we will have to limp along and get on the best we can; but this crude narrative will not have been written in vain, if it succeeds in awakening any sympathy with the young men who are coming on, and whom we will leave behind us, or if it awakens with those who give employment any increased tolerance or respect for soldiers whose convictions meant, for one out of every three—DEATH!

This narrative will be rather of the cheerful or careless sort—one not intended to awaken foolish feeling about our struggle, or which had better be forgotten. It will pick away, Old Mortality-like, a little of the mildew and moss from the graves of martyrs of conviction; but it will be tempered with the reflection that the surviving comrades, who marched barefooted and without food, have since had better days; and that their adventures in hard straights will be read with something of the same interest as that of those princes of romance, whose lives are no longer cared for the moment they become happy and comfortable. But enough: when we came back from the wars our friends treated us with so much sympathy, that we preferred entering by quiet streets to witnessing their generosity or tears; and the monument recently erected in Greenwood, tells us that our heroes have not been forgotten. I believe that the services of our troops deserve to be recorded not only in monumental marble, but in the page of history; in such works as those of "the grand old masters," as well as of the humblest scribes. Not as belonging to any regiment or batallion, but as illustrating what our beloved State did when we were all placed in the balance—as showing what the LOUISIANA SOLDIER did in times that tried men's souls. My belief is that it is a great misfortune for a State not to recall the names of her great dead—not to hold them up as models for the old and young, and to keep them from falling into obscurity. We are made good and useful more by example than by the pulpit or schoolhouse; and if Louisiana had preserved the legacy of great names which she has produced, she would have escaped much of the misery into which she is now plunged; her men of ability would prefer glory to the thrift which follows fawning; and she would probably, as is the case with Georgia or Virginia, be again on the road to prosperity.

The man who gives his life doing what he believes to be his duty, makes a bequest which has an actual value to a State not exceeded by that of lands and money. The day of her ruin is when we regard the time serving and corrupt with equal favor with the good man and hero.

CHAPTER I.
THE ROLL CALL

I went out to the war with a large number of young men in the Batallion of Washington Artillery, and as the reader is henceforth to be familiar with the name, a word will here be said as to its early history.

In 1839, Gen. Persifer F. Smith gave the first decided

impetus to the volunteer companies of the city, and contributed greatly to their organization. He was really the founder of nearly all above Canal street. It was by his efforts that the Washington Regiment was organized, and it remained under his command until the breaking out of the Mexican war, at which time he was appointed General of the brigade composed of it and three other regiments. Eleven days after the call for volunteers, the Washington Regiment was descending the river in transports on its way to Mexico.

Previous to its departure the regiment partook of the nature of a legion in its organization: that is was composed of horse, foot and artillery.

General Smith distinguished himself at Monterey—rose to be Brevet Major General, and by his talents caused himself to be retained in the U. S. Army in spite of the absence of a military education. He died in command of the Department of the Pacific shortly before the war.

The company of the Washington Regiment which more than any other bequeathed its organization to the Washington Artillery Batallion, first appeared as an organized company in 1840; but this organization dwindled down to seventeen men in 1852. In those days the company, then known as the "Native American Artillery," afterwards as the Marion, was drilled by Capt. R. O. Smith, and subsequently by Brig. Gen. E. L. Tracey. James Beggs, Capt. H. M. Isaacson, Gunnegle,* Bannister and

* Lieut. N. G. Gunnegle is the oldest member of the organization known to be alive. He joined in 1840, when the Artillery went by the name of the 1st Company Native American Artillery. The well known Armory on Girod street was then a blacksmith shop, but was gradually adapted to military purposes. In 1845 $30 a month was appropriated by the State to maintaining an armorer. Capt. Forno, who was a few years since killed by a railroad accident on the Jackson Railroad, had, up to the date of the Mexican War been its captain; but at that time he resigned or perhaps was promoted to be Lieut. Colonel. Forno was succeeded by Capt. Isaac Stockton, much to the surprise of Gunnegle's friends, who had wasted their time and money in advancing his claims.

some others are names that are still associated with the old organization.

Then Soria became its Captain and the honor cost him his life. That is, the Artillery on the occasion of some rejoicing had carried out to the Levee at the foot of Canal street, four guns which were fired to the four points of the compass in honor of the event. It was while ramming a cartridge home that the piece he was loading prematurely exploded. His arms were torn from his body, and he sustained such other injury as to occasion his death shortly after. Until the Batallion went to Virginia, the coat and equipments of Captain Soria hung as a memento of his services in its Arsenal or drill-room.

The company still numbered not over fifteen members, with H. J. Hunting, 1st Lieutenant, and Dan. Harrison, 2d. The Captaincy was now offered to Leeds, who declined, and afterwards to Col. J. B. Walton, then Secretary to Mayor Waterman, and who had served in the war with Mexico, as the Colonel of the Washington regiment. This was two or three years prior to the war.

A growing interest in military matters now became prevalent as sectional passions increased in intensity, and the feeling was increased and encouraged by leading men*

The latter went as 3d Sergt. and ultimately was courtmartialed for refusing to fill a position to which he had never been elected, but was ultimately acquitted. Stockton, whose company in the Mexican War was the first of the Washington Regiment, enlisted 64 men, and died after his return. At the time he went out the old privates in the company furnished officers for four or five regiments. Add was then Adjutant and Breedlove Major of the Washington Regiment, Jas. Strawbridge, 1st Lieut. and Greene 2nd. The regiment advanced as far as Barita in Mexico, and has still some twenty-five members alive, several of whom went out with the Batallion to Virginia.

Gunnegle served as Treasurer, Secretary, keeper of the Arsenal, and 2nd Lieut. till 1857. He applied for leave to serve in Virginia, but was refused on account of age.

*" With the commencement of the year '61 a stranger visiting our city would have deemed its streets the parade ground of one vast encampment. At every step a soldier is met, and martial music fills the air. The tramp of armed men is heard by day and night, and the reverberation of the drill room assails the ear upon every side."—*True Delta.*

who foresaw the approach of war. Partly from this cause, partly because the men began to work with a will, and through the talents of Col. Walton as an officer, the Artillery steadily increased in number and reputation.

A fine armory had been given it by the city, situated on Girod between St. Charles and Carondelet, and from this the Batallion armed as infantry, marched to assist in the capture of Baton Rouge from the U. S. authorities, previous to the commencement of hostilities.*

In the month of May† the Batallion was accepted "for the war" by President Davis, an arrangement which caused us to be classed as Confederate instead of State troops contributed by Louisiana. This arrangement, had afterwards the effect of giving us some advantages over other troops, or disadvantages (for both were contended

*On Jan. 10th, 1861, the first active steps towards separation were taken, and the steamer National started for Baton Rouge after midnight for the capture of that place with a strong force of citizen soldiers. They were "young men mostly of hot blood, and determined to do the State some service." An expedition down the river got off at 10 o'clock the day after. At Baton Rouge, Jan. 11, P. M., Major Haskins commanding at the arsenal capitulated 50,000 stand of arms and other munitions. The companies from New Orleans now held the barracks. Some of the Baton Rouge companies deemed themselves slighted by not being sent to take charge of the place, and intimated that they would disband. Great excitement in consequence.

Three companies afterwards disbanded, retiring in high dudgeon. The volunteer troops of Baton Rouge finally took charge of the Barracks. Capt. Voories during the expedition commanded the Washington Artillery, Captain Charles D. Dreux, the New Orleans Cadets, and the Orleans Guards were under Captain S. M. Todd and Lieut. Girardey. The whole expedition was under the command of Col. Walton.

†As early as the month of December, 1860, a requisition was sent to Governor Moore for guns, stores, battery, horses, forges, etc., in order to put the Batallion in a condition for service in the field. On the 27th of March the petition was renewed, and subsequently made to the Secretary of War at Montgomery. The following extract quoted from the application of the commanding officer will show what was then its condition:

"The Batallion Washington Artillery, under my command, numbering upon the rolls over three hundred men, two hundred and fifty for service, and divided into four companies, with a battery complete in all respects, of six bronze six pounder guns, two twelve pounder howitzers, and one eight pounder rifled cannon, is ready and desirous to take the field. The Batallion can take the field within a very few days after being notified, and provided with horses, camp and garrison equipage, etc., which of course I will be obliged to make requisition for upon the Confederate States."

for) among which was the appointment instead of the election by the men of their officers.

We were mustered into service on the 26th,* and then marched in a body to Christ's Church, and preached to by Rev. Mr. Leacock, who recommended us to remember that we had been educated to be gentlemen, and to bring back our characters with our arms. This advice of the worthy Doctor caused us afterwards some mental discussion in settling in our own minds whether a soldier could or ought to be any thing of the sort, and whether it was not better to leave his society manners, pride, prejudices about birth, education and modes of living, and nearly every thing that makes up the word, behind. However it may have been, and this is what we suppose the Doctor intended to advise. They, most of them, retained their cheerfulness and a disposition to do their duty in camp or society, and probably gained more in manly feeling than they could have ever acquired any where else.

To complete its outfit the citizens of New Orleans contributed $7,000—the Ladies' Association alone giving

---

* The Washington Artillery were out in full dress uniform yesterday with fine band. After delighting the spectators who lined the streets, with a display of their accurate maneuvering, they were drawn up at Mr. T. C. Twichell's, St. Charles street, and presented with a beautiful Camp flag of the Confederate States. "You take with you," said the speaker for the ladies who presented it, "their blessings and the Godspeed of every loyal heart in the entire community." This morning at 8 o'clock, the Battalion—every man—will be mustered into service by Lieut. Phifer. On Monday at 6 o'clock they will take their departure for Virginia. The reserve corps of the Batallion will be left here until further notice. Lieut. W. Irving Hodgson has been detailed on special duty as an agent and resident quartermaster of the Batallion: also in command of those detailed from the corps for home duty. The honorary members will escort the Batallion to the Railroad depot on Monday evening. In the course of a little while from now the reserve will probably be on the way to some other point of action than Virginia.—*N. O. Crescent, May* 26, 1861.

This prediction came true. Under the call of Gen. Beauregard for ninety days men for the army of the West, Capt. Slocomb, or rather Capt. W. I. Hodgson, at that time taking out the 5th Company of Washington Artillery, 250 strong, and with them gaining full as many laurels as were obtained by the first four companies in Virginia.

$500, and the large houses and corporations aiding with equal liberality.

The following were the names of the officers and of those who on Sunday morning May 26th, 1861, answered to Lieut. Phifer's roll-call—a very solemn moment—and who thus became mustered into the Confederate service:*

STAFF.

Major............	J. B. WALTON,	Adjutant............	LIEUT. W. M. OWEN,
Surgeon............	DR. E. S. DREW,	Quarter Master......	LIEUT. C. H. SLOCOMB.

NON-COMMISSIONED STAFF.

Sergt. Major............C. L. C. DUPUY, Quarter Master Sergt. STRINGER KENNEDY,
Color Sergeant......................LOUIS M. MONTGOMERY.

COLOR GUARD.

Corporal............GEORGE W. WOOD, Corporal....................E. L. JEWELL,
   "   ....A. H. PEALE,   "   ....J. H. DEARIE.

BUGLERS.

F. P. Villavasana,   Jo. Kingslow.

ROLL OF FIRST COMPANY.

Captain....................H. M. Isaacson, *Jr. First Lieutenant,*....J. B. Richardson,
First Lieutenant............C. W. Squires, *Second Lieutenant*...........H. G. Geiger.
First Sergeant...............Edward Owen, *First Corporal*............F. D. Ruggles,
Second Sergeant............J. M. Galbraith, *Second Corporal*............E. C. Payne,
Third Sergeant............C. H. C. Brown, *Third Corporal*...............W. Fellows,
         Fourth Corporal......................F. F. Case.

Thomas S. Turner,	C. Chambers,	W. T. Hardie,
G. M. Judd,	G. W. Muse,	H. Chambers,
E. J. Kursheedt,	L. Labarre,	E. V. Wiltz,
J. W. Kearney,	M. Mount,	J. P. Manico,
C. Rossiter,	P. A. J. Michel,	L. E. Zebal,
W. Chambers,	J. M. Payne,	H. L. Zebal,
W. F. Perry,	R. McK. Spearing,	W. R. Falconer,
J. E. Rodd,	A. F. Coste,	G. B. DeRussy,
M. E. Jarreau,	J. R. McGaughy,	F. Lobrano,
J. A. Tarlton,	E. A. Cowen,	C. A. Everett.
T. Y. Aby,	F. A. St. Amand,	

* The Batallion, when in Virginia, was several times recruited to fill the places of the killed, wounded and disabled, who averaged about one hundred to each company.

ARTIFICERS.

S. G. Stewart, W. D. Holmes, Israel Scott,

DRIVERS.

Geo. Bernard, Sergt,	Pat. Mooney,	Fred. Lester,
Michael Hock,	H. Meyer,	R. Nicholas,
Charles Rush,	Jno. Jacobs,	Jno. Charlesworth,
Jno. E. Scheman,	Thos. Kerwin,	Jno. Anderson,
Jno. O'Neil,	David Nolan,	Mathew Burns,
W. K. Dirke,	Wm. Forrest,	Jas. Heflogh.

ROLL OF SECOND COMPANY.

First Lieutenan........C. C. Lewis Com'dg,   *Third Sergeant*................H. C. Wood,
First Lieutenant......Sam'l J. McPherson,   *Fourth Sergeant*.................C. Huchez,
Second Lieutenant..........C. H. Slocomb,   *First Corporal*...............J. D. Edwards,
First Sergeant...............J. H. DeGrange,   *Second Corporal*...........C. E. Leverich,
Second Sergeant............ Gustave Aime,   *Third Corporal*...............Jules Freret,
Fourth Corporal..............................B. V. L. Hutton.

H. N. Payne,	R. Axson,	F. Alewelt,
J. S. Meyers,	Wm. Roth,	F. P. Buckner,
Tracey Twichell,	E. D. Patton,	G. E. Strawbridge,
T. J. Land,	A. G. Knight,	A. R. Blakely,
J. W. Emmett,	J. D. Britton,	R. Bannister, Jr.
J. A. Hall,	W. A. Randolph,	R. C. Lewis,
G. Humphrey,	W. F. Florence,	H. B. Berthelot,
W. C. Giffen,	J. W. Parsons,	W. J. Hare,
J. C. Woodville,	J. Howard Goodin,	J. H. Randolph,
A. A. Brinsmade,	Thomas H. Suter,	W. H. Wilkins.
E. L. Hall,		Sam'l Hawes.

ARTIFICERS.

John Montgomery,   Leonard Craig.

DRIVERS.

John Weber,	William Little,	James Brown,
Toney Hulby,	James Crilly,	W. F. Lynch,
John Fagan,	John Cannon,	Louis Roach,
George Barr,	Jas. Leyden,	William Oliver,
Wm. Carey,	Ed. Loftus,	Corn'l McGregor,
B. B. F. McKesson,	Ewin Lake,	Alex. Bucher.

ROLL OF THIRD COMPANY.

Captain.......................... M. B. Miller,
First Lieutenant.........J. B. Whittington,
Second Lieutenant.............L. A. Adam,
First Sergeant............ ..Frank McElroy,
Second Sergeant................A.. Hero, Jr.
Third Sergeant.....................L. Prados,
Fourth Sergeant................ J. T. Handy,
First Corporal...................E. L. Jewell,
Second Corporal...............A. H. Peale,
Third Corporal................. W. H. Ellis,
Fourth Corporal..............................W. A Collins.

Napier Bartlett,
H. D. Summers,
J. H. Moore,
W. Mills,
Robert Bruce,
J. H. Holmes, Jr.
T. H. Fuqua,
O. N. DeBlanc,
E. W. Morgan,
P. W. Pettis,
E. Riviere,
F. Kremelberg,
Chas. Hart,
Sam'l C. Boush,
Geo. McNeil,
J. H. Colles,
Frank Shaw, Jr.
E. Toledano,
W. S. Toledano,

Jos. Blanchard,

P. O. Fazende,
Fred. L. Hubbard,
Jos. H. DeMeza,
L. E. Guyot,
J. F. Randolph,
S. Chalaron,
J. T. Brenford,
C: W. Deacon,
Stringer Kennedy,
Howard Tully,
Wm. Leefe,
I. W. Brewer,
C. H. Stocker,
J. R. Porter,
S. G. Sanders,
B. L. Braselman,
R. P. Many,
F. A. Carl.

ARTIFICERS.

C. E. Fortier,
R. Maxwell,
E. Avril,
E. Charpiaux,
T. M. Mc.Fall,
M. W. Cloney,
Ed. Duncan,
C. A. Falconer,
H. J. Phelps,
T. Ballantine,
E. W. Noyes,
M. W. Chapman,
W. P. Noble,
W. G. Coyle,
L. P. Forshee,
George H. Meek,
J. C. Bloomfield.
A. B. Martin,
R. Turnell.

Jas. Keating,

ROLL OF FOURTH COMPANY.

Captain..................B. F.Eshleman,
First Lieutenant.................Jos. Norcom,
Second Lieutenant.......Harry A. Battles,
Second Sergeant................W. J. Behan
Third Sergeant ....G. E. Apps,
Fourth Sergeant............J. D. Reynolds,
First Corporal..................Geo. Wood,
Second Corporal..............J. W. Dearie

A. D. Augustus,
B. F. Widler,
J. R. McGowan,
J. M. Rohbock,
H. F. Wilson,
C. C. Bier,

G. L. Crutcher,
J. F. Lilly,
T. J. Stewart,
Sam'l A. Knox,
Wm. Palfrey,
L. C. Lewis,

H. N. White,
Jno. B. Chastant,
W. Snead,
H. D. Seaman,
F. H. Bee,
C. W. Marston,

J. C. Wood,
Jno. S. Fish,
F. A. Brodie,
E. Lauer,
G. Beck,
R. F. F. Moore,
H. H. Baker,
J. W. Burke,
Jno. Meux,
J. B. Valentine,
Phil. Von Coln,
T. B. White,
Bernard Hufft,

J. H. Smith,
G. Montgomery,
Isaac Jessup,
A. F. Vass.
W. W. Jones,
P. C Lane,
T. Carey,
W. P. S. Crecy,
W. C. Morrell,
W. T. O'Neill,
A. Banksmith,
Frank Williams,

C. A. Deval,
E. A. Mellard,
J. W. Wilcox,
V. D. Terrebonne.
E. F. Reichart,
Thos. H. Cummings,
R. H. Gray,
S. T. Hale,
J. W. Lesene,
Chas. Hardenburg,
J. C. Purdy,
E. Jaubert.

ARTIFICERS.

Levy Callahan,

Jno. McDonnell.

BAND.

J. V. Gessner, *Leader*,
T. Gutzler,
Ch. W. Struxe,
J. Arnold,

Jno. Deutsch,
Jno. Geches,
Peter Trum,
Jno. Lorbs,

Thos. Kostmel,
J. H. Sporer,
Charles Meir,

CHAPTER II.

DEPARTURE FOR VIRGINIA.

THERE will never be a time of such intense public feeling in the history of New Orleans, or perhaps in that of the country generally, as that which attended the departure of the first troops at the commencement of the late civil war. Writing at this day, one is almost inclined to doubt the impressions which still remain in his memory, not to speak of those half effaced, which are occasionally brought to mind by the conversation of old comrades or friends, or by glancing over old letters or files of papers. Can it be possible, you say to yourself, that business men, though always in our city known for generosity, would give away clothing, arms or horses, without scarcely thinking of the matter: or that salaries were continued, by liberal houses, even after the employees had enlisted for the war;

that the stores were closed on the day of our departure, the streets were crowded to suffocation, the balconies lined with smiling and crying women, and that those were esteemed most happy who had departing friends upon whom to lavish their gifts, or bestow their flowers?* That certainly is the only time we can remember when citizens walked along the lines offering their pocket books to men whom they did not know; that fair women bestowed their floral offerings and kisses ungrudgingly and with equal favor among all classes of friends and suitors; when the distinctions of society, wealth and station were forgotten, and each departing soldier was equally honored as a hero.

On the day of our departure we certainly had a little touch of the millenium of good feeling, and it was nearer like Utopia than one generation can ever live to see a second time.†

---

* The Washington Artillery embraces as large a representation of our old and permanent population, the sons of our old citizens, as any military organization in the city. Every member of it is a gentleman; many occupy high positions in social and commercial circles, and the parting scenes were most affecting—*Delta, May* 28.

† Rev. Dr. Palmer delivered from the steps of the City Hall an address from which we quote the final passage:

"The alternative now before us is subjugation and absolute anarchy—a despotism which will put its iron heel upon all that the human heart holds most dear. The mighty issue is to be submitted to the ordeal of battle, with the nations of the earth as spectators, and with the God of Heaven as umpire.

"With such an issue we have no doubt of the part that will be assigned you to play, and when we hear the thunders of your cannon echoing from the mountain passes of Virginia will understand that you mean in the language of Cromwell 'to cut this war to the heart.' It is little to say that you will be remembered. And should the frequent fate of the soldier befal you in a soldier's death, you shall find your graves in thousands of hearts, and the pen of history shall write your martyrdom. Soldiers farewell! And may the Lord of Hosts be round about you as a wall of fire, and shield your heads in the day of battle." We make room for an equally touching farewell from the sermon of Rev. Dr. Leacock of the Sunday previous:

"Remember that the first convert to Christ from the Gentiles was a soldier. Inscribe the cross upon your banners, for you are fighting for liberty. In but a few hours more you will dare the toils of the battle field, and may God protect you in your absence. Our hearts will follow you—our ears will be open for tidings of your condition, and our prayers ascend for your safety, success and return. Let us, as the last thing that we can do, commend you to the care of Him who alone can assist."

But though the route to the depot was scattered with flowers, the thought also began to enter our minds that we had assumed the hard and unprosaic duties of soldiers, and that individual freedom and happiness were now to be left behind. The day too, in spite of our glory and the enthusiasm of our friends, was suffocatingly hot—so much so as to cause the death of two of our men,* as it were, in the ranks, from sunstroke; and although every other military organization turned out in honor of those whom they envied the priority of departure, and allowed us to go to the cars through their divided ranks, it would have added greatly to our bodily comfort to have had more air, even at the sacrifice of some of the music of the brass bands, proffers of gifts, sympathy and excitement. We suffered the torture of unaccustomed heavy clothing, knapsacks, and the dusty march of three hours duration, but meanwhile were being equally suffocated with roses; but what young man or soldier who has just enlisted ever cares for fatigue, when compared with such glory; or would exchange the happiness of seeing his whole past life brought out, as it were in tableau, at the moment of leaving it probably for ever, for ten times as much fatigue?

Our Batallion, at starting, consisted of three hundred men, who, most of them, had parents or other friends to bid them good-bye. Had they known that an interval of four years would separate them—that thirty battle fields were to be strewn with their bones, and that every other man of their number would be crippled or killed, the scene would not have been more affecting than it really was.†

* One of them F. A. Carl, singularly enough was an old soldier who besides speaking five languages, had served three years in the Russian Royal Artillery and fought in the Hungarian struggle.
†Israel Gibbons, himself an excellent soldier, and at that time writing on the *Crescent*, thus describes the scene:
"The departure yesterday was a perfect ovation. No previous military

A great many fathers, in shaking hands with the men, would ask us to look after and keep an eye on their sons. It generally turned out that the parties recommended would be the first to be killed, or that difference of temperament prevented an opportunity of acquaintance, much less doing the solicited service.

departure has been honored with so tumultuous a demonstration. The Batallion moved in four columns, with the drivers as a fifth or auxiliary, and with a large turn out of honorary members. Their escort were the Orleans Light Horse, Capt. Leeds, the Orleans Guard, 500 strong, Capt. Theard, and the Louisiana Cadets. All along this route the scene was one of the most unexampled enthusiasm. The men made noise with cheers and huzzas, and the ladies silently expressed their feelings with their flowers and handkerchiefs. The scene at the Depot was indescribable. All the carriages of the town were here filled with loads of beauty, and the balconies, windows and house-tops were filled with people.

"We never before saw ladies of fashion, respectability and wealth do as much as they did last evening for a final view, leaving their carriages, dodging under mules heads, and wading ancle-deep in dust. The crowd extended a half a mile beyond the Depot—to the edge of the swamp. They gave all sorts of evidence of the very highest heart-feeling, and everybody had wet eyes. As the twilight faded into dark, the train rumbled off, groups of people were seen sitting about on the piles of lumber, waiting for the ladies to have their cry out, before starting for home.

The Honorary Members who turned out upon this occasion, were :
Brig. Gen'l E. L. Tracey, Col. A. H. Gladden, Hon. Gerard Stith, W. A. Freret, Esq., John D. Foster, M. D., E. T. Parker, Adam Giffen, Norbert Trepagnier, Hon. P. H. Morgan, M. A. Foute, Jules Tuyes, Hon. Wm. G. Austin, M. D., D. Maupay, Alfred Munroe, E. B. Smedes, John Holmes, Col. C. A. Taylor, A. S. Withers, Hon. C. M. Bradford, T. S. McCay, Hon. John T. Monroe, E. C. Hancock, A. P. Harrison, Mark F. Bigney, E. F. Schmidt, H. G. Stetson, John Calhoun, Hon. John B. Leefe, Wm. G. Hewes, Maj. Thomas F. Walker, John Pemberton, R. L. Pugh, Jacob J. Herr, Hon. J. O. Nixon, J. C. Ferriday, A. P. Avegno, Dan'l E. Colton, Charles T. Nash, T. L. Leeds, H. W. Reynolds, B. F. Voorhies, R. L. Outlaw, G. H. Chaplain, W. B. Bowles, W. L. Allen, Col. S. H. Peck, T. L. Bayne, P. N. Wood, H. Doane, Geo. W. Hynson, Col. Geo. W. Race, Wm. H. Hunt, W. C. Lipscomb, Col. Daniel Edwards, R. Esterbrook, J. M. Davidson, C. F. White, F. Wing, Howard Smith, M. D., W. M. Pinckard, Wm. Ellis, A. W. Bosworth, George Connelly. J. D. Dameron, G. S. Hawkins.

The names of the members of the Batallion who went as officers in various regiments or who continued the existence of the organization in the city, were Capt. O. Voorhies, Jr. First Lieutenant, T. A. James, Second Lieutenant, M. S. Squires, First Sergeant, O. F. Peck, Third Sergeant, A. Luria, Color Sergeant, J. Thomas Wheat, Quarter Master Sergeant, E. L. Hews, First Corporal, Charles Thompson, First Artificers, C. H. Waldo, D. Kelly, Treasurer (afterwards Capt. W. Irving Hogdson.

PRIVATES.—Anderson J. B., Bruce N. M., Baker Marion A., Blair J. C., Blow R. A., Butts E. S., Brand F. A., Bisland J. J., Bloomfield Benj., Barton R. G., Culbertson C. W., Caldwell A. F., Correjolles G., Churchill W. E., Carey F. S., Calmes W. N., Dudley L., DeMerritt J. W., Delamore Jas., Evans Geo. P., Estella M., Easton T. B., Finley L. A., Jr. Fisk John S., Ferriday W. M., Grayson J. B., Jr. Graham L., Grandpre P., Gordon W. E., Goldsmith F., Halsey W. S., Hutton B. V., Henning Wm. H., Hanlon Jos., Harrington S., Hawthorn

The leave-taking of the young men, generally with their relatives, it must be admitted was much more hurried than with their wives, or more often with their sweet-hearts, (for we were nearly all at that age when it is difficult to keep from having at least one.) Some of us were compelled to remain in ranks and be witness to these tender leave-takings—to watch the lustrous eyes, suffusing cheeks, the heaving breasts, the last fond smile, and the concluding kiss—all taking place in less time than it takes to relate it; and to become, as it were, each of us, by sympathy, an actor and *particeps criminis* in the love-making or love.ending tableau that was going on. It did not take a great many minutes to complete this part of the drama—though it was curious in one respect—that of bringing together so many couples of education and refinement and making them act out the drama of their loves, or at least a specimen chapter. All these little incidents were remembered long after and frequently talked over in camp, and very often when we had all become growlers, not much to the credit of the *dramatis personœ*. The fact is, there was some little forgetfulness about these vows after the arrival of the Batallion in Virginia, while the fond and trusting hearts that were left behind, subsequently found themselves so situated, after the capture of the city, as to render any such remembrance inconvenient.

These little love episodes, too, as we soldiered further

A. T., Harvey C. M., Hedges J. H. H., Hemines D. P., Johnson F. A., Johnston T. G., Johnston D. C., Jones O. G., Kennedy John, Lipscomb, A. A., Leverich Chas, E., Lonsdale H. H., Lowe B. M. Jr., Lange F. G., Morell W. C., McLearn John G., McNair H. M., Miller J. H., Norris J. B., O'Brien R. M., Pierson, J. G. Prados J. B., Phelps W. V., Perkins J. A., Quirk Wm. C., Rodgers, J. C. Rocquet A., Robira A., Reid W. A., Smith Alex. Jr., St. Amant ——, Spedden E., Speoring C. F., Sambola A., Steven W., Stewart ——, Stroud George. Sanford C. H., Savage A., Seymour J. W., Simpson G. W., Summers H. D., Tisdale B. F., Tisdale E. K., Tracy M., Vaught W. C. D., West Geo., Wingate W. W., Wingate E. H., Walshe B. T., Willard E. O., Webb J. V., Wolf O. B., Wyche J. F., Wordall F., Ximines W. A.

on, were destined to have their influence, in a remote and indirect way on all of the Batallion, even those most indifferent to the sentiment, and so far from the fond absent being remembered with sympathy, was the cause not unfrequently of loud swearing. For instance, the first detail made of a member to return home (naturally enough) was the man who had just married a bran new wife. Then there were faithful spouses who found opportunities to overtake the Batallion in its various marches, who were either obtaining or entreating to obtain, their husband excused from some camp service, and which, if obtained, would throw the wearisome duty on some less fortunate batchelor comrade. While on the other hand, the latter class would either be absent from camp at every turn, when the presence of the fair was to be obtained, or writing love-letters home, or seeking for furloughs, mostly, of course, with reference to attractions left behind.

At length we were marched into the cars by companies and assigned our places for the journey. The knapsacks, belts and other useless plunder of one sort and another with which we were all more or less burdened, was quickly disposed of upon the hooks over head, or under the seats, (Damocles swords were suspended above,) and every man made himself as comfortable as could be done in a car crowded to its utmost capacity, and on the hottest night of the year.

It need hardly be stated that there was too much excitement for the first half of the night to allow of much sleep. The men laughed, and danced and sung as if possessed by hysteria. The sardine boxes which we had brought along to be eaten when rations run short, were opened before we reached the first station, and the various flasks much sooner.

CHAPTER III.

ALL ABOARD—A CAR WHEEL ANABASIS.

IN spite of all of the heat and dust, and the drawback of having no place or opportunity for comfortable sleep, we were most of us in excellent spirits, and our upward journey to Richmond was one all the way through of wild excitement.

But gradually the older and more serious members began to settle down to pipes and tobacco—to staring out at the trees which seemed to rush homewards like an army of giant phantoms, and to realizing that their past habits were cut off from their future. The loud talkers, who had indefatigably told heavy stories which the noise of the train prevented any one but themselves from hearing, began to show signs of exhaustion; and as the night wore on there would sometimes be a brief lull, undisturbed by anything except the heavy breathing of the sleepers. Then the train would stop at a station—one man would be heard complaining of the oppressive boots of his vis-a-vis neighbor against the pit of his stomach, while another would expostulate at the length of legs from behind which projected over the top of the seats and inconvenienced the complainant's head.

We were now made to realize that those with whom we would be most thrown together were the comrades who resembled each other in the single matter of height, and were in character and tastes the most widely different, and that our first study would be to learn to adapt ourselves to each other's ways. And a very difficult lesson to learn that subsequently proved.

For instance, the next morning about day light when the train stopped for water, a clear branch was discovered running near the railroad embankment, and the men began to tumble out, considerably worn and pulled down, to profit by the best opportunity we would have of washing. The provident soldiers now would produce towels, soaps, combs, etc., and save for the trouble of bending on their knees and bathing like Diana with the brook for a mirror, would manage to make their toilet about as well as if they were at home, or in a fashionable barber's saloon. The only trouble would be that the man who came after would be unprovided, or was too lazy to go down into his own knapsack, and consequently would have to borrow. Before the first borrower had concluded, a second application to borrow would be filled, with similar requests following in rapid order from others, until the owner becoming wearied with waiting would timidly request that the articles be returned when all were through. An hour or so afterwards when the matter was under investigation, it would be made to appear that the soap was regarded as Batallion soap, and that there was nothing more to be heard of it; that the tin wash basin which its fastidious owner had fondly fancied would accompany him in all of his campaigns, had been left behind at the halting station; that the towel had been hung out to dry; and as for the comb somebody had brought it along, but precisely who, nobody could tell!

Of course it need not be said that the owner of the wash basin felt ruined and discontented for the balance of the day, and the day after; for when the time for ablutions came again, he found no friend that was willing to lend him any of the articles before mentioned, and so his satisfaction and happiness at leading the life of a soldier would receive its first check and begin to wane.

"It's not that I care about a d—d little cake of soap," he

would feelingly growl, as his Alnashar visions of soldiering began to disappear like the bubbles that were made from the missing cube; "it's not that I can't make a raise of another towel and comb; but it's the principle of the thing. I begin to believe that about one half of the Batallion are beats that intend to live off the other half, and I want it understood that they won't work that game any more with me. I've got at any rate a bag of good perique tobacco left," (says the speaker filling his pipe and anticipating a movement among the crowd) and if you hear of any body inquiring for any, send them to me, and they will find out where they *can't* get it.

And so far from receiving the sympathy which his misfortunes merited, the victim was affectedly condoled with and taken aside by some one of every group in which he happened to enter, for the purpose of drawing from him a further recital of his wrongs.

We dozed on through the following day, pulled out a novel now and then, or talked in a somewhat more quiet strain than on the night before. Some of the men had still enough enthusiasm left to occupy their time in scouring their sabres; others who had not left civilization entirely behind, produced cards and an ear of corn, which, such is the wickedness of the times, need not be explained to any body, meant a mild game of poker. This included for several days quite a large circle, but this gradually contracted with the pocket books of the players. The game always remained popular, particularly after pay day, though owing to certain difficulties about chips, the number who kept constantly occupied at it was limited. There was a small devoted circle who applied themselves faithfully to it on the cars and off, at night at the guard tent—around the bivouac fire, and sometimes before and after the bloody carnage of battle. The counters were of gold not unfrequently, at starting—the cards gilt-edged. But the last time I saw the game in camp, the players looked unwashed and ragged, and the papers taken from a bloody knapsack were dealt on an old red cotton handkerchief. The prize that was contended for was a chicken which had been pressed into service, and the loser was to have the privilege of cooking and eating this, and sucking the bones. There is nothing like having a passion or mission in life; and except for the difficulty of paying for the chips, card playing seemed to be as popular a way of killing time as any.

As we journeyed on, we passed through several towns where we were welcomed with great eclat by the population, and indeed the same might be said about every village and isolated house. There was always a sign, as was the case with all the troops who first went out, that the sight of the soldier touched some profound and sympathetic cord. At every depot there would be gathered the most beautiful ladies of the place, who would enthusiastically stream out and welcome us as Calypso and her nymphs did Telemachus, giving us at leaving, flowers, cold chicken, gloves, aprons and knic-nacs of every sort. Sometimes the reception would be at a regularly laid table, as it was at Huntsville—sometimes in a ball room, as at Iuka Springs, and then after fifteen minutes of waltzing of fast city youth and bashful girls (who thought much to the astonishment of the former, that it looked nicer to be held by the arms instead of being encircled around the waist,) the cars would again move on.

Knoxville and Chattanooga each furnished impressions, but our pride had been humbled along that portion of our route by having to ride all night in box cars. Our special glory was reserved for Lynchburg, and in after years we never grew weary of gloating over the honors there bestowed upon us. It was on Sunday about noon that we first stood drawn up in line in the principal street, and there were many carriages filled with ladies who lent the charm of their presence to the occasion. One of them was a gorgeous looking beauty who seemed from the glances she bestowed, to have fallen in love with some one of us at first sight. We each of us flattered ourselves with having wrought the charm, and doubtless thenceforth would have recounted around camp fires a good many Arabian night romances, or stories of ourselves, similar to that of Queen Christiana and Ronzares, promoted from a coming soldier, to be a Spanish grandee. But a civilian who was standing by her carriage, dashed these hopes by bringing a message of invitation to one of the color corporals, and this was followed up by an introduction, exchange of rings, correspondence, and all that. Possibly the romantic meeting would have ended in something else, had not death swept away both before the second year of the war.

We passed the remainder of the day and night in Lynchburg, the citizens entertaining us at their houses— that is, all with the exception of the Zenophon of this narrative and a dozen other unfortunate wretches. These were detailed on a very dark, chilly night, to stand guard over the cars on the railroad—none of us well knew which. The first guard mounting, proved as dangerous as it was irksome. Having been placed on the embankment, the sentinel was ordered to march forward on the side of the cars fifty feet and return, keeping meanwhile a bright look out for the enemy. He started to march, as directed, on the track by the side of the train, but had not proceeded fifty feet before his path (owing to the narrowness of the embankment suddenly ended.) As it was very dark, he was not made aware of this state of things, until he found himself about twenty feet below, with his sabre sticking in the ground, and very much wondering how he so suddenly reached there.

We stood our guard watch of two hours and were then allowed to crawl among some sacks of corn in one of the freight cars, and sleep there until again wanted. By the time we had got through our second dose of guard mounting, there were a dozen of their country's defenders who began to have a low opinion about soldiering.

The only other incident I shall now stop to relate, previous to the arrival at Richmond, was that performed by a young private of that day, and a well known merchant of this. While the train was in motion, proceeding to the last point of our week's journey, a very pretty and patriotic young girl appeared near the track with a bouquet of flowers in her hands, of which to her evident regret, she had no opportunity of disposing. The rear of our long train was composed of platform cars, laden with the guns which were afterwards to accompany us into the field, and underneath whose rattling chains at night the men would crawl and sleep. Upon the last of these platform cars a sentinel was standing, who thought it a pity that such a pretty bouquet should be left behind. The train was going slowly around a curve. Acting up to his idea, he jumped down without accident, took the bouquet, and the moment after succeeded in regaining the train. In fact, he did more—he not only gallantly took the bouquet, but a kiss besides, from the lips of the astonished donor. The same sort of thing happened at a way station where a young lady locked in a room on the second story, offered a bouquet, then a ring, and finally a kiss to anybody that would climb after them. The work had to be done on a shutter and the outside of a window sash, nevertheless, we had such a variety of talent, that the work was accomplished.

CHAPTER IV.

THE CONFEDERATE CAPITOL.

We were very much disgusted on arrival at Richmond, for arrive there we at last did, to find that instead of being allowed to take a run around and see the place we were shut up in a tobacco warehouse and a sentinel placed at the gate. While some of us were meditating an imitation of the too lively Zouaves who had been shut up temporarily in an upper hall, and who made a very practical use of their new sashes to let themselves down to the ground, the welcome order came to march to a hotel breakfast. This was our breakfast of adieu, the last we were ever to eat altogether, and when finished, we moved toward camp.

We were now marched in a comfortable frame of mind through the streets of Richmond, led on by the exhilerating notes of Gessner's brass band, which accompanied us from New Orleans, and we spread to the breeze the most costly and beautiful standard borne by any of the Confederate or holiday troops.*

*This standard made of very costly silk, yellow upon one side and red upon the other, represented the coat of arms of Louisiana and of the Batallion. It was said to have been made in Paris at a cost of $750, was heavily mounted in silver and was presented by the ladies of New Orleans, in a speech delivered by Senator Benjamin in which he predicted the war.

It was replied to by the gallant Capt. Wheat, then the color bearer of the Batallion. Towards the close of the war when its preservation became difficult

The uniforming of the members which was done by first class city tailors, had been an item of something like $20,000 and with brass scales, white belts and gloves and flashing sabres, no organization in the world, as was afterwards told us by President Davis and Lee (to which latter we reported,) ever presented a braver appearance.

Still, in spite of our ardor, there appeared a certain coolness on the part of spectators, which had been previously lacking in our reviews. We did not understand it then, but did afterwards. The fact was, the town was overrun with soldiers, till, as the phrase then was, you could not rest. This was the meditative view taken by the business population, who were occupied rather in thinking of the additional amount of money that would be spent in the city than our showy appearance, and in the few words that we were permitted to exchange in ranks, the people of Richmond began to descend to a low figure. But we soon had cause to change this opinion in every respect; and certainly the ladies of the city, when in the afternoon our camp had been pitched, and who came to see us by thousands, magnificently atoned for any lack of enthusiam during the day.

It need not be added that there was no city of the Confederacy with which we became so familiar, or to which we became so much attached, as Richmond. It was in

amidst incessant marching, it was sent to grace the Louisiana table of Mrs. Slocomb, at a fair given at Columbia, S. C. The colors were however stolen, before its arrival from the valise of the soldier who had been entrusted with it, together with the valise itself; and though rewards have been offered nothing has ever been heard of it from that day to this. Several of the battle flags that went with the different batteries were brought back. The silver socket was all that was ever brought back of the standard.

It was displayed for the last time on the works in front of Petersburg, on the morning of July 4th, 1864, as a sort of defiance suggested by the day. The production of this flag was speedily responded to, by the hoisting of apparently all of the regim ntal colors along both Federal and Confederate lines. It was of course subject to a heavy cannonade during the day, though without once being struck.

4

reality for the next four years our second home, and became the permanent one for a good many of the members, who there contracted ties of marriage and of business, and never returned to the Crescent City. There were none of us but what formed a large circle of friends of every class among the inhabitants, and as time wore on, we found a very large population from our own city gathered there, and in the surrounding camps. To take a Virginia soldier's impressions of Richmond from his pleasant recollections, would be the play of Hamlet with the part of the young lord of Denmark omitted. They were our gleams of sunshine.

But to return to camp. After the work of putting up tents, which we found to be a tremendous bore, the hour for evening drill had arrived, and a very large crowd had gathered to witness our manœuvres, including President Davis himself. We were overwhelmed with invitations to houses, and received them just as readily without any introductions, and inside of camp lines, as we did in private salons. I used to wonder how Romulus and his fellow-robbers, when they seized on the Sabine women—how they managed in the short time they had for acquaintance, to adapt their booty to individual taste—whether, for instance, the white whiskered robber, who had been compelled to take a sentimental prize, did not afterwards have to swap her off to some young comrade, in exchange for another that was domestic and who had no nonsense about her. But as far as making acquaintances went in our experience, it was astonishing how the different cliques and classes seemed almost instinctively or naturally to find out and adapt themselves to their own kind, whether they believed in blood, money, talent or education, whether carefully brought up or fond of a wild life, of a religious or business turn, or fond of intrigue and adventure. One of the latter sort, I remember who was on guard at the time of the parade, made a lady acquaintance which made him leave his post to accompany her home; which kept him in all sorts of scrapes for the balance of the war, and which years after led to the singular fainting away of "a star," (for she finally went on the stage,) in a way that the audience could not understand. By a singular sort of coincidence a second lady of the same party became attached and afterwards married to a soldier who was never once absent without leave, and is now well known in our city for his business capacity.

Discipline was very rigidly enforced, and the guard tent was the centre of intelligence, partly because of the details for duty from the various companies, partly because it was generally filled with offenders who had gone off to town without leave, and the narrative of whose adventures about every class of city society was fully as lively as the average newspaper chronicles. Though the guards were very strict (rendered doubly so because they themselves had probably already been caught and made to do extra duty) there never was any means found out for keeping the men in camp when there was no prospect of battle. They would cross the lines, apparently to go after water to bathe, or wash their clothes, (for we were already commencing to do this) and would show no alacrity about coming back. As the sight of a soldier dressed to go to the city would have been enough to have led to his arrest, the plan would be to start badly dressed with a bundle as if for washing, but which in reality contained the best suit. The washing in reality was mostly done by colored *blanchisseuses* who were constantly about camp. When this plan could not be worked at night, some such ruse as turning a horse loose and rushing after it would be resorted to.

Meanwhile in the matter of sleeping accommodations, we fared rather roughly, for a time. Our blankets were of the thinnest sort, and hardly large enough to envelope a cat. When you covered your feet, your breast would be uncovered, or a gentle zephyr would be playing about your ears or back. Besides, for the first night there was nothing between us and the ground, and we could not well get to sleep without undressing. If ever there was a thoroughly disgusted crowd when the bugle summoned us at day break to roll call, ours was that one. The complaints went to the officers, and the one especially in command could be heard harshly swearing about everybody and everything all through camp. That was the worst day we ever had for growling and rough talk. Then too we had nothing to eat but very tough fried beef, cut in small rhomboids, instead of the magnificent flaps of porter-house steak to which many of us had been accustomed. One of the companies had an excellent cook, J. H. Ingraham, who has since become conspicuous among the colored members of the Legislature;* but Joe, the one we had, was such a travesty upon the noble *chefs* of the Crescent City, dressed in paper caps and white aprons, that it made us furious to hear him lying, chattering and frying, as if in defiance of our misery. Joe subsequently gratified us by deserting to the enemy, and figuring very largely as an intelligent and well informed contraband. In some of McClellan's reports the northern papers spoke about giving him an important command.

―――――――――

*Dick Kenner, one of our cooks, has also since been a member of the Legislature.

CHAPTER V.

SURE-ENOUGH SOLDIERING.

WE remained about Richmond, awaiting orders, several weeks,* undergoing daily a good deal of hard drilling,

* The following is a letter written by Fishback to the N. O. Crescent, dated July 7, 1861 :
"The third and fourth companies of the Washington Batallion artillery leave to-day for Manassas Gap, whither the first two companies have already preceded them.
A delay in obtaining the cannon, harness and drivers, the latter still wanting, has thus far detained them from what is known as "the scene of action." We leave Camp Beauregard with few regrets. Heat, cold, dust, rains, flies—each tent looked as if a swarm of bees had been hived in it—altogether, contributed to make us the most wretched band of patriots upon whose heads ever descended a hot sun or drenching rain. It was a soldier's life with all its hardships, with none of its pleasures or excitements. Our only amusement was cleaning sabres, mounting guard, going through the motion of loading cannon, and lastly, sleeping under the shade of two stunted trees—the only chance for shade there was in the camp. And then, too, to be so near town, and not be able to get there oftener on an average than once a week! The old steeples and roof-tops, as looked down from our camp upon the southern metropolis, was for us an enchanted city—something about which we might sigh, dream about, and form strange fancies, but could not often see. Any one who obtained two "permits" during the week was viewed with considerable envy and jealousy, and when he returned with his pockets filled with candy, sweetmeats and whisky, and told big stories of having dined with Jeff. Davis, and advised his Cabinet officers, we regarded him in the light of a distinguished traveler just returned from some remote land.
I do not know what we should have done, if we had not at length grown weary of so much camp life, and learned to pass the sentinels' lines without always remembering to give the countersign. We began to make acquaintances, to accept invitations to houses, and there were vague rumors which hinted at successes among the fair sex of a more enduring kind.
For myself, my modesty led me to be satisfied with the friendship of a pretty widow, the relict, I think, of some deceased butcher; and I can't boast that I ever succeeded in obtaining from her partiality more than an occasional beefsteak or mutton chop
Returning late one night, I concluded to sleep till tattoo upon a long bench which occupied the side of our stable, stealing from a horse his bundle of hay for a pillow. I suffered considerably from nightmare, and on awakening was not a little astonished to find pillow, straw hat, and the best part even of my flannel shirt, all gone.
The streets of Richmond are crowded with almost as many soldiers in uniforms as were those of Paris in the Allied Occupations of 1815. I walked all over the city without counting more than ten young men who were not dressed *a la militaire*. Bar rooms and hotels are coining money—your plain drinks, (whiskeys, for instance, which cost, perhaps, twenty-five cents per gallon) sell for fifteen cents a glass, and mint juleps and sherry cobblers at twenty-five cents, so that a campaign of six months would be in what the soldier gets for pay worth exactly three hundred and sixty-five drinks!
We are limbering up our cannon ("Key up that sponge-staff there") for the last time here, and the men are filing off ("Never make the turn until the word, march")

and becoming accustomed to our new duties, (which at first we found extremely irksome, and which took up most of our time) as best we could. The men when not on guard duty, drilling, policeing camp, loading the ammunition chests, would hunt the shade of small trees, and only move with the shadow, or would be seen stretched out in the tents, like so many sullen, discontented animals, in the depths of a cave, glaring out angrily and selfishly from their limited quarters at every intruder.*

By this time, having in our leisure nothing to do but sleep, notice and comment on individual character, we had come to be pretty well acquainted with each other's failings and strong points. Like every other organization, the Batallion had its aristocracy and popular favorites, and coming, as we did, from a large business centre, those who had been previously engaged in commercial pursuits gave the tone to the balance of the organization—the book-keepers and *attachés* of the large cotton, commission and grocery houses assuming, or having accorded to themselves the first rank. Those whose opportunities as clerks had thrown them much with the every day world, had sufficient powers of self-assertion to claim probably the next grade, while, as likely as not, the men with the most learning, the deepest experience, rarest talent, and eccentricities, generally were regarded rather shyly in the mess

for the last drill; and now having packed our knapsacks, pitched our tents, and kissed the sweethearts we leave behind, you will see us for the future more actively employed, with the scowl of battle upon our face, and hanging upon the flying ranks of the foe."

*Some such speech as the following, was very commonly heard : "Now don't all of you come piling in here, unless you want to knock the tent down; there's some cussed galoot that makes it a point to stumble over the tent ropes and pins every time he passes, who has nearly done it already."

"Come, Tom, take a rest, and dry up. You've managed to smuggle in the best canteen of whiskey brought into camp, and you can't throw off on old friends that way. Out with it."

And after one more growl about bringing around the whole Batallion, the coveted canteen would be reluctantly handed over.

and social relations of camp. For instance, a French Colonel who had accompanied us as a volunteer, hardly became known by name, and would never have been promoted to the rank of a Corporal. The same was true of one or two Prussian officers. Of the half dozen lawyers, and the same number of writers, none of them were much thought of—that is in the first year of soldiering. But the truth was, that the men of most ability had no opportunity of showing their special talent, and had but little of any other kind—generally becoming disgusted with camp life among the first, and too contemptuous or despairing of the scanty honors within their reach, to take the trouble to obtain them. "The world is full of the successes of common place men," says the proverb, and undoubtedly the working characters of every day life made the best soldiers with us.

The real aristocracy, however, in the harsh life of a camp—as well as everywhere else—which outranks all others, is that which can always command money, and which knows how to spend it. On a long march in after years, it is astonishing, when provisions are scarce, how much respect we can have for a comrade who has money enough to buy a loaf of bread for himself as well as his poorer mess-mate. Such a man would be forthwith invited to join the best messes, and be allowed to shirk, if not the entire mess work, at least its roughest parts; and his influence in obtaining leave of absence, a horse to ride, or some body to stand his extra guards, would extend throughout the camp.

The best men would frequently fail of commanding much influence, through modesty and the absence of a stirring, bustling disposition. There, for instance, was Professor Gessner, well known now in our city as an accomplished teacher, who was scarcely known in camp, except as a faithful, brave soldier; and the same remark would apply to Ernest Byer, the present Prussian Consul at Mobile, and who has since made a fortune in buying cotton. Corporal Coyle has since found it easier to control the coal or towboat business than he did in four years service, to get made Sergeant; while our well known Notary of the present day, A. J. Hero, though the smallest man in the company, through his vigilance, energy and unremitting attention to his duties, became Captain of the Third Company.

In what has been said in our social distinctions, reference is had rather to the make up and material of the Batallion as we started out, than to its character, as we soldiered on. The young snob who believed implicitly in blood, in his father's wealth, family position, or felt elevated above ordinary mortality from having obtained a fat situation in a banking house or insurance company, got bravely over these ideas as he soldiered further on—forgot to part his hair in the middle, and learned to regard men rather by their worth than their artificial position. On the other hand, those who were not known at all at starting, in many instances continued to obtain influential places in the Quartermaster's or Commissary department, and make their influence felt in the distribution of rations. The tendency of this class, who were generally thought to be partial, and were therefore unpopular, was to assume style and airs in proportion to their power; however small and insignificant our honors, we liked to have them recognized for what they were worth.

In the last year of the war, when the provisions given out for three days could have been easily consumed at one meal, I received with several others, an invitation to take dinner with the Commissary of our company. Although we had nothing but fried middling and baker's bread for our repast, no reader at this day can realize how much awe the hospitality of our Amphytrion inspired, even in the breasts of some of the higher officers who happened to be present. As each guest present felt in honor bound to eat only a fair share of the delicacies spread before us, one can judge how much of the company's rations had been actually stolen; the effect however of these gorgeous spreads, was to create the impression that the detailed commissaries were reveling in the luxury of Lucullus; or something like the celebrated banquet given years ago in this city, where a politician on the verge of ruin, spent in one night $40,000 in entertaining his friends.

There were a good many other classes that might be named, such as the class who continued to obtain soft places, and to shirk duty by flattery and playing in a very modest role as courtiers—such too as the musical choirs—a class much envied, who through their talents were always welcomed, not unfrequently to the exclusion of less fortunate rivals.

Having stated thus much of the critisisms which soldiers, for absence of other employment, passed upon each other, it is but just to add, that with no hope of glory or of doing more than what every man ought to do for his country, they bore their trials, the meanest of them, with excellent spirit. Their miseries which were indeed great, were met with no discontent. There was no crime— there were no murmurs—and there waa a patient acquiescence in orders, except when men were detailed to be away from the battle field, and these were hardly ever obeyed.

CHAPTER VI.

OUR FIRST BATTLE.

Having bade adieu to civilization and comfort at Richmond, a dusty day and night of travel brought us to Manassas. I remember nothing of this, except that there were two or three ill-natured disputes among the men who were out of humor about seats, and that the farther we traveled, the less impressed seemed the world, at the sight of a soldier's uniform. It was evident that the farmers, so far from regarding us as patriots, were concerned only about the best means of preserving their fences and crops; our predecessors in soldiering had taught them this much already. Instead of fair women to welcome us with flowers, we saw if we got out of the cars, only cynical landlords who regarded with an evil eye any attempt at a free use of his water or towels, or who would indulge in sneering remarks in reference to a lavish extravagance in the matter of soap.

Arrived at the depot, which was afterwards to become so identified with our recollections of Virginia, we were set to work in the hot sun at getting off our guns, horses, and ammunition chests. We had then to take the road to "Camp Louisiana," whither two of our companies, 1st and 2nd, had already preceded us. We found them pleasantly entrenched on the south bank of Bull Run, in rows of tents connected by an arbor shade, and which latter was as great a luxury to us as Jonah's Gourd was to the much complaining prophet. Our comrades who preceded us consoled us for our fatigue and travel, by welcoming us to a dinner on beans—equivalent on the field to covers at Fritz's or John's at this day. Still it was not without some agony and depression of soul, that we came down to sheet-iron crackers, or hard-tack, or reconciled ourselves to the afterwards familiar smell of fried bacon, with which, to tell the truth, I have, ever since the war, associated military glory. Now commenced those longings for sweetmeats and vegetables with which our soldiers for four years were consumed, and so hardly, indeed, did it fare with us in diet, that the most intellectual men in the Batallion probably spent more time in painful or envious thought as to the best means of obtaining pies, chickens and eggs than we did on any other subject—patriotism, danger, home and sweethearts, all included.

Those were the days when alarms were of very frequent occurrence—when the imagination was excited by talk of masked batteries, black horse cavalry, "Tigers," Zouave slaughters, and the like—when cautious sentinels would watch the ears of horses to discern the first tread of the foe, (thirty miles distant) or when the return of the battery-horses from watering, would lead to a rush of the guard to arms, or to the prancing around of the officer of the day with a drawn sabre, and a tremendous shout to the off-duty men to "Fall in." I remember one fine looking officer, dark, bushy whiskered, and covered with a red-lined cloak, who went through the pantomime of rushing to meet the whole of McDowell's army, so dramatically—in the style of Forrest, say—that we all voted him, in camp talk, promotion at once.

But at last the alarm which we had felt in our bones for days previous did come—a rocket had been seen—as well as a pillar of smoke, and these marked the approach of the enemy. The most prudent betook ourselves to packing and looking after rations—bathers came in from the Run; idlers quit lazing in the shade, and even the cooks who were dancing or singing around the camp fires, became silent and watchful. We did not wait long—soon came the bugle sound to "Hitch up," and of "Boots and saddle," and in a moment all was confusion. In less than an hour afterwards the white tents had disappeared and we were galloping off to positions assigned us at the various fords.*

I was lying on a caisson the next day, reading an old farmhouse novel, when we saw the enemy appear on the opposite heights. I did not believe then it was worth while turning down a leaf, even when we could see the gleam of the sun on their brass pieces or arms. A light curl of smoke, followed by a shot, which we could see coming towards us, and which looked like an India rubber ball thrown through the air, convinced us that the first shot had been actually fired. We shifted our position—as their guns were of longer range—and soon saw our line of infantry moving towards the Run. The regiments that then moved forward were mostly composed of sanguine impetuous young men, the pick of the fighting material of the South, who moved forward with loud shouts and an exultant swing at the prospective combat, and who were so impulsive and imprudent, that they threw away their knapsacks and blankets in order to have more freedom of movement. They felt the need of them badly before we were through with our fighting.

As the day advanced (the 18th of June) the enemy made an attempt to cross the Run—our batteries were shoved forward, the infantry opened fire, which rattled

*General Evans of South Carolina, was the first to lead his Brigade into action at Stone Bridge. It consisted of the Fourth South Carolina Regiment and Wheat's Louisiana Batallion. Sustaining them, was General Cocke's Brigade, consisting of the 17th, 19th and 28th Virginia Regiments, commanded respectively by Cols. Cocke, Withers, and Robert T. Preston. These Brigades were the first to bear the brunt of the action, as they were exposed to a concentric fire, the object of the enemy being to turn our left flank while we were endeavoring to turn his right. These regiments of infantry were sustaining the famous Washington Artillery, of New Orleans, who had two of their guns at this point, which made terrible havoc in the ranks of the enemy.—*Richmond Dispatch*, July 6th.

along the line in murderous volleys, and the skirmish or battle of Bull Run was brought on.

It was just as much of a battle, so far as our artillery was concerned, as any we afterwards were in, as we were under heavy fire and continued in action until the fight was decided. It had been commenced, according to Swinton, through the "silly ambition" of Gen. Tyler, "who got it into his head that the enemy would run whenever seriously menaced." In pursuance of a belief that the man that got Manassas would be the great man of the war, and of an intention, as he expressed it, "to go through that night," he drew up his forces on Bull Run parallel to the Confederate troops, and opened an unmeaning fusillade. The result did not correspond to his expectations. The Confederates did not scare worth a cent; on the contrary, they suddenly charged across with a loud yell, and astonished Tyler by completely disrupting his left flank. Meanwhile the guns of the Washington Artillery, which had been distributed about, at the various fords, kept up an active fire until the foe had disappeared.

The following memoranda of the affair of the 18th, was made by Adjutant (afterwards Lieut Colonel) Owen, to whose journal frequent reference will be made in these pages:

"Camp was broken up on the 17th, owing to the driving in of our pickets and the advance of the enemy. Troops withdrawn from north side of Bull Run. Baggage was ordered to Manassas; bivouacked in a pine thicket, near McLean's. Guns placed at McLean's and Blackburn's Fords; we were roused on the 18th, before day, the batteries getting closer to the fords, and one detachment being sent to Union Mills. Zouaves seen moving about in the woods on opposite heights."

A portion of the second and third companies were ordered to Blackburn's ford. Geo. W. Muse, a young man of much promise and amiability was the first victim of the war in the Batallion. Gen. Beauregard, after the engagement, sent us word that we had behaved "like veterans."

The troops kept about their same positions during the following day, though subject to frequent movements and alarms. At a consultation of our Generals, held at McLean's house, afterwards used as a hospital, Beauregard said on the 20th, " Let to-morrow be our Waterloo." If his prediction had been carried out, for which the Confederate Army had every facility in the route of Manassas, it is not too much to suppose that the history of the Confederate war would have been somewhat different from what it is.

The following was the report of Gen. Beauregard, of the action of the Washington Artillery upon the 18th of July:

"It was at this stage of the affair that a remarkable artillery duel was commenced and maintained on our side with a long trained professional opponent, superior in character as well as in the number of his weapons, provided with improved munitions and every artillery appliance, and at the same time occupying the commanding position. The results were marvelous and fitting precursors to the artillery achievements of the 21st of July. In the outset, our fire was directed against the enemy's Infantry, whose bayonets, gleaming above the tree-tops, alone indicated their presence and force. This drew the attention of a battery placed on a high, commanding ridge, and the duel began in earnest. For a time, the aim of the adversary was inaccurate, but this was quickly corrected, and shot fell and shells burst thick and fast in the very midst of our battery, wounding in the course of the combat, Capt. Eshleman, five privates, and the horse of Lieut. Richardson. From the position of our pieces, and the nature of the ground, their aim could only be directed at the smoke of the enemy's artillery; how skilfully and with what execution this was done, can only be realized by an eye witness. For a few moments their guns were silenced, but soon reopened. By direction of Gen. Longstreet, his battery was then advanced by hand, out of the range now ascertained by the enemy, and a shower of spherical case, shell and round shot flew over the heads of our gunners; but one of our pieces had become *hors de combat* from an enlarged vent. From the new position our guns fired as before, with no other aim than the smoke and flash of their adversaries' pieces, renewed and urged the conflict with such signal vigor and effect, that gradually the fire of the enemy slackened, the interval between their discharges grew longer and longer, finally to cease, and we fired a last gun at a baffled, flying foe, whose heavy masses in the distance were plainly seen to break and scatter in wild confusion and utter rout, strewing the ground with cast away guns, hats, blankets and knapsacks, as our parting shells were thrown among them. In their retreat one of their pieces was abandoned, but, from the nature of the ground, it was not sent for that night, and under cover of darkness the enemy recovered it."

The guns engaged in this singular conflict on our side, were three 6-pounder rifle pieces, and four ordinary 6-pounders, all of Walton's battery—the Washington Artillery of New Orleans. The officers immediately attached, were Capt. Eshleman, Lieuts. C. W. Squires, Richardson, Garnet and Whittington. At the same time our infantry held the bank of the stream, in advance of our guns, as the missiles of the combatants flew to and fro above them; as cool and veteran-like, for more than an hour, they steadily awaited the moment and signal for the advance.

CHAPTER VII.

BATTLE OF MANASSAS.

The battle of Manassas was, in many respects, the most curious, and at the same time, the least eventful of the war. If the Federals had given battle on Saturday instead of Sunday, (the 21st of July,) they would have encountered the Confederate army without Johnston's command, whose men, as it was, only arrived at the most critical moment. If the Federals had delayed their attack a few hours longer, Beauregard, dreading Patterson's arrival, would have attacked them, with all the advantages of position on their side. In no battle of the war was there so much of the heroic element developed; the leading generals fought like private soldiers. Gen. Johnston threw himself into the thickest of the fight, and led the gallant 8th Georgia Regiment on with their glorious colors in his hand; Beauregard charged at the head of Hampton's Legion. He was riding up and down the lines between the enemy and our men, thoroughly combative, shouting them on with desperate ardor. Still the battle was going against us. Bee, Bartow, Fisher, Branch and all the field officers of some regiments were killed while struggling to maintain the Confederate line. This was being slowly driven back a mile and a half. But now the quick eye of Jackson discovers a weakly guarded battery and swoops down upon it; Beauregard at the same time pushed forward to regain his line, and so the chances went balancing from one side to the other—the Confederates at one moment driving, at the next being driven. Finally, while Johnston, like Wellington about Blucher, was sighing for his additional regiments to appear in sight, Kirby Smith, who had come fifteen miles since the battle commenced, now rushes forward, and though he falls wounded, cheer after cheer from the Confederates tells that the battle is won.* The rest was but the stampede of a panic-stricken army towards Washington.†

We make the following further extracts from Adjutant Owen's report:

"Gen. Kirby Smith coming up on the left, the enemy are routed; we firing the last gun. At 4 P. M. I rode over the field and saw the effects of battle for the first time. Men lay killed and wounded on every side—broken muskets, pieces of clothing and dead horses and disabled cannon were scattered about.

"We had been fighting Sherman's, Griffin's and Sprague's Rhode Island Batteries. In the panic they left all their guns where they had been fighting, near Mrs. Henry's

---

*His coming up, I heard one soldier remark, was like the throwing of four aces upon a poker table. There was nothing more to be done but to sweep in the stakes.

†JULY 21.—Enemy shelling different portions of our line from the high ground on the other side of Bull Run; it is evident we will have another battle to-day.

7 A. M.—Five guns under Capt. Squires ordered to Lewis House, near the Stone Bridge. Enemy moving towards our left; Evans and Wheat fighting there and falling back. Two rifle guns ordered forward. Enemy still pushing us, and it now becomes evident, from the clouds of dust which rise over their line of march, that the enemy's main attack will be directed here. Gens. Beauregard and Johnston ride by us; fresh troops ordered up; our guns ordered in. We go into position under heavy fire, and fight the enemy's batteries around Henry House. Jos. Reynolds falls mortally wounded. In the thickest of the battle Gen. Beauregard, Capts. Chisholm and Hayward ride up. Gen. B. said to Col. Walton, in passing,

"Hold this position there, and the day is ours. Three cheers for Louisiana."

The cheer was taken up on our right and left and ran the whole length of the battle line. At this instant the General's horse had his head shot off, and his Aid took Sergt. Owen's mare, much to the latter's disgust.—*Batallion Journal.*

house. She, poor old lady, was between two fires, and was killed in bed. We buried her in her garden.

"Lieut. Dearing and I brought in the colors of the 2d Michigan Regiment, and gave them to Gen. Beauregard. 5 P. M. President Davis arrives from Richmond—is received with great cheering. The pursuit has been checked; why we cannot tell. It is reported the enemy are going at "double" for Washington. Bivouac on the field."

The fact that the last gun of the day was fired by our battery will be confirmed by the following from the Petersburg *Daily Express*, July 26th, 1861:

"The Washington Artillery, who had drawn their guns up the hill and in front of the house known as Mr. Lewis'—Gen. Cocke's and Gen. Johnston's headquarters, and which was riddled with shot—commanded by Major J. B. Walton in person, gave the enemy about this time a parting salute.   *   *

"Before the ball had well reached the point aimed at, a whole regiment of the enemy appeared in sight, going at the "double quick" down the Centreville road. Major Walton immediately ordered another shot "to help them along," as he said, and two were sent without delay right at them. There was no obstruction, and the whole front of the regiment was exposed. One-half were seen to fall, and if Gen. Johnston had not at that moment sent an aid to Major Walton, with an order to cease firing, nearly the whole regiment would have been killed."

Draper, in his history of the war, says that the panic was produced by the jam over one of the bridges, and the unexpected explosion of a shell in the midst of the fugitives.

Considering that the route of the Federal army was complete, the most astonishing thing in the world was that none of the desperate ardor that had characterized the generals and troops came to the surface now. The promptness of Evans, on our left flank, in forming a new line of battle with a handful of men, different from what he had anticipated, together with the resistance of Wheat's (La.) Battalion, the 4th Alabama, and 8th Georgia, had stemmed the tide until the other Confederate troops, who were totally unprepared for the situation, could come up; in other words, about all the generalship that was displayed or much needed, was to animate the troops on the ground, and to shove in the balance as fast as they arrived on the field. But when the battle was over, the leading actors were either killed, worn out, or ignorant of their victory, or incapable of profiting by it. I remember seeing some officers stop, before charging, to read the news of the glorious victory to a brigade who had not been in the fight at all, and the slowness with which the brigade moved off in pursuit, contrasted strongly with the impetuous rushes which the men learned at a later day to make. It is hardly credible to think of our attacking afterwards impregnable positions like Gettysburg and Malvern Hill, and showing lack of the requisite fire in the moment of victory. A little of the daring of Cortes or Pizarro was what we needed. Jackson, who had been pointed out as standing like a stonewall, and whose cry of, "We must give them the bayonet," had largely decided the battle, earlier in the day—Jackson had too little influence to control, and neither he nor Longstreet (the men on whom Lee afterwards principally relied,) had fairly come to the surface. We had three commanders-in-chief during the day, and it was to the weakness of some one of them that our cavalry charged only for a mile or two. As Greeley truly states, "there were hours of daylight when our troops rushed madly from the field like frightened sheep, yet their pursuit amounted to nothing." The truth was that the Federal army was in a great deal worse condition than Lee in his final retreat, (who took two hundred prisoners a few moments before surrendering at Appomatox Court-House,) and if the cavalry of Manassas had corresponded to that of our enemy's in the last fight, there is no reason why the whole of the Federal army should not have been bagged.

As for what followed after the battle,* all of the military rules were observed, and by ordinary prudential lights the war was prolonged as well this way as perhaps by any other means that could have been adopted. But this policy did not correspond to the wishes and dreams of the men, who were, from impatience of camp life and disci-

* *Extract from the Adjutant's Journal.*

JULY 22d—Raining this morning ; rode down the turnpike towards Centreville, the route of the fleeing column ; we pass large numbers of prisoners coming in; the road is strewn with guns, clothing and dead men ; abandoned ambulances and wagons—some filled with wine and luxuries of every kind. Many citizens, members of Congress and others, came with the Federal Army to "see the fun ;" ladies came as far as Centreville—we have seen several carriages coming in. At Cub Run suspension bridge, everything is jammed and smashed up. Capu red here a good supply of red blankets and overcoats, which were distributed o the men on returning to camp.

24—The enemy has fallen back to Washington, and everything is supposed to be in a great confusion. In fact, persons coming from there say, all organization is gone ; why we don't move on and enter Washington, Pres. Davis and Gen. Beauregard best know.

AUGUST 1st—Still encamped at our old camp-ground, going through the dull routine of camp life. We see many visitors daily who have come on to visit the battle field ; we are kept busy riding about and pointing out objects of interest ; enough of the exploded caissons belonging to Sherman's Battery, has been carried away to build a house ; we live splendidly : Chickens, eggs, vegetables, milk, ice, and claret, paté de foi gras, sardines, etc. Mr. Slidell of New Orleans, visits our camp ; we are now according to the papers, the *famous* Washington Artillery.

SEPT.—Change our camp to Centreville, call it Camp Orleans—it is laid out beautifully, and the Third Company has its streets covered by an arbor of branches and leaves.

OCT.—Move camp to Fairfax C. H., (Camp Benjamin.)

NOV.—The Army falls back to Centreville; fortification thrown up on the height; our camp is near Gen. Beauregard ; a new supply of tents have been sent us from New Orleans ; our camp looks very pretty.

DEC. 25—Begin building winter quarters on Bull Run, on the old battle field of the 18th July.

30—The winter quarter camp is laid out, regularly, with a street for each Company ; the houses are of logs, and are roofed with planks, and all have glass windows ; the officers have double houses, two rooms on a line and at right angles with the Company Street, the staff on a line in rear of the Company's Officers, the long stable for the horses are in front of the camp, as is also the park of Guns..

JAN.—Gen. Beauregard and Staff have left us : have been ordered to the West; much regret is felt at his being removed. Gen. Joe Johnston is in command ; we have but 30,000 men here, and learn that McClellan is massing a large force at Alexandria ; we anticipate a retreat from our present position ; we have some sport; one day it was fighting a snow ball battle with St. Paul's Chasseurs Battalion.

MARCH 6—Attached to Gen. Longstreet's Division by order of Gen. Johnston.

pline, compelled to die a thousand deaths, and rot away in idleness. In the same way that in times of revolution, the public prefers the bloodiest tragedies on the stage, or that the soldier selects the wildest and most bizarre novel for camp reading—in the same way ought our generals to have found work for an army, upon whose ranks, inaction was more fatal than the bullets of the enemy. For a cause that from the first could not hope for success, if continued on until one side or the other was exhausted, appeals to extraordinary motives should have been made, daring chances should have been encountered, the feelings and passions which make a frenzied people superior to all military force, should have been stirred up. To do something was the true policy of the Confederacy. Our troops were then the flower of the South, men capable of extraordinary things. They could have been made to disperse and re-assemble, in and out of the enemy's country—as was once done by a Roman conspirator who, finding his six hundred men surrounded, ordered each man to shift for himself and report at Rome, hundreds of miles distant. Any plan as wild for instance, as that of Mahomet and his few followers who broke down the Eastern Roman Empire, would have been better than slow strategy, where our enemy had every advantage in military resources, in the facility of filling up their regiments with foreigners, and in the more patient temper of the troops. The fact that the South sent so many men of education and accomplishments into the ranks, lying about camps idle for months, was an evidence of the devotion of her people, and at the same time of the heavy strain there was upon her. A man ignorant of fencing, and who fights without rules, will frequently disconcert his experienced antagonist; on the same principle having to meet a foe who would always be better prepared than himself for standing a long war, the South ought to have adopted a policy which savored rather of madness and desperation than one of retreats.

Possibly the war in this way would have been ended in a few months. If so the means suggested were the best. If otherwise, it ought to have been the best reason for preventing the total destruction of property in the South.*

*Col. J. B. Walton, states that the Batallion carried into various portions of the line on the 21st, thirteen guns under the commands of Miller, Lewis, Richardson, Squires, Rosser, Slocomb, Battles, Norcom, Garnett, and Whittington, three rifled six pounders, and the balance 4 twelve pound howitzers and smooth six pounders. The battery under Lieut. Squires, received the first fire from the enemy's guns. Fire was shortly after opened by Lieut. Richardson; Sergeant Owen dismounted one of the enemy's guns. About 10 A. M., the artillery was upon the crest struggled for during the day, subject to a terrific fire, the men working as silently and composedly as when on ordinary drill, until the fire of the enemy was silenced. About 1 P. M., Lieut. Squires took position on the Stone Bridge Road, and opened fire upon the retreating columns of the enemy until ordered (momentarily) by Gen. Johnston to save our ammunition; soon after, having obtained their range, our shots fell like target practice upon an enemy retreating by thousands. "The last gun of the 21st was fired from one of the rifles of my battery." Sergeant. J. D. Reynolds, killed—wounded, Corporal E. C. Payne, 1st Company; G. L. Crutcher, 4th Company.

Gen. Beauregard in his report says, that two pieces of the Washington Artillery under Richardson, four under Imboden, confronted Hentzleman's Division, and another at about 11 A. M. The Confederates then had only Evans, (Wheat's gallant Batallion,) Bee and Bartow, and two Companies of the 11th Miss. Against this odds, scarcely credible, our advanced position was for a while maintained, and the enemy's ranks constantly broken and shattered under the scorching fire of our men. Col. Early, with the 7th Va., and Hay's 7th La., came on the ground immediately after Elzy, and took position near the Chinn House, under a severe fire, outflanking the enemy's right. At this moment, under a combined attack all along the line, and by the aid of the fresh troops, we finally carried the contested plateau, and "Early's Brigade pursued the now panic-stricken enemy."—*Beauregard's report, battle of Manassas.*

Telegram sent of the Battle of Manassas.

RICHMOND, July 24—(*Crescent* 25th.) Out of the four hundred of Wheat's Command engaged, less than a hundred escaped being either killed or wounded. The Catahoula Guerillas, Capt. Bahoup, belonging to the Batallion, fought with desperation.

Letter from a member of Wheat's Batallion.

(*Crescent*, August 1st 1861.) On Sunday 21st, at sunrise, the enemy commenced throwing shot and shell among us; the enemy fired as if all hell had been set loose. Flat upon our faces we received their showers of balls; a moment's pause, and we rose, closed upon them with fierce yells, clubbing our rifles and using our long knives. This hand to hand fight lasted until fresh reinforcements drove us back—we carrying our wounded with us. Major Wheat was here

CHAPTER VIII.
CAMP LIFE.

After the battle, we had for some months* no other inci-

shot from his horse; Capt. White's horse was shot under him; our 1st. Lieut. Dick Hawkins, was wounded, shot through the breast and wrist, and any number of killed and wounded were strewn all about.

The New York Fire Zouaves, seeing our momentary confusion, gave three cheers and started for us, but it was the last shout that most of them ever gave. We covered the ground with their dead and dying, and had driven them beyond their first position, when just then we heard, three cheers for the Tigers, and Louisiana. The struggle was decided. The gallant Seventh had "double-quicked" it for nine miles, and came rushing into the fight. They fired as they came within point blank range, and charged with fixed bayonets.

When the fight and pursuit were over, we were drawn up in line and received the thanks of Gen. Johnston, for what he termed our extraordinary and desperate stand; Gen. Beauregard sent word to Major Wheat, "you, and your Batallion, for this day's work, shall never be forgotten, whether you live or die."

CAMP AND GENERAL RECORD.

*Our Batallion sustained, during its first year, a severe loss in the resignation of some of its best officers, among whom were Capt. Isaacson and Lieutenants Lewis, Slocomb, Whittington and Adams, whose talents had greatly contributed to the successful organization of the Batallion in its infancy, and most of whom afterwards did good service in other companies. The truth was, that an officers' duties involved so much constant care and trouble, that the position was scarcely to be envied, and we had a good many instances of officers from other corps who honored us by entering our ranks, and like D'Artagnon and his friends of the "Three Guardsmen," were contented to do the duty of a private soldier in preference to holding command.

AUG. 7.—The Louisiana troops now concentrated at Brenville, near Centreville. The 6th and 7th Regiments and Wheat's Batallion near by, Col. Seymour commanding. The time is now arrived for concentrating them all in one brigade. Hon. John Slidell and Warren Stone among the visitors.

AUG. 24th.—The Washington Artillery in New Orleans, turn over $1280 as the result of a concert given to assist destitute families.

AUG. 16.—Prince Napoleon (Plon-Plon) a guest of Beauregard for two days. The news was soon transmitted by some waggish skirmisher that "Old Fuss and Feathers" had been bagged at last, and the Prince enjoyed the joke largely, until a Georgia regiment was met, which manifested a disposition to anticipate the action of a court martial.

OCT. 20th, 1861.—The first and second company stationed on Munson's Hill. The first had been sent to different points on secret expeditions, one of which was going thirteen miles in the enemy's lines, surprising a camp, etc.

Nov. 26.—Amount expended and due for equipping State soldiers up to date, beside private contributions, $2,300,000. Gov. Moore states that "the Secretary of the Confederate States made his first requisition on me for three thousand volunteers in April. Before this was filled, the Secretary made a second requisition for five thousand men. In July a third was made for three thousand more. Eight of these regiments and two batallions are now in Virginia, one in Mississippi, three in Kentucky, and five within our own State. There have been besides fourteen companies of infantry mustered in for the special defence of this State, and four companies of artillery. Thirteen other companies are at Camp Lewis—making an aggregate of 20,202, raised by the State, besides, as I believe, 3891 men of independent organizations, or 24,003 in all."—*Governor Moore's Message*, Nov. 26, 1861.

dents in our life than the changing from one camp to another—the distribution of uniforms, drill, guard-mounting and an occasional detail to go with the wagons to Manassas Station to get corn and provisions. This latter duty or privilege, of riding in a six-mule wagon, driven at full speed, which almost jolted the teeth out of you, was regarded in somewhat the same light at that day as a drive over the shell road would be now. It was a happiness to get a half a dozen miles from camp, and besides that we had a chance of meeting up with friends from other organizations; and, if we had any money, of spending it. These meetings were not, however, generally very satisfactory, and resulted only in showing how men let down as they soldiered on. If the writer of the "Guide to Politeness" had had his rations of water limited to what he could carry in his canteen, it is doubtful whether he would have insisted so strongly that no man could be a gentleman who did not wash his face at least once every day. Possibly, too, in time he would have had his views modified as to the amount of mud upon a man's back or straw in his hair admissible in strictest drawing room etiquette. Count D'Orsay and Beau Brummel would in the end have become disgusted at having to substitute a tin plate, *a la* Jack Strop, for a Venitian mirror—to trying to imagine that his frying pan at dinner represented costly plate or Sevres china, or to using clothes brushes to which the backs of the battery horses might have advanced superior claims. We were so overwhelmed with absurd changes and variations upon all ordinary modes of living, that things became, after a while, as was said by the Texan (when he saw every thing he owned burned down or destroyed) "perfectly ridiculous."

The worst of it was, too, that though somebody was

always falling a victim to these *contre temps* or innovations, the jokes gotten off about them would not always be of the most original or outrageously funny sort. They seldom, for many of us, amounted to much beyond awakening a sad smile, the first time they were told; and they did not pan out any better as they grew in age. But with the majority they wore well, like army clothing; and they were a well-spring of joy to a good many old buffers, whose hearty haw-haws would at the same time reward the narrators, each time they were told, and threaten the stability of our rather rickety tents.

One of these standing camp jokes I may as well mention here, as an illustration of what tent-life is in summer, rather than from any fondness for inflicting old stories. It was about some man who went dead in some particularly hot camp, and whose ghost, some nights after, haunted his old comrades; not because of any remorse, or for the reasons that ghosts usually come. The ghost's real reason, he stated in answer to a cross-examination upon the subject was, that hell was so cold compared with the heat of camp, that the place seemed to have burned down and frozen over, and he had consequently got a leave of absence to come back for his blanket. This joke had a big run in both armies; in fact there was only one other that was oftener quoted; that of the sutler who found he had to compete in selling whisky with a chap who had gone behind his tent, and who, with aid of a gimlet, was underselling him from the sutler's own barrel. One of the yarns said to have secured the passage of the conscript law, was told of an officer who had leave of absence to go home and raise a volunteer regiment, six months after we learned what soldiering was. When the Secretary of State inquired how he was getting on, the officer reported that he had not yet made any enlistments, but that he had had his eye on a d—d fine looking recruit.

In the days when it began to be said that one had to take a good wallow in the mud to make himself respectable, the visitor who had the hardihood to appear in camp in citizen's clothes had a terrible gauntlet to run in the way of advice, suggestions and comments. How many kind voices would extend him invitations to "Come out of that hat," with such corroborative hints thrown out to convince him that he ought to act promptly, as that his legs were "sticking out." It would be pointed out that his Parrot shell hat might explode; and if a timid turn, he would be agonizingly warned for "God sake to lie down, we are going to explode a cap." The joke was not always confined to the civilian; it was just as exasperating if you were a grand officer and prancing around in gold lace, to create no other effect than the shout of, "Here's your mule."

But as has already been said, a soldier's life is too hard, too much like that of a frontiersman or gambler's, to admit of much sentiment or generosity. The instinct of self-preservation prevails; "everything for me—nothing for you" was the rule generally carried out. Men in those days who had been accustomed at home to jovial dissipation in midnight suppers, with a crowd of similar spirits, bent on amusement or excitement, would sometimes go off alone to the station, from the various regiments and make a small investment in fire water. Now, happiness! This would consist in stealing off to the shade of a fence corner, or of getting under the wagon, if its protection had not already been previously pre-empted, and the happy proprietor would then think that happiness consisted in having a full canteen, and being untroubled by flies. Soldiering, which is founded on rough military rule inculcates the principle of looking very carefully after self, and it is not easy to remember many names who very often lost sight of this rule—possibly because they had nothing to give, but there were times when, in spite of the hard life by which we were surrounded, their better nature would crop out. We could give our lives for our country, but found it hard frequently to divide some trifling comfort.

But once in a while the old spirit would flash up, and the generous disposition shine forth. For instance, it was the fortune of one of us at the battle of Manassas to get run over by a caisson full of ammunition, and with eight or ten men on it besides. The battle was not over, and any one who had a flask of liquor, was likely enough to need it himself. This fact, however, did not keep Jack C—— from generously extending the last drink in his flask. To know the value of this act, one must have soldiered or traveled across the plains.

On the other hand a wounded man of an adjoining regiment was carried off by a comrade from where he was, bleeding to death, and sent to a hospital, where he recovered. The two men came together again in Pizini's Restaurant—the wounded man eating ice-cream, his brother soldier without a cent of money, and as hungry as a thirty miles march could make him. The man who had been wounded did take the trouble to lay down his spoon long enough to shake hands, but that was all. His omission to offer his comrade a crnst of bread probably arose from forgetfulness or lack of more money, as he at any rate gave his life to his country.

Once a man who had one of his legs shot off, begged so hard for his life that some of us picked him up and carried him away, although it was rather a neglect of duty, as the firing might at any moment have recommenced. This poor fellow had a pocket book containing $2.50 which he gave to one of us to carry, and which was handed back to him when he was put down. The man counted over the Confederate money attentively, in spite of the pain he must have suffered from his wound, and rather intimated that twenty-five cents were missing. But he got over this feeling presently, and then offered us about fifteen cents a piece for having saved his life. It was a noble offer on his part, as he proceeded to tell us that he was wounded and helpless, and would need the money more than we did.

Some of us helped off a Federal soldier who was similarly wounded; he afterwards met one of our command as a prisoner, and gave him a piece of tobacco, and an old knife, both of which he begged from somebody else, by way of showing that he wished to do what was right. Some such gossiping comments as those above made, would occur as likely as not, while we were marching side by side on the road, when some comrade had been sufficiently rich and generous to buy a flask of liquor and divide its contents with his friends, or where a detail had purchased the article by forming a joint stock association. I shall tell, and then proceed, one more incident which I heard in a similar crowd, by way of showing that we sometimes become hard-feeling and brutal, but afterwards saw our selfishness in its truest light: Tom C—— was a gallant Louisiana Sergeant, who had been wounded in every fight he went into, and whose position near the colors made it certain in his own mind that he always would have the same luck. Passing through Atlanta towards the close of the war, on his way to Chattanooga, he mentioned his presentment to a relative, who told him to telegraph back any casualty he might meet with, if he had a chance. C—— went into battle, his color-sergeant was wounded and the colors fell on C——. He had not proceeded far with them, before he was shot through both hips. A friend gave him a plug of tobacco and a canteen of water, promised to send his telegram, and the regiment moved on. The doctor came around and refused to move him or dress his wound, as it appeared beyond cure, and thousands of others were suffering. Tom lay there for two days, was carried from the field by his relative, and ultimately recovered enough to hobble about on crutches.

About the time he had recovered enough for him to take the cars and go home, a comrade came to the same house whom Tom had once helped when in great danger, and which comrade, if he had been so disposed, could now have rendered Tom a good many little services. But his friend did nothing of the sort. Tom, who was not only very polite and respectful, but almost reverent towards every woman, had found warm friends in the household among the lady inmates, who rightly regarded him as a hero, and had it not been for the coming of his handsome and showy comrade, probably Tom, in spite of his crippled condition, would have carried away the heart of one of the party. But after his fellow soldier's arrival a cloud came over Tom's fortunes; his simple stories, and honest, artless comments upon life lost their freshness and charm; his sweetheart took or seemed to take a fancy for his comrade, and he began to suspect that his friends were getting weary of rendering service to a cripple. He left one morning with a heavy heart. He had to start at daylight on a chilly, tempestuous morning, and as it was with the utmost difficulty Tom could drag one foot along after the other, he had hoped that his comrade would take interest enough in him to help him into the carriage, and assist him at the cars. But this comrade who had been talking to the ladies late the night before, and who was very sleepy at the moment of departure, did nothing of the sort. He simply rubbed off enough sleep from his eyes to be able to yawn a "Good bye, old fellow—if I wasn't so d—d sleepy I'd go and help you off." This was the last that the two men saw of each other.

But if Tom had seen the ladies at the breakfast table, and seen especially the flashing eyes of the young lady he loved, he would not have been unavenged. His comrade was told plainly that she could not see how one soldier could be so profoundly selfish and indifferent to a wounded fellow soldier; and there were no more smiles henceforth for him in that house.

The man that told the story said it was himself that had treated Tom C. so badly; and he thought his conduct was as shabby as the ladies had represented, when he had been a little while longer out of camp, and began to look at things unbiassed by the selfishness which soldiering naturally makes.

I speak about such little incidents, because every man worth speaking of, had to do or see some practical soldiering, and in all probability held an obscure position and has a hundred little remembrances in his own history similar to the above. Nearly every reader knows how it was himself, because in all likelihood he as a good citizen, "just went along," without bothering much about the matter, whether he was a soldier, or held high position. There are other and better narratives, which tell of our brilliant officers who were every moment galloping by with jingling spurs, gold lace and scarlet sashes; and who for all mention made of the soldier in their pages—did pretty much all the service and hard fighting by themselves. It deserves however to be stated, while confining myself mainly to an outline of a soldier's life, that nearly all of our Southern officers, were too proud to fare any better than their men; and practically in their lives, carried out the example of Alexander, when he threw away a cup of water in presence of his thirsty troops.

It deserves to be said that they went in with all of their combativeness to the surface—bracing themselves in the stirrup, with a lusty wave of their sword, and using a musket like a soldier; or later in the war, sitting still on horseback meditatively, as if each man in a regiment had learned what to do, and as if it was better not to bother it with any interference in action, or interruption. The latter was really the style of fighting that prevailed with the veteran regiments. The men kept on as long as they felt that they were doing any good, and then if not satisfied, as if putting it to a vote, would stalk disgustedly off. The tone of the officers in the few cases, when no general command had been given to fall back, would be that of obstinate jurors, or that of a man in a stage-coach who has been detained, and asks his fellow-passengers to wait with him a little while longer, till he gets through with his dinner. An officer's troops would always stay with him, when there seemed to them any sense in the men keeping on, and sometimes would refuse to retire, when ordered to fall back. The best evidence of this, is the fact in such battles as Malvern Hill and Gettysburg, the storming brigades of the Confederate troops lost forty-four per ct. more than Napoleon ever lost or than was lost in the Franco-German war. The official reports of Gen. Gordon showed that the losses amounted to one man in every three wounded—one man in every ten, killed in one battle, not to speak of absentees or prisoners.. There were brigades where the killed and wounded were over one half.

CHAPTER IX.

A WARLIKE HOTEL.

I OUGHT not to have left so far behind all mention of Manassas station, which point every soldier had more or less occasion to visit during the first year of the war, and about which every one who then did duty has probably a thousand recollections to relate. Apart from its military value, it was the most uninteresting place in existence. In rainy weather, when the wagon trains of the whole army came to it every day, the mud was at least two feet deep— so deep that a horse would sink up to his belly, or in walking a square on foot, one would have his boots pulled off his feet, at least a half dozen times. Beside the cake and pie stands, the most conspicuous feature about the station was Belcher's Hotel—a building almost as large as the City Hotel, though the prices for meals and lodging were rather higher. The walls were rushed up very much like a barn or stable, where the wind on cold nights would whistle through the cracks or intervals of the planks, which were at least a half inch apart. The building was too stories high, and was heated when cold weather came on by an immense stove whose smoke all settled inside.

There was always a large crowd surrounding the stove, though they never remained in their seats more than ten minutes at a time, on account of the smoke. Most of the men who surrounded it appeared like the Blind Calendars mentioned in the Arabian Nights story, and sat with their eyes firmly closed. Candles about the building were consequently of no use. The last thing you did at night was to wash your eyes in cold water, if you could find any, and the first thing in the morning—to get out of the building as quick as you could, strike for camp, and swear you would never enter it again. It was destroyed, with everything about Manasses, when Gen. Johnston made the first of his everlasting retreats, together with a very large amount of Commissary stores, and every other building there was about the place.

We had occasion to do some hard fighting in a few miles of this famous depot, when Lee was chasing Pope out of his "Head-quarters (or hind-quarters as the joke was) in the saddle;" but we never got to see it again until after the war. At that time the innumerable wagon roads that seemed to lead everywhere, had disappeared, though the fences were still absent. But the town of Manassas has sprung up more prosperously than it had ever been known to be before. A new quarry of red sandstone had been discovered—new stores had been erected from this, as well as a printing office, and a comfortable hotel. Faint traces of the old breast-works could just be discovered, overgrown with grass, and that was all.

One of the pleasantest of our resting places I can remember, was one known as Camp Orleans. This was, perhaps, on account of the shade—perhaps because we had some distance to go for water, and thus had a better opportunity of getting out of camp limits. The spring was the great centre of attraction for our own batallion, two or three Louisiana regiments, and the Tigers, Guerrillas and other companies, who composed the gallant Colonel Wheat's Batallion. A little distance off was a little village, known as Centreville, pretty much abandoned by its ancient inhabitants to sutlers, ready made forts, quaker guns and all the paraphernalia of war. I remember nothing in the way of incident connected with the place, except the pleasure we all experienced at the commencement of the Indian Summer, at sometimes having to stand guard over the Commissary tent, where there were sometimes a few perquisites of office, and at once having an opportunity of rescuing a couple of ladies from a runaway team of horses. That is, the horses actually ran away, and by rescuing them, I mean that one of us had the honor of helping them from the carriage after the horses had stopped and the danger was over.

Then the whole army went to Fairfax and did nothing particularly worthy of mention, except to execute a beautiful retreat, which was much gloated over at the time, and which simply amounted to striking our tents and burning everything we did not want to carry back with us, immediately after firing off a sky-rocket. It took us all night and part of the next day to get back to camp from about the same place where we started.

Our next camp was called Camp Hollins, and here we were again getting into all sorts of scrapes. We kept our quarters in excellent condition, cutting broom-straw, which grew plentifully, for pallets, and generally having a rather pleasant time around camp fires, dodging smoke, telling stories, and borrowing from our comrade's tobacco pouch, where there was an opening. We had some drills and fancy parades, but these were almost the last we were to have. Once in a while some improvidential youth would be detected in furtively making use of a government horse to visit friends at a distance, and sometimes there would be a court-martial or two, resulting from this grave violation of discipline. The same party of ladies who had been rescued from the runaway chariot, were the cause of the exercise of one of these exhibitions of camp discipline; and if the reader will picture to himself the difficulty of obtaining a horse under patrol of two or three guardsmen—riding a dozen miles during a snow storm, where your horse would fall down three and four times in descending long and slippery hills, he will have an idea of the restless feeling produced when you are kept a long time inactive in camp. Then we were ordered all of a sudden to go to cutting down trees, chopping them off in prescribed lengths, and then hauling them to a new camping ground, preparatory to building winter quarters. We soon acquired sufficient experience to lay those notched logs one upon the other, and cover them over with shingles prepared for the purpose; and when this was done, with the addition of a rough puncheon floor, window sash, brought in by parties on horseback from some remote abandoned house, and a door, the habitation of a dozen men was in short measure completed.

LETTER WRITTEN IN TENT.

CENTREVILLE, Dec. 6th, 1861.—This will be my last letter from this place, so at least our officers encourage us so to believe, and feeling that we are thus encouraged for some wise purpose, we give fancy free rein in laying out plans for the future, quartering ourselves for instance in Richmond, and dancing and reveling through the winter solstice with the natives. Meanwhile, time drags wearily enough. Our only amusement is to build air castles (I wish it was winter quarters) around a big fire and dodge the smoke, and should we remain here, I think more of us will die from too much Centreville on the brain, than from all other causes whatever. I don't say that the town is any more dull and sensationless than many others that we both have probably passed through; but it seems so to us. I doubt if an incident or adventure ever took place within its dreary limits, unless the necessity of passing through or of staying all night, of some benighted traveler in such a God-forsaken collection of boards, might be regarded in that light. Society of the softer sex, there is none, coffee-houses, there are none. A blacksmith shop, a few stores kept by men who swindle the careless soldier at extremely cheap rates, and the ghost of a hotel so unredeemably dismal, that a night spent in a snow bank would be preferable to entering its portals; these and a few other houses, built upon an almost perpendicular street, constitute the town.

From this atmosphere, a few friends of different regiments, together with myself, resolved for one day to escape. Freedom, though only for a few hours, was a sufficient motive for me, but with my friends, a determination to obtain a lost dog, was an additional inducement. Our conversation naturally turned upon the qualities of this faithful follower of man, and from my friends I learned that his complexion was a billious, soap colored yellow, that his body was bereft of its tail, and that his legs were disproportionately long for his body, had it not been curtailed of its narrative already. What the use of this sorry cur was, I was unable to ascertain, as the mere asking of such a question might have been construed by a soldier's mind, into an affront. But, I learned that the mere permission to hunt for him required the signatures of half the officers in the regiment, besides one or two Brigadier-Generals, in order to pass the pickets.

Gradually the conversation subsided into subjects of

less interest, (excepting of course, inquiries of every wayfarer, in reference to the lost animal,) and one of the party, who seemed familiar with localities, and anxious to talk, pointed out surrounding objects of interest. Among others he described the occupant of a small house—two rooms and a small garret, which was, he said, familiar to soldiers as the "Widow's," and where those who were fortunate enough to have fifty cents were wont to repair for their meals.

The doorway, continued my informant, is always thronged with a hungry crowd, under the eye of a sentinel, of officers and privates, who restrain their impatience until the board is spread, by wallowing on the beds, or smoking pipes, with their legs above the kitchen mantlepieces, ejecting saliva at the hissing stove. Whether the guests visit the widow from admiration of the sex, or the culinary art, my friend thought impossible to say, her pretensions to beauty and skill being about evenly balanced. But eating or love making, no one seems able to boast of much preference, her smiles being distributed with the same impartiality as the tit-bits, gizzards and livers of her table.

Conspicuous at one time among the widow's admirers, was a sandy-haired youth with a "coming stomach," whom you may know as Charles. Charles's parti-colored ties, moccasin vests, bear greased locks, and glittering appearance generally, had constituted him at one time the cynosure of the bar-rooms and banquettes of your city; but the sun of his glory has long since set, and nought remained of his former splendor, but a dirty shirt. His face bore but little evidence of a familiarity with water, while the tangled jungles of his head were equally untroubled with the inroads of brush or comb. His hands dangled at his side, coarse and dirty, like a couple of smoked hams, and in short, as mouldy and wilted a looking bird was Charles, as was to be found in the Confederate camp. It was about this time that chance led him to the widow's door. The visit awakened old memories, and was attended with purchase of a comb. The second interview involved the washing of his face and hands, and each succeeding visit was succeeded by a similar change and transformation. Whether this brilliant metamorphosis was wholly due to the humanizing influence of woman, or partly to his month's pay, and the holding of strong hands at poker, my informant did not take it upon him to say; but at any rate, the moments of Charles, which are not absorbed in painting a pair of tremendous boots—tops, soles and all, are generally whiled away in the widow's salons.

Thus discoursing and listening to the statistics of another soldier, whose mind appeared to have been much occupied with the study of mules, wagons, and other means of conveyancing not mentioned in law writers, not forgetting meanwhile, to make constant inquiries in reference to the missing dog, we passed through a country war-scathed, exhausted of almost every supply, and almost depopulated of its native inhabitants. No traces of anything like an inclosure were to be seen.

The zig-zag worm fences had disappeared at the first appearance of winter, and a rail is now almost as much an object of curiosity as would be the presence of the great rail-splitter himself. Much was said at the time by the few farmers, who remained, about the destruction of their property, and stringent orders were issued from camp. But the soldiers, whose blood was freezing, were not in a condition to weigh calmly the difference between *meum* and *teum*. It was doubtless good that farmers should have fences, thought the soldiers; but it was also good that patriots should keep warm, and so the last sign of one has long since disappeared.

Our roads led us over the black waters of Bull Run, by the famous stone bridge and stone house, (the Hougomont Chateau of our Waterloo,) and through the memorable battle-field itself. The fallen trunks of the trees which were cut down to intercept the enemy's path near the bridge, are still remaining, and the broken, splintered tops of others attest where the whirlwind of battle has passed; otherwise, a few shreds and patches of cotton which mark the position of the batteries, a house almost destroyed by the balls and, lastly the graves of the dead, are the sole remaining indications of the greatest battle ever fought upon this continent.

We had not proceeded many miles farther before we came to a house, which appeared to be still inhabited by its owners, and whose external appearance, and the savory smell from the kitchen, gave us some encouragement to hope for dinner. It is not generally thought necessary by the soldier to waste much time in knocking or pulling at the bell, and so we entered the parlor without further ceremony. By way of announcing our arrival, one of the party, in a large, broad-brimmed hat, and with blanket thrown around him, in Indian style, seated himself at the piano, and favored us with some music, with a touch about as light as would have been produced by a horse galloping across the keys. We had sung or rather shouted the Marseillaise and other airs, and one or two couple were waltzing in bonnets and other articles of female paraphernalia which we found in the room, when just at that moment the door opened, and through the dust which had been kicked out of the carpet, we saw the angry face of the lady of the house. There was evidently no use of apologizing or attempting to mitigate her wrath. So putting on a courageous face, we told her we wanted dinner—we were ready to pay for it, and were obliged to have it—that we were not particular, and that anything in the way of chickens, eggs, butter, and other light dishes of that sort, would easily satisfy us. This we finally persuaded her to give us, and before we had finished the meal, she admitted we were not as hard-looking cases as she at first thought us to be, and that we might, if we chose, return. Meanwhile, one of the party who had been out on the back porch, discovered the lost dog Tige, lying sleeping in the sun, and was beckoning, whistling, and employing all the endearing names which are generally found most successful in attracting a dog's attention, but without avail. Tige seemed to be afflicted with the aristocratic affectation of deafness; but at the first movement that was made by the soldier in his direction, he uttered an indignant yelp, and sought refuge under the kitchen floor. His retreat was, however, useless. The lady of the house abandoned him to his fate, and the remainder of the party coming to the rescue, a part of the flooring was removed, and Tige was ignominiously dragged from his hiding place. His captor now took his prize under his arm, and bidding adieu to our hostess, we all started for camp.

Our return was not attended with many incidents. The soldier who was so well informed on the subject of mules had rashly exhausted his stock of ideas in the morning, and so we trudged on through the mud in silence, by the side of the heavily laden wagon. Once, upon the way, one of us ventured to enter at the back of one of those wains, and had appropriated a seat beside what appeared to be a closely muffled soldier, but was not a little astonished to find, as he crowded into one-half of the seat, that it was in reality a lady. He was about to vacate the premises, with a profusion of apologies, when she laughingly told him he might stay—that she wanted some one to talk to and would be glad of his company. She was the wife of an officer, who, she proceeded to inform me, (I might as well admit it was myself,) had come on a flying visit to look after her truant husband.

But the road soon forked. I had besides to get down and show my pass to the sentinel, who examined it very carefully up side down. Here, too, our faithless cur availed himself of a moment's freedom, and took to his heels, and although we made the air vocal with Tige's name, we soon found, as one of my disappointed comrades gravely observed, "all hell couldn't whistle him back."

We gained our camp without further adventure, and I soon fell asleep, dreaming that I led the hostess of the day to the altar in the dress of a Vivandier, and that your Fat Contributor acted as grooms-man, in a flannel shirt and red-topped boots. FISHBACK.

CHAPTER X.

IN WINTER QUARTERS.

THERE is nothing about which soldiers more pride themselves, or about which they show more jealousy, than in retaining the few fair acquaintances it was their fortune, during their marches, to make. Whether it was the pastry cook and her little girls who sold pies at Centreville, the village teacher, elderly, motherly old ladies, or dashing, showy belles, who would move around on horseback, or travel in the ambulance wagon, most of the young men were keenly sensitive to their good opinion, and however awkward, backward or indifferent to ladies' society at home, would always put the best foot forward, where the presence of the fair was to be met with about camp. For them the immaculate collar, which had only been worn on a half dozen state occasions, would be carefully extracted and adjusted—your neighbor's high-top boots would be borrowed, and a contribution generally levied on the slender stock of effects admitted by camp wardrobes.

The most amusing part of the matter was the way in which the old soldier would continue to adapt their appearance, manners, or past history to the ideas of their new friends, and it need hardly be said that the traveler's privilege of relating wonderful and marvelous stories was not forgotten. Old sporting characters soon learned how to dandle babies in their arms, or rock cradles in the most domestic manner in the world, or to sanctimoniously join in hymns with as much fervor as they had in times past trolled out bacchanal songs. Some of these old soldiers acquired extraordinary proficiency in the use of the long bow, however it might be with the artillery practice. We had a saturnine, red-faced company commissary, who was with the Washington Regiment in the Mexican war, a thorough martinet in all military matters, and who never wearied of relating wild and hair-breadth narratives of personal adventure—all with the most gloomy composure. As showing what this gallant soldier had achieved, it may be stated that he was present at one massacre, and was the only man who escaped. It ought to be recorded, too, as a part of history, that he once had a *conducta* of Mex- can wagons and mule trains, laden with gold, to bring through a mountain pass, and was almost certain his convoy would be attacked and captured by robbers. What was he to do? Why, to make up a party at Monte at the first *pueblo* with a Mexican *propriedor* of the richest mine in the world, and who happened very conveniently to be on hand at the time. The game was made—the unhappy old soldier soon found to his chagrin that somehow he could not lose—that he won as many wagon loads as he already held, and that he was now burthened with a dozen more *impedimenta*. His apprehensions proved well founded— just as he had finished acquiring this *embaras de richesse*, the guerrillas "struck the train, as he all along expected, and had captured every thing. And worse than that," would the old soldier conclude with great energy, " d—n my Confederate soul if they did not take every rag from our backs—even from a party of young ladies who were along with the *conducta*, on their way to a convent. We made a pretty figure, let me tell you, when at the end of our journey we were all carried into a *posada*, wrapped up in sheets and horse blankets."

There were plenty others, like Henry Phelps, who had a good deal to say about Mexico, or like the Hon. Ned Riviere (of the last legislature,) and Sam Rousseau, (the brother of the Federal General,) who had soldiered in Central America, under Walker, and who were accorded the privilege of distinguished travelers in telling of a hundred mile march made in one day, or of having rations of monkey meat distributed out, as our armies did bacon. But they were overawed when Commissary Hart was about, and never put forth their full strength or quite did themselves justice in his presence.

Then there would be another heavy **conversationalist** who had had some experience at sea, and who finding the land well occupied, was compelled to take to salt water, and told as exciting sea-stories about Confederate rams, blockade runners and submarine boats, as Sinbad and Maryatt could have done. We had several of that sort, who used to practice and polish up their yarns at night, around camp fires, preparatory to the next "pirout;" and these artless *raconteurs* would have a queer group of eccentricities gathered around in long blanket coats, with cowls, one here and there in a Mexican jacket or red flannel drawers, while a third would be tink-a-tinking at the guitar. There was a mess of queer fish, who from having some defects of temper, were forced to occupy the same winter quarters—an eccentric poet in one case, in another a cynical prodigal, who had spent a pretty fortune in a few months, on friends who had politely laughed in his face when his money was gone; another, singular to state, was the nice man at home, who played on the piano and parted his hair in the middle. But defects are developed in other ways in camp than with a comb, and the musician, though engaged to marry a beautiful and wealthy girl at home, (perhaps on account of it,) finally left us with a never-ending furlough.

One night there came a singular report in camp. It was whispered that a move the next morning was to be the word, and there was an immense amount of bustle and packing in consequence. When we went to bed we were only permitted to sleep till three the next morning, and were then aroused without bugle call. And after cooking, as was done by the Grand Army at Moscow, over the flames of our burning quarters, and eating (in part) our rations and good many baker's dozen of biscuit, and drinking a tin cup of coffee each man, we took our places rather silently at the pieces and moved off.

We are now upon the first of our retreats—the retreat from Manassas to Richmond. A frosty morning shows us the whole Confederate army drawn up in the road, the men facing towards Richmond. There is a slight tremor or depression at first, indicative of a fear that something has gone wrong, or else we would not have to fall back; this soon wears away; and the infantry meanwhile march with arms at will, and the air of men who carry heavy burthens, and with that movement which indicates that long marching is before them At the head, or in front of their divisions and regiments, ride the men whose names occupy the page—sometimes the lying page—of history, flanked by cavalry outriders and a cloud of skirmishers. Then come the slow moving trains of ammunition, supplies, and ambulances containing the sick and wounded.

As the day advances, and we discern that the retreat is not the result of any anticipated misfortune, the men, who are glad of any break in camp monotony, regain their spirits.

To understand the first comment frequently made about this and other long retreats, the resident of New Orleans should take a look at the large. life-sized picture, which represents Napoleon's retreat from Moscow. The dead horse, and attendant scavengers—the broken down wagon or forge—abandoned equipments, the sick and wounded by the wayside, make up some of the details at which many of us looked very hard before enlisting, and of which we thought very frequently afterwards. This picture was brought to mind by one of the dreary sights about camp, especially during the winter season and on a long march, that is by the number of dead horses who perish from hunger, cold, bad treatment, or exhaustion.

In this and other marches it was sometimes said that we could have walked all day upon the prostrate bodies of the horses which fell by the wayside. The mule was a much more hardy animal—his carcass was very rarely seen. He endured so well that in time he took the place of the battery horse, (as at Drury's bluff) and we all laughed at the manner in which a mule would shake himself when struck by a bullet, as if divesting himself of some superfluous hornet or gadfly. But a horse once down was like Lucifer—he fell to rise no more. A smooth place would be worn in the mud by the moving to and fro of his head and neck, or where he had thrown out convulsively his legs; and then a lingering death, a swollen and bloated carcass, or bones covered with collapsed hide, with the crows holding a coroner's inquest upon the neighboring tree tops.

To see these serviceable friends of man, and almost indispensable adjuncts of a good army, lying by the wayside, was very depressing, for the reason well known to a soldier, that dull, sluggish horses can never be trained to the point requisite for efficient cavalry horses. Almost as much depends, in a successful charge of cavalry, on the horse as on the man. Raw recruits mounted on well-drilled horses, are more serviceable than veteran troops mounted on clumsy, low-spirited animals. At the battle of the Pyramids, the horses of Muzod Bey's cavalry charged repeatedly in squadrons after their riders were killed. So did the French horses at Waterloo on the English under the same circumstances.

And after the Marquis Romana was compelled to leave his horses on the shore of Denmark, at the embarkation of the troops for Spain, they formed themselves into two hostile armies, as the ships of their late masters faded in the distance, and charged upon each other with such fury that the earth shook for miles around, and the terrified inhabitants of the country fled panic stricken to their houses. So terrible was the slaughter of these fine Andalusian horses, that out of a body of 10,000 but a few hundred remained alive.

I have always thought in reading this in history, that this was the way in which the inhabitants accounted to the government for some of the missing chargers. This supposition is supported by a remark I once heard dropped by a quarter-master, that the mortality was always heavier with horses when near the cities, and that the deaths reported would sometimes be excessive when in close proximity to a faro bank. There was a great deal of mortality among the horses too, at the close of the war, especially among the cavalry. Capt. G——, upon being questioned by the Federal Commander as to what in the deuce had become of all his stock, reported that "Ze buffalo gnat—he eats them all."

By the time that McClellan had discovered the uses of Quaker guns in forts, we were far away on our retreat towards Richmond. I leave it for abler judges to decide as to the policy of keeping an army inactive for months at a time—composed as that one was, of the flower of the South—of retreating to the peninsula, and then retreating from there. What Jackson did in the valley, ought, it seemed to us, to have been done with the army about Manassas; and it seemed to us that if a General has enough inventive genius, he could always find opportunities, like Napoleon, for striking blows with his force whether large or small. But General Johnston probably knew best—he was a cautious, prudent, and thoroughly able commander, who never was caught unawares, but a little long in finding his opportunity.

We had some terrible weather in getting down to Orange Court-House, and the most perfect picture ever made on my mind of blissful sleep occurred on this march. Next to the cooks, who as the men of genius of a mess, gave themselves more airs and made themselves more disagreeable than anybody else, were those who superintended the erection of quarters, purchased supplies, etc. On the occasion referred to, after long and tedious marches and counter marches, making feints upon one place and then on the other, the army was overtaken about dusk by a tremendous storm. The leader of the mess, who exercised great tyranny about having all mess-work done exactly right, was absent when our tent was put up, and some of the lazy ones had contented themselves with a hasty structure, made of rails propped against a fence, that ran at the bottom of the hill. The consequence was, besides what fell over us, the water ran under our blankets from the hill above. Sleep was impossible for many—we were drowned literally out.

"A quarter less twain—six feet scant," and similar soundings out was the cry, and there was nothing to do but to get up, build large fires of the rails, and keep as warm and dry as we best could.

While standing thus before the fire, miserable and discontented, we were compelled to regard, and this with great envy, a comrade notorious for his indolence, who had laid a rail foundation for his bed, and who, covered with his gum cloth, and undisturbed by the underground streams which worked such misery to the balance of us, contrived to sleep like an infant during the whole of the terrible storm. If he had once turned over, or he had discovered the uproar among the elements, he would have been drowned out too; and it certainly showed a great deal of forbearance to let him sleep on, and merely step in between him and his share of the fire, without molesting him.

This storm brought about another accident. The musical characters had rigged themselves up with extraordinary splendor, to make a serenade outside of a hospitable mansion, or rather to lay the foundation to giving a little musical soiree inside. Nothing favored them, not even the weather—the crowd were wet and disagreeable, when they arrived, and what was still more exasperating, the comrade who had floated around the world was inside—had got possession of the field, was telling all of the yarns he had rehearsed in camp, and was singing with perfect indifference to the arrival of the chorus. It was in vain the latter tried to snub him, and give him the cold shoulder, and intimate that he did not belong to the select few. The first comer held his ground; and whenever any music was called for, would, while the chorus was affecting bashfulness, plant himself absent-mindedly and dreamily at the piano, and nothing but a torpedo or bomb-shell would ever have moved him until he got through. The part of the joke however, which made the chorus most swear was, the young lady of the house hung on his lips as if he had been a god, and the submissive subject of the admiration, so far from having shown any repentance for having crowded out those tip-top fellows, the musical chorus, got desperately wounded in the next battle, and then married the lady.

CHAPTER XI.
ON THE ROAD.

WE camped a week at Orange Court House, and this left no other impression upon us than that our three day's rations of bread at starting, were heavier than the balance of our baggage. Most of the rest of the journey to Richmond was made by cars. Previous to entering one of these, one of the messes had bargained for a small supply of fluids, which the treacherous Boniface, after receiving our money, and finding the men on board of the cars, neglected to produce. He failed, however, to carry his point. An impromptu detachment was immediately started back to his hotel, the humorous George Meek, was placed in command, and made for the next half hour, as fierce a looking non-commissioned officer as one would wish to see. The order to "arrest that man, seize on him," was given to the great terror of the treacherous Boniface; (who would probably at that moment, have given a thousand dollars to be out of the scrape,) to the accompaniment of drawn sabres. However, before carrying him before the Commanding General, whom our host supposed had sent us, we consented to listen to his prayers. Any quantity of canteens would be given us, or the money returned. The sound of the locomotive whistle, made us contented to take the latter.*

*Extract from the Adjutant's Journal.

MARCH 8.—Began our retreat from Bull Run, at 8 P. M. Marched to Suspension Bridge; distance three miles, and reported to Gen. Longstreet.
   9.—Marched to Gainsville.
  10.—Marched to Warrenton.
  11.—Marched to camp in Jones' Wood.
  12.—March to, and camp near Woodville.
  13.—We are near Hazle River.
  14 and 15.—Still near Hazle River.
  16.—Three miles from Culpepper Court House.
  17.—Marched ten miles past Culpepper.
  18.—Crossed the Rapidan at Barnett's ford, and camped one mile from Orange Court House.

But arriving at the next station, our good genius came to the rescue. A South Carolina Lieutenant who had been to a still and came back laden with twenty canteens, wished to travel on our train. The orders were positive to allow no one but the companies to come aboard. This was however deemed an exceptional case, and although the officer of the day was shouting and gesturing to "put him off," some of the men contrived to keep the order from being obeyed, the officer of the day meanwhile making wrathful imprecations and signs which hinted at court-martial. The storm however was foreseen and anticipated. The principal offender, as soon as the train stopped, hastened forward to his Captain with one of the canteens in his hand, and affected to believe that no officer of the day in the world could have wanted to put off a man laden down with whiskey. The Captain kept the canteen, and admitted that his command had perhaps been misunderstood, owing to the noise of the train. No other incident until our arrival at Richmond.

Our Batallion camped nominally the first night at the Depot, but the understanding seemed to be that we could sleep where we chose, and there were not many who did not avail themselves of the extraordinary opportunity of sleeping in a civilized bed. There were too, some precious moments of freedom vouchsafed to us after we had gone formally in camp, in which we were permitted to renew

22.—Marched through Orange Court House. and camped on Terrell Farm, five miles from Orange Court House. We halt here for the present.
APRIL.—We have enjoyed our camp near Orange Court House very much; the ladies are pretty—we have formed a dancing club which meets twice a week at the Hotel, Orange Court House. The band of the 1st Regiment furnishes fine music. Among the members, are Gen. Longstreet, A. P. Hill, and the officers of the Washington Artillery.
Received orders in Church, to prepare to march. Began 8 P. M.; marched down plank-road to Fredericksburg. Very wearisome marching.
12.—Shipped seven Guns by rail to Richmond; horses and wagons go by Turnpike.

old friendships, and witness a very curious and motley gathering from every part of the world. As nearly every one was only temporarily absent from home or camp, in search of a commission, or enjoyment of a short furlough, the city was naturally in the gayest of spirits, and every one lived extravagantly, while his money lasted; and when gone, did not have much difficulty about hunting up a friend who would divide his table, purse, or medical supplies with him. So that each stratum of visitors became thoroughly impecunious about the time its furlough expired, and would be succeeded by another, whom military accidents or necessities brought within the radius of the city.

The population of the town at that time was extraordinarily large, for the amount of accommodations, and no one under the rank of a Colonel, could hope ever to obtain a room at a hotel, or portion of one; and very frequently at late hours, a dozen distinguished officers were seen stretched out by envious callers about the entries. These latter would be denied the luxury of even a seat in chairs, from scarcity of room, and sometimes unceremoniously be invited to skip off by the diamonded clerks, or previous claimants of the space. During my night in the city—at a very late hour—happening to think about going to bed, I was put in possession for the first time, of this information. There was nothing to do but sally into the streets and meditate over my homeless condition, for which I had abundant leisure, or to endeavor to meet with some adventures that would kill time until day break.

I had not proceeded far, before I discovered that the population was far from having all gone to bed, and upon inquiry of a soldier, I found that he was as badly situated in the matter of sleeping quarters as myself. The previous night he had managed to find some sort of couch about a livery stable; but upon returning, he found another occupant ahead of him. The night was chilly, and what made the matter worse, we had many of us in marching worn overcoats and double suits of uniform, on account of the smallness of our knapsacks. This extra clothing, through vanity or comfort was soon disposed of, once we had arrived at Richmond, but at night, with no lodging, was much regretted.

Happening to pass the theatre, I entered. It was at that time owned by M'me. ——, who was an old actress herself, and who, from scarcity of talent or infatuation, placed in leading parts a half crazy actor named Dorsey Ogden. One of Otway's old plays (Venice Preserved) was at that time on the boards, and one of the incidents of this was the dragging of the heroine around the stage by her back hair. The poetry of the play was so antiquated or inverted that the soldier audience did not even stop eating ground peas to try to catch it. But the back-hair dragging magnificently atoned for Ogden's absurd acting and absence of everything, except a very fine wardrobe; so much so, that the poor heroine was encored and had to be dragged a second time.

A very beautiful theatre was built during the war, and furnished extravagantly. It was always largely crowded —so much so on the first night, that I lost both hat and overcoat in making my entrance.

What had suggested the idea of my entering the theatre at that time, was the hope of meeting up with some friend who would get me shelter. I did not get this, but did manage to join a pretty large crowd of soldiers who were moving towards obscure lodgings, and in keeping in company with these I proceeded to an attic room containing eight unattractive beds, and succeeded, without opposition, in getting the whole of one of these.

Feeling out of danger in the morning, I ventured to inquire of one of my new acquaintances how it happened that I alone had occupied a whole bed. The soldier told me that for his part he would not have occupied any such couch at all, if he never got any sleep; and in answer to further inquiries explained that a man had been killed in it a night or two previous, growing out of a quarrel as to who had the right of ownership for the occasion. I saw something of the case afterwards in the papers, but the tribunals could obtain no evidence, either through the ignorance, or disinclination to speak, of the witnesses.

Going down to breakfast, I met up with an old Louisiana friend, who, different from every one else, was dressed in an elegant civil costume—a thing at that day regarded with great envy, and the certain index of a soft situation and a plethoric purse. My friend was Jim Morris, (who used to be well known on St. Charles street, and in the army in Violet Guard circles,) and on scanning his costume I discovered that it all probably belonged to its wearer; that is, it was not a mosaic gala, composed of the temporary loans of a half dozen messmates, which we, like the first Napeleon in his days of poverty, were compelled to wear.

I need not state that I felt exceedingly flattered at finding a friend thus dressed, who seemed glad to see me, and in the fervor of my delight I shook him by the hand until the breakfast began to get cold.

Jim had once been a young doctor of much promise, but became seduced by fast company. At some sort of supper or entertainment one night he had won $1500 at gaming; and this success or misfortune gave him a ruling passion, to which he devoted his time henceforth—neglected medicine, and for some years his old friends lost sight of him. When I next saw him, he hunted up all of his old friends. At first glance, from certain hard lines about his face, it was easy to see that Jim had not fared well with the world. His object in coming to see us was to borrow $10 a-piece, which he was confident he could raise the next day. We succeeded with some work in raising the money, and took the opportunity of trying to persuade him to settle down to his profession. He listened attentively, went away with the money, and beyond the raillery of friends, who smiled at our innocence in wasting both money and breath, we heard nothing more of Jim or his promise until the meeting referred to.

As soon as we had shaken hands, instead of sitting down to the table, he made me put on my hat and carried me off to a restaurant near the Spotswood, picking up more comrades on the way, among whom were Kingslow, Handy and Ballantine; we obtained the best breakfast the market afforded. He told me it was worth his money in the way of getting up an appetite, to see an army friend eat, and upon this calculation, he probably ought to have been well repaid and stimulated by our example. After returning the borrowed money, and showing a good deal of curiosity as to whether I had ever entertained any doubts about repayment (which I was forced to confess I had,) he invited us to make his room our headquarters, and to always come there when we were in town from camp. Dr. Jim now held the rank of surgeon, but I don't think my excellent advice about reform had had much of a beneficial effect; but he showed that he had been immensely pleased at having a friend that took that much interest in him, and never afterwards tired of doing me little services.

I left my friends in the doctor's company, after dropping a hint of caution. When I saw them again their features were overcast with what was then known as a flour-barrel expression of countenance, and their manner was very sad. The explanation was soon made. The doctor's company had been found so pleasant, that they had not had the heart to tear themselves away, until our accomplished bugler had lost $150, and the others more than twice enough to pay for the breakfast.

CHAPTER XII.

THE PENINSULA.

AT the end of April, we proceeded down the James River to the Peninsula, and encamped near the Yorktown lines of fortification of the Revolutionary War. We did not see the cave in which George (according to the authentic old darkey's story) slipped up on Cornwallis and took him in out of the cold, while asleep; but the old lines of fortification, as evidence that the event really occurred, are still easily to be discerned.

Williamsport, we found to be a queer old place, and at that time singularly blended the cobwebs of antiquity and scholastic lore with the bare and stripped appearance of a beleaguered town. There were some college buildings still in good condition, and a statue of Botetourt, who seemed to have had things pretty much his own way in his day, (he was Governor or something). And there too was an Insane Asylum, where was to be seen a beautiful young lady, who after getting twenty beaux, went crazy from disappointed love for the twenty-first—a soldier in a Gulf Regiment who did not know enough English to learn what was the matter, or who was prevented by the movement of his regiment from saying so, if he did. But at any rate, there was the poor woman incessantly wringing her hands, or occupied in restlessly rolling up and twisting around a red scarf or mantle, which seemed in some way associated with her misfortune. The town had long since been stripped as bare of everything as a barbecue table is, fifteen minutes after a political speech is finished.

A few days after our arrival, on going to a hospital to see a friend, I found the chaplain growling at having to perform an unusual number of burial services, just at the time when it was the most inconvenient. This statement led to the further explanation that the hospital had been ordered to the rear, and supported the inference that there would be another retreat. We had arrived on the peninsula on a damp, raw evening, but we had beautiful weather most of the time returning, and it naturally put us all in excellent spirits to get once more near Richmond. We had a beautiful country to go through as we approached the city, but the fact was we enjoyed nearly all scenery, when we were kept in motion, particularly the mountainous regions of Virginia and Pennsylvania, and we never heard the order given to go into camp without a sigh.

Extract from the Adjutant's Journal.

APRIL 20.—Left Richmond for the Peninsula, with batteries on transport.

21.—Arrived this afternoon at King's Wharf. Before we had our camp arranged, we had an awful storm, wetting everything and every body.

22.—Camped at Blow's Mill, seven miles from King's Wharf.

25.—Marched to Williamsburg—bivouacked two miles beyond.

MAY 2.—Ordnance wagons pass, which means orders for us. March at 3:30; bivouac at Burnt Ordinary Tavern, 50 miles from Richmond.

4.—Move on the Diascund Road and camp. Report to Gen. Magruder, who commands rear guard.

5.—March through a heavy rain all day, and with axles deep in mud. Met the gallant color-bearer of a La. Regiment, with no clothing except his shirt, and everlastingly splashing mud. Camped near Windsor Shades, at 1:30 P. M.

CHAPTER XIII.

THE BIVOUAC.

THE word which heads the chapter is one which occurs frequently in this narrative, and is one which will awaken a host of recollections from old soldiers, mostly of a pleasant character—that is of the comfort which follows from rest and food after a long march, and the enjoyment of pleasant gossip after the supper has been cooked and eaten.

To bring up freshly such a picture again, let us suppose about twilight that the bugle has sounded the halt—that the pieces have been parked, and the horses watered and fed. All is animation and work now, and those who fail in the duties assigned them in the mess, will soon have to sleep by themselves or make new arrangements. One man provides the wood, another the water, while a third makes ready with the cooking utensils. Meanwhile those whose duty it is to construct the temporary habitations—for the reader must remember that tents have become partially obsolete—are preparing a couple of notched posts to be stuck up in the ground. Across these extends a pole 12 feet long, to the top of which smaller ones are laid, with one end resting upon the ground ; over this is thrown a piece of canvass, where we have one, or a large number of twigs and boughs, or even the rotten bark of trees. This answers as a covering for the head ; the next thing to be done is to scrape away the mud, hail or snow, cut away damp grass, and to cover the interior with boughs, where straw or planks are impossible to be obtained. The fireman has by this time cut some heavy logs, the fire is kindled against a huge spreading tree at the immediate front of the tent, the cold and darkness disappear, and the sparks shoot merrily upward through the shadows. The rays extend out through the trees of the forest, lighting up leaf and bough with ghostly lights and shadows, and throwing the melodramatic lurid tints over gnarled trunks, or sleet-fringed stems which are found so attractive in the Christmas theatrical performances. As the aroma from simmering cauldrons or coffee-pots mounts into the air, the men who have extended their blankets inside of the tent and stretched themselves thereon, begin to recover from their languor; their spirits adapt themselves to the fantastic shadows—to the innumerable lights which glimmer in every direction through the trees, and reflecting that the entertainment is to last at this spot for "Positively one night only," begin to enter into the zest of the thing. It need hardly be added, that the truant comrade who comes back with additions to our slender larder, in the shape of chickens or eggs, or better than all, a drop of something to drink, soon has all his sins forgiven, and by the time we have consumed our hot biscuits, a delicious ration of bacon, coffee, and other et ceteras, and smoked a pipe of old Virginny, the soldier finds himself in about as comfortable a frame of mind as any other living mortal.

The most beautiful bivouac I have ever seen, was where the whole army encamped in a valley and at the sides of a mountain with the bivouac fires close together, as had happened already in our retreat from Manassas. There is no need to dwell upon the magnificent panorama of the improvised city that was spread out around us, or the dancing lights, the thousand different calls and cries. But such was not always the life of a bivouac, especially during a storm. Then the tents, says one camp writer, swelling inward beneath the blast, left no slant sufficient to repel the water, which was caught in the hollows and filtered through. Then the wind would increase to a hurricane, in which the canvass would flap and flutter, and the tent pole quiver like a vibrating harpstring.

Finally the pole and the canvass would fall with a crash across your whole bed, your effects dispersed on the wings of the wind; and all around you, would be seen half clad men, grasping their fluttering blankets, and sitting amid the ruins of their beds.

But in good weather, the men were all in splendid humor, and the laugh and shout over some of the ridiculous incidents and mishaps of the day were long and uproarious, and the patriotic songs were rung out with the sound of "clashing steel and clanging trumpet." Then the men would come forward who had yarns or curious histories to relate—of sudden fortunes made or lost in commerce—of the vicissitudes of trade, bringing some men forward and ruining others, or of some of the darker tragedies which make up city histories. We would give the travelers an opportunity of again crossing the plains, shooting buffaloes while on horseback at full speed, with arrows which would go *through*, or sometimes with guns—the slowest way where a man would use his mouth as a bullet-pouch, and ram down the ball without wadding, by striking the butt end of the gun on the pummel of the saddle. There would be some little badgering about some of these statements, and the "Old Soldier" (before referred to) resented these narratives as a special intrusion, by reciting his own adventures, say, among Mexican Indians, where every body was as virtuous as Hebe and as naked as Venus. Then there were singular gossiping stories which the men had picked up about some of the old houses or villages through which we had passed, which began to have a tendency to ghost spectres and apparitions, as the hours advanced.

One of the unflagging talkers of the occasion was a certain sergeant with a noble air and beautiful side whiskers, whose faults were not those which arise from over-shrinking modesty. He came by some of his sins honestly; he had been an old newspaper reporter, and it was not expected that he should come down to plain truth-telling the moment that printer's ink was beyond his reach. But there was another stirring young man present, of an imaginative turn (Joe L——) who was mixed up with half of the deviltry of the Batallion, and who (merely to show his style,) once sent half the population of Clinton to the woods, by riding through the town while on a furlough, and shouting out that the enemy were coming or just behind. Old Judge Semple, managing editor of the Crescent for many years, and at that time refugeeing, was one of his victims, and every one who remembers the Judge's girth, and knows the distance that had to be run, will admit that the Judge was quite right for abusing Joe for the balance of his days.

These two untiring talkers had been having a good deal to say, and the audience was looking for an avenger. This was found in the person of one of the smallest and most quiet of the group, George M——, who, with the wicked, cynical smile, which every one who knew him will remember, proceeded to relate an incident of the night before. George went on to state that after eating a very square meal, he had laid down to pleasant dreams until he should be called to go on guard. He had, however, not more than comfortably coiled himself in his blanket, before he was wanted. He got up, a little mad at the interruption, and found sitting on a log by the fire, what seemed some new non-commissioned officer—somebody that he had never seen before about the batallion. George started to let into the officer, with a good deal of bitterness, for calling him too soon, but there was something about the looks of the stranger that took him aback and repressed familiarity. Instead of so doing, he began staring very hard at the visitor, and wondering at what seemed a difference in his uniform.

Meanwhile the stranger lit his pipe very deliberately, taking the end of a burning fence rail to do so, and occasionally glancing at George in a way that made the latter feel uncomfortable and impatient.

"Well, what are you waiting for—what do you want?" said George, who began to feel nervous, his tone becoming coaxing instead of irritable, as he ended his inquiry.

The stranger went on puffing, with the immense coal near his cheek, which gave, as George expressed it, "a demoniacal look" to his face; he only, however, glanced furtively out of his eye as much as to say, "It's strange you don't know who I am."

George answered his look rather than his words, and

inquired if he really knew him, or if he was down for any particular detail.

"Detail—I should think you were." Here he took from his side pocket a queer looking roster, or muster roll, and commenced reading out the names of a good many men that had enlisted in Louisiana companies. This reading was listened to with great interest by George; for he began to remark as something singular, that after reading out the statements of age, nativity and other details placed upon muster rolls, the "Remarks" would invariably end with "died," or "killed at Blackburn's Ford, Manassas," or other battle field. In other words, only those were read out who had died or been killed in some previous engagement. George began to think this sort of reading had an ugly look, and he waited and sat thinking that he had had a very strange visitor indeed.

However, the stranger at last came to his name, and began to run his forefinger slowly out to the end of the roll.

"Well, how does it all end?—you've got nothing to say about my name, have you?" said George, with a quavering voice.

The stranger passed his forefinger over his line twice, as if he had possibly made a mistake, and then added:

"No; you are right. The name is not fully run out. But now that I am here, I may as well tell you I'm around, and there is no telling when I'll want you. All I care is to know where to find you, in case you should be called. And this reminds me that there are some others in this camp that I shall want to report right away, and whom I had perhaps better take in my rounds."

The stranger inquired where some others were sleeping, made a sort of military salute, and stopped a moment to glance at the remaining names by the light of the fire.

Meanwhile George had dropped off, glad to find that he was not wanted, and more determined than ever to get a good night's rest.

He was again mistaken. Before George had fairly closed his eyes, the stranger was back to his tent, and again disturbing him.

"I beg your pardon for again bothering you, but the fact is your name *is* down on my detail, after all. I am afraid you will have to come along."

George's heart misgave him. He, however, concluded to crawl out of his blanket and fall in.

"Have you got many down on your list?" he inquired as they proceeded.

"Not so many as we have had—though there were a good many after the last battle, whom I carried off armed and equipped as the law directs."

"That must mean that a good many went to heaven with their boots on," as we say now, thought George, but he only inquired if any body else had been detailed from the batallion.

"Oh, yes! There's the Sergeant —— and Joe L——, and notoriously hard cases they are too. They were detailed to go along too, and have already passed on. But here we are—we've got *two doors* by which we can now enter, and I hardly know which is the proper one for you."

"Do you know which one Joe and the Sergeant went in at?" anxiously inquired George, endeavoring himself to guess which would be the best one for him.

"Which gate? Why, the directions were plain enough in their case. They went in here—*at the left*. They are in there now, and likely to stay some time."

"In that case say no more. If men who never tell the

truth went in that way, I know I can't fare any worse, and probably will a great deal better, by taking the road that leads in the other direction."

And so the result would have turned out, if I had not at that moment been shaken up out of a sound sleep and told in good earnest to go on guard.

The point of the narrative, in spite of the clumsy way in which I have told it, would now appear so obviously to be at the expense of the two preceding truthful speakers, that the narrative ended in the indignant growls of the victims, and the laugh of the rest of the listeners. It was then too late to tell any more stories: besides half of the men had fallen asleep before it was concluded; and soon the whole camp was buried in profound slumber.

CHAPTER XIV.

THE BELEAGUERED CITY.

We were suddenly marched off, late one night* down to Drury's Bluff, and in anticipation of the coming up of the Federal monitors, placed in position upon the bank.

*The following were the orders of our movements:
MAY 6.—Ordered to move at once to the forks of the road, near Forge Bridge. Camped in a beautiful pine grove at 5 P. M.
Enemy pursuing—infantry ordered back. We remain on account of the badness of the road.
7.—Ordered to cross the Chickahominy, at Long Bridge. March ten miles and bivouac.
8.—Marched at a little before 6 A. M. Camp at Blakey's Mill Pond at 12 M.; having made 23 miles in 6 hours—the quickest marching, with perhaps one exception, done during the war.
13.—Capt. Miller's 3d Company ordered to meet gun boats coming up the river at Drury's Bluff.
14.—The rest of the batallion march at 6 A. M. to Bottom's Bridge to report to Gen. Johnston. At 11½ A. M., ordered in camp. At 5 ordered by Gen. Johnston to go two miles back. Bivouac at Savage Station and rejoined by the 3d Co.
16.—Camp six miles from Richmond, at New Bridge.
17.—Back to Blakey's Mill Pond. Whole army in position and invested by McClellan.

I was placed on guard, on a high bluff overlooking the river, though it really was not necessary, as every one was awake and expecting every moment to open fire. The monitors were indeed so near, that we could hear their subdued puffing, and even see the gleam of lights or furnaces on board of the black hulls. Those were the days when the imagination of soldiers were greatly affected by the novelty of the danger we were called upon to meet, and it seemed more terrible, the idea of being killed by a shot as big as a water cooler, than by ordinary musketry fire. It is not a particularly pleasant business any way to be worn out with marching, and then to be forced to meditate upon your chances for the morrow's battle, especially as I can remember was the case at Gettysburg, when the dead and dying of the two days preceding fights are lying on every side of you; when you are compelled to witness every stage of the death saturnalia from the unhappy victim trembling with the last shiver of dissolution to that of the corpse who sits upright with staring eyes, or whose stiffened arm seems to point you yourself the road to perdition on the morrow. A corpse of the latter description passed by us in a wagon while we were at the Bluff, whose hand could not be forced down, and which the soldiers declared was protesting to heaven against the rations we were compelled to eat.

After waiting, or rather changing position twenty times during the following day and digging fortifications in the rain, the batteries were hurried off at midnight, fifteen miles back to Richmond, then down to Chickahominy Swamp, then back to the city again.

Thus we continued to move around the city* with Gen.

―――――

*MAY 31.—Battle of Seven Pines. Longstreet routes Gen. Casey; Capt. Miller brings off a battery of four Napoleons which we are allowed to keep. Capt. Dearing loses nearly all his horses and men.

Johnston's army, having sometimes to be under heavy fire as at Malvern Hill, but at the same time having to hold ourselves in readiness as reserve, to gallop off at the top of our horse's speed, as the tide of battle ebbed and flowed. I walked over nearly all of the battle-fields about Richmond, and found them as well, as those afterwards of North Virginia, Maryland and Pennsylvania—pretty much the same—bloated corpses and carcasses of horses—scattered commissary stores. The hotness with

JUNE 26.—Ordered to the Mechanicsville Road, and held in reserve while A. P. Hill drives the enemy. Standing in the road all day, ready at a moment's notice, and the men all impatient.

27.—Still in reserve.

28.—Move to Mechanicsville Bridge, on Chickahominy. 1st and 3d Company report to Longstreet, on the field. 2nd and 4th, bivouac at bridge. Desperate fighting day before.

29.—At Battery No. 3, Williamsburg Road. At 5 P. M. we (with the whole army) move down the Darbytown Road after McClellan. Bivouacked at night in rain.

30.—Marched at daylight—went into park in advance of Longstreet, who promises to put us in to-day.

JULY 1.—Hear the terrible guns pounding away at Malvern Hill. Order comes from Longstreet to come at once. Batteries galloped over four miles in less than half an hour afterwards. Parked in a field where shells whistle over our heads, and some fall about us; but not ordered to open fire, and otherwise doomed to disappointment. As we dashed down the road at full speed in the afternoon, we were cheered by the troops, as if they had been betting on us in a race; and in truth there are few finer things than to see 32 completely equipped guns and caissons, racing with the men on the seats to the battle ground, and stimulated by the smell of powder from the field.

2.—Move across the battle-field of yesterday; dead and wounded lying thickly around. One man was seen dead in a sitting posture, who had been skulking behind a great oak tree, and who was killed by a cannon ball penetrating through it. The enemy had a splendid position, and covered it with guns; but our troops instead of being hurled forward, were put in by Regiments, and cut to pieces in detail. Still in spite of the terrific fire, many of the Georgia and Alabama troops fell among the enemy's guns. The 8th Ga. and 3d Ala. from Mobile, were terribly mangled.

Bivouac in the rain, near Poindexter's House, which is used as headquarters by Lee. President Davis covered with a Mexican *serape*, which he perhaps captured in the war of '45, passed by amid great cheering.

3.—Move in pursuit, and bivouac on Waterloo Farm.

4.—1st and 3d Companies take position nearer the enemy. 2nd and 4th with Anderson. Capt. Squires, with 1st goes below McClellan's position, with S. D. Lee's Cavalry, and fire into the gunboats and transports. First instance of attack on gunboats by light batteries.

8.—Back to Richmond.

12.—Artillery of the right wing on Almond Creek. We call our camp, "Camp Longstreet." We rest and refit.

which the battle was contested, was of course to be judged by the number of dead and wounded, and their proximity to each other. About thirty feet apart meant heavy work, though where the breastworks had to be stormed, as was the case in some of Grant's battles, the dead would lie in piles. The most effective artillery firing done during the war, was in an artillery duel between our first company and an opposing battery of the enemy. In this, beside exploding the caissons and almost annihilating their enemy, they killed every horse on a piece. The unhappy animals were all tangled up by their harness, in one inextricable pile. One of the men came across a beautiful spaniel at Malvern Hill, whom it was difficult to persuade to quit his dead master's side. The offer of rations, however, finally triumphed over his virtue. The dog was alive at Richmond, and apparently infected with strong Confederate prejudices when last seen; though he made a narrow escape for having indulged in a vitiated taste for gnawing off all the buttons off a $500 coat. This was the property of one of those fierce Majors, whose marches extended only through the streets of Richmond. The feelings of this gallant soldier may be imagined, when upon awakening the morning after a debauch, he discovered the extent of his misfortunes. His fury and agony of mind conld only find relief by asking such questions, and failing to understand, "as what in the deuce anybody wanted to keep any such a d—d flop-eared hound around for anyhow."

There was another homely looking yellow dog on the same battle field (who might have been a relation of Tige's,) who could not understand how the battle had gone, or who had had no offers of bacon to corrupt his principles. In an evil moment he attempted to bite a soldier, detailed to bury the dead, and the attempt cost him a bayonet thrust and his life. The soldier was too much exasperated, and out of humor at the heavy slaughter of our men, to waste any time "fooling around an old dawg."

We were given a number of new guns which had been captured in the fights around Richmond, and had to eat so much of dried vegetables, that the smell of soup Julienne to this day brings to mind the sight of swollen and blackened corpses scattered about for miles over a Virginia battlefield.

It was after McClellan had incautiously placed his army astraddle of Chicahominy swamp (where as Lincoln expressed it, he was like a bull caught on a fence who could neither kick nor gore,) and where the Federal army was bogged up like Captain John Smith, by a sudden rise in the stream—that the cautious General Johnston found his true chance. Here he hastened to deal his enemy a blow, which would have been much more staggering to the Federal general than it was, but for Johnston's having been severely wounded early in the action. The wound might have won promotion and honor for a soldier born under a more fortunate star; but it virtually ended his Virginia career, before he had a fair opportunity of developing his talents. Gen. Lee now came upon the scene with the startling and joyous intelligence that old Stonewall had outwitted his enemies in the Valley, and was on McClellan's flank.

I write the hero's name with pride, and am happy to remember our Batallion ever took orders from him. History will probably give Stonewall the reputation for more genius and achievement, than any general the civil war brought forth, and had he been at the head of affairs and remained alive, the war would have ended differently. Our batteries reported to him at the battle of Manassas, and a crowd of us once sat upon the pieces watching him talk; once afterwards, for a half an hour, in consultation with Lee and Longstreet. Jackson was then dressed in a sort of grey homespun suit, with a broken-brimmed cap, and looked like a good driving overseer or manager, with plenty of hard, horse sense, but no accomplishments or other talent—nothing but plain, direct sense. It was because his manners had so little of the air of a man of the world, or because he repressed all expression, that he had the appearance of being a man of not above average ability. The remark was then made by one of us, after staring at him a long time, that there must be some mistake about him—if he was an able man, he showed it less than any man any of us had ever seen.

Gen. Lee first appeared before us in citizen's dress—that is in white duck, with a bob-tailed coat; jogging along without our suspecting who he was. We thought at first, he was a jolly, easy-going miller or distiller, on a visit as a civilian, to the front, and perhaps carrying out a canteen of whiskey for the boys. He showed himself always a good natured, kind-hearted man, as well as a great general—stopping once to reprove though very gently, the drivers for unmercifully beating their horses when they had stalled; and another day walking about and laughing over one of Artemus Ward's stories, and kept in a good humor about it, the rest of the day. He got put out one day, however, with one of our men who took possession of a shady spot, that had been previously occupied by the General; but which had been temporarily abandoned by him to hurry across the James. The young man was asked what made him appropriate his headquarters, and what annoyed the General was, the idea that he had abandoned the place for good. As the result turned out, we fought more battles in that neighborhood, and stayed there longer than we had done about any other place in Virginia.

CHAPTER XV.
THE DRUMHEAD.

SOMETIMES in the course of our marches our enterprising explorers would come across an odd volume, and for reading this in camp there would be abundant opportunity. For instance, if you were of an indolent turn, you could smoke and read by the tent fire-place, criticising the cook, who was working up to his elbows in dough, or watching the boiling and baking, between the interesting passages. The volume would pass from one mess or dirty hand to another, and the most unreading men in camp, as soon as they found that books were in demand and that they had it in their power to read a coveted volume, would violently claim the right, and set to work in good earnest to cry at or laugh, as the fashion was, over its sentiment or jokes; just the same as men did who never cared for the society of woman previously, or who never cared to drink liquor before entering the army. As soon as it was understood that a canteen, a book or a woman had its value, every body wanted them all; and would study up the art of acquiring them, the same as we did at making brier-root pipes afterwards.

On one of the battle fields about Richmond we came across a volume which had probably gone the rounds of the Federal camp as it did ours, and from one of its chapters, with a view to escaping statistics, and with an object which will be explained further on, I propose to quote in substance, as remembered.

This chapter touched upon a very sensitive chord for a soldier—the fate of a regiment that had disgraced itself in battle, and by shameful cowardice and lack of discipline communicated their panic and exposed the other troops, thus converting a half won victory into a disastrous defeat. The time was in the Thirty Years War of Germany, and the name of the regiment was "Madelon's Cuirassiers." When the remnant of the beaten army had rallied under the walls of Prague, sometime after, the regiment which had lost the battle was seen to approach that city; but its ranks are thinned less by the sword than by desertion. It is understood among them that the matter will be inquired into, and as they come in view, deep shame sits upon the bearded faces of the men; the soldiers declaring that reform should commence at the top of the stairs; the officers conversing in low whispers as to how best to excuse their own conduct.

Arrived at the gates a message is received, ordering the men to dismount, lead their horses, and enter with lowered colors and without sound of trumpet. This ominous reception made the remainder of the regiment regret that they had not followed the example of desertion which had been abundantly set them at the close of the battle; nevertheless, with downcast eyes and with wide intervals between the files, they marched on through the narrow streets.

Suddenly, dismounted dragoons, with mousqueton, appeared behind them—the windows and balconies are seen to be lined with carabineers, who carry their weapons at the recover. In the public square they are ordered to "Halt;" "Draw swords." Then follows the command, "Ground arms." The hearts of the now disarmed men, who are formed up as prisoners, misgive them. The arms and colors are carried off, and every thing appeared ready for an approaching execution. For there in the centre of the square stands the solemn headsman, with his red cloak and black feather, with an iron vice upon one side and a pile of fagots upon the other. A glittering circle of bayonets appears all around, while on one side sit on horseback the military officers who are to try the offenders, if trial there be for men manifestly already condemned. There is but one question—whether the cowardice is the fault of the officers or men; and after the question has been debated violently for two hours, by officers and men, and the prisoners are coming to blows, the clamor of voices ceases, at the blast of the trumpet. The judges consult—the prisoners draw back, and an abrupt, uneasy movement commences among them—behind and in front. In a moment more the cause becomes evident to the spectators—the hands of the officers are being bound behind their backs—they are separating the soldiers by tens. While these latter are made to throw dice on drumheads for their lives, the executioner is burning at the stake the regimental flags and decorations, or snapping the sword blades in his iron vice. With mournful eyes and sad hearts they see their flags consumed and weapons broken at the hands of the headsman—they witness it with an agony to which death would have been sweet.

Meanwhile the soldier of the ten who has thrown the lowest die is being seized and bound and placed with the group of already handcuffed officers. And now comes the closing and most terrible act of all. The gallows appears on the scene, and the unhappy tenth man and all the officers are strung up by their necks, on a scaffold made ready for the purpose, the balance being condemned to labor on fortifications; and the town-crier solemnly proclaims the whole regiment, from colonel down to the last dragoon, to be "Infamous Poltroons."*

I have brought to mind this picture of a regiment which has disgraced its colors, by way of making those who have never thought of the subject, realize how great a misfortune a soldier considers it to be, to be disgraced in battle, and what dejection and downcast looks settle upon his face where the reputation of his regiment has in any degree been tarnished.

Some such picture, in many of its details as the one above given, was constantly coming before every soldier's imagination. He was hearing the words "miserable poltroons" pronounced in the shambling and straggling march of certain regiments who had been disgraced, in the

---

*A similar scene is given in a number of the New York Tribune of 1861 of the mutiny of the 79th New York Regiment which will be suggested by the above. In this 400 men flatly refused to move from camp. The non-commissioned officers took from the men their arms. One hundred men alone stood firm, and kept the mutineers confined until surrounded by cavalry, infantry and artillery. The leaders were handcuffed, an act was read reciting their many instances of insubordination, and the leaders, some seventy in number, who were disarmed and marched to the guard house, declared amenable to the articles of war. The regimental colors were then taken away, and every man ordered to be shot down who refused to obey.

Another misunderstanding between officers and men is thus given in a letter of I. G., from Columbus, Kentucky, to the Crescent, in the same year:

"Serious difficulties have arisen in the — Artillery from your State. Owing to treatment, which is explained—they tore the initial of their Captain from their caps, whom they repudiated, and since this a difficulty has occurred with their new commander. The men complained of rough, unfeeling treatment; open expressions of dissatisfaction led to an altercation between the captain and one of the non-commissioned officers, which resulted in the latter drawing a dagger and the former using a sword. The non-commissioned officer had his hand badly injured in clutching the officer's sword, and is now under arrest. One hundred men made affidavit of grievance, which Polk refused to receive, but offered instead a transfer. This was declined, and a big trouble the consequence; though ultimately settled by a transfer of forty of the members to another artillery."

depressed looks of the men themselves, and in the free criticism of onlooking soldiers. He could see the words of disgrace betrayed in ambiguous reports of battles, where no amount of explanation could conceal what had been bad and cowardly conduct; and at night by camp fires he would hear discussed the reputation of those regiments who had first broken—at Gettysburg or elsewhere, and thus caused the loss of victory and death to the overwhelmed brigades who remained behind.

A company or regiment that once showed signs of weakness, makes its own soldiers ten times more distrustful of each other's valor in the next engagement, and unless the demoralization has been cured, and confidence restored, is a source of danger rather than of strength to an army, and will inevitably damn the reputation of any good men who happen to be connected with it.* As I write this now, there rises before me the picture of a brave old friend from the 8th Georgia Regiment, who was half lamenting, half crying, over the repulse his command and the Confederate troops had met with at Malvern Hill, under the 150 guns with which McClellan on that day swept the Confederate line. "We had nothing but our reputation," said he, "and now we'll never want to go home, as we've lost that." In this latter statement he was mistaken. As for tears, a great many soldiers shed them at Gettysburg, though there had been no lack of courage,

*In so speaking, I am far from recommending the frequent enforcement of the death penalty, as a remedy. Anthony Sambola, Esq., who was detailed from the Fifth Company of Washington Artillery, as clerk to a court-martial, tells me there were 150 men shot between Chickamauga and Atlanta. Desertions on a large scale showed the discontent or hopelessness of the troops from certain States, and wholesale shootings (as for instance, 22 at a time) only made the men more disaffected. My information is that Gen. Lee never signed the death penalty but once, and only then with the greatest reluctance. The penalty might have been just to the men who deserted, or to the officers who did not do their full duty; but at the same time it destroyed the *esprit* of the regiments from whom the men were taken.

and there were no dry eyes at all, though not from a sense of shame, on the day at Appomatox Court House, when General Lee, for the first time, dressed himself in full uniform, and told his few followers, good bye.

The trials which took place in the Confederate army, were mostly regimental, that is were trivial and for which no court-martials should have been ordered at all, and were much more merciful in their awards than the one above recorded—seldom amounting to more than extra guard duty or loss of pay for a month, and for offences, which were really crimes, to confinement at Castle Thunder, with the ball and chain. The only case I can now remember where the death penalty was inflicted, was in the time following the first battle of Manassas, when two of the "Tigers" were tried for insubordination, and for striking their officers. The finding of the Court was—Death.

And so death it was, the spot for the tragedy being but a little distance from our camp. At the appointed hour, a very large crowd of officers and men were there assembled. A hollow square had been previously formed of troops from the same brigade. At about 10, the prisoners who had been sustained in the previous interval by the consolations of liquor and champagne, contributed by generous comrades, were brought upon the field. They were dressed in striped blouse and white Zouave breeches, and in the full eccentric uniform of the Company—the whole command being similarly dressed. The arms of the condemned men were pinioned behind their backs; but their steps were elastic and showed no sign of dejection. Now the officer in command orders the finding of the court-martial to be read, and then the dramatic interest in the scene is increased, when the doomed prisoners are confronted with their own coffins. The remaining details are very simple—bandaging their eyes, and causing them to get upon their knees, before the twelve motionless statues (or friends representing duty,) who stand with loaded guns. The command is given, "make ready, aim, fire," and the strong men of the moment before roll back corpses.

I saw afterwards, several prisoners taken out and shot at Richmond, for various offenses. They were generally carefully dressed in black, and did not greatly differ in appearance from that of a man who is going to appear in public on a formal occasion—who is going to get married in his best suit, or who has some public duty to perform. We had too in our camp, a driver who had been at West Point, enlisted for his knowledge about driving battery horses; but who fell into disgrace. He however, had no greater misfortune than to be driven from camp, by order of court-martial, after having had his head shaved; or in other words, to be drummed out of the army. The man shortly after was elected or appointed major of a Batallion, and did good service. There were a great many more victims of war all through the South, than those who were killed in battles; for instance, those who gave all their time to drilling and equipping their men, who spent all their own fortunes in the work, and that of their friends, and who after all, were ruthlessly shoved aside for some new favorite, kept behind or constantly placed in obscurity. The South would have fared none the worse, if the men of education, who volunteered from duty, had been permitted to go home, and give their talents and experience as officers to new regiments. The fighting of the regiments raised towards the close of the war would have been much better, if such a rule had been adopted.

A tragic incident which awakened much less feeling, as

the guilty party was not one of our own men, occurred on our march after Pope in 1862.

During the march of the army, September 21, 1862, a spy dressed in Confederate uniform, or rather an imitation of it, rode up to Gen. D. R. Jones, commanding division, and told him he had been sent by Gen. Jackson, to tell him to halt his division where it then was. Suspicion was aroused, from the fact that Jones was under Longstreet, and cypher alphabets and memoranda were found upon his person. It was now remembered that one of Longstreet's couriers had been shot on the night previous, while carrying a dispatch, by a man answering the pretended messenger's description. It was now found too, on examination, that one of the barrels of his revolver was empty. A drum head court-martial was immediately called—papers examined, and his guilt clearly proved by his own confession. The unhappy wretch was taken into the woods—his hands tied behind him, and placed astride of a mule; a rope was then tied around his neck—the end thrown over a limb of a tree. Then the mule was struck with a stick by one of Longstreet's couriers; away went the mule, and with it went the soul of Charles Mason, spy, of Terryville, Pa. The column was detained by this interruption three hours. The body of the dangling corpse presented a ghastly spectacle, as we marched by; his boots had disappeared, and it was then said that these were the perquisites of the officiating Jack Ketch. The man died defiantly, claiming to have given his life for his country.

All further that need be said upon this head, is that the talents, or one talent of a great general, consists in knowing profoundly the character of his men—their prejudices and sympathies, and where discipline should be sternly enforced, or wisely relaxed. For instance, one of our Generals in a Western Army, was at one time immensely unpopular by allowing, as was reported in the army, soldiers to be shot for chicken and hog-stealing; though Cromwell, Napoleon, and other great and popular Generals had in the enforcement of discipline, inflicted equally great penalties. But the idea of shooting a soldier in North Georgia, or Tennessee, for hog-stealing, a crime to which the people of those States have the same sort of temptation that a Texan has to get away with a horse or cattle! Such a sentence, though there doubtless was great need of making private property respected, was absurdly unjust, in view of the fact that the army was nearly always half-fed and frequently starving. To shoot a man born on American soil, who has a natural tendency to steal, as a quartermaster or office-holder, but to die like a man when he is fed, was felt to be an outrage on every brave man who had given his life to the issue.

Of a similar character was much of the discipline enforced during the first year of the war. Until officers and men had come to understand each other, and were forced to accord esteem and respect to great qualities shown in battle, we were like animals badly broken or harnessed, galled jades wincing under needless restriction. The gentleman of the salon or parlor retains in the every day life of a camp, but little trace of breeding or civility, but his sensibilities and pride were very easily touched; and probably a stricter and more cheerful discipline would have been kept up, if careful attention had been paid to these facts. Probably, too, there would have been less of the weariness and heart sickness which made so many spirited men sink off, from a feeling that they had not elected rigid and just officers, but selfish and insolent oppressors. But this feeling died out as the war advanced

—the officers who were reserved, more because of their unfamiliarity with their new duties, than from being inflated with vanity, gradually learned their true duty to their men, and to retain at the same time their respect, while the soldiers were not slow in appreciating the deserving ones at their true worth.

It's human nature to abuse more or less, your privileges and advantages of fortune—by keeping the tit-bits for yourself, the soft places for your friends, and by putting on rough duty those whom you do not like; for instance, in putting one soldier to assist in making fortifications under heavy fire, with a spade (as I once saw one officer of the day do) in place of a lazier or more cowardly comrade. But on the other hand, selfishness would crop out just as often in the soldier, as already previously explained.

CHAPTER XVI.

BATTLE OF THE RAPPAHANNOCK.

We laid around Richmond from the thirteenth to the twenty-fifth of July. The life would have been slow suicide a year previous; but after witnessing the desperate fighting at Mechanicsville and Malvern Hill, and seeing thirty thousand men killed, wounded and taken prisoners in the two armies in the Seven Day's Fight alone, we were contented to bide our time—to accept a sort of happiness similar to that of our battery horses, fully assured that we would not have long to wait for hot work.

On the 25th the 3d Company were ordered off with Gen. Anderson to New Market Heights; on the 5th of

August an attack having been made by the enemy on Malvern Hill we got ready to meet him. The First and Fourth Companies were at Laurel Hill Church.

Evans now commenced pressing McClellan and taking prisoners at Malvern Hill, which soon led to its abandonment, and our being sent back to camp (Longstreet.)

General Lee thinking that McClellan's army was no longer worth watching, commenced moving North, and our batteries received marching orders on the 10th. When we passed through Richmond, as an evidence of the change that had commenced, the people looked on Lee's army silently and a little sadly, dimly comprehending that in spite of recent victories many more hecatombs of bodies would be made before the end was yet to come, and that victory for us meant but little more than the showy uniforms in which the volunteer troops had first come on. Here were all the regiments marching through, except those already dead and crippled; and those still alive and now marching on would still have to furnish 100,000 skeletons, as if for a corduroy road, from Gettysburg to Petersburg. There were at any rate 500,000 corpses to be furnished to order as if on requisition from the two armies; and the number taken from those who died or were killed in Virginia would have exceeded Tamerlane's pyramid of 300,000 skulls.

We camped the first night out on the Chickahominy, 12 miles beyond Richmond, while the infantry were shoved forward to Gordonsville by rail. Jackson had been up to his usual thimble-rigging tricks upon Gen. Pope, (who was now trying to see what he could make out of the office of Federal Commander) holding before his blindly-groping enemy at one moment a Jack-o'-lantern light, and the next presenting him with a St. Anthony number of temptations. The first of the military blunders into which Pope was invited, was to attempt attacking our railroad line of communication with Richmond. To do this he pushed Gen. Banks forward to Cedar Mountain, with the caution given many times, through Pope's Chief of Staff, according to Greeley, "that there must be no backing out *this* day." And so there was not to be, he found, when he started onward; for Lee's troops meanwhile arriving, Jackson stealthily pushed forward Ewell's Division, scattering the Federal cavalry, and creeping through the woods along the western base of Cedar Mountain. Having taken up a strong position, fixed his batteries, and generally made himself comfortable, there was nothing more to be done but wait until Banks should come along and carry out his intention of not backing out.

Banks' attack was, however, very heavy upon Early's brigade of Ewell's Division, who held the road, and Taliaferro was assailed at one time in flank and rear. "But the best Union blood," says Greeley, "poured like water; Gen. Geary was wounded, Price taken prisoner, Crawford's brigade was a mere skeleton, and the others lost half their number in killed and wounded—more than two thousand in all." After several day's maneuvering, Pope captured a letter which showed that Lee's whole army was upon him, and immediately struck the back track across the Rappahannock.

Meanwhile our batteries had marched to Montpelier—traveling early in the morning and late in the evening, on account of the heat, and bivouacking at Hope's Tavern. The next day carried us to Louisa Court-House, and the day after to Gordonsville.

We were ordered forward again when Pope fell back to Orange Court-House, (Aug. 16,) and found the enemy directly in our front. On the following day at noon, we moved cautiously forward, and camped near midnight on the Rapidan. The companies were assigned, Eshelman's to Pickett's brigade, Richardson's to Toombs'.

On the night of the 2d it was understood that we were to prepare for hot work the next day, and at daylight the following morning, Col. Walton posted the guns on the South side of the Rappahannock, at the Railroad bridge, and at Beverly's Ford—the design being to threaten a crossing at these points, while the army meanwhile should move up the Rappahannock and get behind Pope's right. At 6.30, Capt. Miller of the 3d company, who had the strain of the firing upon him, discharged the signal gun, and before a third could be fired, obtained a reply from the enemy's batteries upon the opposite side. And a dreadfully hot reply it was. The enemy had as much the advantage in position and guns as Jackson had had at Cedar Mountain. Every shot they fired tore through our ranks, killing and wounding the men, and smashing the pieces. The fire became so hot that a battery who had been assigned position to the left of the Washington Artillery forgot to imitate the boy who stood on the burning deck, and moved off without awaiting orders. In the progress of the battle twenty-three of our horses were killed, and nine men killed and twelve wounded. Lieut. Brewer's horse went galloping back, with an empty saddle, (leaving his rider dying on the field) to the very officer to whom it had been promised that day, in case its owner should be killed; which arrival happened just as a shell exploded at the side of Col. Walton, killing the horse of bugler Frank Villasano, and wounding that of Adjutant Owen. Lieut. Brewer sent word to his friends at home that he had tried to live like a Christian and die like a soldier. He was buried at night in St. James Church yard, with the bodies of other of our own men, who died on the same battle field.

Private R. T. Marshall was the brother of Gen. Lee's private secretary—the latter assisting at the funeral with a clergyman. The grave of the latter is now marked at Warrenton, with a piece of the Richmond-made gun which caused his death. The further details of this battle will be found in the following reports of the battle of the Rappahannock:

REPORT OF GEN. LEE.

On the 23d of August, Gen. Longstreet directed Col. Walton, with part of the Washington Artillery and other batteries of his command, to drive back a force of the enemy that had crossed to the South bank of the Rappahannock, near the railroad bridge, upon the withdrawal of Gen. Jackson on the previous day. Fire was opened about sunrise, and continued with great vigor for several hours, the enemy being compelled to withdraw with loss. Some of the batteries of Col. S. D. Lee's batallion were ordered to aid those of Col. Walton, and under their united fire, the enemy was forced to abandon his position on the north side of the river, burning in his retreat the railroad bridge and the neighboring dwellings.

REPORT OF GEN. LONGSTREET.

I had ordered Col. Walton to place his batteries in position at Rappahannock station, and to drive the enemy from his positions on both sides of the river. The batteries were opened at sunrise on the 23d, and a severe cannonade continued for several hours. In about two hours, however, the enemy was driven across the river, abandoning his tête-de-pont. The brigades of Brigadier Gen. Evans and D. R. Jones, the latter under Col. G. F. Anderson, moved forward to occupy this position. It was found untenable, however, being exposed to a cross-fire of artillery from the other bank. The troops were therefore partially withdrawn, and Col. S. D. Lee was ordered to select position for his batteries, and joined in the combat. The enemy's position was soon rendered too warm for him, and he took advantage of a severe rain storm to retreat in haste, after firing the bridge and the private dwellings in its vicinity. Col. Walton deserves much credit for skill in the management of his batteries; and Col. Lee got into position in time for some good practice.

REPORT OF COL. WALTON.

HEADQUARTERS ARTILLERY CORPS, RIGHT WING,
Dept. Northern Virginia, Aug. 25, 1862.

I have the honor to report that, in obedience to an order received from Major General Longstreet, on the evening of the 22d instant, accompanied by Major

J. J. Garnett, Chief of Artillery on the Staff of Brig. Gen. D. R. Jones, and Capt. C. W. Squires, commanding the first Company of Washington Artillery, I made a reconnoissance of the position of the enemy in the vicinity of Beverly's Ford and Rappahannock station, on the Rappahannock river, with the view, as instructed, to place the long-range guns under my command, in position to open upon the enemy's batteries early on the following morning. Having, during the night, made all necessary preparation, at daybreak, on the morning of the 23d, I placed in position on the left, at Beverly's Ford, Capt. Miller's battery Washington Artillery, four light twelve-pounder Napoleon guns; a section of two ten-pounder Parrott guns under Capt. Rogers, and one ten-pounder Parrott gun under Capt. Anderson; and on the right, Capt. Squires' Battery, Washington Artillery, four three-inch rifles; Capt. Stribling's Battery, one three inch rifle and three light twelve-pounder Napoleon guns; a section of Capt. Chapman's Battery, one three-inch rifle and one light twelve-pounder Napoleon gun under Lieut. Chapman, and two Blakely guns of Capt. Maurin's Battery under Lieut. Landry.

The heavy fog prevailing obscured the opposite bank of the river, and the enemy's positions entirely from view, until about six o'clock, A. M., at which hour, the sun having partially dispelled the fog, I opened fire from Capt. Miller's Battery upon a battery of long-range guns of the enemy, directly in front, at a range of about one thousand yards. By previous arrangements, the batteries on the right and left of Capt. Miller's position immediately opened, and the fire became general along the line. We had not long to wait for the response of the enemy, he immediately opening upon all our positions a rapid and vigorous fire from all his batteries, some in position, until then undiscovered by us. The battery of the enemy engaged by Capt. Miller, was silenced in about forty minutes. Notwithstanding the long range guns under Capt. Rodgers and Anderson, on the left, had, shortly after the commencement of the engagement been withdrawn from action and placed under shelter of the hill on which they had been posted. thus leaving the battery of the enemy, which it was intended these guns should engage, free to direct against Miller, and the batteries on the hill on the right, a most destructive fire. At this time Capt. Miller changed position and directed his fire against the opposing battery, when one on the right of that which had been silenced, opened upon him, subjecting him to a cross fire, and causing him to lose heavily in men and horses. The fire was continued by Miller's Battery alone on the left until seven o'clock, when after consultation with Gen. Jones, and the fire of the enemy having greatly slackened, I ordered him to retire by half battery, which was handsomely done, in good order.

At this time Lieut. Brewer fell, mortally wounded. The combat on the right was gallantly fought by the batteries there placed in position.

Capt. Squires assumed command of that part of the field, and won for himself renewed honors by the handsome manner in which he handled his batteries, and for the good judgment and coolness he displayed under the heavy fire of the enemy, to which he was subjected during four hours without intermission.

The object sought to be obtained by this engagement, I am happy to say was fully accomplished by driving the enemy from all his positions before nightfall, and causing him to withdraw from our front entirely during the night.

I have to lament the loss, in this engagement of a zealous, brave and most efficient officer in Lieut. Brewer, Third Company Washington Artillery, who fell at the head of his section at the moment it was being withdrawn from the field, and of many non-commissioned officers and privates. The officers and men in all the batteries engaged, are deserving the highest praise for their gallantry upon the field. The attention of the General commanding is respectfully directed to those named particularly in the reports of Capts. Miller and Squires. Too much praise cannot be awarded to Capt. Miller and his brave Company for the stubborn and unflinching manner in which they fought the enemy's battery in such superior force and position on the left, and to Capt. Squires and Stribling, and Lieuts. Landry and Chapman on the right. I am indebted to Capt. Middle-

ton, of Brig. Gen. Drayton's Staff, to Lieut. Williams, of Gen. D. R. Jones Staff, and to Lieut. William Owen, Adjutant, Washington Artillery, all of whom were constantly with me under fire during the engagement, for their valuable assistance and zealous conduct on the field—there are none more brave or more deserving consideration than these gentlemen. I annex a list of casualties, and have the honor to be,
J. B. WALTON,
Col. and Chief of Art., Right Wing.

REPORT OF CAPT. MILLER.

I proceeded with my battery of four smooth-bore 12-pound Napoleons to Beverly's Ford on the Rappahannock, 1000 yards from the river. My position, on a hill sloping towards the river, was not such a one as I would have desired, though doubtless the best the locality afforded. At sunrise I discovered a battery of the enemy in position, immediately in front of us, on a hill on the north side of the river, and I opened on it with spherical case. The enemy replied briskly, and for half an hour the firing was very spirited. During this time I was considerably annoyed by an enfilading fire of a long-ranged battery, posted to our right, and entirely beyond our range. After nearly an hour's engagement I was gratified to notice that the fire in our front had perceptibly slackened, indeed had almost entirely ceased. Up to this time but one of my men had been wounded, and two horses killed. The batteries supporting me at this time retired from the field, subjecting me to a galling cross-fire from the enemy's rifle battery in their front. I immediately changed front on the left and replied. The enemy having our exact range, replied with terrible precision and effect. For sometime we maintained this unequal conflict, when having nearly exhausted my ammunition, and agreeably to your orders, I retired by half battery from the field.

My casualties were: Killed—First Lieutenant Brewer, privates Thompson, McDonald, Joubert (mortally wounded) and Dolan.

Wounded—Corpl. P. W. Pettiss; privates James Tully, Levy, Fourshee, Maxwell, Crilly, Kerwin, Lynch—eight.

Twenty-one horses killed—356 rounds of ammunition expended.

I would be pleased to pay a tribute to the coolness and intrepidity of my command; but where all acted so well, it would be invidious to particularize. I should be wanting in my duty, however, were I not to mention Lieuts. Hero and McElroy, and my non-commissioned officers, Sergeants McNeil, Handy, Collins, Ellis and Stocker, and Corporals Coyle, Kremmelburg, Pettiss and DeBlanc, who by their coolness and close attention to duty, contributed not a little to the efficiency of my battery. Respectfully,
M. B. MILLER,
Capt. Commanding 3d Co. B. W. A.

REPORT OF CAPT. SQUIRES.

Early on the morning of the 23d of August, the artillery, composed of the first company of Washington Artillery, (four three-inch rifles) and Captain Stribling's battery, (three Napoleon guns and one three-inch rifle) marched in the direction of the hill opposite to Rappahannock station. * * * The batteries were formed in line from right to left in the following order: First Company Washington Artillery, four three-inch rifle guns: Dixie Artillery, one Napoleon gun and one three-inch rifle ; Stribling's battery, three Napoleon guns and one three-inch rifle; this had scarcely been accomplished when the signal was given from your position to "commence firing," which was quickly responded to by the enemy. The combat was briskly carried on by the artillery directly in our front for half an hour, when the enemy placed a battery on the extreme left, and had partly succeeded in enfilading our batteries, when I withdrew the section of Lieut. Galbraith, and directed him to engage the enemy on the left. Lieut. G. accomplished this under a heavy fire, and was partly forced from his first position when Lieut. Landry, with a section of Capt. Maurin's Battery reported, and was sent to assist Lieut. G., the four guns being placed under Lieut. G., who managed to keep a heavy enfilading fire from the main batteries, by the coolness and bravery with which he manœuvred this battery. The fire on both sides now became general and rapid. The enemy placed more artillery in position, and for some time I thought I should have to retire; but the enemy soon after slackened his fire, and it was evident he was worsted by the projectiles with which our artillerists assailed him. An officer now came from the right and informed me that the infantry were preparing to charge, and to cease firing as soon as they appeared. I kept up the fire, returning shot for shot with the enemy, who appeared willing to give up the combat.

Seeing this, and being informed that Gen. Evans (commanding the infantry,) was advancing to attack the enemy, I ordered the four (reserve) guns of Lieut. Galbraith in position to engage the enemy's artillery, and draw his attention while our troops were advancing. The enemy finally gave up his position, retired across the Rappahannock, and only replied occasionally to our fire, and in an hour after ceased firing altogether.

It is with pleasure I am enabled to speak of the gallantry with which Capt. Stribling, officers and men, behaved on this occasion. Lieut. Chapman, with his section of Dixie Artillery, behaved with great coolness, and handled his guns with effect. To Lieut. E. Owen, J. M. Galbraith, and those under their command, I would especially call your attention. Both officers commanded full batteries, and handled them with coolness, bravery and good judgment, which has so often on previous occasions won the confidence of their men. Sergeants T. Y. Abby, C. L. C. Dupuy and L. M. Montgomery rendered me efficient service: the latter, on previous occasions, has placed me under many obligations for his voluntary services.

First Company, Battery Washington Artillery, killed: Privates, W. Chambers, R. T. Marshall, J. Reddington and H. Koss. Wounded, Coporal W. H. West, Privates, John R. Fell, T. S. Turner, M. Mount and W. R. Falconer.

Dixie Artillery, wounded: Privates, John Eddins, Westley Pence, John Knight and Daniel Martin.

Stribling's Battery, wounded: Lieut. Archer, and one Private.

First Company Battery Washington Artillery, horses killed, 1, wounded, 1.

Stribling's Battery, horses killed, 4, wounded, 0.

Dixie Battery, horses killed, 1, wounded, 0.—Total, 6 killed, 1 wounded.

One three inch rifle gun exploded during action. The batteries were engaged from about seven o'clock, A. M., to eleven o'clock, A. M., and expended the following amunition:

First Company Washington Artillery, 400; Section of Dixie Artillery, 209; Section of Maurin's Artillery, 119; Stribling's Artillery, 354; Leake's Artillery, one gun.—Total, 1,182.

Captain Leake reported after the enemy had retired with one rifle and three smooth-bore guns. He sustained no loss. About two o'clock, P. M., Major Garnett rode up and requested me to send four rifle guns to Col. S. D. Lee, who was on the right, near Central railroad. For this purpose I detached Lieutenant Owen with one section of the Washington Artillery, and one section of Mann's Battery. In obedience to your orders, at half past five P. M. I ordered all the guns back to their respective commands.

Very respectfully, Colonel, your obedient servant,

C. W. SQUIRES,
Capt. Commanding First Co. Bat. W. A

CHAPTER XVII.

SECOND BATTLE OF MANASSAS.

While Pope's attention was thus occupied with Longstreet, Jackson was pushing on up the Rappahannock to make a crossing at one of the upper fords, (Hinson's Mills,) move around Pope's army in the rear, and strike the railroad to Alexandria. The first day of his rapid march he reached Selma, and as McClellan was coming on from the Peninsula with more troops, and no time was to be lost, Jackson pushed on to Bristow Station, striking the railroad about dark—Hay's Brigade in the front, and Forno in command—capturing two trains of cars. He had thus forced himself between Pope and Washington without meeting any resistance, or without any suspicion upon Pope's part that so daring and dangerous a move would ever have been attempted. His position is now indeed critical—foot-sore and weary as his men are, he must divide off two regiments (21st Georgia and 21st North Carolina) and send them with Stuart's cavalry, seven miles further on to Manassas. This expedition crept cautiously through the dark and struck the place from behind. It might have been warned by the dashing by of an engine from Bristow, which soon after ran into a train of cars, but was not.

At this point he captured immense supplies of provisions, guns, engines, and other munitions of war, for which latter Pope's army will soon have sore need. But the alarm has been given now, and the enemy are closing around Jackson on every side. First, the little force at Manassas must beat off Scammon across Bull Run, and take his bridge away from him; then Stuart's cavalry must raid up and down and destroy everything about Fairfax and Burke's station. Then (for the moments grow more and more precious) Jackson must push up his own and Hill's divisions from Bristow, and rout the Federal Taylor who goes one leg on the encounter, and has much difficulty in hobbling off on the other. But Pope's whole army is being spread out now, and they hold the gap by which Jackson came in. As the afternoon of this eventful day (the 27th) wears away, Hooker comes up on Ewell, (left behind at Bristow,) and after hard fighting Gen. Ewell* burns everything behind—the Louisiana regiments being "hotly engaged"—and destroys the bridges. He must now rejoin Jackson, whose only chance is to move westward, towards Longstreet. There was not much sleeping that night for the weary soldier; and at 3 o'clock the next morning, (28th) Jackson makes a detour by way of Centreville and Sudley Springs, followed behind by great masses of the enemy, whom he impeded by de-

*The following is extracted from the report of Gen. Early:
Hays' Louisiana brigade was on the right of the railroad, and my own brigade to the right of Hays' in a pine wood.
Col. Forno, with four regiments of Hays' brigade and one of Lawton's, and one piece of d'Aquin's battery, was then ordered to the front to reconnoitre and destroy the bridge over Kettle run, and tear up the track of the railroad. He found the enemy had brought up on a train of cars a body of infantry sufficient to fill nine cars; but having doubtless discovered our force to be larger than was thought, was re-embarking it. A few shots from the piece of artillery were fired at the train and it made its way back again, after receiving some damage. The 6th Louisiana, under Col. Strong, was left on picket two miles in front, on the railroad, and the 8th Louisiana was put to work destroying the railroad bridge and tearing up the track, and Col Forno returned with the rest of the forces.
The enemy was seen approaching on the right of the railroad and in front of Hays' brigade, the 6th and 8th Louisiana regiments falling back and taking position in a wood three or four hundred yards in front of the brigade. The enemy's force consisted of heavy columns of infantry, with artillery. As soon as the enemy came in range our artillery, from its several positions, opened on him, as did the 6th and 8th Louisiana. By this combined fire, two columns of the enemy, of not less than a brigade each, were driven back, and the 5th Louisiana regiment was sent forward to reinforce the sixth and eighth. At this time the Louisiana regiments were actively engaged, and a large body of the enemy was moving up, and the experiment had to be tried whether our troops could be withdrawn in good order. Gen. Ewell directed me to cover the retiring of the troops with my brigade. Lawton's was the first withdrawn across the ford at the railroad bridge, and then Hays' Brigade followed—all without much loss.

stroying the bridges and moving on back towards Sudley Mills Ford, where he must encounter in a sanguinary fight a fresh division, (King's) only to be terminated by darkness—Ewell and Taliaferro both being wounded.

It certainly looks as if the game for Jackson is ended now: so General Pope believes, for on the 29th Jackson will be assailed by 25,000 troops, and from every quarter, at the same time. But meanwhile Lee and Longstreet had been following Pope closely behind—so closely that at Jefferson, where we bivouacked about sundown on the 24th, the two hostile camps came in sight of each other, and the enemy commenced shelling our position. In crossing at Waterloo bridge, (26th) Longstreet had felt our need, and made our batteries follow immediately after him.

Moving through woods and fields to keep out of sight of the signal corps, through Annanville and over the Warrenton Turnpike, we crossed the Rappahannock and camped near Orleans. On the 27th, during a halt for rest near Salem, the town was suddenly dashed into by Federal Cavalry, and a number of stragglers absent for water or food barely escaped, came rushing back and gave the alarm, though it did not prevent Gen. Lee from great risk of capture. Our trouble was we had no cavalry at hand to give any news; and I remember seeing Gen. Lee enquire of us, so difficult was it to see or obtain information, whether some horsemen in front were the enemy or our own men. At any rate, the infantry with us were ordered into line—Gen. Anderson getting them stirred up with the cry of "Put on your shirts, men, there's no time to lose now."

The same night we marched to Thoroughfare Gap, a very narrow pass, with precipitous sides, and through

Bull Run Mountains. We were here delayed by the enemy in force, (McDowell) who, it seemed to us might have, with a hundred men, achieved among the gloomy precipices as much as Leonidas. The Persian king, however, did not have Hood's Texas Brigade to do his flanking over the mountains; and so Jackson, whose destiny now hangs on a thread, and the booming of whose guns our vanguard can hear, will soon be reinforced. At about mid-day, (29th) Longstreet, who had been pressing hotly forward, came in on the right of Jackson, and the crisis for him had passed. Pope's efforts to overwhelm Jackson had been a failure. There remained now nothing to do but to turn upon Pope, twine around his army although still the largest, and to leisurely beat him back in two days fighting, across Bull Run, to the heights of Centreville. The reports of our Commanders, given below, tells the rest of the story:

REPORT OF COL. WALTON,

OF SECOND BATTLE OF MANASSAS.

HEADQUARTERS BATALLION WASHINGTON ARTILLERY, }
November 30th, 1862. }

TO MAJOR G. W. SORRELL,
Assistant Adjutaut General, Right Wing, A. N. V.

I have the honor to transmit the following report of the operations of the Batallion Washington Artillery of New Orleans, under my command, on the 29th, 30th, and 31st August last, at and after the second battle of Manassas. On the 29th August, 1862, the four batteries composing the batallion were assigned and served as follows: The fourth company, consisting of two six-pounder bronze guns, and two twelve-pounder howitzers, under Capt. B. F. Eshleman, Lieuts. Norcòmb, Battles and Apps, with Pickett's brigade; the second company with two six-pound bronze guns, and two twelve-pound howitzers, under Capt. Richardson, Lieuts. Hawes, DeRussey and Britton, with Toombs' brigade; the first company, with three three-inch rifle guns, under Capt. C. W. Squires, Lieuts. E. Owens, Galbraith and Brown, and the third company, with four light twelve-pound guns, (Napoleons) under Capt. M. B. Miller, Lieuts. McElroy and Hero in reserve.

About noon on the 29th, the two batteries in reserve having halted near the village of Gainesville on the Warrenton and Centreville turnpike, were ordered forward by Gen. Longstreet, to engage the enemy then in our front, and near the village of Groveton. Captains Miller and Squires at once proceeded to the position indicated by the General, and opened fire upon the enemy's batteries. Immediately in Captain Miller's front he discovered a battery of the enemy, distant about twelve hundred yards. Beyond this battery, and on a more elevated position, were posted the enemy's rifle batteries. He opened upon the battery nearest him, and after a spirited engagement of three quarters of an hour, completely silenced it and compelled it to leave the field. He then turned his attention to the enemy's rifle batteries, and engaged them until having exhausted his ammunition he retired from the field.

Capt. Squires, on reaching his position on the left of Capt. Miller's battery, at once opened with his usual accuracy upon the enemy's batteries. Unfortunately, after the first fire, one of his guns having become disabled by the blowing out of the bushing of the vent, was sent from the field.

Captain Squires then placed the remaining section of his battery under command of Lieut. Owen, and rode to the left, to place additional guns (that had been sent forward to his assistance) in position. At this time the enemy's infantry were engaged by the forces on the left of the position occupied by our batteries, and, while the enemy retreated in confusion before the charge of our veterans, the section under Lieut. Owen poured a destructive fire into their affrighted ranks.

Scores were seen to fall, until finally the once beautiful line melted confusedly into the woods.

The enemy's artillery having withdrawn beyond our range, the section was ordered from the field. Both batteries, the first and third, in this action, fully maintained their well-earned reputation for skilful practice and gallant behavior. With this duel ended the operations on the left of our line for the day.

The next morning, 30th August, the second company of Captain J. B. Richardson was ordered forward from its position on the Manassas Gap railroad, to join its brigade (Toombs') then moving forward towards the enemy. Captain Richardson pushed forward until, arriving near the Chinn House, he was informed that our infantry had charged and taken a battery near that position, but, owing to heavy reinforcements thrown forward by the enemy, were unable to hold it without the assistance of artillery. He immediately took position on the left of the Chinn House and opened on the enemy, who were advancing rapidly, in large numbers. After firing a short time, he moved his battery forward about four hundred yards, and succeeded in holding the captured battery of four Napoleons, forcing the enemy back, and compelling a battery immediately in his front, and which was annoying our infantry greatly, to retire. He then turned the captured guns upon their late owners, and at night brought them from the field with their horses and harness.

Captain Richardson, in his report, makes special mention for gallantry of privates J. B. Cleveland and W. W. Davis, who were the first to reach the captured battery, and with the assistance of some infantry, fired nearly twenty-five rounds before being relieved by their comrades. Lieutenant Hawes had his horse shot under him during this battle. While Richardson, with the second, was doing such gallant services near Chinn House, Eshleman, with the fourth, with his short range guns, was doing good work in the same neighborhood. Following his brigade, (Pickett's) he shelled the woods in their front, while they advanced in line of battle against the enemy, whose skirmishers were seen on the edge of the wood. Finding it would be impracticable to follow the brigade, owing to the broken nature of the ground, he passed rapidly to the right and front, going into battery and firing from every elevated position from which he could enfilade the enemy, until he had passed entirely to the right of General Jones' position, (overlooking nearly the whole space in front of Chinn House) from which his shells fell into the ranks of the enemy with great execution. A persistent attack on the front and flank drove the enemy back into the woods, and now the immense clouds of dust rising from Centreville road indicated that he was in full retreat. He was directed by General D. R. Jones to move forward and shell the wood and road, which he continued to do until directed by Gen. J. E. B. Stuart to send a section of his battery to the hills in front of the Conrad House, and to fire into a column of cavalry advancing in his rear. The section under Lieut. Norcom was detached, took position on the left of the Conrad House, and fired into the enemy until directed to cease by Gen. Stuart, his object having been accomplished.

The remaining section of the battery, under Lieut. Battles, was then ordered by Captain Eshleman across the Sudley road, firing as it advanced, into the retreating enemy. At this time, Captain Eshleman's only support was one company of sixty men of Gen. Jackson's sharpshooters, under Capt. Lee.

After a short interval, the enemy again appeared in force near the edge of the wood. Capt. E. immediately changed his front to the left, and poured into the enemy's ranks two rounds of canister, with deadly effect. Those not killed or wounded ran in disorder. After throwing a few shells into the woods, Captain E. retired about two hundred yards to the rear, being unwilling to risk his section with such meagre support. In a few minutes an order was brought from Gen. Stuart directing the section to be brought again to the vicinity of the Conrad House.

It was now dark, and Capt. E. kept up from this last position, a moderate fire until nine o'clock, in the direction of the Centreville road, when he was directed to retire, with Lieut. Norcom's section, that had joined him on the field, and rest his men. Capt. E., in his report, applauds highly the conduct of his officers, non-commissioned officers and men, to whose coolness and judgment he was indebted for the rapid evolutions of his battery and precision of his fire.

The next day, August 31, 1862, Lieut. Owen, with two guns of the first Company, accompanied Gen. Stuart, commanding Cavalry in pursuit of the enemy to and beyond Germantown. They came up with the enemy at several points, driving him ahead of them and capturing five hundred prisoners.

Capt. Squires on the same day, with one gun accompanied Col. Rosser, to Manassas, going in rear of the enemy, capturing a large amount of stores, (Quartermasters and Surgical) ambulances, horses, etc.

My casualties in this battle were one killed, Private, H. N. White, of second Company, and nine wounded.

Thus ended the operations of this batallion in this great second battle of Manassas, fought almost on the same ground and in sight of the field where our guns first pealed forth a little more than a year before.

I have the satisfaction in conclusion, to say that all the officers and men gave in this important battle renewed evidence of their devotion, judgment and cool bravery, in most trying positions. No eulogy of mine can add to the reputation they so worthily enjoy, earned upon bloody battle fields.

I am under obligations to Lieut. W. M. Owen, my always devoted and brave Adjutant, for distinguished services under fire. I have the honor to be your obedient servant,

J. B. WALTON,
Col. Commanding.

Gen. Longstreet, in his official report, describes the excitement of battle as giving new life to the men—says that the Washington Artillery was placed midway between Jackson and his line, "and engaged the enemy for several hours in a severe and successful artillery duel."

CHAPTER XVIII.

THE MARYLAND CAMPAIGN.

To go a little more into detail, the turning point, on the 29th of August, of the battle on Jackson's flank was brought about by a heavy attack of Kearney upon that portion of the line, about 6 o'clock in the afternoon. For a while it was successful enough to double up Jackson's left upon his centre. Though the troops had been exhausted by many days previous fighting, by one attack after another during seven hours of struggle, and had hardly a round of ammunition, "Yet," says General Early in his report, "My brigade and the Eighth Louisiana advanced upon the enemy through a field, and drove him from the woods and out of the railroad cut, crossing the latter and following in pursuit several hundred yards beyond."

The lines of the two armies, however, were but little affected on the 30th by the battle of the 29th, but the fight of the last day was renewed by Pope under the absurd error that Lee was seeking to escape. McDowell was ordered to "press the enemy vigorously the whole day." But once the pressing process was commenced, it was very quickly shown what the supposed retreat amounted to.

"Line after line," says Swinton, "was swept away by the enemy's artillery and infantry fire; and so destructive was its effect that Porter's troops finally were compelled to withdraw. Porter's attack had been directed against Jackson; but Longstreet, on Jackson's right, found a commanding point of ground, whence he could rake the assaulting columns with an enfilading fire of Artillery." "From an eminence near by," says Gen.

Longstreet, "one portion of the enemy's masses, attacking Gen. Jackson, were in easy range of batteries in that position. It gave me an advantage I had not expected to have, and I made haste to use it. Two batteries were ordered for the purpose, and one placed in position immediately and opened.

"Just as this fire began, I received a message from the Commanding General informing me of Gen. Jackson's condition and his wants. As it was evident that the attack against Gen. Jackson could not be continued ten minutes under the fire of these batteries, I made no movements with my troops. Before the second battery could be placed in position, the enemy began to retire, and in less than ten minutes the ranks were broken, and that portion of his army put to flight."—*Longstreet's Report.*

Batallion Journal: We silenced the enemy's guns at 3:30 P. M., and broke up a line of advancing infantry. The practice was splendid—our batteries in time occupying the ground held previously during the day by the enemy. Gen. Jackson who served in the Mexican war with great distinction as an artillery officer, remarked while standing near Longstreet: "General, your artillery is superior to mine."

"The head of Longstreet's column having come upon the field, in the rear of the enemy's left, found the battle already opened with artillery on Jackson's right. Longstreet immediately placed some of his batteries in position; but before he could complete his dispositions to attack, the enemy withdrew; not however without loss from our artillery. The enemy now changed his position—Col. Walton placed a part of his artillery upon a commanding position between Jackson and Longstreet, by order of the latter, and engaged the enemy vigorously for several hours."—*Gen. Lee's Report.*

Gen. Warren, one of the best of Pope's Generals, "held on stoutly against fearful loss, till the enemy had advanced so close as to fire in the very faces of his men." The rest of the day's work consisted of an advance and pursuit by Lee—the remainder of Pope's army being saved by the resistance of a body of Regulars who held the Henry House Hill till Pope could cross his men in the darkness to the further side of Bull Run. The disordered masses of the Federal army presented the same scene that they did at the same river the year before; and the victory was just as complete—Lee capturing 9000 prisoners, 30 pieces of artillery, and 20,000 stand of arms, besides putting 40,000 of Pope's army *hors du combat.* This victory however was like the first in a still more important respect—it was no more decisive than any that preceded it, and the fighting and marching had to be commenced on the morrow the same as if nothing had yet been done.*

---

* *Report of Colonel Stafford commanding Second Louisiana Brigade, of the Battles of the Second Manassas.*

"The Brigade, consisting of the first, second, ninth, tenth, fifteenth, and Coppens' bataillon Louisiana Volunteers, reported near Gordonsville, on or about the 12th August, 1862, and was assigned to duty in the division of Major General T. J. Jackson. Being the senior Colonel in the Brigade, the command devolved upon me. I had command but one week, when Brigadier General W. E. Starke, reported for duty and took command. Shortly after Gen. Starke's arriva, we took up the line of march and continued it until we reached the ford on the Rappahannock, near Brandy Station, on or about the 21st August, at which period we found the enemy strongly posted on the opposite bank. On the morning of the 22d we resumed the march, and crossed the Rappahannock at Major's Mill, on Hazel fork on the 25th; passed through Thoroughfare Gap on the morning of the 27th, and reached Manassas the same day. That night we fell back, and took position near the little farm called Groveton. On the afternoon of the 28th, the enemy appearing in sight, we formed our line of battle on the crest of the hill overlooking Groveton, and awaited his attack. The battle commenced at five o'clock, P. M. and lasted until nine o'clock, P. M. resulting in the repulse of the enemy, we holding the battle ground. In the engagement, the Brigadier General commanding the division, receiving a severe wound, the command devolved upon Brig. Gen. Starke, and the command of the brigade fell upon me. On the morning of the 29th being in reserve, we were not thrown forward until

The marches of Jackson and Longstreet afforded during this week a good idea of what soldiering was. It was hard work with all, but with the Louisiana troops under Jackson, it was 35 miles forced marching, for two days, from the Rappahannock to Manassas, rounded off with a fight and railroad burning, two or three fights the day after, and the same work continued for ten days—all of the time with almost certain destruction awaiting the corps.

It deserves also to be stated—with many members of the Washington Artillery, as soon as it was discovered that there was no immediate demand for their guns—from having exhausted their ammunition or other cause, that they went into the action with other batteries, and that their services were gladly received. At the second Manassas, some of the men were in action at three different points, and with three different batteries during the same day.

One of the horrors of such a system of ten days fighting, may be cited in what the troops suffered in the battles just alluded to.

They were all day exposed to a broiling sun, and to

about twelve o'clock, at which time we received an order to charge. Driving the enemy before us, we again fell back to our position, remaining in it during the night. On the morning of the 30th, Brig. Gen. Starke ordered me to send half of one of my regiments forward, and occupy the Rail Road ut cas a point of observation, to be held at all hazards. About eight o'clock in the morning, the enemy commenced throwing forward large bodies of skirmishers, into the woods on our left, who quickly formed themselves into regiments, and moved forward by brigade to the attack, and massing a large body of troops at this point, with the evident design of forcing us from our position. They made repeated charges on us while in this position; but but were compelled to retire in confusion, sustaining heavy loss and gaining nothing. It was at this point that the ammunition gave out, the men procured some *from the dead bodies of their comrades*, but the supply was not sufficient, and in the absence of ammunition, the men *fought with rocks and held their position*. The enemy retreated, and we pressed forward to the turnpike road; then halted and camped for the night. On the 31st, we took up the line of march, and on the 1st of September at Chantilly, we again met the enemy and repulsed them.

great suffering from scarcity of water. Added to this, was the ghastly sight of the men slain in the previous day's fights, and, what was worse to a soldier, the intolerable stink emanating from 10,000 bloated and festering corpses.

On our march to the rescue of Jackson from Thoroughfare Gap, the men drank from stagnant pools, and their sufferings were so great, that Gen. Lee was heard to inquire of some of his officers, if there were no roads by which to save his poor soldiers in their forced marches, from so much dust and heat.

As showing what the slaughter of such a battle field is, I may mention that being detailed as a driver, when our artillery moved across the field, it was found impossible for the drivers to prevent their wheels from passing over more than one prostrate corpse, particularly over those of the red legged Zouaves, nearly annihilated on this field, by the Texas Brigade. It was just such a scene as the old pictures in republican Geographies used to represent of the carriage of the Emperors of Austria or of Russia, passing over the cripples and beggars who stood in the way.

Among other singularities of the First Manassas, was the fact that both armies were preparing to attack on their right at the same time. As the storm burst first upon the Confederate left flank, the consequence was that the battle was gained by the 7000 Confederate troops who could be brought to that wing—by their almost incredible stand against five times their superior force. In the Second Manassas, a year after, the two armies as if by mutual agreement had changed to opposite sides, as if to decide whether the first had been won owing to some advantage in the facings or the ground. In the first, the hottest portion of the fight had been around the house of Mrs. McHenry, who was there killed and buried. In the following year, two soldiers were found stretched over her grave—as if to show that they had fought over some Belle Helene, or rather over an old woman's quarrel, and by some sort of retribution, after marching always in opposition over and around Virginia, had finally come back by a poetic coincidence, to die face to face over the grave of the first innocent victim of the war.

Practically stated, the Second Manassas may be defined as the culminating effort of Pope to capture Jackson, who in the moment his prey was completely in the toils, removed himself, his men from the entrance to the trap, and allowed Lee to come through Thoroughfare Gap* to his assistance. The blunder here made, of which every battle affords instances on one side or the other, culminated in Pope trying to flank the right wing of Jackson, and never being able to find the end of it, for the reason that Lee and Longstreet had in the very nick of time been added on to it. Failing in capturing Jackson, his last blunder was his attempted pursuit of Lee.

*The following is from the *Batallion Journal*, Aug. 29th: A little after the Texas and Georgia Brigades had taken possession of the cow paths of Bull Run Mountains, and driven the enemy therefrom, a squadron of horse emerged as we advanced, from the woods on our left, and caused a halt, and a momentary doubt was entertained as to whether it was friend or foe; but soon the red banner with the blue cross was discerned through a glass, and a horseman with flowing beard, (who turned out to be Gen. Beverly Robinson) advanced rapidly. "What of Jackson," said Lee. "He has fallen back and is holding the enemy at Sudley's Mills." "Let us press on to his assistance," said Lee; and the booming of Jackson's guns told us that we would be none too soon: we went on the battlefield of the 29th on the right flank of Jackson, at 11:30—six hours before Pope or Porter knew that Lee's army was present; the 3d Company being the first to be ordered in.

If Pope who had the superiority of men had held the gap, and kept his troops on the road therefrom, everything else being equal, he ought to have succeeded in crushing Jackson.

OFFICIAL REPORT OF THE KILLED AND WOUNDED AT THE BATTLES OF THE SECOND MANASSAS, 29TH AND 30TH OF AUGUST, 1862.

Wounded:—Third Company, Sergeant W. A. Collins. Private, E. Chapiaux, Driver, James Bloom.

SECOND COMPANY.

Killed:—Private, Henry N. White.   *Wounded:*—Privates, A. R. Blakely, Douglas Ware, H. D. Summers.

FOURTH COMPANY, (Groveton).

Wounded:—Privates, Jos. W. Lescene, E. S. Burke, Driver, Davis Nolan. Batallion horses killed in the three battles—41.

Meanwhile, the head of the column was again to the front—Jackson once more creeping around and behind Pope with a drawn sword, or rather fixed bayonet, and appearing, for many a Federal regiment and division predestined to Hades, as the executioner of the Fates—little occupied as to what particular body of men to smite first. Marching north by Germantown, he struck the enemy at Chantilly, during a tremendous thunder storm, and the roar of the elements and the fall of the rain on that chilly afternoon was so great that the men could scarcely handle their guns, nor could the armies, three miles distant, distinguish the booming of the cannon. The number of killed and wounded was considerable upon both sides (among other dead was Gen. Kearney,[*] of the United States Army, whose body was brought into our lines;) but the move otherwise bore no fruit, Pope retiring without further struggle within the lines about Washington.

Shortly after our army moved towards the Potomac, for which event we had been dreaming ever since the first Manassas.

On the 3d of September we marched with three days rations and bivouacked at Dranesville, with the whole

---

[*] Gen. Kearney was once asked by the colonel of a re-enforcing regiment in one of the battles of '62 where to go in? "Oh'anywhere!" was the answer, "anywhere! It's all the same. Lovely fighting along the whole line."

army. The order was given on the following day for Jackson to cross the Potomac, and the word was, "On to Maryland!"

On the 5th we marched through Leesburg and bivouacked in a half a mile of the Potomac, which stream was next morning crossed.

As full of hope as the soldiers of Hannibal going over the Alps—many of whose battles, by the way, those of Lee and Jackson resembled—the men splashed through the water, too happy to be moving forward to trouble themselves about wet clothing. The careful artillerists who were by the side of their pieces, mounted the caissons—the laggards behind shouted frantically for a little delay, and in vain attempted to obviate a wet skin by extra speed.

It was with a deep heaving of the chest and expansion of the lungs with us all that we stood at last upon the Maryland shore, and thought of the battle fields behind and before. At all of the farm houses near the river the people appeared hospitable and reb down to their boots, and crazy to see Lee. Adjutant Owen brought back a string of ladies, who overwhelmed the old man with kisses and welcomes.

On the following day we crossed the Monocosy and camped near Frederick City. Jackson's troops had pretty much swept the town; but the troops were paid in Maryland, and grocers were found with sufficient sympathy to take Confederate money in return for a variety of eatables and drinkables. Our supplies were replenished and that night there was a Sardanapalan feast, on a limited scale, which effectually banished the memory of hard marches (however it might have been with headache) from every couch that night.

Our marches led us through Frederick City, Hagerstown, and Boonsboro. But little opportunity was afforded us for seeing the country, as hard fighting was evidently before us in the not remote perspective, and it was necessary that the men should stand close to their guns; besides we were in Maryland only two weeks. An advance after the First Manassas, (which there can be no question would have been made, if Gen. Lee had been in command) would have carried Maryland to the cause of the Confederacy, but it was now too late. Her refined population could only see as the result of long soldiering, rags and filth, and barefooted soldiers (totally indifferent or indisposed to the bright muskets,) and so the sentiment of " My Maryland" evaporated in poetry and paper. The number of recruits (300) did not begin to compensate for the heavy drain upon Lee's Regiments from forced marching; which cut the number of his men down one-half, and so there was to be no interest of any practical value felt in us— and but little enthusiasm; that is with a few very noble exceptions. One of these I now remember, was that of a kind-hearted woman who offered one of our weary soldiers some fruit. Before she had ended in making this good natured evidence of friendship, a mob of her own sex invaded her house and overwhelmed her with every reproach. The intelligent soldier whom she tried to benefit, seeing how the land lay, pretended to have taken the fruit without asking, and hastened to relieve his well-wisher of what must have been at the time embarrassing company.

To a soldier, whose pleasures like that of the clergy, are almost limited to eating and drinking, a rare opportunity of this sort was viewed by our Generals with an indulgent eye, and the men were allowed to forget, for at least one day, wearisome marches, watches and privations, and the bloody tragedies which were looming up in the future.

During the short time that we were camped about the towns of Maryland, the streets were full of soldiers, not to say the drinking saloons, which from time to time would mysteriously open and shut, though contrary to orders, and the jingling of spurs, sabres and glasses, and the faint aroma of tempting drinks, would be borne to the senses of the envious lookers on, compelled to remain upon the outside. A hotel of limited accommodations was the great point of attraction. The guests, however, had only Confederate money, and the unpatriotic landlord (though he affected the very reverse) was unwilling to accept this currency in payment. Besides, he was completely overslaughed by the number of his guests, whose appetites more than corresponded to the contents of his larder. A party of our men went there one day, fully determined to eat a square meal before going into another fight; but it soon became evident that if they did so, it would be without any assistance from our host, who affected the greatest pleasure in our company, but frankly told us that two hundred other guests stood a much better chance.

He however, did not hesitate to sell us our dinner tickets, while good naturedly laughing and telling us at the same time that there was no chance.

Once provided with these documents, there was only need for watchfulness and attention—the entrance of the select ‹crowd beforehand, meaning of course no dinner for the balance of us. The danger was guarded against by dividing ourselves up into corps of observation, and keeping a bright look out, especially in the neighborhood of the kitchen.

Our vigilance met with its reward. We found out the precise moment for action—through the friendship of a French *chef* or waiter we discovered the secret entrance reserved for the favored few, and better than all the watchword that would permit us to pass the closely guarded door. To the infinite astonishment of our landlord, the soldiers of the Louisiana regiments went in with the first move, and some of their acquaintances among the officers and generals were indebted to our timely discovery to getting anything to eat at all.

I have always thought that the two hundred guests assembled that day, did the heaviest knife and fork work ever performed in that hotel, or indeed in the whole State.

In the careless meetings which took place between the higher officers on such occasions, and the soldiers whom they had previously known, the conduct of the former was always manly and good-natured, and an evident disposition was shown to forget their rank; whether it was at a wayside dinner, or when a train of provisions or army clothing was struck, and every one with great glee, would rig himself out to his fancy, or according to the length of his arms or legs would cast the unsuitable clothing to his next friend, or some of his men. Some of us in the midst of one such toilette, were with Gen. Gordon, the most gallant and dauntless officer in the Confederate Army, and almost as popular with the Louisiana Brigades as Jackson; and a sudden alarm came very near causing him to lead his men into action, minus both his old costume and his new.

On one such occasion, Gen. Jackson had succeeded in getting hold of a rasher of bacon. One of his men who had bread, offered to divide with him, and the offer was accepted, on condition that he received half of the General's slice of meat.

It must be confessed that the fields of fruit and grain in our marches Northward, were of invaluable assistance to our army, as may be judged by a remark which I heard a soldier make when we afterwards invaded Pennsylvania, that he could not understand how the movement at that time could succeed, as it was too late in the year for green apples or roasting ears, to live upon during the march. But in the Rappahannock and Maryland Campaign, the man who owned a frying pan, was possessed of no little influence, and various sorts of flattery were frequently resorted to, to gain temporary possession of it. With this, in a half an hour, and with the aid of a few sticks or splinters from rails, and a small cut of bacon, an impromptu meal could be hatched up whenever the line halted. The owner of so useful an article was allowed to assume a certain dignity and style, somewhat comparable to that of the chief officer of a regiment, so long as the corn remained tender; but as all human honors are fleeting, he was afterwards forced to yield to the messmate who discovered a way of manufacturing a grater out of a canteen, and of thus making out of an otherwise indigestible food, a dish of first-class hominy.

CHAPTER XIX.

SHARPSBURG.

From that time until we had passed Boonsboro, we journeyed on quietly enough through a delightful mountain country, but finally halted about midday, as it seemed to us, in order to rest our horses. While we were quietly dozing by the side of these, the faint sound of cannon was heard, which gradually increased in loudness, and it now became evident that an attack by the enemy was being made upon our rear column—upon the men who were holding the passes; now, as it seemed, with much less success than we had at Thoroughfare Gap. We formed the impression without being able to learn much about the matter, that fortune had suddenly given the enemy the trump card; and that so far from advancing, that we would have to turn back.

We subsequently learned that our success had been decided by an accident of the most trivial nature—by a scrap of paper, which falling in the mud and being left behind, had been picked up, after the Confederate army left Frederick city. The scrap contained the marching orders of Gen. Lee, and McClellan now knew the disposition of all his corps. The most important information he in this way gained, was that Jackson had branched off to swoop down on a depot of supplies, and 12,000 Federal troops who had been left behind, in spite of all the rules of war, at Harper's Ferry, and that Lee's forces were divided in the enemy's country.

By this time almost every soldier had acquired sufficient experience to know what the heavy prolonged firing to the rear meant. We did not hear of the captured letter, or the precise cause of our check, until years afterwards, but our faculties were sufficiently keen to couple the booming of the guns with the absence of Jackson, and to know what it meant.

If at that juncture McClellan had done what Jackson was doing, without any chance assistance from fortune—had pressed forward his troops through the passes or over the mountains, Gen. Lee's army would have been in a bad way. But instead, Lee held the Thermopylæ—time was lost in making a wrong flanking movement by his enemies, and the few hours thus gained (at the cost of some desperate fighting by the small divisions left behind,) enabled Lee to regain the mastery of the situation. While the rear was holding its ground, Jackson, who conquered as much by the legs of his troops as by their arms, was returning.

Meanwhile, our retreat towards the Potomac had commenced a little after midnight—(on the 15th,) and part of our duties was to guard the rear of the army, by taking positions upon every commanding eminence, and preparing for an attack until the remainder of the troops had filed by. This operation was kept up till mid-day, at which time we took position definitely at Sharpsburg.

A little while after, while the men were cooking or sleeping, as we happened to be suffering most with hunger or lack of sleep, we were called to our guns and ordered to reply to some of the guns of position,* in which we were always excelled by the enemy. It is needless to say that our firing was for the same object with which Lee had made an ostentatious display of his infantry—with a view of deterring the enemy, and gaining time until the arrival of Jackson. The firing did not amount to much, or rather was a sheer farce as Gen. Hill called it, and we were soon permitted to go back and prepare for the serious work before us. McClellan meanwhile lost his opportunity by postponing his attack until the 17th, though his fire continued during the 15th, and the following day.

*Guns of position—viz. those of large calibre and long range. The enemy's plan of operations, as it was with the Russians in the Crimean War, who had confessedly the same superiority over the English and French, was to plant a number of guns upon some commanding forts or hills, and then open a converging fire, to which from lack of sufficient range and calibre, the Confederate Army could make no adequate reply. As to what our Artillery could do in a pitched battle, at Sharpsburg or elsewhere, even with badly made guns and ammunition, all of the reports are sufficient evidence.

Our line was about a mile from Sharpsburg, then undergoing shelling, and though a battle was obviously to be fought on the 17th, we were willing to visit the town in order to add to the scanty rations of camp. Soldiers being naturally of an indolent turn, it was easier to find volunteers who would encounter the danger, than those who were ready about bringing water, cooking, borrowing and washing our limited number of cooking utensils. Those who went into Sharpsburg, found much difficulty in coming across a store-keeper, sufficiently daring to do business under the circumstances, and only threats of helping ourselves, induced traders to return and receive our greenbacks.

Most of us wanted sugar, coffee, and similar supplies; but there was more than the average number, who hang around corner-groceries, ready to stand an unlimited quantity of shelling, provided they could thereby gratify what most soldiers acquire, a craving for liquor. But by this time we had all of us became so indifferent to balls, that the men of the two armies when picketed in sight of each other, and exposed to fire, would not only pay but little attention to the shots, but frequently be kind enough to point out to the enemy where their balls had gone to, and tell them to fire more to the right or left.

The duty of having the coffee now purchased ground at an adjacent house, brought me in company with an elderly Maryland lady, whose nature seemed to have become as much absorbed in the war, as that of Flora McIvor in the hopes of the Scottish Pretender. She sat softly singing before the fire as I entered, rocking herself to and fro in her chair, and apparently heedless of the shells which were passing over her house. When she ceased, it would be to launch out in fond praises of her son, whom she thought the bravest man in Stonewall's army, and whose death she apparently regarded as certain—something to which she had long since made up her mind. While having a look of fixed despair and resignation at his probable fate, she never seemed to admit to herself that this only son and relative could be any where but in a soldier's place. No entreaties could induce her to accept any of the coffee, though she was evidently much affected by the smell, and if she had possessed any would have probably sent it off to her son.

The intensity of the devotion of this poor woman, was painfully brought to mind the next day, by the fate of a soldier who was killed before the battle had fairly commenced, and who from her description, might have been her son. This man was shot down right by the side of a surgeon, who was behind the crest of the hill to avoid the enemy's fire, and in the presence of a number of soldiers, this medical officer refused to dress the man's wounds, or give him a chance for his life because he did not belong to his regiment. The old woman and the Doctor were pretty good types of the noble class upon one side, and those whose cowardly or selfish instincts were always coming to the surface.

The principal battle of Sharpsburg, next to Gettysburg the hardest fought battle of the war, occurred the next day, Sept. 17th.

The following taken from Gen. Early's, report of the Battle of Sharpsburg, will show how it fared with the Louisiana Infantry :

"About sunrise, the enemy advanced in line, driving in our skirmishers, and advancing to the edge of the woods. About this time, batteries opened in front from the woods with shell and canister, and these brigades were exposed to a terrible carnage. After a short time, Gen. Hays advanced with his brigade, to the support of Col. Douglas, under a terrific fire and passed to the front. About this time Gen. Lawton, who had been superintending the operation, received a very severe wound and was borne from the field. Col. Walker by moving two of his regiments, 21st Georgia and 21st North Carolina, and concentrating their fire and that of the 12th Georgia upon a part of the enemy's line in front of the latter, succeeded in breaking it and as a brigade of fresh troops came up to the support of Lawton's and Hays' brigades just in time, Walker ordered an advance; but the brigade which came up having fallen back, he was compelled to halt, and finally to fall back to his first position. His brigade, (Trimble's,) had suffered terribly, his own horse was killed under him, and he had himself been struck by a piece of shell. Col. Douglas, whose brigade had been hotly engaged during the whole time, was killed, and about half the men had been killed and wounded. Hays' brigade, which had advanced to Col. Douglas' support, had also suffered terribly, having more than half killed and wounded, (both Gen. Hays and Staff being disabled); and Gen. Hood having come up to their relief, these three brigades which were reduced to mere fragments, their ammunition being exhausted, retired to the rear. The terrible nature of the conflict in which these three brigades had been engaged, and the steadiness with which they maintained their position, is shown by the losses they sustained. They did not retire from the field, until General Lawton had been wounded and borne from the field; Col. Douglas, commanding Lawton's brigade had been killed, and the brigade had sustained a loss of five hundred and fifty-four killed and wounded out of eleven-hundred and fifty, losing five Regimental Commanders out of six. Hays' brigade had sustained a loss of three hundred and twenty-three out of five hundred and fifty, including every Regimental Commander, and all of his Staff; and Col. Walker and one of his Staff had been disabled, and the brigade he was commanding had sustained a loss of two-hundred and twenty-eight, out of less than seven hundred present, including three out of four Regimental Commanders. I am sorry that I am not able to do justice to the individual cases of gallantry displayed in this terrible conflict.

"I deem it proper to state that all the killed and wounded of my own brigade were inside of my lines, as I established them after the fight, and that the killed and wounded of the enemy on this part of the field, were also within the same lines. All my killed were buried, and all my wounded were carried to the hospital in the rear."

One line of the enemy's infantry came so near us, that we could see their Colonel on horseback waiving his men on, and then even the stripes on the Corporal's arms. How it made our blood dance and nerves quiver as we saw their colors floating steadily forward, and how heroically and madly we toiled at and double-shotted our guns. Our men worked that day desperately, almost despairingly, because it looked for a time as if we could not stop the blue wave from coming forward, although we were tearing it to pieces with canister and shell. Longstreet was on horseback at our side, sitting side-saddle fashion, and occasionally making some practical remark about the situation. He talked earnestly and gesticulated to encourage us, as the men of the detachments began to fall around our guns, and told us he would have given us a lift if he had not that day crippled his hand. But crippled or not, we noticed that he had strength enough left to carry his flask to his mouth, as probably everybody else did on that terribly hot day, who had any supplies at command, to bring to a carry.*

Finally the blue line disappeared from our front, and we managed to hobble off with our pieces, though with the loss of a good many men, horses, and some wheels to our gun carriages. Then we loaded our chests with

---

*Gen. Longstreet says in his report, that the enemy on the 17th, renewed an attack commenced the night before on Hood's brigade—a handful compared with those before him. Hood fought desperately until Jackson and Walker came to his relief—the former soon moving off to flank the enemy's right. The enemy "now threw forward his masses against my left: met by Walker, two pieces of Captain Miller's battery of the Washington Artillery, and two of Birce's battery. The enemy was driven back in some confusion; an effort was made to pursue, but our line was too weak. From this moment our centre was extremely weak. The enemy's masses again moved forward, and Cook's regiment stood with empty guns, moving his colors to show his regiment was in position. The artillery played upon the enemy with canister—their lines hesitated and after an hour and a half retired.

"Another attack was quickly made a little to the right of the last, Capt. Miller turning his pieces upon these lines, and playing upon them with round shot (over the heads of R. H. Anderson's men) checked the advance, and Anderson's division, with the artillery, held the enemy in check until night. This attack was followed by the final assault, about four o'clock P. M., when the enemy crossed the bridge in front of Sharpsburg, and made his desperate attack upon my right. He drove back our right several times, and was himself made to retire several times—badly crippled; but his strong reinforcements finally enabled him to drive in my right, and occupy this part of my ground.

"Thus advanced, the enemy's line was placed in such position as to enable Gen. Toombs to move his brigade directly against their flank. Gen. Jones seized the opportunity and threw Toombs against the enemy's flank, drove him back and recovered our lost ground. Two of the brigades of Major Gen. A. P. Hill's division advanced against the enemy's front as Gen. Toombs made his flank attack. The enemy took shelter behind a stone wall, and another line was, advanced to the crest of a hill in support of his first line. Capt. Richardson's, Brown's, and Moody's batteries, were placed in position to play upon the second line, and both lines were eventually driven back by their batteries.

"Before it was entirely dark, the hundred thousand men that had been threatening our destruction for twelve hours, had melted away into a few stragglers.

"In one month, these troops had marched over two hundred miles upon little more than half rations, and fought nine battles and skirmishes, killed, wounded and captured nearly as many men as we had in our ranks, besides taking arms and other ammunition of war in large quantities."

Gen. Toombs in his report, gives a very laudatory account of Richardson's battery of the Washington Artillery at Sharpsburg.

ammunition, and reappeared at two or three different points of the fray during the day. At one time about dusk, the hostile lines became so blended that no one could tell friend from foe, and we were afraid of firing for fear of doing harm to our friends.

The following is from Gen. Lee's report of the battle of Sharpsburg :

> "The advance of the enemy [on the 15th,] was delayed by the brave opposition he encountered from Fitz Lee's cavalry. During the afternoon the batteries were slightly engaged.
> " [On the 17th,] the firm front presented by the 27th N. C. standing boldly in line without a cartridge, and the well directed fire of the artillery under Capt. Miller of the Washington Artillery, and Capt. Bryce's S. C. Battery, checked the progress of the enemy. Another attack was made soon afterwards, a little further to the right, but was repulsed by Miller's guns of the Washington Artillery.
> "Our artillery though much inferior to that of the enemy in the number of guns and weight of metal, rendered efficient and most gallant service throughout the day, and contributed greatly to the repulse of the attacks upon every part of the line."

We held our ground until darkness put an end to the fight; but the army had been hardly pressed, and we were not sorry when the night after, the order came for the army to recross the Potomac.

Now followed some of the most tiresome and fatiguing work it was ever the lot of an army to do—the getting across the immense train of commissary wagons, needlessly and perilously large, as was shown in the fact that it ultimately led to the capture of Lee's army itself, in the retreat to Appomattox Courthouse. Some overloaded wagon or leatherheaded mule driver (the M. D.'s as they were called,) was everlastingly blocking the road, until these conveyances would be compelled by impatient cursing from behind, to vomit up their contents. To see the road strewed with heavy old trunks and useless plunder belonging to a favored few, was very exasperating, and at the same time much enjoyed by every one, except the owners, especially when every one knew that the critical position of the army was embarrassed by an already too long wagon train.

The scene on the Maryland side on the night of the crossing rivaled Bedlam. The wagon train had to go down a very high and almost perpendicular bank, and except for the still greater danger from behind, was such a descent as no prudent wagoner would ever have attempted to make. Although it was as precipitous as the road to perdition, the teamsters had to make an elbow half way down, at the imminent risk of an overturn—some of the wagons actually meeting with such a calamity. These were set fire to, partly for warmth, partly for the purpose of seeing; and these and the flaring torches held about by different hands, gave a weird Rembrandt touch to the scene. Then there was a large number of officers and men who had come forward from behind, and who had to stand around all night—the ground being too muddy to admit of seats.

Some who were mounted went to sleep in their saddles All of this time there would be a confused shouting among the wagoners, and the cry of "Pull around to the right and then swing to the left," was to be heard with each descent.

One of the men who was holding a torch, who shouted out this explanation, was almost ridden down by an angry General who wanted to know who commanded that regiment —himself or some one else. The General was afterwards just enough to ride back and thank the soldier for saving his baggage. Then there were two batteries that approached the bank at the same moment, and who actually kept the army, worn down and in danger, as it was for some time, delayed, because neither would yield the precedence to the other. One rash headstrong General took possession of the only wagon road, for his infantry men, who could have got down to the water's edge, any where else, and when the instructions were that they should cross at a ford a little below.

The strangest feature of the whole affair, was the grotesque appearance of our army who had stripped off most of their clothes, and who went shuddering and shivering in the cold water. Altogether, it was a torch-light procession of the most fantastic sort. Some hints were thrown out to the brass band to strike up a lively air as they marched through; but the musicians were very little in the humor for joking that night. Indeed, this was the case with most of us.

By daylight the next morning, we were all pretty well stove up and fagged out, and most of us felt that we had our belly-full of fighting for some time to come. That campaign certainly added pretty largely to the army of stragglers, (one-half of Lee's army in Maryland, though there the men had been simply marched to death,) who never cared about getting nearer than the baggage wagons to the front.

We marched through Bunkerhill to Winchester, Virginia, where we stayed forty days (to Oct. 30th, 1862.) The place must have been a delightful town, full of fine shade trees, tasteful gardens, old stone buildings, and with a very hospitable, easy going population. It came though, in course of time, with Jackson and Milroy always changing ownership, or with Lee marching through it, to have the hard, tarnished and jaded look which military quarters generally have. Fair faces were more meditative in the second year, than sympathetic—and thought rather of the probability of losing their spoons, or the price of a square meal, than over the pleasure inspired by soldiers' compliments. There was one noble exception however, (though exception is not the word, as the residents were after all right); this was a lady who came near to being a heroine in her way: nearer than any other whose name has yet been in print. I allude to Miss Josephine Carson, a lady of fine social position and many attractions, who merits mention on account of her devotion to the sick and wounded, who had been sent back from Sharpsburg, and who deserved the reputation of having won the admiration and good-will of our soldiers as much as any lady whom we met in Virginia; a reputation to which she was entitled, from her dignity of demeanor, and from a good nature and natural largeness of heart which interested her in every soldier who passed by her.

The truth is, the same might be said of a very large number of Virginia women, who almost every one of them did an incredible number of kindnesses to soldiers. The soldiers from Louisiana were ready to dispute the palm on the battle-field, with the troops from Virginia or any other State; but we all of us became infatuated with the patience and devotion of the ladies of that State—as well as of those who claimed no pretensions to that title; and I never heard a soldier worthy of that name, speak in other than tones of the highest commendation of the mothers and daughters of that State. None of us ever met with any other reception from the women of the South, who were always our best friends, and who would always realize and pity a soldier's misery a long time before it would occur to their male relatives or friends, and who when they did a kindness, did so in such a way as to mollify many proud spirits, who were unwilling to accept any evidences of good-will for doing only what they considered their duty.

Let us now return, while the soldiers and battery horses

of Gen. Lee's army are resting, after the fatigues of their past battles and long marches, to New Orleans, and relate what has meanwhile transpired at the old Washington Artillery Armory. For the chapter which follows, this work is indebted to the pen of one of the officers high in command of the Fifth Company.

CHAPTER XXI.

BATALLION WASHINGTON ARTILLERY—FIFTH COMPANY.

On the departure for the seat of war in Virginia, of the first four companies of the Batallion, on the 27th of April, 1861, the following order was promulgated by the Major Commanding, the last issued by him previous to mustering into the service of the Confederate States.

HEADQUARTERS BATALLION WASHINGTON ARTILLERY, }
New Orleans, April, 1861. }

* * * * * * * *

VII—1st Lieut. W. I. Hodgson, of the 4th Company, is hereby specially detailed to remain in New Orleans on recruiting service, and will forward from time to time, to the seat of war, such recruits as may be required, and hold himself subject to any further orders from these headquarters.

* * * * * * * *

By order,   J. B. WALTON,
WM. M. OWEN, *Adjutant*.   *Major Commanding.*

A reserve force of about twenty men was all left behind of the original command, and Lieut. Hodgson, with their assistance, rapidly organized a Fifth Company; and in one month from the day of the departure of the Batallion, held an election for officers, casting over 150 votes, with the following result:

Captain—W. Irving Hodgson;
Senior First Lieutenant—Theo. A. James;
Junior First Lieutenant—Rinaldo Banister;
Senior Second Lieutenant—Jerry G. Pierson;
Junior Second Lieutenant—E. L. Hews.

When the batallion left for Virginia, they left the arsenal on Girod Street, in an unfinished condition, the roof not yet put on, the floors torn up, and everything in the way of camp and garrison equipage, artillery and ordinance stores taken with them. Yet in order to supply their place, the reserves went to work with a will. They sent special committees to Baton Rouge to the Legislature, to the City Council of New Orleans, and the merchants and capitalists of the City and State. Through handsome donations from the former, a generous appropriation from the Council, and the unbounded liberality of the latter, (including the present of a piece of artillery and caisson complete from Governor Thos. Overton Moore, and a similar gift from John I. Adams, a prominent merchant of New Orleans,) they were able within ninety days to complete the arsenal, and pay for it.

They besides perfected the organization of six handsome brass field pieces, with limbers, caissons and harness all complete, with a serviceable and complete stock of camp and garrison equipage for 160 men; all this without owing a dollar.

From time to time during the first year of the war, they sent to their comrades in Virginia, reinforcements[*] of men and drivers, artificers, etc., always forwarding under the command of an officer of the Fifth Company, and always sending them off fully clothed and equipped, free of expense to the batallion.

A semi-weekly mail was regularly sent also to the command in the field, the cases being packed not only with mail matter, but with clothing, edibles and everything intended for any member of the command, sent him by

---

[*]Lieut. J. G. Pierson, came on in charge of two detachments consisting of about fifteen men each during the first year of the war.

his family or friends, and with no expense to the soldier of transportation.

Early in the year 1862, the members of the 5th Company exhibited much military ardor, and felt unwilling to remain longer at home, while their comrades, friends and brothers were sharing the dangers and toils of camp life.

In February of that year, Captain Hodgson addressed a communication to Brig. Gen. E. L. Tracy, commanding the 1st brigade, 1st division Louisiana State Militia, to which his battery was attached, asking for a new election of officers, intended for active service in field; in conformity to which, Gen. Tracy ordered an election on the 24th day of that month; and under the supervision and direction of Majors Ignatius Caulfield, and John B. Prados, of his staff, the election took place as directed. There were 185 votes cast, with the following result:

Captain—W. Irving Hodgson;
Senior First Lieutenant—Cuthbert H. Slocomb;
Junior First Lieutenant—Wm. C. D. Vaught;
Senior Second Lieutenant—Edson L. Hews;
Junior Second Lieutenant—J. A. Chalaron.

On the 1st day of March 1862, the following dispatch from Gen. G. T. Beauregard, was published in all of the New Orleans daily papers:

DISPATCH FROM GEN. BEAUREGARD.

JACKSON, *Tenn.*, February 28, 1862.

To Gov. THOS. O. MOORE:

Will accept all good equipped troops under the act of 21st August that will offer, and for ninety days.

Let the people of Louisiana understand that here is the proper place to defend Louisiana.

G. T. BEAUREGARD.

Captain Hodgson immediately called a meeting of his command, which was held on the 2nd day of the month, when it was shown that there was one unanimous voice to at once offer their services for ninety days, or the war. All necessary arrangements having been made for their immediate departure for the field, the following order was issued and published in the daily papers :*

HEADQUARTERS 5TH Co., BAT. WASHINGTON ARTILLERY,
NEW ORLEANS, March 5th, '62.

[Order No. 44.]

I—The officers and members of this corps are hereby ordered to appear at their Arsenal on Thursday morning, the 6th inst., at 10 o'clock, punctually, fully equipped, with knapsacks packed, for the purpose of being mustered into the Confederate States service.

II—Every member of the command is expected to be present. Those failing to appear will not be allowed to leave with the command.

By order of

W. IRVING HODGSON, *Captain.*

A. GORDON BAKEWELL, *O. S.*

On Thursday morning, March 6th, 1862, at 11 o'clock, the Fifth Company were regularly mustered into the service by the enrolling officer of Gen. Mansfield Lovell's staff, in Lafayette Square, with 166 men, rank and file; they left New Orleans for the seat of war in Mississippi and Tennessee via the N. O. J. & G. N. R. R. on Saturday March 8th, 1862, carrying with them their six guns, with everything perfect and complete, including their camp

---

* Among the many flattering comments of the press, was the following, taken from the Picayune of March 3rd, 1862.

THE WASHINGTON ARTILLERY—The 5th Company of this fine battalion, Capt. W. Irving Hodgson, have with extreme unanimity determined on responding forthwith to the call of Gen. Beauregard, whom they go to join on Thursday next. The company is in perfect order for immediate and efficient service, and will take the field with their battery of six guns, with full ranks, and with every thing necessary in the way of equipment.

The Battalion of Washington Artillery, Major J. B. Walton, consisting of four companies, have been in the Confederate service from the commencement of the war, and have done good service in Virginia where they are still encamped, ready to do more, when called upon. The 5th Company, which, when the battalion left, was composed of some thirty members, now numbers in its ranks over a hundred young, vigorous and enthusiastic men, who have been sedulously fitting themselves for active duty. Emulating the zeal and promptitude of the four first companies, in responding to the call made upon them for their services, Company No. 5 have also entered the Confederate army, for ninety days, to "fight the battle of New Orleans," in the place where Beauregard tells us it is to be fought.

We doubt not they will prove worthy of their membership of a battalion which has been mentioned in Beauregard's general orders in terms of the highest eulogium.

and garrison equipage, and without the cost of one dollar to the general government.* The following is the "Roster" of the Fifth Company, as mustered, into service :

Officers—Capt. W. Irving Hodgson ; Senior 1st Lieut., C. H. Slocomb; Junior 1st Lieut., W. C. D. Vaught; Senior 2d Lieut. Edson L. Hews; Junior 2d Lieut., J. A. Chalaron ; Assistant Surgeon J. Cecil LeGaré.

Non-Commissioned Staff—Orderly Sergeant, A. Gordon Bakewell ; Ordnance Sergeant, J. H. H. Hedges ; Quartermaster's Sergeant, J. B. Wolfe ; Commissary Sergeant, W. A. Barstow.

1st Sergeant J. W. De Merritt, 2d Sergeant B. H. Green Jr., 3d Sergeant A. J. Leverich, 4th Sergeant W. B. Giffen, 5th Sergeant John Bartley, 6th Sergeant Thos. M. Blair.

1st Corporal John J. Jamison, 2d Corporal S. Higgins, 3d Coporal W. N. Calmes, 4th Corporal R. W. Frazer, 5th Corporal Emmet Putnam, 6th Corporal N. L. Bruce.

1st Caisson Corporal D. W. Smith, 2d Caisson Corporal E. J. O'Brien, 3d Caisson Corporal A. S. Winston, 4th Caisson Corporal L. Macready, 5th Caisson Corporal Alf. Bellanger, 6th Caisson Corporal E. Charles.

Sergeant Drivers J. H. Smith, Corporal Drivers F. N. Thayer.

1st Artificer W. A. Freret, 2d Artificer J. F. Spearing, 3d Artificer W. A. Jourdan, 4th Artificer John Beggs, 5th Artificer John Davidson, 6th Artificer Fred. Holmes.

Privates—Alex. Allain, V. F. Allain, T. C. Allenn, C. A. Adams, N. Buckner, Jos. Banfil, Ben Bridge, A. T. Bennett, Jr.. B. Boyden, A. J. Blaffer, John Boardman, Marcus J. Beebe, C. B. Broadwell, T. L. Bayne, Jas. Clarke, J. T. Crawford, W. W. Clayton, Joseph Denegre, J. H. Duggan. J. M. Davidson, A. M. Fahenstock, E. C. Feinour, E. Fehrenbach, John Fraser, Charles W. Fox, Robert Gibson, James F. Giffen, C. J. Hartnett, C. M. Harvey, W. D. Henderson, H. L. Henderson, Curtis Holmes, John B. Humphreys, Charles G. Johnson, C. B. Jones, Gabriel Kaiser, W. B. Krumbharr, Minor Kenner, Jr., H. H. Lonsdale, H. Leckie, L. L. Levy, Martin Mathis, Lewis Mathis, H. G. Mather, E. Mussina, Eugene May, E. S. McIlhenny, Milton McKnight, H. D. McCown, J. C. Miller, W. R. Murphy, F. Maillieu, G. W. Palfrey, Robert Pugh, Richard L. Pugh, E. F. Reichert, S. F. Russell, E. Rickett, J. M. Seixas, W. W. Sewell, G. W. Skidmore, L. Seicbrecht, George H. Shotwell, R. P. Salter, W. B. Stuart, Robert Strong, W. Steven, J. H. Scott, J. T. Skillman, John Slaymaker, Warren Stone, Jr., J. H. Simmons, R. W. Simmons, A. Sambola, E. K. Tisdale, Hiram Tomlin, C. Weingart, T. B. Winston, James White, John W. Watson, C. S. Wing, J. A. Walsh, Charles B. Watt, Charles Withan, Willis P. Williams.

Drivers—Byrnes Joseph, Bale James, Clayton John, Farrell Richard, Dooly William, Lynch Thomas, Long Patrick, Leary John, Moore Daniel, Jordan James, Davis Sam. J., Kelly Pat., Norris Robert, Turner Geo. A., White William, Williams Thomas, Young John, Farrel Michel, Abbott John, Leary Thomas.

Bugler—Carl Valanconi.

* The following is from the Picayune of March 7th, 1862.

THE WASHINGTON ARTILLERY, COMPANY 5.—This fine company, under Capt. W. Irving Hodgson, was mustered into the service of the Confederate States, yesterday, for ninety days. There were 160 men all told. They made, as usual, a most admirable appearance.

On Saturday next, (to-morrow) they leave for Jackson, Tenn., and will attend divine service to-day, at 11 o'clock, A. M., at the First Presbyterian Church, Dr. Palmer's, where they will be addressed by the eloquent pastor.

We have heard it suggested that on their arrival at the seat of war they will

A Soldier's Story of the War.

The following was the organization of the other troops who left New Orleans under the same call :

Crescent Regiment.—Colonel, M. J. Smith; Lieut. Col., G. P. McPheeters; Major, A. W. Bosworth; Adjutant, Richard S. Venables; Surgeon, B. Stille; Assistant Surgeon, S. R. Chambers; Quartermaster, R. D. Gribble. Crescent City Guards, Company B.—Captain, George Soulé; 1st Lieut., H. B. Stevens; 2d Lieut., B. E. Handy; Junior 2d Lieut., L. N. LeGay. Crescent Rifles, Company D.—Captain, A. F. Haynes; 1st Lieut., W. C. C. Claiborne, Jr.; 2d Lieut., C. G. Southmayd; Junior 2d Lieut., W. F. Howell. Company C., Louisiana Guards.—Captain, G. H. Graham; 1st Lieut., Wm. Bullit; 2d Lieut. Alex. Trolford; Junior 2d Lieut., C. A. Wood. Beauregard Rangers.—Captain, Jules Vienne; 1st Lieut., E. G. Meslier; 2d Lieut., ———; Junior 2d Lieut., N. C. Forstall. Twiggs' Guards.—Captain, M. A. Tarleton; 1st Lieut., Thos. L. Airey; 2d Lieut., E. F. L'Hoste; Junior 2d Lieut., Eugene Holmes. Crescent City Guards, Company C.—Captain, W. S. Austin; 1st Lieut., Chas. Guillet; 2d Lieut., R. Green, Jr.; Junior 2d Lieut., A. H. F. Smith. Ruggles Guards.—Captain, Geo. W. Helme; 1st Lieut., G. H. Braughn; 2d Lieut., J. J. Mellon; Junior 2d Lieut., W. C Shepperd. Orleans Cadets, Company E.—Captain, S. F. Parmele; 1st Lieut., H. Perry, Jr.; 2d Lieut., S. Fisher, Jr.; Junior 2d Lieut., T. A. Enderle. Crescent Blues.—Captain, John Knight; 1st Lieut., ———; 2d Lieut., W. H. Mackay; Junior 2d Lieut., W. H. Seaman. Sumpter Rifles.—Captain, C. C. Campbell; 1st Lieut., M. McDougale; 2d Lieut., J. E. Garretson;\Junior 2d Lieut., David Collie. Alexandria Rifles.—Captain, J. P. Davidson; 1st Lieut., A. D. Lewis; 2d Lieut., R. Legras; Junior 2d. Lieut., Jos Fellows.—Total, 945.

Batallion Orleans Guards.—Major, Leon Querouse. Company A.—Captain, Charles Roman; 1st Lieut., J. B. Sorapuru; 2d Lieut., Francis Moreno; Junior 2d Lieut. F. O. Trepagnier. Company B.—Captain, Eugene Staes; 1st Lieut., Emile DeBuys; 2d Lieut., O. Carriere; Junior 2d Lieut., P. O. Labatut. Company C.—Captain, August Roche; 1st Lieut., Fred. Thomas; 2d Lieut., Eug.

be divided into two companies, while, as we understand, there is material here almost sufficient for the formation of a third.

Also the following remarks from the same paper:
The Fifth Company of the Batallion of Washington Artillery attended divine service yesterday, at 11 o'clock, A. M., in the First Presbyterian Church, on Lafayette Square, where a very impressive and eloquent address was delivered to them by Rev. Dr. Palmer, the pastor of that church.

He vindicated, in the most able and convincing manner, the justness and righteousness of the cause in which this Confederacy in arms is now engaged. I. is a war purely defensive, in resistance to an invasion by a foe that would subjugate us to his despotic will, and deprive us of all our dearest rights. Should the war, on our part, be hereafter aggressive, it would be equally a just and righteous one, as a means of depriving our enemy of the means of carrying into effect his hostile purposes. In this confidence of the rectitude of the cause i 1 whose defence they are engaged, the reverend speaker bade the members of the Artillery to go forth in the trust of God. He bade them rely, too, on the fidelity with which the people of this city would care for their interests, as well as pray for their success, and contribute to their support and comfort while absent. He told them that they were going forth to discharge for Louisiana and this city the debt that, for nearly fifty years, has been due to Tennessee, for the prompt and efficient aid she rendered to both, on the plains of Chalmette. He concluded his eloquent address with an invitation to the corps and the congregation to unite with him in prayer, which being concluded, he dismissed them with a solemn benediction.

The services were exceedingly interesting, and were participated in by a large assemblage.

Tourné; Junior 2d Lieut., L. Charvet. Company D.—Captain, Charles Tertrou; 1st Lieut., Paul Declouet; 2d Lieut., Alfred Voorhies; Junior 2d Lieut., B. St. Clair, (from Parish of St. Martin.)—Total, 411.
 Batallion Confederate Guards.—Major, F. H. Clack; Captains, D. H. Fowler; G. P. McMurdo; 1st Lieuts., W. R. Macbeth, A. W. H. Hyatt; 2d Lieuts. H. H. Price, J. W. Bonner; Junior 2d Lieuts., R. H. Browne, J. W Hardie.—Total, 201.
 Cavalry—Jefferson Mounted Guards.—Captain, Guy. Dreux; Lieuts., B. Toledano, H. P. Janvier; Cornet, J. Chambers. Orleans Light Horse.—Captain, T. L. Leeds; Lieuts. W. A. Gordon and Geo. Foster; Cornet, Greenleaf.—Total, 150.
 Orleans Guards Battery—Captain, H. Ducatel; 1st Lieut., F. Livaudais; Jr. 1st Lieut., M. A. Calogne; 2d Lieut., G. Legardeur, Jr.; Jr. 2d Lieut., F. Lange.
 Total number of soldiers who left New Orleans, under the 90 days' call, 1948.

The following notice of the departure of the command, appeared in the Picayune of Sunday, March 9th, 1862:

" OFF FOR THE SEAT OF WAR.—The vicinity of the Jackson Railroad Depot was yesterday afternoon the scene of intense interest. The 5th Company of the Washington Artillery, Capt. Hodgson, and four companies, forming the left wing of the Crescent Regiment, Col. Smith, left in a special train, and thousands of men, women and children literally thronged the streets on their march to the depot, and swarmed around the cars at the station to take leave of their friends and relatives and acquaintances. The scene was interesting beyond description. The brave fellows went off with buoyant spirits, though occasionally could be seen the starting tear in their eyes, as they took a farewell of some loved one, or some dearly attached friend. They looked in fine order, and will doubtless make a good report of themselves within a short time. Good luck, health, prosperity, victory and a safe and glorious return to them, one and all!"

Arriving at Grand Junction, Tennessee, on Monday evening, March 10th, 1862, the battery immediately went into camp, under the instructions of Gen. John K. Jackson, Commander of the Post. They were here supplied with their battery horses, and began drilling, and otherwise actively preparing for service. On the 27th day of March, the tents were struck, and the command started over land for Corinth, Mississippi, arriving there on the 1st day of April, 1862, and were immediately assigned to the Brigade of Brig. Gen. Patton Anderson, of Ruggles' Division, Bragg's (2d) Army Corps, and went into camp the same day.

On Thursday, the 3d day of April, the battery filed out through the fortifications with its brigade, and the army, destined for the battle field of Shiloh.

For the full details of this battle, reference can be

made to the "Confederate Reports of Battles," officially published by order of Congress, a few extracts from which are herewith appended, having special reference to the part taken by the Fifth Company Washington Artillery, and to the official report of Captain Hodgson, with reference to the same subject matter:

OFFICIAL REPORT OF CAPTAIN HODGSON.
[Page 323 to 327.]

HEADQUARTERS 5TH CO., BAT. WASHINGTON ARTILLERY,
CAMP MOORE, *Corinth, Miss.*, April 9th, '62.

TO BRIG. GEN. PATTON ANDERSON,
Commanding Second Brigade, Ruggles' Division, Army Miss.

GENERAL:—In accordance with usage, I hereby report to you the "action" of my battery, in the battles of the 6th and 7th instant.

My battery, consisting of two 6-pounder smooth bore guns, two 6-pounder rifled guns, and two 12-pounder howitzers,—total 6 pieces, fully equipped with ammunition, horses, and men, entered the field, just in the rear of the 20th Louisiana regiment, (the right regiment of your brigade,) on Sunday morning, the 6th inst., on the hill, overlooking from the Southwest, the encampments of the enemy immediately to the front of it, and to the Northeast, being the first camp attacked, and taken by our army.

At 7 o'clock, A. M., we opened fire on their camp, with our full battery of six guns, firing shell and spherical case shot, soon silencing one of their batteries, and filling the enemy with consternation. After firing some forty (40) rounds thus, we were directed by General Ruggles, to shell a camp immediately upon the left of the one mentioned, and in which there was a battery, from which the shot and shell were thrown on all sides of us.

With two howitzers and two rifled guns, under Lieuts. Slocomb and Vaught, assisted by two pieces from Capt. Sharp's battery, we soon silenced their guns, and had the gratification of seeing our brave and gallant troops charge through these two camps, running the enemy before them at the point of the bayonet.

At this point I lost your command, and on the order of General Ruggles to "go where I heard most firing" I passed over the first camp captured, through a third, and on to a fourth, in which your troops were doing sad havoc to the enemy.

I formed in battery, on your extreme left, in the avenue of the camp, and commenced firing with canister from four (4) guns, into the tents of the enemy, only fifty (50) yards off. It was at this point, I suffered most. The skirmishers of the enemy lying in their tents, only a stone's throw from us, cut holes through their tents near the ground, and with "white powder" or some preparation which discharged their arms without report, played a deadly fire in among my cannoniers, killing three men, wounding seven or eight, besides killing some of our most valuable horses, mine among the rest. As soon as we were well formed in battery, and got well to work, we saw them creeping from their tents, and making for the woods, and immediately afterwards saw your column charge the whole of them in ambush, and put them to flight.

A visit through that portion of their camp, at a subsequent hour, satisfied me from the number of the dead, and the nature of their wounds, that my battery had done its duty.

Losing you again at this point, on account of the heavy brushwood through which you charged, I was requested by Gen. Trudeau, to plant two guns further down the avenue, say two hundred yards off, to shell a fifth camp further on, which I did, and after firing a dozen or more shells, had the satisfaction of seeing the cavalry charge the camp, putting the enemy to flight—killing many, and capturing many wounded prisoners.

Being again without a commanding General, and not knowing your exact position, I received and executed orders from General Hardee and his aid, Col. Kearney, also from Col. Chisholm of Gen. Beauregard's Staff, and in fact from other aids, whose names I do not know, going to points threatened and exposed, and where firing was continual, rendering cheerfully all the assistance I could with my battery, now reduced in men and horses—all fatigued and hungry.

At about 2 o'clock, P. M., at the instance of Gen. Hardee, I opened from the fifth camp we had entered, firing upon a sixth camp, due north. Silencing the battery and driving the enemy from their tents—said portion of the army of the enemy, were charged and their battery captured—afterwards lost again—by the Guard Orleans and other troops on our left, under Col. Preston Pond, Jr.

This was about the last firing of my battery on the 6th instant. Taking the main road to Pittsburg Landing, we followed, on the heels of our men, after a retreating and badly whipped army, until within three fourths of a mile of the Tennessee River, when the enemy began to shell the woods from their Gunboats. General Ruggles ordered us to the enemy's camp, where we bivouacked for the night.

I received orders on the morning of the 7th, at about half-past five o'clock to follow your command with my battery, and at six o'clock being ready to move, could not ascertain your position—so took position on the extreme right of our army, supported by the Crescent Regiment, of Col. Pond's Brigade, in our rear, and an Arkansas Regiment on my front, and I think the 21st Tennessee Regiment on my left flank; all under Gen. Hardee, for in fact, he seemed to be the master spirit, giving all orders and seeing that they were properly executed.

At about 9 o'clock, Gen. Breckenridge's command, on our extreme front had pushed the enemy up and on, to within several hundred yards of our front, when we opened fire with shell and shot with our full battery; after firing some (70) seventy rounds, we took position further on, just on the edge of the open space ahead, and with our full battery, assisted by two pieces from McClung's battery, we poured some sixty (60) rounds into the enemy, who continued to advance upon us, until within some (20) twenty yards of us, when Col. Marshall J. Smith, of the Crescent Regiment, gallantly came to our rescue, charging the enemy at the point of the bayonet, putting them to flight, and saving our three extreme right pieces, which would have been captured but for them.

It was at this point, I again met with some losses. Lieut. Slocomb, Sergt. Green, several privates, and many horses fell at this point, either killed or badly wounded.

After the enemy had retreated well in the woods, I had my guns limbered and taken from the field. My men broken down, my horses nearly all slain, ammunition out, and sponges all broken and gone, I was in the act of making repairs, and preparing for another attack, when I was ordered by Gen. Beauregard to retire in order, to Monterey, which I did that evening—and afterwards to this point, arriving last evening, with my battery all complete, with the exception of three (3) caissons, a battery wagon, and forge, which I had to abandon on the road, for want of fresh horses to draw them in.

At the request of Gen. Beauregard, I detailed from my command, twelve men, under a non-commissioned officer, to remain and act with Capt. Byrne's (or Burns') battery, on a prominent hill on the Pea Ridge road, overlooking the battle field, to cover the retirement of our army. They all came in to-day, safe and sound.

We captured two stands of United States colors, which were handed over to

Gen. Beauregard; we also captured several U. S. horses and mules, some of which we have now, others we have lost.

I cannot close this report, without again calling to your favorable notice, the names of my Lieuts. Slocomb, Vaught and Chalaron, for their coolness and bravery on the field. Their conduct was daring and gallant, and worthy of your consideration.

I have the honor to be,
Yours, very truly,
W. IRVING HODGSON, Captain.

SUPPLEMENTARY REPORT OF CAPTAIN HODGSON.
[Page 326 and 327.]

HEADQUARTERS 5TH CO., BAT. WASHINGTON ARTILLERY,
CAMP MOORE, Corinth Miss., April 11th, '62.

To CAPT. WM. G. BERTH,
Acting Asst. Adjutant General:

CAPTAIN :—I herewith tender to you a supplemental report, in regard to matters connected with the battles of the 6th and 7th inst.

My battery fired during said actions, from the six guns, seven hundred and twenty-three (723) rounds, mostly from the smooth bore guns and the howitzers, a large proportion of which was canister. Some of our ammunition chests, being repacked from a captured caisson, and other canister borrowed from Captain Robertson's battery, which he kindly loaned.

The badly torn wheels and carriages of my battery from minie balls, will convince any one of the close proximity to the enemy in which we were. I had twenty-eight (28) horses slain in the battery, exclusive of officers' horses.

I cannot refrain from applauding to you, the gallant actions of the rank and file of my command, all of whom behaved so gallantly on these occasions, that it would be invidious to mention names, suffice it, they all remained at their posts during the action, and behaved most gallantly, many of them, for the first time under fire, conducted themselves as veterans.

I have the honor to be,
Yours, very truly,
W. IRVING HODGSON, Capt.

In connection with the battle of Shiloh, the following extracts are taken from the same work :

Extract from official report of Col. Marshall J. Smith, Commanding Crescent Regiment of La.—page 344.

* * * * *

As the army advanced, the forces in front of us retired, and the Washington Artillery, Captain Hodgson, forming his battery in front of us, we supported him. This battery gallantly maintained their position, dealing destruction upon the foe, until the artillery on their left retired, leaving them alone.

At this moment, the enemy advanced in heavy force, and the artillery properly fearing such odds, limbered up and filed off to our left. We then advanced, covering the movement of the artillery, saving several of their pieces, and driving the enemy before us.

* * * * *

Extract from official report of Col. W. A. Stanley, Commanding 9th Texas Infantry—page 312.

* * * *

On the morning of the 6th, we advanced in line of battle, under a heavy fire of artillery and musketry, from the enemy's first encampment. Being ordered to charge the enemy with our bayonets, we made two successive attempts, but finding as well as our comrades in arms on our right and left, it almost impossible to withstand the heavy fire directed at our ranks, we were compelled to withdraw for a short time, with considerable loss. Being then ordered, we proceeded immediately to the support of the Washington Artillery which, from their battery's well directed fire, soon silenced the battery of the enemy.

* * * * *

Extract from official report of Col. Daniel W. Adams, Commanding 1st Regiment La. Infantry—page 243.

* * * * *

During this time, the enemy opened upon us again with their artillery, when I directed Captain Robertson to return their fire, which he did with great effect. Capt. Hodgson's battery of artillery also came up and rendered valuable services and assistance.

* * * * *

Extract from official report of Brig. Gen. Patton Anderson, Commanding 2nd Brigade, Ruggles' Division, 2nd Corps, Army of the Mississippi—page 300.

* * * * *

The 5th Company Washington Artillery, 155 men, commanded by Captain W. Irving Hodgson, following the centre, as nea:ly as the nature of the ground would permit, ready to occupy an interval, either between the Florida Battailon and the 9th Texas, or between the 9th Texas and 20th Louisinna, as necessity or convenience might require; the whole composing a force of 1634 men.

* * * * *

The most favorable position attainable by our field pieces, was selected, and Capt. Hodgson was directed to open fire upon the enemy's battery, (now playing vigorously upon us) with solid shot and shrapnel, and when occasion offered without danger to our own troops, to use canister upon his infantry. This order was obeyed with alacrity. Taking advantage of this diversion in our favor, the infantry was directed to pass through the swamp and drive the enemy before it, until Capt. Hodgson could either silence his battery, or an opportunity be presented of taking it with the bayonet.

The movement was made with spirit and vigor.

* * * * *

Page 302. The perceptibly diminishing fire from the enemy's battery, was soon, by Capt. Hodgson's superior practice, entirely silenced.

* * * *

Page 304. Gen. Ruggles had now placed our battery in position. Col. Smith, of the Crescent Regiment, had driven the enemy's sharpshooters from the cover of a log cabin, and a few cotton bales on the extreme left and near the road, and the enemy was being sorely pressed upon the extreme right by our columns upon that flank, and I felt the importance of pressing forward at this point. The troops too seemed to be inspired with the same feeling. Our battery opened rapidly, but every shot told. To the command "Forward," the infantry responded with a shout, and in less than five minutes after our artillery commenced playing, and before the infantry had advanced within shot range of the enemy's lines, we had the satisfaction of seeing his proud banner lowered, and a white one hoisted in its stead.

* * * *

Page 309. Captain W. Irving Hodgson, commanding the Fifth Company Washington Artillery, added fresh lustre to the fame of this already renowned corps. It was his fine practice from the brow of the hill overlooking the enemy's first camp, that enabled our infantry to rout them in the outset, thus giving confidence to our troops, which was never afterwards once shaken.

Although the nature of the ground, over which my infantry fought, was such as frequently to preclude the use of artillery, yet Captain Hodgson was not idle.

I could hear of his battery whenever artillery was needed. On several occasions I witnessed the effect which his canister and round shot produced upon the enemy's masses, and once saw his cannoniers stand to their pieces under a deadly fire, when there was no support at hand, and when to have retired, would have left that part of the field to the enemy.

When a full history of the battles of Shiloh shall have been written, the heroic deeds of the Washington Artillery will illustrate one of its brightest pages, and the names of Hodgson and Slocomb, will be held in grateful remembrance by a free people, long after the sod has grown green, upon the bloody hills of Shiloh.

* * * * *

Extract from official report of Brig Gen. Daniel Ruggles, Commanding Ruggles' Division, 2nd Corps.

* * * * *

Page 281. The Washington Artillery, under Captain Hodgson, was then brought forward, and two howitzers and two rifled guns commanded by Lieut. Slocomb, and two guns under Major Hoop were put in position on the crest of a ridge near an almost impenetrable boggy thicket, ranging along our front, and opened a destructive fire in response to the enemy's batteries then sweeping our lines at long range. I also sent orders to Brig Gen. Anderson to advance rapidly with his 2nd brigade, and as soon as he came up, I directed a charge against the enemy, in which some of the 6th Mississippi and 2nd Tennessee joined; at the same time I directed other troops to move rapidly by the right to turn the enemy's position beyond the swamp, and that the field artillery follow, as soon as masked by the movement of the infantry.

Under these movements, vigorously executed, after a spirited contest, the enemy's whole line gave way, and our advance took possession of the camp and batteries against which the charge was made.

* * * *

Page 282. The enemy's camps on our left, being apparently cleared, I endeavored to concentrate forces on his right flank in this new position, and directed Captain Hodgson's Battery into action there; the fire of his battery and a charge from the 2nd brigade, put the enemy to flight. Even after having been driven back from this position, the enemy rallied and disputed the ground with remarkable tenacity for some two or three hours, against our forces in front and his right flank, where cavalry, infantry and artillery mingled in the conflict.

* * * *

Extract from official report of Major General Braxton Bragg, Commanding 2nd Corps, Army of the Mississippi—page 232.

* * * *

Brig. Gen. D. Ruggles, commanding second division, was conspicuous throughout both days, for the gallantry with which he led his troops. Brig. Gen. Patton Anderson, commanding a brigade of this division, was also among the foremost where the fighting was hardest, and never failed to overcome whatever resistance was opposed to him.

With a brigade composed almost entirely of raw troops, his personal gallantry and soldierly bearing, supplied the place of instruction and discipline.

* * * *

Extract from official report of Gen. G. T. Beauregard, Commanding Army of the Mississippi.

* * *

Page 215. For the services of their gallant subordinate commanders, and their officers under them, as well as for the details of the battle-field, I must refer to the reports of corps, divisions and brigade commanders, which shall be forwarded as soon as received.

* * * *

List of killed and wounded at the battles of Shiloh, fought on the 6th and 7th days of April, 1862, *in the Fifth Company Washington Artillery.*

KILLED—1st Sergeant, John W. Demerith ; 2nd Sergeant, Benj. H. Green, Jr.;

4th Sergeant, Wm. B. Giffen; wounded in leg, suffered amputation and died; Private, C. J. Hartnett; Drivers, John Leary, Patrick Long, John O'Donnell—total, 7 killed.

WOUNDED—1st Lieutenant, C. H. Slocomb, shot in breast; 2nd Corporal, S. Higgins, spent ball in neck; 6th Corporal, W. L. Bruce, spent ball in side; 4th C. Corporal, L. Macready, shot in the leg; 5th C. Corporal, Alfred Bellanger, lost left hand; Corporal Drivers, F. N. Thayer, injured in hand; Privates, Thos. L. Bayne, shot in right arm; J. M. Davidson, shot in thigh; Octave Hopkins, Curtis Holmes, Milton McKnight, wounded; Robert Strong, William Steven, John W. Watson, John A. Walsh, wounded in leg; Drivers, Jas. Byrnes, Wm. Dooley, Samuel J. Davis, M. Campbell, John Clayton—total, 20. Killed, 7, wounded, 20—total casualties, 27.

After the battle of Shiloh, the following men were honorably discharged from the service :

Second Lieutenant, Edson L. Hews, resigned; 6th Corporal, W. L. Bruce, doctor's certificate; 5th C. Corporal, Alfred Bellanger, wounds received; 5th C. Corporal, F. N. Thayer, doctor's certificate; Privates, T. L. Bayne, wounds received; W. W. Clayton, doctor's certificate; J. M. Davidson, wounds received; J. M. Seixas, by order Gen. Bragg; Robert Strong, wounds received; Middleton Eastman, by order Gen. Bragg; John A. Walsh, wounds received; C. S. Wing, H. H. Lonsdale, doctor's certificate.

The resignation of Lieut, Ed. L. Hews, having been accepted, Gen. Bragg attached to the battery Mr. J. M. Seixas, and appointed him Lieut. in the 5th Company, to fill vacancy.

The following names were added to the roll of the battery, after it left the City of New Orleans, and previous to the battle of Shiloh, and were regularly mustered into service :

Privates: Middleton Eastman, Octave Hopkins, Wallace Ogden, Henry V. Ogden, Dr. John Pugh, George Pugh, William Pugh.
Drivers : M. Campbell, and John O'Donnell.

EVACUATION OF CORINTH, MISS.

On the 30th day of May, 1862, the army of the Mississippi evacuated Corinth, the 5th Company Washington Artillery, with its brigade, covering the retreat of the army.

The retrograde movement began at about 8 o'clock. P. M., continuing during that night, and by 3 o'clock, A. M. the last of the troops had passed through the town, on their way to Tupelo, Miss., via Clear Creek, a point about 40 miles south of Corinth, which latter place they reached on the morning of June the 1st, and immediately went into temporary camp.

The enemy did not pursue the retreating Confederate army more than 10 or 15 miles south of Corinth, and finding the Confederate forces ready to give battle, they returned to Corinth and went into camp.

On the 5th day of June, ascertaining the Federal army would not pursue or risk a further engagement in this vicinity, the Confederate army, now under the command of Gen. Braxton Bragg, determined to change their base to Chattanooga, Tennessee, for a resumption of hostilities, resulting in the famous Kentucky campaign—with a view to a long overland march. The army fell back to Tupelo, where there was an abundance of good water and forage, and went into regular camp, preparatory to said grand movement.

On the eve of the departure from Clear Creek, an order was issued from the Headquarters of the Army, that all officers and men, who were unable to march 20 miles a day, would go to Okalona, Miss., on surgeon's certificate, into the general hospital at that point by a special train, at 5 o'clock the following morning.

It was at this point, that Captain Hodgson, who had been sick and confined to his bed for some days, turned over the command to Lieut. Vaught, as Senior Lieut., (1st Lieut. Slocomb, being absent on sick leave, from wounds received at the battle of Shiloh,) and went to Okalona.

It was while the battery was in camp at Tupelo, (June 6th, 1862,) Capt. Hodgson, then in hospital at Okalona, forwarded his resignation to Gen. Bragg, commanding the army, which was accepted, and Lieut. C. H. Slocomb, was appointed Captain in his stead.

CHAPTER XXII.

THE BATTLE OF FREDERICKSBURG.

We spent a pleasant month and over at Winchester, during the period of the Indian summer, living on bacon and autumn corn, getting new clothing—reading books aloud, or telling camp-fire stories, and generally enjoying the superb climate of Virginia, as much as if there were no bloody battle-fields to dream of in the future. But the boots-and-saddle call came at last; and having welcomed the bugle blast with a shout, and packed up, there was nothing to be done but stretch out, Oct. 30th, in the direction of the Richmond Capitol. The most singular event that happened at this camp, was the killing of two of the 3rd Company, who had escaped all of the perils of battle, by the falling of a tree.

The move southward ended at Culpepper C. H., and was intended to meet a feint made in that direction by the Federal army; but their real intention having soon after been discovered, we continued our march, (Nov. 19th,) down the plank road to Fredericksburg, and appeared upon the south bank simultaneously with their arrival upon the right.

Adjutant's Journal.—Nov. 20. Cold rain all day. Forded Rapidan, at Racoon Ford. Camped on Mine Run, at Bartely's Mill. Dreadful night and impossible for the men to sleep dry.
21. Rained in torrents all night. Camp at Chancellorsville.
22. Reached Fredericksburg.

As we moved down the dreary plank road—past the old Chancellor Hotel or Mansion-house, around which only wounded guests linger—past the gloomy wilderness in whose depths the Federal army will soon be entangled and leave behind half its number for corpses or spectres, we met the inhabitants of Fredericksburg pouring out, and each one bearing in his or her arms, what was considered most valuable. The advances of the two armies already confronted the doomed city, and the inhabitants fled from it as if stricken with the plague. Delicate women who had been frightened from their homes, half clothed and badly shod, were trudging along, wondering where they would find shelter for themselves and little ones for the coming winter. The men gazed at them with great pity, and doubtless the same feeling was entertained by them for us; seeing that many times their number of soldiers would take their places in the town—that is in the cemeteries.

On our arrival there, I mean at Fredericksburg, many stores and houses were found abandoned—one of them containing fruit, fish, and barrels of oysters, which some of us felt ourselves after a long march, and under the circumstances justified in consuming. An occasional shell from the enemy which came crashing in, gave some little interest to the scene; but otherwise the sight of the crowded resorts of business abandoned and unoccupied, awoke a very melancholy feeling. The place seemed enchanted or cursed by a spell, and reminded us of Hood's Haunted House. We conversed in low tones while we remained inside of the town, and curious sight-seers did not think it worth risking their lives to prolong the visit.

Our appearance, it is now proper to state, in this neighborhood, was accounted for by the fact that McClellan had been removed as too slow a coach, and Burnside assigned the duty of trying to wriggle into Richmond, by some new and unguarded route. With great secrecy, he had transported his army to Fredericksburg, to cross at that point before Lee could discover his profound strategy. His feelings may be imagined, when after many days hard marching, he found his old enemy quietly on hand, on the opposite heights, with the air of having come there by appointment. This air of quiet expectation was sufficiently exasperating, to cause Burnside to open on us a few shots, very much as if inquiring through the cannon's mouth—" Who in the deuce would have ever thought you were there?"

Still as Lee would not go away, and something was expected to be done, Burnside finally resolved to cross the river, and either persuade Lee to change his mind, or go to Richmond without his consent. It was an unfortunate conclusion, as the result turned out, for the Federal General, and still more for some 20,000 of his troops, who in consequence of this decision were soon after left behind, dead or wounded, on the battle plain.

Blundering along with this idea, Burnside spent a day and a half, (the 11th,) in trying to get down his pontoon boats, and when the Confederate sharpshooters picked off his engineer corps, he bombarded Fredericksburg with one hundred guns, and set it on fire, though without incommoding the skirmishers on the river banks, or effecting much else than give warning and concentration to the Confederate army. A subordinate Federal General at nightfall, finally suggested the happy idea of crossing a regiment in boats, and thus capturing or driving in the picket line. This plan was carried out a little before day-break, on the 12th, after his design in crossing had become known, and there was no earthly chance of executing it. Both armies bivouacked on the cold ground—preparatory to the final and eternal rest on the morrow. At 3 o'clock, P. M., Stafford's heights were seen to be covered with troops, who moved to the pontoons under our heavy fire. Our batteries dispersed a mass of troops near the gas works.*

On the 13th Burnside had thrown over Franklin still lower down, who with one half of the Federal army attacked Lee's right, under Jackson, and at the time resting on Massaponax Creek.

Here the enemy had at first borne back a part of our lines; but he was met further back by a withering fire from Gregg's S. C. Brigade, and by a double quick charge from Early with the La. troops, which according to Northern historians "instantly turned the tide." "Early pursued with great slaughter," says the Federal General Birney, "to within 50 yards of my guns." The Federal army lost 40 per cent. of its men in this portion of the battle.

But meanwhile through a dense fog their advance also is on the 13th made—12:30 P. M.—upon Longstreet, up the steep plain upon whose top rested the Confederate batteries. The advance was made in fine style, the walls and fences falling before it like paper or frostwork.

"The Washington Artillery," says Gen. Lee "under Col. Walton, occupied the redoubts on the crest of Marye's Hill—the heights to the right and left being held by the reserve. The Washington Artillery here sustained the heavy fire of artillery and infantry with unshaken steadiness." About 11 A. M. says Gen. Longstreet, "I sent orders for the Washington Artillery to play upon the streets and bridges beyond the city, by way of a diversion to our right. The batteries had hardly opened when the enemy began to move out towards my line. Our pickets, in front of the Marye house were soon driven

*Sergeant Woods was wounded by this fire.

in, and the enemy began to deploy his forces in front of that point. Our artillery opened fire upon them as soon as the masses became dense enough to warrant it. This fire was very destructive and demoralizing in its effects, and frequently made gaps in the enemy's ranks that could be seen at the distance of a mile. The attack was again renewed and again repulsed. Col. Walton was particularly distinguished." Conspicuous among the enemy were the green flag of Meagher's Irish Brigade and the red bag breeches of the Zouaves. We hammered away at them as fast as we could load and fire, but on they came. They became confused as they advanced and when in range of the Georgians and Mississippians under Gen. Cobb, wheeled about and fled in confusion to the town. The attack lasted an hour. At 2 P. M. another line came on with deafening firing; line after line was pushed forward only to be mown down. We remained firing at our guns until 5 P. M. A note from Longstreet declared the firing of the batallion to be splendid.

Loss during the day, three killed and twenty-four wounded. The position was a very hot one, the minies flying around like hail. A brick house which was white at the commencement of the fight was red at its end. Ruggles received his mortal wound while ramming his piece. He exposed his body at the embrasure in spite of caution, and soon fell. Out of eight men at that embrasure, six were killed or wounded: infantry volunteers then assisted in manning the guns.

Maj. Gen. Ransom, says in his report, that "the gallantry and efficacy of the famous Washington Artillery*

---

*The report of Col. Cabell and several other Confederate officers, not to mention those published at the time in leading journals, assign equal importance to the work done by the Washington Artillery, or as Col. Cabell expressed it "the gallant corps who occupied the crest of Marye's Hill."

who drove back the enemy in triple lines, fighting heroically and under a heavy fire, is worthy of all praise."*

The force of the enemy at Marye's Hill was 30,000. There were only two brigades of 1500 men, who can be said to have taken part in this battle—on the Confederate side—that of R. R. Cobb, (the brother of Howell and a noble representative of Georgia in every way, who here lost his life) and Ransom's. These, placed behind a stone wall on the Telegraph road, constituted the advanced line. The honor of the fight on Marye's Heights, or what was the principal part of the battle of Fredericksburg, were yielded without any dissent to the artillery. The first who came under their fire, was French's Federal Division, who went down under a frightful fire, and close behind came Hancock, who left two men behind of every three; and then three other divisions. Lastly, about nightfall, Hooker led his men up the same avenue of death—only suspending his attack when he "had lost as many men as he was required to lose."

The Federal loss (by actual count there were 1500 bodies immediately around our pieces,) was more than 12,000; on the part of the Confederates on both wings, it was a little more than a third of that number.

In this battle Lieut. W. J. Behan, who had won his spurs at Sharpsburg, and who had since commanded one of the fine volunteer regiments of the city, first assisted in the command of the fourth company. Besides being a good officer, he enjoyed the honor of never having missed a roll call, or battle during the war.

---

*Lieut. Landry, of Capt. Maurin's battery, (the Donelson (La.) Artillery) took his piece from behind the epaulment to dislodge a body of the enemy. Most effectually he performed this service; but in doing so, lost several of his men, and had his piece disabled. His conduct was admirable, for during the time he was exposed to a direct fire of six and an enfilade fire of four guns. *Ransom's Report.*

Adjutant's Journal—December 16. Enemy abandoned the town, leaving their dead in our hands. Prisoners estimate their entire loss as 20,000. An Irishman of Meagher's Brigade fell nearest to our line.

17th. To-day a detailed Federal regiment came over from the enemy to bury the dead. The 1500 bodies were all thrown into a long trench with no more ceremonies than to so many brutes. The ice house on the edge of town was full of dead. These were temporarily laid in rows and covered with earth.

19th. Big jollification over captured supplies; all hands jolly; war dance, and songs.

31st. Batallion goes to Pole Cat Creek. Ordered with Col. Walton, to go to Mobile to recruit.

CHAPTER XXIII.

WINTER-QUARTER AMUSEMENTS—INCIDENTS OF A VISIT TO RICHMOND.

We went into winter-quarters—always a terrible drag to the men, a short distance from Chesterfield Station, in Caroline County, most of us having no other shelter than canvass or tarpaulin tents (with fire places at one end) affording the best of ventilation, and a rather too free an entrance for rain and snow. There was a charm about living under canvass which made them preferable with many to occupying a badly lighted log house, with a dozen others, which in reality were but little superior to negro quarters on a plantation.

We would have been happier if the talents of the men had been employed, as was the case with the Roman, and is to-day with the Spanish armies, in some sort of way where skill would have increased our scanty rations. Failing however in this, the men who did not contrive, under some excuse or leave of absence to get to Richmond, a not very difficult affair, were mostly occupied in building a theatre. The walls of this were composed of pine tree branches, and in representing on the stage some of the popular farces and dramas, every one was suited to his bent, and was detailed to some appropriate duty.

Dempsy, one of our Artificers, who had previously had some experience as a stage carpenter, and Nugent, who is now regarded as the best blacksmith in the city, made what was under the circumstances an admirable stage, and the accessories of light, scenery and artificial thunder, were all ingeniously provided for. The audiences from surrounding corps, including in many cases distinguished Generals and their staff, were as large as those gathered together in a city theatre on a benefit night, and probably more delighted.*

*We had in this camp but little to do or talk of except of the eccentricities which soldiering had begun to develop, peculiarities to which every one was keenly alive, except their possessor. The musical genius for instance, was Otto Frank—the traditional German professor in every respect—gold spectacles, a touch of sentiment and bad English, a fondness for ladies' society, and a general impatience (though a good soldier,) of the harsh outlines of camp life. Otto was constantly falling into the hands of the tormentors, who would beguile him into an artless recital of his impressions of war by the show of a grave and melancholy interest which awoke no suspicion of treachery in his manly bosom. Another victim was a *naveï* soldier who became vain of his talents for shaving. His vanity was still further stimulated one day by bets as to the number of chins he could scrape in a given time. The consequence was that he had the batallion on his hands. It was not a little amusing to hear him bawling out the name of every one to "Come and get shaved—*viens donc.*" A young lawyer was one day overheard relating some curious facts about the only client he had ever probably had—Joins, or (as he called him) *Jines.* The boys betrayed great interest in the history of this wonderful suitor, and the point or *pint* would be to make him pronounce *Jines'* name and words with similar dipthongs, as often as possible. A young soldier was detected later along, writing verses—which were highly complimented by some of our generals, but at the same time would perhaps have been improved by fuller rations and the burning sky of Louisiana. The poetic spirit had long since died out in camp. What increased the enormity of the offence of a poetical description was, that the author read some of his lines—he, a young recruit—to old veterans, about patriotism and glory. The thing could not be passed by. A court-martial was convened with John Porter, presiding judge, Sam Bland, as prosecutor, (representing an old farmer, whose chickens had been stolen,) and severe jurors, sheriff's officers and clerks, in proportion.

The poet in vain endeavored to prove that he was meditating about and gazing at the stars, and not chickens, and it was not until he had consented to buy up the jury with a promise to pay for the "incidental expenses" that a verdict was found of "not guilty." Previous to Fredericksburg, the fancy seized us to make all the talking men step forward on a given night and say what they had got to say before a formal audience. Noble (afterwards of the Legislature,) was in this way embarked in a metaphysical lecture on the Diaphanous Properties of Mud, or something similar, and no one at its conclusion could tell whether the joke was on the speaker or the audience. They gave him a historic cane with a flourish. Cleveland, (one of the men who captured the battery and worked it on their own hook, but who had the least conception of

I succeeded in escaping most of the monotony which attended the long months in winter and the opening of spring, by a short detail from the medical board to Richmond. The order from the Department came at night, just as we had concluded a march of thirty miles, and while the men were lying in front of their bivouac fires, awaiting supper. But as no soldier cares to lie rotting around camp, where dysentery and weariness carried off more men than battle, or when he knew the dangers to which such furloughs were liable, I lost no time the night the order from the Secretary was handed to me, in immediately rolling up my blankets and limping over the same wearisome thirty miles at night, in the direction of the Gordonsville R. R. that I had just passed over. I might have taken the cars at Fredericksburg, the next morning; but the travel on a terribly cold frosty night was nothing to the happiness of feeling a little sooner, that you were your own master, and of knowing that a military order could scarcely reach you. As showing how such instructions were respected in Bragg's army, an order from the Secretary was repeated three times, and the messenger was then recommended to keep out of the way if he did not wish to be shot.

My journey back, therefore, though I would frequently fall down with fatigue, hunger and weakness, and I might too have perhaps frozen, but for the way side bivouac camp fires, was under the actual circumstances, the hap-

a joke of any man in the batalliou) was suddenly confronted with a long series of adventures, which could not have happened inside of a hundred years, and was offered a discharge, as too old for military service. The bores, after the musicians and humorous talkers had been disposed of, were summoned forward for judgment, and not allowed to go unpunished.

The success of this impromptu gathering, led to the organization of a theatrical corps, which first performed a little before the battle of Fredericksburg —one of the leading characters (Spearing,) losing his life in the battle which followed shortly after.

piest march I ever made. No ceremony would be used in stepping in between the sleepers and the burnt down fires of glowing coals. The only objections in such cases raised by the courtesy of camps, was when the sleeper turning over uneasily, and becoming indignant at the coldness of his feet, would complain that you were outstaying your welcome. It would then be necessary to trudge on to the next glowing log fire, and so on through the night and following morning. There were several similar adventures—one that of traveling, Mazeppa-like, on one of a body of horse, (without bridle or saddle,) which was being carried back to the rear at a slapping pace. When I reached the train, I had to rely more upon my skill in elbowing past sentinels, than upon the order of the Secretary of War; and before entering Richmond, preferred, with other soldiers, to be shot at rather than be marched off to some rough camp or hospital, where you would be placed with bounty jumpers, or small-pox patients, and be pulled and jerked around by any idle officer who had nothing else to do.

Once in the city, I proceeded with a very serious fear about quarters to the room of a friend from the army, already mentioned. but had scarcely entered and commenced undressing, which I did very quickly, before a feminine scream warned me of my error. My next attempt was something more successful. After getting confused in marching about in a blinding snow storm, and mistaking a statue of Washington, for an evil-disposed sentinel, I at length entered my friend's room. But this was full of beds, in each of which there was a couple of immense soldiers from Hood's Brigade, I believe, with arms, legs, and mouths spread open to their widest extent, and with bowie knives and revolvers half concealed by the pillows.

I struck a match, but the light went out—the prospect

did not look encouraging. I determined to grope my way out as silently as I came in. Unfortunately a chair was knocked over.

"Who's there?" shouted a voice. "What in the h—l are you doing with them clothes?" Before I could explain a pistol was discharged.

"Kill 'em as you catch 'em!" cried another voice, and off went another barrel.

Supposing that these might be followed by others, I took the prudential step of crawling under a bed and awaiting till the barrels were all emptied.

Another startled inmate, thinking the Federals had reached the city, jumped out of a window—I believe into a cistern. When the firing had at length ceased I made an explanation which was accepted without gainsaying.

Half of the inmates were now sitting up in bed; a light was again struck. There were the remains of a fire still burning in the fire place, and two or three getting out of bed in their night blouses, stirred up the chunks, and resting their tremendous limbs upon the mantle-piece, began to meditatively squirt tobacco juice at the flames. It struck me at the time as being a queer crowd altogether, although I had become so accustomed to new sights, and ways of thinking and acting, that I was prepared for almost anything.

"I wish you d—d fellers would quit your foolishness and go to bed," here sung out a petulant voice; "I always save one or two barrels in case of accident, and if you don't dry up and go to bed, hang me, if I don't blaze away right in the crowd."

But the complaint was unheeded. One of the watchers gave me permission, or rather ordered me off to his bed, perhaps as occupying too much of the fire. A pack of cards was produced, a bottle of liquor and a plug of tobacco, the table was covered with corns for counters—and I dozed off into an uneasy slumber. The game, however, I imagined, was fiercely contested; and each player, as he led a strong card, would bring his fist down with a blow which would make the glasses jingle. When the hands were particularly good, they fell thick and fast. I could not help regarding the table in the morning, and was not surprised to see its leg looking rickety.

About day-break I woke up with a sudden start caused by a tremendous thump. The tobacco had almost disappeared, the bottle was empty, and one of the players was sweeping up a pile of Confederate bills into his handkerchief. The rest of the inmates now commenced dressing, or gazed from beneath the bed clothes with a half sleepy, half sullen expression, preparatory to doing the same. They were all soldiers on furlough, and I need not say we had a pretty wild, rattling set in that room; every body was on the hurrah-style, and lived as recklessly as if pay day in greenbacks came every day, and there was to be no to-morrow. Especially was this the case with a brave captain from North Louisiana, who had just bought a $500 coat, as gorgeous as gold lace could make it. He played on a guitar, and affected a pensive style of singing, which was somewhat interfered with by the loudness of his voice and the prominence of his jaw, and he told all manner of impossible and fearful stories. At breakfast he made love to the landlady's daughter, and would have been helped doubtless to the best dishes, if there had been anything to eat but fried bacon and corn coffee.

At the same table, was another lady who came from New Orleans, and after getting sent out of the city by Butler, was equally unfortunate in being taken for a

Federal spy. However, she had been allowed to go to Richmond on parole, and had become not a little soured at the number of visits necessary to be made before obtaining her release. She gave the Captain who condoled with her, a beautiful lace handkerchief to bathe in somebody's blood, on the battle-field. The Captain, however, never got much closer to the enemy, than the nearest faro-bank, and in that classic quarter, boasted of the gift in a manner which would hardly have pleased its fair donor had she heard it.

My first day in town brought me in contact with the Provost Marshal, who treated me with American civility, but allowed his eyes to droop when speaking of the necessity of reporting for detail duty, and the sentinels too, began to find fault with my pass.

Under such pressure, I soon found myself making out pay rolls, or following rather humbly behind a paymaster with bundles of Confederate shinplasters, and assisting him in paying off the various hospitals about Richmond.

This brought me acquainted with the matrons, who at that day represented as much address, experience of the world, knowledge of human nature, personal attraction, and kind-heartedness, as any other class of southern women who came to the surface. They were by no means the ideal of the domestic woman, and sometimes were possessed of much more wit and liveliness of manner than refinement; but they were better adapted to taking care of soldiers, than ladies with less restlessness, vanity, jealousy, and love of power; a class with which every soldier during his time of sickness or wounds became familiar. As an illustration of this, I may mention what happened at my boarding house, to the brave Captain. He had been going about a good deal, boasting of his handkerchief, and generally carried things with rather a high hand in the parlor.

One day as I passed by the door, I found him talking in his usual loud, hectoring, pleasant manner to two ladies. By way of giving animation to the scene, he would walk up and down the floor, singing "I'm the boy that's gay and happy." One of the ladies had once traveled in our ambulance wagon, and as the principal part of my costume was an old blanket with a hole cut in the middle, (except about dinner time when it was a dressing gown,) it was with much distress, that I saw that I could not escape bowing and speaking. I arrived just in time to see that the Captain was not received with much favor—that he had encountered a Tartar in the second of the two ladies. She had become weary with his freedom of manners, and was now turning on him a very handsome, satirical face, vicious black eyes, and the keenest tongue that any camp absentee had ever heard wagged at his expense. She snubbed him still further, after a dubious glance at my costume, by inviting me, instead of the Captain, to escort her home; and to add still more to his discomfiture during a momentary absence, I contrived to become possessed of one of his beautiful blue and gold coats which he had rashly left in our room unguarded. My new acquaintance after a rather liberal abuse of the Captain, whom she thought not worthy to look a lady of education in the face, allowed me to assist her in an ambulance which was in waiting. Entering after her she proceeded to inform me that there was but one thing that ladies in the South could do who were not of a domestic turn —become officers of the government—devote themselves to wounded soldiers, learning how to command in their departments and to defend themselves from imposition. She thought there was especial danger from the Doctors, whom she maintained could boast of but little more knowledge than that of knowing how to potter at simple pills, and whose services were counterbalanced by drinking up most of the medical supplies when so permitted. She had lived very gaily in New Orleans society, she told me; but a hospital and soldiers was now the thing for a lady who had always been accustomed to a stirring and exciting life—books, society, dancing being out of the question. However the denial on her part did not prevent her from showing by her gestures that her arms were still finely shaped, that her back hair, which she moved, grew on her head as in the antique models, and that her shoe, which she took off (probably from pride at that day in having a new pair) was of the smallest pattern. She now took a philosophical tack, and told me her character grew out of the war like everything else—that the soldiers she met were frequently the first gentlemen in the land, and having no competition they admired her as much, if not more, than she had been in ten years previous. She couldn't be a *vivandière* as they had in French armies, or ride about from one line in male attire like Bell Boyd, or fight with a musket in a soldier's uniform, as some heroines were doing—so long as they behaved themselves; or do as Gen. Gordon's wife did, rally his brigade when her husband was absent; but she had traveled hundreds of miles as a refugee through the lines, without money and friends; sometimes in a soldier train where she would be concealed in the mail car and surrounded with mail matter for days and so on. The ambulance stopped at the house of one of the secretaries with whom she was staying, and as the ground was covered with snow, I had the courage, instead of putting her on the ground, to carry her to the doorsteps. The result was that it fared worse with me in the way of epithets and abuse, than it had with the Captain. However, when I went with the paymaster, she gave me a laughing invitation to take dinner with her, to the great indignation of the local doctors, whom she wanted to feel miserable—in the very room that contained the envied stores.

CHAPTER XXIV.

CHANCELLORVILLE.

The spring of '63 has meanwhile passed, and the roads have commenced to harden. The men absent from camp have grown weary of cities, and the old soldiers about winter-quarters, shout lustily when a popular general passes by—a sure sign that they have regained their old combative feeling, and a sign, too, that they will soon be called upon, to make use of it. The battery forges are kept constantly busy, and the ringing of Callahan's blacksmith's hammer in his labors, for the benefit of the battery horses, and the flying sparks which gayly shoot upward, begin to intoxicate the blood of men.

During the close of April, the rumbling of the artillery wheels, and the weary tramp of the infantry are once more heard. Hooker has daringly thrown his army across the Rappahannock, and waded them through the Rapidan, a deep tributary, and has made a move which causes Lee rather to open his eyes. However, the advantage lasts but a moment. The Confederate troops are promptly gathered up, and boldly moved forward—Jackson being thrust out in the same way, on the enemy's flank, as the one-armed Captain Cuttle would his hook—to drag the enemy in. Hooker, meanwhile, has occupied the ground, which, if he only knew it, and would hold on to it, would gain him the battle; but he becomes timid, with a greatly superior force, as Lee becomes daring, and meanwhile, his army is like one of those read of in the classic page, which gets bogged up in a swamp, or trembling prairie, or overwhelmed by the Lybian or Arabian sands; or as in the "Shipwreck," where the whole of the Duke's Court are wandering about on an unknown land, encountering enemies, and coming across friends—in all manner of fantastic ways. At one end of the line—Hooker's left, which faces towards Richmond, is the old Chancellor House. It will soon be dripping with more blood than ever was put in a sensational tragedy or novel. Against one of its pillars Hooker is leaning in the battle, when stunned by the concussion against it of a shell.

On Friday morning, (May 1st,) the opposing columns began to jostle each other, and Hooker now can emerge from the tangled thicket in which he has been so far groping; but it is his last chance. It is one thing to mark out a campaign brilliantly, and to execute it unflinchingly, with new difficulties to be provided for on the battle field, at every step. As the Irish duelist explained it, to hit the stem of a wine glass with a bullet, is not difficult—provided the wine glass has no pistol.

Hooker once had emerged from his dangerous position, where his army could not manœuvre, but was either driven back, or took up from choice, according to Northern accounts, a line with rising ground in front, and with impenetrable thickets behind, from which the Confederate attacks could readily be formed. The night which followed, passed silently in both armies—silently, so far as the guns were concerned; but faint noises told of the shoveling up of rifle pits; thousands of midnight woodcutters, as if suddenly possessed with a superstitious fancy for making a clearing, were causing the Wilderness, on both sides, to resound with their blows, or bringing to the ground some of the huge trunks, with a noise equal to cannon.

The falling of these trees meant for Hooker, that he would await an attack; for Lee that he knew Hooker's plan, and would go off and make an attack somewhere else. He will act upon Jackson's last and most brilliant idea, and send the latter around by an obscure farm road on Hooker's right, between him and his river communications. This move of Jackson, thought to be a retreat to Richmond—strikes the Federal right at 5 o'clock on the afternoon of May 2nd, and by dark it has put a whole corps to utter route. Jackson has got on the reverse side of the enemy, to within half a mile of headquarters. He is now about to deal his finishing blow, and while anxiously seeking the precise situation of the enemy, gets his death wound in the dark, at the hands of some of his own pickets. His loss left the battle incomplete, in spite of its stunning blow, and the melancholy news affected the Confederates in the same way that the fulfillment of the various omens predicted, before Troy could be captured, affected that city's defenders. On the other hand, if Jackson had not been wounded, as he said on his dying bed, "the enemy would have been obliged to surrender or cut his way out."

On the next day, Stuart, in Jackson's place, bore down and pressed back the Federal right wing, while Lee on the opposite side, hammered away at Hooker's centre and left—forcing back two corps; or as a Northern* historian expresses it, "the line melted away, and the front appeared to pass out." Hancock, who alone held out, began to waver at 10 A. M., when "the Confederates sprang forward, and seized Chancellorville."

Fredericksburg during this time had been left with a small force of five brigades, including the 1st and 2d La., and three companies of the Washington Artillery, who had been ordered from Chesterfield three days before, to the crest of Marye's Hill—their old battle ground. Barksdale was still with us. The latter, Sunday morning, in view of a movement by Sedgwick's corps, on this part of the line, were reinforced by Hays' Brigade. After three failures in other directions, a powerful assaulting column was formed to carry the hill by storm, which feat was finally achieved, though "under a very severe fire that cost Sedgwick a thousand men. The Confederates made a savage hand-to-hand fight on the crest, and over the 8 guns." As there was only in reality two regiments, (less than 2000 men) assigned to the support of our artillery, and the attack was made by twenty-two thousand of the enemy, (according to Sedgwick's report,) it will not appear surprising that the works were finally captured. The guns were worked desperately to the last, and were faithfully manned by their cannoniers, when six pieces were surrounded, and the guns and cannoniers made prisoners—most of them under the command of Capt. Squires and Lieut. E. Owen. A large proportion of the gallant 18th and a part of the 21st Miss., were taken prisoners at the same time.

Sedgwick now commenced moving on the slender brigades who had been retained here by Lee to make up a show

---

*Swinton's History of the Army of the Potomac.

before the enemy, and retain his line of communications with Richmond—Early meanwhile retreating slowly towards Lee. He did not do so long—before the day was over, a sufficient force, McLaw's and Anderson, were promptly sent back to Early's support. The shock occurred at Salem Chapel, and all that need be said about it, was that Sedgwick was checked that day, "with a total loss of 5000 men."* Marye's Hill was re-occupied the next day without any difficulty by its former possessors.

On Monday night, May 4th, Sedgwick being surrounded on three sides, and hard pressed as to his communications with the river, took advantage of the darkness, and was fortunate enough to safely withdraw his troops.

Lee having cleared, as it were, the brushwood from his path, was now (May 6th) with the troops whom he had recalled, prepared to attend to the case of Hooker; but that General was found to have lost all stomach for a fight, and had put the Rappahannock between himself and the enemy.

The result of the matter, and this was about the whole result, except that new material for powder had to be provided—was that the Union loss was 17,197, and the Confederate, 10,281. All of the spoils in the way of artillery, prisoners, and 20,000 stand of arms, fell to the Confederate army. The victory in short, was a glorious one, but really amounted to nothing, as Jackson disappeared from the scene, at the moment when most needed, and the result was incomplete.

*Swinton, page 299.

CHAPTER XXV.

THE STORMING OF WINCHESTER BY GEN. HAYS' BRIGADE.

There being no other work before him, the army of Gen. Lee began to stretch out and lengthen towards the Potomac. Longstreet came up from the James.

A dim suspicion of some move on foot led to an attack on Stuart's cavalry, which was in the advance, at Brandy Station, and led to one of the few regular cavalry engagements which took place during the Confederate war—the loss being something between five and eight hundred on a side. This engagement, where the men remained on horseback, and used their sabres, instead of dismounting and "grabbing hold of roots," as the infantry would sometimes derisively speak of what they called the "Butter-milk Rangers," did much to raise the popularity of the cavalry, though it waned afterwards in spite of hard and arduous service, with the wearing out of horseflesh and the increase of Company Q.

Our line having meanwhile lengthened until it reached from Fredericksburg to the Valley, Ewell suddenly pounced down on Winchester and stormed its heights, taking 4000 prisoners, and a large amount of war material.

The way in which this was accomplished, according to Gen. Early's report, was by an assault made on a hill to the Northwest of the enemy's works. A position having been selected—that is, the side from which the attack should be made, Early led his guns and infantry by obscure paths to within a short distance of the hill to be stormed. His movements thus far had been concealed by the woods, and he had been fortunate enough to miss meeting any of the enemy's scouts. Meanwhile Gordon had been making an advance from the opposite side of the town.

Jones' Artillery (twenty guns) were now put in readiness to support the charge on the storming side, and Gen. Hays' Louisiana Brigade, which had many times before enjoyed the honor of being selected for similar work, was put under cover, and allowed to gaze at the hill in front, covered with recently felled timber, at the bastion works with which the fort was crowned, and at the two lines of breast work further beyond.

It was now an hour by sun, and the men were burning with impatience. Twice Gen. Hays made ready to move, and was detained by Early's orders; a third time the detaining order was sent to him by Early, who could not believe but what the enemy were keeping a better look out than they did. But finally the twenty guns opened simultaneously, which was the *laisser faire* for action, and the next moment, before the enemy had recovered from his astonishment at seeing troops in this direction, and in spite of orders, Hays and his men were crawling through the brushwood, and up the steep slope. "He drove, says Gen. Early, the enemy from his fortifications in fine style," and with some of his infantry who had been purposely for such occasions, trained as cannoniers, he opened with the enemy's own rifled pieces, thus preventing all efforts at recapture. The enemy abandoned the whole town the next morning—Gordon's Ga. brigade being the first to reach the main fort, and pull down the flag flying over it. The infamous Milroy fled towards the Potomac, but too late to save his infantry, who now found themselves intercepted by Johnson's division. Twenty-five guns were captured, and only a few horsemen, who were with Milroy, succeeded in reaching the opposite side of the Potomac. Gen. Early justly speaks of it, as "a most brilliant exploit."

CHAPTER XXVI.

THE GETTYSBURG CAMPAIGN.

Meanwhile, our batteries remained a few days at Stannard's Farm, grazing the horses. We then marched (5th,) past the old Wilderness Tavern, and crossed the Rapidan at Racoon Ford, with Gen. Longstreet's corps. Our road led us on towards Woodville and Winchester, and through Sperryville and Little Washington. After then crossing the Blue Ridge at Chester Gap, we passed through Front Royal, to the banks of the Shenandoah. Meanwhile, rumors of another invasion campaign were daily increasing in probability, which the victory at Winchester tended to confirm. After crossing at Morgan's Ford, we remained at Millwood, which was with the surrounding scenery the paradise of all camps, and soon after took up the line of march through Bunker Hill, and again into Maryland. The move north of the Potomac, was regarded with much questioning by the army, though its danger gave it a risk that soldiering on a worn out soil, did not possess. At any rate, we crossed the river in *sans culotte* style, like so many King Dagoberts, and then marched through Hagerstown, to Greencastle, Penn.

It was difficult to say which was the most surprised, the farmers who scarcely knew of the war, or the Southern army, at the worldly thrift, agricultural comfort, and at the same time thoroughly Bœotian spirit of these (as we then called them,) "Pennsylvania Dutchmen." There was nothing of course to correspond with the magnificent cotton and sugar plantations of the South, which sometimes were tilled by a thousand hands before the war; nor, with those old plantation chateaux, which the traveler on the Mississippi sees nestling among orange groves and tropical foliage. But the farmers we now saw, though not possessed of great means, had excellent habitations. Their ignorance of anything but tilling the soil, to a soldier appeared astonishing; it was however exceeded by their prejudice and bitterness.

Lee's orders, much to the disgust of the army, were not to plunder or in any way destroy private property, and passes when we reached the neighborhood of Chambersburg, which we did the next day, were now not easy to obtain. It need not however be stated that all of the cheese, whiskey, and other articles with which the country abounded, were not entirely left behind. For several days indeed, our commissaries tolerably well supplied us with food.

It was raining torrents all day, on the 30th, as we marched over splendid roads, and through fine mountain scenery; but on the first of July, we followed Hill and Ewell towards Gettysburg, who were then driving the enemy through the town, and while awaiting orders, our men watched with great anxiety the battle, which we could partially see, in front of us.*

---

*Extract from the note book of one of our men: "Part of the time during our halt, I was talking to a scowling farmer. He asked me in response to some remark about climate or health, if I knew anything of medicine, and when I shook my head, he attributed my denial to unwillingness to do him any service. I then, observing his disappointment, told him what was the truth, that I had read medicine to some extent, but was no practitioner, and asked him what he wanted done. He led the way silently to a room where a young lady was reclining, and asked me to assist her, if I knew how. Both the young girl and the old man himself were obviously only half dead with terror, and I thought it most good-natured to assume all the dignity of an experienced M. D., and in this way endeavor to alleviate her terror. I accordingly examined her tongue with great importance, felt of her pulse, and talked learnedly about valerian and *digitalis*,

CHAPTER XXVII.

THE DECISIVE STRUGGLE.

The battle of Gettysburg was brought on without being anticipated by either of the contending Generals. It was like an accidental fight which starts at a street corner, and which becomes "free" all around. It was decided opportunely, though with but little in the way of result, by the lucky arrival of Hays' and Gordon's Brigades, under Ewell, from Yorktown, when affairs were in a very critical condition. By their desperate charge, and by the penetration of a weak point in the Federal line, they with Rhodes' Division captured or totally routed all the Federal troops on hand. Those who escaped, were driven back and huddled together on the heights, north of Gettysburg.* This was the first feature of the fight. The most important consequences, the fruits of most value, which should have been gathered, were lost by a neglect to seize the Cemetery Ridge, which commanded the situation, and which was the turning point of the battle.

neither of which I knew was in the house; and as a last resource I suggested, like David Copperfield's housekeeper, to restore her forces, with a little weak brandy and water. The old man hunted up the brandy with alacrity, while I meanwhile showed the young lady that she was in no danger, either from the balls or the rebels themselves. I think I proved to both that I was an excellent physician, and to show that I had confidence in my remedy, I very readily consented to drinking myself what remained.

*The following is from Gen. Ewell.

The enemy were moving large bodies of troops from the town, and affairs were in a very critical condition, when Maj. Gen. Early coming up, ordered forward Gordon, who broke Barlow's Division, captured Gen. Barlow, and drove the whole back in a second line, when it was halted. Gen. Early now ordered up Hays' and Hokes' Brigades, on Gordon's left, and then drove the enemy precipitately towards and through the town, just as Ransom broke those in his front. Three hundred dead were left on the ground, passed over by Gordon's Brigade. Early and Rhodes together, captured 4000 prisoners; two pieces of artillery fell in the hands of Early's Division. No other troops than those of this corps entered the town at all. [See Gen. Ewell's report of the second army corps, Gettysburg Campaign.] His statement about Cemetery Hill, and the reason why the attack was delayed, is substantially the same as is here given further on, excepting in not mentioning the earnest appeal made by Hays, for a prompt attack.

This halt and neglect to take the afterwards so famous crescent-shaped ridge, after Hays had marched straight into the town, when fifteen minutes further of advance would have finished the business at a blow, is thus explained:

Hays had received orders through Early from Ewell (though Lee's general instructions subsequently were the reverse,) to halt at Gettysburg and advance no further than that point, in case he should be successful in capturing the place. But Hays now saw that the enemy were coming around by what was known as the Baltimore road, and were obviously making for the strong Cemetery ridge, immediately north of Gettysburg. The ridge in question meant life or death, and for the mastery of it, the battles of the 2nd and 3rd of July, the days following, will have to be fought. The Baltimore road referred to ran at the foot of the hill for several miles. Consequently, owing to the long detour which the enemy were compelled to make, it was obvious that they would not be able to get their artillery in position on Cemetery Hill for one or two hours. The immediate occupation of the hill by the Confederate army, who were in a position to get there at the time referred to, without much opposition, was a matter of vital importance. Hays recognized it as such, and promptly sent word to Early. The latter thought as Hays, but declined to disobey orders. At the urgent solicitation of Gen. Hays, however, he sent for Gen. Ewell: when the latter arrived, many precious moments had been lost. But the enemy who did not see its value until the arrival of Hancock on the scene, had not yet appeared in force.

If Gen. Ewell will now act, the Confederates will have the frowning hills, against which brave men may throw away their lives by the thousands without success, for their own fortifications, and the two days of bloody fighting, will either take place at Philadelphia or Harrisburg, the Capital of Pennsylvania; or the result will be on the Gettysburg ground a certain victory. If Ewell makes the right decision, there will be an overwhelming feeling in favor of allowing the Southern States separation, without further war.

Unfortunately, Gen. Ewell, while sharing Hays' convictions, thought it better to wait a little, until Johnson came up, and meantime the precious moments, whose value Jackson knew better than any man, are flying.

Johnson gets up finally, and Lee is pressing for an attack. But now, there is a new delay: the enemy appear to be making a demonstration, to one side or the other. At last, this is discovered to amount to nothing. Still the evening has come, and so the attack must be postponed until to-morrow.

Ewell laughed at Hays, when he appeared so anxious to make the attack, and wanted to know if his men would never have their bellyful of fighting—if they could not wait a day. Hays' answer was, that it was with a view to prevent the slaughter of his men, that he wanted to make the attack at once—and was unwilling to throw away their lives if the heights were allowed to be defended by guns and breastworks. But so it was to be. That very night, the Louisiana Brigade, as the men threw themselves despondingly on the ground, (for soldiers know now as well as their generals, when a point is lost or made,) were startled by a rumbling noise, faint at first, but which comes nearer. The heavy guns are being dragged up to the crest of the hill, and will tell their own tale on the morrow. The sound of the pickaxe and spade are heard—the enemy are shoveling up breastworks and trenches, which will protect those who are to live. Still useful, when the battle is over, these trenches will answer equally well for the graves of those who are to be left behind.

The following day, (July 2d,) dragged on: it was the last for many thousands, and they waited impatiently to know their fate. An unbroken stillness prevailed until late in the afternoon. But the loss of opportunity‘ yesterday, must now be replaced, and great masses of men are to be put in motion.

The result of this day's struggle, (the 2d,) was an attempt to repair the mistakes made the day before, by a desperate charge of the whole of Longstreet's line. The Texas brigade, sweeping back from Peach Orchard to Round Top, succeeded by a quick movement, in wedging itself in between the Federal left and the latter mountain —thus cutting off the Federal line of retreat, and enfilading the enemy's line, if the brigade could have been sustained. The position was however saved to the Federal army, by a bayonet struggle, led on by Warren. Hood who did not see that Round Top itself was unoccupied, was forced to give back. Longstreet wedged into every crack and crevice of the enemy's ranks, and gained ground ; but the result was unsatisfactory. Meanwhile, at the opposite end of the line, the same attack and repulse were being repeated by Hays' brigade, as will now be shown in detail :

The attack on this wing commenced about dusk, Hays' and Hokes' Brigades being assigned to the work in hand. and moving directly forward against Cemetery Hill in their front.

Hays thereupon charged over a hill, into a ravine.

where they broke a line of the enemy's infantry, posted behind a stone wall—up the steep face of another hill, and over two lines of breastworks, capturing several batteries of artillery. These works were held until finding that no attack was made on the right, and heavy masses of the enemy advancing, they reluctantly fell back, bringing away with them, 75 to 100 prisoners, and four stands of captured colors.

Gen. Lane, commanding Pender's Division on the right, was asked by Ewell, at this juncture, to co-operate, but made no reply. Maj. Gen. Rhodes "did not advance for reasons given in his report." Had it been otherwise, from the eminent success attending the assault of Hays and Avery, (though that latter gallant commander of Hokes' Brigade, was the only one of his command, according to his own statement, who went into the enemy's works,) the enemy's lines would have been carried. The above statements are from Ewell's report.

The truth about the charge on Cemetery Hill, on this part of the line, was that Hokes' Brigade advanced only a few hundred yards, breaking on the first hill under an almost infernal fire, in spite of the gallant efforts of Col. Avery to lead them on. Avery himself went into the enemy's lines and said to Gen. Hays: "I am here without my command. I wish you to remember that I at least have reported in person."

This position was finally yielded to superior numbers.

About the hour this attack was made, a little after dusk, the batteries of the Washington Artillery were sent for in hot haste, and as soon as the order was received, we went tearing to the front, over trees and stumps, and with imminent risk to the cannoniers, mounted on the seats, of being crushed. We were not, however, ordered to open fire. Although the enemy had been taught his weak points, and had shown unusual readiness in getting to the point assailed, which was in reality easy to be done with a line of only two miles in length to six on the part of the assailant, yet as the Confederates had driven back the enemy and all the trophies of victory were with them, it was resolved to make one more final throw of the die, and to renew the fearful assaults of the two preceding days. The point aimed at now—the attack on the wings having failed of decided results—was to pierce the enemy's centre.

At two o'clock on the morning of the eventful day, (July 3d) our batteries were ordered to take what proved to be our final position for the great battle. The ground was covered with the slain of the preceding days' fights, who had been left behind in the forcing back of the Federal army, and their groans would have been enough to have disturbed the consciences of even those who had no risks themselves on the morrow to encounter.

One of the statements made to me afterwards, by Lieutenant H——, of the way in which he passed the night, was that having no blanket, he had concluded to crawl, as was frequently done, under the covering of another soldier. He remarked during the night, that the man seemed very cold blooded, and the next morning when he woke up and looked around, he thought so more than ever. He understood the situation at a glance. He had been sleeping all night with a corpse.

The fight commenced in the morning, at an early hour, with the roar of artillery from the enemy's guns, and was as hot as any we had ever previously encountered—the more so because our own guns meanwhile remained silent.

In a few moments, two of the Third company's finest

horses, and Smith, their driver, were killed.* Joe Norcomb of the Fourth, was wounded. The fence behind us was finally torn down, and the internals of the caissons and pieces widened. At a given signal, it was arranged about 1 o'clock P. M., that all the guns of Longstreet's corps, (135) should open, and that Pickett's Virginia Division, supported by Heath Wilcox, and Pettigrew *en echelon*, were to storm the enemy's work, while the latter, meanwhile, would be demoralized by our artillery fire.

At 1:30 Longstreet ordered Col. Walton (now chief of his artillery,) "to open fire with all the guns from right to left." The signal guns previously agreed upon—"two fired in rapid succession by the Washington Artillery," were now discharged, and were promptly answered by the roar of 220 others—one of the greatest cannonades ever made in the world's history, and the greatest on this continent. The enemy's fire slackened after thirty minutes from the number, as officially reported, of caissons and ammunition wagons we exploded; but shells still ploughed through our ranks with terrible effect, one of them setting fire to a hospital and burning up in the flames a great many wounded. Many of their guns were disabled, and soon the blinding battle-smoke gave place to the stillness of death. Now had come the decisive moment when the gloomy presentiments which had been pressing upon Gen. Lee's men were to become facts, or be dissipated like the sulphurous wreaths above us.

I speak of presentiments, because the night before, when we had taken our place for bivouac on the corpse-covered battle field, there rose before us, what we at first thought was a cloud, black and threatening, but which we soon

---

*Later in the day Adolphe Dupre was carried back wounded, and the two cannoniers, who gave him their places, were killed simultaneously by the same shell.

discovered were the mountains behind, or on which the Federal left was posted; protected, we discovered, too, on the morrow, by breastworks. In regarding this we stared at each other in amazement. Still the men believed so much in themselves, that when the storming divisions moved off, we did not fear the treachery of fortune.

As Pickett's Division pressed on by us, or rather along side of us part of the way, the men realizing the certain death that awaited them, and too proud to falter in doing what they considered their duty, were heard some of them, saying "good-bye" and the fixed look in their face, showed that they had steeled themselves to certain death. Then the flag station signaled, and the whole lined moved. McDonald at Wagram, was eclipsed. There was a mile of ground to get over, and the storm of lead from their enemies in the breastworks, laid them down by scores. Meanwhile what was the most extraordinary feat of the war, the third company battery charged as far as the ground admitted, with Pickett, finally maintaining a position far in advance of any other Confederate guns.*

Heath's Division emerged from the woods, *en echelon*, as was ordered, just as we heard a yell which told that our colors had been successfully planted over the enemy's fortifications, and eleven captured cannons. At that moment, Pettigrew's men, who were raw troops, and soon after, Heath's Division, broke under a flank fire, and retreated in confusion. Pickett's position, which is now being charged by a fresh division of the enemy becoming critical, and his men being unable to hold their ground fell back by order.

This settled the day, and the hopes of many of the

---

*A battery from another State moved with us, but soon left both the Third company, and their own guns.

Confederate army. The crest of the hill soon became almost deserted—there being present only four pieces of cannon from the Washington Artillery which still retained their original position. These about dusk fired a shower of shots at what appeared to be an advance movement of the enemy—the last shots that were fired upon that fatal day.*

CHAPTER XXVIII.

THE RETREAT.

During the whole of this memorable day, and part of the preceding, the men had nothing to eat, and were very often without water. I succeeded at one time, in satisfying the pangs of hunger, by eating the fruit from a cherry tree, which either hung close to the ground,

---

*At 6 P. M., we heard a long and continuous Yankee cheer, which we at first imagined was an indication of an advance; but it turned out to be their reception of a general officer, whom we saw riding down the line, followed by about thirty horsemen. Soon afterwards I rode to the extreme front, where there were four pieces of rifled cannon, almost without any infantry support. To the non-withdrawal of these guns is to be attributed the otherwise surprising inactivity of the enemy. I was immediately surrounded by a sergeant, and about half-a-dozen gunners, who seemed in excellent spirits, and full of confidence, in spite of their exposed situation. The sergeant, [Corporal Coyle] expressed his ardent hope that the Yankees might have spirit enough to advance and receive the dose he had in readiness for them.

Whilst we were talking, the enemy's skirmishers began to advance slowly, and several ominous sounds in quick succession told us that we were attracting their attention, and that it was necessary to break up the conclave. I therefore turned round and took leave of these cheery and plucky gunners.
* * * * *
It was difficult to exaggerate the critical state of affairs as they appeared about this time. If the enemy or their general had shown any enterprise, there is no saying what might have happened. Gen. Lee and his officers were evidently fully impressed with a sense of the situation.
* * * * *
Gen. Longstreet said the mistake they had made, was in not concentrating the army more, and making the attack on the 2d, with 30,000 men instead of 15,000. The advance had been in three lines, and the troops of Hill's corps, who gave way, were young soldiers who had never been under fire before. The enemy would have attacked, had the guns been withdrawn. Had they done so at that particular moment, immediately after the repulse, it would have been awkward.
—*Freemantle.*

or whose boughs had been struck off by the bullets and shell. The last bread we tasted was obtained by some of us who, to preserve the strength of the men, were detailed by Capt. Hero to gather food from the dead Federal infantry, whose haversacks were furnished with three day's ration. It was not the kind of food that fastidious stomachs could endure. But a soldier's first motto is to take care of his material wants, and the men who resolutely satisfied the cravings of nature, probably did the best service in marching and fighting, and preserved longest their health.

The day altogether, was productive of different emotions, from any ever experienced on any other battle field. The sight of the dying and wounded, who were lying by the thousand between the two lines, and compelled amid their sufferings, to witness and be exposed to the cannonade of over 200 guns, and later in the day, the reckless charges, and the subsequent destruction or demoralization of Lee's best corps—the fury, tears or savage irony of the commanders—the patient waiting, which would occasionally break out into sardonic laughter at the ruin of our hopes seen everywhere around us, and finally, the decisive moment, when the enemy seemed to be launching his cavalry to sweep the remaining handful of men from the face of the earth: These were all incidents which settled, and will forever remain in the memory. We all remember Gettysburg, though we do not remember and do not care to remember many other of the remaining incidents of the war. Of this latter kind, were for instance, our marches a short time afterwards from the Potomac, the campaign on Mine Run, the battle of Bristow Station, (or the third Manassas, as it might be more properly called.)

But to return to the battle field, from which at a little distance we bivouacked that night. It is true that many of us shed tears at the way in which our dreams of liberty had ended, and then and there gave them a much more careful burial than most of the dead received; yet when we were permitted at length to lie down under the caissons, or in the fence corners, and realized that we had escaped the death that had snatched away so many others, we felt too well satisfied at our good fortune—in spite of the enemy still near us, not to sleep the soundest sleep it is permitted on earth for mortals to enjoy.

On the following day during a heavy and continuous rain, the army commenced its retreat to the Potomac.*

Gen. Imboden was put in the van, in charge of the immense amount of captured plunder, and the many thousand prisoners who had been taken, and our batteries were temporarily assigned to his command. His duty it need not be said, was a very arduous one, as it exposed us constantly to a sudden swooping down of the cavalry. Once they actually dashed down on us, and compelled us

---

*July 4th. The army commence moving this evening from want of ammunition. It was hoped that the enemy might attack during the day, especially as this is the 4th of July, and it was calculated that there was still ammunition for one day's fighting. The ordnance train had already commenced moving back towards Cashtown, and Ewell's immense train of plunder had been proceeding towards Hagerstown by the Fairfield road ever since an early hour this morning.

July 5th, Sunday.—The night was very bad—thunder and lightning, torrents of rain—the road knee deep in mud and water, and often blocked up with wagons "come to grief." I pitied the wretched plight of the unfortunate soldiers who were to follow us. Our progress was naturally very slow indeed, and we took eight hours to go as many miles.

At 8 A. M. we halted a little beyond the village of Fairfield, near the entrance to a mountain pass. No sooner had we done so and lit a fire, than an alarm was spread that Yankee cavalry were upon us. Several shots flew over our heads, but we never could discover from whence they came. News also arrived of the capture of the whole of Ewell's beautiful wagons. At 6 o'clock we traveled on again (by the Hagerstown road). The road was full of soldiers marching in a particularly lively manner—the wet and mud seemed to have produced no effect whatever on their spirits, which were as boisterous as ever. The same old chaff was going on of "Come out of that hat—I know you're in it—I sees your legs a-dangling down," &c. When we halted for the night, skirmishing was going on in front and rear—Stuart in front and Ewell in rear.

to get our pieces unlimbered. Never had the men and horses been so jaded, and stove up. One of our men who dropped at the foot of a tree in a sort of hollow, went to sleep, and continued sleeping until the water rose to his waist. It was only then that he could be awakened with the greatest difficulty. Battery horses would drop down dead. So important was our movement that no halt for bivouac, though we marched scarcely two miles an hour, was made during the route from Gettysburg to Williamsport—a march of over 40 miles. The men and officers on horseback would go to sleep without knowing it, and at one time there was a halt occasioned by all of the drivers—or at least those whose business was to attend to it, being asleep in their saddles. In fact the whole of the army was dozing while marching and moved as if under enchantment or a spell—were asleep and at the same time walking.

Over the rocky turnpike road some of us had to march barefooted, our shoes having been destroyed by the rough Macadamized road, or the heavy mud; and those were especially sufferers whose feet, my own among the number, were inconveniently larger than those of the passing Dutchmen whom we would meet on the road.

Scarcely had we arrived at Williamsport, before we were attacked by Kirkpatrick with a body of Federal cavalry who had already harrassed us at Hagerstown, on our retreat, and captured some of our wagons. At Williamsport, the morning after our arrival, there was a sudden dash and hotly contested fight. These assailants were however, ultimately driven off, with the assistance of the wagoners, who now shouldered the muskets they had been hauling, and fought like Trojans. In this teamsters' fight, the enemy were driven away without doing any serious damage.

Lee's army a few days after reached the Potomac without opposition, and although his pontoons were destroyed, and the Potomac unfordable, a bridge was constructed, and the army on the 13th of July, passed over very quietly—the bridges having been covered with bushes to prevent the rumbling of the wheels. Ewell's corps by this time had managed to ford the river.

CHAPTER XXIX.

CAPUA.

The events that now need only be glanced at in this narrative, are, that large detachments were taken from the Federal army of the Potomac, to reinforce those of the West, and to assist in the North, in making the draft. On the other hand, the climate of Virginia, not allowing a very active campaign, induced Lee, following this example, to send Longstreet South. This general took part in the battle of Chickamauga, with our 5th Company of Washington Artillery, and his troops greatly contributed to the victory at that time gained. The strategical movement that followed in Virginia, resulted only in showing either that none of Jackson's brilliant flank movements could now be aimed at, or that the times and the hopes of the Southern people had changed, and that Lee's army never replenished, and always decreasing, could, henceforth, hope for but little, in the way of an aggressive movement. Lee's subsequent defense of Richmond, formed the brightest part of his military reputation, but it differed essentially in its character, from that of the preceding campaigns.

With the coming of Grant into power, it became

obvious that some new movement to Richmond would be attempted, and the defence of that city and of Petersburg, from attack by way of the James, became a matter of increasing importance. It was with a view to this, and to the preservation of our horses that our Batallion was ordered to Richmond, and subsequently to Petersburg. Our campaigning, henceforth, until the following June, alternated from one side of the James to the other— from Richmond to Petersburg, and finally to the various forts or breastworks of that closely guarded town. Previous to going to the Cockade City, we were detailed around Richmond a few days, not for the purpose of refreshing the men, but of resting the battery horses, which became appreciated with their scarcity, and whose good condition was a matter of much more consideration than that of a private. In spite of this depreciation, the old soldiers improved what little opportunity was afforded them to renew their friendships, and to affect as much style in eating, living and dressing, as their somewhat limited opportunities admitted. To show how times changed men's conduct, I may mention an incident which happened to an old soldier, whose courage was only exceeded by his vanity. He cared as little for being complimented for the former quality, as Richelieu, or Frederick the Great did, for being flattered as statesmen. When it came however, to his dress, he was vulnerable as Achilles. What pleased him best of all, was to be promenading the streets with a neat walking cane, and to be reproached as a hanger-on about Richmond, who had not sufficient manhood to do his duty. The more he was cursed by sentinels or mud-covered soldiers, who did not know him, the more he was delighted.*

*A—, one of the recruits who had recently joined us and who came to the surface

Our camp life at Petersburg was a new revelation to nearly all of us. The place had not yet seen soldiering, and we were so many Telemaques welcomed by Calypsos. One of the latter, a tall fine-looking young lady of Petersburg, was enthusiastic enough to take the baggage from the weary back of a poor soldier, and to insist upon carrying it upon her own ivory shoulders. It was thought among us for a little while that this romantic acquaintance would terminate in marriage; but perhaps it was just as well that she married instead one of the first Federal officers who came into the city, after its capture.

We were very advantageously placed, upon our arrival, in a camp a mile east of town, and which commanded a very large extent of turnip producing country. The influence this fertile region and short rations exerted on the principles of some of the younger and less scrupulous members may be guessed at from the fact that one of them declined joining the church, during a religious revival, on account of the too great temptation exerted upon his morality by a neighboring vegetable garden.

The citizens all received us with great hospitality, not only at this camp but when we were moved four miles

during this short stay, put in an equally magnificent appearance, and developed a different sort of talent. He dressed in what was considered gorgeous raiment at the time, and secured a table at the best restaurant in the town. At one time he was upon the point of marrying a beautiful girl who heard with rapture of his plantation, where the flavor of pork was improved by feeding a hog on oranges; so much so that she was ready to agree to live forever, upon such remarkable breakfast bacon. But the order for the batallion came to move to Petersburg —and the marriage was postponed, the fascinating recruit lingering so long in the lap of beauty that he scarcely had time to return his borrowed suit, much less pay his restaurant bill. He however lingered long enough for both parties to discover there was some mistake not only about the orange-fed hogs, and the plantation, but about the character of the lady. During the march to Petersburg, he consumed his time in swearing he would get even with the wags of the batallion who had introduced him and let him so badly in, if it was the last military act of his life; and his excitement and the condition of the roads may be judged of when it is stated that, by actual count of time, he and two or three similar characters, shook the Richmond dust off their feet at the rate of 20 miles, for four hours marching.

further away—that is received those who had horses and could come frequently to town. Ultimately we were encamped at "Model Farm," though it might have been the model of almost anything else, at the time we occupied it.

Our life here in these winter quarters, barring short commons, was the pleasantest experience we had yet had of soldiering. Petersburg was large enough to admit of every variety of society, embracing, as Pierre Soulé once declared, some of the most beautiful ladies he had ever seen anywhere. Richmond too was but a little ways off, and there was an excellent public library. Lastly, the amateur performers gave an entertainment— "Pocahontas" and "Toodles" in the theatre of the town, which drew a packed house, ladies not only from Petersburg, but Richmond; and such was the preternatural splendor of the occasion, that one of the ushers refulged through the evening in a pair of $150 white kid gloves.

What great places of resort were the two hotels and one or two coffee houses, the bridge and river bank; and towards the last, some of the noble residences richly furnished, which a few of us from time to time were permitted to roam through and enjoy—not in any wise to molest or disturb; simply by staring very hard at the carved oak, carpet and curtains, to bring to our minds that we had once led some other life, than the one under canvass or in bunks.

The winter months passed away, with some disagreeable work in the shape of guard mounting and wood cutting, and in the labor of getting the latter to the camp habitations. The men did not much like the idea of carrying great logs over steep or rugged ground on their shoulders, and besides were thinking of the pleasant times they might have had in elegant society in Petersburg. Disagreeable contrasts were naturally enough instituted between the bruised muscles and blistered hands of one existence, and the refined drawing rooms, abounding with gay company, music and dancing on the other. We had become such sybarites before the winter passed, not only with our own batallion, but with Pickett's Division, and a few other old veterans who were thus afforded a month or so of rest, that what with church going, visiting or reading by the pleasant fires of winter-quarters, we began to imagine, (after one or two little interruptions towards North Carolina and Lynchburg) that our Capua would last forever. It was true that the rations from week to week became scarcer, and that anything like hospitality became from day to day of more difficult occurrence.

One day there was what might be called, for the times, a grand carousal, a sort of one-horse Belshazzar's display, made up mostly of brilliant officers from the army, and at which the display of demijohns was as great as in the Irish hospitality described by Lever. A distinguished hospital surgeon from Georgia, was the worst victim; so much so, that he was stretched upon the table, the cloth thrown over his motionless body, and the burial service read and chanted over him with great emphasis and ceremony. We had not seen enough of that sort of thing in reality, and had to do some of it as a joke, by way of refreshing our recollection. Besides, we were half inclined, on general principles, to send the doctor to keep company with a good many of his patients. However, nothing in the way of reminders was needed long. Couriers, as the spring advanced, began to arrive in camp, and the men were put through, though not without loud growling and swearing, a regular course of inspection and drill.

Suddenly, at all sorts of hours, we began to be called upon to "hitch up" to cross the Appomattox or the James. We could hear, too, the faint booming of the guns of Lee's and Grant's armies, who were now starting up from their winter-quarters north of Richmond, and swinging around towards Petersburg—smiting and rending each other as they marched, and making ready for the final death grapple which was to be completed during the following year.

With the first guns that were fired about Petersburg, the brilliant society which had hitherto remained about that city commenced to melt away. But it was not until the small trenches had become great mounds and had been lengthened into miles of fortifications—and until the shot from the enemy's guns began not only to deafen the population by their roar but to penetrate their houses, that the streets became altogether deserted by their former gay frequenters. The spurs of brilliant horsemen ceased to echo so frequently through fashionable church aisles; and about the only resort for which soldiers showed much predilection, was one of the old finely furnished saloons. The traditional coffee-house pictures, with their voluptuous and impossible beauties still hung on the walls; the glasses and bottles still glittered; and it is pleasant to reflect that during all of those long months of bombardment one man still remained behind the counter with neat cuffs and hair parted in the middle, ready to administer to the wants of his thirsty fellow-man.

Nevertheless, the supply of stimulants was at a low ebb; and it was only in the days when there did not seem to be a hundred people in the streets, or under circumstances of the most mysterious secrecy, that one could penetrate into the spirituous twilight of the inner side, and only one or two at a time. It was like waiting at the pool for the troubling of the waters; and once the visitor had paid his two or three dollars, and swallowed the moderate amount of Nepenthe allowed him, a door in the rear opened and he was expected to foot it back or gallop back to camp forthwith. It might perhaps be thought that the necessity of passing over a field a mile wide, in which shells and bombs were constantly exploding, would have some influence in keeping the men from having such longings. Such however was not the case.

One of the most singular features about Petersburg, as month after month passed on, and the anaconda-folds of Grant's army hugged closer and closer the doomed city, was the way in which the hill-side embankments would be honeycombed into human dens and places of shelter and refuge. In one place it was like a glimpse of Petrea, with the houses excavated in rock; in another the ground would be cut up with such a maze of alleys and streets of trench work, that as you went through them, crouching down and with bent shoulders, you could never tell at what end you would come out of this Dædalus labyrinth. What made the matter more difficult, was that a regiment of soldiers, with fireplaces and cooking utensils, would be sometimes encamped inside of these narrow avenues, whose heads, if they ever stood erect, were certain marks for the Federal sharpshooters. Stumbling or falling over men who were wasting away under a siege that was kept up more than a year, all of the finer and nobler traits of the old soldiers seemed to disappear, and their thoughts to be only occupied by their ever present misery and wretchedness. But the roll of the drum, or the order "Fall in men," would waken them, and as General Longstreet recently told me in conversation, he believed· they steadily improved in soldiering to the end of the war.

CHAPTER XXX.

THE LAST YEAR.

But notwithstanding the spirit of the men, it would have seemed, at first blush, after the decisive battle of Gettysburg, the loss of Vicksburg, with the South doomed to certain starvation, in a fixed time, and opposed by a pertinacious general having absolute power over 1,200,000 troops, that the leaders of the South would have sought to hedge in or compromise, and preserve to the land some little vestige of property. Considering that the loss of the game was now absolutely certain in a given number of moves, the question was whether it was worth while to play it out and submit to the brutality of a checkmate; or to get at once the best terms the situation admitted. It is very probable that the latter was what Gen. Lee thought about the matter, and it is certain from his statements to Gen. Gordon, that he had ceased to see any hope, some time before retreating from Petersburg.

But another year of hard fighting was to be gone through with, and Lee will now have to keep Grant's main army from Richmond by the overland route, and at the same time defend that city on the South from an approach of Butler in that direction with 30,000 men.

The struggle between Lee and Grant opened with the battle of the Wilderness, which was fought on nearly the same ground as that of Chancellorville. In this, Lee attempted to shut up the Federal army, consisting of 100,000 men, in the forest well described by its name, where movement was as difficult as in a cane brake. Lee succeeded to the extent of putting 30,000 of the enemy *hors du combat.*

It was here, where the enemy, by the suddenness of his

attack, had broken the line of Hill, that Gen. Lee temporarily closed up the breach by leading on the Texas Brigade in person, riding himself in front of the lines. It was not until the men dragged his horse back by the bridle, and until the brigade shouted that they would do the fighting if he would stay in the rear, that Lee consented to remain behind. The brigade was cut to pieces, but Longstreet now had time to get up, and the line was saved. The movements of both armies were thoroughly aggressive, and as the ground admitted of no manœuvering, Grant's orders were substantially to fight it out as if in a promiscuous row, to strike at everything going. The log breastworks in front of Hancock caught fire, and the fight had to be continued through smoke and flame, the crippled and wounded being many of them burnt to death or suffocated before they could escape. The fight lasted two days and Lee's loss was 8,000.

Grant's second encounter (May 12th, Spottsylvania) was still less fortunate for the Federal Commander. Its general character was the same, in the nature of the ground, as that of the Wilderness. Here too the woods caught fire, and the direction of advance through the forest could only be told by compass. One line of Lee's works having been taken, was in turn re-assaulted by him in five terrific charges. Confederate bodies bayoneted in these assaults, lay piled upon each other, so Federal accounts say, and the woods were black with corpses. The fight at Spottsylvania was of twelve days' duration, at the end of which time, Grant who had now lost 40,000 men, gave it up in despair, of here making an impression on Lee, and commenced flanking towards Richmond.

After thirty days' marching, flanking, racing and fighting, Grant's army attempted to drive Lee back, June 3d, from the Chickahominy. His plan was simply an attack along the whole line. His troops having lost 15,000 men in a short time at this battle, and his men remembering that they had now lost 60,000 by this free-fight system of tactics, stood still in ranks when ordered to advance. Grant's loss in this campaign was greater than what the whole force of Lee amounted to. Still Lee lost 18,000 men, and there was no way of filling up his ranks.

Our victories, brilliant as they were, did not deceive old soldiers. They were sometimes compared to the winnings of a poker player, who, in those days, was heard growling at his luck, because, after winning $3,000 in Confederate money, he lost twenty-five cents in silver.

On the night of the 12th of June, the movement to the Southern side of the James was begun.

Having said this much by way of general explanation, I shall here introduce the concise record of Lieut. Col. Miller Owen, (whose former place was supplied by Adjutant E. J. Kursheedt,) of the military movements made by the Washington Artillery, for the following year:

Batallion Journal: APRIL 15. The command has had no service since August last, and things have gotten a little loose and rusty. Winter quarters near such a pleasant place as Petersburg, has demoralized the boys a little. They are now well clad in gray jackets and pants, and every one has at least one sweet-heart among the pretty girls of the city. Trust a W. A. for that.

Horses and harness in miserable order; drills and inspections have been neglected all winter. Too much leisure in camp will spoil the discipline of the best soldiers. The men are not disposed to have what they consider needlessly, their liberty restricted, but are all anxious to join Gen. Lee at Gordonsville— Lieut. Col. Eshleman in command, in place of Col. J. B. Walton, resigned.

April 16. In camp at Model Farm, drilling commenced, bugle and roll call resumed. Tall swearing among the men who regard all this as an outrage.

21. In Richmond. Hotel board $50 a day. A month's pay can be eaten up in three days.

23. Mr. Davis will not let us go to Gordonsville, but suggests that we be placed in the works around Richmond.

25. Drilling and putting everything in order.

May 4. Looking for the Yankees to begin operations every day.

5. Action at last. Ordered by Gen. Pickett to move our guns to City Point road. All the horses in the city are pressed and sent to us to be converted into

battery horses; buggy horses, express horses, in fact trotters and all are made to do service.*

30. Transport full of Federals and five Monitors are reported at Bermudas Hundreds. Butler in command; we can look for hot work now. After much trouble with our new horses, we go into position north of the Appomattox, as follows:

3rd Company, in Battery No. 2, City Point Road.
2nd Company, in Battery No. 5, City Point Road.
1st Company, in Battery No. 8, City Point Road.

The Fourth Company under Norcom and Behan were placed with the 2nd.

May 6. Enemy reported coming up the City Point Road. 1st Company ordered back to Petersburg with his four guns.

5 P. M. Firing heard North of the Appomattox river. Enemy have landed on the south bank of the James, pushed out to Walthal Junction on the Richmond Railroad, and have been attacked and repulsed. Six guns placed opposite them in position on the Prince George road and Lieut. McElroy in command.

The enemy is in great force, and we have nothing to support our guns except the militia from the town of Petersburg, and a portion of the 31st Regiment, North Carolina troops.

The militia are jolly cases and have plenty to eat and drink; they seem to look upon the whole thing as a good joke.

May 7. All quiet along the lines this morning. Grant is reported fighting Gen. Lee somewhere near the Rappahannock. We are going to have it now "hot and heavy." Placed at 12 M. two guns under Lieut. Britton, on the Baxter road; two under Richardson on Jerusalem road. 1 P. M. two Companies Militia sent to Batteries 9, 10, 11. N. C. troops to Baxter and Jerusalem roads.

May 8, 2 A. M. Two guns in battery 16, under Lieut. Britton, removed to battery 40. 5 P. M. Go on reconnoissance towards Broadway. No signs of the enemy.

Monday, May 9, 2 A. M. One section under Captain Hero of the 3rd Company, is ordered to report to Capt. Sturtevant, to attack gunboats on the Appomattox River. 1 P. M. heavy firing in the direction of Fort Clifton.

Col. Jones placed in command of the Washington Artillery and Reid's Batallion, by order Gen. Beauregard.

May 10. Gen. Beauregard arrives at Petersburg from battle Drury's Bluff.

May 14, 2 A. M. Our whole force falls back to second line of works.

Gen. Beauregard, with Colquitt's Brigade and Macon Battery, arrives from Petersburg. Heavy skirmishing all day along the lines, 4 cannoniers killed, 4 wounded.

May 14. President Davis rides down from Richmond this afternoon and visits Beauregard.

May 15. Skirmishing all day along the lines. The enemy have occupied our outer abandoned works, and keep our lines completely swept with sharp-shooting. Assault made on 4th Company's position repulsed.

May 16, 5 A. M. Artillery opens all along our lines. At 5:45 A. M. our infantry advance over our works and fall upon the enemy all along the line.

May 16. The 1st Company, Capt. E. Owen, sent down the turnpike in rear of B. Johnson's Brigade, and engage the enemy's batteries in the road. Enemy badly whipped.†

1 P. M. With horses belonging to 1st Company Washington Artillery, I brought in the battery captured by Haygood's S. C. Brigade in the Turnpike, and presented by Gen. Haygood to Capt. Owen, three 20-pounder Parrotts, two

---

*An ingenious lady of Petersburg who could not make up her mind to part with a fine pair of carriage horses had them hid in her dining room or parlor until the danger had passed. It was the first time probably since Nero—if then, that horses have been accommodated with Brussels carpets.

†The fight here referred to was one of the hottest engagements of the war—the guns being separated by a very small interval, and the battery horses of the enemy killed in heaps.

12-pounder Napoleons. General Beauregard commanded in person. 1600 prisoners taken.

Enemy retreat to Bermuda Hundreds, leaving their dead and wounded on the field, baggage wagons and arms. President Davis visits the field.

[Losses at Drury's Bluff, on the 13th, 14th and 15th of May: 1st Company, Killed—H. Peychaud, Geo. Chambers, T. G. Simmons. Wounded—Capt. E Owen, slightly ; Lieut. J. M. Galbraith, mortally ; Corporal S. Turner, Ed. Peychaud, J. J. Norment, C. Rossiter, T. J. Wilson, Jos. Myers, Captured—Sergt. P. O. Fazende.* 2d Company, Wounded—M. J. Lapham, Geo. Gessner, J. N. Greenman. 3d Company, killed—H. Madden. Wounded—G. Guillotte, A. Guillotte, A. Leefe, Jas. Crilly. 4th Company, Killed—R. G. McDonald, John Faulkes, E. A. Mallard, Ed. Condon. Wounded, Sergt. John B. Valentine, J. S. Hood, A. Norcomb, Wm. Martin.—Total loss, 30. The above is the official report of Adjt. C. J. Kursheedt.]

May 17, 8:30 A. M. Pursuit begins. We march towards Petersburg. Counted twenty-five dead horses in front of position occupied yesterday by the 1st Company Washington Artillery. Bivouacked eight miles from Petersburg; Wise and Martin's Brigades join us to-day, commanded by D. H. Hill.

May 18. Heavy skirmishing in front.

May 19. Ordered to construct works, put guns in position, and shell out enemy's skirmish line.

May 20. Assault made on enemy's line to-day. First line of fortification carried.

May 21. The 2d, 3d and 4th Companies relieved from duty on the lines, and sent back to the rear.

May 22, 10:30 A. M. Monitors shelling again.

May 22, 5 P. M. Flag of truce to bring in the dead lying between the lines.

28. Return to Petersburg.

June 2. Reported that Grant was repulsed yesterday by Gen. Lee.

1:15 P. M. Whole command ordered to Richmond by Secretary of War to report to Gen. Ransom.

3. Ordered to Bottom's Bridge, Chickahominy.

4. Third anniversary of our arrival in Virginia. All quiet on the lines.

15. We apply to Mr. Davis to go over to Petersburg.

16. Firing in the direction of Petersburg. Reported that the enemy carried the outer line of works last night.

*The latter made his escape from a northern train, while in rapid motion.

At that time in June, Gen. Wise was in command at Petersburg—2200 troops. Bushrod Johnson was guarding Bermuda Hundreds' line from Howletts' on the James to the distance of four miles. The Petersburg line was then seven miles long.

On the 15th of June, Gen. Baldy Smith attacked Petersburg from the south, and meeting but slight resistance would certainly have taken it, but for his lack of enterprise and loss of time. The attack was renewed the next day—40,000 troops against 11,000, the latter commanded by Gen. Beauregard. Petersburg could still have been taken, if Smith had divided his troops and attacked on the unguarded Confederate right. The Federals now brought up a third corps and broke like an avalanche through Johnson's lines, which had been placed on the Confederate left. He was here met by Gen. Gracie's Brigade who, by Beauregard's order, had left the Bermuda Hundreds line abandoned. It was while Gracie's Brigade was forming about sundown, that they found the Federals sweeping down upon them, and Beauregard "now thought" according to his own statement "that the last hour of the Confederacy had arrived." But the orders of Gracie "forward" and "charge," were never given to a braver set of men. They routed everything before them, and captured twice their own number of prisoners, which was 2300. The battle raged furiously until 12 o'clock at night, and meanwhile the road to Richmond at Bermuda Hundreds was left unguarded. At that hour the three Federal corps, according to captured dispatches, were *hors du combat*. Beauregard had previously seized the opportunity to mark out a new line, 500 yards to the rear, with white stakes so that the brigades could find it, and this became the celebrated line of fortifications which were defended to the end of the war. "The enemy in this days' fight," says Gen. Beauregard, "lost 13,000 men, or more than I had in my whole force."

A fourth corps under Warren had arrived, when Gen. Lee started his whole army forward. Kershaw's Division coming up first, such a warm reception was given to the Federals, that they commence forthwith the siege of Petersburg.

Beauregard then wanted to push Grant into a corner of the Appomattox and James; but Lee after almost consenting to this plan, decided to let Grant wear himself out by a costly series of attacks. Grant's previous experience however prevented him from doing anything of the sort. His quickest method would have been to have continued his wheel around Richmond, destroying the railroads, by which, with the utmost difficulty, Lee's army obtained its supplies. But Grant who had not forgotten Lee's strategy, decided on the wearing out and attrition process, involving the construction of regular breastworks and forts, and a steady firing and bombardment which lasted a year.*

A chance, which was lost at this time to the Confederate arms, was the neglect of Early, who made a diversion into Maryland, to capture Washington. "Early had then," says Swinton " an opportunity to dash into the city, the works being very slightly defended. The hope at headquarters, that the capital could be saved from capture, were very slender. But his conduct was feeble. Lee founded his hopes on the menace he supposed this move to Washington would have." In spite of the opportune arrival of the 19th Corps at Washington, it required all of Grant's moral firmness to withstand the severe pressure brought upon him to remove his army to Washington.

June 17. Nine Federals came into camp this morning—all German, French and Irish.
18. Ordered to South side of the James. Reach Petersburg on 19th, and put in position in the works at batteries, 34 to 38, on the 20th.
25, 10 P. M. Enemy shelling the city; several women reported killed. Many buildings struck. No notice was given of the shelling of the city.
27. Rain. Enemy continues shelling the city.
June 28, to July 3. Sharp-shooting and shelling has been going on. Women and children nearly all left. Hospitals have been removed. Our horses have not had a feed of corn this week.
July 4. Enemy in our front display all their flags along the lines, shelling the city at intervals.
July 9. Morgan Harris, 1st Company, mortally wounded.

* Letter of Gen. Beauregard to Gen. C. M. Wilcox.

24. Kremelburg, 3d Company, killed last night while sleeping in the works.*
30, 5 A. M. Mine sprung on the line, blowing up Pegram Battery, four guns, twenty men and eighteen of the S. C. Regiment. Enemy makes an assault and occupies our line. We took ten stands of colors and many prisoners, black and white. Whitcomb and Maines, 1st Company, and O. J. Toledano, 3d Company, killed.†
[The casualties along the line to the close of 1864, were: 1st Company, Killed—M. E. Harris, H. Whitcomb and W. Maines. 2nd Company—Wm Almindinger. 3d Company—Sergt. Kremelburg, O. Toledano. Wounded—Corporal Grimmer, D. Kobleur. 4th Company—Died, P. Mooney.
Murville, the twin-brother of Lecestiere Labarre, (both of the 3rd,) died about this time. He was a good soldier, and his mental attainments made him charming company in spite of a slight impediment in his speech. Another young soldier greatly regretted, and of more than ordinary promise, was Henry Peychaud.]
August 1st. Gen. Lee allows Gen. Grant an armistice of three hours to bury his dead, lying between the two armies.
Estimated loss of the enemy 4000; walked over to the Crater, and met the flag of truce. The Federal officers bring out plenty of good wine and brandy, luxuries unknown to us poor Confederates in the trench. Negro prisoners bury the dead in the trench between the lines.
Flag withdrawn and all retire to respective posts, and bang away again.
August 3. W. M. Owen, was shot in the face by sharpshooters, while directing the charging of a gun.
Oct. 12. One-half our artillery drivers are armed with muskets, to put on duty at Fort Gregg. Our supernumeraries will help in the same way, defend the lines if attacked.
Oct. 27. Fighting on our right; heavy fighting all day. At dark, a regiment of Federals, that our men on the lines took for our relief picket, entered—a bold move—the line at our left gun, nearest the Crater, and for a time created some little excitement. They were soon driven out.
Oct. 28. The attack yesterday by the enemy was evidently intended as a *coup de main* to gain the Southside railroad and the Appomattox river. Northern newspaper correspondents say the troops carried six days' rations and plenty of ammunition. It proved a failure; so Grant of course calls it a "Reconnoissance"; dead and wounded Federals left on the field.
March 29, 1865, 10 P. M. Heavy firing in front of Petersburg. Our lines are very weak, having a front of forty miles to cover; our men in the trenches.

*Kremelburg was one of the most honorable men and best soldiers we had. A short time before lying down for the last time, he had borrowed a spade from an infantryman. Without knowing of this circumstance, the same spade was taken to dig K.'s grave, and never afterwards came to hand. When the thick-headed owner came to inquire for it, we never could, after two hours explanation, get it into his head that our dead comrade could have borrowed a spade for shoveling out his own grave, or why he or his ghost, after showing so much foresight in borrowing, could not have been equally thoughtful about returning.
†Oswald Toledano, was a mere stripling when he with his father, old Ben Toledano, joined the bata lion—very amiable and faithful to his duties, as a messmate and soldier. On the morning of the crater explosion, the heat had been so great in the trenches, that some of the men though exposed to an enfilading fire, went back to get under shade. I was sitting down under a tent shelter when a shell tore through it, killing T. who was standing, almost instantaneously. He had but time to make the sign of the cross and utter a half finished word of a prayer, before falling lifeless into my arms. He was much attached to a lady of this city, of whom he was never tired of speaking, and whose ring he wore upon his finger. After his death, faithful to his memory, she entered a religious order and died a few months after, in the performance of her new duties.

CHAPTER XXXI.

THE GAME ENDED.

The buoyant, hopeful tone of the army has now disappeared. Short rations and the conscript law have done their worst; most of the old leaders are dead, and no one could discover in Lee's old veterans, more than the smouldering embers of their former fire.*

The 2nd of April, 1865, virtually ended the Confederate war, though the surrender of Lee was not made until eight days after.

The concluding battle had been brought on near Petersburg, by a desperate and last effort on the part of Gen. Lee to assume the offensive. The movement was entrusted at the time to Gen. Gordon, and was spoken of by both leaders as almost hopeless, and the last that could in any case be made without extraordinary success. It was probably a reconnoissance, or intended to open the road to North Carolina for a retreat, by causing Grant to withdraw from Lee's right flank.†

---

*Gen. Longstreet says, the men improved in fighting qualities to the end of the war. My own observation was, that they were pretty well starved and fought out. The high strung young men who went out with picked companies, went into the fight with just as much determination to acquit themselves with credit, and do themselves justice. as in their maiden fight.

† The account of Lee's last attack at Petersburg has been given so variously, that I cannot do better here than to record what Gen. Gordon once told me of an interview which passed between himself and Gen. Lee, some time preceding the attack.

Gordon having been sent for, was asked, when he reached Lee's quarters, what he thought of the chances for the Confederate cause. He told Gen. Lee frankly, that he could see no chance at all. Lee admitted that he was equally hopeless. Gordon then inquired why, if he held these convictions, he did not urge them upon Mr. Davis. Gen. Lee replied that he was then about to visit Richmond, and left the impression that Mr. Davis would be made to understand what were the convictions of the army. When Gen. Lee returned, Gen. Gordon in his next interview, inquired if he had told Mr. Davis, of the true condition of affairs. Gen. Lee said no, and in further conversation, gave as an excuse—" You know what sort of man Mr. Davis is "—referring doubtless to the well known impossibility of shaking Mr. Davis in any of his convictions. Gen. Lee then inquired if he could see no loop-hole where an advantage could be gained, or a blow

The move was attempted by a midnight attack with two divisions, who succeeded in capturing the abattis of the enemy, for the distance of a quarter of a mile without loss. This opportunity was not improved, either on account of the darkness and the difficulty, from the disappearance of scouts, the Confederates had of discovering their way, or from natural weakness. While the latter were hugging the captured picket line in disorder, the artillery in the forts to the right and left opened on them, fresh troops were brought up, and the storming party were compelled to take refuge under the breastworks they had captured.

The decisive battle which followed two days after, was preluded with firing of cannon on the extreme right and left, and by the buzz and hum of arriving reinforcements, and a great addition to their drum corps and trumpeters. Every available man from the Confederate left and centre was hurried to the right, leaving only artillerymen in the trenches and pickets in front. The firing grew hotter— the water batteries on the left boomed incessantly, and the earth shook under the jar of the sound. This booming signified that Grant had opened his formal attack, March 27th, on our lines, and it caused Lee to send large bodies of troops to the aid of Gens. Pickett and Johnston. The old spirit of the men flamed up, and Lee now dealt Grant's Brigades, in their advanced positions on his left, a staggering blow, and at one moment there was "a great fear of another Chancellorville disaster in the Federal lines." *

---

dealt. Gordon was more than ever convinced that any advantage gained would be only momentary, but at last entered into the spirit of leading the assault on the enemy's net work of entrenchments on the 29th.

The object of this was doubtless, if it had succeeded, to cause Grant to leave a road open for Lee to concentrate with Johnson, in North Carolina.

*Greeley.

In the next, Lee was repulsed, and Sheridan* who had coveted Five Forks, and several times been repelled in trying to seize it, made the most of his opportunity. Pickett and Johnston were now overwhelmed by double their force, losing heavily in killed, wounded and prisoners, when their flank was turned.

The night which followed was made lurid with death-dealing missiles, and the earth shook under the jar. The next day (April 2d) decided the fate of Richmond and the Confederacy. At 3:30 o'clock in the morning, the firing commenced from one end of the line to the other. Then ensued desperate charges from Grant's line. The attacking force here, Parkes' 9th Corps, succeeded in taking a portion of the breast-works to the right of the Crater; a capture which was really of no advantage as our men could retreat into a line of breastworks a few yards beyond, and an individual warfare was kept up until dark.†

---

*Sheridan's presence at the time on Lee's right flank was one of the curious accidents of the war. In a fight in the Valley the Federal troops had been dispersed by Early with a greatly inferior force with the exception of one corps; just as Early began to lose ground and in turn be hard pressed, Sheridan arrived on the field by making the famous ride of which so much has been heard, and was just in time to receive the credit of Early's defeat. He continued a riding expedition towards Lynchburg which did not succeed, and having nothing else that he could well do, he came in by the only route open to him which was on Grant's left; the second time arriving just at the lucky moment which makes reputations.

†The following is the narrative of the occurrences of April 2nd by a member of the Batallion: I was in bed about 9 o'clock when I heard the order given to the infantry to sleep on their arms, as there might be a fight at any moment. I became so much impressed by this, that I immediately folded up my blanket, and made preparations for what I regarded as certain, the evacuation of Petersburg. I had scarcely done so, when a shot burst through my house, and the cry of "To arms—get to your pieces" was heard. The firing lasted from about midnight until next morning, our cannoniers replying.

About day-break we began to see the enemy and their flag, the latter on our front and flanks waving unsteadily, as if the color sergeant found difficulty in advancing or getting into lines of breastworks. All the time the firing continued. By this time we had two pieces disabled in the third company, Lieut. Stocker was knocked senseless, and shortly after Capt. Hero had been shot from the top of the breastworks by a ball in his leg. A piece was now taken from the embrasure and fired at the enemy who had already penetrated our line, or were

The Federal Army in advancing upon Petersburg found our artillery corps in the various places that had been assigned them, doing their duty probably a little more steadily, from the force of habit, in their last field fight, than ever before, repelling charges—arming their spare men with muskets, and each man working with the same pride and conviction as when first mustered in. But the time had now come for us to abandon the underground bomb-proofs that had been built; or the tents and huts which would every night be filled with a new supply of bullets.

The Federal right, as already stated, had struck the Confederate line on the western side of Petersburg. Meanwhile, the next corps (Wright's 6th,) swept, after a hard struggle, the scanty brigades before them, turning to the right, and then with Ord's Corps, who had also penetrated, swung to the left nearly up to Fort Gregg, a half a mile in front of the main line of Petersburg entrenchments. The small force towards Hatch's Run had been driven back and into the Appomattox. Besides the Federal Corps already mentioned, Humphrey entered still further to the Confederate right. There is some severe fighting in front until 2 o'clock P. M., at which time

coming over the breastworks. We had now become reduced to only two rounds of ammunition, and as the enemy were within fifty yards of us, our case seemed hopeless. Just then a fresh supply of ammunition arrived, which lasted until dark, at which time the firing gradually ceased. About that time, the order was given to leave the breastworks with as much secrecy as possible—which was done. The bodies of our dead, Coyle, and some others whose names are not now remembered, were placed upon the caissons, and as we passed through Petersburg interred in the Cemetery. The last rations I ever drew were cooked while the firing was going on, the latter being so long and continuous that the men would take turns, except when hotly pushed, and relieve each other at the guns. If anything else was given to us to eat until the surrender, I do not now remember it. A handful of corn, or a scrap of almost anything to eat that we found by the way was all I saw. The sheet-iron crackers that we found on the Yankee dead at Gettysburg, and which some of us then disdained to eat, I thought of with envy now, the more so, as, during the time when we were in the trenches, rations were so scarce that many of the men made themselves sick by swallowing tobacco, in order to experience nausea or indifference to food.

the enemy are seen to be advancing upon Fort Gregg and Whitworth. There will now be no further opposition to their forward move than can be made by a very small body of men in these two fortifications.

CHAPTER XXXII.

WHAT TWO HUNDRED MEN CAN DO.

A dramatic interest attached to the defence of the forts, aside from the fact that here was to be the last stand for Petersburg. This was because of the necessity of here detaining the enemy, who were advancing, wave after wave around the works, until Longstreet could get across the James; secondly, the attack on Gregg was followed by a lull along other portions of the line, and the men rested upon their weapons to witness, as at a spectacle of great national interest, the struggle of Secessia, and the last angry glare of her guns on a formal field of battle. The number of men on the two sides, 214 in Fort Gregg, about the same in Whitworth, and 5000 advancing against them, illustrated the comparative strength of the combatants. Fort Gregg was the Confederate LaTourgue. When it falls all of the old traditions and usages of the South fall with it; when the Federal standards wave over it, there is then to be centralization, negro government, and four times the ruin inflicted on the South, as was put by Germany on France.

The two forts stand 250 yards in the rear of the captured line, and were built for precisely such an occasion as is suggested by the cheers of the advancing enemy, namely, for use as an inner defence when disaster should overtake the Confederate line. Fronting Gregg, is a little fort, the last built by Lee, and called by the men Fort "Owen," after the Lieut. Col. of that name from the Washington Artillery, who was assigned to the command of Fort Gregg, and the surrounding works. Lieut. Battles of the W. A. is in "Owen" with two guns, and Lieut. McElroy of the same batallion has charge of a company of 62 artillerymen who have been doing duty here most of the winter.

The night had been strangely quiet upon this portion of the lines, but towards daybreak the silence gave place to a little touch of skirmishing to the right of Gregg— sufficient to cause the ordering of the infantry and artillerymen into Fort Owen, although it was then so dark, that scarcely anything could be seen. Our infantry there could be barely detected moving in the trenches, towards what seemed to be the picket firing. As the men peered into the darkness in the direction of the flashes, solid shots commenced to plough up the earth—the infantry began quitting the trenches and taking to the fields, leaving the cannoniers under the impression that the troops were chasing small game of some sort.

Lieut. Col. Owen, in his report says he gave orders to withdraw to Fort Gregg, and hurried off to rally fugitives —a no easy matter—who had already been dispersed by the Federal attack. McElroy reached the latter with his men, but Battles not receiving his horses in time, found himself suddenly surrounded, and his command captured by the enemy. McElroy immediately opened fire from Fort Gregg with his artillery-infantry, drove them away, and then turning his infantry once more back to artillery, ran down into Fort Owen and opened fire with the recaptured pieces on the enemy, two hundred yards to his right. Horses having been procured, the pieces by order were moved forward a mile, where the guns fired thirty-five rounds each, and were then retired to Fort Gregg. Lieut. McElroy says, in his report, there were two hundred men in the Fort, who were, with the exception of his command, of Harris' Miss. Brigade, and that his loss was six killed, two wounded and thirty-two prisoners. Col. Owen proceeds to say :

At the time McElroy was put in position in " Gregg" some guns were placed in Fort Whitworth, a detached work like "Gregg" and to its right and rear.

Major Gen. Wilcox, who was then in Gregg, seeing Harris' Brigade in what he thought a dangerous position in front, sent his Aid to the General to recall his men to the two forts, Harris himself going into Whitworth, and Lieut. Col. Jas. H. Duncan, of the 19th Mississippi, into Gregg.

As the enemy advanced, McElroy was cautioned to have his ammunition as handy as possible upon the platform for quick work. Under orders, Capt. Walker hurriedly withdrew the guns from Fort Whitworth.

The enemy, a full corps of at least 5000 men, advanced in three lines of battle. Three times the little garrison repulsed them. The Fort seemed fringed with fire from the rifles of the Mississippians.

The cannoniers bravely and skilfully used their guns. The enemy fell on the clear field around the Fort by scores.

The capture of the work was but a question of time. The blue coats finally jumped into the ditch surrounding the Fort, and presently climbed over each others backs to gain the summit of the Parapets. There was a weak point on the side of Gregg, where the ditch was incomplete, and over this a body of the enemy rushed. Presently six regimental standards were distinctly seen waving on the Parapet.

*   *   *   *   *

The part taken in the defence of Gregg, by the Mississippians, is thus described in the " Vicksburg Times":

"Fort Gregg was held by the 12th and 16th Mississippi Regiments, Harris' Brigade, numbering about 150 muskets, under command of Lieut. Col. Jas. H. Duncan, of the 19th Mississippi, who had been assigned by Gen. Harris, to the immediate command of that work. The artillery in the Fort was a section of 3d Co. Washington Artillery, commanded by Lieut. Frank McElroy. General Harris, with his two other regiments, 19th and 48th Mississippi, occupied 'Fort Whitworth,' distant about 100 yards, and between that work and the Southside Railroad."

Gen. Harris, in a letter designed to be an official report, says, "Gen. Wilcox ordered me to take position in front of the enemy, and detain them as long as possible. With this object in view I advanced about 400 yards, and formed at right angles with the Boydton Plank Road. The ground being undulating, I threw both flanks behind the crest on which I formed, and exposed my center, in order that I might induce the enemy to believe that there was a continuous line of battle behind the ridge. I then advanced a line of skirmishers well to the front. The enemy being misled by this device, made the most careful dispositions, two lines of battle, and advancing with the utmost caution, my position was held until the enemy was in close range, when a heavy fire was opened upon both sides.

"The enemy pressing me heavily and out-reaching me on my flanks. I fell back upon Fort Gregg and Whitworth, the 12th and 16th under Col. Duncan, being ordered to Fort Gregg, and to hold it at all hazards.

"The 19th and 48th were placed in Whitworth. In Gregg there was a section of the 3d Company Washington Artillery, commanded by Lieut. Frank McElroy. Preparations were now made by the enemy for the assault, and this time Capt. Walker, A. and I. G. of Gen. Walker, Chief of Artillery, came with orders to withdraw the artillery, and against this I most earnestly protested.

"The four guns were withdrawn from Whitworth under protest; but the enemy were too close to permit the withdrawal of the guns from Gregg. Perceiving the guns of Whitworth leaving, the enemy moved forward to assault us in both works. He assaulted in columns of brigades, completely enveloping Gregg, and approaching Whitworth only in front. Gregg repulsed assault after assault; the two remnants of regiments, which had won glorious honor on so many fields, fighting this, their last battle, with most terrible enthusiasm, as if feeling this to be the last act in the drama for them ; and the officers and men of the Washington Artillery fighting their guns to the last, preserved untarnished the brilliancy of reputation acquired by their Corps. Gregg raged like the crater of a volcano, emitting its flashes of deadly fires, enveloped in flame and cloud, wreathing our Flag as well in honor as in the smoke of death. It was a glorious struggle. Louisiana represented by these noble artillerists, and Mississippi by her shattered bands, stood there side by side, together, holding the last regularly fortified lines around Petersburg."

While Gregg and Whitworth were holding out, Longstreet was hastening with Fields' Division, from the north side of the James, to form an inner line for the purpose of covering Gen. Lee's withdrawal that night. As soon as Harris heard of the formation of that line, he withdrew with his little band, cutting his way through.

At 12 o'clock that night the last man and the last gun of the brave army that had defended the lines of Petersburg for one year, passed over the Pontoon Bridges, and the march commenced, that ended at Appomattox Court House. I have been induced to write the foregoing, of which I was an eye witness, in the hope of *correcting History*. Many accounts have been published of the defence of Fort "Gregg," but all that I have seen have been generally far from the truth. Pollard, who showed but little disposition to waste compliments on the troops from the Gulf States, says, Capt. Chew of the fourth Maryland Battery of Artillery was in command of the work, and his account is reiterated by many others. If he was, it is strange we did not know it. A battery of Marylanders had in reality been disbanded a short time before the fight, their time having expired, and they were awaiting their discharge papers to enable them to go to their homes. If Capt. Chew was in the fort at all, he was simply there as a volunteer or a spectator.

We should give the honor to those who earned it in this fierce fight of three hours against such fearful odds. Swinton, in his "Army of the Potomac," in his description of the breaking through the lines on this historic Sunday, says:

"On reaching the lines immediately around Petersburg, a part of Ord's command under Gibbon, began an assault directed against Fort Gregg and Whitworth, two strong enclosed works, the most salient and commanding south of Petersburg. The former of these redoubts was manned by Harris' Mississippi Brigade, numbering two hundred and fifty men, and this handful of skilled marksmen conducted the defence with such intrepidity, that Gibbons' force surging repeatedly against it, was each time thrown back; at length a renewed charge carried the work, but not till its two hundred and fifty defenders had been reduced to thirty. * * Gibbons' loss was four hundred men "

Swinton does not mention the Washington Artillery in the fort: he also errs in putting the number of Mississippians at 250. Gen. Harris says there were 150, these with the 64 artillerists make a total of 214 men, and these men put *hors du combat* 500 of the enemy, or an average of more than two men each.

CHAPTER XXXIII.

FIRING THE LAST GUN.

The close of the day (April 2nd,) the most anxious that most of the men had ever passed, found Grant's lines touching on both sides of the Appomattox, and Lee completely hemmed in.* A retreat from Petersburg north of the Appomattox, which all feel is a foregone conclusion, is now necessary, and Longstreet's troops can only be useful in covering Lee's flank, while he withdraws from his breastworks. The firing meanwhile continues during the night from the Federal batteries. At 9 P. M. all of the guns were ordered to be moved across the Appomattox,† and this was done without any delay, and as quietly as if the skeleton army had been one of spectres and phantoms. The whole of the night was spent in getting out wagons, artillery and infantry, and a large

---

*As soon as Gregg was captured, the Federal signal corps were at work, and the cannonading and sharp-shooting were renewed on the other part of the line. In a moment heavy bodies of cavalry were seen emerging from the Federal's former lines, moving rapidly over the captured works and galloping in squadrons towards the Appomattox, which was some four or five miles off. Their track could be traced by the heavy columns of black smoke that rose from the various farmhouses on their route, which had been set on fire. The infantry who had succeeded in capturing the fort formed line fronting the Confederates' right flank, and looked as if they intended marching by the rear into Petersburg. New dispositions were also made along the Confederate front. Regiments were detached from their positions along the line (whose place had to be filled by deployment of those remaining) and sent to the right flank and rear, confronting the new line of the Federals. Artillery galloped into position, and soon Fields' Division, with the Texans in the lead, joined the right flank and formed a defensive line in the rear towards the river. A narrow creek only divided the opposing forces, but the Federals seemed satisfied with their success now and did not advance. *Lee's Last Campaign, Capt. J. C. Gorman.*

† Lieut. John R. McGaughey, of the first company, was captured while working away at his gun when our lines were broken. John was a strongly made, manly looking soldier, never absent from battle, and always popular with the men. Among some of our worthiest and most kindhearted officers, and whose consideration for their men deserve mention, before this narrative is concluded, were Lieut. Stocker, DeRussy, Apps, Britton, Battles, and Brown. During all of our long four years of fighting and hard marching, I do not remember the time when they did not show themselves more thoughtful for their men, than their own comfort. Britton was wounded at Sharpsburg, DeRussy at Chancellorville, and all received honorable mention in various battles.

mass of army plunder, which as the result showed would have been much better left behind.

The Washington Artillery crossed at midnight, Gordon bringing up the rear. The crossing of the bridge occupied three hours—quick time, and no delay was given to stragglers, before applying the torch. Petersburg had been previously almost abandoned; but a few sad faces appeared at the windows, and sent out sorrowful adieus —to the men who had so long remained about the city, that seemed almost their home. To the despondent reflections which the midnight retreat suggested, the flame and smoke which hung over the depots and warehouses, and the glare from the exploding magazine, gave an additional sombre tint. Still the men experienced a sense of relief—that of getting rid of some hideous dream, in leaving behind the trenches, and once more moving in column on the road.

The most singular feature of the retreat, was the noiseless manner in which Lee's army moved from the works, and the fact that the withdrawal was not known until revealed, as it were, to the world, by the blowing up of the siege guns and batteries, which had protected Richmond, and which by innumerable explosions proclaim, as with an Apocalyptic emphasis, that the Confederate Capital was and is, but shall be no more.*

---

* According to Pollard, Gorman, and "An Officer of the Rear-guard," a similar scene was meanwhile transpiring at Richmond, which, so tranquil when Mr. Davis receives the fatal dispatch, and walks composedly out of Church, will in a few moments be perturbed from top to bottom, and a few hours later be wrapped in flames. Late in the afternoon, wagon loads of Confederate boxes and trunks reach the Danville depot—hangers on imitating the example set them; $100 for a wagon, in gold. All over the city, hurrying fugitives. Confederate money is destroyed—gold removed, the liquor is poured out as on board of a sinking ship—the gutters running with it. Still retreating stragglers, and roving pillagers get hold of it—open stores, and cover the side-walk with glass. Ewell is firing the four principal quarters, or as might be said the four tobacco warehouses—and the rams and shipping are blown up or scuttled; the bridges are burnt. Rioters are plundering, and despairing women shrieking,

The army, now pushed through the darkness in the direction of Amelia C. H.—the different army corps making good progress by different roads, though the wagon loads of plunder when united on one road almost destroyed all movement. One ominous feature was, that there was nothing to eat for man or beast, and occasionally pieces of artillery showed that the horses were giving out. Another thing to be noted was, that upon our arrival at Amelia C. H., the enemy's cavalry commenced dashing upon our wagon trains, whose canvass covers they readily ignited. Their plan of operation, was to strike the train, several miles long, fire a number of wagons, and then making a circuit, strike it again. Three hundred cavalrymen supported by large bodies moving parallel, thus destroyed or confused the whole train. The burning caissons which had been sent on in advance of the artillery, were anything but pleasant neighbors.*

while at the government stores such a break is made upon the provisions, as causes the building to totter to its foundations.

Then the Federal General Weitzel, who in addition to the other horrors of the situation, had been playing "Yankee Doodle" and similar airs, was startled at last by the tremendous explosions of powder magazines; and like Blue Beard and some other historical characters, made his sentinel ascend his seventy feet watch tower, to see what it was all about. A great light in the direction of Richmond, is the answer. A rebel picket was now captured who could tell nothing about his commander—then a contraband, and finally, after daybreak with a sharp lookout for torpedoes, and amid exploding shells, Weitzel, on the 3rd rode into Richmond, just as the last rebel soldiers were going, and Butler's flag, which he had planted over the St. Charles Hotel of New Orleans, was now placed over the Confederate Capitol. President Davis had left with the Confederate Congress at 10 A. M., though why he thought it worth while to carry them off has never been ascertained; and meanwhile, as if to mark the commencement of a new regime, the fire is burning out the city, that is one-third of old Richmond.

It was Babylon the Great fallen, for the North, when the telegraph flashed the news. "No unmanly exultation was indulged in over those who had so nearly destroyed the Republic." Greeley here paid a tribute to a noble touch of feeling on the part of the North—one that he had not always previously been careful to observe.

*The Falling Flag. "By the road-side was a lady from Mississippi, who had been in our ambulance wagon, and whose horses had been carried off. She was more mad than scared as she stood there in the mud—young, pretty, and gesticulating, and she made a picture striking and peculiar. As the advance

Reaching Amelia, it was discovered that the provisions which should have been in readiness for the army, were missing. They had, by some accident, been carried on to Richmond, and the army was now without food. Besides, the great wagon train sent by a different road was destroyed. Our doom was now staring us in the face. Instead of halting to give battle to Grant, there was nothing that could be done, but push on and try to reach Danville.

Demoralization, which the accursed slow wagons were enough to have effected alone, had now begun; the men straggled off to get something to eat at the farmhouses, and the commands had dwindled to hundreds;* while at night as if to increase the desperation of the situation, the strains of triumphant music would float over from the enemy's brass bands. As we proceeded into the hilly country, it began to be hoped that the many fine military positions on either side, would afford us some chance of escape; and so (April 6th,) we marched all day and all night. It was a race for life, for men who were hungry, and for gaunt-looking horses who were dropping by the road side; but we had to push on. Still the enemy was all the time close behind. The rear guard commanded by Gen. Lee in person is attacked, while cavalry are formed in front and a few shots are fired. Gen. Rosser

---

guard rounded the bend of the road, it was swept by the enemy who wheeled as soon as he delivered fire. Four out of five were hit—one of them, an approved scout, in the spine ; throwing his arms over his head, with a yell of agony wrung from him by intense pain, he pitched backwards off his horse which was going at full speed. When I saw him again, years afterwards, he was a preacher."

* At one of the burnt down bivouac fires, two men attracted by its warmth were discovered sitting, cold and weary. One was a colonel of Pickett's Division and another a lieutenant, and the destruction of this famous fighting command may be guessed at when a regimental officer did not know where to look for his standard. * * * When the troops passed on, a number of tender girls stood gathered in a piazza, and greeted us with waving handkerchiefs and moist eyes, while cheer after cheer arose from the men.—*The Falling Flag.*

(one of our W. A. captains of the first year,) who meanwhile was ahead guarding Longbridge, at Farmville, here succeeded in capturing 800 men.

The column had now to keep up a retreating fight to Farmville, impeded by wagons which hurried forward regardless of contents. Ewell was cut off. The roads were axle-deep with mud. A *triste noche* for Lee's army was the night which followed. We reached Farmville early on the 7th, and bivouacked, after crossing the bridge with some show of provisions. But by some misfortune, the bridge over the Appomattox was not destroyed after us, and the enemy's cavalry followed closely. We were soon ordered to get under way, and the Federal cavalry, who were now becoming rampant, were taught a lesson which they were in no haste to forget. The cavalry charged them at a double-quick and captured 200 prisoners. Gen. Lee took off his hat, at the spirit shown by the men as he passed, and was in turn welcomed with one of the rousing cheers of old.

The wagons were then devoted to destruction, and the Chief Q. M. had the heart to apply the torch himself. The whole army were now marching by an out-of-the-way path, and fooling any longer with wagons was out of the question. If Gen. Lee had never sent his last dispatch to Richmond and given them timely notice, he would have succeeded in gaining the mountains. We made rapid progress; but matters were very blue indeed.

Late in the afternoon, horsemen from the front announced the rapid approach of the enemy. We quickly threw the guns in position, and gave the enemy such a reception as induced him to wheel and not stand on the order of his going. Our cavalry gave chase, and Gen. Gregg, of the U. S. A., was brought in prisoner And now comes the hour when our artillery fires the last gun, and ends its military record. The account which follows is substantially taken from the excellent narrative of a S. C. officer of the Rear Guard, entitled the "Falling Flag:"

The army lay down to rest, and to watch—a very interesting process to a hungry man—a little modest cooking. Sleep was the great thing in view. We woke in a half hour, to eat what there was, and were about tumbling over again, when an officer came around, in a quiet way, and ordered us to be ready to move. Now for a weary march that ends only at Appomattox!

The line of retreat had been changed—a push was being made for the mountains at Lynchburg. On before us was a long line of wagons and artillery, splashing through ruts and mudholes. Pickets were posted under the immediate direction of Gen. R. E. Lee. When we moved again, time was lost in watering the horses—the wagons moved in double lines. The order now was, to get on past Appomattox, a little village of three or four houses, a mile from the Lynchburg railroad. The regiments were closing up, when suddenly the scream of a shell developed artillery practice in the neighborhood of the depot.

It was hammer and tongs down there—shell at short range. Custar was after the artillery train in advance, sixty pieces, and the three batteries left to hold it were the La. Washington Artillery; the Donaldsonville cannoniers, Creoles, exclusively of La., and a Virginia battery attached to our brigade.

The roar of the batteries was incessant. They were holding the dismounted cavalry in check. By the light of the moon there seemed to be a lull in the attack; but before our men could get to the guns, the enemy charged among them suddenly, but were driven back by the fire and rush, though taking some of our men prisoners—among others, Capt. Hankins of the Va Battery, who got away. Our men fell in between the guns, and then begun one of the closest artillery fights for the number engaged and the time it lasted, that occurred during the war. The guns were fought literally to the muzzles. It was dark by this time, and every cannon was ablaze from touch hole to mouth, as well as the small arms of some three or four hundred men packed in among the guns, in a very confined space. It seemed like the very jaws of the lower regions. They made three distinct charges, preluding always with the bugle on the right, left and centre, and thus confusing the point of attack; then a cheer and up they came. It was too dark to see anything under the shadows of the trees, but the long dark lines. They would get within thirty or forty yards from the gun and then roll back, under the deadly fire that was poured upon them from the artillery and small arms. In addition to the other extraordinary and infernal noises of the occasion, the scream of an engine was heard as a train rushed up almost among us, and sounded on the night air as if the devil himself had come up, and was about to join in what was going on. Then came a lull; our friends in front seemed to have had the wire edge taken off.

The great object that remained for us, was to draw off the guns, if possible, now night had set in, from the depot, and get them back with the rest of the train, in the line of retreat.

The guns were limbered up and moved off at once, it being but a few hundred yards to the main road. The silence of the guns soon told the enemy what was going on, and they were not long in following after; our men facing to the rear, delivered their fire steadily, effectually keeping off a rush; they pressed us, but cautiously. The darkness concealed our numbers.

We were going through an open field, and came now to a road through a narrow piece of woods, where we broke from line into column, and double quicked it through the woods, so as to get to the road beyond. Before we got to the turnpike, we heard the bugles of the enemy down it, and as the head of our column came into the road, their cavalry charged the train, some two or three hundred yards below us.

Sixty pieces of cannon (the remainder of Lee's guns,) were at the point when we came into the road. The drivers were attempting to turn back towards the Court House—had got entangled with one another, and presented a scene of utter confusion.

In passing from the old field, where the guns had been at work, into the woods that separated it from the turnpike, two men were walking just in front of me, following their guns, which were on before. I heard one say, "*Tout perdu.*" I asked at once "What battery do you belong to?" "Donaldsonville." It was the Creole Company: and they might well have added the other words of the great Francis, after the battle of Pavia, " *Tout perdu fors l'honneur,*" all lost but honor; for well had they done their work from sixty-one, when they came to Virginia until now, when all was lost, " *Tout perdu.*" It was the motto of the occasion.

The stag was in the toils, but the end was not yet: we would hear the rush, the shouts and pistol shots, when the enemy mounted and in force had attacked the train; the artillerymen having no arms could make no fight, as they could not use their pieces. We could do nothing (being closely pressed by a superior force of their dismounted men,) but fall back upon the town toward our main body, making the best front we could, leaving the road and marching under cover of the timber on the side. Being on foot, gave us a better position to resist any attack that might be made upon us by the cavalry.

The following, is from Lt. Col. W. M. Owen's Journal from which much of the preceding details of the retreat, has already been drawn :

On the 8th, we halted just before day, to rest an hour or two, near New Store—in road to Lynchburg. We resumed march at day light, and camped at night on Rocky Run, one mile from Appomattox. C. H.

At Amelia Court House, most of the Army was sent off by another road, under charge of Gen. Walker, Chief of Artillery, to try to reach Danville to recruit horses.

This afternoon, heavy firing heard in the direction of Appomattox Station. After bivouacking—Lieut. Norcomb, 4th Co. Washington Artillery, and other officers of same Battalion, rode up and reported the whole artillery reserve under Walker, cut off and destroyed near A·pomattox Station. The Washington Artillery have buried and destroyed their guns, and gone to the mountains. No formal surrender of the men with Gen. Lee took place. Some of them succeeded in reaching President Davis, and acting as his body guard.*

The names of the Louisiana Artillery, who acted as Presidential body-guard, were; C. H. C. Brown, Lieut. Commanding; Sergeant, W. G. Coyle, 3rd Company; Corporals. J. F. Lilly, 4th Company; W. A. McRay. 1st Company; L. D. Porter, La. Guards Artillery; W. R. Payne, C. A. Longue, La. Guard Artillery; G. A. Weber. 2nd Company; T. J. Lazzare, 4th Company; T. J Domerty. La. Guard Artillery; R. Wilkerson, J. B. McMullun, 1st Company; McDonald, Webster, Davis. 4th Company.

*WASHINGTON, GA., May 3rd, 1865.

LIEUT. BROWN, *Washington Artillery.*

MY DEAR SIR,

The President directs me to return to you his heartfelt thanks for the valuable services rendered him, by yourself and the gallant men under your comm·n l, as part of his es·ort.
Very Truly Yours,
WM. PRESTON JOHNSTON,
Col. and A. D. C.

We fired our last shot to day, after three years nine months service, since the first shot was fired at Bull-Run.
Gen. Gordon is fighting the enemy in front. We are massed in a sort of natural basin. High land encircles us.
Gordon captures two Napaleon Guns from the Federals.
Gordon can't hold out any longer, and Lee orders the token of surrender, the white flag," to be raised.
The Army of Northern Virginia is no more.*
Lee had but 8000 men with arms in their hands this morning. We are surrounded by more than 100,000 of the enemy.

*The Louisiana troops at the surrender, were extremely reduced in number, as indeed was the case with every other brigade. This was owing partly to the many desperate charges which they had made, partly to having once neglected while on picket duty on the Rapidan, the etiquette of retiring when confronted by the enemy in overwhelming force. The picket line was overrun, held by them and N. C. troops after they had been cut off from the pontoon bridge, and the men were all gobbled up who could not swim back. Hays who had been presiding at a court-martial, gal oped over the pontoon, under a heavy fire, just at the right moment to be regular y in for it. His horse had become meanwhile so frantic, from the bullets, or frem the sword in H.ys' hand, that he cou d not have surrendered if he would. There was nothing left him but to pop spurs to the beast and ride through the enemy's line and over the bridge, which was now in the enemy's hands. His escape from the volleys fired at him was almost miraculous. Col. Eugene Waggaman, who marched straight up to the enemy's batteries at Malvern Hill, was in command on the day of Lee's surrender, and the addresses of Gen. Gordon and Evans, made to the command through him were extremely touching.

To show what service these troops did, it may be stated, that about 16,000 men all told, followed the brigade colors. Of those who can now be found in the city, it is thought that 800 would l e a large estimate. Lt. Col. L. Power of that command, has kindly furnished the subjoined addition l list of names—all he could remember, ten years after the Brigade's disbandment, of those who followed its marches: Col. Monaghan, killed; Col. Jos. Hanlon, since dead; Col. D. B. Penn, Col. James Neligan, since dead; Col. Noland, killed; Col. T. G. Hunt; Col. Henry Forno, since dead; Col. Peck; Col. Alcibiade DeBlanc; Capt. Louis Prados, commanding much of the time from loss of life of regimental and brigade officers of 2nd Brigade; John M. Leggett, killed; Lt. Col. H. D. Monier; Adjutant Mills, 10th; Adjutant A. Marks, now pastor of Tr nity Church; Capt. Wm. P. Harper, Adjutant General; Capt. Dave Merrick, Adjutant General; Major New; Capt. Jos Witherup, since dead; Capt. Levi T. Jennings, since dead; Capt. McClellan, killed in battle; Major Andrew Brady; Lieut. Col. R. A. Wilkinson, killed in battle; Brig. Gen. Nicho s; Brig. Gen. Stafford, killed in battle; Col. Williams of 2nd Regiment, killed in battle; Capt. Ashbridge; Capt. Bowman; Lieuts., Condon, Lockwood, Cady; Capt. McChesney; Capt. W. T. Scovell; Lieut. Crain; Capt. Brigham; Lieut. Davenport; Capt. Jonte, killed in battle; Col. Zebulon Yorke, aft rwards Brig. General; Col V. Zulakowski; Capts. Thomas G. Morgan, and George Morgan; Major Toler; Capts. John Leach, Egan, and Murphy.

MUSTER ROLL

OF THE

WASHINGTON ARTILLERY

OF THE ARMY OF VIRGINIA.

From May 27th, 1861, to April 8th, 1865.

STAFF.

J. B. Walton, Major; promoted to Colonel; made Chief of Artillery Army of the Potomac; Nov. '61, Chief of Artillery Longstreet's Corps; appointed by Secretary of War Inspector-General of Field Artillery; recommended twice by Generals Beauregard and Longstreet for promotion to Brig. Gen. of Artillery; resigned July, 1864.

B. F. Eshleman, Captain Fourth Company; May, 1861, wounded at Bull Run; promoted Major of Artillery, 1863; promoted Lieut. Colonel of Artillery, vice Colonel Walton, April, 1864.

W. M. Owen, Adjutant First Lieut.; promoted Major of Artillery, August, '63; assigned Chief of Artillery Preston's Division, Army of Tennessee; reassigned to Washington Artillery, April '64, as second field officer; wounded at Petersburg, August, 1864; promoted to Lieut. Colonel, '65.

M. B. Miller, Captain Third Company; May '61, promoted to Major of Artillery; assigned to Va. Batallion; re-assigned to B. W. A. January, 1864.

E. J. Kursheedt, promoted Adjutant B. W. A.

E. S. Drew, Surgeon, present with the command in all its marches and battles to the close of the war

Thos. Y. Aby, promoted Assistant Surgeon, Feb., '63.

C. H. Slocomb, Q. M. May, '61; resigned Nov., '61; Captain commanding Fifth Company W. A. of Western Army.

H. G. Geiger, A. Q. M. May, '61.

C. L. C. Dupuy, Sergt. Major; May, '61, promoted to Lieut. of Artillery at Vicksburg.

W. A. Randolph, promoted Sergt. Major.

B. L. Braselman, Ordnance Officer, May, '61.

ROLL OF FIRST COMPANY.

Captain Harry M. Isaacson, resigned August, '61. First Lieutenant, C. W. Squires, promoted to Captain, September, '61; to Major, January, '64. First Lieutenant, John B. Richardson, promoted to Captain; assigned to Second Company, June, '62. Second Lieutenant Geiger, detailed in Q. M. Dept. First Sergeant, Ed. Owen, promoted to First Lieut. September, '61; promoted to Captain, January, '64. Sergeant John M. Galbraith, promoted to Second Lieut. Nov. '61; promoted First Lieut. December, '61; died of wound received at battle of Drury's Bluff, May, '61. Sergeant C. H. C. Brown, promoted to First Sergeant, October, '61; to Second Lieut., May, '61. Sergeant C. L. C. Dupuy, promoted Sergeant-Major, May, '61. Corporal Frank D. Ruggles, killed at Fredericksburg, Dec. '62. Corporal E. C. Payne, Jr., promoted Second Sergeant, Oct. '61; discharged Feb. '62. Corporal Wm. Fellowes, Jr., returned to his ranks at his own request, Aug. '61. F. F. Case, returned to his ranks at his own request, Oct. '61; promoted to Corporal, April,' 63; to Sergeant, October, '64. Private Thos. Y. Aby, promoted to Corporal, Oct. '61; to Sergeant, Oct. '61; to First Sergeant, July, '62; to Assistant Surgeon, Feb. '63. Richard Aby. Saml. Aby. R. H. Alsobrook, blown up on a caisson in Maryland, Sept. '62, severely wounded. Jos. H. Berthelot, discharged Feb. '64. R. J. Ball, transferred to McGregor's Hose Artillery, Nov. '64. S. A. Baillio. H. P. Bayley. W. H. Blount, promoted to Corporal, Oct. '64. Jno. Bozant. L. L. Brown. Jno. Bare. W. Chambers, killed at Rappahannock Station, Aug. '62. H. Chambers, died at Camp Hollins, Va., Dec. '61. C. Chambers, wounded at Sharpsburg, Sept. '62; lost portion of his hand. Geo. Chambers, killed at Drury's Bluff, May, '64. A. F. Coste, wounded at Fredericksburg; died Dec. '62. E. A. Cowen, promoted Capt. Q. M., B. W. A. Nov. '61; resigned, June, '62. J. B. Cleveland, transferred to Second Company, Dec. '61. S. M. D. Clark. W. L. Clark. W. T. Cummings, detailed in Richmond. E. Collins. Thos. Carter, captured at Petersburg, Sept. '64. C. E. Caylat. Geo. B. DeRussy, promoted to Sergeant, Oct. '61; to Second Lieut. July, '62; transferred to Second Company. R. N. Davis, Jr., transferred to Fourth Company. Geo. Dupré. C. W. Deacon, transferred from Third Company, April, '62; promoted to Q. M. Sergeant, and captured June, '64, at Petersburg. C. A. Every, wounded at Fredericksburg, Dec. '62; at Fredericksburg, May, 1863; at Drury's Bluff, May, 1864. L. G. Elfer, transferred to Third Company. W. R. Falconer, promoted to Corporal, April, '62; transferred to Second Louisiana Cavalry, February, '64. C. A. Falconer, transferred from Third Company, June, '61; killed December, '62, at Fredericksburg. P. O. Fazende, transferred from Third Company, June, '61; promoted to Corporal. April, '63; to Sergeant, July, '63; captured at Drury's Bluff, May, 1864; returned having escaped, November, '64. John R. Fell, wounded at Rappahannock, Aug., '62; discharged. H. C. Florence. J. E. Florence, killed at Fredericksburg, May, '63. F. H. Fowler, wounded at Sharpsburg, Sept., '62; detailed, Q. M. Dept. M. Fisher. J. Frolick, jr. Paul Grima, G. B. Genin, promoted to Corporal, April, '64. D. H. Garland. Wm. H. Hardie, promoted to Corporal, Oct., '61; to Sergt., July, '62; to First Sergt., Sept., '64. S. Harrison, promoted to Corporal, Oct., '64. J. R. Harby. T. P. Hall. E. Morgan Harris, killed at Petersburg, July, '64. J. Horrock. G. M. Judd, promoted to Sergt., Oct. '61; killed at Sharpsburg, Sept., '62 J. E. Jarreau, promoted, Feb., '62; J. U. Jarreau. H. O. Janin, wounded at Fredericksburg. G. D. P. Jones. Thos. P. Jones. E. T. Kursheedt, promoted to Corporal, Oct., '61; to Sergeant-Major, April, '63; to Adjutant, with rank of Lieutenant. J. W. Kearny, discharged, April, '62. Herman Ross, killed at Rappahannock, August, '62.

E. F. Keplinger. D. Kilpatrick. L. Labarre, transferred to Third Company. Frank Lobrano. T. J. Lutman, promoted to Corporal, April, '63; killed at Fredericksburg, May, '63. A. M. Lappington, detailed in Montgomery, Alabama. E. Levy. P. Leahy. John R. McGaughy, promoted to Sergeant, March, '62; to First Sergeant, April, '63; to Second Lieutenant, September, '64. S. M. G. Mount, caisson ran over his leg, August, '63; retired by Medical Executive Board, October, '64. J. P. Manico, discharged, January, '62. J. Muntinger, wounded at Sharpsburg, September, '62; died October at Winchester. A. M. Moore. R. F. Marshall, killed at Rappahannock, Aug. '62, by explosion of his gun. Geo. Maxent. Geo. W. Muse, killed at Bull Run, July, '61. W. Moran. P. A. J. Michel, wounded at Sharpsburg. T. M. McRobert, discharged Aug. '62. W. Mains, killed, July, '64. A Micou, promoted to First Lieut. on Gen. Fry's Staff, May, '64. H. H. Marks. J. L. Mathews, detailed to Med. Dep. B. W. A. N. Milhardo, discharged July, '62. Jos. Meyers, detailed to Med. Dep. B. W. A. J. McCormick. W. J. McLean. J. B. McCutcheon, wounded at Sharpsburg, lost his arm. W. P. McGehee. J. B. McMillan. H. C. McClellan, died at Petersburg, Nov. '64. A. G. McCorkle. W. A. McRae, promoted to Corporal, Oct. '64. C. M. McIntire. W. T. Norment, promoted to Sergeant, April, '63. E. S. Ogden, promoted Second Lieutenant First La. Artillery, April, '64 J. W. Outlaw, captured at Gettysburg, July, '64. W. F. Perry, discharged by Medical Board, April, '64. J. N. Payne, promoted to Sergeant, July, '62; transferred to Major Byren's Batallion Artillery, March, 1864. L. Parson. N. B. Phelps, detailed Nov. '64. D. Pendegrass. R. Pollard, detailed Nov. '64. E. Peychaud, wounded at Drury's Bluff, det. in Richmond. H. Peychaud, killed at Drury's Bluff. C. Peychaud, detailed by Med. Board. C. Rossiter, wounded at Drury's Bluff, retired by Medical Board, Oct. '64. J. E. Rodd, wounded at Fredericksburg, detailed. M. Ranch. E. Niviere, captured at Gettysburg. John Richardson, det. Q. M. D. Jas. Reddington, killed at Rappahannock, Aug. '62. R. McK. Spearing, promoted to Corporal, '62: killed at Fredericksburg, Dec., '62. F. A. St. Amant, discharged, July, '61; disability. W. T. Saul. C. N. B. Street, transferred to Moody's Battery, July, '62. Ph. Seibrecht. P. D. Simmons, killed at Drury's Bluff, '64. W. W. Spencer. Frank Sagee. T. S. Turner, promoted Corporal, '63. S. Turner, promoted Corporal, April, '64; wounded at Drewry's Bluff. John A. Tarleton, discharged, July, '62, special order Secretary war. J. M. Turpin. W. E. Fowles, killed, Railroad accident, March, '63. F. Villasana. Van Vinson, promoted to Corporal, July, '63; to Sergt., April, '64. H. Whitcomb, killed, July, '64. E. V. Wiltz, discharged. C. R. Walden, killed at Drury's Bluff, May, '64. W. H. West, promoted to Corporal, May, '62; to Sergt., April, '63; killed at Fredericksburg, May, '63. John A. Wayne. J. V. Webb, discharged, May, '62. T. J. Wilson. B. Woodward. J. P. Woodward. H. S. Wilkinson. J. N. White, detailed. H. L. Zebal, discharged by Med. Board, May, '64. L. E. Zebal, discharged, furnished a substitute. S. G. Stewart, J. Scott. J. A. O'Neal, discharged, April, '64. John Charlesworth. H. Collins. John Eshman. John Earls, died in hospital. John Farrell. W. Farrell. E. Gallagher. J. L. Heck, promoted to Quarter Master Sergeant, September, '64. M. Hock, detailed in Ord. Department. J. Hammel, discharged, June, '62; Surgeon's certificate. J. Jacobs, detailed Medical Department. Jas. Kinney, died from wound received at Fredericksburg, December, 62. John Krafts, detailed to Ordnance Department. F. Lester. J. S. Lehman, transferred to Second Company. J. Lenon, transferred to Second Company. B. D. F. McKesson. J. A. McCormick. Wm. Oliver. Chas. Rush, transferred to Second Company. E. W. Smith. Jas. Smith. A. Szar. F. Schmarbeck. H. L. Allain. John Bachr. J. J. Norment, promoted to Corporal, October, '64; wounded at Drury's Bluff.

Names of Wounded omitted in above Roll.

Captain E. Owen, at Sharpsburg and Drury's Bluff. Lieutenant C. H. C.

Brown, severely wounded, left on the field, and captured at Gettysburg. W. R. Falkner, at Rappahannock and Fredericksburg. W. R. Fell, at Sharpsburg and Fredericksburg. W. H. Hardie, at Fredericksburg. J. R. Harby, at Fredericksburg. C. J. Kursheedt, Sharpsburg, '62. A. Micou, Fredericksburg, '62. Jos. Myers, Drury's Bluff. N. B. Phelps, at Drury's Bluff. C. Rossiter, Fredericksburg and at Drury's Bluff. P. S. Turner at Rappahannock Station. Van Vinson, at Gettysburg. T. J. Wilson, at Drury's Bluff. H. S. Wilkinson, Drury's Bluff. A. L. Zebal, at Bull Run and at Williamsport, Md. John Charlesworth, at Fredericksburg, '62. C. Rush, Fredericksburg, '62.

The above statement has been taken from the Historical Record furnished to the War Department C. S., January 1st, 1865, and is correct and as full as can possibly be made from that Record.

          Lt. C. H. C. BROWN,
          Ranking Officer 1st Co. B. W. A.

New Orleans, Oct. 2d, 1874.

ROLL OF SECOND COMPANY.

Lieutenant C. C. Lewis, commanding Company, May, '61; resigned, Aug. '61. Capt. Thos. L. Rosser, promoted to Lieutenant Colonel of Artillery; wounded at Mechanicsville. Captain J. B. Richardson, assigned to Company, June, '62. First Lieutenant Sam. J. McPherson, resigned August, 1861. Cuthbert H. Slocomb, promoted to First Lieutenant; resigned November, 1861. Second Lieutenant Samuel Hawes, promoted to First Lieutenant, December 1861. Second Lieutenant J. D. Britton, wounded at Sharpsburg, September, 1862. Second Lieut. Geo. B. DeRussy, promoted from Sergeant First Company, and assigned by Col. Walton, July, '62; wounded at Chancellorville, May, 1863. (Cadet) F. H. Wigfall, relieved from duty with company, June, 1862, by order No. 137. First Sergeant Jos. H. DeGrange. First Sergeant A. A. Brinsmade, promoted to Second Lieut. of Artillery. First Sergeant A. G. Knight. Serg. Gustave Aime. Sergeant H. C. Wood, discharged October, 1861, by order of Secretary of War. Sergeant C. Huchez. Sergeant Charles E. Leverich, appointed First Lieutenant P.A. C. S. July, 1863, by order of Secretary of War. Sergeant Jules Freret. J. W. Emmett, appointed First Lieut. P. A. C. S., July, '63, by Sec'y of War. A. G. Knight, promoted to Orderly, Nov. 1863. Geo. E. Strawbridge, appointed Second Lieutenant P. A. C. S., March, '68, by Sec'y of War. Sergeant W. A. Randolph, promoted to Sergeant Major, Sept. '63. Sergeant Walter J. Hare, wounded at Sharpsburg. Sergeant Ed. L. Hall. Sergeant Thos. H. Fuqua. Sergeant John W. Parsons. Corporal James D. Edwards, discharged December, 1861. B. N. L. Hutton, discharged July, 1861, by order of Gen. Beauregard, Samuel Hawes, promoted Second Lieut. Nov. '61. Corporal T. B. White, discharged Nov'r '62. A. G. Knight, promoted to Sergt. Feb., '62. W. A. Randolph, promoted to Sergt., April, '63. Ed. L. Hall, promoted to Sergt., August, '63; wounded at Williamsport, July, '63. Thos. H. Fuqua, promoted to Sergt., Nov., '63. Jno. W. Parsons, captured at Gettysburg, July, 5th, exchanged; promoted to Sergt., Nov. '63. S. Isaac Meyers, killed at Petersburg, August, '64. E. J. Jewell, wounded at Williamsport, July, 6th, '63; died at Williamsport, July, 19th, '63. Stephen Chalaron, wounded at Gettysburg, July, '63; captured, exchanged; promoted to First Lieut. in Nit. & Min. Bureau. May, '64. L. C. Woodville, wounded at Petersburg, June, '64. Jno. Howard Goodin, wounded at Drury's Bluff, May, 1864; promoted to Ordnance Sergt.. June, '64. C. C. Twichell. Thos. H. Suter. J. F. Randolph. E. D. Patton.

Phil. A. Clagett. John C. Woodville. G. W. Humphries. Q. M. Sergeant Josh DeMeza. J. S. Bradley. Artificers—Leonard Craig. James Keating. Jno. W. Dempsey, transferred to Third Company, June, '63. Privates—Fred. Alewelt, wounded at Sharpsburg, died at Shepardstown, Sept., '62. Randolph Axon, detailed in Richmond, Oct., '62. E. D. Augustus. Geo. Alpin. — Almundinger, killed at Petersburg. F. P. Buckner, transferred to Fifth Regiment, April, '62. A. R. Blakely, wounded Second Manassas, August, 30th, '63; captured August, '63; exchanged and detailed in Treasury Department. R. J. Banister, wounded at Williamsport, July, '63; captured, exchanged; drowned while on furlough in Mississippi River, February 8th, '64. J. T. Brentford. E. M. Bee, discharged, Oct. '62. James Brown. James Byrnes. Joe Barr. Patrick Brooks, wounded at Sharpsburg, July, '63. Frank Baker. John S. Bradly, promoted Q. M. Sergt. April, '61. John A. Bloom. Henry Brooks. Stephen W. Britton. J. B. Cleveland, transferred from First Company, appointed Second Lieutenant, P. A. C. S. March, 1863, by Secretary War. W. P. Curtis, discharged. H. D. Coleman, captured at Chancellorville, May, '63; exchanged. Phil. A. Clagett, promoted to Corporal, Oct. '63. H. S. Carey, detailed in Ordnance Department. John A. Coakley, wounded at Williamsport, July, 1863. J. W. Cross, wounded at Williamsport, July, 1863; died August, 1863. W. H. Cantzon, detailed clerk, Gen. Lee's Headquarters, Nov. '64. N. J. Clark. C. A. Duvall, transferred from Fourth Company, July, '61; appointed Second Lieutenant P. A. C. S., March, 1863. A. DeValcourt. Wm. Davis, honorable mention at Second Manassas, August, 1862; wounded at Williamsport, July, 1863. Theo. O. Dyer. Charles Dougherty. Dan J. Driscoll. Thos. W. Dyer. W. E. Florance. Wm. Forest, wounded at Williamsport, July, 1863. Thos. H. Fuqua, transferred from Third Company, July, '61; promoted to Corporal, Nov. '62. L. C. Fallon, wounded. Geo. A. Frierson, wounded at Williamsport, July, '63. Armand Freret, wounded at Sharpsburg, September, 1862; died at Winchester, September, 1862. Jules Freret, wounded at Gettysburg, July '63; died same place. John H. Forshee. Wm. M Francis, transferred from Watson's Battery, July, '64. Wm. C. Giffen, captured at Chancellorville, May, '63; exchanged. John H. Goodin, promoted to Corporal, August, '63. John M. Greenman, wounded at Bermuda Hundreds, May, 1864. John F. Giffen, wounded at Williamsport, July, 1863. D. Gleason. Geo. Gessner, wounded at Drury's Bluff, May, '64. F. M. Gillespie. Hugh S. Gookin. E. E. Gookin. Jas. A Hall. Geo. Humphrey, wounded at Williamsport, July, '63; captured, exchanged May, '64. S. C. Hartman, discharged, Oct., '62. J. Hefleigh. Chas. Harris. Chas. Hurley. Alex. Anderson. C. M. Harvey. I. Ichstien. O. Jewell, died, February 1863. J. Jackson, detailed, May, 1864. D. E. Giggetts, discharged by order, May, 1864. B. C. Jacques. T. R. James. M. Kelly, discharged, May, 1862. B. F. Kirk, wounded at Chancellorville, May, 1863. Wm. Kirk, transferred, June, 1864. R. H. Knox, appointed cadet, P. A. C. S. November, 1864. T. F. Land, discharged. Wm. Little. B. Lynch, discharged, December, 1861. W. Layman, wounded at Gettysburg, died. L. S. Lehman. James Lennon, transferred Feb. '64, A. G. Lobdell, retired December, 1864. M. P. Lapham, wounded, and died at Drury's Bluff. May, '64. P. B. Lynch. J. S. Meyers. J. R. McGowen. W. Mills, detailed Oct. 1863. John Meux, transferred from Fourth Company, July, '61. W. Maroney. J. McCormack. D. T. Moore, died Aug. '64. J. Madden, detailed Feb. '65. L. Miller. B. A. McDonald. W. O. Mallory. W. E. Maynard. H. McGill. H. M. Payne. retired Aug. '64. A. H. Peale, discharged Nov. '61, by order of Gen. Beauregard. William Palfrey, promoted Second Lieut. First Louisiana Artillery. J. C. Purdy, appointed Second Lieut. P. A. C. S., March, '63. W. A. Perrin. J. H. Peebles. I. H. Randolph, killed at Williamsport, July, '63. W. Roth, discharged August, '61. Wm. Rockwell, discharged Dec. '61. J. W. Ridgill. A. G. Ridgill. W. G. Raoul, appointed Capt. A. Q. M., March, 1864. J. L. Richardson. H. D. Summers, captured at Chancellorville, detailed with wounded' captured at Williamsport; exchanged May, 1864. W. D. Sayre. A. D. R. Sutton. D. Self. W. H. Simpson. H. C. Twichell, discharged October, '61.

C. C. Twichell, wounded at Williamsport, promoted Corporal, August, 1863. C. A. D. Theineman, discharged, Aug. '62. G. J. Thomas. R. Urquhart, wounded at Petersburg, June, 1864. P. Von Colln, wounded at Chancellorville. L. C. Woodville, promoted to Corporal, April, 1863. W. H. Wilkins. J. Weber. F. Wilson. H. N. White, killed at Second Manassas. T. B. White, promoted to Corporal, December, 1861. F. M. Williams, appointed Second Lieutenant, P. A. C. S. April, 1863. B. Ward, wounded Second Manassas, captured; exchanged. G. Watterston, wounded at Williamsport, captured and died, August, 1863. T. E. Williams, wounded at Gettysburg. G. A. Webre. Chas. Waterson. D. P. White, wounded at Williamsport. —— Winter. F. H. H. Walker. H. Berthelot. F. H. Sawyer.

The above statement has been taken from the Historical Record furnished to the War Department C. S., January 1st, 1865, and is correct and as full as can possibly be made from that Record.

JOHN B. RICHARDSON,
Captain Commanding at surrender.

NEW ORLEANS, Oct. 5, 1874.

ROLL OF THIRD COMPANY.

Merritt B. Miller, Captain, May, '61; promoted to Major of Artillery, Feb. '64. Andrew Hero, jr., Second Serg. May '61; First Serg. Nov. '61; Second Lieut. May '62; First Lieut. Aug. '62; Capt. Feb. '64; wounded at Sharpsburg, Sept. '62; at Petersburg, April, '65. Jos B. Whittington, First Lieutenant, resigned Louis A. Adam, Second Lieut. resigned Aug. '61; re-enlisted as private. Aug. '61. James Dearing, Second Lieut,. promoted to Captain Art'y, April 8, '62. J. J. Garnet, First Lieutenant, assigned to Company July, '61; transferred to Signal Corps, June, '63. Isaac W. Brewer, First Lieutenant, killed at Rappahannock Station. Frank McElroy, First Lieutenant; Geo. McNeill, Second Lieutenant; Charles H. Stocker, Second Lieutenant, wounded at Petersburg, April, '65. First Sergeant John T. Handy. Sergeant Louis Prados, promoted to Lieut. La. Brigade. Sergeant W. A. Collins. Sergeant R. Maxwell, discharged from command. Sergeant W. H. Ellis. Sergeant O. N. DeBlanc. Sergeant W. G. Coyle. Sergeant F. Kremelberg, killed at Petersburg. Sergeant P. W. Pettis. Corporal Ed. J. Jewell. Corporal A. H. Peale. Corporal C. E. Fortier. discharged. Corporal E. W. Morgan. Corporal R. P. Many, died of wounds. Corporal W. Leefe, died in Louisiana Hospital. Corporal A. E. Grimmer. Corporal N. Bartlett. Corporal T. Ballantine. Corporal Samuel Bland. Corporal R. Ballauf. Corporal M. B. Cantrelle. Corporal I. C. Dick. Corporal John R. Porter. Corporal H. J. Phelps. William A. Collins, wounded at Second Manassas, August, 1863. E. Avril, wounded at Sharpsburg, Sept. 61; discharged Dec. '62. John Anderson, transferred from First Company, July, '61. Henry J. Atkins, killed at Sharpsburg, Sept. 1862. Frank M. Andress. J. A. Adde. S. S. Andress. B L. Braselman, promoted to Ordnance Sergeant Battalion. Robert Bruce, discharged April, '64. Samuel C. Boush, on duty in Quarter Master's Department. J. D. Blanchard, died March, 1864. James C. Bloomfield, promoted to Lieut in Magruder's army. Michel A. Becnel, discharged December 1861, by order of Secretary of War. Geo. Bernard, detailed with ambulance. M. Burke. J. P. Benton, captured by enemy, June, '64. Samuel Bland, wounded at Rappahannock, Aug.' 62. James

S. Behan, died at Mobile, Ala. Wm. Barton. Jos. Bloom. Rudolph Ballauf, promoted to Corporal, April, '64. Geo. Brady. Geo. B. Behan, died at Culpeper, Sept. '62. C. Bush, injured by falling of a tree, Oct. '62; detailed in Richmond. Ernest Beyer. Charles Brady. Henry G. Brooks. John H. Benton, wounded at Petersburg, Sept, '64; died Sept. '64. Geo. H. Bryens, killed at Gettysburg, July '63. Lawrence Berry. Richard Bryens. Wm. P. Brewer, promoted to Assistant Surgeon. B. F. Bryan. Robert J. Ball, transferred to First Company. Steve Burke. F. A. Carl, died May 27, 1861. M. W. Cloney, wounded at Sharpsburg, Sept. '62; captured at Gettysburg, July, '63. John H. Colles, discharged Nov. '61, by order Secretary of War. Ernest Charpieux, wounded at Manassas, August 1862; detailed Q. M. Dept., April, '64. W. G. Coyle, promoted to Corporal, Nov. 1861; to Sergt., Oct. 1863. Stephen Chalaron, transferred to Second Company, July, 1861. Wm. Casey, transferred from Second Company, July, 1861. James Crilly, transferred from Second Company, wounded at Rappahannock Station, August, 1862. Frank E. Coyle, wounded at Gettysburg, July, 1863; killed at Petersburg, April, '65. W. Campbell. Geo. W. Charlton. L. W. Cressy, killed by falling of a tree at Winchester. C. W. Deacon, transferred to First Company. Edward A. Clark. W. W. Charlton. T. S. Collins. J. F. Clark, killed at Gettysburg, July, '63. Jos H. DeMeza, transferred to Second Company, July, '61. Edward Duncan, captured at Petersburg and exchanged. Fred. Douber, killed at Sharpsburg. J. F. Davis. A. Dumas. James Dolan, died from wound at Rappahannock. August DeBlanc, Isaac C. Dick, promoted to Corporal, October, '64. H. Dietz. Benj. E. Dick, captured at Fredericksburg and exchanged. Armand DeBlanc, discharged May, '63. W. Dennison. Wm. DeLacy. Honoré Doussan. Adolphe Dupré, Jr., wounded and captured at Gettysburg. Louis G. Elfer. Edgar D. Evans. P. O. Fazende. Charles E. Fortier, promoted to Corporal, July, '61; discharged, Sept. 1861. F. P. Fourshee, wounded at Rappahannock. T. H. Fuqua, transferred to Second Company. Otto Frank, wounded at Fredericksburg. René Faisans. Auguste Faisans. Louis E. Guyot. A. E. Grimmer, wounded at Fredericksburg; promoted to Corporal November, '63. Fred. W Gras. Jno. W. Gore. J. B. Gretter. C. A. Gough, wounded at Gettysburg, and died. S. R. Givens, discharged January, '63. Leon M. Gerard. Philibert Gerard. G. A. Grimes. Henry Guillote. F. L. Hubbard, right arm injured, and discharged October, '61. C. Hart, discharged February, '62. John Holmes, jr., wounded at Sharpsburg, and discharged May, '64. John Huisson. John G. Hottinger. Ed. D. Hubbell. Wm. Jones. Wm. N. Johnson. Eugene Joubert, wounded at Rappahannock, and died. Jos. H. Jagot. F. Jourdan. John Jones, captured and escaped July, '64. Joseph Kinslow. S. Kennedy, transferred to Twenty-eighth Louisiana Regiment; resigned, '64. Thos. Kerwin. Damas Kobleur, wounded at Petersburg, October, '64. W. H. Kitchen. R. H. Kitchen. M. Kent. Wm. Leefe, promoted Corporal April, '63; died October, 1864. Ed. Loftus. died February, '63. M. F. Lynch. James Little, died June, '62. G. Leytze, missing after battle off Gettysburg. S. Levy, wounded at Rappahannock; discharged September, '62. J. T. Luddy. John Land. Geo. Land. Gustave Leclere. Eugene Leclere. Charles Lombard, transferred to Fourth Company June, '63. T. Lazarre, died at Petersburg, December, 64. Murville Labarre, died at Petersburg, December 31, '64; E. Labarre, discharged October, '63. Lacestiere Labarre, transferred from First Company September, '63. P. E. Laresche. A. Leefe, wounded at Drury's Bluff. N. Lighthouse. T. M. McFall. promoted to Q. M. Sergeant April, '63. O. McDonald, killed at Rappahannock. J. H. McCartney, wounded at Sharpsburg. J. H. Moore, transferred to 7th Brigade. W. Mills, tranferred to Second Company. E. W. Morgan, discharged July, 1861. Robert Maxwell, promoted to Sergeant November, '61; wounded at Rappahannock and discharged '63. A. B. Martin. G. H. Meek, promoted to Ord. Serg. Nov., '63. R. P. Many, Corporal, April, '63; wounded, captured and died at Fredericksburg, May, '63. C. B. Marmillon, discharged '62, by Secretary of War. G. W. Massy, wounded at Sharpsburg; died September, '62. John C.

Murphy. Henry A. Madden, killed at Drury's Bluff, May, '64, E. L. Mahen. S. W. Noyes. Albert Norcom, transferred to Fourth Company. J. S. Nesbitt. discharged May, '62. L. T. Noyes. W. P. Noble. T. Nulty. F. Ozanne, captured and escaped at Hagerstown, '63. Peyton W. Pettis, promoted Corporal July, '62; wounded at Rappahannock and Sharpsbnrg; promoted Sergeant, '64. Jno. R. Porter, promoted Corporal August, '64; wounded at Petersburg, Oct. '64. H. J. Phelps, Corporal, April 1863; wounded at Fredericksburg, 1862. Abraham B. Philips. Geo. A Peirce. Paul T. Patin. Jas. W. Price. Wm. F. Pinckard, wounded at Petersburg. Wm. M. Pinckard. C. P. Russell. Sam'l Rousseau, wounded at Petersburg. J. F. Randolph, transferred to Second Company. Charles Raymond. H. Rideau, killed at Gettysburg. F. Ruleau, wounded and died at Gettysburg. E. Riviere. Jules A. A. Rousseau. G. D. Robinson, severely wounded by capsizing of a cannon, fourth of July, 1863. Frank Shaw, jr., discharged by Secretary of War. Chas. H. Stocker, promoted Corporal. June, 1862; Sergeant, July, 1862; captured at Gettysburg, July, '63; elected Second Lieutenant, March, '63. S. G. Saunders, wounded at Sharpsburg. Charles Smith, captured at Petersburg, June, 1864. A. Seicshnaydre, Leon Seicshnaydre. S. B. Slade. C. G. Smelser. T. W. Smith. R. Smith. H. D. Summers, transferred to Second Company. Wm. S. Toledano, discharged September, 1861. E. Toledano, discharged September, 1861. Howard Tully, wounded at Bull Run and Fredericksburg. Ralph Turnell, discharged November, 1862. Hugh Thompson, killed at Rappahannock. James Tully, wounded at Rappahannock. G. J. Thomas. Walter A. Tew. Victor R. Tisdale. John Trémé. Oswald J. Toledano, killed at Petersburg. Ernest Vidal. J. W. White. Thos. E. Williamson. W. Williamson. W. J. B. Watson, transferred to Fourth Company. J. N. White, transferred to Fourth Company. J. W. Dempsey, transferred to Second Company. Geo. Pielert. W. D. Holmes, transferred to Second Company. Tom Nugent. James Keating, transferred to Second Company.

The above roll is copied correctly from the historical records of the Third Company of the Washington Artillery, and contains all details as to members of the Company.

A. HERO, JR.,
late Capt. Com'd'g 3d Co. B. W. A.

ROLL OF FOURTH COMPANY.

Captain Jos. Norcom; First Lieut. H. A. Battles; Second Lieuts., G. E. Apps, W. J. Behan; Sergeants—1st, J. S. Fish; 2d, J. C. Wood; 3d, J. W. Wilcox; 4th, B. F. Weidler; 5th, J. B. Valentine. Quartermaster—S. T. Haile. Corporals—F. A. Brode, O. S. Babcock, B. Hufft, J. F. Lilly, Geo. Montgomery. R. S. Burke, F. W. Ames, Geo. E. W. Wilkinson. Privates—Geo. Anderson, J. S. Allen, Jos. Adams, O. W. Adams, P. M. Baker, Lewis Baker, H. H. Baker, A. Banksmith, Jas. Bateman, F. A. Behan, Jas. Borland, Chas. M. Byrne, A. Boucher, J. W. Burke, L. W Clayton, W. P. Creecy, O. E. Cook, Thos. Carey, Wm. Cary, Wm. Curley, J. M. Cox, Denis J. Cronan, E. Condon, A. S. Cowand, Chas. Cowand, B. Chapman, R. N. Davis, W. Deninson, W. R. Dirke, R. Davidson, Jas. D. Edwards, Jno. Fowlkes, Jno. Fagan, W. S. Fell, J. J. Farrell, R. H. Gray, G. C. Gregory, E. F. Gubernator, J. G. Hood, Thos. Herbert, Sam'l E. Holt, W. McC. Holmes, W. W. Jones, A. C. Jones, I. Jessup, F. Jordan, M. J. Kinney, M. Keegan, F. Langdon, Chas. Lake, J. R. Land, Theo. Lazarre, Dupre Lazarre, P. J. Lavery, C. W. Marston, E. A. Mellard, Wm. Martin, R. F.

MUSTER ROLL OF THE WASHINGTON ARTILLERY.

F. Moore, R. McDonald, Jno. McManus, B. Marisoli, H. Mayer, C. McGregor, A. Norcom, D. Nolan, Thos. Norris, A. L. Plattsmier, Chas. Palfrey, D. W. Pipes, H. T. Peak, Jno. Pheiffer, J. M. Rohbock, M. J. Ryan, G. Reynolds, W. Redmond, L. Reney, Louis Roesch, J. H. Smith, J. H. Stone, Jno. Schekler, A. Soniat, Chas. Smelzer, A. Shew, W. N. Stuart, E. Terrebonne, A. F. Vass, H. F. Wilson, Geo. Walker, G. W. Wood, P. N. Wood, J. J. Wall, Jno. Wilson, W. J. B. Watson. Artificers—Levi Callahan, J. McDonald.

The above roll has been taken by me from the records of the Washington Artillery, and I certify that the same is as full and correct as it can be made.

WM. J. BEHAN,
Ranking Officer of 4th Co. B. W. A.

For the muster roll of the Fifth Company, see p. 150. Of the remnants of the four companies in Virginia, forty-five escaped under Major Miller, (the horses having been cut from their harness,) by way of Lynchburg and the mountains, to Johnston's army in North Carolina, Capt. Chas. A. Green, of the Louisiana Guard Artillery, and some of the Donaldsonville Artillery, under Lieutenant Prospere Landry, among the number. Major Moses says, in reference to the Confederate gold which was placed in his hands, and which had followed President Davis to Washington, Ga.: " I employed four young men of the Washington Artillery, to guard the gold and accompany me to Augusta. There were a great many cavalry and straggling soldiers prowling about, and on the train they made what was then called several 'charges' upon the gold, which, with the assistance of Col. Sanford, of Montgomery, and Private Shepherd, of Texas, were successfully resisted." Whatever became of the gold, after it was honorably placed by Major Moses in Federal hands for the relief of wounded soldiers, has never yet been ascertained.

The very last battle fought, or regular engagement during the war, took place on the night of the 16th of April, at Columbus, Ga., at which time that town was captured and 1,200 Confederate soldiers made prisoners. Three of the Washington Artillery,[*] Adams, Cummings and Bartlett, the first and last of whom had fired the first guns at Bull Run, were present at the night attack, and made prisoners, the last named three times during the night.

[*] The following is one of the orders still in existence :

HEADQUARTERS CAMP RENDEZVOUS, BATTERY DIVISION,
COLUMBUS, GA., April, 16th, 1865.

Corporal N. Bartlett, having reported to me for duty, will hold himself subject to my orders, mounted.

V. H. TALIAFERRO.
Colonel Commanding.

REPORT TO THE LOUISIANA LEGISLATURE

OF

ADJUTANT GENERAL M. GRIVOT,

UPON STATE TROOPS,

FOR THE YEARS 1860, '61 AND '62.

1860.

Abstract Statement of the Officers in Commission preceding the War.

FIRST DIVISION

Major General John L. Lewis, Commanding; Col. L. E. Forstall, Division Inspector; Lieut. Colonel Chas. A. Labuzan, Division Quartermaster; Lieut. Colonel Thomas Cripps, Division Paymaster; Major W. P. Williams, Division Surgeon; Major E. L. Forstall, Aid; Major U. Lavillebeuvre, Aid; Major A. Trudeau, Aid; Major N. Gunari, Aid; Major L. Stein, Aid; Major L. Lay, Aid; Major Jos. M. Kennedy, Jr., Aid.

LOUISIANA LEGION BRIGADE.

Brigadier General H. W. Palfrey, Commanding; Major J. F. Chatry, Brigade Inspector; Captain R. Beltran, Aid; Captain P. O'Rorke, Aid; Captain W. B. Cook, Aid; Captain Chas. A. Janvier, Aid.

ORLEANS BATALLION OF ARTILLERY.

First Company—Captain, F. Gomez; Senior First Lieutenant, A. D. Garcia; Junior First Lieutenant, P. A. Gomez; Second Lieutenant, P. Marrero.

Third Company—Captain, F. Stromeyer; Senior First Lieutenant, G. Berluchaux; Junior First Lieutenant, A. A. Canon; Second Lieutenant, Alexander Diogenes.

Sixth Company—Senior First Lieutenant, Theo. Morano, Commanding; Junior First Lieutenant, N. Rivera; Second Lieutenant, Jean Schweitzer.

Fourth Company, attached to Legion—Captain, J. L. Lamothe; Senior First Lieutenant, A. Abadie; Junior First Lieutenant, G. Raymond; Second Lieut. I. Erard.

REGIMENT OF LIGHT INFANTRY.

Colonel Chas. F. Sturcken, Commanding; Lieutenant Colonel, C. L. Mathes; Major, H. Blaize; Lieutenant E. H. Bœlitz, Adjutant; Lieutenant Herdsfelder, Quartermaster; Lieutenant G. Lugenbuhl, Paymaster; Lieutenant Loisenger, Surgeon.

CHASSEURS, 1814–15.

First Lieutenant, F. Ecrot, Commanding; Second Lieutenant, L. Honidobre.

YAGERS.

Captain, F. Peters; First Lieutenant, Henry Fassbinder; Second Lieutenant, Jacob Huth.

SHARPSHOOTER.—Captain F. Christen.

FUSILIERS NO. 1.—Captain, F. Sievers; First Lieutenant, H. Gerdes.

FUSILIERS NO. 2.—Second Lieut., Henry Waflbrech.

LAFAYETTE GUARDS.

Capt. F. Kœnig; First Lieutenant. G. Hollenbach, Second Lieutenant, A. Frideback.

JEFFERSON GUARDS.—Captain, F. Wollrath; Second Lieut., G. Lehman,

BATALLION CHASSEURS A PIED DE LA LOUISIANE.—Major —— ——

First Company.—Captain, Henry St. Paul; First Lieutenant, Oscar Aleix; Second Lieutenant, Nemours Lauve.

Second Company.—Captain, Simeon Meilleur; First Lieut., Isidore Esclapon; Second Lieutenant, Raphael Painpare.

FIRST BRIGADE.

Brigadier General, E. L. Tracy, Commanding; Major Thomas F. Walker, Brigade Inspector; Captain R. Hooper, Aid; Captain I. J. Daniels, Aid; Captain J. G. McLearn, Aid; Captain J. F. Caldwell, Aid.

WASHINGTON ARTILLERY.

Capt. J. B. Walton; Senior First Lieutenant, O. Voorhies; Junior First Lieutenant, Theo. A. James, Second Lieutenant, R. Bannister.

WASHINGTON REGIMENT.—Major John Cavanaugh.

LOUISIANA GREYS.—Capt., Edmund Kennedy; First Lieut., A. D. Caulfield.

REGIMENT NATIONAL GUARDS.—Colonel, H. Forno; Major, G. Stith.

COMPANY C., NATIONAL GUARDS.

Captain, Charles D. Drew; First Lieutenant, J. P. Nesbit.

CITY GUARDS.—Captain, W. T. Dean; First Lieutenant, C. R. Fagot.

ORLEANS RIFLE GUARDS.

Captain, John A. Jacques; First Lieutenant, Erastus Stevens.

CONTINENTAL GUARDS.—Capt. George Clark; Second Lieut., A. W. Merriam.

MISSISSIPPI RIFLES NO. 2.

Captain, F. Camerden; First Lieutenant, Chas. C. Campbell: Second Lieut. Lea F. Bakewell.

FIRST REGIMENT.

First Brigade.—Colonel Louis Lay.

SECOND REGIMENT.—Colonel J. J. Daniels.

FOUTH REGIMENT.—Colonel John Price.

EIGHTH REGIMENT.

Colonel, Chas. De Choiseul; Lieutenant Colonel, James De Baum.

NINTH REGIMENT.—Colonel, R. Hooper; Lieut. Colonel, C. C. Miller.

SECOND BRIGADE.

Brigadier General, D. Cronan ; Major, John Stroud, Brigade Inspector.

FOURTH REGIMENT.

Colonel, Daniel Edwards; Lieut. Colonel, Samuel McBurney ; Major, Chas. J. Murphy.

SECOND DIVISION.

Major General, R. C. Camp.

FIRST BRIGADE.—Brigadier General, R. C. Martin.

PARISH ST. CHARLES REGIMENT.

Colonel, Ezra Davis ; Lieut. Colonel, Ad. Rost, Jr.

PARISH ST. JAMES REGIMENT.

Company Chasseurs de St. Jacques.—Captain, Alfred Roman ; First Lieutenant. Camille Mire ; Second Lieut. K. Gaudet ; Cornet, Florent Fortier.

Company Chasseurs St. Michel.—Captain, Narcisse Landry, Jr. ; First Lieutenant. Francis L. Haydel ; Second Lieutenant, Emile Jacobs ; Cornet, Nicholle Tecle,

ASCENSION REGIMENT.—Colonel, John S. Minor.

DONALDSONVILLE ARTILLERY.

Captain, V. Maurin ; Senior First Lieutenant, J. C. Dannequin ; Junior First Lieutenant, Villeor Dugas ; Senior Second Lieutenant, L. D. Nicholls ; Junior Second Lieutenant, Lestang Fortier.

LAFOURCHE REGIMENT.

Company Lafourche Dragoons—Captain, R. G. Darden ; First Lieutenant. Ed. Cross ; Second Lieutenant, John A. Collins ; Cornet, M. King.

SECOND BRIGADE.—Brigadier General, C. N. Rowley.

TERREBONNE REGIMENT.

Colonel, Albert G. Cage ; Lieutenant Colonel, F. S. Goode ; Major, James Daspit.

HOUMA RIFLES.

Captain, Joseph Aycock ; First Lieutenant, V. A. Righter ; Second Lieutenant, Sulakoski.

ST. MARY REGIMENT.

Colonel, A. L. Tucker ; Lieutenant-Colonel, H. C. Wilson ; Major, R. N. McMillan.

TECHE GUARDS.

Captain, W. F. Haiflegh ; First Lieutenant, Louis F. Smith ; Second Lieut., Newman Trowbridge.

THIRD DIVISION.

Major General, George W. Munday.

FIRST BRIGADE.—Brigadier General, W. E. Walker.

SECOND BRIGADE.—Brigadier General, R. Barrow.

PARISH EAST FELICIANA REGIMENT.—Colonel, Preston Pond.

EAST BATON ROUGE REGIMENT.

Colonel, Louis Hébert; Lieutenant Colonel, F. M. Kent.

EAST BATON ROUGE DRAGOONS.

Captain, H. M. Pierce; First Lieutenant, Chas. Chenette; Second Lieutenant, Thomas Gilbert.

PELICAN RIFLES.

Captain, W. F. Tunnard; First Lieutenant, H. B. Monteith; Second Lieut., Ernest Gourier.

COMPANY C.—Captain L. J. Freemaux.

FOURTH DIVISION.

Major General, L. G. De Russey; Lieut. Colonel, Oscar Chaler, Paymaster; Major F. Johnson, Surgeon; Major W. H. Levy, Aid.

FIRST BRIGADE.

Brigadier General, P. Keary; Captain D. C. Goodman, Aid.

PARISH ST. LANDRY REGIMENT.

Colonel, A. M. Perrault; Lieut. Colonel, André Meynier; Major, Lewis Stagg.

OPELOUSAS RIFLES.

Captain, J. D. Israel; Second Lieutenant, J. J. Beauchamp.

SECOND BRIGADE.—Brigadier General, Alfred Mouton.

PARISH RAPIDES REGIMENT.

Colonel, B. F. Fulton; Lieutenant Colonel, A. N. Ogden; Major, Louis Stafford.

PARISH NATCHITOCHES REGIMENT.

Colonel, Thomas Herzog; Lieutenant Colonel, Thomas C. Hunt; Major, Felix Metoyer.

FIFTH DIVISION.

Major General, Jacob Humble; Major Newton Guice, Aid.

FIRST BRIGADE.

Brigadier General, F. A. F. Harper; Major G. W. Hendrick, Brigade Inspector.

TENSAS REGIMENT.—Colonel, L. V. Reeves.

PARISH FRANKLIN REGIMENT.

Colonel, Asa Hawthorn; Lieutenant Colonel, Isaac Doyal.

SECOND BRIGADE.—Brigadier General, Felix Lewis.

PARISH CLAIBORNE REGIMENT.

Colonel, James W. Berry; Lieutenant Colonel, John W. Hays; Major, James Duke.

PARISH BOSSIER REGIMENT.

Colonel, E. W. Herring; Lieutenant Colonel, Austin Miller; Major, David J. Elder.

ANNUAL REPORT MADE NOVEMBER 22, 1861.

CONDENSED MEMORANDA.

Feb. 5, 1861. Two regiments of regulars of the State army organized.

March 13. Transfer made of these to Provisional Army of the Confederate States. Artillery stationed in the State forts : infantry at Pensacola. The Colonel of the latter, A. H. Gladden, made Brigadier General, and succeeded by Col. Daniel W. Adams. The regiment was suddenly called to Pensacola.

Dec. 14, 1861. Volunteer companies ordered to organize into regiments. To complete the companies, it became necessary to call upon volunteers. Five companies tendered their services and were accepted: The Orleans Cadets, of New Orleans, Captain C. D. Dreux. The Louisiana Guards, of New Orleans, Captain S. M. Todd. The Crescent Rifles, of New Orleans, Captain S. H. Fisk. The Grivot Guards, of Lafourche, Captain V. G. Rightor. The Shreveport Greys, of Caddo, Captain J. H. Beard. They were with the regiment stationed at Warrington, up to June last, when the regiment, having received its complement of regular companies, these companies were relieved from duty at Warrington. They formed themselves into a special battalion, under the command of Lieut. Colonel Charles D. Dreux, and Major V. H. Rightor, and were ordered to Yorktown, Virginia. Lieutenant Colonel Dreux was killed whilst in the performance of his duties, and the battalion is now under the command of Lieut. Colonel V. H. Rightor.

18th of April, 1861 requisition from the Secretary of War, for three thousand infantry for twelve months service, received.

As soon as this made its appearance, in all parts of the State companies were organizing and tendering their services in less than five days, the number of troops offering exceeded five thousand.

This requisition did not state whether they were to be received by companies, battalions or regiments; a subsequent requisition for 5000 additional troops, received on the 21st April, 1861, gave the authority to organize them into battalions and regiments.

The troops were arriving rapidly; it was found expedient to establish a camp in the neighborhood of the City, and by order No. 188, issued on the 29th April, 1861, Camp Walker was established on the Metaire Course, under the command of Brigadier General E. L. Tracy, first Division Louisiana Militia, detailed for that purpose. The number of troops increasing, the fear of disease in camps, and owing to the scarcity of water, it was deemed advisable to transfer the camp to Tangipahoa, on the Jackson Railroad. This camp was called camp Moore.

The 1st Regiment Louisiana Volunteers was organized on the 25th of April by the election of Albert G. Blanchard as Colonel, Wm. G. Vincent Lieutenant; Colonel, and Wm. R. Shiver as Major, and transferred to the Confederate States on the 29th April and ordered to Virginia. Col. Blanchard has since been appointed Brigadier General in the Confederate Army, and Lieutenant-Colonel Vincent elected Colonel of the Regiment.

The 2d Regiment was organized with Lewis G. DeRussy as Colonel, John W. Young as Lieutenant-Colonel, and J. T. Norwood as Major, mustered into the service on the 11th May, 1861, and ordered to Virginia. Colonel DeRussy having resigned, Captain Wm. M. Levy was elected to fill the vacancy.

The 3d Regiment organized with Lewis Hebert as Colonel, S. M. Hyams as Lieutenant-Colonel, and W. F. Tunnard as Major; was mustered into service on 11th May, ordered to Arkansas, and from thence to Missouri. It participated in the battle of Oak Hill, performing deeds of valor.

The 4th Regiment organized with R. J. Barrow as Colonel, H. W. Allen as Lieutenant-Colonel, and S. E. Hunter as Major.

The 5th Regiment organized with Theo. G. Hunt Colonel, Henry Forno as Lieutenant-Colonel, and W. T. Dean Major.

At this period, whilst other regiments were in process of organization, the companies having mustered into the State service, to be transferred to the Confederate States, for the period of twelve months, under the Proclamations, after the transfer of the 3d Regiment, a communication from the War Department was received, declining to accept any more regiments unless for the term of the war. To this communication the governor earnestly protested, and urged upon the Secretary of War the necessity of accepting the regiments already organized for twelve months service, but with no success.

This act of the Secretary of War created considerable excitement both at the camp and in the country. The men who had volunteered, sacrificing their all, believed they were being trifled with, and had the effect of disorganizing the whole system for awhile.

After some difficulty, the 4th Regiment was accepted for the twelve months service, and was transferred on the 25th May, 1861. All the influence that could be brought to bear upon the War Department was exercised by your Excellency to obtain the acceptance of the 5th Regiment, and all the corps at Camp Moore, for the twelve months service, but with no success. Still entertaining hopes that the Secretary of War would reflect upon the injury about to be inflicted upon the troops, by not accepting their services except for the war term, would reverse and order them to be received, as originally mustered in, for twelve months, granted a delay in which the companies were to decide whether they would volunteer for the war or be disbanded. This delay was extended to the 25th May. This delay having expired, and the companies still refusing to muster in for the term of the war, were disbanded. On the 26th May, the governor received a dispatch from the War Department announcing the fact that the regiments and companies would be accepted for the twelve months term. It was received at a late hour—the morning train of the Jackson Railroad had left. Upon application to Capt. J. S. Williams, Superintendent of the road, he kindly offered his services to convey, by an express train, to Camp Moore, the orders countermanding the disbanding of the troops, but it was too late, the mischief had been done. A large number of companies had been disbanded, and were on their way home.

Shortly after it was ascertained that twelve months troops would be received, both in the country and city, the organization recommenced with redoubled vigor. The 5th Regiment, which had received a check, completed its organization, and was mustered into service on the 25th May, 1861, and was immediately ordered to Virginia.

The 6th Regiment, organized with I. G. Seymour as Colonel, Louis Lay as Lieutenant-Colonel, and S. S. James as Major, was mustered into service on the 4th June, 1861, and ordered to Virginia.

The 7th Regiment, organized with Harry T. Hays as Colonel, Charles De Choiseul as Lieutenant-Colonel, and D. H. Penn, Major, was mustered into service on the 5th June, 1861, and ordered to Virginia.

The 8th Regiment, organized with Henry B. Kelly as Colonel, F. T. Nicholls as Lieutenant-Colonel, and J. B. Prados as Major, was mustered into service on the 15th June.

The 6th, 7th and 8th Regiments were engaged in the memorable battles of Bull Run on the 18th, and of Manassas on the 21st July, 1861, and rendered important service.

The 9th Regiment, organized with Richard Taylor as Colonel, E. G. Randolph as Lieutenant-Colonel, and N. J. Walker, Major, was mustered into service on the 6th July, 1861, and ordered to Virginia.

The 10th Regiment, organized with Mandeville Marigny as Colonel, J. C. Denis as Lieutenant-Colonel, and Felix Du Monteil as Major, was mustered into service on the 22d July, 1861, and ordered to Virginia.

The 11th Regiment, organized with S. F. Marks as Colonel, Robert H. Barrow as Lieutenant-Colonel, and E. G. W. Butler as Major, was mustered into service on the 18th August, 1861, and ordered to Columbus, Kentucky. This regiment was in the battle of Belmont, and was mainly instrumental in gaining the victory. Major Butler fell while gallantly leading his men.

The 12th Regiment, organized with Thomas M. Scott as Colonel, Wade Hough as Lieutenant-Colonel, and John C. Nott as Major, was mustered into service on the 13th August, 1861, and ordered to Columbus, Kentucky.

The 13th Regiment, organized with R. L. Gibson as Colonel, Aristide Gerard as Lieutenant-Colonel, and A. P. Avegno as Major—transferred to the Confederate service on the 9th September, 1861, stationed for a long time at the fortifications below the city—and on the 22d November was ordered to Columbus.

The 14th and 15th Regiments, were so designated by the War Department, and are composed of the troops known as the Polish Brigade. They were not mustered into service of the State and transferred to the Confederate States, and consequently I have no record of the names of the companies or officers, or number of men composing it.

The 16th Regiment was organized with Preston Pond, Jr., as Colonel, Enoch Mason as Lieutenant-Colonel, and Daniel Gober as Major; was mustered into Confederate service on the 29th September, 1861.

The 17th Regiment, organized with S. S. Heard as Colonel, Charles Jones as Lieutenant-Colonel, and R. B. Jones as Major, mustered into the Confederate service on the 29th September, 1861, and is now at Camp Moore.

The 18th Regiment, organized with Alfred Mouton as Colonel, Alfred Roman as Lieutenant-Colonel, and Louis Bush as Major, was mustered into Confederate service on the 5th October, 1861, and is stationed above Carrollton.

The 19th Regiment, organized with B. L. Hodge as Colonel, D. M. Hollingsworth as Lieutenant-Colonel, and ——— Major, and is stationed at Camp Moore.

Five companies in May last organized as a special battalion with C. R. Wheat as Major, was accepted and mustered into service on 6th June, 1861, and ordered to Virginia. This battalion was in the battle of Manassas, and is reported as having performed deeds of valor.

The foregoing regiments and battalions have been fully armed and equipped.

The regiments and battalions mustered into the State service and transferred to the Confederacy, with the names of the companies, the parishes from which they come, the names of the officers and number of men of each company, amounted to a total of 19,152 men.

The President having the appointment of Surgeons and Quartermasters, the names of these do not figure therein. The names of some officers of companies do not appear on the list owing to the fact that changes being made by promotions or otherwise, the officers to fill the vacancies were elected after the transfer to the Confederate States.

On the 19th April, 1861, the Secretary of War made a requisition for the 1st Company Louisiana Foot Rifles, under command of Capt. Henry St. Paul.

The parishes bordering on the Gulf coast were unprotected, and the enemy's fleet had been committing depredations, and threatening attack. Maj. Gen. Twiggs, commanding the Department, deemed it necessary to call for troops, to be stationed at the forts and at various points, so as to guard and protect the coast. Eighteen companies transferred for that purpose.

Companies have been mustered for service within the State. Camp of Instruction near Carrollton, on the Carrollton Railroad, under the command of Brigadier General C. A. Labuzan.

A recapitulation of the forces as above stated shows:

Regiment of Artillery (Regulars.)	740
do. " Infantry "	1,033
1st, 2d, 3d, 4th, 5th, 6th, 7th, 8th, 9th, 10th, 11th, 12th, 13th, 16th, 17th, 18th and 19th, Regiments of Louisiana Volunteers	14,949
Wheat's Battalion	415

Dreux's Battalion		480
14 Companies transferred to the Confederate service, for State service		1,231
4 Companies of Orleans Artillery		304
Number of troops in service of the Confederate States		19,152
13 Companies for service within the State, at Camp Lewis		1,050
Total number of troops thus far organized by the State		20,202
1 Company Orleans Chasseurs	95	
Soulakouski's Regiment, (14th Regiment.)	850	
Lieut. Col. Bradford's Regiment, (15th Regiment.)	450	
Point Coupee Light Artillery	90	
Washington Artillery	320	
Crescent Blues	80	
Donaldsonville Artillery	85	
Marion Infantry	129	
Watson's Artillery	100	
Carroll Guards	76	
Jackson Regiment	450	
Zouaves	650	3,375
Force in the field from Louisiana, Nov. 22d, 1861		23,577

To prevent trafficking between the enemies fleet and a large number of small boats and luggers trading in the various bays, bayous, lakes, etc., in the parishes bordering on the sea-shore, order issued to arrest all offenders 12th June. Captain A. O. Murphy appointed and placed in charge of the schooner Antonio with full authority to arrest all persons dealing with the enemy, or persons of a suspicious character found within the limits of Barrell Keys and Texas, and who could not prove themselves loyal to the government

Similar authority given to Captain R. G. Darden, of Thibodaux, and Captain Murphy, who made some important arrests.

14th of January, 1861, an order issued for the organization of the militia throughout the State; considerable opposition made thereto,—officers met with serious difficulties in compelling attendance to drills and obedience to their orders, and organization turned into a farce. In many parishes no objections raised, and militia organized.

September 28th, 1861—stringent order issued from Gov. Moore, regulating, organizing and drilling militia. Black List ordered for shirkers and permanent Court Martial for trial of military offences. Drills ordered after 3 o'clock twice a week.

First Division returns		30,499
Confederate Guards		752
Total		31,251
The following parishes have made their returns, to-wit:		
Parish of Iberville	634	
" Natchitoches	1,031	
" Livingston	754	
" St. Tammany	442	
" St. Charles	210	
" Washington	441	
" Carroll	691	
" East Baton Rouge	1,200	
" East Feliciana	495	5,898

17th November, 1861, order issued for a review of all the volunteer and regular militia of the 1st Division, under command of Major General John L. Lewis.

RELATIVE TO STATE TROOPS. 243

The troops assembled on Canal street, on Saturday the 23d November, 1861, were passed in review by Gov. Moore, accompanied by Major General M. Lovell, commanding Department No. 1 C. S. A., Brigadier General Ruggles, C. S. A., and staffs. This assemblage was the largest and most imposing that had as yet taken place. The force out on that occasion numbered 24,551; absent 6402.

REGIMENT OF ARTILLERY.

Colonel—P. O.Hebert, (appointed Brigadier General C. S. A., 14 August, 1861.)
Lieut. Colonel—C. A. Fuller, (promoted to Colonel, vice P. O. Hebert, 14th August, 1861.)
Major—D. Beltzhoover, (promoted to Lieutenant Colonel, vice Fuller, 14th August, 1861.)
Captains—H. A. Clinch, (promoted to Major, vice Beltzhoover, 14th August, 1861;) F. B. Brand; J. B. Anderson; Ed. Higgins; W. C. Capers; R. L. Gibson, (elected Colonel of 13th Regiment Louisiana Volunteers;) E. W. Rawle; M. T. Squires; R. C. Bond; W. B. Robertson; J. B. Grayson, Jr., (promotion from 1st Lieutenant; J. B. Lamon, (promoted from 1st Lieutenant, 6th September, 1861.)
First Lieutenants—J. B. Grayson, Jr., (promoted to Captain, vice Church, Major;) J. H. Lamon, (promoted to Captain, vice Gibson, elected Colonel) R. J. Bruce; E. G. Butler; L. P. Haynes; E. W. Baylor; A. V. Ogden; J. H. Stith; W. H. Holmes, resigned 24th June, 1861; Carlton Hunt; Wm. C. Pinckney; Claude Gibson; H. W. Fowler; W. C. Ellis; L. V. Taylor; J. M. Johnson, resigned; G. R. Wilson; R. Agar; C. A. Conrad; J. F. Fuller; Jno. G. Eustis, rank 13th July, 1861; Bev. C. Kennedy; J. W. Gaines, rank 14th August, 1861; Jno. G. Devereux, rank 6th September, 1861.
Second Lieutenants—John G. Eustis, promoted to 1st Lieutenant, 13th July, 1861; Bev. C. Kennedy, promoted to 1st Lieutenant; R. M. Hewitt, resigned, June 9th, 1861; J. W. Gaines, promoted to 1st Lieutenant; C. H. Sanford; J. G. Devereux, promoted to 1st Lieutenant; G. M. Tureaud, resigned; W. M. Bridges; B. M. Harrod; C. N. Morse; George Crane, appointed 5th July, 1861; A. J. Quigley, appointed 5th July, 1861; Francis McManus, appointed 5th July, 1861; Richard Charles Cammack, appointed 13th July, 1861; Wm. Bullitt Jones, appointed 27th Aug., 1861; Wm. Taylor Mumford, appointed 27th August, 1861.

REGIMENT OF INFANTRY.

Colonel—A. H. Gladden, appointed Brigadier General C. S. A.
Lieut. Colonel—D. Adams, promoted to Colonel, vice Gladden.
Major—C. M. Bradford, resigned, 23d July, 1861.
Captains—J. A. Jacques; promoted to Major, vice Bradford, resigned, thence to Lieut. Colonel, vice Adams; F. H. Farrar, promoted to Major, vice J. A. Jacques; Wm. H. Scott; F. M. Kent; James Strawbridge; J. T. Wheat; Thos. Overton, resigned, 27th May, 1861, S. S. Batchelor; Douglas West; C. A. Taylor; P. H. Thompson; J. H. Trevezant, appointed 23d July, 1861; Taylor Beatty, appointed 30th September, 1861.
First Lieutenants—P. H Thompson, promoted to Captain, 1st June, 1861; J. S. Hyams, resigned; J. H. Trevezant, promoted to Captain, 23d July, 1861; Taylor Beatty, promoted to Captain, 30th September, 1861; James Cooper; E. Preston; W. H. Sparks; J. W. Stringfellow; W. N. Starke, B. C. Cenas; Thomas Butler. promoted from 2d Lieutenant, 21st May, 1861; C. H. Tew, promoted from 2d Lieutenant, 1st June, 1861; Louis Guion, promoted from 2d Lieutenant, 23d July, 1861; W. A. Reid, promoted from 2d Lieutenant, 30th September, 1861.
Second Lieutenants—Thos Butler, promoted to 1st Lieutenant, 21st May, 1861; C. H. Tew, promoted to 1st Lieutenant, 1st June, 1861; L. Guion, promoted to 1st Lieutenant, 23d August, 1861; W. A. Reid, promoted to 1st Lieutenant, 30th

September, 1861; C. R. Benton; L. N. Olivier; R. C. Kennedy; Wm. Quirk; G. W. Simpson; G. W. Mader; R. Marston; James Goode; J. C. Stafford; A. Kent; E. Eastman, elected Captain in Louisiana Volunteers; S. S. Semmes ι James Nelson; John E. Austin, resigned, July 25th, 1861; T. W. Behan; G. L. Bond; Louis West, appointed 21st May, 1861; M. Caruthers Gladden, appointed 1st June, 1861; Paul Wm. Barbarin, appointed 30th June, 1861; Wm Paul Grivot; appointed 23d August 1861; Alfred Joshua Lewis, appointed 21st October, 1861; John C. Golden, appointed 21st October, 1861.

FIRST REGIMENT OF LOUISIANA VOLUNTEERS.

A. G. Blanchard, Colonel; W. G. Vincent, Lieut.-Colonel; W. R. Shivers, Major.

Montgomery Guards.—Michael Nolan, Captain; M. B. Gilmore, First Lieut.; Wm. Hart, Second Lieut.; Sam. McLelland, Jr. Second Lieut.

Louisiana Guards Co. B.—C. E. Girardey, Captain; Edgar Daquin, First Lieut.; S. McC. Montgomery, Second Lieut.; V. Murphy, Jr. Second Lieut.

Davis Guards.—Ben. W. Anderson, Captain; Robt. L. Vanortern, First Lieut.; J. E. Burthe, Second Lieut.; A. G. Duncan, Jr. Second Lieut.

Louisiana Guards, Co. C.—Frank Rawle, Captain; H. W. Montgomery, First Lieut.; R. H. Kenna, Second Lieut.; P. W. Semmes, Jr. Second Lieut.

Caddo Rifles.—C. Dailee, Captain; C. W. Lewis, First Lieut.; J. Kashmore, Second Lieut.; A. Brannon, Jr. Second Lieut.

Orleans Light Guards, Co. A.—Chas. E. Cormien, Captain; E. Cucullu, First Lieut.; H. C. Parker, Jr. Second Lieut.

Orleans Light Guards, Co. B.—T. M. Dean, Captain; E. D. Willet, First Lieut.; A. Blaffer, Second Lieut.; E. A. Chadwick, Jr. Second Lieut.

Orleans Light Guards, Co. C.—Chas. N. Frost, Captain; Sam. R. Harrison, First Lieut.; W. C. Tavener, Second Lieut.; A. A. Cummings, Jr. Second Lieut.

Orleans Light Guards, Co. D.—P. O'Rourke, Captain; W. L. Randall, First Lieut.; Hortaire Audry, Second Lieut.; J. J. Molaire, Jr. Second Lieut.

Emmet Guards.—James Nelligan, Captain; Geo. M. Morgan, First Lieut.; A. A. Wilkins, Second Lieut.; P. Bedell, Jr. Second Lieut.

SECOND REGIMENT OF LOUISIANA VOLUNTEERS.

Louis G. De Russy, Colonel; John Young, Lieut.-Colonel; J. T. Norwood. Major.

Pelican Greys—A. H. Martin, Captain; E. B. Stubbs, First Lieut.; S. D. Mc Enery, Second Lieut.; H. B. Holmes, Jr. Second Lieut.

Vienna Rifles—H. W. Perrin, Captain; J. J. Neilson, First Lieut.; J. Henry, Second Lieut., A. G. Cobb, Jr. Second Lieut.

Moore Guards—Jno. Kelso, Captain; W. A. Croghan, First Lieut.; W. L. Ridge, Second Lieut.; J. Delahauty, Jr. Second Lieut.

Vernon Guards—Oscar M. Watkins, Captain; Nat. Rives, First Lieut.; E. Davis, Second Lieut.; H. H. Stevens, Jr. Second Lieut.

Claiborne Guards—Jno. W. Andrews, Captain; J. B. Parham, First Lieut.; Isaac L. Leonard, Second Lieut.; Jno. L. Young, Jr. Second Lieut.

Floyd Guards—Jno. W. Dunn, Captain; G. W. Dougherty, First Lieut.; D. W. Kelly, Second Lieut.: W. A. Draughton, Jr. Second Lieut.

Greenwood Guards—Wm. Flournoy, Captain; Alfred Flournoy, Jr., First Lieut.; S. D. Waddell, Second Lieut.; Lucien Flournoy, Jr. Second Lieut.

Lecompte Guards—Wm. M. Levy, Captain; Ross E. Burke, First Lieut.; J. F. Scarborough, Second Lieut.; S. B. Robertson, Jr. Second Lieut.

Atchafalaya Guards—R. M. Boone, Captain; John J. McRae, First Lieut., J. T. Norwood, Second Lieut.; T. P. Harmanson, Jr. Second Lieut.

Pelican Rifles—Jno. M. Williams, Captain; R. W. Ashton, First Lieut.; L. C. Furmau, Second Lieut.; J. S. Ashton, Jr. Second Lieut.

THIRD REGIMENT OF LOUISIANA VOLUNTEERS.

Louis Hebert, Colonel; Sam'l M. Hyams, Lieut.-Colonel Wm. F. Tunnard, Major.
Pelican Rifles—J. B. Viglini, Captain; John B. Irving, First Lieut.; F. D. Tunnard, Second Lieut.; Felix Brunot, Jr. Second Lieut.
Pelican Rangers No. 1—Winter W. Breazeale, Captain; W. Overton Breazeale, First Lieut.; Geo. Halloway, Second Lieut.; L. Caspri, Jr. Second Lieut.
Pelican Rangers No. 2—J. D. Blair, Captain; S. D. Russell, First Lieut.; Wm. E. Russell, Second Lieut.; J. M. Hyams, Jr., Jr. Second Lieut.
Caldwell Guards—W. L. Gunnell, Captain; J. T. Evans, First Lieut.; L. B. Fluitt, Second Lieut.; Thos. J. Humble, Jr. Second Lieut.
Iberville Greys—C. A. Brusle, Captain; Thos C. Brown, First Lieut.; Thos. G. Stringer, Second Lieut.; T. R. Verbois, Jr. Second Lieut.
Winn Rifles—D. Pierson, Captain; Asa Emanuel, First Lieut.; Wm. Strother, Second Lieut.; W. C. Luny, Jr. Second Lieut.
Morehouse Fencibles—J. F. Harris, Captain; P. C. Bringham, First Lieut.; P. Brooks, Second Lieut.; W. D. Bringham, Jr. Second Lieut.
Morehouse Guards—R. M. Hinson, Captain; W. S. Hall. First Lieut.; D. C. Morgan, Second Lieut.; J. H. Bringham, Jr. Second Lieut.
Shreveport Rangers—J. B. Gilmer, Captain; W. A. Lacy, First Lieut.; Oscar J. Wells, Second Lieut.; A. Wall Jewell, Jr. Second Lieut.
Monticello Rifles—John S. Richards, Captain; W. D. Hardeman, First Lieut.; W. C. Corbin, Second Lieut.; C. A. Hearick, Jr. Second Lieut.

FOURTH REGIMENT OF LOUISIANA VOLUNTEERS.

Robert I. Barrow, Colonel; H. W. Allen, Lieut.-Colonel; S. E. Hunter, Major C. Becher, Adjutant.
Beaver Creek Rifles—J. H. Wingfield, Captain; R. M. Amaker, First Lieut.; R. H. Turnbull, Second Lieut.; R. Y. Burton, Jr. Second Lieut.
St. Helena Rifles—J. B. Taylor, Captain; H. M. Carter, First Lieut.; J. B Corkeran, Second Lieut.; Thos. Spiller, Jr. Second Lieut.
Hunter Rifles, Co. A—E J. Pullen, Captain; Geo. A. Neafus, First Lieu t.; N B. Barfield, Second Lieut.; Henry Marston, Jr., Jr. Second Lieut.
Hunter Rifles, Co. B—John T. Hilliard, Captain; J. P. Adams, First Lieut.; E. C. Holmes, Second Lieut.; F. F. Huston, Jr. Second Lieut.
West Feliciana Rifles—Chas. E. Toorean, Captain; J. S. Wooster, First Lieut.; Wm. Hearsy, Second Lieut.; James Read, Jr. Second Lieut.
Lafourche Guards—Thos. E. Vick, Captain; C. Belcher, First Lieut.; H. Dansereau, Second Lieut.; John S. Billieu, Jr. Second Lieut.
W. B'n Ro'e Tirailleurs—F. A. Williams, Captain; J. A. Levesque, First Lieut., tA. J. Bird, Second Lieut.; B. Landry, Jr. Second Lieut.
Delta Rifles—H. M. Favrot, Captain; O. M. Leblanc, First Lieut.; L. S. Hereford, Second Lieut.; N. W. Pope, Jr. Second Lieut.
National Guards—H. A. Richman, Captain; J. S. Woolf, First Lieut.; A. Blum. Second Lieut.; Ed. Riedel, Jr. Second Lieut.
Lake Providence Cadets—F. V. Whicher, Captain; W. F. Pennington, First Lieut.; D. C. Jenkins, Second Lieut.; C. R. Purdy, Jr. Second Lieut.

FIFTH REGIMENT OF LOUISIANA VOLUNTEERS.

Theodore G. Hunt, Colonel; Henry Forno, Lieut.-Colonel; W. T. Dean, Major; J. B. Norris, Adjutant.
Bienville Guards—Mark L. Moore, Captain; Jas. M. Coffee, First Lieut.; Thos. J. Williams, Second Lieut.; James C. Wilson, Jr. Second Lieut.
Orleans Cadets—Chas. Hobday, Captain; Alex. Hart, First Lieut.; J. T. Beach Second Lieut.; J. B. Norris, Jr. Second Lieut.

La. Swamp Rangers—E. J. Jones, Captain; C. H. Allen, First Lieut.; A. A. Bredow. Second Lieut.; F. Wary, Jr. Second Lieut.
Orleans Southrons—O. F. Peck, Captain; Fred. Richardson, First Lieut.; N. A. Caulfield, Second Lieut.; D. M. Sory, Jr. Second Lieut.
Crescent City Guards—John A. Hall, Captain; R. G. Wingate, First Lieut.; W. W. Marsh, Second Lieut.; L. Sawyer, Jr. Second Lient.
Perret Guards—Arthur Connor, Captain; Rufus A. Hunt, First Lieut.; Thos. F. Evans, Second Lieut.; A. J. Laughlin, Jr. Second Lieut.
Chalmette Guards—A. E. Shaw, Captain; Alex. Riouffé, First Lieut.; John McGurk, Second Lieut.; W. H. Pendall, Jr. Second Lieut.
Carondelet Invincibles—Bruce Menger, Captain; J. S. Charles, First Lieut.; Geo. F. White, Second Lieut.; J. H. Haworth, Jr. Second Lieut.
DeSoto Rifles—W. B. Koontz, Captain; Geo. Seymour, First Lieut.; W. S. E. Sevey, Second Lieut.; A. H. Jones, Jr. Second Lieut.
Monroe Guards—Thos. Dolan, Captain; T. H. Biscoe, First Lieut.; Geo. H. Hinchey, Second Lieut.; R. B. Watkins, Jr. Second Lieut.

SIXTH REGIMENT OF LOUISIANA VOLUNTEERS.

I. G. Seymour, Colonel; Louis Lay, Lieut.-Colonel; S. L. James, Major.
Irish Brigade, Co. A—James Hanlon, Captain; B. Walsh, First Lieut.; J. B. Bressman, Second Lieut.; W. C. Quirk, Jr. Second Lieut.
Irish Brigade, Co. B—Wm. Monahan, Captain; Michael O'Connor, First Lieut.; James O. Martin, Second Lieut.; John Orr, Jr. Second Lieut.
Mercer Guards—Thos. F. Walker, Captain; Robert Lynne, First Lieut.; Geo. M. Brisbin, Second Lieut.; John G. Rivera, Jr. Second Lieut.
Violet Guards—W. H. Manning, Captain; Geo. P. King, First Lieut.; Sam. O. Kirk, Second Lieut.; Edward Flood, Jr. Second Lieut.
St. Landry Light Guards—Nat. Offut, Captain; H. Hickman, First Lieut.; H. B. Ritchie, Second Lieut.; J. D. McCawley, Jr. Second Lieut.
Orleans Rifles—Thos. F. Fisher, Captain; W. H. Butrick, First Lieut; Lewis Graham, Second Lieut.; C. M. Pilcher, Jr. Second Lieut.
Tensas Rifles—Chas. B. Tenney, Captain; David F. Buckner, First Lieut.; T. P. Farrar, Jr., Second Lieut.; Isaac A. Reed, Jr. Second Lieut.
Pemberton Rangers—Isaac A. Smith, Captain; Geo. W. Christy, First Lieut.; Frank Clarke, Second Lieut.; W. P. Brewer, Jr. Second Lieut.
Union and Sabine Rifles—Arthur McArthur, Captain; D. M. Calliway, First Lieut.; J. F. Phillips, Second Lieut.; J. F. Smith, Jr. Second Lieut.
Calhoun Guards—Henry Strong, Captain; Thos. O'Neil, First Lieut.; J. Hogan, Second Lieut.; G. J. Summers, Jr. Second Lieut.

SEVENTH REGIMENT OF LOUISIANA VOLUNTEERS.

Harry T. Hays, Colonel; Chas. De Choiseul, Lieut.-Colonel; D. B. Penn, Major.
American Rifles—W. D. Rickarby, Captain; Sam. Flower, First Lieut.; Samuel Brewer, Second Lieut.; Jno. Rowan, Jr. Second Lieut.
Livingston Rifles—T. M. Terry, Captain; A. G. Tucker, First Lieut.; Wm. Patterson, Second Lieut.; W. F. Ogden, Jr. Second Lieut.
Virginia Guards—Robert Scott, Captain; H. Doussan, First Lieut.; P. Grandpre, Second Lieut.; L. H. Malarshé, Jr. Second Lieut.
Virginia Blues—D. A Wilson, Jr., Captain; C. E. Bellinger, First Lieut.; H. C. Thompson, Second Lieut.; E. A. Brown, Jr. Second Lieut.
Sarsfield Rangers—J. Marc Wilson, Captain; West Steever; First Lieut.; Henry Carthy, Second Lieut.; T. G. Morgan, Jr., Jr. Second Lieut.
Crescent Rifles, Co. B—G. T. Jett, Captain; W. P. Harper, First Lieut.; Andrew E. Knox, Second Lieut.; Henry Grimshaw, Jr. Second Lieut.

RELATIVE TO STATE TROOPS. 247

Crescent Rifles, Co. C—S. H. Gilman, Captain; W. C. Driver, First Lieut. ; J. H. Dawson, Second Lieut.; Conrad Green, Jr. Second Lieut.
Coutinental Guards—George Clark, Captain; A. W. Merriam, First Lieut.; E. McFarlane, Second Lieut.; Aaron Davis, Jr. Second Lieut.
Baton Rouge Fencibles—Andrew S. Herron, Captain, J. Duncan Stuart, First Lieut.; Oscar H. Foreman, Second Lieut.; Jno. H. New, Jr. Second Lieut.
Irish Volunteers—W. R. Ratliff, Captain; L. N. Hewit, First Lieut.; S. Reynaud, Second Lieut.; Thos. Kenegan, Jr. Second Lieut.

EIGHTH REGIMENT OF LOUISIANA VOLUNTEERS.

H. B. Kelly, Colonel; F. T. Nicholls, Lieut.-Colonel; J. B. Prados, Major.
Rapides Invincibles—Lee Crandell, Captain; Henry Hine, First Lieut.; A. W. Davis, Second Lieut.; W. K. Johnson, Jr. Second Lieut.
Phœnix Company—L. D. Nicholls, Captain; Vr. St. Martin, First Lieut.; W. W. Martin, Second Lieut.; Wm. Simms, Jr. Second Lieut.
Bienville Rifles—Aug. Larose, Captain; Wm. Crayon, First Lieut.; P. L. Mailloux, Second Lieut.; F. Borges, Jr. Second Lieut.
Creole Guards—J. L. Fremaux, Captain; A. L. Gusman, First Lieut.; T. D. Lewis, Second Lieut.; G. W. McGimsey, Jr. Second Lieut.
Franklin Sharp Shooters—G. A. Lester, Captain; Newton Z. Guice, First Lieut.; Robt. Montgomery, Second Lieut.: Jos. Bryan, Jr. Second Lieut.
Sumter Guards—F. Newman, Captain; F. M. Harvey, First Lieut,; Wm. DeBolla, Second Lieut.; F. F. Wilder, Jr. Second Lieut.
Attakapas Guards—Alex. DeBlanc, Captain; E. LeBlanc, First Lieut.; Geo. N. Stubinger, Second Lieut.; Chas. Duchamp, Jr. Second Lieut.
Cheneyville Rifles—P. F. Keary, Captain; J. M. Burgess, First Lieut.; W. H. Oliver, Second Lieut.; Jno. M. Murphy, Jr. Second Lieut.
Opelousas Guards—James C. Pratt, Captain; John Taylor, First Lieut.; G. W. Hudspeth, Second Lieut.; Albert Dejean, Jr. Second Lieut.
Minden Blues—Jno. L. Lewis, Captain; B. F. Simms, First Lieut.; J. B. Tompkins, Second Lieut.; W. C. Rockwell, Jr. Second Lieut.

NINTH REGIMENT OF LOUISIANA VOLUNTEERS.

Richard Taylor, Colonel; E. G. Randolph, Lieut.-Colonel; W. J. Walker, Major.
Bossier Volunteers—John H. Hodges, Captain; F. Y. Hughes, First Lieut,; R. T. Crawford, Second Lieut.; R. J. Hancock, Jr. Second Lieut.
Bienville Blues—W. B. Pearce, Captain; J. Cronan Eagan, First Lieut.; C. W. Ardis, Second Lieut.; J. C. Theus, Jr. Second Lieut.
Brush Valley Guards—W. F. Gray, Captain; Grove Cook, First Lieut.; J. W. Milton, Second Lieut.; John Potts, Jr. Second Lieut.
DeSoto Blues—H. L. Williams, Captain; W. F. T. Bennett, First Lieut.; P. F. Jackson, Second Lieut.; N. A. Sutherlan, Jr. Second Lieut.
Colyell Guards—J. S. Gardner, Captain; J. B. Dunn, First Lieut.; A. A. Schneltory, Second Lieut.; P. S. Gardner, Jr. Second Lieut.
Jackson Greys—J. R. Cavanaugh, Captain; G. W. McCranie, First Lieut.; M. B. Kidd, Second Lieut.; G. S. McBride, Jr. Second Lieut.
Washington Rifles—Hardy Richardson, Captain; Jno. J. Slocomb, First Lieut.: Flut Magee, Second Lieut.; John Wadsworth, Jr. Second Lieut.
Moore Fencibles—R. L. Capers, Captain; Alfred Blackman, First Lieut.; R. Grigsby, Second Lieut.; Wilber F. Blackman, Jr. Second Lieut.
Stafford Guards—L. A. Stafford, Captain; Smith Gordon, First Lieut.; C. D. Waters, Second Lieut.; W. T. Cummings, Jr., Jr. Second Lieut.
Milliken Bend Guards—W. R. Peck, Captain; Geo. D. Shadburne, First Lieut.: R. G. Reading, Second Lieut.; Z. C. Williams, Jr. Second Lieut.

TENTH REGIMENT OF LOUISIANA VOLUNTEERS.

Mandeville Marigny, Colonel; J. C. Denis, Lieut.-Colonel; Felix DuMonteil' Major.

Shepherd Guards—Alex. Phillips, Captain, Jacob A. Cohen, First Lieut.; Morris Greenwall, Second Lieut.; Isaac L. Lyons, Jr. Secood Lieut.

Hewitt Guards—R. M. Hewitt, Captain; L. L. Conrad, First Lieut.; Patrick Woods, Second Lieut.; Thos. N. Powell, Jr. Second Lieut.

Confederate States Rangers—W. H. Spencer, Captain; M. J. Prudhomme, First Lieut.; L. Prudhomme, Second Lieut.; E. A. Seaton, Jr. Second Lieut.

Louisiana Rebels—John M. Leggett, Captain; J. E. Cuculu, First Lieut.; E. Miltenberger, Second Lieut.; Albert Pagnier, Jr. Second Lieut.

Orleans Blues—W. B. Barnett, Captain; Chas. Roussell, First Lieut.; E. A. Bozonier, Second Lieut.; B. Clague, Jr. Second Lieut.

Derbigny Guards—L. T. Bakewell, Captain; E. W. Huntington, First Lieut.; E. Fellows, Second Lieut.; H. C. Marks, Jr. Second Lieut.

Louisiana Swamp Rifles—D. W. Dickey, Captain; Albert Fabre, First Lieut.; P. K. Merrill, Second Lieut.; S. Cucullu, Jr. Second Lieut.

Tirailleurs d'Orleans—Eugene Waggaman, Captain; Alph. Canonge, First Lieut.; H. Monier, Second Lieut.; Paul Forstall, Jr. Second Lieut.

Orleans Rangers—Edward Crevon, Captain; G. A. Renaud, First Lieut.; J. P. Montamat, Second Lieut.; L. A. Revolle, Jr. Second Lieut.

Hawkins Guards—Chas. F. White, Captain; J. H. Williams, First Lieut.; Ernest Webre, Second Lieut; W. L. Hawkins, Jr. Second Lieut.

ELEVENTH REGIMENT OF LOUISIANA VOLUNTEERS.

Samuel Marks, Colonel; Robert H. Barrow, Lieut.-Colonel; E. G. W. Butler, Major.

Cannon Guards—J. E. Austin, Captain; R. J. Alexander, First Lieutenant; James Lingan, Second Lieut.; Robert L. Hughes, Jr. Second Lieut.

Dillon Guards—M. W. Murphy, Captain; J. P. Fallon, First Lieut.; A. F. Martin, Second Lieut.; R. K. Broderick, Jr. Second Lieut.

Holmes Light Guards—J. H. McCann, Captain; J. G. White, First Lieut.; M. Cunningham, Second Lieut.; John Cunningham, Jr. Second Lieut.

Rosale Guards—John J. Barrow, Captain; G. M. Miller, First Lieut.; C. J. Johnson, Second Lieut.; O. B. Haynes, Jr. Second Lieut.

Point Coupee Volunteers—Willie Barrow, Captain; T. J. Bird, First Lieut.; C. D. Favrot, Second Lieut.; A. LeBlanc, Jr. Second Lieut.

Westbrook Guards—W. Westbrook, Captain; A. Cazebat, First Lieut.; Ben Turner, Second Lieut.; Rob. R. Dennison, Jr. Second Lieut.

Labauve Guards—J. A. Ventress, Jr. Captain; J. R. Mims, First Lieut.; John Marcot, Second Lieut.; Jos. Warro, Jr. Second Lieut.

Shreveport Rebels—A. Schafner, Captain; L. L. Butler, First Lieut.; J. R. Hyams, Second Lieut.; Jos. Strauss, Jr. Second Lieut.

Continental Guards Company C—J. G. Fleming, Captain; T. W. Peyton, First Lieut.; F. H. Babin, Second Lieut.; L. M. Sones, Jr. Second Lieut.

Catahoula Greys—Alex. Mason, Captain; Richard H. Harris, First Lieut.; S. F. Routh, Second Lieut.; A. N. Spencer, Jr. Second Lieut.

TWELFTH REGIMENT OF LOUISIANA VOLUNTEERS.

Thos. Moore Scott, Colonel; W. H. Hough, Lieut.-Colonel; J. C. Knott, Major.

Claiborne Guards—Isaiah Lennard, Captain; Noel L. Wilson, First Lieut.; R. Evans, Second Lieut.; R. A. Crow, Jr. Second Lieut.

Independent Rangers—D. L. Hicks, Captain; J. W. Dutz, First Lieut.; T. C. Johnson, Second Lieut.; E. McN. Graham, Jr. Second Lieut.

Jackson Sharpshooters—J. H. Seale, Captain; J. S. Reno, First Lieut.; J. W. Jackson, Second Lieut.; W. P. Garr, Jr. Second Lieut.
Farmer Guards—C. W. Hodge, Captain; J. E. Woodward, First Lieut.; E. T. Sellers, Second Lieut.; W. L. Amonett, Jr. Second Lieut.
North Louisiana Cadets—J. T. Jourdan, Captain; H. J. Chapman, First Lieut.; J. W. Sandeford, Second Lieut.; J. N. Atkins, Jr. Second Lieut.
Arcadia Invincibles—C. T. Standifer, Captain; B. W. Glover, First Lieut.; D. S. Butler, Second Lieut.; J. D. Givens, Jr. Second Lieut.
Caldwell Invincibles—James A. Boyd, Captain; F. A. Blanks, First Lieut.; T. C. Hill, Second Lieut.; Jno. Myers, Jr. Second Lieut.
Southern Sentinels—John A. Dixon, Captain; J. R. Bevell, First Lieut.; Thos. J. Tiddlie, Second Lieut.; Wm. Miles, Jr. Second Lieut.
Beauregard Fencibles—Henry McCain, Captain; B. H. Meam, First Lieut.; Jno. F. Brantley, Second Lieut.; Isaiah H. Lacey, Jr. Second Lieut.
Farmer Rangers—B. D. Owen, Captain; W. M. Fuller, First Lieut.; W. A. Ponder, Second Lieut.; G. T. Johnston, Jr. Second Lieut.

THIRTEENTH REGIMENT OF LOUISIANA VOLUNTEERS.

Randall Gibson, Colonel; Aristide Gerard, Lieut-Colonel; Anatole P. Avegno, Major.
First Company Governor Guards—Auguste Cassard, Captain; Chas. Richard First Lieut.; Victor Mossy, Second Lieut.; Victor Olivier Jr. Second Lieut.
Second Company Governor Guards—J. Fremaux, Captain; B. Bennett, First Lieut.; C. H. Luzenburg, Second Lieut.; Chas. Hepburn, Jr. Second Lieut.
Third Company Governor Guards—Bernard Avegno, Captain; St. Leon Deetez, First Lieut.; Henry Castillo, Second Lieut.; Eugene Lagarique, Jr. Second Lieut.,
Fourth Company Governor Guards—M. O. Tracy, Captain; Hugh H. Bein, First Lieut.; Eugene Blasco, Second Lieut.; Geo. W. Boylon, Jr. Second Lieut.
Fifth Company Governor Guards—F. Lee Campbell, Captain; John M. King, First Lieut.; J. B. Sallaude, Second Lieut.; Norman Story, Jr. Second Lieut.
Sixth Company Governor Guards—E. W. Dubroca, Captain; John McGrath, First Lieut.; A. M. Dubroca, Second Lieut.; Robert Cade, Jr. Second Lieut.
St. Mary Volunteers—Thos. G. Wilson, Captain; James Murphy, First Lieut.; H. H. Strawbridge, Second Lieut., Adolph Dumartrait, Jr. Second Lieut.
Gladden Rifles—Wm. A. Metcalfe, Captain; John W. Labuisse, First Lieut.; Walter V. Crouch, Second Lieut.; E. B. Musgrove, Jr. Second Lieut.
Southern Celts—Stephen O'Leary, Captain; John Daly, First Lieut.; E. J. Connolly, Second Lieut.; John Dooley, Jr. Second Lieut.
Norton Guards—Geo. W. Norton, Captain; M. Hurdy, First Lieut.; A. S. Stuart, Second Lieut.; Geo. Cammack, Jr. Second Lieut.

SIXTEENTH REGIMENT OF LOUISIANA VOLUNTEERS.

Preston Pond, Jr., Colonel; Enoch Mason, Lieut.-Colonel; Daniel Gober, Major.
Caddo Fençibles—R. H. Lindsey, Captain; C. Ford, First Lieut.; T. G. Pegues, Second Lieut.; P. H. Kyes, Jr. Second Lieut.
East Feliciana Guards—James O. Fuqua, Captain; L. G. Chapman, First Lieut.; Oliver O. Cobb, Second Lieut.; Thos. J. Fuqua, Jr. Second Lieut.
Edward Guards—M. S. Edwards, Captain; S. A. Haden, First Lieut.; A. A. Harvey, Second Lieut.; Isaac Roberts, Jr. Second Lieut.
Pine Wood Sharp Shooters—Calvin E. Hosea, Captain; L. J. Seawell, First Lieut.; Neal C. Regan, Second Lieut., Adam G. Johnson, Jr. Second Lieut.
St. Helena Rebels—D. W. Thompson, Captain; E. J. Ellis, First Lieut.; J. F. Kent, Second Lieut.; W. G. Williams, Jr. Second Lieut.
Walker Roughs—W. E. Walker, Captain; J. W. Addison, First Lieut.; Horner E. Cozzens, Second Lieut.; Hiram Tumage, Jr. Second Lieut.

Rapides Tigers—F. L. Ragsdale, Captain; J. M. McFeeley, First Lieut.; Stephen Lynck, Second Lieut.; J. McArthur, Jr. Second Lieut.
Castor Guards—W. T. Mabry, Captain; K. E. Cockerham, First Lieut.; J.'A. Kooner, Second Lieut.; J. W. Noling, Jr. Second Lieut.
Big Cane Rifles—Wm. G. Ellerbe, Captain; Louis Stagg, First Lieut.; John P. Davis, Second Lieut.; Paulin Stagg, Jr. Second Lieut.
Evergreen Invincibles—Fred. White, Captain; R. P. Oliver, First Lieut.; W. T. Fuqua, Second Lieut.; Cephus Thompson, Jr. Second Lieut.

SEVENTEENTH REGIMENT OF LOUISIANA VOLUNTEERS.

S. S. Heard, Colonel; Charles Jones, Lieut.-Colonel; B. B. Jones, Major.
Sabine Rifles—D. W. Self, Captain; L. J. Nash, First Lieut.; M. A. Thompson, Second Lieut.; S. T. Sibley, Jr. Second Lieut.
Catahoula Guards—W. A. Reddett, Captain; T. O. Hynes, First Lieut.; J. S. Jones, Second Lieut.; Wm Scott, Jr. Second Lieut.
Phœnix Rifles—J. G. Taylor, Captain; S. Sawyer, First Lieut.; S. W. Taylor, Second Lieut.; R. W. Futch, Jr. Second Lieut.
Morehouse Southrons—W. M. Otterson, Captain; F. M. Grant, First Lieut. R. J. Stevens, Second Lieut.; M. S. Hunter, Jr Second Lieut.
Catahoula Rebels—R. H. Cuny, Captain; J. Q. A. Talliaferro, First Lieut.; Carter Beaman, Second Lieut.; A. Whitehead, Jr. Second Lieut.
Simmons Stars—T. P. Richardson, Captain; W. A. Simmons, First Lieut.; W. Raymond, Second Lieut.; G. W. Webb, Jr. Second Lieut.
Ouachita Southrons—M. Rogers, Captain; B. W. Burrough, First Lieut.; D. M. Garlington, Second Lieut.; S. G. McGuire, Jr. Second Lieut.
Caddo Lake Boys—J. A. Jeter, Captain; F. G. Sperman, First Lieut.; F. G. Bickam, Second Lieut.; J. C. Allen, Jr. Second Lieut.
Landrum Guards—Thos. A. Sharp, Captain; T. H. Triplet, First Lieut., J. C. Kenney, Second Lieut.; H. E. Allen, Jr. Second Lieut.
Claiborne Invincibles—W. A. Maddox, Captain; Jno. G. Heard, First Lieut.; G. M. Killgone, Second Lieut.; J. A. Simmons, Jr. Second Lieut.

EIGHTEENTH REGIMENT OF LOUISIANA VOLUNTEERS.

Alfred Mouton, Colonel; Alfred Roman, Lieut.-Colonel; Louis Bush, Major.
Chasseurs St. Jacques—E. Camille Mire, Captain; L. L. Armand, First Lieut.; S. Alex Poche, Second Lieut.; Ben S. Webre, Jr. Second Lieut.
St. James Rifles—Jules A. Druilhet, Captain; Emile Jacob, First Lieut.; C. M. Shepperd, Second Lieut.; Oct. Jacob, Jr. Second Lieut.
Arcadian Guards—Wm. Mouton, Captain; A. P. Bailey, First Lieut.; F. T. Comeau, Second Lieut.; O. Broussard, Jr. Second Lieut.
St. Landry Volunteers—H. L. Garland, Capt.; Chas. D. Ballard, First Lieut.; Jacob Anselm, Second Lieut.; Ad. Debaillon, Jr. Second Lieut.
Natchitoches Rebels—J. D. Wood, Captain; W. P. Owens, First Lieut.; Theo. Lettier, Second Lieut.; Emile Cloutier, Jr. Second Lieut.
Lafourche Creoles—J. K. Gourdain, Captain; John A. Collins,. First Lieut.; J. B. Tucker, Second Lieut.; C. Gautreau, Jr. Second Lieut.
Hays Champions—J. D. Hayes, Captain; R. M. Sanders, First Lieut.; J. D. Elie, Second Lieut.; Dudley Avery, Jr. Second Lieut.
Confederate Guards—Henry Huntingtion, Captain; Paul B. Leeds, First Lieut.; B. S. Story, Second Lieut.; A. J. Wall, Jr. Second Lieut.

NINETEENTH REGIMENT OF LOUISIANA VOLUNTEERS.

B. L. Hodge, Colonel; J. M. Hollingsworth, Lieut.-Colonel.
Vance Guards—Richard W. Turner, Captain; E. C. Anderson, First Lieut.; A. B. Broughton, Second Lieut.; M. C. Cavett, Jr. Second Lieut.

Henry Marshall Guards—H. J. Fortson, Capt; H. H. Handley, First Lieut.; J. H. Eastham, Second Lieut.; W. H. Turill, Jr. Second Lieut.

Keachi Warriors—D. S. Wells, Captain; George Headrick, First Lieut.; E. M. Woodruff, Second Lieut.; J. W. Jones, Jr. Second Lieut.

Robins Greys—Loudon Butler, Captain; E. E. Robins, First Lieut.; J. L. Mapples, Second Lieut.; A. B. Skannal, Jr. Second Lleut.

Claiborne Volunteers—H. A, Kennedy, Captain; Jno. P. Spears, First Lieut.; S. A. Hightower, Second Lieut.; J. W. Obanivore, Jr. Second Lieut.

Stars of Equality—H. H. Ham, Captain; J. B. Sanders, First Lieut.; Toddy Robinson, Second Lieut.; W. R. Robert, Jr. Second Lieut.

Caddo 10th—W. P. Winans, Captain; Camp Flournoy, First Lieut.; J. P. Bridges, Second Lieut.; Silas Flournoy. Jr. Second Lieut.

Claiborne Greys—W. B. Scott Captain; R. P. Webb, First Lieut.; C. L. Weldin, Second Lieut.; J. N. Leverett, Jr. Second Lieut

WHEAT'S SPECIAL BATTALION LOUISIANA VOLUNTEERS.

Major—C. R. WHEAT

Walker Guards—Robt. A. Harris, Captain; E. B. Sloane, First Lieut.; W. H. Kernan, Second Lieut.; Jno. Coyle, Jr. Second Lieut.

Old Dominion Guards—O. P. Miller, Captain; W. D. Tobin, First Lieut.; A. C. Dickinson, Second Lieut.; A. E. Read, Jr. Second Lieut.

Tiger Rifles—Alex White, Captain; T. W. Adrian, First Lieut.; Edward Hewitt, Second Lieut.; Sam P. Duchene, Jr. Second Lieut.

Delta Rangers—H. C. Gardner, Captain; T. A. Ripley, First Lieut.; M. Eastman, Second Lieut.; C. A. Petman, Jr. Second Lieut.

Catahoula Guerrillas—J W. Buhoup, Captain; J. W. Spencer, First Lieut.; Wm. Guss, Second Lieut.; M. J. Liddell, Jr. Second Lieut.

FIRST SPECIAL BATTALION LOUISIANA VOLUNTEERS.

Orleans Cadets—Charles D. Dreux, Captain; H. F. Bond, First Lieut.; W. R. Collins, Second Lieut.; Theo. Zacharie, Jr. Second Lieut.

Shreveport Greys—J. H. Beard, Captain; George Williamson, First Lieut.; Leon D. Marks, Second Lieut.; B. L. Hodge, Jr. Second Lieut.

Grivot Guards—V. H. Rightor, Captain; F. S. Goode, First Lieut.; D. B. Dunn, Second Lieut; Jos. A. Gagné, Jr. Second Lieut.

Crescent Rifles, Co. A—S. F. Fisk, Captain; Thaddeus Smith, First Lieut.; W. T. N. Robertson, Second Lieut.; Thos. A. Farris, Jr. Second Lieut.

Louisiana Guards—S. M. Todd, Captain; Chs. E. Fenner, First Lieut.; Henry Pierson, Second Lieut.; V. J. B. Girardey, Jr. Second Lieut.

BATTALION OF INFANTRY,

Commanded by Major A. REICHARD, *for* 12 *Months Service* (*at Camp Lewis.*)

Turner Guards—Fred. Bahucke, Captain; Thos Von Arnulinsen, First Lieut.; Th. Eicholz, Second Lieut.; Th. Schneider, Jr. Second Lieut.

Steuben Guards—F. Burger, Captain; G. Kehrwald, First Lieut.; S. Rosenbaum, Second Lieut.; Jno. Hausner, Jr. Second Lieut.

Reichard Rifles—F. Reitmeyer, Captain; Otto Weise, First Lieut.; Charles DePetz, Second Lieut.; F. H. Müller, Jr. Second Lieut.

Louisiana Volunteers—Chas. Assenheimer, Captain; P. Ruhl, First Lieut.; L. VonZinken, Second Lieut.; Julius Durrel, Jr. Second Lieut.

BATTALION OF ARTILLERY,

For 12 *Months State Service.*

First Co. Orleans Artillery—F. Gomez, Captain; P. A. Gomez, First Lieut.; E. R. Lehman, Second Lieut.; P. Marrero, Jr. Second Lieut.

Second Co. Orleans Artillery—Jas. P. Merlot, Captain; Fred. Latil, First Lieut.; Geo. F. Burthe, Second Lieut.
Third Co. Orleans Artillery—G. Stromeyer, Captain; A. A. Canon, First Lieut.; C. R. Fagot, Second Lieut.; A. Selle, Jr. Second Lieut.
Fourth Co. Orleans Artillery—J. T. Theard, Captain; E. Volaire, First Lieut.; L. E. Lemarie, Second Lieut.

COMPANIES FOR ACTIVE STATE SERVICE.

Perseverance Guards—John Rareshide, Captain; Henry L. Blow, First Lieut.; Henry Rareshide, Second Lieut.; E. P. Rareshide, Jr. Second Lieut.
Black Yagers—C. Rabenhorst, Captain; J. Hullet, First Lieut.; H. Miller, Second Lieut.; H. B. Chandler, Jr. Second Lieut.
Co. A. Sappers and Miners—John Ryan, Captain; Geo. Nungesser, First Lieut.; Geo. H. Moran, Second Lieut.; Thos. J. Royster, Jr. Second Lieut.
Washington Light Infantry—James T. Plattsmier, Captain; A. A. Plattsmier, First Lieut.; James L. Lambert, Jr. Second Lieut.
Co. C. Orleans Cadets—Joseph Collins, Captain; John T. Savery, First Lieut.; Jno. G. Wire, Jr. Second Lieut.
Co. A. Screwmen Guards—Sam. G. Risk, Captain; James Gibney, First Lieut.; Wm. McGregor, Second Lieut.; Nicholas Phelan, Jr. Second Lieut.
Marion Guards—R. L. Robertson, Jr. Captain; W. H. Wells, First Lieut.; Ben. Oppenheim, Second Lieut.; C. Fitzenreter, Jr. Second Lieut.
Yager Company—F. Peters, Captain; D. Simon, First Lieut.; Chas. Wermes, Second Lieut.; C. Yacobs, Jr. Second Lieut.
Scotch Rifle Guards—George Purvis, Captain; J. L. Henderson, First Lieut.; J. R. Dickson, Second Lieut; Thos. Fraser, Jr. Second Lieut.
Co. B. Screwmen Guards—J. C. Batchelor, Captain; R. W. Stanley, First Lieut.; D. O'Sullivan Second Lieut.; A. R. Sellars, Jr. Second Lieut.
Allen Guards—S. Jones, Captain; Thos. K. Pearson, First Lieut.; W. S. Jones, Second Lieut.; Robert Manser, Jr. Second Lieut.
Twiggs Rifles—D. H. Marks, Captain; Henry T. Hepp, First Lieut.; W. C. Morrell, Second Lieut.; Lewis L. Ellis, Jr. Second Lieut.
St. Mary Cannoniers—F. O. Cornay, Captain; Jules G. Olivier, First Lieut.; Geo. O. Foote, Second Lieut.; M. T. Gordy, Jr. Second Lieut.
Co. A. Orleans Blues—Richard Herrick, Captain; E. F. Stevens, First Lieut.; S. L. Bishop, Second Lieut.; A. Bobet, Jr. Second Lieut.
Florence Guards—H. Brummerstadt, Captain; E. Lachenmeyer, First Lieut.; B. Wasserogel, Second Lieut.; Ed. Warburg, Jr. Second Lieut.
McCall Guards—Chas. H. Herrick, Captain; Emile Bloom, First Lieut.; J. D. Scott, Second Lieut.; Leon LeGardeur, Jr. Second Lieut.
Co. B. Orleans Blues—Sam. Boyd, Captain; Robt. R. Breeden, First Lieut.; Jno. Baker, Second Lieut.; Patrick Clarke, Jr. Second Lieut.
Tirailleurs d'Orleans—A. Tissot, Captain; P. Canonge, Jr. First Lieut.; Louis Barron, Second Lieut.; J. L. Bargae, Jr. Second Lieut.
Co. B. Twiggs Rifles—Washington Marks, Captain; Oliver Locke, First Lieut.; M. H. Marks, Second Lieut.; Sam. Barnes, Jr. Second Lieut.
Ventress Life Guards—Jos. Goldman, Captain, Ed. Thomas, First Lieut.; Wm. Sylvester, Second Lieut.; Chas. Calhoun, Jr. Second Lieut.

ANNUAL REPORT MADE DECEMBER 10, 1862.

January 27th, 1862.—Gov. Moore issues an order for the celebration of the anniversary of the day the State seceded (27th Jan , '61), by military and civil authorities.

February 17th.—First aud Second Brigade, volunteer troops, ordered to be ready for marching on twenty-four hours notice.

February 23d.—First Brigade, volunteer troops, and Second La. Militia, ordered to report to Gen. Lovell.

March 4th.—Captain W. G. Mullen, stationed near the forts to harrass the enemy and furnished with pirogues for penetrating lakes and bayous.

The resident foreigners formed into the European and French Brigades—numbering altogether 5138 and 3804 men, who did duty when the city fell, and for several days afterwards maintained peace and order.

Sanitary corps of 800 men organized under Dr. W. E. Stone.

March 24th, 1862.—A regiment of free colored natives, tender their services to the State, and are accepted. Gen. Butler, subsequently, after the fall of the city, attempted to revive it, but prior to Dec. '62, only fifty of the old organization responded to the call. A call made for shot guns and other fire arms, which was responded to. Chains, cables and anchors seized from extortioners' for making rafts near the forts, under order by L. E. Forstall and Thos. E. Adams, and Geo. H. Bier, of C. S. Navy. A large number exempted by the State from military duty for government work—the contractors for these works using freely the right of exempting all persons in public employ, especially those building the Louisiana and Mississippi.

February 24th.—Gen. Lovell has the Galveston and Charles Morgan which have been seized, fitted out as gunboats, and named respectively the Gen. Quitman and Gov. Moore, Beverly Kennon, Commander of the latter, James Duke, and Fred. Frame, officers. Engineers: G. Wetter, R. P. Fortune, A. Gleason, B. O. Brien, of the Gen. Quitman ; A. Grant, jr. Commander, S. Marcey, First Officer ; W. J. Irvine, Second Engineer ; H. Behrens, A. Smith, P. Thompson, J. Smith; these participated in the naval battle and behaved gallantly.

Judge J. W. Andrews, Major John Stroud, jr., Maj. E. C. Hancock, and Ph. B. Boisfontaine, put in charge of the Passport Bureau. Lieutenants U. Lewis, W. E. Gordon, R. L. Butler, R. E. McKreevy, A. Chalaire, jr., J. H. Bernos and F. Toca, were appointed to examine passports on the different roads.

March 15th.—Martial law proclaimed in Orleans, Jefferson and St. Bernard. Crescent Artillery, Company A, placed on the Louisiana.

April 11th.—The enemy with a large fleet have crossed the bar off the Balize and are operating with gunboats and mortar fleet. Bombardment continued without cessation, until April 25th, and subsequently thereto. The troops in the fort act heroically. The Ram Mississippi—a mystery thus far, was not finished.

April 24th.—Three gunboats have passed the forts and are on their way up. The people have not anticipated the event, and the excitement is great. Militia placed under arms—the city filled with startling rumors, as to whether the advance would be made by water or land. Gov. Moore left with the archives. Militia, in the midst of great consternation and excitement, detached to perform police duty.

April 25th.—Twenty Federal gunboats at Packwood's Plantation, 20 miles below the city. Gen. Lovell calls at 9 o'clock, and invites Gens. Lewis and Grivot, to proceed to the fortifications. Before reaching there the enemy make the attack, and the State troops forced to abandon the guns. An order was now given to evacuate the city, and State troops were making their way out. The Federal gun boats reach the city ; the rain meanwhile pouring down in torrents. All of the drays and carts impressed to ship off to stores to Camp Moore and Monroe. All cotton ordered to be destroyed and few bales escaped.

April 30th.—State government fixed at Opelousas, which place Gov. Moore and Gen. Grivot, reached on the 18th of May.

May 19th.—Gen. John G. Pratt, in command at New Iberia. Enemy in possession of the road from Algiers to Berwick's Bay.

Sixty-four of the 21st Indiana, take a schooner in the Grande Caillou with arms. The Colonel of the Terrebonne Regiment called a meeting, and proposed an attack, which was not made. Seven or eight young men captured a wagon with Federal soldiers, two of the latter killed, and two wounded. The following day four-hundred of the 21st Indiana, commanded by Col. Keith, seized fourteen citizens, and in front of their prison a rope was suspended. J. B. Bond, 60 years of age, and an invalid. together with his family was driven from his house, which was then burned. The jail was burned, and the property of Dr. Jenning.

May 25th—Capt. E. W. Fuller, of the St. Martin Rangers, to get rid of them, captured a train at Brashear, and immediately put his men on board, and moved towards New Orleans. He captured an uptrain at Raceville, and another at Des Allemands. There still remained one locomotive in Algiers, opposite New Orleans. To prevent this from leaving, Capt. Fuller double-quicked ten miles to Jefferson, and cut a 100 foot crevasse, took up the rails of the track and carried them off. He also burned the bridges, doing much of his work in sight of an armed vessel. The enemy again appearing at Thibodeaux.

June 3d—Lieut. Colonel V. A.Fournet with the Yellow-Jacket Batallion, laid in wait for their train and killed 60, causing them to retreat. Large numbers of river boats, which in ordinary times ran up and down the Mississippi and its innumerable tributaries, took refuge by way of Red River and Achafalaya, in the innumerable net work of lagunes and bayous, whose names and course were hardly well-known, even by hunters and fishermen. Among other boats was the Tow Boat, J. L. Webb, fitted out as a sea-going Steamer, at that time hidden back, and stealthily taking on board 300 bales of cotton. She was seized, and afterwards kept the bayous back to Red River, clear of any Federal Boats, drawing only 7½ feet of water. Capt. Jas. McCloskey, and subsequently Major A. W. McKee, were her commanders.

June 4th—Lieut. Woods, the only person who could be found who had any practical knowledge of the matter employed at the Franklin Foundry to make shot and cannister. Agents sent out to hunt rifle powder. An impromptu battery rigged out from a few old howitzers damaged about the rims, which have been picked up from various points, and which only want harness and carriages to be made useful in the field. They can also be made serviceable by dismounting them as occasion may demand for the boats. The greatest trouble was to find an officer who could organize and drill a company. Major Octave Voohries, formerly of the Washington Artillery, and Buisson's Brigade, and Lieut. Ed. Crow, of De Clout's Regiment were recommended by Gen. Pratt to this work.

May 10th—The Conscript Act of April 10th, ordered to be put in force. Foreigners and Partisan Rangers exempted. Camps of instruction at Monroe and Opelousas.

Thirty-eight parishes have reported a force of 8,690 Conscripts. The parishes of Plaquemine, St. Bernard, Orleans, Jefferson, St. Charles, St. John the Baptist, West Baton Rouge, Madison, Carroll and Caldwell not reporting—say ten parishes.

Returns of Conscripts between the ages of 18 and 35 years, made to the Office of the Adjutant and Inspector General of the State to 1st December, 1862.

EASTERN LOUISIANA.

Camp of Instruction, Camp Moore, Parish of St. Helena.—East Baton Rouge, 79; East Feliciana, 37; West Feliciana, 92; Livingston, 102; St. Helena, 26; Washington, 11; St. Tammany, 54. Total, 401.

WESTERN LOUISIANA—SOUTH RED RIVER.

Camp of Instruction, Camp Pratt, Parish St. Martin.—Assumption, 636; Ascension, 170; Avoyelles, 476; Calcasieu, 340; Iberville, 252; Lafayette, 343; Lafourche, 559; Natchitoches, 446; Pointe Coupee, 376; Rapides, 536; St.

Mary, 202; St. Martin, 196; St. James, 262; St. Landry, 1,148; Sabine, 125; Vermillion, 367; Winn 141; Terrebonne, 501. Total, 6,876.

WESTERN LOUISIANA—NORTH RED RIVER.

Camp of Instruction, Monroe, Ouachita Parish.—Bossier, 179; Bienville, 32; Caddo, 191; Claiborne 150; Catahoula, 235; Concordia; 46; DeSoto, 9; Franklin, 87; Jackson, 00; Morehouse, 59; Ouachita, 212; Tensas, 89; Union, 124; Total, 1,413.

RECAPITULATION:

Eastern Louisiana—7 parishes, 401. Western Louisiana—S. Red River, 18 parishes, 6,876. Western Louisiana—N. Red River, 13 parishes, 1.413. Total 38 parishes, 8,690.

No returns from Plaquemine, St. Bernard, Orleans, Jefferson, St. Charles, St. John the Baptist, West Baton Rouge, Madison, Carroll and Caldwell—10 parishes.

June 20th, 1862.—Trafic with the enemy or any attempt to get out cotton or sugar furtively, or travel to or from New Orleans, made amenable to Court-Martial. River steamboats ordered to be burned when in danger of capture. Mail facilities extremely difficult from the Trans-Mississippi to Richmond.

Applications made for the formation of Partisan Rangers. A few companies formed under command of Simeon Belden, A. L. Hayes and others.

A large amount of specie belonging to the Bank of America, $700,000 or upwards had been transferred from the vaults and brought out from New Orleans upon the approach of the Federal fleet. After some adventures, it was determined by those having it in charge to carry it back to New Orleans. As soon as this determination was ascertained orders were issued to Lieut. Col., Cheney, of Avoyelles, Ralph Smith, Esq., Chiarman of the Committee of Public Safety of Alexandria, and a company under command of Capt. S. M. Todd, [not the officer of the same name from New Orleans] who were sent to seize the parties ostensibly conducting it to New Orleans. The order however was not delivered to Mr. Smith before the specie had reached Alexandria, and had been carried off on the Steamer Moro. [Whatever became of it afterwards is still involved in mystery].

The Steamer J. A. Cotten seized, and with the Anna Perret mounted with two guns assisted in protecting the movement, and after driving the enemy captured a large number of prisoners.

October 22.—Seven deserters executed. Sundry goods and a lot of beeves brought towards New Orleans, seized and confiscated. The enemy make an incursion up to Lake Charles and are opposed by Col. W. W. Johnson. 40,000 troops up to date, sent from the State all armed, with no assistance whatever from the Richmond government.

TWENTY-SIXTH REGIMENT LOUISIANA VOLUNTEERS.

Alexander DeClouet, Colonel; D. S. Cage, Lieut.-Colonel; Winchester Hall, Major.

Allen Rifles—Caleb J. Tucker, Captain; L. A. Webre, First Lieut.; Clay Knoblock, Jr. Second Lieut.

Assumption Creoles—W. Whitnel Martin, Captain; L. Himel, First Lieut.; Numa Arrieux, Second Lieut.; Leon Achee, Jr. Second Lieut.

Bragg Cadets—Cleaphas Lagarde, Captain; Lewis Guion, First Lieut.; Sylvere Navarre, Second Lieut.; M. Aug. Legendre, Jr. Second Lieut.

Grivot Guards, Co. B—W. A. Bisland, Captain; Joseph Aycock, First Lieut.; Homer Lirette, Jr. Second Lieut.

Grivot Guards, Co. C—J. J. Shaffer, Captain; J. A. Leonard, First Lieut.; Thos. J. Shaffer, Second Lieut.; E. L. Aycock, Jr. Second Lieut.

Lovell Rifles—W. W. Bateman Captain; A. S. Lawes, First Lieut.; D. C. Daniels, Second Lieut.; J. Y. Sanders, Jr. Second Lieut.

Grivot Fancy Guards—W. C. Crow, Captain; E. B. Crow, First Lieut.; James C. Rice, Second Lieut.; Jos. Louviere, Jr. Second Lieut.

Prudhomme Guards—Octave Metoyer, Captain; G. W. Cobb, First Lieut.; S. Pace, Second Lieut.; S. W. Bossier, Jr. Second Lieut.

Lafayette Prairie Boys—Eraste Mouton, Captain; Hazard Easten, First Lieut.; Wm. Campbell, Second Lieut.; F. Martin, Jr. Second Lieut.

Pickett Guards—C. O. Delahoussaye, Captain; Aubin Bourg, First Lieut.; Thos. J. Hargis, Second Lieut.; B. Cooper, Jr. Second Lieut.

TWENTY-SEVENTH REGIMENT LOUISIANA VOLUNTEERS.

Leon D. Marks, Colonel; L. L. McLaurin, Lieut.-Colonel; Geo. Tucker, Major.

Skipwith Guards—A. S. Norwood, Captain; Thos. L. East, First Lieut.; L. P. Talbert, Second Lieut.; J. A. Norwood, Jr. Second Lieut.

Iberville Guards—E. W. Robertson, Captain; E. D. Woods, First Lieut.; F. Arbour, Jr., Second Lieut.; Victor Blanchard, Jr. Second Lieut.

Caddo Pioneers—C. D. G. Williams, Captain; J. M. Christen, First Lieut.

Spencer Guards—John T. Spencer, Captain; T. O. S. Robertson, First Lieut.; W. K. Strickland, Second Lieut.; Abner Womack, Jr. Second Lieut.

Rapides Terribles—Jos. T. Hatch, Captain; W. M. McCormick, First Lieut.; A. J. McCranie, Second Lieut.; A. G. Baillio, Jr. Second Lieut.

Sparta Guards—R. W. Campbell, Captain; J. P. Webb, First Lieut.; T. E. Paxton, Second Lieut; R. S. Allums, Jr. Second Lieut.

Winn Rebels—J. R. Cooper, Captain; W. B. Stovall, First Lieut.; J. W. Cockerham, Second Lieut.; F. L. Gregg, Jr. Second Lieut.

McLaurin Invincibles—J. H. Garret, First Lieut.; J. B. Davenport, Second Lieut.; A. J. Gibson, Jr. Second Lieut.

Dixie Rebels—O. L. Durham, Captain; C. J. Foster, First Lieut.; J. H. Tucker, Second Lieut.; G. W. Graves, Jr. Second Lieut.

Caddo Confederates—T. C. Lewis, First Lieut.; J. B. Smith, Second Lieut.; Saml. Beckwith, Jr. Second Lieut.

BATTALION LOUISIANA DEFENDERS—LOUISIANA VOLUNTEERS.

Juan Miangolara, Major; E. Basseli, Adjutant.

First Company—T. Viade, First Lieut.; Jose Ferry, Second Lieut.; T. Alberti, Jr. Second Lieut.

Second Company—Arthur Picolet, Captain; E. N. Ganucheau, Second Lieut.; J. D. Sourdes, Jr. Second Lieut.

Third Company—Jose Domingo, Captain; Leon Prats, First Lieut.; Jose Mora, Second Lieut.; J. Roses, Jr. Second Lieut.

BATTALION YELLOW JACKETS—LOUISIANA VOLUNTEERS.

V. A. Fournet, Lieut.-Colonel; G. A. Fournet, Major; E. DeBlanc, Surgeon; L. A. Laloire, Quartermaster; L. P. Briant, Adjutant.

Company A—Alex. Thibodeaux, Captain; Valery Thibodaux, First Lieut.; Leon Gillard, Second Lieut.; Omer Martin, Jr. Second Lieut.

Company B—Desire Beraud, Captain; Arthur Simon, First Lieut.; Alcee Castille, Second Lieut.; Alf. Gradenigo, Jr. Second Lieut.

Company C—C. DeBlanc, Captain; Nicolas Cormier, First Lieut.; Pierre Lasalle, Second Lieut.; L. T. Smith, Jr. Second Lieut.

Company D—B. D. Dauterive, Captain; Louis Fournet, First Lieut.; J. Z. Boutte, Second Lieut.; V. Dauterive, Jr. Second Lieut.

Company E—A. Berard Captain; Mozart Bernard, First Lieut.; Jos. Nunez, Second Lieut.; V. Lemoine, Jr. Second Lieut.

RELATIVE TO STATE TROOPS

Forces Volunteer State Troops transferred to Major Gen. M. Lovell. Commanding Department No 1, C. S. A.

FIRST BRIGADE VOLUNTEER TROOPS.

Brigadier General—BENJAMIN BUISSON.

Orleans Guards—Numa Augustin, Colonel; Charles Massieu, Lieut.-Colonel.
Chasseurs-a-Pied—J. Simon Meilleur, Colonel; *Chas. A. Janvier, Lieut.-Colonel; *H. J. Rivet, Major.
Chalmette—*Szymanski, Colonel; *Geo. W. Logan, Lieut.-Colonel; *Eugene Soniat, Major.
Cazadores Espagnoles—Nelvil Soule, Lieut.-Colonel; G. Marzoni, Major.

SECOND BRIGADE VOLUNTEER TROOPS.

Brigadier General—E. L. TRACY.

Beauregard—*F. A. Bartlett, Colonel; Geo. S. Lacey, Lieut.-Colonel; *Geo McKnight, Major.
Jeff Davis—Alex. Smith, Colonel; *W. P. Freret Lieut.-Colonel; *Jno. B. Cotton, Major.
Continental—*Geo. Clark, Colonel; *A. W. Merriam, Lieut.-Colonel; *Geo. W. Hynson, Major.
Sumpter—*G. A. Breaux, Colonel; *T. H. Shields, Lieut.-Colonel; — Bell, Major.
Battalions—Johnson Special.—W. W. Johnson, Lieut.-Colonel; *W. H. Winn, Major.
Battalions—King's Special—*J. E. King, Lieut.-Colonel.

THIRD BRIGADE VOLUNTEER TROOPS.

Brigadier General—S. M. WESTMORE.

Confederate Guards—*J. F. Girault, Colonel; C. R. Railey, Lieut.-Colonel; J. J. Noble, Major.
Louisiana Irish—P. B. O'Brien, Colonel; W. J. Castell, Lieut.-Colonel.
Leeds Guards—Chas. J. Leeds, Colonel; E. Grinnell, Lieut.-Colonel.; A. G. Brice, Major.

RECAPITULATION OF FORCES.

Fisrt Brigade, 2815; Second Brigade, 3818; Third Brigade, 2480. Total 9113.

These regiments were mustered into Confederate States Service, and when the gunboats passed the forts and Lovell carried off all transportation, were disbanded by Gen. Tracy. When Butler arrived, the officers and men were arrested as prisoners of war, paroled, and those who did not take the oath, were exchanged on the 8th of October following, being delivered at Vicksburg. Those marked thus* are known to have bsen exchanged, and did good service afterwards.

www.ingramcontent.com/pod-product-compliance
Lightning Source LLC
Chambersburg PA
CBHW051802230426
43672CB00012B/2603